P9-BBU-965

Crossing Boundaries with Children's Books

Sponsored by the United States Board
on Books for Youn

**Other Scarecrow Press Books Sponsored by the
United States Board for Books on Young People**

Children's Books from Other Countries, edited by Carl M. Tomlinson, 1998

The World through Children's Books, edited by Susan Stan, 2002

Crossing Boundaries with Children's Books

Edited by
Doris Gebel

The Scarecrow Press, Inc.
Lanham, Maryland • Toronto • Oxford
2006

SCARECROW PRESS, INC.

Published in the United States of America
by Scarecrow Press, Inc.
A wholly owned subsidiary of
The Rowman & Littlefield Publishing Group, Inc.
4501 Forbes Boulevard, Suite 200, Lanham, Maryland 20706
www.scarecrowpress.com

PO Box 317
Oxford
OX2 9RU, UK

Copyright © 2006 by Scarecrow Press, Inc.

Photo of Lygia Bojuna-Nunes (p. 28) used with permission of the Swedish National Council for Cultural Affairs. Book covers used with permission: p. 36: *Popul Vuh*, Groundwood © 2005; p. 36: *Messengers of Rain*, Groundwood © 2002; p. 131: *The Letters*, Farrar, Straus and Giroux © 2002; p. 240: *The Bremen Town Musicians*, Roaring Brook Press © 2004; p. 240: *Daniel, Half-Human and the Good Nazi*, Atheneum © 2004. Line drawings as follows: (p. xi) Gepetto and (p. xiii) Pinochio, the fox and the cat from the book *Pinocchio, the Adventures of a Marionette* by C. Collodi, Ginn and Company, 1904; p. 212: cover illustration from *Conrad*, F. Watts, 1977; p. 222: Moomintrolls from *Moominpappa's Memoirs*, Farrar, Straus and Giroux, 1994; p. 232: *Book of Coupons*, Viking, 2001; p. 277: Mrs. Pepperpot from *Little Old Mrs. Pepperpot*, Clio Press, 1989; p. 285: Nils from *The Wonderful Adventures of Nils*, Pantheon, 1947; p. 302: Wolves from *The Wolves of Willoughby Chase*, Dell, 1962. Cover art by Peter Sis and used by permission of the artist.

British Library Cataloguing in Publication Information Available

Library of Congress Cataloging-in-Publication Data

Crossing boundaries with children's books / edited by Doris Gebel.
    p. cm.
  Includes bibliographical references and index.
  ISBN-13: 978-0-8108-5203-7 (pbk. : alk. paper)
  ISBN-10: 0-8108-5203-9
  1. Children—Books and reading—United States. 2. Multiculturalism—United States. 3. Children—Books and reading—United States—Bibliography. 4. Children's literature—Bibliography. I. Gebel, Doris, 1953–

Z1037.A1C825 2006
028.5'50973—dc22

2005032774

∞™ The paper used in this publication meets the minimum requirements of American National Standard for Information Sciences—Permanence of Paper for Printed Library Materials, ANSI/NISO Z39.48-1992.
Manufactured in the United States of America.

Contents

Foreword

When I am asked, as I often am, about my favorite books, I always mention the books of Sigrid Undset. Then it occurs to me that I have never really read these books. What I have read (and re-read) are translations of the books I call my favorites. I cannot read Norwegian, and I'm never likely to learn. So I owe an enormous debt to translators. My life would be immeasurably poorer if I had never been able to read *The Master of Hestviken* or *Kristen Lavransdatter.*

In her preface to *Crossing Boundaries with Children's Books,* the editor, Doris Gebel tells how books and stories from other countries enriched her childhood, and yet it is an almost foregone conclusion that very few American children will read books from other countries and cultures. Librarians lament the scarcity of such books, and publishers protest that those they dare to publish do not sell.

The United States Board of Books for Young People (USBBY) is devoted to promoting the cause of peace through children's books that cross boundaries of nationality, race, and creed. A first step in this effort is education. Why should children read books that cross boundaries, which deal with issues outside their cultural comfort zones? Once convinced of the need, where does one find such books? *Crossing Boundaries* will help answer both of these questions with essays by scholars and translators as well as an extensive annotated bibliography.

When former President Jimmy Carter was asked what event during his presidency had had the most profound effect on him, he answered: "My friendship with Anwar Sadat." He went on to tell how he, a devout Baptist, and President Sadat, a devout Muslin, would spend hours talking to each other about their faiths, not seeking to convert, but to understand.

Most of us will not have the privilege of a personal friendship with a world leader, but we can make friendships across boundaries through books. To go to war against ones friends is unthinkable. If you have friends in another country, you will seek every opportunity to understand them better and to work for their well-being. Read this book. Study the bibliography. Share the books annotated there. Take a giant step towards peace.

Katherine Paterson
Hans Christian Anderson Award winner for writing, 1998

Acknowledgments

This book has been in the making for many years and I am indebted to so many people. I wish I could thank each one individually, but the list would be as long as the book and no one would want to read it. To my family, friends and colleagues, you know who you are, thank you for your inspiration and support.

How do I know hundreds of Mother Goose rhymes? Certainly not because I studied the Opie's collection of rhymes. Why, "I had a mother who read to me."[1] When my mother, Joan Zauner, read to us from her childhood copy of *Pinocchio*,[2] in which she crayoned as a little girl, did I know this story was translated from Italian? One of the first books I owned was *Folk Tales from the Far East*[3], a book my mother gave me from her own mother's bookshelf. I read it over and over, as it was one of the few books I actually owned. In my mind's eye, I sat in the shade of the banyan tree and could only imagine this far-off place.

Many years later, my grandmother, Connie Sehrig, gave me her copy of *The Book of Folk Stories*[4] and told me this was one of the few things she brought to this country from England in 1913. Did she know that she was bringing this book on its second trip across the ocean, having been printed in Cambridge, Massachusetts in 1887? Of course not. How stories travel, from here to there and back again. It is this heritage of world literature, planted in early childhood that shapes our tastes and reading habits and grows in ways that should not surprise us.

This is what Margaret Poarch made clear to me when she introduced me to USBBY and the formal study of International Children's Literature. Books like Jella Lepman's *Bridge of Children's Books*[5] and Paul Hazard's *Books, Children and Men*[6] opened the door to new worlds. *Babies Need Books*[7] by New Zealander Dorothy Butler and *Only Connect*[8] by Canadian Sheila Egoff, which I read in Margaret's class in 1975, have continued to be revised and updated and reinforce the notion that children the world over can enjoy each other's national literature.

Awareness of literature from countries that may not have the means to publish books that can be translated is heightened by the tireless efforts of Anne Pellowski in encouraging literacy projects in countries around the world. I first learned about her efforts while working at the Information Center for Children's Cultures at the U.S. Committee for UNICEF and most recently in reading about her cloth book project at the IBBY Congress in South Africa in September 2004. When you read through the bibliographies and realize how many countries are under-represented or not represented at all, you will know that there is still much work to be done.

When I met my friend Barb Barstow at ALA in 1996 and told her I was teaching a class about international children's literature and wanted to write a book, she asked if I knew that Carl Tomlinson was writing a book for USBBY and might need another annotator. And so he did. It was my privilege to write annotations for Carl's book *Children's Book's from other Countries*[9] and again for *The World through Children's Book*,[10] edited by Susan Stan. I thank USBBY for the opportunity to edit the third edition *Crossing Boundaries with Children's Books* and hope that you, the reader, will benefit from the essays and bibliographies contained herein.

A heartfelt thank you goes to Peter Sis, who drew the beautiful cover for this book. Thank you to Katherine Paterson, a great friend of USBBY, who wrote the foreword. To Jeffrey Garrett, Stephen Roxburgh, and Simon Boughton, this book is richer for your contributions. Translators Doris Orgel, David Unger, Cathy Hirano and editor Jill Davis have added insights into their efforts in bringing books to us from other languages. Thank you to Hadley Dyer, children's book editor at James Lorimer & Co., Brenda Halliday, librarian at the Canadian Children's Book Centre, and Deidre Baker, co-author of *A Guide to Canadian Children's Books,* for advice and annotations in the chapter on Canada. Judith Ridge graciously corresponded with me via e-mail and added suggestions for the Australian chapter. Julie K. Kline, Outreach and Academic Program Coordinator, Center for Latin American and Caribbean Studies, University of Wisconsin-Milwaukee, read the chapter on Latin America and Dr. Meena Khorana, editor of *Sankofa*, read the chapter on Africa south of the Sahara and I appreciate their advice. I would also like to thank Grace W. Ruth who compiled the list of sources for foreign-language and bilingual publishers. Any errors of inclusion or omission are, of course, my own.

A huge debt of gratitude is owed to the many hard working annotators who have contributed to this edition. I want to especially recognize Linda Staskus who contributed the most annotations. I also want to recognize my Long Island colleagues Kristine Casper and Alison O'Reilly who helped with proof reading and were so willing to pitch in to help in so many ways. Thank you to Mary Lois Nicholls, who has been a sounding board and traveling buddy to the USBBY Regional Conferences. Most especially I want to thank Susan Stan, current president of USBBY, editor of *The World through Children's Books*, and advisor for this edition. I could not have completed this task without you.

NOTES

1. "The Reading Mother" by Strickland W. Gillian.

2. Collodi, C. *Pinocchio: The Adventures of a Marionette*. Translated from the Italian by Walter S. Cramp. With editorial revision by Sara E.H. Lockwood. Many original drawings by Charles Copeland. New York: Ginn and Company, 1904.

3. Meeker, Charles H. *Folk Tales from the Far East*. Illustrated by Frederick Richardson. Philedelphia: The John C. Winston Co., 1927.

4. *The Book of Folk Stories*. Rewritten by Horace E. Scudder. Cambridge, MA: Houghton Mifflin Co., 1887.

5. Lepman, Jella. *Bridge of Children's Books: The Inspiring Autobiography of a Remarkable Woman*. Dublin: O'Brien Press, 2002. Originally published by ALA, 1969.

6. Hazard, Paul. *Books, Children, and Men*. Boston: Horn Book, 1960, 1983.

7. Butler, Dorothy. *Babies Need Books: Sharing the Joy of Books with Children from Birth to Six*. Portsmouth, NH: Heineman reprint edition, 1998. Originally published by Atheneum, 1969.

8. Egoff, Sheila. *Only Connect: Readings on Children's Literature*. Toronto: Oxford University Press, 1969, 1996.

9. Tomlinson, Carl. *Children's Books from Other Countries*. Lanham, MD: Scarecrow, 1998.

10. Stan, Susan. *The World through Children's Books*. Lanham, MD: Scarecrow, 2002.

Part 1

CROSSING BOUNDARIES

Chapter 1

Introduction

Children's books keep alive a sense of nationality; but they also keep alive a sense of humanity. They describe their native land lovingly, but they also describe faraway lands where unknown brothers live. They understand the essential quality of their own race; but each of them is a messenger that goes beyond mountains and rivers, beyond the seas, to the very ends of the world in search of new friendships. Every country gives and every country receives—innumerable are the exchanges—and so it comes about that in our first impressionable years the universal republic of childhood is born.[1]

Crossing Boundaries with Children's Books is the third volume sponsored by the United States Board on Books for Young People. The first, *Children's Books from Other Countries*, edited by Carl M. Tomlinson (Scarecrow, 1998) is a compendium of international children's literature with annotations of both in- and out-of-print books published between 1950 and 1996. Susan Stan's *The World through Children's Books* was the second, and it included books published between the years 1997 and 2000. *Crossing Boundaries* includes books published between 2000 and 2004. Like the second volume, this book includes books published in the United States, but set in another country.

There is little duplication between the volumes and they are intended to be used together. Carl Tomlinson's comprehensive introduction to international children's literature in volume one and revised in the second is not included in this volume and I commend it to you for your consideration.

The title for the book *Crossing Boundaries* was inspired by the fifth IBBY Regional Conference sponsored by USBBY and held at the Chautauqua Institute in October 2003. Chapter two includes two essays edited from speeches presented at that conference. Stephen Roxburgh encourages us to leave the American sector, crossing the boundaries of the familiar and leaving our comfort zone. Jeffrey

Garrett challenges us to understand that there are other ways of being and seeing which are not ours and yet are worthy of our respect, understanding, and tolerance. A third original essay by Simon Boughton describes how a children's book publisher finds international titles and brings them to the United States. Together these articles create the backdrop for part 2, which is a listing of quality international and domestic books organized by regions of the world. This section is the core of the book and is the work of people who have volunteered their time and energy because they believe in the value of international literature for children. Part 3 identifies resources that will help readers find books with an international focus.

As you select books to share with children from part 2, it is important to remember that no one book is meant to adequately represent the national literature of a country or to present a complete picture of a culture or geographic region. It is through a multiplicity of books that a young reader becomes familiar with new ideas and styles of writing and illustration. Use the titles annotated in this volume along with those in the first two editions to round out the picture. Take off your "American glasses" and read these books without preconceptions about what is comfortable in books for children. It is in this way that, as Paul Hazard tells us, the universal republic of childhood will be born.

Once you have crossed the boundaries into that universal republic, you will use the standard guides for evaluating children's literature that can be found in most textbooks about children's literature. *From Cover to Cover* (1997) by Kathleen T. Horning[2] is another useful resource. The same standards for judging children's literature apply to all books. But Carl Tomlinson adds insights about evaluating translated literature when he says that "translated works should exhibit a good, fluent writing style that is not stilted or awkward. Some flavor of the country should remain. Place and character names should usually remain true to the original text to foster in children a tolerance for and an appreciation of other languages and customs."[3]

NOTES

1. Hazard, Paul. *Books, Children, and Men*. Boston: Horn Book, 1983: 146.
2. Horning, Kathleen T. *From Cover to Cover: Evaluating and Reviewing Children's Books*. New York: HarperCollins, 1997.
3. Lynch-Brown, Carol and Carl M. Tomlinson. *Essentials of Children's Literature*. New York: Pearson, 2005: 196.

Chapter 2

Essays

SI SIE MÜSSEN DEN AMERIKANISCHEN SEKTOR VERLASSEN: CROSSING BOUNDARIES BY STEPHEN ROXBURGH

Boundaries have been much on my mind lately having just returned from a trip to Berlin. For my generation the mother of all boundaries was the Berlin Wall. Since unification, what Germans call *die Wende*—literally, the turning point—that wall has been demolished. Berlin is now one city, rather than two, and it is a tremendously exciting place. But 1,800 miles southeast of what was West Berlin is the West Bank and there another wall is being built. This new boundary is dividing Israelis from Israelis and Palestinians from Palestinians as much as it is dividing Israelis and Palestinians from each other.

Walls are physical boundaries and stand as a recurring testimony to our efforts to separate from each other. But we can't build walls everywhere to separate people. And besides, as the poet said, "Something there is that doesn't love a wall." Dismantling boundaries may be the better way to go, and language is one of the greatest means we have for doing so, even though working with language can be tricky business.

There was a warning sign posted at Checkpoint Charlie, the border crossing between West and East Berlin, which said, "Sie verlassen den Amerikanischen Sektor," that is, "You are leaving the American sector." The warning was posted in four languages—German, Russian, French, and English. Leaving the American sector meant crossing the boundary between the American and Soviet zones, into a heavily fortified and guarded no-man's land, and finally entering "enemy territory"—Soviet-occupied East Berlin. West Berlin was an American enclave, an island, an outpost. In a thousand books and movies crossing that boundary represented moving from safety, comfort, a haven, to danger, discomfort, *and* uncertainty. After the Soviet Union collapsed, the Berlin wall came down, and Germany was unified. The one section of the wall that remains standing is now a tourist attraction. However, on a deep level, the mentality engendered by the cold war lingers in America today. We were brought up knowing the world was divided between them and us. Checkpoint Charlie is in our minds.

The divide between America and the rest of the world is evident in myriad ways. However the primary concern of IBBY is children's books so let us consider for a moment the Mildred Batchelder Award. "This award, established in 1966, is a citation awarded [by the ALSC division of the ALA] to an American publisher for a children's book considered to be the most outstanding of those books originally published in a foreign language in a foreign country, and subsequently translated into English and published in the United States." In recent years the Batchelder committee has been having a hard time finding enough books to evaluate. The sad fact is that very few publishers are commissioning translations. They are expensive, time consuming, and usually unsuccessful in the marketplace. Why is this?

Bad economics are often cited as being the reason not to publish books in translation. Translations cost a bit more to publish. You have to pay the translator, and while grants are available from most European countries to partially subsidize the cost of translation, children's books are supported at about half the level that they subsidize adult books.

A more significant aspect of the economics of publishing translations is what we call the grant of rights. That is, when you license a book you acquire rights for a territory and a language. For example, there are North American English language rights—otherwise known as USCPOM (i.e., the United States, Canada, the Philippines, and the Open Market)—or World English language rights. Most foreign publishers selling the rights don't want to grant World English language rights. They want you to translate the book and then they can use your translation as a tool to license the rights to other English-language publishers. You do get to sell the translation to the other publishers—if they want it—but you have to do all the work first, with no guarantees, and you aren't participating in the level of income that derives from licensing the rights. You haggle over the rights you get but the more you want, *the* more you pay. I've gone into more detail than I expect you to find meaningful or interesting to show that it is the accumulation of expense and work in the face of modest sales and little or no rights income that discourages many publishers from taking on translations. No single factor is overwhelmingly expensive or onerous.

Having said all that, I believe that a far more significant boundary than economics is language. This is obvious and complicated. Let's begin with the English languages. When you are commissioning a translation, do you translate it into British or American English? I've had British and Australian translators tell me that they are perfectly capable of writing American English. I'm here to tell you, they really aren't. The diction, syntax, and rhythm of British English are inherent in the language, thoroughgoing and pervasive, and, in my experience, they can't be disguised or eliminated. Nor, let me hasten to add, should they be. The same is true of American English. I made the pragmatic decision some time ago, after many years and many translations that I would work as often as possible with translators whose first language is American English. I publish for an American audience; I will publish books translated into American English. It isn't better, it isn't worse. It *is* different. The subtle differences among the English languages are smooth going in comparison to translation into another language, a foothill in comparison to the Hindu Kush.

Like me, few editors have other languages. High school French or college Spanish does not constitute "having another language." We are forced to rely on readers who write reports on books that interest us. A good reader—like a good writer and a good friend—is hard to find. Most readers are biased in favor of any book they read in that language. It's what I call the Little Jack Horner syndrome. "He stuck in his thumb and pulled out a plumb and said, 'What a good boy am I!'" I can read this book in a foreign language; it must be good. It takes someone who is very comfortable in a second language not to bring a little bit of self-aggrandizement to the evaluation of a book. Further complicating the matter is, even if you find a good reader, they probably don't know anything about publishing, and it's a rare bird indeed that knows anything about publishing for young readers. Yet part of the publishing decision has to do with the viability of a book in our market. In short, we end up buying books based on readers' reports and, sometimes, when the translation comes in I simply have to hold my head in my hands and weep.

By far and away the most substantial of the boundaries presented by another language is, indeed, the translation. I have worked with a lot of translators. Some translators believe in adhering to the letter of the author's words in order to render something as close to a literal translation as possible. Others are after what *they* perceive to be the author's vision, and they could care less about being literal. It's very hard to adhere to either extreme position, and most translations fall somewhere in the middle.

Think of the process as akin to light passing through a series of filters. One filter—by far and away the most important—is the author's perspective and vision. Another is his or her language. The reader is a third filter. The translator becomes another filter. Readers of the translation are another. That's a lot of filters. Things can get blurry. Or think of the process in terms of the whisper game. You know, someone whispers something to someone else who then whispers it to a third person and so on, around the room. What comes out at the other end doesn't bear much resemblance to the original. Well think of translations as a kind of whisper game but by *very* articulate, *very* attentive players. The end result is more reliable, more faithful, but it won't be exact.

My approach to evaluating and editing a translation is simple and best understood in terms of the filter analogy. All I can hope to do is make sure the filter I'm responsible for—the translation into my language—is transparent. To do that, I have to find the best translator I can and make sure that his or her language is crystal clear. For that I have to trust my eye. I expect a translation to read as if it were originally written in American English. This is very easy to state and very hard to do; only the best translators can achieve it.

I've tried to suggest some of the issues that are relevant. The economic and language factors are big and they dominate discussions of literature in translation. Having said that, I don't think language is the most difficult boundary to cross. The ultimate boundary is culture: the American sector.

All too often, we Americans look at another culture as if we were looking at a mirror. We look for the familiar and when we see something we recognize, we think we've had an insight into that culture. Cultural diversity meets globalization. MacDonald's arches in Tokyo. Sponge Bob dubbed in Italian. CNN on television anywhere, anytime. In fact, when we actually do encounter another culture, we find it a little weird, uncomfortable, possibly dangerous. Be careful! You are leaving the American sector. *Sie verlassen den Amerikanischen sektor.*

Books originally written in another language and published in another country are outside the American sector. They aren't about assimilation into American culture. They don't have anything to do with America. They present lives that are not premised on our assumptions and don't focus on our cultural concerns. Often the world they represent seems strange; sometimes it's hard to understand what's going on or what specific issues are at stake. They can be disorienting and can make many readers uncomfortable.

Translations seem to be off-putting to many American readers. The authors have weird names. Here are some from my list: Ineke Holtwijk, Hanna Kraan, Bart Moeyaert, Anke DeVries, Hannes Binder, Szabinka Dudevszky. I've had sales reps ask me if there is any way we could change the author's name to something more American sounding. Where are John Smith and Mary Brown when you need them? Then, on the title page you have what constitutes a warning label, "Translated from the [pick a language] by [pick a name]." Sometimes translators have to fight to get their name on the title page rather than in 6-point type on the copyright page.

To the best of my knowledge, this aversion to books in translation is not evident in other countries. Some years ago at a conference in Paris in front of an intimate gathering of 500 or so people, I was accosted by Pierre Marchand, the late, great publisher of Gallimard Juenesse. First he described the United States as a desert wasteland littered with television sets. Then he took me personally to task for the fact that American publishers don't publish many French authors but French publishers publish lots of American authors. Before I could respond, Pierre left the room. I don't much like being bludgeoned publicly but, I have to say, he had a point.

Look at any major juvenile list in Western Europe and you will find a substantial, vital selection of literature in translation. There are actually clusters of houses in different countries that tend to publish similar kinds of fiction. Earlier I said that because we are hopelessly monolingual we are forced to make acquisition decisions based on readers' reports. In fact, I have been more successful basing my decision on the specific recommendation of a book's editor, people whom I have known for years and whose taste I know and who know my taste, in conjunction with the cluster of publishers who are publishing the book. It used to be, for example, that if a book was recommended to me by someone whose judgment and taste I knew and shared, and if I saw that the book was being published by, let's say, Querido in the Netherlands, Hanser in Germany, l'ecole des loisirs in France, Alfaguera in Spain, Tokuma in Japan—any combination of these—that would be all I needed to act on. I'd buy the book. Unfortunately much publishing in Europe, once remarkably stable, has over the last decade or more begun to resemble the game of musical chairs that has so diminished American publishing. Editors are no longer with the lists they spent years developing and independent houses are now imprints of conglomerates. Be that as it may, there is much more receptivity to literature in translation outside the American sector.

All of this is, I fear, a pretty grim state-of-literature-in-translation address. It is hard for me to summon up much good news. So why do I keep publishing books in translation? I don't do it for any high-falutin' altruistic reasons. And I don't do it to get rich. And I'm not rich. That, I suppose, means I've been successful. I do it because the books are so exciting. Have you ever been in a place that you'd never been before? Maybe you're a little lost. You're not really in danger but you're definitely not in terra cognita. Maybe you're not quite sure what's going on but you're interested by what you see. When I'm in that situation I get very attentive to my surroundings, hyper-alert, and I proceed carefully. This heightened state of awareness is exhilarating. And gradually I get more comfortable with the situation; I find a way, points of reference that enable me to orient myself. And then, I begin to see things, even familiar things, in a new light.

Literary fiction represents universal human experience in a unique and specific cultural context regardless of the language it's written in. A good translation makes the language transparent enabling the reader to see with the author's eyes. If the author's vision is astigmatic, the reader will see things slightly out of focus. If the cultural orientation is foreign, for a while the reader will be disoriented. This will pass. If the book is any good, if it warrants being called literary fiction, if it is worth translating because it is true, then the vision will be much deeper than the surface where the unfamiliarity lies—so deep in fact, that it transcends cultural differences, offering us a glimpse of our shared human condition. If these books are any good at all, they give us ultimately a new perspective on common experience. And in the process there is discovery—seeing new things—and there is revelation—seeing in a new way.

This is why I keep publishing books in translation. *Twenty-five years* in and I still don't know how to make them more successful in this country. I can't say that I think there's much of a chance that multicultural education will embrace these books. I do believe that they offer a way of seeing that is otherwise un-available to most of us. The only thing I know for sure is that in order to see what these books have to offer, you must leave the American sector. *Sie müssen den Amerikanischen sektor verlassen.*

Note: This essay is edited from a presentation given at the 5th USBBY Regional Conference in Chautauqua, New York, October 10, 2003.

Stephen Roxburgh is the president and publisher of Front Street, Asheville, NC.

OF TRANSLATIONS AND TARANTULAS: WHAT'S AT STAKE WHEN AMERICAN CHILDREN READ BOOKS FROM OTHER COUNTRIES BY JEFFREY GARRETT

Writer William H. Gass said once that Americans like translations about as much as they like tarantulas.[1] Our publishers do in fact keep publishing them, these translations of literary works—though far fewer than in other countries—and for our part we keep not reading them. Wait long enough, and you'll find the most wonderful translated books in the remainder bins at your bookstore or in the catalogs of Daedalus and Labyrinth.[2] Our neglect of translated literature is democratic and does not discriminate between books for adults and books for children. It explains why virtually no winners of the Mildred L. Batchelder Award, our "special" prize category for translations (since translations are excluded from consideration for the important prizes, the Newbery and the Caldecott), are still in print. And why should the publishers bother? Librarians know that translated children's books—the oddball, quirky stuff—are the first to be weeded when space becomes scarce. This is analogous to our kitchens, where we toss out the exotic Indian or Hungarian spices that were so captivating as souvenirs when we picked them up on vacation years ago, but they never really fit in at home. We hang on to the salt, the pepper, and the MSG.

What is it with this national rejection of books in translation? Is our literary culture in fact "severely ethnocentric," as author Howard Norman has said? If so, how does that jibe with our legacy of being so welcoming to immigrants? How does it fit in with America's trademark multiculturalism—a word, incidentally, that originated here and has since gained entry into many of the world's languages. In Spain there is now "literatura multicultural." In Germany and across Scandinavia, we find the word "multikulturen." We ourselves are avid users of this word of our own creation, but its scope and validity—and apparently that of the open, tolerant worldview it appears to represent—seem to stop at our borders.

At the risk of over generalizing—or perhaps doing so on purpose for the sake of argument—I see the rejection of foreign books for children and adults in the context of our national character, a character that is welcoming of peoples from abroad entering our country (providing they are willing to become like us), but that itself ventures abroad with reluctance, fear, and a measure of disdain. And then there is our unspoken and perhaps unrealized belief in the "naturalness" of English, a predilection so profound that we are not even aware of how deeply it influences our response to other national cultures, other national literatures.

Let us put it simply: We Americans expect to be talked to directly, without interpreters. That is why a Hamid Karzai in Afghanistan or the cultivated private school accents of our appointed leaders in Iraq evoke our confidence, our trust, even our affection. Those speaking to us through interpreters in languages such as Arabic or Pashtun we naturally tend to mistrust, even if they are trying to make themselves understood. Why don't they speak English? Is it contempt?

So, on the one hand, we understand that to live together, we must all talk to one another and seek to understand and appreciate each other's differences. But we insist on being talked to, and we expect on the part of members of different cultures seeking integration into ours an acceptance of our values and, if they want to live under the same roof with us, a willingness and indeed an eagerness to embrace our way of life.

The multiculturalism that is the source of such strength within our borders is the source of our weakness internationally, at least in the arena of transcultural understanding. We expect to be talked to, and we expect our interlocutors to be striving for the same goals as we are. Yet internationally that is often just not the case. This difference between "multicultural" and "international" is also at the heart of the difference between multicultural children's books and those we call foreign or, more frequently, "international," which of course they are not, for they are as national as ours are. These books are not created to speak to us, at least not primarily, but often not at all. They do not seek the understanding or affection of Americans. Very often, they even reject, often explicitly, America or our vaunted way of life. And yet these books can contain worlds of richness and of meaning that may be entirely new to us, precisely because they are *not* trying to meet us on our terms. Above all, they can contain the key to a lesson that Americans are today more than ever sorely challenged to learn: that there are other ways of being and other ways of seeing that are not ours, and yet are worthy of our respect or at least our understanding and our tolerance.

I had a lesson a few years ago that showed me how subtly our presumptions of our own cultural normalcy influence how we see the rest of the world—and make it difficult to engage other cultures on their own terms. In 2002, I was preparing a lecture for the Art Institute of Chicago on several children's book illustrators whose works were on display there. One of them was a young Irish artist named Alan Clarke. When I first saw his work, I appreciated his humor, his rich color palette, his playful approach to perspective, and his grotesquerie. I tried to reach him to ask him about his work. I succeeded in contacting his mother by phone in County Wicklow south of Dublin. She gave me an e-mail address for her son with an Internet provider that I dutifully wrote down as "aircom.net". When the message bounced, I called back and asked Mrs. Clarke to spell the address for me letter by letter, and sure enough, "aircom" was actually spelled "e-i-r-c-o-m," incorporating the Irish name of the country, Eire. I thought: isn't this exactly what we do all the time with the cultures of other countries? We think we understand what they are saying or trying to say—with a slur or lisp or stutter—when in fact, without even being aware of it, we bend their statements to fit our preconceptions. We make them make sense in our own context of meanings, when in fact we may completely misunderstand, and our assumed understanding may even appear quite ridiculous in the eyes of the natives. For our part, we attribute our lack of understanding to *the other's* inadequate command of language, technique, or plain reasoning. Most cultures therefore have a word that mixes foreignness with this kind of judgmental censure. The ancient Greeks called everything that wasn't Greek "barbarism," a term that even then was laden with negative connotation. In English we have the equally freighted word "outlandish."

In fact, our struggles with foreign children's books in translation tend to mix our own cultural predispositions with a genuine desire to understand, to learn, and to enjoy. For confirmation of this, go to amazon.com and look at reader reviews of foreign children's books in translation. Take for example Michael Ende's *The Neverending Story*, translated from the German in the early 1980s into at least twenty world languages and perhaps the biggest international children's book bestseller before Harry Potter. At the amazon site, one reviewer titled her review "Um . . . that was weird." She writes: "I liked the movie so I read the book. The book is strange and philosophical and much less concrete than the movie. For now I'm going to chalk it up to being some German thing." This reader ultimately rejects the book because of the otherness of its style, which she finds "monotonous." It is of little consequence to her that German fantasy writing looks back on a long philosophical tradition, beginning perhaps with E.T.A. Hoffmann in the early 1800s, and that Ende's *Neverending Story* is also a work in the tradition of the German *Bildungsroman*. If you go to this work expecting Tolkien, you will inevitably be disappointed. If you can cast aside your expectations and endure the foreignness until it ceases to feel foreign, you may have slipped into another world—and inhabit it, along with all the other worlds you come to know, for the rest of your life.

The danger of misunderstanding something from the outside that I am describing here is what psychologists call *projection*. It applies to both literary works in translation and foreign illustrated works. Both translations into English and illustrations appear to speak to us directly. In images, we recognize human figures, buildings, animals, and we believe we understand what the artist intends to show us. Yet our further understanding of these foreign images is often not just that they are different, but that they are also somehow better or worse, more beautiful or less beautiful than our own, depending on our overall regard for the originating culture—with the default being, perhaps, "less," since we are used to a high level of production standards in our cultural artifacts. Umberto Eco has called this American penchant for the perfect (some might say: the slick) "hyperrealism."[3]

In translations, we encounter in what are *foreign* works words *that we know* such as "grandpa," "dinner," "mosque," all of which mean something to us within our own cultural context, but that inevitably evoke associations from our daily lives, are in harmony with our concepts of normalcy, or, as with the word "mosque," are influenced by recent encounters in the morning newspaper or the evening television news.

What has been said thus far could suggest that the reading experience as it relates to children's books from other countries is a binational phenomenon, an encounter between the cultural baggage of an American child with the cultural baggage of a foreign writer. In fact, the literature of the world does not break down conveniently along national lines. The Irish children's book illustrator Alan Clarke, mentioned above, counts among his strongest influences English, American, and Norwegian artists—but also the Austrian artist Lisbeth Zwerger. The Slovak children's book artist Dušan Kállay is a member of what we might call the Eastern European school of surrealism, but he has also been heavily influenced by the art of the German and Flemish Middle Ages and Renaissance: Brueghel and Bosch, for example, are undeniably present in his work. The Korean illustrator Jong Romano lives in Paris. His interpretation of the Englishman Lewis Carroll's *Alice in Wonderland* incorporates influences of German artists Georg Grosz and Max Beckmann—alongside the French artist Claude Magritte and the Spaniards Pablo Picasso and Salvador Dali. The winner of the 2003 Bratislava Biennale for children's book illustration was the Japanese artist Iku Dekune, who despite her rootedness in Japanese traditions of illustration is a confirmed student and follower of no other than the Slovak Dušan Kállay, but who has recently begun studying and internalizing the work of the great Czech-American children's book creator, Peter Sís.

The complexities of influence and originality in the world of children's book writers are no less enormous.

What we should wish for in our children—as in ourselves—when we approach the books that are introduced on the pages of this volume is, for one, patience, coupled with a willingness to temporarily suspend our American notions of what is "normal" and rational and attractive, with the hoped-for reward of being swept up by literary expressions from cultures that are not our own into worlds that may just turn out to be just as exciting as our own—or more so—in ways that are entirely new to us. We may find things there that are more repellent than what we know at home, but also more noble and appealing: vicarious experiences that cast into relief our own lives, culture, and values. Imparting this patience along with the gift of a temporary suspension of cultural judgment to our children is a goal that we as educators, librarians, and parents should strive for. Success in this endeavor is a desirable end, for we could be leading our children to reading experiences that enrich their lives and inform their worldviews. It could in the end also make us and them, our children and ourselves, better world citizens.[4]

NOTES

1. Quoted (along with the statement following by Howard Norman) on the homepage of Archipelago Books, accessed on January 22, 2005, at http://www.busycreature.com/archipelago/reverberations.html.

2. Cf. Chris Orlet, "Interview with William H. Gass," *Pif Magazine*, January 22, 2005, accessed on January 22, 2005, at http://www.pifmagazine.com/SID/706/.

3. Cf. Umberto Eco, *Travels in Hyper Reality: Essays*. Translated from the Italian by William Weaver. San Diego: Harcourt Brace Jovanovich, 1986.

4. This essay is based in part on presentations delivered at the 28th IBBY Congress in Basel, Switzerland, on October 1, 2002 ("IBBYs Awards and Selections: Can There Be International Standards of Excellence?"), and at the 5th IBBY Regional Conference in Chautauqua, New York, October 11, 2003 ("International Illustrators: On Their Own Terms"). For the texts of these presentations, see Leena Maissen, ed., *Children and Books: A Worldwide Challenge*. Basel: IBBY, 2003: 119–128, and http://www.library.northwestern .edu/collections/garrett/ibby/chautauqua.pdf, respectively.

Jeffrey Garrett is a librarian at Northwestern University in Evanston, Illinois. Between 1983 and 1988, he was head of the English Language Section of the International Youth Library in Munich, Germany. From 1992 until 1995, he was the editor of *Bookbird*, the international children's literature journal of IBBY, the International Board on Books for Young People. He served as president of IBBY's Hans Christian Andersen Awards jury in 2004 and 2006.

SHRINKING WORLD: BOOK FAIRS AND THE CHANGING MARKET BY SIMON BOUGHTON

It's the second week in March, and I'm on my way to the London Book Fair. Like BookExpo in the United States, the London fair is primarily a retail trade show for the UK publishing industry, but the amount of international business transacted there has steadily grown—to the point that the entire second floor gallery of the Olympia exhibition hall is devoted to the International Rights Center, where publishers' rights directors, agents, and editors are found deep in conversation at hundreds of tiny tables.

Just over the horizon, in April, is the Bologna Book Fair. Then at the end of May comes America's BookExpo, which, like London, has become a significant venue for international publishing business. The ALA summer conference in June attracts a trickle of European publishers (in some years more than others, depending upon the conference city), who know that they can find many of their U.S. counterparts in one place and catch up on business not finished at Bologna or BEA. Later in the year comes Frankfurt, the biggest and best known of the calendar's procession of international book fairs, and there are important regional book fairs emerging in Asia and elsewhere. And procession is what it is: these events, with their growing attendance, the ease of international travel, and technology that makes it a simple matter to email a complete layout of a full-color book halfway around the world, have made international publishing year-round business.

Hence, I travelled to London. Roaring Brook is launching a new imprint devoted to graphic novels. The imprint was born, in part, of international publishing: European and—in particular—Asian comics have found a huge readership in the United States and helped create a new interest in graphic storytelling. The authors and artists contributing work to the new imprint come from all over the world: the United States, France, Britain, Malaysia, Korea, even Africa. Now, a year or more before the first books are published, we're presenting the program to overseas publishers, seeking interest and a commitment to publishing them in their territories. Gaining such commitments at this early stage of course makes good business sense: it helps to underwrite some of the investment involved in starting the new imprint. But beyond business sense, it also makes publishing sense: it's in the nature of these books to cross national and cultural boundaries.

This is the world we live in: increasingly international, boundary-less, and frenetically busy. Many trade publishers are global in reach—and all pay careful and increasing attention to overseas markets, whether directly, through export sales, or indirectly, through the licensing of rights to overseas publishers. Nonetheless, for all the global and frantic pace of the publishing industry, the Bologna Children's Book Fair, held in northern Italy in April, stands apart as a separate and quite special event. Naturally, the words "northern Italy in April" go some way to account for this: Bologna is a lovely city—a modern, working metropolis under a beautiful medieval skin, with the best cuisine in Europe. For an averagely bibulous, culturally attuned industry, it's a setting and an atmosphere that's good for business, and smiles always seem to break out on publishers' faces the minute the airplane wheels touch the ground at Marconi Airport.

Bologna is also unique in being devoted to the children's sector of the industry. The fair offers a focus and concentration quite different to the Frankfurt Book Fair in October, where corporate CEOs are in attendance and much attention is paid to the glamour and celebrity of adult trade publishing. For children's publishers, Bologna is an opportunity to meet with their peers around the world without distraction, and to take snapshots of the children's publishing industry around the world. Although the fair has changed significantly over the past decade or so, a great deal of good business is still accomplished there.

Bologna is, essentially, a marketplace, at which the stallholders are publishers and the wares set out for inspection and sale are books to which those publishers hold international publishing rights. For an acquiring editor visiting the fair, the two essentials are a good pair of shoes, and a good breakfast: the fair is spread over a large area, with different countries or regions occupying different exhibit halls, so there's a lot of hurrying from one appointment to the next. And with as many as 15 or 16 half-hour-long appointments packed into a day, there's not a lot of time for lunch.

The majority of those appointments proceed in similar fashion: a rights sales person will run through a selection of new books on offer from his or her publishing house, showing proofs or covers or offering synopses to the acquiring editor across the table. As a "customer" in this situation, it pays to know one's mind, and to be able to say "no" quickly—there's little time for, and little point in, expressing polite interest, and most rights sales people appreciate a firm, unambiguous response.

At its simplest, I look at potential new acquisitions at Bologna in the same way that I look at them from any source, domestic or foreign—which is to say that I'm looking for a book that I think I can publish successfully. Is there an audience for this book in the United States? Is my publishing house equipped to reach that audience? Does the book have a voice—does it speak to its audience in a way that is interesting, entertaining, original, or otherwise distinctive and likely to attract attention? Is it timely? (Always a hard question to answer, given the ups and downs of literary fashion.) What's the price tag, and does this acquisition make business sense? And underlying all these, there's a question of taste—simply, do I like the book enough? Does it appeal to me and can I support it when it gets cast in with a crowd of other books on a busy schedule a year or two from now?

These are the same questions that confront any acquisition decision, but they are shaded a little differently for foreign acquisitions. For all that the world is shrinking and cultural boundaries becoming blurred, the audience for a book in, say, France or Germany, or even other English-speaking countries, is quite different from that in the United States. This is at its simplest a matter of setting. Schools are different in different countries. Clothes, buildings, machines, sports, the music kids listen to, and the shows they watch on TV—the basic fabric of life differs remarkably from one country to the next, and children are very attuned to their surroundings. Readers expect to recognize the world they are familiar with in what they read. This is true of picture books: if the world in the book looks like Europe, it may not make sense to an American toddler. And it's true of fiction. A novel set in the daily surroundings of school, say, will differ from country to country, where customs, fashion, and young people's preoccupations vary greatly. With setting, goes language. Kids speak differently in Australia and Britain and the United States. Will the unfamiliar idiom seem interesting, exotic—or simply odd to an American reader?

Sometimes the question of whether a book's setting will be an obstacle to travel is moot, either because the setting is unspecific, or because it's invented. I find I'm rarely taken with books that are unspecific—that don't have that essential sense of place. Too often they feel like they've been written for everyone, and the result is bland, pleasing no one. It's perhaps surprising how stories built from the most universal themes and characters depend on setting for their life. Think of the toys in a toy box. Think of *Winnie the Pooh*.

Books that invent their own setting don't carry any local baggage, and if they're convincing they travel easily. It's no accident that fantasy fiction—from C.S. Lewis to Philip Pullman to J.K. Rowling to Garth Nix—is internationally popular: in creating their own worlds, they have a universal setting. And successful fantasy deals in large, universal themes: moral authority, good and evil, and children growing up and learning to tell one from the other. But it's striking that many of these books also have distinctly local flavor. What could be more British than Harry Potter's boarding school, or Lyra's Oxford? Along with their large universal themes, the books are exotic—and that's the other side of the penny when it comes to judging a book by its setting. Books that tackle everyday life, that are concerned with daily matters and the world of the reader, have to be at some level recognizable and familiar. Books that offer the reader a place to escape to are not constrained in the same way—they can, indeed must be, exotic.

Stories are told differently in different places. The 32-page full-color picture book format is an international standard, but its use varies greatly. Picture books originating in Britain frequently have a good deal of descriptive text, with the art functioning as illustration to the story—illustrated storybooks, if you will, recognizably different from the U.S. picture book tradition, which is generally shorter on text and in which the art is integral to the storytelling and does more of the narrative work. There are great differences in artistic sensibility from territory to territory. A lot of European picture book illustration falls into one of two categories: either sophisticated, cerebral work with its roots in the world of editorial cartoons, or cute, rather bland characters that seem to come out of the world of toys and animation. The former, although fascinating, is frequently quite foreign to American sensibilities—and we originate plenty of the latter on our own side of the Atlantic.

There are differences in the way books are sold in different places that have an impact on the way books are published. For a long time—although this is no longer so obviously the case—European and Australian teen fiction was able to deal more frankly and directly with sex, drug use, and other "difficult" topics than American fiction written for the same age group. Part of the reason American publishers were more cautious in this area was because libraries form a large part of their market, and sales to libraries are mediated by reviews.

Sorting through these differences and looking for the book that stands out and that will find an audience in the United States is both the fun and the challenge of an event like Bologna. Almost all books are essentially local—as of course they should be: they belong to a particular place and time. Paradoxically, almost all books for young readers are also at some level universal: whether European, Asian, or American, they deal with common themes and experiences—of development, growing up, coming of age, experiencing the world and finding a place in it. How do we choose—decide which books will travel and which will not?

Inevitably, the answer lies with an acquiring editor's instinct and experience—an educated hunch about which books will speak to American readers. The challenge, and the opportunity, to my mind, is to not steer clear of the differences between American and other sensibilities, but to look for those books that work in spite of them; to find books that express themselves powerfully and distinctively enough that they transcend their local origins. The task any book faces is to suspend the reader's lack of interest. Will this book do that? Does the book have something to say to the reader? Is the voice and the vision strong enough?

Every acquisition is part editorial decision, part business decision. The basic business considerations are the same whether buying at home or abroad: at its simplest, what does a book cost, and what sort of return will if offer on the investment? But like the editorial considerations, the business considerations involved in buying in a book from a foreign publisher differ slightly from those involved in a domestic acquisition. A U.S. publisher buying rights to a book from an overseas publisher is likely to be getting significantly limited territorial and other rights as compared to a book it originates. It is also likely that a licensing publisher will have less control over the final form of a book. Translations and "Americanized" versions of British texts are generally required by contract to be faithful to the original edition, so the opportunity to make significant editorial changes to a book doesn't arise. With fewer places to sell a book, and fewer opportunities to make editorial suggestions that might strengthen it for the home market, one has to feel that much more strongly about its merits and about one's ability to publish it well. It is, I think, a slightly higher bar, and a book has to be that much more special to clear it.

One of the most interesting things about having attended Bologna regularly over the past decade or so has been seeing the business change. There's a consistent bedrock to the industry in the work of finding and publishing new and talented authors and artists, but the way in which children's books are bought and sold internationally has changed significantly. When I started going to Bologna, at the beginning of the 1990s, a great deal of the fair was devoted to selling not just rights, but "co-editions." The term refers to the business of lining up multiple editions of a book on a single print run. European—and in particular, British—publishers became very good at this. They would bring proofs of a new picture book or illustrated nonfiction series to the fair and arrange to print for foreign licensees—some thousands for a U.S. publisher, a few thousand for a French publisher, a few thousand more for a German or a Scandanavian or an Italian publisher—and so on. The expensive part of the printing—the color illustrations—remained the same across all editions and could all be printed together, changing from one language to another required only a relatively inexpensive change to the black text plate on the press. The publishers originating these co-editions made money marking up the print price, and the volume gained from long print runs meant they could support a book that might not otherwise get published in their own relatively small domestic market. It wasn't uncommon for books to be auctioned at the fair on the basis of print quantity, and for the bidding to become quite intense. By lunchtime on the opening day, there'd be whispers about "the book of the fair"—and the inevitable anxiety about missing it.

The co-edition business hasn't gone away, but it has declined—and it's certainly less frenzied. Co-edition runs are likely to be built up in smaller quantities, and over weeks and months, rather than during the fair. This change has a lot to do with the decline in the U.S. market for the two categories of books best suited to co-editions: picture books, for which sales have been flat for several years because of changing demographics, and illustrated nonfiction, which has suffered with the steep decline in school library book sales. The axis of the co-edition market has swung—away from the Atlantic and toward the east. With U.S. publishers buying fewer illustrated books, European publishers are looking toward emerging markets in eastern Europe and Asia for their print runs.

Simultaneously with the change in the co-edition market has come a change in the way territorial rights to children's books are held and handled. It's not so long since it was common—almost customary—for the originating publisher of a children's book to be able to acquire world rights. Today, territorial rights are much more likely to be sold separately, and the major publishing houses are coming to Bologna and other book fairs with fewer rights to sell.

This is partly a result of a change in focus: a decade ago, there was a strong market for picture books. Because there's often a separate author and artist involved, and because illustrated books are expensive and complicated to manufacture, publishers could make a good case that they were better equipped than authors or their agents to handle foreign sales. Today the industry is focused more on fiction than on illustrated books. Novels are rarely printed in co-editions, and rarely have multiple authors, and it's easy—and frequently more lucrative—for a good agent to sell off separate territories one by one.

It's also partly a result of the way the children's book industry has matured. Children's publishing is big business; advances paid to authors have escalated, and competition for new talent is fierce. In the world after Philip Pullman, Harry Potter, and Lemony Snicket, agents are seeing a great deal more value in children's publishing, and retaining a great deal more interest in control. In consequence, the "book of the fair" is now as likely to be found in the Agents' Center as in the booths of overseas publishers, and acquiring editors visiting Bologna do well to take the opportunity to establish relationships with agents from overseas.

Publishing is both a local and a global business. As I move from appointment to appointment at Bologna, I'm looking at both—I'm looking for that special, individual title originating in one place that I think will travel and find an audience in my place. And I'm looking to see where the world at large is moving: what kinds of books will work the world over. Recently, fantasy fiction has been a tremendously buoyant international category. A few years ago, Dorling Kindersley opened a huge international market for high-quality, illustrated nonfiction with its "Eyewitness" books. What is the next "global" opportunity? Graphic novels, perhaps, with their international heritage and readership. One never knows for certain, but the likelihood is that the answer is being incubated somewhere among the stands at Bologna.

Meanwhile, a less tangible but at least as significant benefit of traveling the aisles at the fair is simply how stimulating it is. Walking from hall to hall, from territory to territory, opens a window on the world. Publishers everywhere are occupied with the common themes of childhood, but the way they are represented, the ways books are designed, the way they are marketed and sold—these things vary greatly. Seeing how publishers in other regions think and operate casts a light—sometimes flattering, sometimes not—on one's own work, and there are always ideas to be found.

Simon Boughton is the vice president and publisher of Roaring Brook Press.

Part 2

BIBLIOGRAPHY

International literature in the United States has been defined as books that were originally published for children in a country other than the United States in the language of that country and later published in the United States.[1] These books may have been translated into English or written in English, but published outside the United States. This is the third edition of a series of books sponsored by the United States Board on Books for Young People (USBBY). The first, Carl Tomlinson's *Children's Books from Other Countries* included books published between the years 1950–1996 and selected books that are defined as above. Susan Stan's second edition, *The World through Children's Books*, included the years 1996–2000 and expanded the scope to include books published in the United States and set in another country.

This third edition annotates books published in the years 2000–2004. I have again included books published in the United States and set in another country. That is because, for some countries listed here, the only books available were those written by American authors. These books are identified by the line "Author from United States." In the same way, you will find books by International authors, setting their stories in countries other than their own. In this case the author's heritage will be identified. Older titles that have been reissued have been included in this edition. I have added eight "Author Spotlights" to highlight significant authors: authors who have achieved special awards in recent years, or my personal favorites. Additionally you will find four features, written by writers who translate children's literature. It is my hope that these features, found in chapters three, five, and nine will add depth to the coverage.

Chapters in the bibliography are arranged by geographic region. For the most part, books are placed in a geographic region because they represent the national literature of that country. To the extent that it is possible, books are listed in this bibliography by the author's native country. For example, the works of Joan

21

Aiken are placed in chapter nine in the section for the United Kingdom. Occasionally, the author and illustrator are from different countries and the book is published in yet another country. In this case, the book is placed in the country in which the book was published with cross references to country. For example, the book *Cousins*—written by Elisa Amado, a Guatemalan writer and translator now living in Toronto, illustrated by Luis Garay, born in Nicaragua—is published in Canada by Groundwood. Though the book is about a family of Latino heritage, the exact setting is unknown and I have placed it in chapter four, Canada, with a reference in chapter three, Latin America. Finally, Susan Stan reminds us that "national borders are arbitrary distinctions and that it is our cultures—customs, traditions, beliefs, behaviors—that distinguish communities of people from one another."[2] An index for author, illustrator, translator, title, and subject are provided to assist in locating books.

Each entry includes author, title, and publication information, as well as the number of pages followed by the age range of the target reader in parentheses. Awards received by the book or author are noted at the end of the annotations. Initials of the annotator are in italic. As in previous editions of this book, selection for this bibliography is based on literary and artistic quality, worthy and up-to-date treatment of people and their cultures, interesting presentation of information specific to a country other then the United States, unique quality of illustrations, and appropriateness for readers aged 0–14. In some cases Young Adult literature has been included.

Whenever possible, each country concludes with a section titled "Related Information" that includes organizations, awards, websites, and print and online resources which will lead the interested reader to more information about the literature of each country.

ANNOTATORS

Carolyn Angus *(ca)*
Stone Center for Children's Books
Claremont, CA

Roslyn Beitler *(rb)*
Children's Literature Specialist
Washington, DC

Dr. Patricia L. Bloem *(plb)*
Grand Valley State University
Michigan

Kristine M. Casper *(kmc)*
Huntington Public Library
Huntington, NY

Chris Desai *(cd)*
Southern Illinois University
Carbondale, IL

Doris Joan Gebel *(djg)*
Northport-East Northport Public Library
Northport, NY

Joan Glazer *(jig)*
Professor Emerita,
Rhode Island College

Susan L. Golden *(sg)*
Appalachian State University
North Carolina

Karen K. Kabrich *(kk)*
Paradise Valley Community College
Phoenix, AZ

Abbey Nowak Kaczorowski *(ank)*
Allendale Columbia School
Rochester, NY

Helen Kay Kennedy *(hk)*
Kent District Library
Michigan

Barbara Killian *(bk)*
Webster, NY

Oksana Kraus *(ok)*
Cleveland Public Library
Cleveland, OH

Michelle Kuhonta *(mk)*
IBBY, Augsburg, Germany

Catherine LaStella *(cbl)*
Hauppauge Public Library
Hauppauge, NY

Judith V. Lechner *(jvl)*
Auburn University
Auburn, AL

Susan Link *(sl)*
Colony Bend School
Texas

JoAn Martin *(jm)*
Children's Book Reviewer
Baytown, TX

Barbara Nelson *(bn)*
Auburn University Library
Auburn, AL

Mary Lois Nicholls *(mln)*
Children's Librarian
Port Jefferson, NY

Nancy Ryan Nussbaum *(nrn)*
Goshen College
Goshen, IN

Alison O'Reilly *(aao)*
Hauppauge Public Library
Hauppauge, NY

Linda M. Pavonetti, Ed.D. *(lmp)*
Oakland University
Rochester, MI

Jennifer Smith, Ph.D. *(js)*
Northern Kentucky University
Highland Heights, KY

Susan Stan *(ss)*
Central Michigan University
Michigan

Linda Staskus *(ls)*
Cuyahoga County Public Library
Parma, OH

Maureen White *(mw)*
University of Houston–Clear Lake,
   Texas

Dr. Daniel Woolsey *(dw)*
Houghton College
Houghton, NY

NOTES

1. Tomlinson, Carl. *Children's Books from Other Countries*. Lanham, MD: Scarecrow, 1998: 4.

2. Stan, Susan. *The World through Children's Books*. Lanham, MD: Scarecrow, 2002: 41.

Chapter 3

Latin America and the Caribbean

ARGENTINA

Comino, Sandra. **The Little Blue House**. Translated by Beatriz Hausner and Susana Wald. Toronto: Groundwood Books, 2003. Originally published as *La casita azul*. ISBN 0-88899-503-2. 156 p. (11 up). Novel.

In a small Argentine village, there is an abandoned house that mysteriously turns blue once a year. Every Saturday evening, the villagers listen to a storyteller on the radio telling a story of loss and love. Cintia loves to spend time at the abandoned house. She is also the subject of her father's anger and is severely beaten. Cintia finds love and protection at her grandmother's house. When Cintia and her best friend Bruno discover who tells the stories on the radio, they become involved in solving the mystery of the little house that leads to the town being rid of its criminal element. This is an unusual story about friendship and love. *Winner of the 2001 Papa Leer el XXI Prize awarded at the Cuba IBBY Regional Congress.* ls
Author from Argentina

Lamm, C. Drew. **Gauchada**. Illustrated by Fabian Negrin. New York: Knopf, 2002. ISBN 0-375-81267-9; 0-375-91267-3. 31 p. 32 p. (6–8). Picture book.

In Argentina the expression "to make a *gauchada*" means to do something kind without expecting anything in return. In this story, a gaucho carves an old bone into a crescent moon shape, mounts it on silver, and creates a necklace. He gives the necklace to his grandmother, and page by page the necklace travels to new owners, always with love. The illustrations by Negrin are glowing, stylized paintings, and the use of specific terms in Spanish give the sense of place. Argentinean expressions are explained on the page before the story begins. *jig and bn*
Author from United States. Illustrator from Argentina.

Sagastizábal, Patricia. **A Secret for Julia**. Translated by Asa Zatz. New York: W.W. Norton & Co., 2001. Originally published in Spanish as *Un Secreto Para Julia*. ISBN 0-393-05044-0. 250 p. (14 up). Novel.

Though structured as a mystery, this is a psychological coming-of-age tale. Told from the point of view of Julia's mother, this novel examines the effects of the politically tumultuous time in Argentina when 30,000 people "disappeared." Though she survived and escaped to exile in England, the events scared her emotionally and had profound effects on her daughter, Julia. *Premio La Naci¢n prize, 2000. Author from Argentina*

Vidal, Beatiz. **Federico and the Magi's Gift: A Latin American Christmas Story**. Illustrated by Beatriz Vidal. New York: Knopf/Random House, 2004. ISBN 0-375-82518-5 (trade); 0-375-92518-X (lib. bdg.). 32 p. (4–8). Picture book.

Based on Vidal's childhood in Argentina, this picture book tells of little Federico, who worries that that his misbehavior will dissuade the Magi from leaving a gift in his shoes for Twelfth Night. After his sisters fall asleep, Federico slips into the starlit garden, gazing at the constellations until he sees the Wise Men flying through the sky on their camels. Glowing with gentle colors, the watercolor and gouache paintings portray Federico's story in an inviting way. An author's note discusses the Feast of the Three Kings, and a glossary defines Spanish words used in the text. *Kirkus Book Review Stars. cp Author/illustrator from Argentina*

Related Information

Bookfairs

Buenos Aires Book Fair–Argentina
http://www.el-libro.com.ar/

Buenos Aires International Book Fair
Buenos Aires, Argentina
http://www.el-libro.com.ar
April–May

Online Resources

Imaginaria. This is a monthly electronic journal from the Argentina Association of Children's Literature and is available in Spanish.
http://www.imaginaria.com.ar/index.htm

BELIZE

Crandell, Rachel. **Hands of the Maya: Villagers at Work and Play**. New York: Henry Holt & Co., 2002. ISBN 0-8050-6687-X. 29 p. (5–8). Picture book.

Through photographs and a simple text, the author describes life in the day of a Mayan village in Belize. Each two-page spread features a small photo illustrating the activity and a larger close-up focusing on the use of hands in that task. The book begins with a map and an explanation by the author of her contact with the village and it ends with a glossary of terms. *Children's Book Award Notable Book; Notable Social Studies Trade Books, 2003.* bn
Author from United States

BRAZIL

Ibbotson, Eva. **Journey to the River Sea**. Illustrated by Kevin Hawkes. New York: Dutton Children's books, 2001. ISBN 0-52546739-4. 298 p. (10 up). Novel.
See Europe/UK for description.

Lago, Angela. **Street Scene**. In: **The Best Children's Books in the World: A Treasury of Illustrated Stories**. Edited by Byron Preiss. New York: Harry N. Abrams, 1996. ISBN 0-8109-1246-5. 319 p. Picture book anthology.
This collection of fifteen picture books from as many countries reprints the text and illustrations and includes the story of the book *Street Scene* that wordlessly depicts a day in the life of a homeless boy trying to sell fruit in the street. Vibrant acrylic colors portray the plight of this child with sympathy. The reduced size of the pages in this anthology does not allow the reader to fully experience the impact of the book, however it is easy to understand why this book received the award for *Best Picture Book in 1994 from the Brazilian Section of IBBY* and the award for *Best Picture Book in 1994 from APCA (the Association of Critics and Journalists).* djg

Machado, Ana Maria. **Me in the Middle**. Translated by David Unger. Illustrated by Caroline Merola Buffalo. New York: Groundwood/Douglas & MacIntyre, 2002. First published as *Bisa Bia, Bisa Bel* by Salamandra Consultoria Editorial in 1990, c1982. 0-8889-9463-X; 0-8889-9467-2 (paperback) 110 p. 10 p. (8–11). Novel.
Isabel (Bea) discovers a photograph of her great-grandmother Bisa Bea. Excited at the resemblance between herself and her great-grandmother, and about the old photograph from the 1890s, Bea talks her mother into letting her take the picture to school, where she loses it. While trying to find the picture, Bea notices that Bisa Bea seems to have come alive, inside herself, and is now beginning to not only tell her what life used to be like, but to boss her around. Bea finally finds the photograph with help from her own future great-granddaughter, rounding out this multigenerational fantasy with a glimpse into the past and speculation about the future. *Hans Christian Andersen Award.* jvl
Author from Brazil

Machado, Ana Maria. **Nina Bonita**. Translated from Spanish by Elena Irrabarren. Illustrated by Rosana Faría. New York: Kane/Miller Book Publishers, 1996

(2001). Translated into English from the Spanish *Niña Bonita* by Ediciones Ekaré, 1994. Original Portuguese version was published as *Menina Bonita do laço de fita* (Pretty girl with the bright colored bow). São Paulo: Melhoramentos, 1986. ISBN 0-916291-63-4; 1-929132-11-5 (pbk.) 24 p. (4–7). Picture book.

As far as the little white rabbit was concerned, Nina Bonita, the girl next door, with her shiny, olive black eyes, her curly pitch black hair, which looked "as if made of unwoven threads of the night," and her glossy black skin, was the most beautiful girl in the world. He longed for a daughter as beautifully black as Nina Bonita. After several ineffectual trials to find out the secret of her beauty, he learns that Nina Bonita was born this way, because one of her grandmothers is just as beautifully black. The white rabbit obtains his wish when he marries a black rabbit. The illustrations show Nina Bonita's multiracial family as well as that of the white rabbit, along with lively street scenes from Brazil. *Americas Award—Commended List for 1996. Hans Christian Andersen Award, 2000.   jvl*
Author from Brazil

Lygia Bojunga-Nunes was born in Brazil. She started writing for children in 1972 and has won every major Brazilian award for children's literature as well as several International awards including the Jabuti Award (1973), the prestigious Hans Christian Andersen Award (1982), and the Rattenfänger Literaturpreis (1986). *The Companions* was her first book to appear in English in 1989 and was followed by *My Friend the Painter* in 1991. Her books have been translated into a number of languages including English, French, German, Italian, Spanish, Norwegian, Swedish, Icelandic, Bulgarian, Czech, and Hebrew. In 2004 she was awarded the second Astrid Lindgren Memorial Award. The jury's reasoning for giving the award to Bojunga:

> Lygia Bojunga (Brazil) dissolves the boundaries between fantasy and reality with all the exhilarating ease of a child at play. In her dramatic and word of mouth-style narratives the reader is always enabled to enter directly into the dreams and fantasies that her principal characters draw on for survival. In a deeply original way she fuses playfulness, poetic beauty and absurd humour with social critique, a love of freedom and a strong empathy with the vulnerable child.
> http://www.alma.se/page.php?pid=1760

*An interview with the author can be read at the Astrid Lindgren Memorial Award Website at http://www.alma.se/page.php?pid=538.

> *You can read an interview with Ana Maria Machado on The Cooperative Children's Book Center website at http://www.soemadison.wisc.edu/ccbc/authors/machado.asp.

Related Information

Organizations

IBBY Brazil IBBY Brazil
http://www.fnlij.org.br/

CARIBBEAN

Agard, John, and Grace Nichols, eds. **Under the Moon and over the Sea: A Collection of Caribbean Poems**. Illustrated by Cathie Felstead, Jane Ray, Christopher Corr, Satoshi Kitamura, and Sara Fanelli. Cambridge, MA: Candlewick, 2003. ISBN 0-7636-1861-6. 77 p. (8–12). Poetry.
   See Europe/UK for description.

Berry, James. **A Nest Full of Stars**. Illustrations by Ashley Bryan. Greenwillow, 2004. Originally published in Great Britain by Macmillan in 2002. 96 p. (8–12). Poetry.
   Sixty poems from a child's perspective are gathered under six broad headings by the Jamaican-born poet. Many reflect universal experiences but add the extra flavor and texture of Caribbean culture. Most of the poems are in standard English, while some are in the Caribbean Creole speech. Berry writes in his foreword that he loved school but was derided, which he now pours into poems about his childhood and schooling. Occasional unfamiliar British or island terms are explained at the bottom of the poems. Bryan's black-and-white illustrations, resembling woodcuts, are strongly patterned and rhythmic and much to the cultural feeling of the poems. *sg*
   Author born and raised in Jamaica, now lives in England

Keens-Douglas, Richardo. **Mama God, Papa God: A Caribbean Tale**. Illustrated by Stefan Czernecki. New York: Crocodile Books, 1999. ISBN 1-56656-307-1. 32 p. (5–8). Folktale.
   Papa God was tired of living in the dark so he created light. In the light, Papa God saw how beautiful Mama God was. He wanted to give her something beautiful. He created the world. Mama God liked the world but she thought it needed to be fixed up. Both Mama God and Papa God filled the world with people, plants, animals, water, and wind. They filled the sky with the sun, moon, and stars. A very gentle, joyous creation story supported by bold, dramatic illustrations inspired by the religion and folk art of Haiti. *ls*
   Author from Canada

McLean, Dirk. **Play Mas'! A Carnival ABC**. Illustrated by Ras Stone. Toronto: Tundra Books, 2000. ISBN 0-88776-486-X. 32 p. (8–12). Picture book.

Rather than functioning as a vehicle for learning the alphabet, *Play Mas'!* is an introduction to the riotous, raucous, days-long party that precedes Lent in some locations, and New Years in others. Endnotes explain the sometimes-elusive text on each page and list the multiple hidden words and illustrations for each letter. Stone's frenetic watercolor illustrations suggest some of the color and confusion that accompany these masquerades.
Author and illustrator from Trinidad, live in Toronto, Canada

San Souci, Robert D. **The Twins and the Bird of Darkness: A Hero Tale from the Caribbean**. Illustrated by Terry Widener. New York: Simon & Schuster, 2002. ISBN 0-689-83343-1. 40 p. (8–11). Picture book.

San Souci based his hero tale about the courageous and honorable twin, Soliday, who rescues the island's princess from the Bird of Darkness, and whose greedy brother tries to wrest his glory and bride from him, on seven Caribbean versions of the story. The lushly colored illustrations with their deep blues and greens, menacing Bird of Darkness, and a childlike innocent hero evoke the Caribbean land and seascapes. *Notable Social Studies Trade Books, 2003.   jvl*
Author from United States

CHILE

Lourie, Peter. **Tierra del Fuego: A Journey to the End of the Earth**. Honesdale, PA: Boyds Mills Press, 2002. ISBN 1-56397-973-X. 48 p. (7–10). Informational book.

This beautiful photo-essay explores this island off the southern coast of South America. Explorations by Magellan, Charles Darwin, and Joshua Slocum are described with period maps and drawings. The ecology and island life are portrayed in a appealing way in this travelogue, sure to inspire young explorers. *Best Children's Books of the Year, 2003; Bank Street College of Education; Children's Catalog, Eighteenth Edition, 2003.   djg*

Related Information

Book fairs

Feria Internacional del Libro de Santiago
Santiago, Chile
phone: 52 8328 4328
e-mail: filmty@filmty.itesm.mx
http://www.camlibro.cl/
October–November

Organizations

IBBY Chile
www.ibbychile.cl

COLOMBIA

Cameron, Sara. **Out of War: True Stories from the Front Lines of the Children's Movement for Peace in Columbia**. New York: Scholastic, 2001. A UNICEF publication to celebrate the U.N. special session on children in September 2001. ISBN 0-439-29721-4. 186 p. (12 up). Informational book.

Nine young people from Columbia relate their stories about living in a war-torn country. Each young person shares how they are personally affected by the war and violence in Columbia. They describe how family and friends have been executed, kidnapped, victims of gang violence, and many other atrocities. Each teenager also tells what inspired them to become involved in the Children's Movement for Peace in Colombia and how that decision has changed their lives. *js*
Author lives in New York

Torres, Leyla. **The Kite Festival**. New York: Farrar, Straus, Giroux, 2004. ISBN 0-374-38054-6. 32 p. (5–9). Picture book.

For their weekly Sunday drive and picnic, Fernando and his extended family travel to San Vicente. When the family arrives, they discover that the town is hosting a kite festival. Fernando and his grandfather soon discover that no one in San Vicente has a kite to sell. In order to participate in the festivities, Fernando and his family create a kite from everyday materials they have with them and win a prize for having the most original kite. The soft, pastel-like illustrations capture and reinforce the tone of this very satisfying "every child" story. *js*
Author from Colombia, lives in United States

Related Information

Organizations

IBBY Columbia
http://www.fundalectura.org.co/

CUBA

Barrios, Flor Fernandez. **Blessed by Thunder: Memoir of a Cuban Girlhood**. Seattle, WA: Seal Press, 1999. ISBN 1-58005-021-2. 244 p. (14 up). Biography.

Through the child's eye of Flor Teresa Barrios the reader witnesses the rise to power of Fidel Castro, and the events of the revolution in Cuba. Her grandparent's

farm is confiscated and her family comes under suspicion when her father applies to immigrate. At the age of 11, she is sent along with the other school children to camp to pick tobacco and sugar cane. Through the years of hardship, she gains wisdom and strength from the elder women in her family. When, at last, her family is granted permission to emigrate, she draws on this strength to cope with the sadness of separation from them.   *djg*
Author from Cuba, lives in United States

Brown, Monica. **My Name Is Celia: The Life of Celia Cruz**. **Me Llamo Celia: La Vida de Celia Cruz**. Illustrated by Rafael Lopez. Flagstaff, AZ: Rising Moon, 2004. ISBN 0-87358-872-X. unpaged. (10 up). Picture book biography.

"When we sing together our words are like smiles flying across the sky." Celia Cruz was born in Havana in 1924 but emigrated to Mexico during the Cuban revolution. During her life she surmounted racial and economic bigotry, earning for herself the title Queen of Salsa. The language of this biography reverberates with the timbre of Celia's voice and the rhythm of her band. "My voice climbs and rocks and dips and flips with the sounds of congas beating and trumpets blaring." Rafael López's vibrant, folk art illustrations infuse a sense of place and rhythm to this energetic biography.   *lmp*
Author and illustrator live in United States

Figueredo, D.H. **The Road to Santiago**. Illustrated by Pablo Torrecilla. New York: Lee & Low Books, 2002. ISBN 1-58430-059-0. unpaged. (6 up). Picture book.

War is difficult for young children to contextualize so author Figueredo relates it to something familiar: a family gathering on Christmas Eve—*Noche Buena*, 1958. The young narrator tells of his disappointment when rebels dynamite railroad tracks so that his family cannot leave Havana by train. The remainder of the book describes a torturous trip cross-island by bus and broken-down automobile that is accomplished only because the family shares their gifts and food with strangers. Set in pre-Castro Cuba, this story is based on an incident in the author's life. A glossary of Spanish words appears on the copyright page.   *lmp*
Author from Cuba, lives in the United States

Leiner, Katherine. **Mama Does the Mambo**. Illustrated by Edel Rodriguez. New York: Hyperion Books, 2001. ISBN 0-7868-0646-X. 36 p. (5–8). Picture book.

After Papa died, Mama stopped dancing. But Papa's been gone a long time now and Sofia wonders if she will ever again see her Mama's skirts swirl. Told in the voice of a young girl yearning to see her mama happy again this story is illustrated in brilliant mixed media that reflect the dance movements and energy of Havana, Cuba.   *djg*

Veciana-Suarez, Ana. **Flight to Freedom**. New York: Orchard Books, 2002. ISBN 0-43938199-1. 197 p. (10 up). Novel.

Writing in her diary, thirteen-year-old Yara Garcia begins with how her family is living in Cuba in 1967. The Castro government is becoming more oppressive and controlling. Yara's parents have applied to leave Cuba for the United States. They feel that their sojourn in the United States will be short because they are sure Castro's government will not last long. The family does leave Cuba and struggles to survive in Miami with the help of relatives. Conflicts arise in the family because of differences in cultural expectations. A heart-wrenching story in which a temporary exile turns into permanent residence. *Best Children's Books of the Year, 2003; Bank Street College; United States; Growing Up Latino in the U.S.A., 2004.   ls Author from United States*

DOMINICAN REPUBLIC

Alvarez, Julia. **Before We Were Free**. New York: Alfred A. Knopf, 2002. ISBN 0-375-81544-9. 167 p. (10 up). Novel.

Twelve-year-old Anita de la Torre relates, through narrative and her secret diary, the overthrow of Rafael Trujillo—*El Jefe*—the dictator whose power and secret police controlled the Dominican Republic until 1961. The book opens as Anita and her cousins hurriedly flee their school so her cousins can escape on a waiting airplane. Life becomes increasingly more difficult and dangerous for Anita and her family. When she discovers her father, uncle, and brother are planning to assassinate *El Jefe*, Anita elects muteness. This griping account of the early 1960s in the Dominican Republic is a novelized reminiscence of the author's own childhood and experiences. *2004 Pura Belpre Award for Author.   lmp and bn Author lives in United States*

ECUADOR

Haycak, Cara. **Red Palms**. New York: Wendy Lamb Books/Random House, 2004. ISBN 0-385-74648-2. 328 p. (14 up). Novel.

Benita is fourteen when she learns that the depression of the 1930s has bankrupted her fathers business in their city of Guayaquil, Ecuador. In an effort to start over, the family moves to a small, primitive island called Paíta. The father's arrogance and bigotry nearly bring the family to ruin. Benita, desperate to escape, agrees to marry Raúl, and goes to live with him in the jungle as is the island premarital custom. Through hardship and adversity, this young woman gains strength, compassion, and the courage to help heal the rift her father has created with the islanders. This compelling coming-of-age story with a strong cultural setting leaves the reader with much to think about.   *djg Author lives in United States and this novel is drawn from her experience working with the tribal people of Brazil.*

EL SALVADOR

Argueta, Jorge. **A Movie in My Pillow/*Una película en mi almohada***. Illustrated by Elizabeth Gómez. San Francisco: Children's Book Press, 2001. ISBN 0-89239-165-0. 32 p. (6–10). Poetry.
A young boy misses his family and remembers his life in El Salvador in this collection of poems written in English and Spanish. Papa keeps him safe from the war and comforts him with images of his rural home while they adjust to their new life in the city. Jorgito remembers it all in his dreams—the movie in his pillow. Paintings in brilliant colors and striking details fill the page with authenticity and charm. *Americas Award—Children's and Young Adult Literature Winner 2001 Picture Book.* djg

Argueta, Jorge. **Zipitio**. Pictures by Gloria Calderón. Translated by Elisa Amado. Toronto: Groundwood/Douglas & McIntyre, 2003. ISBN 0-88899-487-7. 32 p. (5–10). Picture book.
See Canada for description.

GUATEMALA

Cameron, Ann. **Colibri**. New York: Farrar, Straus and Giroux, 2003. ISBN 0-374-31519-1. 227 p. (11 up). Novel.
Tzunún Chumil, whose name means Hummingbird in her native Mayan language, and whose loving parents used her Spanish name, Colibri, as a nickname, vaguely remembers life with her parents, before she was kidnapped and began her wanderings with "Uncle." From her earliest childhood, she helped him beg in Guatemalan villages and towns, traveling across Guatemala with this unscrupulous man. Rosa performs her duties obediently until she meets Doña Celestina and learns her real name, Tzunún Chumil, her nickname, "Colibri," which means "hummingbird," and that she has a "split heart" that must be mended. By discovering her true name, Tzunún is able to break free of Uncle's abusive custody and reunite with her lost parents. Readers are introduced to the political violence that was a reality under Guatemala's military dictatorship in the 1970s and 1980s. *Booklist Starred Review. Notable Books for a Global Society, 2004; IRA; United States; Notable Children's Books, 2004.* aao and jvl
Author from United States, has been living in Guatemala for the past 20 years.

Ichikawa, Satomi. **My Pig Amarillo**. New York: Philomel Books, 2003. First published in France as *Mon Cochon Amarillo* in 2002 by l'ecole des loisirs, Paris. ISBN 0-399-23768-2. 32 p. (3–5). Picture book.
See Europe/France for description.

Mikaelsen, Ben. **Red Midnight**. New York: Harper Collins, 2002. ISBN 0-380-97745-1. 212p. (10 up). Novel.

During the 1980s, many military massacres took place in Central America; in Guatemala alone more that 450 villages were torched and tens of thousands massacred. As the only survivors from their small village, twelve-year-old Santiago and his four-year-old sister flee to their uncle's seashore home where they set sail for the United States in a tiny sailing kayak. Doggedly determined to tell the world of the atrocities they witnessed, Santiago must use every resource and every ounce of courage to stay alive. *Notable Books for a Global Society, 2003.* mln *Author from United States*

Mikaelsen, Ben. **Tree Girl**. New York: Harper Collins, 2004. ISBN 0-06-009004-9. 225 p. (12 up). Novel.

As one of the few Indio children to receive an education, fifteen-year-old Gabriella is elsewhere when her small village (or cantòn) is massacred by the military. She rescues her little sister and flees to a nearby town, only to witness the same blood bath. Called Tree Girl because of her affinity for tree-climbing, she blames herself for hiding in a tree and being left alive. She eventually finds her way to a refugee camp in Mexico where she atones for her imaginary cowardice by helping the children and the elderly survive. She is responsible for teaching her Quichè Mayan people in the camp and returns to Guatalmala as a teacher. *Author from United States and bases this novel on a true account. He has won the Western Writers of America Golden Spur Award and the International Reading Association Award.* mln

Montejo, Victor. **Popol Vuh: A Sacred Book of the Maya**. Translated by David Unger. Illustrated by Luis Garay. Toronto: Groundwood/Douglas McIntire, 1999. Originally published as *Popol vuj: libro sagrado de los Mayas* by Groundwood, 1999. ISBN 0-88899-334-X. 85 p. (11–14). Mythology.

The "Book of Power," destroyed by the Conquistadores, was recorded in 1558 from memory in Mayan. This beautifully illustrated version relates the Mayan account of creation and the establishment of world order through the exploits of the Amazing Twins, who kill the "monsters" of earlier times, such as the boastful Sipakna, the destructive creator of volcanoes. The Twins' adventures in Xix'al-b'a, the underworld, where they defeat the personified lords of diseases in a deadly ball game, is particularly exciting, while the story and illustration of the ancestor grandmother's creation of humans from cornmeal is lovely to read and view. A glossary is included. *jvl* *Author is a Mayan poet exiled from Guatemala living in United States.*

Ray, Mary Lyn. **Welcome, Brown Bird**. Illustrated by Peter Sylvada. Orlando, FL: Harcourt, 2004. ISBN 0-15-292863-4. 32 p. (4–8). Picture book.

MY EXPERIENCE TRANSLATING INTO ENGLISH
BY DAVID UNGER

This whole business of translation began for me when my parents decided in 1955 to leave Guatemala for the United States. Without warning, I was forced into a double exile, from my birthplace and from my mother tongue. Suddenly I had to navigate in English, a language as foreign to me as the flat Florida landscape of my newly adopted homeland. This happened when I was four, but for many years I operated as a double agent betraying my native and adoptive tongues with equal vigor. I was caught between two languages and two cultures, in the gap, as it were.

Translation, which I discovered in graduate school, offered me a way out of this betrayal. I could use my Spanish language skills, honed by years of spending summers in Guatemala with relatives, to bring into English works that I thought demanded to be in English. Translation also was a way to deepen my own skills as a younger poet, taking T.S. Eliot's dictum "Good poets steal, poor poets imitate" quite literally. As a translator, I found myself deconstructing poems in Spanish as if they were magical timepieces before I could begin the process of reconstruction in another language, English. When I found myself gravitating toward fiction, I felt the urge to translate novels mostly written by Mexican women writers including Bárbara Jacobs, Elena Garro and Silvia Molina.

Patsy Aldana at Groundwood Press contacted me to translate a young adult Spanish version of the *Popol Vuh*, the Sacred Book of the Mayas. It was written by Víctor Montejo, who brought impeccable credentials: himself a Jacaltec Maya with a PhD in Anthropology and a poet/fiction writer—how could I resist? All the existing versions of the *Popol Vuh* were either scholarly, repetitive, or reductive. None was accessible to the general reader. Montejo understood the importance of creating a text that was faithful, accurate, and respectful of his own ancestry and that would be a lively account to read. Since the oldest existing version of the *Popol Vuh* is itself a translation—tainted with human error and based on an oral version of a written text the Spaniards destroyed—I believe that Montejo felt he could take certain liberties regarding placement and repetition. His version is great because it is for adults and young adults as well—and it has great narrative strength.

Since then, I've translated mostly children's books and poetry. This is partly because the work is shorter, but also because translating children's literature is both challenging and rewarding—there's a freshness noticeably absent from much of the adult fiction and poetry that I have recently encountered. I have translated *Me in the Middle* by Ana María Machado and books by Silvia Molina. *Messengers of Rain and other poems from Latin America* included poetry by Humberto A'kabal. For this book, I translated only those poems to which I felt I could do justice. Naturally, I was drawn to those written by Guatemalans. . . . I think that each translator brings his/her own strengths, talents, and limitations to the translation task. Further, depending on the translator's reading, he or she may decide to stress certain images or ideas by either placement or emphasis. Though I think that the translator must feel that he or she is the only one who can translate a particular text, the reality is that there can be many good and valid versions of the same text. There is absolutely nothing better than to read the texts in their original tongue.

A certain degree of arrogance has determined which books I've chosen to translate—I almost feel as if I'm the only person capable of translating these books since only I know what the authors have done in their originals. Arrogance aside, I think it is almost proscriptive that the translator feels that the translation exists and that it is his/her duty to bring it forth into life. The translator must be willing to create in English a version that stands beside the original work—this does not mean that the translation has achieved all the complicated tonalities of the original, but that it can somehow "fool" the reader into believing that he/she is reading the work itself. As Cynthia Ozick has written: the translator "must dare to be equal master of the poem together with the poet."

Translation, for me, has been partly therapy—it has helped me to bridge the gap between my mother tongue and my adopted language in a way that makes me feel integrated and whole.

Two boys, thousands of miles apart, await the arrival of a small songbird—the thrush. In spring, the thrush wends it way north to the woodlands of New Hampshire. In fall, it hurries south to the tropical forests of Central America. Each boy wonders where the bird goes when it flies away. "Only the bird knew they were brothers" who guarded and preserved the bird's habitat. Peter Sylvada's illustrations, rendered in luxurious oils, highlight the simplicity of this spare, poetic text. *lmp* *Author and illustrator live in United States*

HAITI

Danticat, Edwidge. **Behind the Mountains**. New York: Orchard Books, 2002. ISBN 0-439-37299-2. 166 p. (12–14). Novel.

Thirteen-year-old Celiane records her thoughts about her life in Haiti in the new notebook her teacher has given her. She continues the description of her life as she and her mother and brother join her father in Brooklyn where he emigrated five years earlier. *NYPL Best Book for the Teen Age, Americas Award, Book Sense.* *bn* *Author from Haiti, lives in United States*

Youme (Landowne, Youme). **Sélavi, That Is Life: A Haitian Story of Hope**. El Paso: Cinco Puntos, 2004. ISBN 0-938317-84-9. 37 p. (5–9). Picture book.

A homeless young Haitian boy, who is called Sélavi, is befriended by a group of street children in Port-au-Prince. Together they find shelter, share food, and begin to rebuild their lives as a family. The watercolor illustrations convey both the despair and hope of the individual children and a warm sense of community. In an afterword, which includes black-and-white photographs, Youme offers background on the story that is based on the experience of homeless children in

Port-au-Prince. Writer Edwidge Danticat contributes an essay on her childhood in Port-au-Prince and provides historical context for this moving story. *ca Author from United States (Note: The author is identified as Youme on the cover; the CIP identifies the author as Landowne, Youme.)*

MEXICO

Andrews-Goebel, Nancy. **The Pot That Juan Built**. Illustrated by David Diaz. New York: Lee and Low, 2002. ISBN 1-58430-038-8. 32 p. (6–10). Biography.
    The story of Juan Quezada, renowned Mexican potter, is told in several ways in this innovative picture biography. Double page spreads have a cumulative rhyme on the pattern of "House that Jack Built" on the left and informative information about how Quezada makes his pots on the right. Diaz's brilliant, stylized, computer-generated illustrations in desert colors add beauty and excitement to the text. An afterword explains the story of his town's history and the transformation wrought by Quezada's rediscovery of the pottery-making techniques of his people. A U.S. anthropologist introduced Quezada's pottery to art collectors and encouraged him to produce even better pots and teach the craft to villagers, thus starting a community of now famous potters. This is followed by a step-by-step explanation of the craft, with small color photos. The whole package makes a fascinating story with many connections to art, geography, and history. *2002 Pura Belpre Honor Book for Illustration. Notable Books for a Global Society, 2003. djg Author from United States*

Bang, Molly. **Tiger's Fall**. New York: Henry Holt, 2001. (Paperback: New York: Yearling, 2003). ISBN 0-8050-6689-6. 110 p. (9–12). Novel.
    Eleven-year-old Lupe, who lives in a small Mexican village, falls from a tree, is paralyzed from the waist down, and tired of people's pity, loses her desire to live. After she nearly dies from an infected bedsore her father takes her to a center for disabled people where she gradually regains her health and her will to live by helping others. Told in plain, unsentimental prose, this is a somewhat purposive but nonetheless accessible and involving story. It is based on the author's visit to the PROJIMO rehabilitation near Mazatlan, Mexico, and is illustrated with occasional line drawings illustrating Lupe's experiences. *Skipping Stones Honor Awards Winner, 2002, Multicultural and International United States; Notable Social Studies Trade Books for Young People, 2002. sg Author from United States*

Bierhorst, John. **Spirit Child: A Story of the Nativity**. Translated from the Aztec by John Bierhorst. Pictures by Barbara Cooney. New York: William Morrow, 1984. ISBN 0-688-02609-5. 32 p. (5–8). Picture book.
    The story of spirit child was recited by Aztec chanters to the accompaniment of the *huehuetl*, an upright skin drum and the *teponaztli*, a two-toned log drum. It

combines elements of the Biblical account of the Christ child's birth, medieval legend, and traditional Aztec lore. Composed by the missionary Fray Bernardino de Sahagun with the assistance of Aztec poets, the story was preserved in Sahagun's *Psalmodia Christiana* (Mexico, 1583). Originally recited to music, this telling is the first English translation. Before illustrating this Aztec Nativity story, Cooney traveled to Mexico City and did research in small towns and rural settlements. *djg*

Castillo, Ana. **My Daughter, My Son, the Eagle, the Dove: An Aztec Chant/***Mi Hima, Mi Hijo, El Aguila, La Paloma: Un Canto Azteca*. Illustrated by S. Guevara. New York: Dutton, 2000. ISBN 0-525-45856-2. 48 p. (14 up).

Cohn, Diana. **Dream Carver**. Illustrated by Amy Cordova. San Francisco: Chronicle Books, 2002. ISBN 0-8118-1244-8. 32 p. (8–10). Picture book.

In a small village in Mexico's Oaxaca province, Mateo and his family carve and paint small wooden animals that they sell at fiestas. Mateo observes closely the behavior of the animals around his village. He dreams of carving large wooden animals. In time, Mateo learns to carve large animals that cause much excitement and joy at the fiesta, Day of the Dead. Mexican folk art forms the basis of the story and is reflected in the strong, bold acrylic illustrations. *Smithsonian Magazine's Notable Books for Children, 2002. ls*
Author from United States

Endredy, James. **The Journey of Tunuri and the Blue Deer: A Huichol Indian Story**. Illustrated by María Hernández de la Cruz and Casimiro de la Cruz López. Rochester, VT: Bear Cub Books, 2003. ISBN 1-59143-016-X. 32 p. (6–10). Picture book.

The magical blue deer comes to guide Tunuri through a mystical landscape meeting Father Sun, Mother Earth, Brother Wind, and Sister Water after he becomes lost in the forest. But it is Grandfather Fire who tells Tunari the significance of all he has seen on the journey and charges Tunuri to tell his human family of the importance of what he has learned. Beautiful hand drawings made from yarn applied to wood illustrate Huichol sacred symbols. An afterword describes their meaning and also includes information about the Huichol Indians and the method used to create the drawings. *djg*

Geeslin, Campbell. **Elena's Serenade**. Illustrated by Ana Juan. New York: Atheneum, 2004. ISBN 0-689-84908-7. 34 p. (5–9). Picture book.

In this fairy tale–like story set in Mexico, young Elena is determined to become a glassblower like her father, but is refused because of her gender. Dressed as a boy, she has magical adventures on her way to Monterrey where she learns to blow beautiful glass stars and birds. She returns home to a joyful reunion with her father and they work together blowing their creations. Spanish words are sprinkled through the text and there is a Spanish-English glossary. The pictures are luminous and mysterious, lush crayon and acrylics with a folk art quality that

perfectly complements the text. Geeslin's childhood memories of watching Monterrey's glassblowers transform pop bottles into exquisite vases prompted this fanciful tale. *Amelia Bloomer Project, 2005.*   sg and nrn
Author from United States

Johnston, Tony. **The Ancestors Are Singing**. Illustrated by Karen Barbour. New York: Farrar, Straus and Giroux, 2003. ISBN 0-374-30347-9. (10 up). Poetry.

Twenty-nine lively, evocative poems in various forms pay homage to Mexico's mythology, history, and present-day cultural traditions and life. Barbour's black-and-white illustrations carry out the traditional motifs of the poems but sometimes overwhelm the poems on the pages. A helpful glossary of mostly proper names is appended. This is a natural introduction or supplement to the study of Mexican culture. *Best Children's Books of the Year, 2004.*   sg
Author from United States

Johnston, Tony. **Isabel's House of Butterflies**. Illustrated by Susan Guevara. San Francisco: Sierra Club Books for Children, 2003. ISBN 0-87156-409-2. 32 p. (5–8). Picture book.

The *oyamel* tree grows outside eight-year-old Isabel's window in Michoacán, Mexico. It is the tree to which the monarch butterflies return each year. But Isabel's family is poor and it has been a cruel dry year. Like many of his neighbors, Isabel's father is forced to consider chopping down the tree to sell for firewood. *Nautilus Award Finalist 2004.*   djg
Author from United States

Joosse, Barbara. **Ghost Wings**. Illustrated by Giselle Potter. San Francisco: Chronicle Books, 2001. ISBN 0-8118-2164-1. 32 p. (5–8). Picture book.

In Mexico, a little girl and her grandmother visit the Magic Circle, a winter home of the monarch butterflies. The grandmother tells her granddaughter that the butterflies carry the souls of the old ones. When spring comes, the butterflies migrate north and the grandmother dies, leaving the little girl lost and bereft. In the fall, while celebrating the Day of the Dead, the little girl sees a monarch butterfly and she remembers how her grandmother sang, and their visits to the Magic Circle. Clever pairing of the monarch butterflies' winter home and the festival of the Day of the Dead combine to form a poignant story about life, death, and memories. The book concludes with a glossary of information about the Day of the Dead, the migration of the monarch butterflies, and a guide to using the book. *Kirkus Book Review Stars.*   ls
Author from United States and has traveled for nearly thirty years to visit her mother who lives in Mexico.

Luján, Jorge Elias. **Beyond My Hand**. Pictures by Quintana. Toronto: Groundwood, 2000. Originally published in Spanish as *Mas alla de mi brazo* by Petra Ediciones in Mexico in 2000. ISBN 0-88899-460-5. 28 p. Picture book.

See Canada for description.

Author from Argentina, lives in Mexico City, and published poetry and prose. He has won the Americas Award, the Children's Poetry Prize of ALLIJA (the Argentine Association of Children's Literature). He has also received the Premio de Poesía para Niños de ALIJA (IBBY, Argentina, 1995).
Georgina Quintana lives in Mexico City and is primarily a portraitist.

Mora, Pat. **A Library for Juana: The World of Sor Juana Inés**. Illustrated by Beatriz Vidal. New York: Knopf, 2002. ISBN 0-375-80643-I. 34 p. (5–10). Biography.

This picture book biography tells the life of the seventeenth-century Mexican poet, still considered one of the most brilliant writers in Mexico's history. The precocious young girl leaned to read at the age of three and aspired to a university education when this opportunity was denied to young women. Vidal's guache and watercolor illustrations, created in the style of illuminated manuscripts, add to the text. *Américas Award for Children's and Young Adult Literature, Commended 2002; Tomas Rivera Mexican American Children's Book Award Winner 2002 United States.* djg
Author from United States

Morales, Yuyi. **Just a Minute: A Trickster Tale and Counting Book**. San Francisco: Chronicle Books, 2003. ISBN 0811837580. Unpaged. (6–9). Picture book.

Vibrant art combines with playful dialogue in this original trickster tale of Grandma Beetle outsmarting death when he comes calling in the form of a skeleton. With a twinkle in her eye and glitter in her hair, Grandma Beetle cajoles Sr. Calavera into helping her prepare for her birthday party while counting the chores to be done in both English and Spanish. Mexican cultural motifs in bold colors and geometric shapes show the celebration of a special birthday to which Sr. Calavera is invited along with nine beautiful grandchildren. *2004 Pura Belpré Award for Illustration.* rcb

Pérez, Amada Irma. **My Diary from Here to There**. Illustrated by Maya Christina Gonzalez. San Francisco: Children's Book Press, 2002. ISBN 089239-175-8. 32 p. (7–10). Picture book.

This is a bi-lingual book, written in both Spanish and English. The author tells a fictionalized version of her family's emigration from Mexico to Los Angeles in the early 1950s. Her voice portrays the fear of an uncertain future and yearning for friends, family, and a comfortable home left behind. Maya Christina Gonzalez's double-page spreads dance with life, love, and longing. Each page explodes with the colors of the Southwest while beauty and dignity radiate from every face and detail. *2004 Pura Belpré Honor Award for Author.* lmp
Author lives in United States

Ramírez, Antonio. **Napí**. Illustrated by Domi. Toronto, Vancouver, Berkeley: Groundwood, 2004. Published simultaneously in Spanish as *Napí* by Groundwood, 2004. ISBN 0-88899-610-1. 40 p. (4–8). Picture book.
[Spanish edition: ISBN 0-88899-611-X]

Napí, a Mazatecan girl, tells of life in her village, where her family gathers in the shade of a ceiba tree to hear her grandfather's stories. In the evening, Napí dreams of becoming a heron and flying along the nearby river. Vibrant acrylic paintings express Napí's joy in her surroundings: the trees that line the river banks, the fish teeming in the river, the herons in the sky, and the ceiba tree that seems to bring her magical dreams. Domi, who is Mazateca, paints in a distinctive style featuring bold forms and brilliant colors. *cp*
Author and illustrator from Mexico

Ryan, Pam Muñoz. **Esperanza Rising**. New York: Scholastic Press, 2000. ISBN 0-439-12041-1. 262 p. (12–14). Novel.

When fourteen-year-old Esperanza and her mother, who have lived in luxury on a ranch in Mexico, lose everything at the death of her father, they have to move to southern California to work as farm laborers. She is horrified by the conditions and the work that they must do. When her mother becomes ill, Esperanza learns the value of friends. Interwoven in the story is the cultural and political situation of the Great Depression. *Americas Award; Pura Belpré Award Winner 2002; Jane Addams Children's Book Awards Winner 2001.* *bn*
Author from United States

Sobol, Richard. **Adelina's Whales**. New York: Dutton, 2003. ISBN 0-525-47110-3. 32 p. (7–9). Informational book.

Ten-year-old Adelina lives in a remote Baja, Mexico fishing village where she anticipates the winter return of the gray whales to have their calves. This full-color photo essay conveys in a human and accessible way the stories of Adelina's family and their relationship to the mammals, the visitors, and scientists who study the whales, and efforts by all to ensure that the waters of the lagoon stay clean and the whales keep coming. An end page gives basic information about gray whales, but a map would have been welcome. *Best Books for Children, 2004; Science Books & Films; Choices, 2004.* *sg*
Author from United States

Talbert, Marc. **Small Change**. New York: Dorling Kindersley, 2000. ISBN 0-7894-2531-9. 170 p. (10–14). Novel.

Vacationing with his family on a southern Mexican beach, Tom from Minnesota feels uncomfortable and suspicious of the people whose language and customs he does not understand. When an exchange of gunfire between local rebels and the military disrupts the market where he and his sister are shopping, Ignacio, a boy he does not trust, and the boy's father take the American youngsters to their mountain ranch to get them out of harm's way. The warmth of the family and their loyalty in trying to shield Tom and his sister help Tom relax and enter into the rhythms of farm life for a few days and to form a friendship with Igna-

cio. This adventurous coming-of-age story introduces Mexican rural life with vivid details. *Parent's Guide to Children's Media.*   jvl
Author from United States

Winter, Jonah. **Frida**. Illustrated by Ana Juan. New York: Arthur A. Levine Books, 2002. ISBN 0-590-20320-7. 32 p. (8 up). Biography.

   Frida Kahlo, a celebrated Mexican artist, is the subject of this picture book biography. Focus is on her childhood and youth and how she survived both polio and a serious bus accident. While recuperating from these traumas, painting became her therapy. Throughout her life, she surrounded herself with the objects of Mexican folk culture. These items often inspired her work. This influence is reflected in the colorful and active illustrations of this biography. The illustrator has included skeletons, devils, and other traditional characters that are identified with the folk art and culture of Mexico. *Notable Children's Books, 2003.*   js
Author from United States

Related Information

Bookfairs

Guadalajara Book Fair-Mexico
http://www.fil.com.mx/ingles/i_index.asp

Guadalajara International Book Fair
Guadalajara, Mexico
http://www.fil.com.mx/
November–December

Organizations

IBBY Mexico
www.ibbymexico.org.mx

PERU

Allende, Isabel. **City of Beasts**. Translated by Margaret Sayers Peden. New York: HarperCollins, 2002. Simultaneously published as *La Ciudad de las Bestias*. (Paperback: RAYO, 2003). ISBN 0-06-050917-1. 406 p. (10 up). Novel.

   When Alex's mother needs cancer treatment in another city, he is sent to stay with his brusque and eccentric grandmother, Kate, a writer for the *International Geographic*. Alex, 15, has no choice but to accompany her on her latest adventure to the Amazon to document the legendary nine-foot Yeti of the Amazon.

When Alex and Nadia, 12, daughter of their guide, are kidnapped by an invisible Stone Age tribe, they are assisted on their dangerous but life-changing quest by a shaman who takes them deep into the Amazon to the mythical "dwelling of the gods" some call El Dorado. With the help of the tribe and the Beasts, they are able to foil the attempts of those on the expedition who intend to annihilate the natives in order to exploit their lands. *kk*
Author from Peru and raised in Chile

Díaz, Katacha. **Carolina's Gift: A Story of Peru**. Illustrated by Gredna Landolt. Norwalk, CT: Soundprints/Trudy Corp., 2002. ISBN 1-5689-9696-9. 32 p. (3–7). Picture book.

Carolina lives with her family in the village of Pisac in the Andes Mountains. On this Sunday morning she hurries to the market to find a perfect birthday gift for her abuelita. Over the stone bridge and past vendors selling sweet rolls, flowers, hats, and eggs and on past the musicians playing the *quena* with its haunting sounds she goes. They continue on until at last Carolina is satisfied that she has found the perfect gift, a walking stick so she can join them at the next Sunday market. *djg*
Author raised in Peru, lives in United States. Illustrator lives in Lima, Peru, and has illustrated several books for publishers in Peru and other Latin American countries.

Silvano, Wendi. **Just One More**. Illustrated by Ricardo Gamboa. San Jose: All About Kids Publishing, 2002. ISBN 0-9700863-7-7. 32 p. (4–8). Picture book.

On a mountain road high in the Andes, a rickety bus makes its way. Hector gets on the bus and wiggles into the last seat. Although the bus is full, the bus driver still has room for just one more, despite Hector's complaint that there is no more room. Disaster strikes and the overcrowded, overloaded bus crashes into a ditch. Hector avoids being stranded on the road by asking the bus driver if there is room for just one more. A silly cumulative tale illustrated with soft, humorous, pen-and-ink and watercolor paintings. *Children's Choices, 2003*. *ls*
Author from United States

Tompert, Ann. **The Pied Piper of Peru**. Illustrated by Kestutis Kasparavicius. Honesdale, PA: Boyds Mill, 2002. ISBN 1-56397-949-7. 32 p. (5–8). Biography.

This is a picture book retelling of a legend associated with Saint Martin de Porres (1579–1639), a Peruvian lay brother associated with various miracles. An order to rid the priory of mice puts Brother Martin in a quandary. He doesn't want to harm any creature yet he doesn't want to disobey orders either. When he meets a brave little mouse, the teller of the tale, he discovers a happy solution to the problem. Detailed full-color illustrations give a sense of monastery life at the time but don't go well with the pictures of the mice that are portrayed as cute little creatures in aprons. *sg*
Author from United States

Vande Griek, Susan. **A Gift for Ampato**. Illustrated by Mary Jane Gerber. Toronto: Groundwood, 1999. ISBN 0-88899-358-7. 109 p. (9–12). Novel.

In 1995 on Nevadeo Ampato, a mountain in Peru, anthropologists discovered the mummified body of an Inca girl, called the Ice Maiden, who lived during the 15th century. Each chapter of this fictionalized account of her life begins with a passage recounting the details of the discovery followed by the story of Tinta and her friend Karwa, both weavers and "chosen ones," young girls selected by the priests to serve the gods in various capacities. The survival of their village is being threatened by smoke and ash erupting from a nearby mountain, and the villagers' many offerings have failed to appease the mountain gods. The priests choose Tinta to sacrifice as a final offering, but she does not see her death as a great honor. With Karwa's help, Tinta flees the village so that Karwa can willingly take her place on the ceremonial altar. A glossary and a list for further reading are included. *Runner-up, Groundwood Books Twentieth Anniversary First Novel for Children Contest.* kk
Author lives in New Brunswick, Canada

PUERTO RICO

Cofer, Judith Ortiz. **The Meaning of Consuelo**. New York: Farrar, Straus and Giroux, 2003. ISBN 0-374-20509-4. 186 p. (14 up). Novel.

This novel describes the life of a young girl growing up in San Juan in the 1950s. VOYA reviewer Sherry York says, "Although not written specifically for younger readers, this coming-of-age story will expand readers' awareness of Puerto Rican history and culture and will provide an opportunity to view life from a young Latina's point of view. Themes of loss, family, relationships, and culture mingle in this complex, engaging story, which mature teens will relate to and enjoy."

Silva Lee, Alfonso. *Mi isla y yo: La naturaleza de Puerto Rico*/**My Island and I: The Nature of Puerto Rico**. Illustrated by Alexis Lago. Saint Paul: Pangaea, 2002. ISBN 1-929165-06-4. 36 p. Informational book.

The beautiful island of Puerto Rico is simply described in this bilingual book, richly illustrated with watercolor paintings to portray the plant and animal life of forest and sea. The interdependence of the people and the ecology of the island are summed up in the final pages in a poetic celebration of island life: "It is marvelous to sense everything around us." *djg*
Author lives in the mountains of Puerto Rico near Ponce

Wallner, Alexandra. **Sergio and the Hurricane**. New York: Henry Holt, 2000. ISBN 0-8050-6203-3. 28 p. (5–8). Picture book.

Sergio lives in San Juan, Puerto Rico, with his mama, papa, dog Peanut, and cat Misu. He can see the wild choppy waves and knows a storm is coming in. As the adults begin to gather supplies, board up windows, bring patio furniture inside, and pick the coconuts from the tree, he knows that this is no ordinary storm. Never having experienced a hurricane, he is excited and eagerly anticipates its arrival. His parents warn Sergio that a hurricane is a serious thing, but it is only after the devastating storm hits that Sergio can appreciate this. Through his experiences readers learn about hurricanes and the effects they can have on people and communities. *Notable Social Studies Trade Books.*   djg
Author from United States

SAINT LUCIA

Orr, Katherine. **My Grandpa and the Sea**. Minneapolis: Carolrhoda, 1990. (Paperback: First Avenue, 1991). ISBN 0-87614-409-1. 32 p. (5–8). Picture book.

On the island of St. Lucia, Grandpa loves his traditional fishing life but cannot compete with bigger, more powerful new boats and worries about their effect on the fish population. Finally he comes up with the solution to farm seamoss, enabling him to be back on his beloved sea without depleting it of its creatures. This quiet story, told by his young granddaughter, is filled with reverence for Grandpa's wisdom and practicality, and the brilliant paintings in Caribbean hues make the reader appreciate the beauty of the sea and this satisfying lifestyle. *Kaleidoscope, A Multicultural Booklist for Grades K–8.*   sg
Author from United States

VENEZUELA

Maggi, María. **The Great Canoe: A Kariña Legend**. Translated by Elisa Amado. Illustrated by Gloria Calderón. Toronto: Groundwood, 1998. ISBN 0-88899-444-3. Originally published in Spanish as *La gran canoa* by Playco Editores, Venezuela. 38 p. (5–10). Picture book legend.

See Canada for description.

Uribe, Verónica. **Buzz, Buzz, Buzz**. Pictures by Gloria Calderón. Toronto: Groundwood/Douglas & McIntyre, 2001. Originally published in Spanish by Ediciones Ekaré under the title *El Mosquito Zumbador*. ISBN 0-88800-430-3. 28 p. (3–7). Picture book.

A full moon shines in the sky of a bright quiet night and Juliana and Andrés are ready for bed. But suddenly, back and forth, in and out, and round about trying to bite is—a mosquito. The children jump out of bed and try to hide, buzz, buzz,

buzz, out the window and into the jungle; who will help them? Poetic text and vibrant illustrations make this a delightful bedtime story. *djg*
Author from Chile. Colombian illustrator now lives in United States.

Related Information

Organizations

IBBY Venezuela
http://www.bancodellibro.org.ve/

LATIN AMERICA—MIXED OR UNSPECIFIED SETTINGS

Amado, Elisa. **Cousins**. Pictures by Luis Garay. Toronto: Groundwood/Douglas & McIntyre, 2003. ISBN 0-88899-459-1. 32 p. Picture book.
See Canada for description.

Argueta, Jorge. **Trees Are Hanging from the Sky**. Translated by Elisa Amando. Illustrated by Rafael Yockteng. Toronto: Groundwood Books/Douglas & McIntyre, 2003. ISBN 0-88899-509-1. 24 p. Picture book.
See Canada for description.

Delacre, Lulu. **Arroró, mi Niño: Latino Lullabies and Gentle Games**. New York: Lee & Low, 2004. ISBN 1-58430-159-7. 32 p. (0–3). Informational book.
Delacre presents fifteen comforting lullabies and games collected from Latinos in the United States, placing the original Spanish next to her free-verse translations into English. Instructions are given for the hand games, and music is included in the back for eleven of the lullabies. Her warm illustrations portray parents and their children in various loving situations. *sg*
Author from Puerto Rico, lives in United States

Hinojosa, Tish. **Cada Niño: Every Child: A Bilingual Songbook for Kids**. Illustrated by Lucia Angela Perez. Louisville, El Paso, TX: Cinco Puntos Press, 2000. ISBN 0-93817-60-1. 56 p. (4–10). Song Book.
A bilingual mixture of folk and art songs arranged or created by Tish Hinojosa, who wrote the lyrics to most of the songs. The songs include "Cada Niño," a paean to children, who deserve a hopeful, peaceful world. Other songs are a musical memorial to Hinojosa's Mexican grandmother, a humorous song about vegetables having a wild party, and a song Hinojosa wrote to help her children learn and practice Spanish. The bold flat colored illustrations depict the subject of each song giving culturally specific details where appropriate, as in the Mexican home setting accompanying the song about Grandmother. Folkloric images of birds, the

sun, and dancing skeletons accompany other songs. Musical scores and an index of chords for guitar accompaniment are included. Hinojosa's lively renditions can also be heard on a CD by the same title.   *jvl*
Author/performer from United States

Kirwan, Anna. **Lady of Palenque: Flower of Bacal**. New York: Scholastic, 2004. ISBN 0-439-40971-3. 187 p. (9–12). Novel.
    Set in Mesoamerican in 749 A.D., this fictional diary written by ShahnaK'in Yaxchel, 13, an actual princess from the Kingdom of Bacal, records the five months during which she is chosen to marry King Fire Keeper, 33, of Xukpi, and completes her arduous and dangerous journey to his kingdom located in what we know as Honduras. The author's "Historical Notes" discusses the development of the Mayan Empire and includes a map of the Mayan world during the classical period. Photographs of archeological finds and a glossary of Mayan words are appended. This book is one of sixteen in The Royal Diaries series.   *kk*
Author from United States

Lee, Claudia M., ed. **Messengers of Rain and Other Poems from Latin America**. Pictures by Rafael Yockteng. Translations by Andrew C. Leone, Sue Oringel, David Unger, and Beatriz Zeller. Toronto: Groundwood, 2002. ISBN 0-88899-470-2. 80 p. Poetry.
    See Canada for description.

Luján, Jorge Elias. **Beyond My Hand**. Pictures by Quintana. Toronto: Groundwood, 2000. Originally published in Spanish as *Mas alla de mi brazo* by Petra Ediciones in Mexico in 2000. ISBN 0-88899-460-5. 28 p. Picture book.
    See Canada for description.

Luján, Jorge Elias. **Rooster Gallo**. Pictures by Manuel Monroy. Translation by Elisa Amado. Toronto: Groundwood/Douglas & McIntyre, 2004. ISBN 0-88899-558-X. 24 p. (4–7). Picture book.
    See Canada for description.

Orozco, José-Luis. **Fiestas: A Year of Latin American Songs of Celebration**. Selected and translated by José-Luis Orozco. Illustrated by Elisa Kleven. New York: Dutton, 2002. ISBN 0-525-45937-5. 48 p. (4–10). Song book.
    Twenty-one traditional songs with lyrics adapted by Orozco for specific occasions are included, starting with three songs for January. The music is simple and easy to sing with guitar accompaniments (chords are given). The lyrics are in both Spanish and English. Celebratory songs include traditional Christmas, Valentine's Day, Cinco de Mayo, and Day of the Dead songs. While sources are not identified, the introductions to the songs give clues as to their origins, and describe the contexts in which the songs are sung, as well as some of the customs associated

with the occasion. The vibrant illustrations fill in the gap about specific cultures, providing delightful details. An example is the picture for the Day of the Dead celebration, where children and adults in colorful clothes are shown bringing flowers to the ancestors' tombs, setting up altars, and placing colorful candies on a tomb stone. *jvl*
Author from Mexico, lives San Francisco, California

Related Information

Awards

Norma-Fundalectura Latin American Children's Literature Award
Established in 1996 to promote better books for children and young people in Latin America, this award is given to an unpublished work that has not already received another prize and is open to any author who is a citizen of a Latin American country. It carries a cash prize of US $10,000 and ensures publication by Grupo Editorial Norma.

Pura Belpré Award
The Pura Belpré Award, established in 1996, is presented to a Latino/Latina writer and illustrator in the United States whose work best portrays, affirms, and celebrates the Latino cultural experience in an outstanding work of literature for children and youth.

Américas Award for Children's and Young Adult Literature
Sponsored by the National Consortium of Latin American Studies Programs, this award is given in recognition of U.S. works of fiction, poetry, folklore, or nonfiction published in the previous year in English or Spanish that authentically and engagingly portray Latin America, the Caribbean, or Latinos in the United States.

Online Resources

Barahona Center for the Study of Books in Spanish for Children & Adolescents
This academic center at California State University San Marcos promotes literacy in English and Spanish. The center endeavors to inform current and future educational decision-makers about books centered around Latino people and culture and about books in Spanish and their value in education of English-speaking and Spanish-speaking children and adolescents. The website includes two searchable catalogs entitled "Recommended Books in Spanish" and "Recommended Books in English about Latinos."
http://www.csusm.edu/csb/

La Biblioteca de Catalunya, Barcelona
This institution maintains a significant collection of children's literature in Catalan.
http://www.gencat.net/bc/

Passport: South America
http://passport.imaginarylands.org/continents/southamerica.html

Organizations

Banco del Libra
The *Banco del Libro (Book Bank)* is a private Venezuelan non-profit, Civil Association dedicated to investigating, experimenting, innovating and imparting activities dedicated to children and young people for the promotion of reading habits. To this end, the *Banco del Libro* studies, evaluates, recommends, and distributes books and other reading material in Spanish, destined to children and young people. Furthermore, it compiles and disseminates useful information on reading and books for the formation of adult promoters of reading habits, such as parents, teachers, librarians, specialists, editors, book keepers, and others. The goal is to guide parents, teachers, and library personnel in the different ways of creating good reading habits in the homes, schools, and libraries.
http://www.bancodellibro.org.ve/AA0/DETRAS/institucional/institucional.htmo

Print Resources

Schon, Isabel. **The Best of the Latino Heritage: A Guide to the Best Juvenile Books about Latino People and Cultures**. Lanham, MD: Scarecrow Press, 1997. ISBN 0-8108-3221-6.
This book, designed to help teachers and librarians identify books that will provide children and young adults with an understanding of the cultures of Latino people features books from Central and South America, Mexico, Spain, Puerto Rico, and Latin-heritage people in the United States. Schon's criteria for inclusion: overall presentation of the material, the quality of the art and writing, and the appeal to children. Books are listed by country and include complete bibliographic information as well as a summary of content and critical annotations.

Publishers

Arte Público Press
This is the nation's largest and most established publisher of contemporary and recovered literature by U.S. Hispanic authors. Its imprint for children and young adults, Piñata Books, is dedicated to the realistic and authentic portrayal of the themes, languages, characters, and customs of Hispanic culture in the United States.
http://www.arte.uh.edu/

Ediciones Ekaré

This small, independent Latin American Publisher has been publishing children's books for 25 years. Today there are more than 150 titles in their catalogue and their mission is to produce meaningful books, books that children and adults can read with interest, books that will stay in their memories and their hearts. http://www.ekare.com/English/index.cfm

Chapter 4

Canada and the Far North

Barton, Bob. **The Bear Says North: Tales from Northern Lands**. Illustrated by Jirina Marton. Toronto: Groundwood, 2003. ISBN 0-88899-533-4. 71 p. (7–10). Folktales.

This collection of tales grows out of storyteller Barton's fascination with the high Arctic. Images of the harshness, stillness, and silence from northern hemisphere countries that border on the frozen tundra, snowy mountains, and ice fields fill the pages of this collection. Meticulously researched and distilled as only a practiced storyteller can, these stories capture the beauty, mystery, the extraordinary, the funny, and the serious of the places from which they come.   *djg*

Edwardson, Debby Dahl. **Whale Snow**. Illustrated by Annie Patterson. Watertown, MA: Talewinds/Charlesbridge, 2003. ISBN 1-57091-393-5. 32 p. (4–8). Picture Book.

Amiqqaq is at home with grandma frying donuts and waiting for the whale crew to return. When Papa comes in through the door with a flurry of fat snow and the whaling flag, he knows that the hunters have been successful. Permitted to return with his father to the whale camp, they race on the skidoo onto the frozen ocean, out into the strong wind to do the hard work ahead of them. The Inupiat belief that the whales choose to give themselves to worthy whaling crews that have emulated the spirit-of-the-whale is conveyed in this respectful picture book, illustrated with water color paintings.   *djg*

Hesse, Karen. **Aleutian Sparrow**. Illustrations by Evon Zerbetz. New York: Margaret K. McElderry Books, 2003. ISBN 0-689-86189-3. 156 p. Novel.

Seven months after attacking Pearl Harbor, the Japanese navy invaded Alaska's Aleutian Islands. Within days, the entire Aleut population was evacuated to relo-

cation centers in the forests of Alaska's southeast. "Your work is to know the ways of our people" an elder tells the young girl whose first person narration chronicles the events through the spare, chilling prose. This story of the struggle to survive and keep community and heritage intact despite harsh conditions will inspire young readers.   *djg*
Author from United States

Love, Ann, and Jane Drake. **The Kids Book of the Far North**. Illustrated by Jocelyne Bouchard. Toronto: Kids Can Press, 2000. ISBN 1-55074-563-8. 48 p. (8–12). Informational book.

This book about the eight countries that share the top of the world gives information about the arctic environment, plant and animal life, the ancient peoples who lived there, and the everyday life of the Nenet herders, Inuit hunters, and Inupiat whalers, who still live in the frozen north. This accessible book, illustrated in watercolor includes a table of contents and index. *The Norma Fleck Award for Canadian Children's Non-Fiction Honour Book 2001 Canada; Society of School Librarians International Book Awards.*   *djg*

Sullivan, Paul. **Maata's Journal**. New York: Atheneum Books for Young Readers, an imprint of Simon & Schuster, 2003. ISBN 0-689-83463-2. 221 p. (11 up). Novel.

Maata's family were nomadic Inuit people, whom the Canadian government forcibly relocated to a settlement camp at Foster's Bay. Most of the family did not fare well in their new surroundings: violence and alcohol stripped away the honor and principles of the tundra. Through a series of flashbacks, Maata records the events that have shaped her life. Tragedy and death, kindness and respect, sadness and joy quietly emerge through journal entries that also question the religious, educational, and governmental policies that stripped the arctic tribes of their identities during the early twentieth century.   *lmp*
Author lives in United States

Wallace, Mary. **Make Your Own Inuksuk**. Toronto: Owl Books, 2001. ISBN 1-894379-09-8. 32 p. (7–10). Informational book.

In a straightforward way the reader learns that an Inuksuk is a stone structure resembling a human, built by the Inuit to act as signposts or to leave messages. Concise chapters include information on how to put together an Inuksuk, adhesives to use, and how to prepare and balance stones. The young reader learns that an Inuksuk can be built as a symbol of respect and that it embodies the spirit of strength. Clearly illustrated with color photographs of original structures and "how-to" instructions, this is a useful book to share a part of Inuit tradition.   *djg*
Author lives in Canada

CANADA

Aker, Don. **The First Stone**. Toronto: HarperCollins Canada, 2003. ISBN 0-00-639285-7. 224 p. (13–17). Novel.

Unable to cope with his grandmother's death, Reef throws a stone at a girl's oncoming car with life-changing results. Aker tackles the issue of violence in a gritty, yet sensitive way. *Our Choice 2004 starred selection; 2004 Ann Connor Brimer Award; 2004 White Pine Award.* Our Choice*
Author lives in Nova Scotia, Canada

Aldana, Patsy, ed. **Under the Spell of the Moon: Art for Children from the World's Great Illustrators**. With a foreword by Katherine Paterson. Toronto: Groundwood/Douglas & McIntyre, 2004. ISBN 0-88899-559-8. 80 p. (7–12). Illustrated book.

Thirty-three of the world's greatest picture book illustrators have donated a piece of their artwork based on a text of their choice drawn from their childhood and culture. The texts, whether poem, nursery rhyme, song, piece of prose, riddle, or street game were written in each artist's own language and rendered into English by Canadian poet and editor Stan Dragland. Many of the artists selected for this work are winners of the Hans Christian Andersen Award. The Biennial of Illustrations Bratislava (BIB) and the NOMA Concours for Picture Book Illustrations of the Asia/Pacific Cultural Centre for UNESCO (ACCU) helped to identify others. An introduction by Patsy Aldana and a foreword by Katherine Paterson set the stage for this beautiful read-aloud art book. 15% of book sales will be donated to IBBY. *Notable Children's Books, 2005.   djg*

Amado, Elisa. **Cousins**. Pictures by Luis Garay. Toronto: Groundwood, 2004. ISBN 0-88899-459-1. 32 p. (5–8). Picture book.

A little girl comes to understand she is fortunate to live between the two worlds of her grandmothers in this moving story. She has a privileged life with her North American maternal grandmother and her Latin American father, but visits her paternal grandmother's Catholic household several times a week. Her cousin and best friend live with this grandmother and she is intrigued by the Catholic traditions but becomes jealous of her cousin's forthcoming first communion. Wrestling with her emotions, she steals her grandmother's beautiful rosary. Compassionate adults help her understand that she is a very lucky child to enjoy two such wonderful worlds.   *djg*
Author is a Guatemalan writer and translator now living in Toronto.
Illustrator from Nicaragua.

Andrews, Jan. **Out of the Everywhere: Tales for a New World**. Illustrated by Simon Ng. Toronto: Groundwood, 2001. ISBN 0-88899-402-8. 95 p. (8–12). Folktales.

Ten stories retold from around the world are set in Canada, but told within the context of the heritage communities from which they have been derived. The stories from Finland, Greece, Chile, Zimbabwe, Russia, India, and Vietnam seek to answer the question "Where do I come from?" Beautiful paintings illustrate each story and careful source notes are appended. *Our Choice starred selection.* *djg*

Argueta, Jorge. **Trees Are Hanging from the Sky**. Translated by Elisa Amado. Illustrated by Rafael Yockteng. Toronto: Groundwood Books, 2003. ISBN 0-88899-509-1. 24 p. (4–8). Picture book.

A little boy with a fanciful imagination dreams of trees hanging from the sky with snake-like roots dangling down over him. Pink branches become whooshing rivers, and fish leaves play among the branches. Mother warns him that eating before bedtime will give him nightmares, but the lure of the beautiful dream country is powerful. Playful, magic-realistic watercolor illustrations accompany this bedtime poem. *djg*
Author from El Salvador, has been named poet laureate of San Francisco's libraries. He won the Americas Award in 2001.
Illustrator was named winner of the Utopia competition for illustrators held in conjunction with the IBBY Congress in Colombia and lives in Cuba.

Argueta, Jorge. **Zipitio**. Pictures by Gloria Calderón. Translated by Elisa Amado. Toronto: Groundwood, 2003. ISBN 0-88899-487-7. 32 p. (5 up). Picture book.

Rufina Pérez is a young Pipil/Nuhua girl of El Salvador. Her mother tells her about El Zipitio who appears to all girls as they mature into young women. Older than rocks, he is only as tall as a child, he wears a tall black hat, and his feet point backwards. He hides on the banks of the river, afraid to show himself because of his ugliness. But Rufina's mother tells her not to be afraid and what to do when he appears. *djg*
Author is a gifted poet and teacher who was born in El Salvador and now lives in San Francisco. He won the Américas Award for Children's Literature in 2001. Illustrator from Colombia, lives in Boston.

Armstrong, Luanne. **Jeannie and the Gentle Giants**.Vancouver: Ronsdale Press, 2002. ISBN 0-921870-91-4. 150 p. (8–12). Novel.

When Jeannie is placed with foster parents, she develops a friendship with two giant workhorses and gains inner strength. A memorable novel of pain, growth, and fulfillment. *Our Choice 2003 starred selection; Sheila A. Egoff shortlist, 2003.* Our Choice*
Author lives in British Columbia, Canada

Attema, Martha. **Hero**. Victoria, BC: Orca Book Publishers, 2004. ISBN 1-55143-251-X. 130 p. (7–10). Novel.

As World War II draws to a close, eight-year-old Izaak must leave his mother and their hiding place in Amsterdam to assume a new identity on a farm in the northern part of the Netherlands. The farm family is kind, but the Jewish boy is sad and lonely until he gets to know Hero, a beautiful black stallion. Izaak shows resourcefulness and courage in hiding Hero from the Nazis who come to appropriate the horse for their escape from the advancing Allied troops. The story is based on the actual experiences of her great uncle. *Author from the Netherlands, lives in Canada*

Bailey, Linda. **Adventures with the Vikings**. Illustrated by Bill Slavin. Toronto: Kids Can Press, 2001. ISBN 1-55074-544-1. 48 p. (8–12). Informational book.

The Binkertons are stowaways on the Viking ship. Then a fearsome warrior drags Josh along on a Viking raid, and Emma makes a blunder that turns the sibling into slaves. Also by the same author and illustrator: *Adventures in Ancient Egypt, Adventures in the Middle Ages*, and *Adventures in the Ice Age. Our Choice 2002 starred selection; 2003 Hackmatack Children's Choice Award (Non-Fiction category).* Our Choice* *Author lives in British Columbia, Canada. Illustrator lives in Ontario, Canada.*

Bailey, Linda. **The Best Figure Skater in the Whole Wide World**. Illustrated by Alan and Lea Daniel. Toronto: Kids Can Press, 2001. ISBN 1-55074-879-3. 32 p. (4–9). Picture book.

Lizzy wants to be the best skater in the world, but skating isn't as easy as it looks! Then Lizzy uses her imagination and discovers her own way to shine. *Our Choice 2002 starred selection.* Our Choice* *Author lives in British Columbia, Canada. Illustrators live in Ontario, Canada.*

Bailey, Linda. **Stanley's Party**. Illustrated by Bill Slavin. Toronto: Kids Can Press, 2003. ISBN 1-5533-7382-0. (3–8). Picture book.

Stanley has a wonderful time when his owners go out, but soon realizes that the company of his friends makes it more fun. Humorous illustrations will delight dog-lovers of all ages. *Our Choice 2004 starred selection; 2004 Blue Spruce Award; 2004 Tiny Torgi Literary Awards (Print Braille category); Christie Harris Illustrated Children's Literature Prize; 2004 Amelia Frances Howard-Gibbon Award.* Our Choice* *Author lives in British Columbia, Canada. Illustrator lives in Ontario, Canada.*

Bannatyne-Cugnet, Jo. **Heartland: A Prairie Sampler**. Illustrated by Yvette Moore. Toronto: Tundra Books, 2002. ISBN 0-88776-567-X. 40 p. (12 up). Informational book.

Like a quilt, the prairie is composed of many separate elements to create a whole. It is a special environment where the climate and geography mold the inhabitants' lives. The flat expanses are ideal for farming and mining. The variable

temperate climate exhibits extremes with blizzards and tornadoes. People have migrated to the prairie from all over the world and have learned to live together on this vast expanse of grass. Beautiful realistic illustrations extol the beauty of the "big sky" country. *ls*
Author from Canada

Baskwill, Jane. **Touch the Earth**. Peter Fiore. New York: Mondo Publishing, 1999. ISBN 1-57255-428-2 (paper). 32 p. (2–7). Picture book.

Vivid, fluid illustrations accompany patterned language that invites all readers to observe their natural habitat and care for the created world. Yes, the Earth touches you in many ways. How might you touch the Earth? Elegantly written, superbly illustrated and crafted for children to join the litany. A bibliography of resource books for readers interested in nature activities is included on the last page. Baskwill is a former teacher and principal who currently teaches in the education department at Mount Saint Vincent University. She enjoys watching foxes steal pears from her backyard. *nrn*
Author lives near Halifax, Nova Scotia

Batten, Jack. **The Man Who Ran Faster Than Everyone: The Story of Tom Longboat**. Toronto: Tundra Books, 2002. ISBN 0-88776-507-6. 112 p. (12 up). Informational book.

Read how this Six Nations member became one of the world's best runners. Photos compliment his story of triumph over hardship, and his legacy continues to inspire. *Our Choice 2003 starred selection; 2002 Norma Fleck Award for Canadian Children's Non-Fiction.* Our Choice*

Bedard, Michael. **The Wolf of Gubbio**. Illustrated by Murray Kimber. Markham, ON: Fitzhenry & Whiteside, 2000. ISBN 0-7737-3250-0. 24 p. (4–9). Picture book.

A giant wolf threatens the safety of the townsfolk until a miracle man—said to understand animal language—offers the beast a deal. Based on a legend about St. Francis of Assisi. *Our Choice 2001 starred selection.* Our Choice*
Author lives in Ontario, Canada

Bell, William. **Alma**. Toronto: Doubleday Canada, 2003. ISBN 0-385-66008-1. 148 p. (8–14). Novel.

When Alma becomes friends with a reclusive old woman, she is determined to know why the woman is so secretive, but unprepared for what she discovers. *Our Choice 2004 starred selection.* Our Choice*
Author lives in Ontario, Canada

Blair, Marjorie. **Jasper's Day**. Illustrated by Janet Wilson. Toronto: Kids Can Press, 2002. ISBN 1-55074-957-9. 32 p. (5 up). Picture book.

Gentle pastels capture the love shared by a boy and his dog. This sensitive story speaks of acceptance, remembrance, and the importance of cherishing life's every moment. *Our Choice 2003 starred selection; 2003 Amelia Frances Howard-Gibbon shortlist.* Our Choice*
Illustrator lives in Ontario, Canada

Bonder, Dianna. **Accidental Alphabet**. North Vancouver: Whitecap Books, 2002. ISBN 1-55285-394-2. 32 p. (4–6). Picture book.
People and beasts stumble and bumble along in alphabetical order through various incredible and amusing mishaps. Ants steal an apple pie. Dilly dances until he falls down and breaks his toe. Peggy makes pizza with purple cheese. The nonsense verse is supported by colorful caricature-like illustrations, which contain hidden letters. An enjoyable romp through the alphabet. *ls*
Author from Canada

Boraks-Nemetz, Lillian, and Irene N. Watts. **Tapestry of Hope: Holocaust Writing for Young People**. Toronto: Tundra Books, 2003. ISBN 0-88776-638-2. 256 p. (11 up). Novel.
These firsthand accounts are written by survivors and include poetry, drama, and selections from novels and short stories about the Holocaust. The contributors include Mordecai Richler and Leonard Cohen. *Our Choice 2004 starred selection.* Our Choice*
Authors from Canada

Bouchard, David. **Buddha in the Garden**. Illustrated by Zhong-Yang Huang. Vancouver: Raincoast Books, 2001. ISBN 1-55192-452-8. 32 p. (10 up). Legends.
In this retelling of an ancient legend, a boy left at the gates of a Buddhist temple is adopted by monks and discovers the meaning of enlightenment. *Our Choice 2002 selection.* Our Choice*
Author lives in British Columbia, Canada. Illustrator lives in Canada.

Bouchard, David. **The Song within My Heart**. Illustrated by Allen Sapp. Vancouver: Raincoast Books, 2002. ISBN 1-55192-559-1. 32 p. (4–9). Picture book.
Author Bouchard gives words to Allen Sapp's memories of the preparations for his first childhood pow-wow. The text, in rhythmic and simple poetry, and the full-color paintings, celebrate Sapp's Cree heritage. His grandmother helps him to understand all that he hears and sees, and the concluding note provides rich and helpful context. *2003 Governor General's Literary Award (English, Illustration).* *plb*

Bourgeois, Paulette. **Oma's Quilt**. Illustrated by Stephane Jorisch. Toronto: Kids Can Press, 2001. ISBN 1-550774-777-0. 30 p. (10 and up). Novel.

Emily's Oma must move into a retirement home. Although the retirement home is lovely, Oma complains about the food, the residents, and the flowers. One day when Emily and her mother are sorting through Oma's boxes, Emily suggests that they make a quilt for Oma—a memory quilt. The quilt is completed and presented to Oma who is delighted and begins to tell stories, of which each piece of fabric reminds her. Oma has grown accustomed to the retirement home where she makes strudel on the cook's day off. This is a touching story about the difficulties of aging and accepting change. *Ruth and Sylvia Schwartz Children's Book Award.   ls Author from Canada*

Bowers, Vivien. **Wow Canada! Exploring This Land from Coast to Coast to Coast**. Illustrated by Dan Hobbs and Dianne Eastman. Toronto: Owl Books/ Greer de Pencier, 1999. ISBN 1-895688-93-0. 160 p. (8–12). Informational book.

The whole family is going on a trip across Canada, province by province in the travelogue scrapbook. The trip begins in British Columbia and continues east. Illustrated in collage fashion with a combination of photos, slides, postcards, maps, and hand-drawings, this family adventure introduces the young reader to the major sites, wildlife, and points of interest in each province. Sure to encourage a vacation in Canada. *Sheila A. Egoff shortlist, 2001. B.C. Book Prize.   djg*

Bradford, Karleen. **You Can't Rush a Cat**. Illustrated by Leslie Elizabeth Watts. Victoria: Orca Book Publishers, 2003. ISBN 1-55143-247-1. 32 p. (4–8). Picture book.

Jessica's grandfather lives alone until one day a kitty appears. Patiently Jessica woos her in, and eventually, Granddaddy has a new friend. The egg tempera art is a purr-fect match. *Our Choice 2004 selection.* Our Choice*
Author lives in Ontario, Canada. Illustrator lives in Ontario, Canada.

Brooks, Martha. **True Confessions of a Heartless Girl**. New York: Farrar Straus Giroux, 2003. ISBN 0-374-37806-1. 181 p. (14 up). Novel.

During a thunderstorm, seventeen-year-old Noreen rolls into the small prairie town of Pembina Lake. Alone and friendless, Noreen's tough attitude serves to protect her from being hurt. The town's inhabitants take Noreen in and give her opportunities to come to terms with her life. Even when it seems hopeless, they do not give up on Noreen who finds she does have a heart. *Governor General's Literary Award.   ls Author from Canada*

Butcher, Kirstin. **The Gramma War**. Victoria: Orca Book Publishers, 2001. ISBN 1-55143-183-1. 168 p. (9–12). Novel.

Annie learns hard lessons about family ties when her grandma moves in and takes over! A funny, fast-paced story that embraces the family experience, with

all its blemishes. *Our Choice 2002 selection; 2002 CLA Book of the Year short-list*. Our Choice*
Author lives in British Columbia, Canada

Butler, Geoff. **Ode to Newfoundland**. Lyrics by Sir Cavendish Boyle. Toronto and Plattsburgh, NY: Tundra Books, 2003. ISBN 0-88776-631-5. 32 p. (4–8). Informational book.

The official anthem of Newfoundland and Labrador, Canada is introduced and illustrated with glorious full color paintings by Butler, based on his memories of growing up in this maritime province. Each verse, held up by two puffins, is illustrated by scenes exemplifying the hardy way of life and history of the people, so intimately bound to the sea. A two-page spread at the end explains the meaning of the pictures, and the final page gives all the words and music to the Ode.   *sh*
Author lives in Canada

Bynum, Eboni, and Roland Jackson. **Jamari's Drum**. Pictures on Glazed tiles by Baba Wagué Diakité. Toronto: Groundwood/Douglas & McIntyre, 2004. ISBN 0-88800-531-8. 32 p. (5–8). Picture book.

When the faithful drummer Baba becomes too old to carry on the tradition of playing the djembe drum everyday in the village, he passes on the tradition to young Jamari. Soon Jamari gets caught up in the new ways and forgets important traditions. But when the earth begins to shake and the volcano erupts, Jamair remembers what the elder taught him and bravely stands by his village in a time of need. This contemporary fable is co-written by a master drummer and an award-winning Malian illustrator to present a picture of village life and the importance of the great drumming traditions of Africa.   *djg*

Carter, Ann. **Under a Prairie Sky**. Illustrated by Alan and Lea Daniel. Victoria: Orca Book Publishers, 2002. ISBN 1-55143-226-9. 30 p. (6–10). Picture book.

As a storm looms in the prairie sky, a boy rides out to find his wayward younger brother. The courageous story of one boy's exciting rescue adventure. *Our Choice 2003 starred selection; 2002 Mr. Christie's Book Awards (7 years and younger category); 2003 Amelia Frances Howard-Gibbon shortlist*. Our Choice*
Author and illustrators live in Ontario, Canada

Casselman, Grace. **A Hole in the Hedge**. Toronto: Napoleon Publishing, 2003. ISBN 0-929141-99-7. 215 p. (11–14). Novel.

Kaitlin learns to accept her mother's death and her father's new family, while engaging in a bitter rivalry with the boy next door. This is Casselman's first book for young adults. *Our Choice 2004 selection, 2004 Book of the Year shortlist*. Our Choice*
Author from Canada

Chan, Arlene. **Awakening the Dragon: The Dragon Boat Festival**. Illustrated by Song Nan Zhang. Toronto: Tundra Books, 2004. ISBN 0-88776-656-0. 26 p. (5–10). Informational book.

This book is full of information about the Dragon Boat Festival's origins, customs, and the races themselves. Dragon boats raced in an annual rainmaking festival at the beginning of the summer, but it was not until the Han dynasty that it became connected to one of China's famous poets, Qu Yuan. Ancient customs associated with feeding the dragon, Zhong Kui, the demon slayer, are explained. Details about modern dragon boats and contemporary races are described. Beautifully detailed illustrations make this an attractive and useful book.   *djg*
Illustrator from Shanghai, studies at the Beijing Central Institute of Fine Arts, and has won Mr. Christie's Award for A Little Tiger in the Chinese Night *as well as* Five Heavenly Emperors, The Children of China Cowboy on the Steppes, *and* A Time of Golden Dragons.

Clark, Joan. **The Word for Home**. Toronto: Penguin Books, 2003. ISBN 0-670-91121-6. 224 p. (10–13). Novel.

Sadie tries to provide her sister with love, but it's not easy. A moving story, set in pre-Confederation Newfoundland, of one girl's quest to save her family—and to find a home. *Our Choice 2003 starred selection; 2003 Winterset Award; 2003 Geoffrey Bilson Award for Historical Fiction for Young People, Geoffrey Bilson Award for Historical Fiction for Young Readers; 2003 CLA Book of the Year shortlist.* Our Choice*
Author lives in Newfoundland, Canada

Coulman, Valerie. **When Pigs Fly**. Illustrated by Rogé. Montreal: Lobster Press, 2002. ISBN 1-894222-36-9. 32 p. (4–8). Picture book.

Can cows ride bicycles? Can pigs fly? In this story, anything can happen! Readers will delight in the adventures of a young cow who will try about anything for a new bike. *Our Choice 2003 selection; 2002 Blue Spruce Award.* Our Choice*

Cowling, Douglas. **Hallelujah Handel**. Illustrated by Jason Walker. Markham, ON: Scholastic Canada, 2002. ISBN 0-7791-1391-8. 44 p. (8 up). Novel.

The composer and his famous Messiah are brought to life for children. This story follows in the footsteps of *Beethoven Lives Upstairs* and *Tchaikovsky Discovers America. Our Choice 2003 selection; 2003 Amelia Frances Howard-Gibbon shortlist.* Our Choice*
Author and illustrator from Canada

Cumyn, Alan. **After Sylvia**. Toronto: Groundwood, 2004. ISBN 0-88899-612-8. 200 p. (8–12). Novel.

Owen Skye and his two brothers live in a small rural town with their parents and bachelor uncle. The Skye brothers have a knack for turning simple, everyday events into adventures. In the sequel to *The Secret Life of Owen Skye*, his first love moves away, he runs for class president, and learns a few new skills.   *djg*
Author from Canada

Cumyn, Alan. **The Secret Life of Owen Skye**. Toronto: Groundwood Books, 2002. ISBN 0-88899-506-7. 176 p. (10–13). Novel.

Owen and his brothers turn every innocent plan into full-scale mischief! A quirky story about a boy's adventures growing up in a small town, by the acclaimed adult author. *Our Choice 2003 selection; 2002 Mr. Christie's Book Award (8–11 years category); 2004 Hackmatack Children's Choice Award.* Our Choice*
Author from Canada

Czernecki, Stefan. **Buddha under the Bodhi Tree**. Illustrated by author. Calgary, Canada: Bayeaux Arts, Inc., 1998. ISBN 1-896209-15-7 (cloth); 1-896209-19-X (paper). 32 pp. (4–12). Picture book.

After four signs of a wise man's prophecy are revealed, the king's son begins his journey to find happiness. Stefan Czernecki chronicles the life of Buddha with insight, sensitivity, and beauty. The text instructs, while the illustrations illuminate. Czernecki delicately weaves Buddhist symbols into each illustration. Even the end pages and borders whisper to the reader! This book is lovingly illustrated in traditional Indian style with cyclical elements from beginning to end. A brief history of Buddha appears on the last page. Czernecki has won several awards for his books and illustrations. His most recent award is the *2004 Children's Resources Gold Award.*   *nrn*
Author lives in Vancouver, British Columbia

Czernecki, Stefan. **Paper Lanterns**. Illustrations by the author. Watertown, MA: Talewinds, 2001. ISBN 1-57091-410-0. 32 p. (4–7). Picture book.

This modern-day tale set in China tells the story of tired Old Chen, a master of the art of making paper lanterns. Because his two apprentices are uninspired, when Little Mouse comes into his life, he passes on his art and teaches him everything. Little Mouse succeeds because of persistence as well as talent. Heavy watercolor guache paintings are combined with cut paper lanterns. "The depictions of the cut paper lanterns at festival are especially engaging, but the illustrations of the faces feel stereotyped."   *plb*

Debon, Nicholas. **Four Pictures by Emily Carr**. Toronto: Groundwood Books, 2003. ISBN 0-88899-532-6. 32 p. (10 up). Novel.

A highly original book in comic strip format that traces Carr's life through four of her paintings: *Cedar House, Autumn in France, Silhouette,* and *Beloved of the*

Sky. 2004 shortlist for the Norma Fleck Award Award for Canadian Children's Non-Fiction; Our Choice 2004 starred selection. Our Choice*
Author/illustrator from Canada

De Vries, Maggie. **Chance and the Butterfly**. Victoria: Orca Book Publishers, 2001. ISBN 1-55143-208-0. 151 p. (7–11). Novel.

Chance doesn't like reading or math, but he finds science fascinating. Then, one day a box of caterpillars arrives in the classroom, and suddenly school becomes fun again. *Our Choice 2002 starred selection.* Our Choice*
Author lives in British Columbia, Canada

Dodds, Dayle Ann. **Where's Pup**. Illustrated by Pierre Pratt. Toronto: Tundra Books, 2003. ISBN 0-88776-622-6. 32 p. (2–6). Picture book.

"Where's Pup? I give up!" Readers are invited to join this silly circus and help take a look. The rhyming words and the funny, fold-out surprise ending will engage young children. *Our Choice 2004 selection; 2003 Elizabeth Mrazik-Cleaver Canadian Picture Book Award.* Our Choice*
Illustrator from Canada

Doyle, Brian. **Boy O'Boy**. Toronto: Groundwood Books, 2003. ISBN 0-88899-588-1. 161 p. (12 up). Novel.

It is the summer of 1945 and World War II is winding down. Life is difficult for Martin O'Boy who lives in Ottawa's Lowertown. His granny has just died. His parents fight all the time. His twin brother, Phil, is completely incapacitated. When Martin joins the church choir, he attracts the attentions of Mr. George who is the church organist and a child predator. Written with humor and compassion, this is a story of a child looking for love. *Canadian Library Association 2004 Book of the Year; Canadian Children Book Centre's Geoffrey Bilson Award for Historical Fiction for Young Readers; NSK Neustadt Prize for Children's Literature; Ruth and Sylvia Schwartz Children's Book Award.* ls
Author from Canada

Doyle, Brian. **Mary Ann Alice**. Toronto: Groundwood Book, 2002. Originally published in Canada in 2001. ISBN 0-88899-453-2. 168 p. (12 up). Novel.

A dam is being built on the Gatineau River. Mary Ann Alice McCrank, who is named after the bell in the St. Martin Church steeple, is an eyewitness and the storyteller of this historical fiction novel. Through her narration, Mary Ann Alice reveals the impact that the building of the Paugan Dam has on the people she knows along the river. Several new characters such as Patchy Drizzle, the school teacher, join those already known from other Doyle novels set in this area of Canada. The novel provides a sometimes humorous, sometimes poignant, ultimately satisfying look at this historical event. *2002 Geoffrey Bilson honor.* js

Edwards, Wallace. **Alphabeasts**. Toronto: Kids Can Press, 2002. ISBN 1-55337-386-3. 32 p. (6–12). Picture book.

Alphabeasts fulfills readers' expectations and more: twenty-six animals, birds, and reptiles introduce the alphabet in exceptional style. The book opens with a wordless page picturing an enigmatic Victorian mansion—tusks instead of columns, an enormous elephant-foot foundation, and animal-hide roofing material. This urbane, lushly illustrated abecedary is not just for youngsters; the visual pranks display a subtlety that requires more mature understanding. For example, "K is for Kingfisher" displays a fishing tackle box, resplendent with lures and a kingfisher balancing a bobber on its beak. Visual wit, verbal repartee, and hidden mysteries compel readers to return again and again. This is a fantastic tour through the alphabet. *Winner of the 2002 Governor General's Literary Award for Illustration.   lmp and ls*
Author/illustrator lives in Canada

Edwards, Wallace. **Monkey Business**. Toronto: Kids Can Press, 2004. ISBN 1-5533-7462-2. 28 p. (8–12). Picture book.

"Monkey business," "spring chicken," and "lucky duck" are just three of the idioms Wallace Edwards illustrates in his stunning follow-up to *Alphabeasts* (Kids Can Press, 2002). The book commences by defining idiom: "A group of words whose meaning cannot be understood from . . . the individual words. . ." (n.p.). He presents each idiom in a cleverly worded sentence as well as a visual labyrinth. One illustration features a beret-wearing beaver, surrounded by Escheresque sculptures, then explains, "As an artist, Nash was constantly looking for things to sink his teeth into" (n.p.). On the final page, suitably dubbed "Enough Monkeying Around! Here's What It Means," each idiom is clearly defined.   *lmp*
Author/illustrator lives in Canada

Ellis, Deborah. **The Breadwinner**. Toronto: Groundwood Books/Douglas & McIntyre, 2000. ISBN 0-88899-419-2. 170 p. (10–14). Novel.

Parvana lives in war-torn Afghanistan. When her father is arrested for having a foreign education, Parvana must disguise herself as a boy in order to support the family. *Sweden's Peter Pan Prize; 2003 Rocky Mountain Books Award; University of California's Middle East Book Award; Notable Books for a Global Society, 2003; Our Choice 2001 starred selection; 2003 Hackmatack Children's Choice Award; 2002 Manitoba Young Readers' Choice Award; 2003 Red Cedar Book Awards.* Our Choice*
Author lives in Simcoe, Ontario, Canada

Ellis, Deborah. **Parvana's Journey**. Toronto: Groundwood Books/Douglas & McIntyre, 2002. ISBN 0-88899-514-8. 199 p. (9–13). Novel.

Bombs are falling, and Parvana, 13, leaves Kabul to find her family. Masquerading as a boy, she travels across Afghanistan. A sequel to *The Breadwinner*.

Jane Addams Peace Award, 2003; CLA Book of the Year shortlist, 2003; Ruth and Sylvia Schwartz Children's Book Award; Our Choice 2003 starred selection; 2004 Golden Oak Award. Our Choice*
Author lives in Simcoe, Ontario, Canada

Ellis, Deborah. **A Company of Fools**. Markham: Fitzhenry & Whiteside, 2004. ISBN 1-55041-719-3. (10 up). Novel.

The area outside of Paris is recovering from the Plague. Henri, a choirboy, is recording the events of that terrible time in hopes of ridding himself of nightmares. Henri writes of life in the monastery, of making friends with Micah, a street urchin with the voice of an angel, their escapades, and the devastation of the Plague. A glimpse of fourteenth-century life in France and how disasters bring out the worst and the best in people. *2003 CLA Book of the Year shortlist, 2003 Geoffrey Bilson Honor Award. ls.*
Author from Canada

Ellis, Deborah. **The Heaven Shop**. Markham: Fitzhenry & Whiteside, 2004. ISBN 1-55041-908-0. 186 p. (12 up). Novel.

Thirteen-year-old Binti, along with Junie, her older sister, and Kwasi, her younger brother, have worked hard with their father in the Heaven Shop, making coffins. Unfortunately, it is a profitable business in Malawi, where 80% of the people who go to the public hospital have AIDS. Their life takes a terrible turn, when their father becomes ill and the children must take time off from school to assist him in the hospital (there aren't enough nurses). When he dies the children are split up and sent to work with cruel relatives. Junie runs away and falls into a life of prostitution and Kwasi ends up in jail. But Binti is determined to reunite her family in this coming-of-age story that makes readers aware of the tragic conditions under which many of Malawi's children exist. The royalties from this book will be donated to UNICEF. Pair this book with *Chandas Secrets* for a devasting picture of contemporary Africa. *djg*

Ellis, Deborah. **Mud City**. Toronto: Groundwood Books/Douglas & McIntyre, 2003. ISBN 0-88899-518-0. 164 p. (10–13). Novel.

The first two novels focus on Parvana, a young girl who masquerades as a boy in Taliban-controlled Kabul in order to feed the family after her father is taken to prison. After she becomes separated from her family and her father dies, Parvana travels on her own encountering an abandoned baby, a young boy missing a leg, and a young girl living near a field of land mines. The makeshift family endures hunger and thirst and several terrifying situations before arriving at a refugee camp where Parvana finds the remainder of her biological family. The two families blend to become one. The last novel of the trilogy features Parvana's friend, Shauzia. She also dressed as a boy in Kabul. Shauzia leaves Kabul to avoid an arranged marriage to a man 30 years older. Before going their separate ways,

Shauzia and Parvana make a pact to meet at the top of the Eiffel Tower in 20 years. Shauzia finds herself at a refugee camp located near Peshawar, Pakistan. She attempts to make it on her own in the city, but is returned to the camp where she puts her dream of France on hold in order to help others like herself out of Afghanistan. This trilogy was inspired by the stories heard by the author when she visited an Afghan refugee camp. *Our Choice 2004 selection.* js
Author lives in Simcoe, Ontario, Canada

Ellis, Deborah. **Three Wishes: Palestinian and Israeli Children Speak**. Toronto: Groundwood, 2004. ISBN 0-88899-554-7. 112 p. (8 up). Informational book.

Ellis visited Israel and the Palestinian territories in 2002 and interviewed children and teens, asking them to tell her about their lives, what made them happy, what made them afraid and angry, and how the war has affected them. Some of the stories are hopeful, some disturbing or shocking, but they reflect the world in which these children live. Eighteen of the narratives illustrated with black-and-white photographs are included in this book along with a concise explanation of the conflict. A map, a short bibliography, and a list of organizations trying to make a difference in the situation in Israel and Palestine make this book a helpful resource. *djg*

Ellis, Sarah. **Big Ben**. Illustrated by Kim LaFave. Markham: Fitzhenry & Whiteside, 2001. ISBN 1-55041-679-0. 32 p. (3–5). Picture book.

Robin and Joe get report cards. Since Ben is in preschool, he does not get a report card. The family celebrates report card day by going to the swimming pool, but Ben can't swim, and then going to a Chinese restaurant, where Ben cannot eat with chopsticks. Feeling very small and sad, Ben goes to bed. Robin and Joe wake Ben up and create a report card for him. Ben's subjects are feeding the cat, brushing his teeth, and tying his shoes. Ben feels much better and marches off proudly clutching his report card. A clever story where the older siblings perceive a younger one's distress and find a delightful solution to the problem. *ls*
Author from Canada

Ellis, Sarah. **A Prairie as Wide as the Sea: The Immigrant Diary of Ivy Weatherall**. Markham, ON: Scholastic Canada, 2001. ISBN 0-439-98833-0. 205 p. (9–13). Novel.

Upon Ivy's family's arrival on the prairies in 1926, prejudice and a job shortage obstruct their dream. Ivy keeps a diary of their trials and tribulations. *Our Choice 2002 selection; 2002 CLA Best Book of the Year shortlist.* Our Choice*
Author lives in British Columbia, Canada

Ellis, Sarah. **The Several Lives of Orphan Jack**. Illustrated by Bruno St Aubin. Toronto: Groundwood Books, 2003. ISBN 0-88899-529-6. 84 p. (9–12). Novel.

"Well, young man, this is your moment of Opportunity" (17). At age twelve, orphans from the Opportunities School for Orphans and Foundlings are apprenticed

to local merchants. Otherjack—he was the second "wee poor orphan called Jack" (20)—revels in dreams of words and phrases, sentences, chapters, and books. Consequently, Otherjack rejoices when he is apprenticed to a bookkeeper. Joy becomes desolation as Mr. Ledger heaps unpleasant numerical chores on his desk. Jack shudders at "a brain full of arithmetic and no room for a single dream" (31). Jack's "Several Lives" is a funny, fantastical delight for language lovers. *lmp*
Author and illustrator live in Canada

Ellis, Sarah, and David Suzuki. **Salmon Forest**. Illustrated by Sheena Lott. Vancouver: Greystone Books, 2003. ISBN 1-55054-937-5. 18 p. (5–9). Picture book.
   Readers are invited to walk in the woods with Kate and her family. Beautiful watercolours and a fascinating story reveal the connection between forest, sea, and all of life. *Our Choice 2004 selection; 2003 Science in Society Book Award.* Our Choice*
Authors and illustrator live in British Columbia, Canada

Fitch, Sheree. **No Two Snowflakes**. Illustrated by Janet Wilson. Victoria: Orca Book Publishers, 2002. ISBN 1-55143-206-4. 32 p. (4–11). Picture book.
   "What is snow?" a Ghanaian child asks her Canadian pen pal. The response unfolds as a letter in poetry. Wilson's glowing pastel drawings revel in all the sensory experiences. *Our Choice 2002 selection.* Our Choice*
Author from Canada.

Fitch, Sheree. **One More Step**. Victoria: Orca Book Publishers, 2002. ISBN 1-55143-248-X. 96 p. (12 up). Novel.
   Julian's parents separated when he was a baby, and he is still hurt. On a road trip with his mother and her new beau, Julian finds that love comes in many different guises. *Our Choice 2003 starred selection.* Our Choice*
Author from Canada

Foon, Dennis. **Skud**. Toronto: Groundwood Books, 2003. ISBN 0-88899-549-0. 171 p. (14 up). Novel.
   Four young men face an uncertain world—the last year of high school. Each is trying to become a man, and coping with violent situations. *Our Choice 2004 selection; 2004 Sheila A. Egoff Children's Literature Prize.* Our Choice*
Author lives in British Columbia

Friesen, Gayle. **Losing Forever**. Toronto: Kids Can Press, 2002. ISBN 1-55337-031-7. 248 p. (13 up). Novel.
   A half-crazed mother, a lovesick friend, a perfectly evil stepsister—could things for Jes get any worse? *Our Choice 2003 starred selection; 2003 Red Maple Award; Sheila A. Egoff shortlist, 2003.* Our Choice*
Author lives in British Columbia, Canada

Friesen, Gayle. **Men of Stone**. Toronto: Kids Can Press, 2000. ISBN 1-55074-782-7. 216 p. (6–10). Novel.

Harassment causes fifteen-year-old Ben to give up dance—the one thing he's good at. When his great-aunt tells her powerful story, Ben begins to see the route he must take. *Our Choice 2001 starred selection.* Our Choice*
Author lives in British Columbia, Canada.

Galloway, Priscilla. **Archers, Alchemists, and 98 Other Medieval Jobs You Might Have Loved or Loathed**. Illustrated by Martha Newbigging. Toronto: Annick Press, 2003. ISBN 1-55037-811-2. 96 p. (8 up). Informational book.

A fascinating guide to 100 olden occupations, described with historical accuracy and wit. Amusing comic-style illustrations capture the imagination. *Our Choice 2004 starred selection.* Our Choice*
Author and illustrator from Canada

Galloway, Priscilla. **The Courtesan's Daughter**. New York: Delacorte, 2002. (Paperback: Laurel Leaf, 2004). ISBN 0-385-72907-3. 254 p. (12–16). Novel.

Ancient Greece (350 B.C.E.) comes alive in this story about Phano, the fourteen-year-old daughter of a citizen of Athens and stepdaughter of a former courtesan, Nera. Phano's quiet existence is shattered by Phrynion, a powerful, but evil man, whose accusations that Phano is Nera's real daughter threaten both Phano's impending marriage to Theo, an elected high official of the ruling council of Athens, and Theo's career. Set during the time Philip of Macedon threatened war on Athens, the story reveals fascinating and well-researched political, social, and cultural details. In the "Acknowledgments," the author reveals that the book was inspired by an actual prosecutor's speech delivered around 340 B.C.E. A glossary is included. *2002 ALA's Best Books for Young People.* kk
Author lives in Canada

Galloway, Priscilla. **Too Young to Fight: Memories from Our Youth during World War II**. Markham, ON: Fitzhenry & Whiteside, 1999. ISBN 0-7737-3190-3. 207 p. (12 up). Biography.

Twelve Canadian authors of children's literature describe their experiences during World War II. Although they were too young to fight, the war affected their lives on many levels. They remember the lack of consumer goods, victory gardens, friends and relatives being killed, the bravery of the English children who came to Canada as "War Guests," and the celebrations on V-E Day. Poignant stories, that give fascinating insight into the effects of war and how it shape the lives of of these authors. *2000 Bologna Ragazzi Award of Nonfiction.* ls and kk
Author from Canada

Garay, Luis. **The Kite**. Toronto: Tundra Books, 2002. ISBN 0-88776-503-3. 32 p. (6–12). Picture book.

Francisco longs for a kite and learns that sometimes dreams do come true! Captivating . . . clear language and distinctive illustrations. *Our Choice 2003 starred selection.* Our Choice*
Author/illustrator from Canada

Gardam, Heather. **Life on the Farm**. Toronto: Penguin Books, 2001. ISBN 0-67089-311-0. 157 p. (8–13). Novel.

Spend a year in the life of Patti, a spunky ten-year-old who wants a horse more than anything. Patti lives with her family on a farm, where she is taking on new responsibilities and thinking more for herself. Annotation provided by publisher. Our Choice*

Gardam, Heather. **Little Guy**. Toronto: Penguin Books, 2001. ISBN 0-14-100444-4. 160 p. (9–13). Novel.

Patti's wish for a horse has finally come true. And even though he has a hurt leg that may never fully heal, and Patti may not get to keep him forever, Little Guy is her horse, and she will do almost anything to ride him—especially in the Fall Fair. *Our Choice 2002 selection.* Our Choice*
Author from Canada

Gay, Marie-Louise. **Good Morning Sam**. Toronto: Groundwood Books, 2003. Distributed in the United States by Publishers Group West. ISBN 0-88899-528-8. 32 p. (3–6). Picture book.

Sam decides he can get dressed all by himself, and he does, with a few delays, and with just a little help from big sister Stella. When he's ready to run out the door, however, Stella reminds him, "Didn't you forget something?" He did. His pants. One more delay, but finally they are ready to leave. As they start skipping down the steps Sam notices Stella is still in her nightgown. With a bit of irony for preschoolers, Sam comments, "Didn't you forget something?" In all the Stella and Sam books the children are portrayed with simple, expressive lines and soft watercolors with the occasional saturated red for Stella's hair and yellow for Sam's. Read more about Sam in *Good Night Sam* (2003).
Author lives in Canada. She has won the Governor General's Literary Award, the Amelia Frances Howard-Gibbon Award, and Mr. Christie's Book Award.   jvl

Gay, Marie-Louise. **Stella, Fairy of the Forest**. Toronto: Groundwood/Douglas & McIntyre, 2002. Distributed in the United States by Publishers Group West. ISBN 0-88899-448-6. 32 p. (3–6). Picture book.

Stella with her flaming red hair takes little brother Sam to look for fairies in the forest. Exhibiting the loving but weary patience of an older sister, Stella answers Sam's endless questions. The children are shown walking, running, and relaxing in a lovely birch forest with birds, flowers, fern, and friendly foxes. Sam, who seems to know very little about the world at first, knows when he sees a fairy, even if it flies away before Stella gets to see it. Both children agree, however, that they would love to stay in this forest paradise. *Governor General's Literary Award; Amelia Frances Howard-Gibbon Award; Mr. Christie's Book Award.   jvl Author lives in Canada*

Gay, Marie-Louise. **Stella, Queen of the Snow**. Toronto: Douglas & McIntyre, 2000. ISBN 0-88899-448-6. 32 p. (5 up). Picture book.
    Stella helps her brother, Sam, explore the wonder of his first snowstorm. Sam is apprehensive and inquisitive. With Stella's patience and imagination, Sam comes to enjoy the snow as much as Stella. An older confident sibling helps out a younger reluctant sibling to enjoy a new phenomenon. Expressive watercolor illustrations make the book especially endearing. *Our Choice starred selection; Elizabeth Mrazik-Cleaver Canadian Picture Book Award.* Stella's adventures continue in *Stella, Fairy of the Forest (2002).*   ls

Ghent, Natale. **No Small Thing**. Toronto: HarperCollins Canada, 2003. ISBN 0-00-639277-6. 176 p. (10–12). Novel.
    When Nat and his sisters see an ad for a free pony, they can't believe their luck. But what will their mother say? A heartwarming journey of self-discovery and love. *Our Choice 2004 selection; 2004 CLA Book of the Year shortlist.* Our Choice*
Author from Canada

Gillmor, Don. **Yuck, a Love Story**. Illustrated by Marie-Louise Gay. Markham, ON: Fitzhenry & Whiteside, 2000. ISBN 0-7737-3218-7. 28 p. (5–8). Picture book.
    A new family with a little girl named Amy moves in next door to Austin. Austin tries impressing Amy by telling her facts about dinosaurs, dressing up as superhero Impossible Man who has x-ray vision, and building a life-sized model of an Apatosaurus out of Popsicle sticks. When Austin receives an invitation to Amy's party, he dresses up as a cowboy and lassoes the moon for Amy then ties it up to the tree in Amy's backyard. The moon really is made of blue cheese to which the children say "Yuck!" and go indoors to eat cake. A whimsical tale of young love that is full of imagination and humor. *Governor-General's Literary Award.*   ls
Author from Canada

Glossop, Jennifer. **The Kids Book of World Religions**. Illustrated by John Mantha. Toronto: Kids Can Press, 2003. ISBN 1-55074-959-5. 64 p. (10–14). Informational book.
    From Judaism to Taoism, children learn about different religions and trace their history. This timely and extensive volume is presented in an objective, engaging manner. *Our Choice 2004 starred selection.* Our Choice*
Author and illustrator from Canada

Goldring, Ann. **Spitfire**. Vancouver: Raincoast Books, 2001. ISBN 1-55192-490-0. 160 p. (9–12). Novel.

Will Kathryn help April beat a gang of bullies when she enters a boys-only soap box derby, even though they'll end up competing against each other? *Our Choice 2003 starred selection; 2002 CLA Best Book of the Year shortlist.* Our Choice*
Author lives in Ontario, Canada

Goobie, Beth. **Before Wings**. Victoria: Orca Books, 2000. ISBN 1-55143-161-0. 203 p. (14 up). Novel.

Having survived an aneurysm two years ago, fifteen-year-old Adrien Wood is spending her summer working at her Aunt's summer camp. She makes contact with the ghosts of five campers who died in a boating accident. Her negative reaction to the camp initiation isolates her from the older camp staff. Adrien's only friend is Paul, a boy with psychic abilities. A suspenseful ghost story where Adrien learns to value life and love over death. *Saskatchawan Book Award; 2000 Canadian Library Association's Young Adult Book Award; 2003 ALA Best Books; Canadian Children's Book Center; Our Choice starred selection.   ls*
Author from Canada

Goobie, Beth. **The Lottery**. Victoria: Orca Books, 2002. ISBN 1-55143-238-2. 264 p. (12 up). Novel.

Every fall the Shadow Council at Saskatoon Collegiate has a lottery to pick a winner, read victim, who will be a gofer for the group and be a scapegoat shunned by the student body. Fifteen-year-old Sally Hanson is selected as the winner. She struggles with her situation, which ends with a strange twist. This eerie story portrays a select secret gang, who terrorizes and bullies an entire student body and get away with it.   *ls*
Author from Canada

Gorrell, Gena K. **Heart and Soul: The Story of Florence Nightingale**. Plattsburgh: Tundra Books, 2000. ISBN 0-88776-494-0. 146 p. (12 up). Biography.

Florence Nightingale was born into a family of privilege with many influential connections. Florence was determined to make a difference. She had a natural talent caring for sick people and received great satisfaction from it. During the Crimean War, soldiers were dying from disease and neglect. Florence stepped in and took effective measures. The story of this intelligent, determined, unconventional woman and all of the changes she instituted in a world run by men is still amazing today. *Our Choice starred selection; Norma Fleck Award for Children's Non-Fiction.   ls*
Author from Canada

Gorrell, Gena K. **Working Like a Dog: The Story of Working Dogs through History**. Toronto: Tundra Books, 2003. ISBN 0-88776-589-0. 160 p. (10 up). Informational book.

This fascinating book describes the working dogs of history, the evolution of breeds for different purposes, and the training involved in preparing these modern-day heroes. *Our Choice 2004 starred selection.* Our Choice*
Author from Canada

Granfield, Linda. **Where Poppies Grow: A World War I Companion**. Markham, ON: Fitzhenry & Whiteside, 2001. ISBN 0-7737-3319-1. 48 p. (8 up). Informational book.

A moving and informative look at those who served during World War I. Topics are presented in scrapbook style with over 180 photographs, articles, and memorabilia. *Our Choice 2002 starred selection; 2002 Information Book Award; Ruth and Sylvia Schwartz Children's Book Award.* Our Choice*
Author lives in Ontario, Canada

Graydon, Shari. **Made You Look: How Advertising Works and Why You Should Know**. Illustrated by Warren Clark. Toronto: Annick Press, 2003. ISBN 1-55037-815-5. 120 p. (11 up). Informational book.

This intriguing and hip exploration of the advertising world will help kids decode all the messages. Witty and engaging illustrations accompany lively text. *Our Choice 2004 starred selection; 2004 Information Book Award.* Our Choice*
Author lives in Ontario, Canada

Gregory, Nan. **Amber Waiting**. Illustrated by Kady MacDonald Denton. Calgary: Red Deer Press, 2002. ISBN 0-88995-258-2. 32 p. (3–6). Picture book.

There's only one thing Amber doesn't like about kindergarten . . . her dad is often late picking her up, so she must wait outside the office. Watercolor art adds a whimsical twist. *Our Choice 2003 selection.* Our Choice*
Author lives in British Columbia, Canada. Illustrator lives in Ontario, Canada.

Gregory, Nan. **Wild Girl and Gran**. Illustrated by Ron Lightburn. Calgary: Red Deer Press, 2000. ISBN 0-88995-221-3. 32 p. (4–10). Picture book.

After the death of her grandmother, a young girl does not feel safe or adventurous anymore. Then one day, she discovers that love passes across generations and her spirit is renewed. *Our Choice 2001 starred selection.* Our Choice*
Author lives in British Columbia, Canada. Illustrator from Canada.

Gugler, Laurel Dee. **There's a Billy Goat in the Garden**. Illustrated by Clare Beaton. Cambridge, MA: Barefoot Books, 2003. ISBN 1-84148-089-4. (2–7). Picture book.

A rowdy group of farmyard animals try to chase away a stubborn old billy goat. Based on a Puerto Rican folktale. The illustrations—handiwork of beads, embroidery, and appliqué—are stunning. *Our Choice 2004 starred selection.* Our Choice*
Author lives in Ontario, Canada

Harrison, Troon. **A Bushel of Light**. Markham, ON: Fitzhenry & Whiteside, 2000. ISBN 0-7737-6140-3. 244 p. (12 up). Novel.
Orphaned, Maggie is working on a farm that is just falling apart. The farmer is more interested in horse racing and his wife is suffering a severe depression. Maggie hears that her twin sister, whom she has been separated from for six years, is living in a nearby town. Maggie leaves the farm to find her sister and ends up finding a new life for herself. *2001 Geoffrey Bilson Honor.* ls
Author from Canada

Harrison, Troon. **Courage to Fly**. Illustrated by Zhong-Yang Huang. Calgary: Red Deer Press, 2002. ISBN 0-88995-273-6. 32 p. (5–10). Picture book.
Striking paintings capture the anxiety of a child who is alone in a new world but whose imagination and courage are nourished by unexpected friendships. *Our Choice 2003 starred selection; 2003 Alberta Book Illustration of the Year Award; 2003 Alberta Children's Book of the Year Award.* Our Choice*
Author and illustrator from Canada

Heneghan, James. **Flood**. New York: Frances Foster Books, Farrar, Straus and Giroux, 2002. ISBN 0-374-35057-4. 182 p. (10–14). Novel.
When his house is swept away in a mudslide, eleven-year-old Andy's mother and step-father disappear, but he is rescued by quick thinking leprechauns who hale from his parents' native Ireland. Taken across Canada to Nova Scotia to live with a stern Aunt and Uncle, Andy runs away to find the father he hasn't seen since he was two. Though loving and charming, Andy's father struggles to keep a job even with the help of the Irish faeries. Seamlessly blending fantasy and reality, *Flood* explores Andy's search for home and for identity. *Sheila A. Egoff Children's Literature Prize.*
Author grew up in Liverpool, England, lives in British Columbia

Heneghan, James. **The Grave**. Toronto: Groundwood Books, 2000. ISBN 0-88899-414-1. 236 p. (12–15). Novel.
Abandoned when he was little, Tom Mullen feels drawn to a mass grave unearthed on his school grounds. Then he is transported back in time and discovers the key to his destiny. *Our Choice 2001 starred selection; 2001 Sheila A. Egoff Children's Literature Prize.* Our Choice*
Author lives in British Columbia, Canada

Highway, Tomson. **Caribou Song**. Illustrated by Brian Deines. Toronto: Harper-Collins Canada, 2001. ISBN 0-00-225522-7. 32 p. (6–10). Picture book.

Joe and Cody are young Cree brothers who follow the caribou all year long. A moment of terror turns mystical and magical as the boys embrace the caribou spirit. *Our Choice 2003 selection.* Our Choice*
Author and illustrator from Canada

Highway, Tomson. **Dragonfly Kites**. Illustrated by Brian Deines. Toronto: HarperCollins, 2002. ISBN 0-00-225527-8. 32 p. (3–7). Picture book.

Joe and Cody, two young Cree brothers, are at their summer home in northern Manitoba. They transform dragonflies into gossamer kites, propelled to the wondrous places found in children's imaginations. The paintings complement text in English and Cree. Annotation provided by publisher. Our Choice*
Author and illustrator from Canada

Highway, Tomson. **Fox on the Ice**. Illustrated by Brian Deines. Toronto: Harper-Collins Canada, 2003. ISBN 0-00-225532-4. 32 p. (3–8). Picture book.

Another lyrical story of celebration—written in both Cree and English by an award-winning team. Masterful, shimmering oils depict the beauty of northern Manitoba. *Our Choice 2004 starred selection.* Our Choice*
Author and illustrator from Canada

Hodge, Deborah. **The Kids Book of Canada and How the CPR Was Built**. Illustrated by John Mantha. Toronto: Kids Can Press, 2000. ISBN 1-55074-526-3. 48 p. (8–12). Informational book.

The story of Canada's first transcontinental railway and many people who made the dream a reality. Also examines the different types of trains and what our railway system looks like today. *Our Choice 2001 starred selection; 2001 Information Book Award.* Our Choice*
Author and illustrator from Canada

Holeman, Linda. **Search of the Moon King's Daughter**. Toronto: Tundra Books, 2002. ISBN 0-88776-592-0. 309 p. (12 up). Novel.

In 1836, Emmaline's mother, Cat, gets her hand crushed in a spinning machine. Emmaline works as a seamstress in her aunt's house and now she is responsible for her family's survival. When Cat sells Emmaline's brother, Tommy, as a way to obtain more opium, Emmaline goes to London to rescue her brother. A rather Dickensian story, which ends on a hopeful note. *2003 Geoffrey Bilson Honor.*   ls.

Horne, Constance. **The Tenth Pupil**. Vancouver: Ronsdale Press, 2001. ISBN 0-921870-86-8. 159 p. (10–14). Novel.

Drawing from life in a British Columbian logging camp in 1934, Horne paints a picture of racial prejudice as witnessed by an eleven-year-old girl and her

Japanese friend. *Our Choice 2002 selection; 2002 CLA Best Book of the Year shortlist.* Our Choice*
Author lives in British Columbia, Canada

Horrocks, Anita. **Topher**. Markham, ON: Fitzhenry & Whiteside, 2000. ISBN 0-7737-6092-X. 211 p. (10–14). Novel.
Stacie and Christopher help their father restore the family's summer cabin. As time passes, the cabin seems cursed. Together, the siblings must stop tragedy from striking again. *Our Choice 2001 starred selection; 2001 R. Ross Annett Award for Children's Literature.* Our Choice*
Author lives in Alberta, Canada

Horvath, Polly. **The Canning Season**. New York: Farrar, Straus and Giroux, 2003. ISBN 0-374-39956-5. 195 p. (12 up). Novel.
One summer, Ratchet trades a lonely existence in a Pensacola basement apartment for life on an isolated farmhouse deep in the bear-infested Maine woods with Aunt Tilly and Aunt Penpen, eccentric twin nonagenarians. This summer vacation gets very interesting when Harper, an outspoken orphan, joins the household. They spend their days swimming in the ocean, taking care of the gardens, the cow, and the bees, and canning blueberries to sell. What began as a summer vacation becomes Ratchet's and Harper's home. *YA Canadian Book of the Year. ls*
Author lives in Canada

Horvath, Polly. **Everything on a Waffle**. New York: Farrar, Straus and Giroux, 2004. ISBN 0-3744-2208-7. 160 p. (8–12). Novel.
Set in the author's town of Coal Harbour, British Columbia, this slim novel tells the story of a plucky girl named Primrose Squarp, whose favorite restaurant, The Girl on the Red Swing, serves absolutely everything on top of a waffle. With her parents lost at sea, Primrose Squarp is technically an orphan. She lives with her crazy babysitter, her uncle, and then foster parents, all the while insisting that her parents will return. This is a charming and funny story, complete with recipes. *Sheila A. Egoff Children's Literature Prize; Newbery Honor Book; International White Ravens; Manitoba Young Readers Choice Award.   plb and ls*
Author lives in Canada

Horvath, Polly. **The Happy Yellow Car**. New York: Farrar, Straus and Giroux, 1994. ISBN 0-374-32845-5. 151 p. (10 up). Novel.
In the midst of the Depression, Gunther Grunt, using his wife's secret college fund for their daughter, Betty, purchases a yellow car and drives it home. This event begins a chain reaction of humorous events. Betty Grunt, a sixth grader, is voted Pork-Fry Queen but needs to pay a dollar for flowers or the honor will go to Janine Woodrow. This warm, humorous story is about one family's struggle for success. *ls*
Author lives in Canada

Horvath, Polly. **The Pepins and Their Problems**. Illustrated by Marylin Hafner. New York: Farrar, Straus Giroux, 2004. ISBN 0-374-35817-6. 179 p. (10 up). Novel.

Readers are invited to help the Pepins and their very fine neighbor, Mr. Bradshaw solve the myriad problems by which they are completely confounded. The assortment of problems includes toads in their shoes, a cow who gives lemonade rather than milk, and a dapper man who makes himself at home. An extraordinarily sly book that is absurd, witty, and nonsensical.   *ls*

Horvath, Polly. **The Trolls**. New York: Farrar, Straus and Giroux, 2001. ISBN 0-3744-7991-7. 144 p. (9–12). Novel.

The children finally get to know their dad's estranged and eccentric sister, Sally, when she helps out in a pinch and replaces an ill babysitter. They are enthralled by her crazy family stories that they've never before heard, especially the incident with the troll, an event that changed their father's life and their family history forever. Skillful writing makes this story alternately funny and poignant. *National Book Finalist; Boston Globe-Horn Book Award Honor Book; ALA Notable Book.*   *plb*

Hughes, Monica. **Keeper of the Isis Light**. Toronto: Tundra Books, 2000; Simon & Schuster, 2000. ISBN 0-6898-3390-3. 160 p. (12 up). Novel.

Olwen's solitary existence on the planet Isis ends when space travelers from earth arrive. *The Keeper of the Isis Light* well deserves the 2000 Phoenix Award and the IBBY Certificate of Honor that it has received since its reissue. This science fiction will be worth the effort to track it down.

Hughes, Vi. **Aziz the Storyteller**. Illustrated by Stefan Czernecki. Vancouver: Tradewind Books, 2002. ISBN 1-896580-45-9. 32 p. (4–8). Picture book.

The tale, set in the Middle East, is the story of "how stories began" and were carried westward by the first storytellers. Based on "1001 Nights," it tells how Aziz took on the mantle of storyteller and how he found the magical carpet. Annotation provided for Our Choice 2003 by publisher.

Huser, Glen. **Stitches**. Toronto: Groundwood Books, 2004. ISBN 0-88899-578-4. 200 p. (12–14). Novel.

As grade nine graduation approaches, Travis's proudest achievement—a puppet production—is overshadowed by taunting and threats. His unconventional interests and sexuality make him a target. *Our Choice 2004 selection; 2003 Governor General's Literary Award (English—Text category); 2004 R. Ross Annett Award for Children's Literature.* Our Choice*
Author lives in Alberta, Canada

Janisch, Heinz. **The Fire: An Ethiopian Folk Tale**. Illustrated by Fabricio VandenBroeck. Toronto: Groundwood, 2002. ISBN 0888994508. 24 p. (5–10). Picture book.

In this traditional Ethiopian tale, a slave who has worked tirelessly for a cruel master asks to be free. The master sets him an impossible task: climb the mountain and spend the night, naked and alone. If he can survive the freezing temperatures and return in the morning, he will win his freedom. In despair, the slave turns to a wise old man who, through an extraordinary act of friendship, helps him. *djg*

Author was the Austrian Honour Book nominee for IBBY in 2000.

Illustrator was the Mexican Honour Book nominee for IBBY 2000 and winner in the Utopia competition for illustrators at the IBBY Congress in Colombia.

Jennings, Sharon. **Priscilla and Rosy**. Illustrated by Linda Hendry. Markham, ON: Fitzhenry & Whiteside, 2001. ISBN 1-55041-676-6. 32 p. (5–8). Picture book.

A charming tale of friendship featuring an alley rat with all-too-human flaws. Hendry's illustrations are delightful in this award-winning book. *Our Choice 2003 selection; 2002 Amelia Frances Howard-Gibbon Honor*. Our Choice*

Author and illustrator live in Ontario, Canada

Jocelyn, Marthe. **Earthly Astonishments**. Toronto: Tundra Books, 2000. ISBN 0-88776-495-9. 179 p. (10–14). Novel.

It's 1884 and Josephine is the world's smallest girl. Her parents charge people to gawk at her. Then she joins a sideshow on Coney Island—an exploitation of a different kind. *Our Choice 2001 starred selection*. Our Choice*

Author from Canada

Jocelyn, Marthe. **Mable Riley**. Toronto: Tundra Books, 2004. ISBN 0-88776-663-3. 288 p. (9–12). Novel.

Set in a town near Stratford, Ontario, during the time of women's early struggles for independence, Marthe Jocelyn's coming-of-age tale about a girl finding her voice—and the courage to make it heard—is as funny as it is inspiring. Annotation provided by publisher. Our Choice*

Author from Canada

Johnston, Julie. **In Spite of Killer Bees**. Toronto: Tundra Books, 2001. ISBN 0-88776-537-8. 253 p. (12 up). Novel.

When three sisters arrive at a village to collect their grandfather's fortune, they are met with suspicion, but no money. A brilliant novel about love, family, and self-discovery. *Our Choice 2002 starred selection*. Our Choice*

Author lives in Ontario, Canada

Johnston, Julie. **Susanna's Quill**. Toronto: Tundra Books, 2004. ISBN 0-88776-706-0. 330 p. (11 up). Novel.

In this fascinating work of historical fiction, Johnston gives Susanna Moodie—writer, woman, pioneer—a face and a voice. Full of memorable characters, hardship, and courage, this compelling novel is told with compassion and humour. Annotation provided by publisher. *Our Choice 2005.* Our Choice*
Author lives in Ontario, Canada

Jorisch, Stephane. **Jabberwocky**. Text by Lewis Carroll. Toronto: Kids Can Press, 2004. ISBN 1-55337-079-1. 40 p. (10 up). Picture book.

The most celebrated nonsense poem in the English language, Lewis Carroll's *Jabberwocky* has delighted readers of all ages since it was first published in *Through the Looking-Glass and What Alice Found There* in 1872. Stéphane Jorisch's stunningly inventive art adds a vibrant, surprising dimension to an already unforgettable poem. Annotation provided by publisher. *2004 Governor General's Literary Award (English Illustration category).* Our Choice*
Illustrator lives in Quebec, Canada

Juby, Susan. **Alice, I Think**. Toronto: HarperCollins, 2003. ISBN 0-00-639-287-3. (13–18). Novel.

In this funny coming-of-age story, Alice is the contemporary equivalent of her famous namesake. Caustic realism blends with keen insight into the daily obstacles facing teens. *Our Choice 2001 starred selection—when published by Thistledown Press.* Our Choice*
Author lives in British Columbia, Canada

Kacer, Kathy. **Clara's War**. Toronto: Second Story Press, 2001. ISBN 1-896764-42-8. 189 p. (10 up). Novel.

It's a dangerous time for thirteen-year-old Clara and her family who have just been imprisoned in Terezin (Terezinstadt), a ghetto in a medieval town near Prague. Clara encounters hunger, disease, and filthy living conditions. Even worse is the constant threat of being deported to concentration camps where the possibility of death awaits her. In the midst of the horror she makes strong friendships with Hanna, a girl from home, and Jacob, an older boy who helps her learn about life in the ghetto. Life takes an unusual turn for them, when a children's opera, Brundibar, written by an inmate, allows them moments of joy and laughter. Inspired by real events, particularly by performances of Brundibar, this compelling work includes historical photographs of the ghetto and of the children on the opening night of the opera. A review of the performance written by a young boy in an underground ghetto newspaper adds further depth to the book. Annotation edited from Second Story Press website www.secondstorypress.ca/booksfs.html. *2002 Red Maple Award; 2002 CLA Best Book of the Year shortlist.* Our Choice*
Author lives in Ontario, Canada

Keefer, Janice Kulyk. **Anna's Goat**. Illustrated by Janet Wilson. Victoria: Orca Book Publishers, 2000. ISBN 1-55143-153-X. 32 p. (6 up). Picture book.
War rages in their homeland and Anna's family takes refuge in a foreign land. When their mother goes to work in a factory, Anna and her sister get an unusual caregiver—a nanny goat! *Our Choice 2001 starred selection.* Our Choice* *Author and illustrator live in Ontario, Canada*

Kositsky, Lynne. **The Thought of High Windows**. Toronto: Kids Can Press, 2004. ISBN 1-55337-621-8. 175 p. (12 up). Novel.
Whenever Esther is trapped or frightened, she escapes through a window. Esther leaves her family in Berlin and travels to Belgium where she thinks she will be safe. When the Germans invade Belgium, Esther and sixty other children escape to the south of France where they live in a filthy barn. When Esther learns that the route to Switzerland has closed, she joins the Jewish Underground and becomes a courier. This novel honestly presents the dangers and uncertainties the Jews faced in France in World War II. *ls*
Author from Canada

Lama, Tenzing Norbu, with Stéphane Frattini. **Secret of the Snow Leopard**. Toronto: Groundwood, 2004. First published in French in 2002 by Éditions Milan as *Himalaya: Le Chemin du Léopard*. ISBN 0-8889-9544-X. 40 p. (4–8). Picture book.
Tsering, the boy from a small Nepali village who was first introduced in the book *Himalaya* (2002), demonstrates that he has courage and persistence in this coming-of-age story. He now must travel through the mountains on a dangerous journey with his new stepfather. He has been warned not to take the mountain pass where his father was killed, but he is compelled to find the shorter path. Hearing the words of his grandfather, "When you are faced with two paths, always choose the most difficult," he is inspired to continue his mission and brings the prayer flag to the mountain summit. Stylized paintings in earth tone watercolors add drama to the telling. CM Magazine reports that Lama, himself from Dolpo, studied painting in a monastery where he prepared to be a lama. *djg*

Lawrence, Iain. **B for Buster**. Delacorte Press, 2004. ISBN 0-385-73086-1. 321 p. (12 up). Novel.
Under-aged and desperate to escape his abusive parents, Kak enlists in the Canadian Air Force in order to fly bombers in World War II. He is trained as a wireless operator and sent to England where he flies bombing raids over Germany. Kak is terrified and can't confide in his buddies for fear that they will find out he is only sixteen. He finds an unlikely confident in Bert, caretaker of the homing pigeons that go out on every flight. A griping story by an award-winning author that portrays the horror of war in the tradition of the *Lord of the Nutcracker Men*. *djg*

Lawrence, Iain. **The Lightkeeper's Daughter**. New York: Delacorte Press, 2002. ISBN 0-385-72925-1. 246 p. (14 up). Novel.

Three years have passed since Squid McCrae last saw her parents and the remote island where she grew up. She returns now at 17, a young woman with a daughter in tow. The visit, she knows, will be rough. *Our Choice 2003 selection.* Our Choice*
Author from Canada

Lawrence, Iain. **Lord of the Nutcracker Men**. New York: Delacorte Press, 2001. ISBN 0-385-72924-3. 210 p. (11 up). Novel.

It's 1914 and Johnny plays at war with nutcracker soldiers his father sends to him from the battlefields in France. Can he control his father's fate, and the war itself? *Our Choice 2003 starred selection.* Our Choice*
Author from Canada

Lawson, Julie. **Arizona Charlie and the Klondike Kid**. Illustrated by Kasia Charko. Victoria, BC and Custer, WA: Orca Books, 2003. ISBN1-155143-250-1. 32 p. (5–8). Picture book.

Young Ben practices his lasso and slingshot tricks in Dawson City, Yukon, just like his idol, Arizona Charlie, who sees him and invites him to be in his Wild West show. When the time comes, though, "the Klondike Kid" gets stage fright when he realizes that Charlie means to shoot a glass ball out of his hand. Ben runs out of the theater where he stops a thief with his lasso, to the approval of the crowd. Colorful, action-packed watercolor and colored pencil illustration bring the times and atmosphere to rip-roaring life. A note gives details on the real-life Arizona Charlie. *ls and sg*
Author lives in Canada

Lawson, Julie. **The Klondike Cat**. Illustrated by Paul Mombourquette. Toronto and Tonawanda, New York: Kids Can Press, 2002. ISBN 1-55337-013-9. (5–8). Picture book.

Despite his father's injunction, Noah smuggles his cat, Shadow, along when he and his father join the 1890s Klondike gold rush. The cat disappears into the steamboat and his father allows the cat to finish their long hard journey when it emerges from the hold. Although all the good claims are gone by the time they arrive, Shadow's kittens, born on the trip, fetch an excellent price as mouse catchers, giving the pair a stake in a new life. Colorful oil paintings detail the hard way of life of the miners and the cold, unforgiving country. An afterword tells about the Klondike River gold rush in 1896 and the growth of Dawson City, which served the miners. This short introduction to the Klondike Gold Rush shows the hardships and disappointments faced by people seeking their fortune. *sg and ls*
Author lives in Canada

Lawson, Julie. **Ribbon of Shining Steel: The Railway Diary of Kate Cameron**. Markham, ON: Scholastic Canada, 2002. ISBN 0-439-98848-9. 208 p. (9–11). Novel.

Will Kate's father be hurt building the Canadian Pacific Railroad? Despite the danger, there is huge excitement as all of Canada eagerly awaits its completion. *Our Choice 2003 selection; 2003 CLA Book of the Year shortlist.* Our Choice*
Author lives in British Columbia, Canada

Leavitt, Martine. **Heck Superhero**. Calgary: Red Deer Press, 2004. ISBN 0-88995-300-7. 144 p. (12 up). Novel.

Throughout a series of harsh and risky encounters, Heck sustains himself (and the reader) with his wit, imagination, and optimism. As he faces the challenges of growing up on the streets, he must come to terms with his perception of himself and others. Annotated by publisher. Our Choice*
Author lives in Alberta, Canada

LeBox, Annette. **Salmon Creek**. Illustrated by Karen Reczuch. Toronto: Groundwood Books, 2002. ISBN 0-88899-458-3. 48 p. (5–10). Picture book.

This lyrical non-fiction book tells the story of a coho, and makes a plea for the protection of salmon. A capsule life cycle presents the factual basis for the poetic text and luminous paintings. *Our Choice 2003 starred selection; 2003 Christie Harris Illustrated Children's Literature Prize.* Our Choice*
Author lives in British Columbia, Canada

LeBox, Annette. **Wild Bog Tea**. Illustrated by Harvey Chan. Toronto: Groundwood Books, 2001. ISBN 0-88899-406-0. 32 p. (6–10). Picture book.

Eloquently written and evocatively illustrated, this book portrays the unique environment of the bog—its flora and fauna—and the importance of landscape of our lives. *Our Choice 2002 starred selection; 2002 Amelia Frances Howard-Gibbon Honor.* Our Choice*
Author lives in British Columbia, Canada. Illustrator lives in Ontario, Canada.

Lee, Claudia M., ed. **Messengers of Rain and Other Poems from Latin America**. Pictures by Rafael Yockteng. Translations by Andrew C. Leone, Sue Oringel, David Unger, and Beatriz Zeller. Toronto: Groundwood, 2002. ISBN 0-88899-470-2. 80 p. (8–12). Poetry.

This anthology contains sixty-four poems from nineteen countries and presents a mix of established and new poets. Themes of the poems range from celebrations of nature to nonsense, from politics to magic, and represent the diversity of Latin America. Beautiful watercolors illustrate this book.   *djg*
Author is a writer and translator from Colombia, lives in United States. Illustrator has won the Utopia competition for illustrators held in conjunction with the

Congress of the International Board on Books for Young People (IBBY) Colombia. He lives in Bogata, Columbia.

Lee, Dennis. **Bubblegum Delicious**. Pictures by David McPhail. New York: HarperCollins, 2001. Originally published by Key Porter Books, Canada. ISBN 0-06-623709-2. 32 p. (5–10). Poetry.

"I think we're gonna laugh, I think we're gonna cry, I think we're gonna love it when the time flies by," and not just at the movies where the big kids go, but you'll laugh all through the day following the activities of a little boy and his dog. Bouncing rhymes and humorous imagery combined with the humorous watercolor illustrations capture the wonder of childhood.   *djg*

Lee, Dennis. **The Cat and the Wizard**. Illustrated by Gillian Johnson. Toronto: Key Porter Books, 2001. ISBN 1-55263-384-5. 32 p. (5–8). Poetry.

A lonesome wizard and a coal-black cat party until dawn—with candlelight, wine, and tuna fish! This rhyming delight is accompanied by whimsical art. A perfect read-aloud. *Our Choice 2003 selection; 2002 CLA Best Book of the Year shortlist.* Our Choice*
Author has also written Jelly Belly, Garbage Delight, *which received the Canadian Library Associations Book of the Year Award. He has been on the Hans Christian Andersen Honor List.*
Author lives in Ontario, Canada

Levert, Mireille. **An Island in the Soup**. Illustrations by the author. Toronto: Groundwood Books, 2001. ISBN 0-88899-403-6. 24 p. (4–7). Picture book.

Uncertain about the strange fish soup that his mom serves him for supper, small Victor, sporting a colander for a battle helmet, sets off on a fantastic journey. He and his mother dodge giant peas and lasso the Bad Fairy until Victor finally downs his soup and gets cake as a reward. The bright and zany illustrations help establish the mood and tell the story. *Governor General Literary Award for illustration.*   *plb*

Levert, Mireille. **Lucy's Secret**. Toronto: Groundwood, 2004. ISBN 0-88899-566-0. 32 p. (4–8). Picture book.

An open gate welcomes the reader into Aunt Zinnia's beautiful garden where bugs are flitting and flying and ferocious wild beasts (two beautiful cats) lie in wait. Aunt Zinnia leads Lucy to a hollow in the tree where she keeps a box filled with shining seeds. While playfully touring through the garden, Aunt Zinnia explains the flowers cycle of growth and together they share the delightful gifts nature has given them.   *djg*
Author is one of Quebec's most talented children's book artists. She has written and illustrated many books including her two Governor General award-wining titles, An Island in the Soup *and* Sleep Tight, Mrs. Ming *as well as* Little Red Riding Hood *and* Rose by Night.

Levine, Karen. **Hana's Suitcase**. Toronto: Second Story Press, 2002. ISBN 1-8967-64-55-X. 112 p. (9 up). Informational book.

In 2000, a mysterious suitcase arrived at a children's Holocaust center in Japan. This remarkable true story follows the curator's international search for clues to the puzzle of a young girl's life. *Our Choice 2003 starred selection; 2003 Canadian Library Association Book of the Year for Children Award; 2003 Golden Oak Award; 2003 Information Book Award; 2003 National Chapter of Canada IODE Violet Downey Book Award; 2003 Silver Birch Award (Non-Fiction category); 2003 Tiny Torgi Literary Awards (Audio category); 2004 Rocky Mountain Book Award; 2004 Hackmatack Children's Choice Award (Non-Fiction category); 2004 IBBY Honour List; It has also won several international awards.* Our Choice*
Author from Canada

Lewis, Wendy. **Graveyard Girl**. Calgary: Red Deer Press, 2000. ISBN 0-888995-202-7. 189 p. (14–18). Novel.

In these linked stories, students re-enact the royal wedding of Charles and Diana. Each seeks out his or her own truth in the years that follow. *Our Choice 2001 starred selection; 2001 Vicky Metcalf Short Story Award for* "Revelations," *in* Graveyard Girl. Our Choice*
Author lives in Ontario, Canada

Little, Jean. **Birdie for Now**. Victoria: Orca Book Publishers, 2002. ISBN 1-55143-203-X. 154 p. (10 up). Novel.

Dickon is looking forward to moving to a new home. Dickon's mother is newly divorced and she is overprotective and smothering in her relationship with her son. The new house is a small box but the Humane Society is right behind it. Dickon volunteers to work at the Humane Society. His hopes to get a dog rise but he needs to convince his mother that she needs to change.   *ls*
Author from Canada

Little, Jean. **Brother Far from Home: The World War I Diary of Eliza Bates**. Markham, ON: Scholastic Canada, 2003. ISBN 0-439-96900-X. 230 p. (9–12). Novel.

Eliza's older brothers are off fighting in the war. Will they return safely? Little's latest addition to this series is the diary of a girl watching her world change as war rages in the distance. *Our Choice 2004 starred selection; 2002 CLA Book of the Year shortlist.* Our Choice*
Author lives in Ontario, Canada

Little, Jean. **Emma's Strange Pet**. Illustrated by Jennifer Plecas. HarperCollins, 2003. ISBN 0-06-028350-5. 64 p. (5–8). Beginning reader.

Emma's four-year-old brother Max really wants a dog for his birthday in this realistic I Can Read book, but he cannot have one because of his sister's allergies to fur. To the family's surprise, Emma decides she wants a pet and chooses a

---

SPOTLIGHT ON JEAN LITTLE

Jean Little was born in 1932 with scarred corneas that impaired her vision. But that never stopped her from reading. For the story of her life from age five to age fifty-five read *Little by Little: a Writer's Education* and *Stars Come Out Within* or go to her website for the years after that, http://www.jeanlittle.com/.

When Ms. Little worked with disabled children, she read classics to them. They were puzzled by the plight of the disabled characters, who either died or were miraculously cured. That is when she decided to write about children with disabilities who coped with their handicaps, conquered their fears, and managed their daily routines (Silvey).

She won a writing contest sponsored by Little Brown and they published *Mine for Keeps* in 1962. This inspirational story is about Sally, a young girl with cerebral palsy. Ms. Little tackled the subject of blindness in *From Anna* and *Listen for the Singing*, which won the Governor General's Literary Award for Children's Literature in 1977 (FBJA).

Selected Works: *Mine for Keeps*, 1962; *Home From Far*, 1965; *Spring Begins in March*, 1966; *Take Wing*, 1968; *When the Pie Was Opened*, 1968; *One to Grow On*, 1969; *Look Through My Window*, 1970; *Kate*, 1971; *From Anna*, 1972; *Stand in the Wind*, 1975; *Listen for the Singing* won the Canada Council Children's Literature Award in 1977; *Hey World, Here I Am!*, 1984; *Mama's Going to buy You a Mockingbird* was the CLA Book of the Year in 1985; *Different Dragons*, 1986; *Revenge of the Small Small*, 1993; *His Banner Over Me*, 1995. Commire, Anne, ed. *Something about the Author*, vol. 2, 1971, vol. 68, 1992. *Fourth Book of Junior Authors and Illustrators*; Electronic, 1978, 1999. Silvey, Anita. *Children's Books and Their Creators*, 1995

---

small lizard called an anole at the pet shop for her birthday. Both children learn about pet care in this involving story and Emma convinces her parents that Max is responsible enough to have his own lizard. Line and watercolor illustrations do a good job of showing the siblings' relationships and their interactions with their pets.   *sg and ls*
Author lives in Canada

Little, Jean. **I Gave My Mom a Castle: Poems**. Illustrated by Kady MacDonald Denton. Victoria, BC: Orca, 2003. ISBN 1-5514-3253-6. 80 p. (9 up). Poetry.

Some days we all need a gift. Jean Little's 43 child-centered poems are a special treat for any reader, on a really bad day or even on a particularly good one. Little's remembrances, both humorous and sad, ring true: "Sticks and stones and names still hurt/And laughing isn't such a great shield. . . ." Others portray the joy (or pain) of holiday gifts: "Every year since I was born/They've given me a book for Christmas. . .Until this year/I never knew Christmas afternoon/Could be so long." This book is a gift, custom-made for every reader.   *lmp and ls*
Author lives in Canada

Little, Jean. **Orphan at My Door: The Home Child Diary of Victoria Cope**. Markham, ON: Scholastic Canada, 2001. ISBN 0-439-98834-9. 221 p. (9–13). Novel.

Victoria's family needs help because of her mother's illness, so they invite Marianna, an orphan from Britain, to live with them. Soon they realize that Marianna needs help too. *Our Choice 2002 selection; 2002 Canadian Library Association Book of the Year for Children Award; 2002 CLA Best Book of the Year shortlist.* Our Choice*
Author lives in Ontario, Canada

Little, Jean. **Pippin the Christmas Pig**. Illustrated by Werner Zimmerman. New York: Scholastic, 2003. 0-439-65062-3. unpaged. (4–7). Picture book.

It is the day before Christmas and the animals in the barn are in an uproar as Pippin's naive questions inspire debate about whose ancestors played the most important role in the nativity story. Feeling ignored and rejected, Pippin runs away, but as she trudges through a blustery snow storm she finds a lost mother and her baby. Pippin leads them to the warmth and safety of the barn, demonstrating to all the seasonal message that we find joy through giving to others. The lively dialogue and humor prevent a descent into the saccharine, and Little's touching tale is well-complemented by animated watercolor-and-pencil illustrations by fellow Ontario resident Zimmerman. *Mr. Christie's Book Award.* dw

Little, Jean. **Willow and Twig**. New York: Viking, 2000. (Paperback: Puffin, 2001). ISBN 0-6708-8856-7. 227 p. (9–12). Novel.

Willow, 10, and her emotionally disturbed brother, Twig, 4, have again been abandoned by their drug-addicted mother. An ailing friend shares what little she has with the two children before she dies leaving Willow and Twig homeless and penniless. Despite fears of being sent to a foster home, Willow goes to the Vancouver police, and soon the children are reunited with their grandmother, Aunt Constance, and Uncle Hum. Nevertheless, Willow remains suspicious that this home, too, will dissolve as all others have. Even though the issues of drug addiction, abandonment, and prejudice are integral to the plot, ultimately this is a warm and sensitive story about the healing power of unwavering love and acceptance. *Mr. Christie's Book Award; CLA Book of the Year for Children finalist; and Violet Downey Book Award shortlist.* kk
Author from Canada

London, Jonathan. **What the Animals Were Waiting For**. Illustrated by Paul Morin. Markham, ON: Scholastic Canada, 2001. ISBN 0-439-98854-3. 32 p. (3–9). Picture book.

Simple, stirring verse and stunning illustrations depict the dramatic cycles of life on the Masai Mara range—one of the last great, wild places on Earth.

Our Choice 2002 starred selection; 2002 CLA Best Book of the Year shortlist.
Our Choice*
Illustrator from Canada

Loyie, Larry. **As Long as the Rivers Flow: A Last Summer before Residential School**. With Constance Brissenden. Illustrated by Heather D. Holmlund. Toronto: Groundwood Books, 2002. ISBN 0-88899-473-7. 48 p. (8–12). Biography.

This autobiographical picture book celebrates a Cree child's tenth summer, an idyllic time of caring for a hurt owl, of picking berries, of braving a scare from a grizzly with his intrepid grandmother, and of becoming a young man. But in the end he and his younger siblings are forced into a truck and must leave their parents behind for boarding school. This last summer in the comfort and security of their family will live in their memories and be a sharp contrast to their lives in the boarding schools. An epilogue explains the sad truth of their experiences and provides helpful historical information, as well as photographs. *Our Choice starred selection; Norma Fleck Award for Children's Non-Fiction.*   *plb and ls*
Author from Alberta, Canada

Luján, Jorge Elias. **Beyond My Hand**. Pictures by Quintana. Toronto: Groundwood, 2000. Originally published in Spanish as *Mas alla de mi brazo* by Petra Ediciones in Mexico in 2000. ISBN 0-88899-460-5. 28 p. (4–8). Picture book.

A simple poem is illustrated with lovely watercolor illustrations to portray a child reaching out its hand to find a surprise: first a coconut that is shaken open to find a lake, which then stirs and swirls and moves to uncover wonders in the world beyond the child's experience.   *djg*

Luján, Jorge Elias. **Rooster Gallo**. Pictures by Manuel Monroy. Translation by Elisa Amado. Toronto: Groundwood, 2004. ISBN 0-88899-558-X. 24 p. (4–7). Picture book.

The rooster opens its beak and up comes the sun. The sun opens its hand and the day is born. Thus begins this simple poem celebrating the dawning of a new day in both Spanish and English. Luminous paintings on wood will delight the youngest reader and captivate older readers with their elegant simplicity.   *djg*
Author from Argentina, lives in Mexico. Among other honors has received the Premio de Poesía para Niños de ALIJA (IBBY, Argentina, 1995).
Illustrator from Mexico and has won several awards, including the Quorum Prize and the NOMA Encouragement Prize in Japan.

Lunn, Janet. **Double Spell**. Toronto: Tundra Books, 2003. Originally published by Peter Martin Associates in 1968. ISBN 0-88776-660-9. 135 p. (10 up). Novel.

Twelve-year-old twins, Jane and Elizabeth, find a small wooden doll in an antique shop on Yonge Street. They purchase the doll for two dollars and fifty-three cents. Soon they begin having the same dreams and seeing visions as if someone from the past was trying to tell them something. When their family moves into a

house, which has been in their family for generations, the girls are determined to find out why they are haunted by memories of the past. This shivery ghost story progresses to a satisfactory conclusion. *ls*
Author from Canada

Maggi, María. **The Great Canoe: A Kariña Legend**. Translated by Elisa Amado. Illustrated by Gloria Calderón. Toronto: Groundwood, 1998. ISBN 0-88899-444-3. Originally published in Spanish as *La gran canoa* by Playco Editores, Venezuela. 38 p. (5–10). Picture book legend.

A very long time ago, Kaputano, the Sky Dweller, told the people that a great rain would soon begin to fall and that they must build a great canoe. Only four families believed Kaputano and they worked together to build the canoe. When they had gathered two of every animal and seed from all the earth, the rains began to fall. The author carefully documents her research in an afterword and includes information about the Kariña culture. *Bulletin Blue Ribbons, 2001; Bulletin of the Center for Children's Books; Capitol Choices, 2001; The Capitol Choices Committee; School Library Journal Book starred review.* *djg*
Author lives in Venezuela. Illustrator from Columbia.

Major, Kevin. **Ann and Seamus**. Illustrated by David Blackwood. Toronto: Groundwood Books, 2003. ISBN 0-88899-561-X. 109 p. (12 up). Poetry.

In 1828, off the shore of Isle des Morts, Newfoundland, the ship Despatch runs aground on a reef during a foul storm. Ann Harvey and her father row out to rescue the survivors. Seamus is one of the ship's passengers. Seamus falls in love with Ann and begs her to come away to seek a new life. This poetic retelling in two voices of a historic event gives a glimpse of the harsh, difficult life the inhabitants of Newfoundland endure. *2004 Geoffrey Bilson Historical Fiction; Our Choice 2004 starred selection.* *ls*
Author lives in Newfoundland, Canada. Illustrator lives in Canada.

Major, Kevin. **Eh? to Zed: A Canadian ABeCedarium**. Illustrated by Alan Daniel. Calgary: Red Deer Press, 2000. ISBN 0-88995-222-1. 32 p. (4–10). Picture book.

An alphabetic, fun-filled tour of Canada set in rhyming verse—with whimsical illustrations. Perfect for visitors to Canada, and an excellent resource for schools and libraries. *Our Choice 2001 starred selection; 2001 Alberta Children's Book of the Year Award.* Our Choice*
Author lives in Newfoundland, Canada. Illustrator lives in Ontario, Canada.

Martini, Clem. **The Mob**. Toronto: Kids Can Press, 2004. ISBN 1-55337-574-2. 239 p. (11 up). Novel.

Every spring a family of crows led by Kalum, the Chooser, migrates to the Gathering Tree to celebrate and reaffirm ancient customs and laws. This year during the Gathering, the family's survival is seriously threatened. First, Kyp, a young

crow, leads an unauthorized revenge attack on a vicious cat and is evicted for six days for endangering the family. Then a fierce blizzard threatens the lives and unity of the family when it forces the crows to split into two groups to search for shelter. All have to reconsider their traditions in order to survive. This novel is the first of three in the series Feather and Bone: The Crow Chronicle.   *kk and jig*
Author from Canada

Matas, Carol. **In My Enemy's House**. New York: Simon and Schuster Books for Young Readers, 1999. ISBN 0-689-81354-6. 167 p. (12 up). Novel.

As the German army continues to invade Poland, the Jews are being methodically persecuted. Miriam, her large extended family, and neighbors are being terrorized. Some members of Miriam's family have been loaded onto boxcars and never heard of again. While some family members plan to join the partisans, a neighbor tells Miriam that she could pass as a Polish girl and work for the Germans. Miriam obtains the papers and spends the war working in the home of a German officer. *2002 Geoffrey Bilson Historical Fiction Honor.   ls*
Author from Canada

Matas, Carol. **Sparks Fly Upward**. New York: Clarion Books, 2002. ISBN 0-618-15964-9. 180 p. (10–13). Novel.

After a devastating fire destroys their house in the Jewish community of Saskatchewan, 12-year-old Rebecca Bernstein and her family struggle to survive in the city of Winnipeg at the turn of the twentieth century. Rebecca's father cannot find work in the theater, so Rebecca is compelled to live with the Kostaniuks, a Ukrainian foster family. Although Sophie Kostaniuk and Rebecca share much in common and would become friends, Sophie's brother Sasha hates Jews, making the living situation uncomfortable and the schoolyard violent. Despite their religious differences, Sophie and Rebecca bond as they struggle to overcome hardships that include scarlet fever, a hospital fire, and knife fights. In the end, friendship and courage prevail over prejudice and fear.   *aao*
Author lives in Canada and United States

Matas, Carol. **The War Within: A Novel of the Civil War**. New York: Simon & Schuster, 2001. ISBN 0-689-82935-3. 151 p. (10–14). Novel.

Wealthy Jewish merchants and their families enjoyed all the social and economic privileges of life in the deep south at the time of the Civil War. Briefly, from December 17, 1862 to January 7, 1863, in a misguided attempt to stop profiteering, General U.S. Grant ordered these families expelled from their homes and marched to Cairo, Illinois. In this narrative, the focus is on thirteen-year-old Hannah Green, a member of such a family, whose struggles during this ordeal lead her to rethink her position on slavery and the purpose of the war. *Geoffrey Bilson Historical Fiction Honor, 2001.   mln*
Author from Canada

McFarlane, Sheryl. **A Pod of Orcas: A Seaside Counting Book**. Illustrated by Kirsti Ann Wakelin. Markham, ON: Fitzhenry & Whiteside, 2002. ISBN 1-55041-681-2. (3 and up). Picture book.

There is lots to count at the seashore—one lighthouse, two freighters, three eagles—exquisite watercolour paintings rounds out this gentle and poetic counting book. *Our Choice 2003 starred selection.* Our Choice*
Author from Canada

McKay, Sharon E. **Charlie Wilcox**. Toronto: Stoddart Kids, 2000. ISBN 0-7737-6093-8. (Penguin, 2003. ISBN 0-14-301470-6). 221 p. (12 up). Novel.

In Newfoundland in the early days of World War I, men either fished or went sealing on the ice. Fourteen-year-old Charlie Wilcox was born frail with a clubfoot. After an operation to correct his disability, Charlie wants to prove himself by going to the ice. Instead, Charlie ends up on a troop ship heading to France where he becomes an orderly and returns home much changed. *Geoffrey Bilson Award for Historical Fiction for Young People; Canada IBBY nominee, 2000.* ls
Author from Canada

McNamee, Graham. **Acceleration**. New York: Random House Children's Books. ISBN 0-385-73119-1. 210 p. (12 up). Novel.

Duncan finds the anonymous journal of a serial killer stalking women in the Toronto subway. Can he stop him before it's too late? *Our Choice 2004 starred selection; 2004 Arthur Ellis Best Juvenile Crime Award.* Our Choice*
Author from Canada

McNaughton, Janet. **An Earthly Knight**. Toronto: HarperCollins Canada, 2003. ISBN 0-0-639188-5. 256 p. (12 up). Novel.

When Isabel disgraces the family of Norman, a nobleman ruling a fiefdom in twelfth-century Scotland, sixteen-year-old Jenny finds herself in the role of the elder daughter. Her father arranges a marriage to redeem the family honor, but the high-spirited girl has fallen in love with Tam Lin, the lands rightful owner. McNaughton blends two legends together in this original tale of love and honor. *Our Choice 2004 starred selection.* djg
Author lives in Newfoundland, Canada

McNaughton, Janet. **Secret under My Skin**. Toronto: HarperCollins Canada, 2000. ISBN 0-00-648522-7. 237 p. (12 up). Novel.

The acclaimed author's novel, set in 2368, chronicles a young girl who learns shocking secrets about her environment and herself. *Our Choice 2002 starred selection; 2001 Ann Connor Brimer Award; 2001 Ruth and Sylvia Schwartz Children's Book Award; 2002 Bruneau Family Children's/YA Award (Newfoundland & Labrardor Book Awards).* Our Choice*
Author lives in Newfoundland, Canada

Munsch, Robert. **Aaron's Hair**. Illustrated by Alan and Lea Daniel. Markham, ON: Scholastic Canada, 2000. ISBN 0-439-19258-7. 32 p. (4–8). Picture book.

Aaron is having the world's worst bad hair day—his hair won't even stay on his head! A hilarious chase ensues. Our Choice*
Author and illustrators live in Ontario, Canada

Munsch, Robert. **Lighthouse: A Story of Remembrance**. Illustrated by Janet Wilson. Markham, ON: Scholastic Canada, 2003. ISBN 0-439-97458-5. 32 p. (5–9). Picture book.

Sarah and her father set off through the darkness and fog, on a special journey. A gentle and poignant story of love and remembrance beautifully illustrated with realistic paintings. *Our Choice 2004 selection; 2004 Amelia Frances Howard-Gibbon shortlist.* Our Choice*
Author and illustrator live in Ontario, Canada

Munsch, Robert. **Up, Up, Down**. Illustrated by Michael Martchenko. Markham, ON: Scholastic Canada, 2001. ISBN 0-439-98815-2. 32 p. (4–8). Picture book.

No matter what her parents say, Anna insists on climbing everything! But getting Anna down is not as easy as it looks. *Our Choice 2002 selection.*
Also by this author/illustrator team is Mmm, Cookies!

Nielsen-Fernlund, Susin. **Hank and Fergus**. Illustrated by Louise-Andrée Laliberté. Victoria: Orca Book Publishers, 2003. ISBN 1-55143-245-5. 32 p. (4–7). Picture book.

Hank has a birthmark on his face, and his best friend is an invisible dog. Now the boy next door is making fun of him. Will they ever become friends? *Our Choice 2004 selection; 2003 Mr. Christie's Book Award—Silver seal (7 years and under category).* Our Choice*

Oberman, Sheldon. **Island of the Minotaur: Greek Myths of Ancient Crete**. Illustrated by Blair Drawson. Vancouver: Tradewind Books, 2003. ISBN 1-8965-8064-5. 104 p. (10–14). Myths.

Famous and forgotten myths of the mysterious Minoans of Crete are retold here as one exciting story. Colourful stylized illustrations capture the drama. *Our Choice 2004 starred selection. Author is deceased.* Our Choice*

Oppel, Kenneth. **Airborn**. Toronto: HarperCollins Canada, 2004. ISBN 0-0020-0537-9. 322 p. (10–14). Novel.

From the author of *Silverwing*, *Sunwing*, and *Firewing* comes a swashbuckling adventure/mystery that is also a tale of growing up and acceptance. Set in an imaginary past, Airborn is the story of fifteen-year-old Matt Cruse, a cabin boy

on a luxury giant airship. Annotation provided by publisher. *2004 Governor General's Literary Award (English-Text category).* Our Choice*
Author lives in Ontario, Canada

Oppel, Kenneth. **Firewing**. Toronto: HarperCollins Canada, 2002. ISBN 0-00-639194-X. 256 p. (8 and up). Novel.

Griffin, a young bat, falls through the earth, and Goth, the evil Vampire bat, is right on his tail! Oppel rounds out the award-winning Silverwing trilogy with this story. *2003 Our Choice starred selection; 2004 Manitoba Young Readers' Choice Award; 2003 CLA Book of the Year shortlist.* Our Choice*
Author lives in Ontario, Canada

Park, Janie Jaehyun. **The Tiger and the Dried Persimmon: A Korean Folk Tale**. Toronto: Groundwood Books/Douglas & McIntyre, 2002. ISBN 0-88899-485-0. (5–8). Folktale.

This exciting, but not too scary, traditional story from Korea, involving mistaken identity, a tiger, a thief, an ox, and a crying child who is quieted with a piece of dried persimmon, will make a great read-aloud. The winning illustrations use gesso to create texture, and add painting over with acrylics. Stylized animals, especially the tiger, which is almost calligraphic in its energy, blend well with the traditional looking backgrounds. Nighttime and daytime colors are well used for contrast, and the text blocks of the nighttime scenes are legible due to the cream color laid under them. A final note explains what persimmons taste like and how they are eaten.   *sg*
Author was raised in Korea, lives in Canada

Parkinson, Curtis. **Storm-Blast**. Toronto: Tundra Books, 2003. ISBN 0-88776-630-7. 160 p. (11–14). Novel.

A day of snorkeling turns to horror as a storm strands three teenagers in the Caribbean. Can this trio—who have never agreed on anything—find a way to survive? *Our Choice 2004 starred selection.* Our Choice*
Author from Canada

Pearson, Kit. **The Sky Is Falling**. Markham: Viking Kestrel, 1989. ISBN 0-6708-2849-1. 248 p. (10 up). Novel.

In the summer of 1940, the threat of a German invasion of Britain seems imminent. Norah and her five-year-old brother, Gavin, are evacuated to Canada for their safety. They endure a long voyage, are placed in a home with wealthy, well-intentioned strangers in Toronto. The children miss their parents and have difficulties adjusting to their new circumstances and unfamiliar surroundings. This is an excellent, poignant account of Canada's war guests who coped with great changes in their young lives. *Mr. Christie's Book Award; Canadian Library Association Children's Book of the Year Award; Geoffrey Bilson Award for Historical Fiction.*   *ls*
Author from Canada

Pendziwol, Jean E. **Dawn Watch**. Pictures by Nicolas Debon. Toronto: Groundwood/Douglas & McIntyre, 2004. ISBN 0-88899-512-1. 32 p. (4–8). Picture book.

Through the darkest part of the night a young girl stands the dawn watch as she crosses Lake Superior with her father on their sail boat. The boat pitches on the waves under the luminous Northern Lights as they travel toward Thunder Bay. Just before the dawn breaks, Dad brings his brave girl a cup of hot chocolate. Beautiful paintings combined with lyrical prose capture the excitement and mystery of this nighttime adventure. *djg*

Perkyns, Dorothy. **Last Days in Africville**. Vancouver: Beach Holme Publishing, 2003. ISBN 0-88878-446-5. 144 p. (9–13). Novel.

Twelve-year-old Selina is growing up in the community of Africville in 1965. The only black student in her grade 6 class, she takes comfort in the fact that every day she goes home to a loving neighborhood. But will the only home she knows be taken away? Annotation provided by publisher. *2004 CLA Book of the Year shortlist.* Our Choice*
Author lives in Nova Scotia, Canada

Pittman, Al. **Down by Jim Long's Stage: Rhymes for Children and Young Fish**. New illustrations by Pam Hall. St. John's, NF: Breakwater, 2001. ISBN 1-55081-163-0. 43 p. (4–8). Poetry.

Vivid award-winning watercolor illustrations give new life to the classic poetry of Al Pittman, an important Newfoundland author. Rodney Cod, Ella Eel, and Donald Dogfish are just some of the sea creatures who live down in the deep on the floor of the sea by Jim Long's stag in this humorous book of sea poems. *djg*

Reid, Barbara. **The Subway Mouse**. Markham, ON: Scholastic Canada, 2003. ISBN 0-439-97468-2. 40 p. (3–11). Picture book.

Nib lives underground in a subway station. He embarks on an adventure and makes a beautiful discovery. Reid incorporates found objects into her acclaimed Plasticine art. *2004 Ruth and Sylvia Schwartz Children's Book Award; 2004 Amelia Frances Howard-Gibbon Award shortlist.* Our Choice*
Author lives in Ontario, Canada

Reynolds, Marilynn. **The Magnificent Piano Recital**. Illustrated by Laura Fernandez and Rick Jacobson. Victoria: Orca Books, 2000. ISBN 1-55143-180-7. 30 p. (10 up). Novel.

One wintry evening, Arabella and her mother arrive in a sawmill town where Arabella's mother plans to teach piano. On her first day at school, Arabella meets her teacher, Mrs. Bat, who dislikes Arabella's frilly dress and ringlets. The first day of school is unpleasant and Arabella arrives home, downcast and teary eyed. She loses herself in practicing on the piano and the cares of the day disappear.

Eventually Arabella's mother gets a number of piano students. In the spring, the whole town attends a piano recital where all the students play and are applauded. When Arabella plays her piece, she receives a standing ovation. Arabella's life in the sawmill town has changed for the best. *Our Choice 2001 starred selection; 2001 Amelia Frances Howard-Gibbon Illustrator's Award.* ls
Author lives in British Columbia, Canada. Illustrators live in Ontario, Canada.

Richardson, Bill. **After Hamelin**. Willowdale, ON: Annick Press, 2000. ISBN 1-55037-628-4. 227 p. (12–15). Novel.

Picking up where the Pied Piper leaves off, Richardson spins a tale through strange lands inhabited by characters both good and evil. Filled with wordplay and imagination. *Our Choice 2001 starred selection; 2001 Silver Birch Award.* Our Choice*

Richardson, Bill. **But If They Do**. Illustrated by Marc Mongeau. Toronto: Annick Press, 2003. ISBN 0-55037-787-6. 24 p. (4–7). Picture book.

A nightly bedtime verse inspires a child's adventurous imagination to conjure up ghouls and monsters until Dad arrives with soothing words and a good-night kiss. Annotation provided by publisher. *Our Choice 2004.* Our Choice*

Ross, Val. **The Road to There: Mapmakers and Their Stories**. Toronto: Tundra Books, 2003. ISBN 0-88776-621-8. 152 p. (12 up). Informational book.

Fascinating stories of history's great mapmakers. Loaded with information and reproductions of historical maps, this extraordinary book is as suspenseful as a novel. *Our Choice 2004 starred selection; 2004 Norma Fleck Award for Children's Non-Fiction; CCBC Choices 2004 (Cooperative Children's Book Center, School of Education, University of Wisconsin-Madison); Notable Book by the International Reading Association's Children's Book Award.* Our Choice*
Author lives in Ontario, Canada

Ruurs, Margriet. **When We Go Camping**. Illustrated by Andrew Kiss. Toronto: Tundra Books, 2001. ISBN 0-88776-476-2. 32 p. (5–10). Picture book.

A family goes camping in the North Woods and revels in nature's beauty. They enjoy eating outdoors, hiking, canoeing, fishing, and swimming. They also enjoy watching the wildlife, which abounds around them. In the evening, the family sits around the campfire telling scary stories. Andrew Kiss's fine wildlife oil paintings convey the majesty of nature plus they include hidden animals, which can be found with the help of a key located at the back of the book. A simple view of a family enjoying and connecting with nature. ls
Author from Canada

Ruurs, Margriet. **Wild Babies**. Illustrated by Andrew Kiss. Toronto: Tundra Books, 2003. ISBN 0-88776-627-7. 32 p. (3–6). Picture book.

Baby woodland animals are shown in their natural habitats. The simple text is accompanied by Andrew Kiss's beautiful oil paintings. At the end of the book, there is a key to the hidden animals in the paintings. This exercise gives children practice in being observers of nature, which requires patience and careful observation.   *ls*
Author from Canada

Sadlier, Rosemary. **The Kids Book of Black Canadian History**. Illustrated by Wang Qijun. Toronto: Kids Can Press, 2003. ISBN 1-55074-892-0. 56 p. (10–14). Informational book.

These inspiring stories are about people who fought oppression. Featuring fact boxes, mini-profiles, a timeline and more, this is a glimpse into an often-overlooked part of Canadian history. *Our Choice 2004 starred selection.* Our Choice* *Author and illustrator from Canada*

Schwartz, Roslyn. **The Mole Sisters and the Question**. Toronto: Annick Press, 2002. ISBN 1-55037-769-X. 32 p. (3–6). Picture book.

The Mole Sisters wonder who they are, and set out to find an answer. The soft-coloured art captures their dreamy optimism. *Our Choice 2004 starred selection.* Our Choice* *Author/illustrator lives in Quebec, Canada*

Schwartz, Virginia Frances. **If I Just Had Two Wings**. Markham, ON: Fitzhenry & Whiteside, 2001. ISBN 0-7737-3302-7. 221 p. (12 up). Novel.

Life is very difficult for the slaves on an Alabama cotton plantation in the early days of the Civil War. Young Phoebe dreams of flying to freedom. When she hears that the master is going to sell her because of the poor cotton crop, Phoebe sets out with some friends on the Underground Railroad to reach Canada and freedom. They travel finding safe houses and being chased by slave catchers. The struggle to survive is hard, but they successfully arrive at their destination. *Geoffrey Bilson Award for Historical Fiction for Young People.*   *ls*
Author from Canada

Schwartz, Virginia Frances. **Messenger**. New York: Holiday House, 2002. ISBN 0-8234-1716-6. 277 p. (12 up). Novel.

Frances was born a week to the day after the tragic death of her father in the mines of Ontario. The hard-working Croatian women of the poor mining town try to convince the grief stricken widow that Frances is a messenger sent to tell her that her husband has safely arrived in heaven. This is the burden that Frances bears as she matures and it is her courage and determination from which her family draws its strength. This is a vivid portrait of the hard life of the miners in the mid 1900s.   *djg*
Author from Canada

Scrimger, Richard. **A Nose for Adventure**. Toronto: Tundra Books, 2000. ISBN 0-88776-499-7. 176 p. (8–13). Novel.

Norbert the alien returns to help the hapless Alan Dingwall out of a jam, after Alan and his new friends Frieda become entangled in an international art smuggling ring. *Our Choice 2001 starred selection.* Our Choice*
Author lives in Ontario, Canada

Sheppard, Mary C. **Seven for a Secret**. Toronto: Douglas & McIntyre, 2001. ISBN 0-88899-437-0. 189 p. (14 up). Novel.

In the early 1960s, three cousins, Melinda, Rebecca, and Kate spend their summers together in Cook's Cove, a small out port in Newfoundland. This summer the cousins seem to be going in different directions with Melinda planning her wedding, Rebecca trying to please her mother, and Kate discovering boys. Melinda must decide whether revealing a family secret is worth the pain that will result. This tale of small town life in an isolated village lacking the modern conveniences is a step back in time. *Ruth and Sylvia Schwartz Children's Book Award (YA-Middle Reader category); Our Choice 2002 starred selection.* ls *Author from Canada*

Siemiatycki, Jack, and Avi Slodovnick. **The Hockey Card**. Illustrated by Doris Barrette. Montreal: Lobster Press, 2002. ISBN 1-894222-65-2. 32 p. (5–12). Picture book.

Jack puts his hockey cards on the line! Will his prized Maurice Richard card be enough to save the day? Inimitable watercolours will stir the interest of any child who loves hockey. *Our Choice 2003 selection; 2003 Amelia Frances Howard-Gibbon shortlist.* Our Choice*

Simmie, Lois. **Mister Got to Go and Arnie**. Illlustrated by Cynthia Nugent. Vancouver: Raincoast Books, 2001. ISBN 1-55192-494-3. (5–12). Picture book.

A cat's pleasant life at the Sylvia Hotel turns upside down when Arnie the dog arrives. This is an amusing sequel to the much-loved bestseller *Mister Got to Go. Our Choice 2003 starred selection; 2002 Shining Willow Award.* Our Choice*
Author and illustrator from Canada

Slade, Arthur. **Dust**. New York: Wendy Lamb, 2003. (Paperback: Laurel Leaf, 2004). ISBN 0-3857-3004-7. 183 p. (12 up). Novel.

Seven-year-old Mathew disappears when he is allowed to walk to the town of Horsho in Saskatchewan by himself. During the 1930s Great Depression, this farming community is in the middle of a devastating drought, and Mathew's disappearance is marked by the appearance of Abram Harsich, who claims to be a meteorologist and can bring them rain if the townspeople help him build a "rainmill." In their excitement, the townspeople quickly forget about Mathew's

disappearance—except for eleven-year-old Robert, Mathew's brother. Robert's persistence and the disappearance of other children finally refocus the community's efforts on their search for all of the missing children. A surprising conclusion ensues. *2001 Governor General's Award for Children's Literature; ALA Best Books for Young Adults. kk*
Author from Canada

Spalding Andrea. **It's Raining, It's Pouring**. Illustrated by Leslie Elizabeth Watts. Victoria: Orca Book Publisher, 2001. ISBN 1551431866. 30 p. (4–6). Picture book.
      A little girl is unhappy because it is raining. Her mother sings the "It's Raining, It's Pouring" song but is unable to answer why the Old Man is in bed. The little girl dons her rain gear, gets out a very long ladder, and climbs into the clouds to see the Old Man. She meets the Old Man who is a giant with a cold and returns home to fetches a wheelbarrow filled with tea, lemon and honey, some warm scarves, and cookies. The Old Man responds very well to the little girl's ministrations and helps the little girl return home. *ls*
Author from Canada

Spalding, Andrea. **Solomon's Tree**. Illustrated by Janet Wilson. Victoria: Orca Books, 2002. ISBN 1-55143-217-X. 32 p. (8–12). Novel.
      The forest is full of cedar trees but Solomon's favorite tree is an old maple. Throughout the year, Solomon's tree shows him nature's secrets. One night, a windstorm blows the maple tree over. Solomon helps with the clean up after the storm but he is grief stricken over the loss of his tree. Solomon's uncle then shows Solomon how to make a Tshimshian mask from a piece of the maple tree. In the spring, Solomon rejoices over his finished mask, and a maple seed begins to sprout. An interesting view of Native American culture and the art of Tshimshian mask carving. *2003 Amelia Frances Howard-Gibbon shortlist; Our Choice 2003 starred selection. ls*
Author from Canada. Illustrator lives in Ontario, Canada.

Sproule, Gail. **Singing the Dark**. Illustrated by Sheena Lott. Markham, ON: Fitzhenry & Whiteside, 2001. ISBN 1-55041-648-0. 32 p. (5–8). Picture book.
      When dew falls, Mother sings a song to the coming dark. The gently rhythmic text and beautiful watercolor paintings of an approaching night make this an ideal bedtime book. *Our Choice 2003 selection; 2002 Amelia Frances Howard-Gibbon shortlist*. Our Choice*
Illustrator lives in British Columbia, Canada

Steiner, Connie Colker. **Shoes for Amélie**. Illustrated by Denis Rodier. Montreal: Lobster Press, 2001. ISBN 1-894222-37-7. 41 p. (8–12). Novel.
      During WWI, Lucien helps his family hide Jews from their persecutors in France. This poignant story—based on a real character—includes beautiful illus-

trations. *Our Choice 2002 starred selection; 2004 McNally Robinson Book for Young People Award (Children's category); 2002 CLA Best Book of the Year shortlist.* Our Choice*
Author lives in Manitoba, Canada

Stenhouse, Ted. **A Dirty Deed**. Toronto: Kids Can Press, 2003. ISBN 1-55337-360-X. 186 p. (12 up). Novel.

In 1952, Grayson, Alberta, Will, and Arthur see Mr. Howe chasing and then beating Catface, a Native American boy. Catface has hidden some papers that Will and Arthur retrieve. It is a deed to some property owned by Wilfred Black. The boys investigate the mystery of the deed ownership. In doing so, the boys are drawn into small town prejudices and one man's greed, deceptions, and family secrets. *2004 Geoffrey Bilson Historical Fiction Honor. ls*
Author from United States

Stewart, Sharon. **Raven Quest**. Markham, ON: Scholastic Canada, 2003. ISBN 0-439-98988-4. 352 p. (11–14). Novel.

Tok the raven is banished from his flock, and must go on a dangerous quest to reclaim his honour. Folklore and fantasy combine in an exciting expedition. *Our Choice 2004 selection.* Our Choice*
Author from Canada

Stratton, Allan. **Chanda's Secrets**. Toronto: Annick Press, 2004. ISBN 1-55037-835-X. 193 p. (14 up). Novel.

In this powerful story, a 16-year-old girl living in Africa must confront the undercurrents of shame and stigma associated with HIV/AIDS. It captures the enduring strength of loyalty, the profound impact of loss, and a fearlessness powered by the heart. Annotation provided by publisher. Our Choice*

Stuchner, Joan Betty. **The Kugel Valley Klezmer Band**. Illustrated by Richard Row. Markham, Ontario: North Winds Press (Scholastic Canada), 1998. ISBN 1566564301. 32 p. (5–8). Picture book.

Ten-year-old Shira yearns to learn to play the fiddle in her father's traveling klezmer band, though her father tells her it is not possible. She secretly watches Isaac, the fiddler, and he makes her a toy fiddle with the admonition to practice. When Isaac falls ill, Shira unexpectedly fills in to everybody's delight and her father buys her a fiddle for Hanukkah. The full-page paintings portray the warmth and joy music brings to small rural communities in the cold of winter. *sg*

Suzuki, David, and Sarah Ellis. **Salmon Forest**. Illustrated by Sheena Lott. New York: Greystone Books, 2003. ISBN 1-55054-937-5. 32 p. (7–10). Novel.

The salmon are running upstream to spawn. A young girl and her father talk about the life cycle of the salmon and the interdependency of nature—how the

forest protects the salmon, how the salmon is food for people and animals. Sheena Lott's watercolor illustrations highlight this story turning a walk in the woods into an ecology lesson.   *ls*
Authors from Canada

Thomas, Ly. **Ha! Ha! Ha! 1,000 Jokes, Riddles, Facts and More**. Illustrated by Dianne Eastman. Toronto: Owl Books, 2001. ISBN 1-894379-15-2. 128 p. (7–12). Anthology.

Jokes, riddles, puns, optical illusions, knock-knock jokes, and visual word games are cleverly arranged on each page, often by a theme introduced by an interesting bit of trivia in a fact box. The unusual black-and-white illustrations add a clever dynamic to the book combining line drawing, photographs, and illustrations credited to anonymous engravers of the nineteenth and twentieth century. *Ontario Library Association's Silver Birch Award.   djg*

Thompson, Richard. **The Follower**. Illustrated by Martin Springett. Markham, ON: Fitzhenry & Whiteside, 2000. ISBN 1-55041-532-8. 32 p. (4–7). Picture book.

What is following the young witch home every night past the frightening statues and life-like trees? The clues are in the shadowy pictures. Young readers will enjoy the repetition and rhyme. *Our Choice 2001 starred selection.* Our Choice*
Author lives in British Columbia, Canada. Illustrator lives in Ontario, Canada.

Thompson, Richard. **The Night Walker**. Illustrated by Martin Springett. Markham, ON: Fitzhenry & Whiteside, 2003. ISBN 1-55041-672-3. 32 p. (4–9). Picture book.

A boy goes exploring, carrying a pouch for his treasures. As it gets dark, he hears strange sounds that get louder and louder. Readers will revel in this rhythmic tale of suspense. *Our Choice 2004 starred selection; 2003 Ruth and Sylvia Schwartz Children's Book Award.* Our Choice*
Author lives in British Columbia, Canada. Illustrator lives in Ontario, Canada.

Tibo, Gilles. **The Cowboy Kid**. Illustrated by Tom Kapas. Toronto: Tundra Books, 2000. ISBN 0-88776-473-8. 32 p. (4–9). Picture book.

A young boy dreams of escaping the city and riding away on a golden steed. Then one night, this dream comes true! A magnificent stallion carries him off on a magical ride. *Our Choice 2001 starred selection. His book* The Grand Journey of Mr. Man *(2001) won the Governor-General Literary Award.* Our Choice*
Author and illustrator from Canada

Tibo, Gilles. **Naomi and Mrs. Lumbago**. Illustrated by Louise-Andrée Laliberté. Toronto: Tundra Books, 2001. ISBN 0-88776-551-3. 86 p. (6–9). Novel.

When Naomi hunts for hidden treasure in Mrs. Lumbago's apartment, her search reaps more than she realizes. A sensitive and funny exploration of intergenerational friendship. Our Choice*

Tibo, Gilles. **Shy Guy**. Translated by Sibylle Kazeroid. Illustrated by Pef. New York: North-South Books, 2002. First published as *Maxi, der Schuchterne* by Nord-Sud Verlag in 2002. ISBN 0-7356-1710-3. 28 p. (3–6). Picture book.

Greg is called Red because of his habit of blushing. His shyness makes it difficult for him to talk with anyone. When his parents let him choose a goldfish as a birthday present, he picks one that is red, names him Shy Guy, and begins to enjoy the fact that they can be shy together. He talks to Shy Guy, begins taking him around town, is able to answer questions about his goldfish that other children ask, and eventually even tells his class about him. The last page shows Greg, now able to play with others, celebrating that he has overcome his shyness.
Author lives in Canada. Illustrator lives in France.

Trottier, Maxine. **Little Dog Moon**. Illustrated by Laura Fernandez and Rick Jacobson. Markham, ON: Fitzhenry & Whiteside, 2000. ISBN 0-7737-3220-9. 23 p. (8–10). Novel.

Moon, a Tibetan terrier, lives in a Tibetan monastery with Tenzin, a young monk. One winter day, two young Tibetan children make their way to the monastery. The children are walking to Nepal where they will be free but the soldiers are guarding the mountain passes and the children don't know where to go next. Tenzin sends Moon with the children to be their guide. One chilly spring day, Moon returns to the monastery with the children's prayer flag tied around his neck. The monks know that Moon's return means the children are safe. *ls*
Author from Canada

Trottier, Maxine. **The Paint Box**. Illustrated by Stella East. Markham, ON: Fitzhenry & Whiteside, 2003. ISBN 1-55041-804-1. 16 p. (5 up). Picture book.

Marietta's father, Jacopo Tintoretto, is a renowned artist living in Venice during the Renaissance era. More than anything, Marietta wants to paint like her father. Annotation provided by publisher. *2004 Amelia Frances Howard-Gibbon shortlist*. Our Choice*
Author and illustrator live in Ontario, Canada

Uegaki, Chieri. **Suki's Kimono**. Illustrated by Stephane Jorisch. Toronto and Tonawanda, NY: Kids Can Press Ltd., 2003. ISBN 1-55337-084-8. 29 p. (5–8). Picture book.

On the first day of school, Suki wears the kimono, which her grandmother brought for her from Japan. At school, Suki's friends are very curious about her kimono. When it is Suki's turn for Show-and-Tell, Suki tells about her grandmother's visit and the festival to which they went—the food, the drumming, and

the dancers. Suki demonstrates how the dancers looked, completely forgetting she is standing in front of the class. The class applauds Suki's dance and after a successful first day of school, Suki dances her way home. The illustrations capture Suki's lively spirit in expressive and colorful watercolor illustrations. A brief list of the Japanese words used in the story precedes the text. This is a lovely intergenerational story of a young girl who is comfortable with her heritage and is willing to share it with others. *ls and sg*
Author lives in Canada

Vande Griek, Susan. **The Art Room**. Illustrated by Pascal Milelli. Toronto: Groundwood Books, 2002. ISBN 0-88899-449-4. 24 p. (8 up). Picture book.
    In the early 1900s, Emily Carr taught children's art classes. This delightful story-poem is filled with Carr's love of animals and her insistence on painting from life and nature. *Our Choice 2003 selection; 2003 Amelia Frances Howard-Gibbon Illustrator's Award; 2004 IBBY Honour List.* Our Choice*

Wallace, Ian. **Duncan's Way**. Toronto: Groundwood Books, 2000. ISBN 0-88899-388-9. 32 p. (5–8). Picture book.
    Duncan's family has always fished off the coast of Newfoundland. Now the fish are gone and his family may have to move away. Then Duncan thinks of a great idea! *Our Choice 2001 starred selection.* Our Choice*
Author lives in Ontario, Canada

Wallace, Ian. **The Man Who Walked the Earth**. Toronto: Groundwood/Douglas & McIntyre, 2003. ISBN 0-88899-545-8. 36 p. (5–8). Picture book.
    André and Elise's father leave home in search of work and it looks like he won't be home for Christmas in this tale reminiscent of the story of Elijah. Their mother instructs them to set an extra plate at the dinner table in the hope that someone will set a place for their father. Eight months pass before a stranger does indeed knock on their door and the family invites him to join them for a hot supper. Their kindness is repaid when Mr. Balzini rewards them with a magic trick and simple gifts. *djg*

Wallace, Mary. **I Can Make That! Fantastic Crafts for Kids**. Toronto: Maple Tree Press, 2002. ISBN 1-894379-41-1. 160 p. Informational book.
    The how-to book contains craft ideas for children and includes clear, step-by-step color photographs and material lists for each project. Award-winning author.

Walsh, Alice. **Heroes of Isle aux Morts**. Illustrated by Geoff Butler. Toronto and Plattsburgh, New York: Tundra Books, 2001. ISBN 0-88776-501-7. 32 p. (7–9). Picture book.
    Based on a true incident, this is the exciting story of young Anne Harvey and her family who hear a distress signal one summer morning in 1832 and row out

in a treacherous storm with her dog, Hairy Man, to see if they can rescue anybody from a foundering ship. The dog, a Newfoundland, is sent by Anne through the waves to the ship and miraculously brings back a rope that Anne and her father use to rescue each of the 163 passengers. The oil paintings convey a sense of the wild seas and storms of Newfoundland province, the desperation of the rescue, and the heroism of the dog. A foreword tells about Newfoundland dogs.   *sg*
Author lives in Canada

Walters, Eric. **Caged Eagles**. Victoria: Orca Books, 2000. ISBN 1-55143-182-3. 256 p. (12 up). Novel.
    In the early days of World War II, fourteen-year-old Tadashi and his family must leave their village in British Columbia and take their fishing boat to Vancouver. The family is sent to an internment center where conditions are primitive and regimented, and their future is uncertain. Tadashi struggles to understand the racism and injustice that his family must endure. Sequel to *War of the Eagles. 2003 finalist—UNESCO.*   *ls*
Author from Canada

Walters, Eric. **Run**. Toronto: Penguin Group (Canada), 2003. ISBN 0-67-004438-5. 224 p. (10–14). Novel.
    In this work of fiction, Winston and his father are on the road with Terry Fox. Winston gains strength and inspiration from the heroic runner. *Our Choice 2004 starred selection; 2004 Tiny Torgi Literary Awards (Audio Category); 2004 CLA Book of the Year shortlist.* Our Choice*
Author lives in Ontario, Canada

Watts, Irene N. **Finding Sophie**. Plattsburgh: Tundra Books of Northern New York, 2002. ISBN 0-88776-613-7. 136 p. (12 up). Novel.
    World War II is over. Fourteen-year-old Sophie Mandel has spent the last seven years living in England with Aunt Em, a friend of her parents. In that time, despite the privations of war, Sophie has made a comfortable life for herself. Sophie's father has survived the war and wants her to rejoin him in Germany. Prospects are dim until a creative solution satisfies everyone involved. *2003 Geoffrey Bilson Historical Fiction Honor.*   *ls*
Author from Canada

Watts, Irene N. **Remember Me**. Toronto: Tundra Books, 2000. ISBN 0-88776-445-2. 174 p. (8–12). Novel.
    Marianne escapes Berlin, but life in England is not easier. She has no friends, doesn't speak the language, and fears for her mother left behind. A sequel to the award-winning *Good-bye Marianne. Our Choice 2001 starred selection; 2003 Chocolate Lilly Young Readers' Choice Award (Chapter Book/Novel Category).* Our Choice*
Author lives in British Columbia, Cana

Wiebe, Ruby. **Hidden Buffalo**. Illustrated by Michael Lonechild. Calgary: Red Deer Press, 2003. ISBN 0-88995-285-X. 32 p. (7–10). Picture book.

Luminous paintings of the early autumn prairie landscape depict this tale of the hidden buffalo. A memorable, mystical story based on an ancient Cree legend. *2004 Alberta Children's Book of the Year Award; Our Choice 2004 selection; 2004 Amelia Frances Howard-Gibbon Award shortlist.* Our Choice*

Wilson, John. **Dancing Elephants and Floating Continents: The Story of the Land beneath Your Feet**. Toronto: Key Porter Books, 2003. ISBN 1-55263-200-8. 48 p. (9–13). Informational book.

A wondrous journey to the center of the Earth—and back! Clear language, illustrations, maps, and photographs of giant earth-pounding trucks (dancing elephants) explain how the earth was formed. *Our Choice 2004 selection.* Our Choice*
Author lives in British Columbia, Canada

Wishinsky, Frieda. **Give Maggie a Chance**. Illustrated by Dean Griffiths. Markham: Fitzhenry & Whiteside, 2002. ISBN 1-55041-682-0. 32 p. (8–10). Picture book.

When the teacher asks who would like to read aloud, Maggie immediately raises her hand. Maggie gets to the front of the class, but not a sound comes out of her. Embarrassed, she wants the floor to swallow her up. The next day, Maggie tries again with the same results. On the third day, Maggie finds her courage in her friend Sam and succeeds in explaining an arithmetic problem to the class. A common problem, which affects many children, is handled with kindness, patience, and encouragement. *ls*
Author from Canada

Wishinsky, Frieda. **Jennifer Jones Won't Leave Me Alone**. Illustrated by Neal Layton. Minneapolis: Carolrhoda Book, 2003. First published by Transworld Publishers Ltd. London, England. ISBN 0-87614-921-2. (Markham, ON: Scholastic Canada, 2004. ISBN 0-439-96981-6). 28 p. (5–8). Picture book.

Jennifer Jones is in pursuit of one thing—the little boy who sits next to her. But the boy is fed up with Jennifer's loving attention and wishes she would go away. One day, she actually does, and he is heartbroken. Annotation provided by publisher.
Author lives in Toronto

Wishinsky, Frieda. **Just Call Me Joe**. Illustrated by Stephen McCallum. Victoria: Orca Book Publishers, 2003. ISBN 1-5514-3249-8. 101 p. (7–10). Novel.

It is 1909 and Joe immigrates to the USA from Russia. Learning English is a challenge, as is resisting the pressure to skip school, steal, and fight. *2004 CLA Book of the Year shortlist; Our Choice 2003 selection.* Our Choice*
Author lives in Ontario, Canada

Wolfe, Frances. **One Wish**. Toronto: Tundra Books, 2004. ISBN 0-88776-662-5. 29 p. (5–8). Picture book.

A young girl has one specific convoluted wish to live in a cottage by the sea where she can walk on the beach, collect seashells, go swimming, build sand castles, or just sit on the shore and gaze out over the water. This simple story is supported by beautifully realistic illustrations done in oil. The story's conclusion is very hopeful. Wishes can come true. *ls*
Author from Canada

Wolfe, Frances. **Where I Live**. Toronto: Tundra Books, 2001. ISBN 0-88776-529-7. 32 p. (4–8). Picture book.

A young girl writes a lyrical poem about where she lives—the seaside. The lush oil painting illustrations provide a view into this girl's world. Gulls flying. Ships sailing. Fireplace flames flickering. Rain falling. The use of perspective in the images creates interest. The images are very immediate. A beautiful, calm, simple book about a girl's love of her home. *2002 Amelia Frances Howard-Gibbon Illustrator's Award; Ann Connor Brimer Award.* *ls*
Author from Canada

Wynne-Jones, Tim. **The Boy in the Burning House**. New York: Melanie Kroupa Books, an imprint of Farrar, Straus and Giroux, 2001. Originally published in 2000 by Groundwood Books/Douglas & McIntyre (paperback: Farrar, Straus and Giroux Sunburst, 2003). ISBN 0-374-30930-2 (paperback: 0-374-40887-4). 213 p. (11 up). Novel.

Jim Hawkins, struggling with his father's mysterious disappearance two years earlier, encounters Ruth Rose Fisher under less than optimal circumstances. She's the moody, unstable, trouble-seeking stepdaughter of the town preacher—one of Jim's father's childhood friends. Ruth Rose accuses her stepfather of murdering Jim's dad because of an incident on New Year's Eve—thirty years earlier. Danger and suspense enshroud Jim and Ruth Rose as they investigate Mr. Hawkins's disappearance and the secrets lurking within their rural Canadian community. *2001 Arthur Ellis Award (Crime Writers of Canada best juvenile mystery); 2002 Edgar Allan Poe Award (Mystery Writers of America best young adult novel); Our Choice starred selection.* *lmp and ls*
Author lives in Canada

Wynne-Jones, Tim. **Ned Mouse Breaks Away**. Illustrated by Dušan Petričić. Toronto: Groundwood Books, 2003. ISBN 0-88899-474-5. 68 p. (7–10). Novel.

Ned Mouse is sent to jail for writing a message in his spinach. Determined to escape, he comes up with a daring plan. Wit and humour fill this gently subversive fable. *Our Choice 2004 starred selection.* Our Choice*
Author and illustrator live in Ontario, Canada

Wynne-Jones, Tim. **A Thief in the House of Memory**. Toronto: Groundwood Books, 2004. ISBN 0-88899-574-1. 180 p. (11 and up). Novel.

Declan Steeple is a 16-year-old who has it all: great grades, dreams of becoming an architect, great friends, and family. Then one day Dec hitches a ride home triggering a chain of events that exposes the not-so-perfect underbelly of his perfect life. Annotation provided by publisher. Our Choice*
Author lives in Ontario, Canada

Yee, Paul. **The Bone Collector's Son**. Vancouver: Tradewind Books, 2003. ISBN 1-896580-25-4. 175 p. (11–13). Novel.

Sinister things start happening when Bing accompanies his father to the graveyard. This ghost story is set in 1907 Vancouver. *Our Choice 2004 selection.* Our Choice*
Author lives in Ontario, Canada

Yee, Paul. **Dead Man's Gold and Other Stories**. Illustrated by Harvey Chan. Toronto: Groundwood Books, 2002. ISBN 0-88899-475-3. 104 p. (9 up). Novel.

Ten original ghost stories dramatize the history of Chinese immigration to North America, from the award-winning creators of *Ghost Train. Our Choice 2003 starred selection; 2003 CLA Book of the Year shortlist.* Our Choice*
Author and illustrator live in Ontario, Canada

Yee, Paul. **The Jade Necklace**. Illustrated by Grace Lin. New York: Crocodile Books, 2002. Published simultaneously in Great Britain and Canada by Tradewind Books. ISBN 1-56656-455-7. 32 p. (4–8). Picture book.

After Yenyee's fisherman father drowns during a typhoon, she throws the jade pendant he had given her into the ocean. The family tries to make a living but finally Yenyee, with her mother's reluctant consent, accepts a position as a caregiver for the young daughter of a merchant. She travels with the family from China to Vancouver. When her young charge falls into the ocean near their new home, Yenyee dives in to save her. When she emerges from the ocean, she finds the pendant entangled in her hair and makes peace with the ocean. *jig*
Author lives in Canada

Yee, Paul. **A Song for Ba**. Pictures by Jan Peng Wang. Toronto: Groundwood/ Douglas & McIntyre, 2004. ISBN 0-88899-492-3. 32 p. (5–10). Picture book.

Wei Lim's father, Ba, is a singer in the Chinese Opera. The company is struggling as the older members emigrate back to China and audiences dwindle. Ba doesn't want his son to learn opera, but grandfather secretly teaches Wei Lim to sing the female parts. Beautiful oil paintings illustrate this story of an ancient art form and the painful transition that Chinese communities endured adapting to the New World, while trying to keep their own culture alive. *djg*

Zeman, Ludmila. **Sindbad in the Land of Giants: From the Tales of the Thousand and One Nights**. Toronto: Tundra Books, 1999. Originally published by McClelland & Stewart Young Readers. ISBN 0-8877-6460-6. 32 p. Picture book.

For 1,000 nights Shahrazad charmed the king with exciting stories of adventure, discovery, and exploration until, forgetting his cruel ways, he ordered his craftsmen to weave the stories into fine silk carpets. Some of the stories are retold by Zeman in this series of books, richly illustrated with patterns reminiscent of the carpets. These stories of Sinbad the Sailor are linked to actual voyages undertaken by the Arabs. Seven centuries before Columbus, the Arabs, who were remarkable sailors, mastered the route to China. The mixture of fact and fiction inspired Zeman's art.   *djg*
Author from Czechoslovakia, lives in Montreal and has written and illustrated many award-winning books including The Quest of Gilgamesh *and* The First Red Maple Leaf.

Zhang, Ange. **Red Land, Yellow River: A Story from the Cultural Revolution**. Toronto: Groundwood, 2004. ISBN 0-88899-489-3. 56 p. (8 up). Informational book.

Ange is a young boy at the time of the cultural revolution in China and wants nothing more to wear than the olive uniform and red arm band of Red Guard. Suddenly he becomes the "black kid" and he understands that it is because his father is a writer and thus a "bad guy." He is sent to a farm and the rest of his family is sent to work camps. Through a child's eye the reader sees the events of Mao's revolution. The mixed media art, a combination of photos of artifacts and posters, and striking watercolors add depth and insight into this tumultuous period of history.   *djg*
Author lives in Ontario, Canada

Our Choice*—These annotations first appeared in *Our Choice*, the annual selection guide published by the Canadian Children's Book Centre. Used by permission of the Canadian Children's Book Centre. I wish to thank Hadley Dyer, past president of IBBY–Canada, Deidre Baker, co-author of *A Guide to Canadian Children's Books* and Brenda Halliday, the librarian at the Canadian Children's Book Centre for their invaluable assistance.

Related Information

Organizations

The Canadian Children's Book Centre
www.bookcentre.ca
40 Orchard View Blvd., Suite 101, Toronto, ON M4R 1B9; tel. 416-975-0010; fax 416-975-8970

Founded in 1976, this national, nonprofit organization promotes and encourages the reading, writing, and illustrating of Canadian children's books through such activities as Children's Book Week and the publications *Children's Book News* and *Our Choice*. The website has links to pages that provide names and addresses of Canadian publishers, bookstores, and related organizations as well as author web pages and an explanation of the Canadian children's books awards.

CANSCAIP
40 Orchard View Blvd, Suite 104, Toronto, ON M4R 1B9; tel: 416-515-1559; fax: 416-515-7022

The Canadian Society of Children's Authors, Illustrators, and Performers (CANSCAIP) is a group of professionals in the field of children's culture with members from all parts of Canada. For over twenty years, CANSCAIP has been instrumental in the support and promotion of children's literature through newsletters, workshops, meetings, and other information programs for authors, parents, teachers, librarians, publishers, and others.

Awards

More information about awards can be found here:
http://www.bookcentre.ca/awards/award_ind/index.shtml

The Amelia Frances Howard-Gibbon Illustrator's Award
Given by the Canadian Association of Children's Librarians (CACL), this annual award is presented to the illustrator of an outstanding children's book (age 0–14) published during the previous calendar year in Canada; the illustrator must be a Canadian citizen or permanent resident of Canada.

Canadian Library Association Book of the Year for Children Award
Given by the Canadian Association of Children's Librarians (CACL), this annual award is presented to the author of an outstanding children's book published during the previous calendar year in Canada; the author must be a Canadian citizen or permanent resident of Canada.

Canadian Library Association Young Adult Canadian Book Award
This award was established in 1980 by the Young Adult Caucus of the Saskatchewan Library Association and is administered by the Young Adult Services Group (YASIG). This prize is awarded to the author of an outstanding English language book for young adults (ages 13–18) published in the preceding calendar year. A CLA member from Saskatchewan is on the selection committee, and the Book Award seal, which was designed by a young adult from Regina, designates the winning title each year. The winning book must be a work of fiction (novel or collection of short stories) written by a Canadian citizen or landed im-

migrant published in Canada. The winner receives a leather bound book with the Award seal embossed on the cover in gold.

Elizabeth Mrazik-Cleaver Canadian Picture Book Award

The award is administered by IBBY Canada and given to a Canadian illustrator of a picture book published in Canada in English or in French during the previous calendar year.

The Geoffrey Bilson Award for Historical Fiction for Young People

This annual prize is awarded to the author of an outstanding work of historical fiction for young people published during the previous year; the author must be Canadian.

Governor General's Literary Awards

Up to four annual awards (one each to an English-language writer, a French-language writer, and illustrator of an English-language book, and to an illustrator of a French-language book) are given by the Canada Council; all books for young people written or illustrated by a Canadian citizen in the previous year are eligible, whether published in Canada or abroad.

IBBY Honour List, administered by IBBY Canada.

http://www.ibby-canada.org/

Information Book Award

Sponsored by the Children's Literature Roundtables of Canada, the Information Book Award is given to recognize an outstanding information book for children and young people five to fifteen years of age written in English by a Canadian citizen.

The Mr. Christie's Book Award

Six awards—three categories (seven and under, eight to eleven, and twelve and up) in English and French—are given, and the books are judged on the content of illustrations and text. Eligible books are published in the previous calendar year written and/or illustrated by a Canadian. Discontinued in 2004.

The Norma Fleck Award for Canadian Children's Non-Fiction

The Norma Fleck Award for Canadian Children's Non-Fiction was established by the Fleck Family Foundation and the Canadian Children's Book Centre in May 1999 to recognize and raise the profile of non-fiction. The $10,000 annual award honors exceptional quality in content and production in children's non-fiction by a Canadian author.

Reader's Choice Awards

There are many reader's choice awards, often known as the "tree" awards, which include the Ontario Library Association's Blue Spruce Hackmatack (Maritimes), Silver Birch, Red Maple, White Pine the Red Cedar (BC), Willow (Sask.), and Manitoba Young Reader's Choice. For more information, see CCBC website below.

Ruth and Sylvia Schwartz Children's Book Award

Administered by the Ontario Arts Council Foundation, the Ontario Arts Council, and the Canadian Booksellers' Association, this prize recognizes authors and illustrators who demonstrate artistic excellence in Canadian children's literature. Winning books are selected by juries of children from a public school in Ontario.

Sheila A. Egoff Children's Literature Prize

The Sheila A. Egoff Children's Literature Prize is awarded annually as part of the British Columbia Book Prize program to what is judged to be the best children's book published in the previous year written by a writer who has been a resident in British Columbia (or the Yukon) for three of the previous five years, published anywhere in the world.

TD Canadian Children's Literature Award

In October 2004 the Canadian Children's Book Centre and the TD Bank Financial Group announced the establishment of a new children's book award for the most distinguished book of the year. All books, in any genre, written by a Canadian and for children aged 1 through 13 are eligible. In the case of picture books, both the author and the illustrator must be Canadian. The grand prize is $20,000 for the most distinguished book written in English and $20,000 for the most distinguished book written in French.

Vicky Metcalf Award

This annual award carries a large cash prize and is presented by the Writers' Trust of Canada to a Canadian writer (citizen or landed immigrant) who has produced a body of work (more than three books) with appeal for children aged seven to seventeen.

Websites

Canadian Children's Book Centre

www.bookcentre.ca

The website of the Canadian Children's Book Centre has links to Canadian children's book publishers, author and illustrator homepages, and a comprehensive listing of all of the Canadian children's book awards.

Canadian Children's Illustrated Books in English
http://www.slais.ubc.ca/saltman/ccib/Welcome.html
[see description on their website]

Children's Literature Web Guide
Created and maintained by David K. Brown of the University of Calgary, this comprehensive site is international in scope and used by people all around the world. Some lists haven't been updated since 1999.
http://www.acs.ucalgary.ca/~dkbrown/index.html

Festivals

Canadian Children's Book Week
Across Canada the first week of November
Organized by the Canadian Children's Book Centre
Phone: 416-975-0010
e-mail: info@bookweek.ca
http://www.bookcentre.ca and www.bookweek.ca

Festival of the Written Arts
Sechelt, BC, Canada
phone: 604-885-9631 or 1-800-565-9631
e-mail: written_arts@sunshine.net
http://www.writersfestival.ca

Journals

CM: Canadian Review of Materials
CM—an electronic reviewing journal published by the Manitoba Library Association—features book reviews, media reviews, news, and author profiles of interest to teachers, librarians, parents, and kids. CM reviews Canadiana of interest to children and young adults, including publications produced in Canada, or published elsewhere but of special interest or significance to Canada, such as those having a Canadian writer, illustrator, or subject.
http://www.umanitoba.ca/cm/

Canadian Children's Book News
Published since 1977 by the Canadian Children's Book Centre, *Canadian Children's Book News* has helped parents, teachers, librarians, and booksellers discover new Canadian children's books and keep up with industry issues and ideas. Each issue is packed with news, book reviews, author and illustrator interviews, profiles of publishers and bookstores, and information about the world of children's books in Canada. Published quarterly in an attractive full-color format, and

distributed nationwide, CCBN is the source for adults who select books for young readers.
http://www.bookcentre.ca/programs/booknews.shtml

Canadian Children's Literature/Littérature canadienne pour la jeunesse

CCL/LCJ: Canadian Children's Literature/Littérature canadienne pour la jeunesse is a bilingual refereed academic journal that advances knowledge and understanding of texts of Canadian children's literature and the literary and cultural contexts from which they emerge in a range of media in both English and French. CCL/LCJ seeks articles from specialists in English and/or French literature, theatre and drama, media studies, literary theory, education, information science, childhood and cultural studies, and other related disciplines. Articles may be submitted as attachments in Word or RTF format to: ccl@uwinnipeg.ca
The current website is:
http://ccl.uwinnipeg.ca/
phone: 1-204-786-9351

The Looking Glass: New Perspective on Children's Books

Founded in 1997, this high-quality electronic journal about children's literature describes itself as combining an interest in the traditional with an eye to the modern. Although its contributors span the globe, they usually have a Canadian connection; the articles are international both in terms of topic and approach. Subscriptions are free but donations are welcome.
www.the-looking-glass.net

Resource Links

Contact: Victoria Pennell
Editor *Resource Links*
P. O. Box 9, Pouch Cove, NL A0A 3L0
Tel: 709-335-2394; Fax: 709-335-2978
e-mail: resourcelinks@nfld.com

Published 5 times a year, Resource Links is Canada's newest national journal devoted to the review and evaluation of Canadian resources for children and young adults. *Resource Links* reviews new information books, picture books and novels for children and young adults, audio-visual materials, CD-ROMs, computer software, and Internet resources for young people and professional literature of interest to teachers and librarians. Written by educators and librarians working with young people across the country, Resource Links also covers Canadian writers, awards, and announcements.
http://www.resourcelinks.ca/

Online Bookstores

Chapters Online

Chapters.indigo.ca

With a separate category called Kids, this online venue of the Canadian bookstore chain makes it easy to browse in the children's section, where author profiles are posted periodically and featured books are described.

Print Resources

Baker, Deirdre, and Ken Setterington. **A Guide to Canadian Children's Books in English**. Illustrated by Kady MacDonald Denton. Toronto: McClelland & Stewart, 2003. ISBN 0-7710-1064-8. 296 p.

Two experts offer guidance in the selection and sharing of the best Canadian children's books. Features over 500 recommended titles organized by age and genre. *Our Choice 2004 starred selection.*

Jones, Raymond E., and Jon C. Stott. **Canadian Children's Books: A Critical Guide to Authors and Illustrators**. Ontario, Canada: Oxford University Press, 2000. ISBN 0-19-541222-2. 538 p.

A thorough introduction to the history of Canadian Children's literature is followed by author entries for all of Canada's major children's book writers. An appendix of major English-language Canadian Book Awards and a bibliography concludes this useful reference work.

Chapter 5

Asia

AFGHANISTAN

Carlsson, Janne. **Camel Bells**. Translated by Angela Barnett-Lindberg. Toronto: Groundwood, 2002, 1989. Originally published in 1987 as *Kamelklockorna* by Rabén & Sjögren. ISBN 0-88899-515-6. 120 p. (10 up). Novel.
See Europe/Sweden for description.

Ellis, Deborah. **The Breadwinner**. Toronto: Groundwood Books/Douglas & McIntyre, 2000. ISBN 0-88899-419-2. 170 p. (9 up). Novel. *Sweden's Peter Pan Prize; Rocky Mountain Books Award; University of California's Middle East Book Award; Notable Books for a Global Society, 2003.*

Ellis, Deborah. **Mud City**. Toronto: Groundwood Books/Douglas & McIntyre, 2003. ISBN 0-88899-518-0. 164 p. (9 up). Novel.
See Canada for description of this award-winning trilogy.

Ellis, Deborah. **Parvana's Journey**. Toronto: Groundwood Books/Douglas & McIntyre, 2002. ISBN 0-88899-514-8. 199 p. (9 up). Novel. *Jane Addams Peace Award.*

Shah, Idries. **The Old Woman and the Eagle**. Illustrated by Natasha Delmar. Cambridge: Hoopoe Books, 2003. ISBN 1-883536-27-8. 32 p. (3–8). Folktale.
There was an old woman who had seen many birds but she had never seen an eagle. When an eagle perches on a tree near her house, the old woman thinks it is a strange pigeon. The old woman trims the eagle's talons, straightens its beak, and smoothes its feathers. The eagle escapes and with another eagle's help, his feath-

ers are ruffled and his beak is re-curved. Both eagles vow to stay away from silly old women who could not tell the difference between a pigeon and an eagle. *ls*
Author from Afghanistan

CAMBODIA

Ho, Minfong. **The Stone Goddess**. New York: Orchard Books, 2003. ISBN 0-439-38197-5. 201 p. (9–12). Novel.

Trained as a classical Cambodian dancer, Nakri and her family must flee their home in Phom Penh for her grandparent's village when the Khmer Rouge takes over the country. Later, Nakri and her brother and sister are sent out into the countryside to plant rice. After four years, the Khmer Rouge regime is defeated and Nakri and her brother begin the long journey to seek out their family and must come to terms with their sister's death. This first person account relates a tragic episode in world history with compassion and sensitivity. *ls*
Author from United States

Lipp, Frederick. **The Caged Birds of Phnom Penh**. Illustrated by Ron Himler. New York: Holiday House, 2001. ISBN 0-8254-1534-1. 32 p. (4–8). Picture book.

Ary feels trapped in the bustling, dusty capital city of Phnom Penh. She wishes her family lived in better circumstances. When Ary saves enough money to purchase one of the colorful caged birds at the market, she celebrates a treasured Cambodian custom. Free a bird and whisper your heart's fondest desires as you guide it skyward. One day your wishes will become reality. After her first bird dutifully returns to the bird woman's cage, Ary hatches a plan to ensure that her next bird remains free. Himler's watercolor illustrations invite us to see the world thru Ary's eight-year-old eyes. Excellent juxtaposition between the first and last illustrations. *2001 Parents' Choice Silver Honor Book.   nrn*
Author from United States, living in UK

Yip, Dora. **Welcome to Cambodia**. Milwaukee, WI: Gareth Stevens, 2001.
See Global/Welcome to My Country for description.

CHINA

Bridges, Shirin Yim. **Ruby's Wish**. Illustrated by Sophie Blackall. San Francisco: Chronicle Books, 2002. ISBN 0-8118 3490-5. 28 p. (7–10). Picture book.

Ruby's wish is based on the author's grandmother's childhood, when, as a young girl, her one fervent wish was to go to the university. Raised in a large, well-to-do family, Ruby's wish came true when her understanding grandfather, the patriarch of the family, listened to her request, and against custom, helped her

enroll as the first female member of the university. This affecting, quietly told story is enhanced by delicate illustrations depicting 19th-century home and family, with authentic appearing clothes, furnishings, and architecture. *Ezra Jack Keats New Writer and Illustrator Award, 2003; Choices, 2003.   jvl*
Author has lived in Malaysia, Singapore, Hong Kong, Australia, New Zealand, and now in the United States. Illustrator from Australia, lives in the United States

Chan, Arlene. **Awakening the Dragon: The Dragon Boat Festival**. Illustrated by Song Nan Zhang. Toronto: Tundra Books, 2004. ISBN 0-88776-656-0. 26 p. (5–10). Informational book.
  See Canada for description.

Chen, Da. **China's Son: Growing Up in the Cultural Revolution**. New York: Delacorte Press, 2001. (Based on *Colors of the Mountain* by the author.) ISBN 0-385-72929-4. 213 pp. (12 up). Autobiography.
  Da Chen and his family become outcasts under the regime of Chairman Mao. Da's father works at a labor camp while Da struggles to survive the inequities he faces daily. Da finds friendship with a gang of boys and abandons his educational pursuits. After Mao Tse Tung dies, the universities reopen. Da's friends and family provide selfless support so Da can study for the highly competitive university exams. This inspirational memoir reminds readers that "genuine pearls shine even in the darkness." The author accurately portrays the stark realities faced by former landlords during the Chinese Cultural Revolution. *Notable Books for a Global Society, 2002.   nrn*
Author from China, lives in United States

Chen, Kerstin. **Lord of the Cranes: A Chinese Tale**. Translated by J. Alison James. Illustrated by Jian Jiang Chen. First published in Switzerland under the title *Der Herr der Kraniche-Ein chinesische Sage*. ISBN 0-7358-1192-X. 32 p. (4–8). Folktale.
  See Europe/Switzerland for description.

Compestine, Ying Chang. **The Story of Chopsticks**. Illustrated by YongSheng Xuan. New York: Holiday House, 2001. ISBN 0-8234-1526-0. 32 p. (5–7). Picture book.
  Striking Chinese cut paper illustrations illustrate this delightful pourquoi tale of youngest child Kuai, who never gets enough to eat: either the food is too hot to hold or he is too slow and it is all gone. Frustrated, he uses two kindling sticks to reach the food and thus chopsticks are invented. The new idea catches on quickly, but the village elders must be convinced that it is acceptable. An author's note tells the true history of chopsticks and its relation to Confucian ideals of good manners. Also included are instructions for using chopsticks and a recipe for

Sweet Eight Treasures Rice Pudding. A similar offering by the pair, *The Story of Noodles* (2002), describes how two boys invent noodles, and is also accompanied by an author's note and recipe. *sg*
Author from China, lives in United States

Compestine, Ying Chang. **The Story of Kites**. Illustrated by YongSheng Xuan. New York: Holiday House, 2003. ISBN 0-8234-1715-8. 32 p. (4–8). Picture book.
Compestine, Ying Chang. **The Story of Paper**. Illustrated by YongSheng Xuan. New York: Holiday House, 2003. ISBN 0-8234-1705-0. 32 p. (4–8). Picture book.
   The mischievous Kang brothers, Ting, Pan, and Kùai, are at the center of these two Chinese pourquoi tales. In *The Story of Paper*, the boys tire of having their teacher write on their hands. Finding inspiration in their mother's rice cakes, they use scraps of silk to create the world's first paper. Similarly, in *The Story of Kites*, when Ting, Pan, and Kùai rebel against scaring birds from their family's rice fields, they devise an almost effortless method—flying paper noisemakers decorated to resemble birds and butterflies. Yong Sheng Xuan's illustrations were created in the traditional Chinese cut-paper style. *lmp*
Author and illustrator from China, live in United States

Demi. **The Greatest Power**. New York: Margaret K. McElderry Books, 2004. ISBN 0-689-84503-0. 32 p. (5–10). Picture book.
   In this companion to *The Empty Pot*, Demi tells of the boy emperor Ping, who sets a challenge before the people: to know the greatest power in the world is to know the greatest peace. Whoever can demonstrate this harmony and show him the greatest power in the world will become the next prime minister. The excited children take up the challenge. Some make swords and shields, some beautiful costumes, some create great technology, but one little girl realizes that great armies fall, beauty fades, and ideas change. It is she who understands the pattern of eternal life and becomes the new prime minister. *djg*
Author from United States

Freedman, Russell. **Confucius: The Golden Rule**. Illustrated by Frederic Clement. New York: Arthur A. Levine Books, c2002. ISBN 0-439-13957-0. 48 p. (8–12). Informational book.
   Freedman tells the story of Confucius' life in the context of the tumultuous time period in which Confucius lived. Although Confucius lived over 2,500 years ago in Ancient China, the author brings Confucius to life through fine descriptive writing. Confucius' teachings are illuminated for young readers by conversations between the teacher and his students that the author expertly weaves into the story. Freedman incorporates quotes from *The Analects of Confucius* not only in the flowing narrative, but on the endpapers, as well. Clement's superb illustrations complement the text with their Chinese style and unique presentation. Each painting is frayed to give it an ancient look but has an overlay of real objects such

as fresh fruit and flower petals. The result is a refreshing combination of old and new, just like this outstanding biography.   *aao*
Author lives in United States

Grimes, Nikki. **Tai Chi Morning: Snapshots of China**. Illustrated by Ed Young. Chicago: Cricket Books, 2004. ISBN 0-8126-2707-5. 51 p. (8–12). Poetry.

The author shares first impressions of traveling to this complex country in an insightful collection of poems. Beginning with the slow, controlled impressions of men and women practicing tai chi in a park in Beijing, Grimes distills her observations into words that convey the beauty and tensions of China in the time leading up to the Tiananmen Square riots. The poetry is illustrated with sketches and drawings by Ed Young. An itinerary of the author's first trip to China is appended along with a map and an index to the illustrations with the titles translated into Chinese. Tai Chi Morning is a unique meeting of two artists, two visions, and one fascinating land. As Nikki's verse and Ed's drawings unfold in counterpoint we are carried on simultaneous journeys that separate, intersect, and run parallel.   *djg*

Grindley, Sally. **Spilled Water**. New York: Bloomsbury, 2004. ISBN 1-58234-937-1. 224 p. (10–14). Novel.

See Europe/UK for description.

Hill, Elizabeth Starr. **Chang and the Bamboo Flute**. Illustrated by Lesley Liu. New York: Farrar, Straus, Giroux, 2002. ISBN 0-374-31238-9. 60 p. (7–9). Novella.

Chang lives on a houseboat on the Li River of southern China with his parents and the nine cormorants his fisherman father has trained to retrieve fish. Though naturally shy, the mute Chang demonstrates courage, resourcefulness, and the ability to communicate when his father's raft is almost swept away on the rain-swollen river. This sequel to the author/illustrator team's *Bird Boy*, which was a Parents' Choice Gold Award Winner, offers a vivid evocation of an unusual way of life as well as a satisfying story of an unexpected and thoroughly likeable child hero. *Bank Street Best Book of the Year, 2003.*

Hong, Chen Jiang. **The Legend of the Kite: A Story of China**. Translated by Jacqueline Miller. Illustrated by Chen Jiang Hong. Norwalk, CT: Soundprints, 1999. Originally printed as *La legende du cer-volant by l'ecole des loisirs*, Paris, 1997. ISBN 1-56899-810-4. 32 p. (5–10). Picture book.

Dan-Long and his grandfather go to the plaza at the Forbidden City to launch their *fēngzheng,* kite. Strong winds take the kite high into the air and the string snaps. Grandfather comforts the boy, telling him the story of Ming-Ming and Ying-Ying and of why there are so many kites flying overhead. A map of China, brief information about the country, and the kite flying are appended.   *djg*

Lee, Jeanne. **Bitter Dumplings**. New York: Farrar, Straus and Giroux, 2002. ISBN 0-374-39966-2. 32 p. (8 up). Picture Book.

When Mei-Mei's father dies, her brothers use her dowry to pay the funeral expenses, then split the inheritance between them. Without dowry or inheritance, Mei-Mei becomes an outcast until she helps out Po Po, an old hunchback woman, who lives alone and makes her living by making and selling bitter dumplings. As they become acquainted, the two women find they have much in common. This is a folktale-like story of compassion, survival, and diligence in thirteenth-century China. *2002 Kiriyama Prize shortlist.* ls
Author from United States

Liu, Siyu, and Orel Protopopescu. **A Thousand Peaks: Poems from China**. Translated by Orel Protopopescu and Siyu Liu. Illustrated by Siyu Liu. Berkeley: Pacific View Press, 2002. ISBN 1-881896-24-2. 52 p. (12 up). Poetry.
This is a welcome, culturally authentic collection of thirty-five poems from 2000 years of Chinese literature presented in an attractively open format. Poems are grouped in three thematic sections. Graceful verse translations, one to a page, are accompanied by the original Chinese characters, pinyin translation, and a literal translation in a sidebar. Poems are illustrated by small black-and-white drawings based on one of the key characters. Information either about the history or setting of the poem, the poetics, or the poet's life follows. Notes on Chinese language and pronunciation, the characters illustrated, and further resources for young readers and teachers conclude the volume. *Independent Publishers Book Award, 2002.* sg
Liu born in China during the Cultural Revolution, lives in United States

Loo, Sanne te. **Ping Li's Kite**. Asheville, NC: Front Street/Lemniscaat, 2002. ISBN 1886910758. Originally published in the Netherlands under the title *Ping Li en zijn vlieger* by Lemniscaat b.v. Rotterdam, 2001. 28 p. (4–7). Picture book.
See Europe/Netherlands for description.

McCaughrean, Geraldine. **The Kite Rider**. New York: HarperCollins, 2002. First published in England by Oxford University Press in 2001. ISBN 0-06-623874-9. 272 p. (9–12). Novel.
See Europe/UK for description.

Pacilio, V. J. **Ling Cho and His Three Friends**. Translated by Elisabeth Kallick Dyssegaard. Illustrated by Scott Cook. New York: Farrar, Straus and Giroux, 2000. ISBN 0-3743-4545-7. 32 p. (7–9). Picture book.
Ling Cho, a wealthy farmer, wishes to help his three friends, who, because their land is poor, are close to starvation. In an attempt to help his friends without embarrassing them, Ling Cho commissions them to take his harvest to market and in return to halve the profits. Upon their return, two of his friends tell unbelievable tales of why they were unable to fulfill their task. The third friend tells the truth: he used the money to feed his starving family. A lesson on honesty is

implied, while Ling Cho spells out another lesson on friends allowing friends to help when they are in need. *jvl*
Author from United States

Pilegard, Virginia Walton. **The Warlord's Fish**. Illustrated by Nicolas Debon. Gretna, LA: Pelican Publishing, 2002. ISBN 1-56554-964-3. 32 p. (8–11). Picture book.

Chuan, a young apprentice to the Warlord's artist, hopes to learn to make everything the artist creates, including the fascinating little goldfish that always point to the south when they are floating on water. When the artist and Chuan are kidnapped and then lost in the desert, along with the kidnapper merchants who had hoped to sell them, Chuan's quick wit saves them all as he produces a little fish and places it on their last remaining bowl of water and is able to identify south. The author's end note describes the invention of the compass in China. The author also wrote *The Warlord's Puppeteers* (2003). *jvl*
Author from United States

Porte, Barbara Ann. **Ma Jiang and the Orange Ants**. Illustrated by Annie Cannon. New York: Orchard Books, 2000. ISBN 0531302415. 32 p. (6–9). Picture book.

Ma Jiang's family earns their money by gathering orange ants to sell to orange growers for their ability to eat the pests that destroy their fruit. When the men in her family are conscripted, times are hard until the girl notices that ants are attracted to honey and invents a low-hanging trap to catch the insects. Her father and brothers return from war, applaud her resourcefulness, and adopt her methods. The author's note explains the use of the citrus ants from ancient days until today. The watercolor, gouache, and ink illustrations beautifully capture the family's lives and emotions. *sg*
Author from United States

Roome, Diana Reynolds. **The Elephant's Pillow**. Pictures by Jude Daly. New York: Farrar, Straus and Giroux, 2003. First published in Great Britain, in somewhat different form by Frances Lincoln Ltd, 2003. ISBN 0-374-32015-2. 28 p. (5–8). Picture book.

See Europe/UK for description.

Simonds, Nina, Leslie Swartz, and the Children's Museum, Boston. **Moonbeams, Dumplings & Dragon Boats: A Treasury of Chinese Holiday Tales, Activities & Recipes**. Illustrated by Meilo So. New York: Gulliver Books/Harcourt, 2002. ISBN 0-15-201983-9. 74 p. (7–10). Informational book.

This compilation of traditional stories, recipes, and activities relates to five major Chinese festivals including Chinese New Year, the Lantern Festival, Qing Ming and the Cold Foods Festival, the Dragon Boat Festival, and the Mid-Autumn Moon Festival. The authors note that there is no definitive way to celebrate any one of these festivals; customs vary from north to south, province to province, and family to family. *Bank Street Best Book of the Year, 2003.* *djg*

Whelan, Gloria. **Chu Ju's House**. New York: Harper Collins, 2004. ISBN 0-06-050724-1. 227 p. (10 up). Novel.

Rather than having her new baby sister sold to an orphanage, Chu Ju runs away from home so that her parents can have another child, hopefully a boy. Chu Ju's odyssey takes her working on a fishing boat, a silk worm factory, and a small farm. In gratitude for her work and devotion, Han Na, the owner of the farm, deeds it to Chu Ju. Chu Ju returns home for a visit where everything is different but still the same. A well-written story about the dynamics and consequences of China's policy to limit the number of births. *ALA Amelia Bloomer Project, 2005.* *ls Author from United States*

Yee, Paul. **The Jade Necklace**. Illustrated by Grace Lin. New York: Crocodile Books, 2002. Published simultaneously in Great Britain and Canada by Tradewind Books. ISBN 1-56656-455-7. 32 p. (4–8). Picture book.

See Canada for description.

Yep, Laurence. **Spring Pearl: The Last Flower**. Middleton, WI: Pleasant Company, 2002. ISBN 1-58485-595-9. 208 p. (10–14). Novel.

Set in 1857 in Canton, China, during the Opium Wars with Britain. Twelve-year-old Spring Pearl, recently orphaned, misses her parents and her home, though she knows she should be grateful to the wealthy Sung family for taking her in. The Booklist reviewer, December 20, 2002, says, "Spring Pearl emerges as a likable character who follows her heart despite challenges, and her descriptive, first-person narrative is personable, often poignant, incorporating both humorous commentary and insightful observations about the events and people around her. Yep does a smooth job of working in historical detail, and there's an afterword describing girls' lives in China, past and present. As with other books in the series, this includes photos and an author's note."

Zhang, Ange. **Red Land, Yellow River: A Story from the Cultural Revolution**. Toronto: Groundwood, 2004. ISBN 0-88899-489-3. 56 p. (10 up). Informational book.

See Canada for description.

Related Information

Awards

Chinese National Book Award

This annual award, established in 1998, is for the most outstanding writing for children and young people in a book published in the preceding year.

Book Fairs

Hong Kong Book Fair
http://www.hkbookfair.com/

Organizations

IBBY China
www.cbby.org

The 2006 IBBY Congress will be held in Bejing, September 20–24, 2006.
The Theme is: "Children's Literature and Social Development." For more information
contact the Chinese Board on Books for Young People (CBBY).
21 Dongsi Shi'er Tiao
Beijing 100708—China
E-mail: cbby@cbby.org
Website: www.cbby.org

Print Resources

Farquhar, Mary Ann. **Children's Literature in China: From Lu Xun to Mao Zedong**. M.E. Sharpe, Inc., 1999. ISBN 0-7656-0344-6.

Winner of the 1999 Children's Literature Book Award, this book introduces the major works and debates in children's literature within the framework of China's revolution and modernization.

INDIA

Demi. **Gandhi**. New York: Margaret K. McElderry Books, 2001. ISBN 0-689-84149-3. 36 p. (8–11). Biography.

This biography focuses on Gandhi's spirituality and philosophy of non-violence in language that is accessible to younger children. Because of the symbolism and delicate illustrations, which add to the text but are not necessarily alluded to in the text, this book would be best as a read-aloud with small groups. Demi's illustrations combine the realism of portraiture, with the stylized art of 17th-century Indian miniatures. *2001 New York Times Best Illustrated. jvl*
Author from United States

Divakaruni, Chitra Banerjee. **The Conch Bearer**. Brookfield, CT: Roaring Book Press, 2003. ISBN 0-7613-1935-2. 265 p. (10–13). Novel.

In India, twelve-year-old Anand struggles to find happiness despite the absence of his missing father, a sister that cannot speak after a mysterious trauma, and an

abusive boss at the tea stall in Bowbajar Market. By stopping to help a man disguised as an old beggar, Anand reveals his kindness to Abhaydatta, a powerful member of the Brotherhood of Healers. Abhaydatta asks Anand to join him on a dangerous journey to return the magical conch to the Silver Valley and keep it safe from the evil Surabhanu, a former student of the Brotherhood. With the help of Nisha, a feisty, streetwise girl from Calcutta, Master Healer Abhaydatta, and the wise conch with a sense of humor, Anand overcomes the perils of his journey, protecting the world from Surabhanu's villainy and finding his own internal peace. *Society of School Librarians, International Book Award, 2003.* *aao*
Author from India, lives in United States

Divakaruni, Chitra Banerjee. **Neela: Victory Song**. Troy Howell. Middleton, WI: Pleasant Company Publications, 2002. ISBN 1-58485-597-5. 196 p. (9 up). Novel.

Neela's father joins Gandhi's March for Freedom in Calcutta, but doesn't return to their rural home. She disguises herself as a peasant boy and sneaks to India's famous city in search of her parent. Twelve-year-old Neela meets members of the Freedom Fighters who invite her to play a role in freeing her father. Intense and moving. This award-winning author portrays passion for her motherland. A brief history of India is included in the afterword. Concise glossary and insightful Author's Note. Part of Girls from Many Lands series. *nrn*
Author from India, lives in United States

Jeyaveeran, Ruth. **The Road to Mumbai**. Boston: Houghton Mifflin, 2004. ISBN 0-618-43419-4. 32 p. (5–8). Picture book.

In the middle of the night, Shoba's Monkey, Fuzzy Patel, wakes her up so they can begin their journey to Mumbai for the wedding of cousin Poori. They begin their journey in a leisurely way, but don't want to be late and so they take a ride with a curious camel; they journey on with a camel, an elephant, and at last a snake. But as the wedding begins, Shoba decides it is the best one she has ever been to. A map of Shoba's route is appended to the back along with a glossary of everyday Indian things. *djg*

Krishnaswami, Uma. **Chachaji's Cup**. Illustrations by Soumya Sitaraman. San Francisco: Children's Book Press, 2003. ISBN 0892391782. 32 p. (4–8). Picture book.

Neel loves to listen to his old uncle Chachaji tell stories of the Hindu gods and of his adventures in the Indian Army over steaming cups of tea. But it is only after he tells of the relocation of his mother's family following the 1947 Partitian that Neel understands the significance of the beautiful rose cup. When Neel drops the cup while washing it and Chachaji becomes ill and goes to the hospital, Neel repairs the cup and learns that while the cup may no longer be good for holding

tea, it can still hold memories. The vibrant paintings reflect elements of the artist's Shivite artistry, and an informative note about the history of India during this time of upheaval in India is appended.   *djg*
Author grew up in India and has won many awards. Her work has been published in anthologies and magazines for children.
Illustrator from Chennai, India, lives in Bangalore, India.

Krishnaswami, Uma. **Monsoon**. Illustrated by Jamel Akib. New York: Farrar, Straus and Giroux, 2003. ISBN 0-374-35015-9. 32 p. (7–10). Picture book.
   In poetic text, Krishnaswami portrays the edgy restlessness of the narrator and her family as they wait for the monsoon rains to arrive. "The heat makes me feel like a crocodile crouching snap-jawed." Taxi drivers honk at obstinate cows, clouds skitter across the sky, leaves rustle, and mangoes ripen, but still the rains don't come. Jarring, grainy pastel illustrations magnify the heat and dusty atmosphere that permeates the text, allowing readers to feel as if they have been deposited on a traffic-laden Delhi thoroughfare. A glossary of Hindi words and historical overview of monsoon rains are also included.   *lmp*
Author from India, lives in the United States. Illustrator lives in England but grew up in Malaysia.

Krishnaswami, Uma. **Naming Maya**. New York: Farrar, Straus & Giroux, 2004. ISBN 0-374-35485-5. 178 p. (10 up). Novel.
   Who is she, *Maya* or *Preeta*? She had always intuited the tension between her parents—and their families—but now they are divorced and memories overwhelm her. She and her mother are in Chennai because Thata, her grandfather, has died. For Maya, it is an opportunity to connect with family, experiencing the abstract India she's only studied in New Jersey. However, her dilemma is that "I'm American here, but in America, I'm Indian" (p. 56). As she discovers her heritage, Maya begins to value herself and examine her life anew.   *lmp and mln*
Author lives in United States

McDonald, Megan. **Baya, Baya, Lulla-by-a**. Illustrated by Vera Rosenberry. New York: Simon & Schuster/Atheneum Books for Young Readers, 2004. ISBN 0-689-84932-X. 32 p. (birth–4). Picture book.
   As a mother baya bird weaves flowers and fireflies into her nest, a mother in India weaves a quilt, decorating it with stars and mirrors "the color of one hundred mornings." The two parallel texts intersect when "mother to mother" the baya bird warns that a cobra is near, threatening their babies. Vera Rosenberry's watercolor illustrations underscore the colorful context and focus attention on the mothers' love for their young. A glossary of Hindi words and descriptions of alternative uses for abandoned nests, as well as the author's inspiration for the lullaby, complete this onomatopoetic text.   *lmp*
Author lives in United States. Illustrator lives in England.

Nagda, Ann Whitehead. **Snake Charmer**. Photographs by the author. New York: Holt, 2002. ISBN 0-8050-6499-0. unpaged. (7–9). Informational book.

Vishnu is a young boy from a small village in northern India who yearns to follow his father and grandfather in the ancient art of snake charming. Focusing on daily life in the village, the engaging conversational voice of the text offers an inviting glimpse into a young boy's life in modern-day India; the book concludes with an informative author's note on snake charmers, their snakes, and how the charming works. Crisp color photographs are artfully interspersed with folk designs within decorative borders. *djg*

Nakagawa, Rieko, and Yuriko Yamawaki. **Guri and Gura**. Translated by Peter Howlett and Richard McNamara. Tokyo: Tuttle, 2003. Originally published in Japan by Fuduinkan-Shoten, 1963. ISBN 0-8048-3352-4. 32 p. (3–7). Picture book.

The singing mice Guri and Gura enjoy the simple pleasures of friendship in four separate picture story books. In *Guri and Gura* the two discover a giant egg and make a cake from it. In *Guri and Gura's Special Gift*, they sing a song as they share with their animal friends. *Guri and Gura's Seaside Adventure* begins when the friends find a bottle and write a message and draw a map inviting the recipient to visit them. *Guri and Gura's Magical Friend* introduces the reader to Bunny Buna who takes them for a ride on a cloud. Simple cartoon style watercolor illustrations make these gentle stories appealing. The books were published in Spanish by Ediciones Ekaré in 2001. Edif. Banco del Libro, Caracas, Venezuela. *djg*

Ravishankar, Anushka. **Excuse Me, Is This India?** Textile art by Anita Leutwiler. Chennai, India: Tara Publishing, 2001. ISBN 81-86211-56-X. 28 p. (7–10). Picture book.

A child snuggles under a quilt sewed from fabrics gathered during Aunt Anna's trip to India and takes off on an aeroplane on a dreamy journey to the beach and to the city, meeting furry bandicoots and elephants. The narrative is told in silly rhyming verse that was inspired by the pictures created by rich Indian fabrics collected by the artist and sewn into quilt squares. *djg*
Author lives in India. Artist lives in Germany.

Ravishankar, Anushka. **Tiger on a Tree**. Illustrated by Pulak Biswas. New York: Farrar, Straus and Giroux, 2004. Originally published by Tara Publishing, 1999. ISBN 8-1862-1135-7. 48 p. (3–7). Picture book.

A tiger is roaming the forest when he hears a loud noise that scares him up a tree. Some village men discover the tiger in the tree and decide to get him down. The men surround the tree with a net. Then they begin blowing horns and banging drums scaring the tiger out of the tree. Once the tiger is in the net, the village men must decide what to do with the tiger. Kill him? Send him to the zoo? Set

him free? This simple story about rural India with award-winning illustrations inspires and delights.   *ls*
Author from India

Robert, Na'ima bint. **The Swirling Hijaab**. Illustrated by Nilesh Mistry. London: Mantra Publishing, 2004. ISBN 1-8526-9910-8. 24 p. (4–8). Picture book.
   A little girl swirls her mum's wide, black hijaab. Its soft fabric makes a perfect fort in which to hide, a comforter when she is away, a tent, a wedding sari, and many other clever imaginings. But covering her mum as part of her faith is what the hijaab does best. The fanciful and colorful illustrations show a young girl, confident and secure in her heritage. This book is available in 20 bilingual editions and is dedicated to the daughters of Islam, past, present, and future.   *djg*

Rumford, James. **The Nine Animals and the Well**. Boston: Houghton Mifflin, 2003. ISBN 0-618-30915-2. unpaged. (6–10). Picture book.
   "In the long-ago . . . days, there lived a very young raja-king . . . who invited nine friends to his birthday party." Fashioned in the tradition of ancient fables and cumulative tales, each animal selects a gift. As other animals join the caravan, the gifts are discarded for successively finer ones. Finally, the troupe arrives at the palace with nothing. But the raja rebuffs their dismay: "What need have I of presents?" Rumford's fiery palette, meandering typography, calligraphy, handmade Indian paper, and collage illustrations extend the fable's tone and setting. Underlying this fable is the numbering system Indians devised more than fifteen hundred years ago.   *lmp*
Author lives in Hawaii

Vijayaraghavan,Vineeta. **Motherland: A Novel**. New York: Soho Press; distributed by Farrar, Straus and Giroux, 2001. ISBN 1-56947-217-3. 232 p. (12 up). Novel.
   The domestic and social contrasts between her two cultures challenges 16-year-old Maya who has returned with her mother from the U.S. to Kerala, India, on a family matter. While there, secrets are revealed and familial differences resolved in this richly descriptive, first person narrative that also explores the political turmoil surrounding the assassination of Raji Gandhi. *Alex Award, 2002; YALSA Best Books, 2002.   mln.*
Author from India, lives in United States

Whelan, Gloria. **Homeless Bird**. New York: HarperCollins, 2000. (paperback: HarperTrophy, 2001). ISBN 0-06-028454-4 (paperback: 0-06-440819-1). 216 p. (11 up). Novel.
   Married and sent to live with her husband, Koly will never see her family again. The circumstances are difficult for the thirteen-year-old, but when her bridegroom dies she must endure her sass's (mother-in-law) resentment and cru-

elty while her sassur secretly teaches her to read. To her new family she's a financial burden. Sass's solution is to abandon her at the temple in Vrindavan. Koly stubbornly refuses to beg but instead sets about fashioning a place among the outcasts. This is a story of hope, strength, courage, and above all, survival—of a girl who won't let life defeat her. *2000 National Book Award.* lmp
Author lives in United States

Related Information

Organizations

Children's Book Trust was founded by Shankar in 1957. Housed in Nehru House since 1965, CBT is the pioneer publisher of children's books in India whose goal is to promote the production of well-written, well-illustrated and well-designed books for children. http://www.hkbookfair.com

Indian Section of IBBY
Association of Writers and Illustrators for Children (AWIC)
Nehru House
4 Bhadur Shah Zafar Marg
IN-New Delhi 110002
e-mail: smberry@vsnl.com

Publishers in India

Balkatha
www. Balkata.com
   This company offers a selection of worthwhile children's books from India in English, Gujarati, Hindi, Tamil, Malayalam, Marathi, and Kannada. Orders can be placed online or by phone or fax to a U.S. number. Balkatha.com

Tulika Publishers
http://www.tulikabooks.com/home.htm—Radhika Menon,
Managing Editor and Sandhya Rao, Editor

Tara Publishing
http://www.tarabooks.com/—established by Gita Wolf

Publications

Khorana, Meena. **The Indian Subcontinent in Literature for Children and Young Adults**. New York: Greenwood Press, 1991. ISBN 3-313-25489-3.
   This bibliography examines literature for young people concerning the Indian subcontinent and associated areas: Bangladesh, the Himalayan kingdoms of

Bhutan, Nepal, Sikkim, Tibet, India, Pakistan, and Sri Lanka. Over 900 entries are organized by country or sub-region. Each chapter is divided by genre.

Writer and Illustrator: Quarterly Journal of the Association of Writers and Illustrators for Children. Nehru House, 4 Bahadur Shah Zafar Marg, New Delhi 110002 India.

Written in English and published by the Indian section of IBBY, this journal contains book-related news as well as reviews of children's books published in India in English and in regional languages.

INDONESIA (BALI)

Fama, Elizabeth. **Overboard**. Chicago: Cricket, 2002. ISBN 0-8126-2652-4. 158 p. (10 up). Novel.

Emily is the fourteen-year-old daughter of American doctors working in a hospital on Sumatra. She knows the importance of her parents work but wants some attention for herself and misses home. Making a rash decision she runs off to meet her uncle, vacationing on a nearby island when the ferry sinks. In the tense night time hours she meets Isman, a small boy. With only Emily's strength and Isman's quiet faith to help them, this is a tense story of survival. Based on a true story, this is a "sensitive portrayal of cross-cultural understanding in a time of crisis." *YALSA Best Books for Young; starred review in KLIATT*. Adults.   *djg*
Author lives in United States

Lewis, Richard. **The Flame Tree**. New York: Simon and Schuster, 2004. ISBN 0-689-86333-0. 276 p. (12 up). Novel.

Isaac Williams is twelve, living in Java, the son of Christian missionary doctors who work at a Baptist hospital there. As anti-American tension builds in this time period surrounding the September 11th attacks on the World Trade Center, his friendship with Ismail, a young Muslim, deteriorates. When Isaac is kidnapped by Islamic fundamentalists intent upon converting him, readers see both the peaceful teachings of the Qur'an and very graphic depictions of terrorists acts, including beheadings and Isaac's forced circumcision. This is a powerful book that explores interpretations of both Islamic and Christian teachings.   *jig*
Author lives in Indonesia

JAPAN

Blumberg, Rhoda. **Shipwrecked! The True Adventures of a Japanese Boy**. New York: Harper Collins, 2001. ISBN 0-06-029365. 80 p. (12 up). Biography.

When an American whaling ship rescues five Japanese fishermen from a desolate Pacific island in June 1841, Manjiro's amazing odyssey begins. Manjiro visits Hawaii, attends school in Massachusetts, and continues to go whaling. In 1852, Manjiro returns to Japan where his knowledge and experiences in the outside world prove valuable in helping open Japan to the outside world. This is a fascinating account of how a series of accidents influenced world history. *Notable Children's Books, 2002.* ls
Author from United States

Godden, Rumer. **Miss Happiness and Miss Flower**. New York: HarperCollins Publishers, 2002. Originally published with drawings by Jean Primrose by Viking Press in 1961. ISBN 0-06029193-1 (pbk. ISBN 0-06-440938-4). 119 p. (8 up). Novel.

When eight-year-old Nona Fells is sent from the warm climate of India to live with her aunt's family in England, not only is the climate cold, but so also is the reception from her cousin Belinda. It is not until a belated Christmas gift of two Japanese dolls arrives from her Great-Aunt Lucy, and Nona assumes the responsibility of making Miss Happiness and Miss Flower feel comfortable in a strange place, that Nona's life becomes more bearable. It is this kinship with the two dolls and the involvement of building a house for them that draws Nona out and establishes a connection between her and her new surroundings. Includes construction plans for a Japanese dollhouse. In 1972 won Whitbread Award for *The Diddakoi*. In 1993 appointed OBE. *ok*
Author from England, lived in India a number of years

Gomi, Taro. **I Lost My Dad**. New York: Kane/Miller, 2001. First published in Japan in 1983 under the title *Tousan Maigo* by Kaisei-sha publishing. ISBN 1-9291-3204-2. 32 p. (4–8). Picture book.

A young boy becomes separated from his father and goes on a search through the department store trying to find him. He catches glimpses of him and leads the reader on a merry chase. Die-cut pages disguise pieces of clothing the boys thinks he recognizes until at last he spots his father on the escalator. "Can we go back to the toys now? I know just what I want" says the boy as the unhappy father leads him by the hand. Colorful, bold, and simple, the illustrations will delight fans of Gomi. *djg*

Kajikawa, Kimiko. **Yoshi's Feast**. Illustrated by Yumi Heo. New York: Dorling Kindersley, 2000. ISBN 0-7894-2607-2. 32 p. (4–8). Picture book.

An old tale is given a new twist in this delightful story set in the old city of Yedo. Yoshi enjoys the smell of Sabu's broiled eels and pays for them with the sound of his money. The neighbors remain stubborn, each one refusing to accommodate the others needs. At last Yoshi dances attracting a crowd that grows hungry enough to buy Sabu's eels. Ultimately, they discover that sniffing broiled eels by yourself is nowhere near as good as eating them with a friend. *Notable Books for a Global Society, 2001; Charlotee Zolotow Award, 2001.*

Kimura, Yuichi. **One Stormy Night . . .** Translation by Lucy North. Pictures by Hiroshi Abe. New York: Kodansha International, 2003. First published in Japanese as *Arashi no yoru ni* by Kodansha Ltd. in 1994. ISBN 4-7700-2970-5. 51 p. (5–10). Picture book.

One stormy night two animals shelter in a small hut: a goat and a wolf. So dark is it that the animals can't see each other and they begin a conversation. It seems they have a lot in common. And the two night companions imagine Breezy Hill where they both find delicious food to eat, where they both have learned the importance of running, where they both were skinny youngsters together. But the reader is not in the dark and the humor of the situation is revealed in the imagined scenes as the animals reminisce.

Scratch board line drawings on black glossy paper, with the imagined scenes in watercolor illustrate this quiet and at times suspenseful story. At the end of the storm, the animals depart agreeing to meet on the next sunny day. The reader anticipates the companion story, *One Sunny Day*, also published in 2003. These stories have a lot to say about the nature of friendship.   *djg*
Author from Tokyo and has written over 300 stories and won numerous prizes. Illustrator from Japan.

McCaughrean, Geraldine. **The Kite Rider**. New York: Harper Collins, 2001. ISBN 0-06-623875-7. 272 p. (12 up). Novel.

In 13th-century China, after saving his mother from a disastrous second marriage, twelve-year-old Haoyou becomes a kite rider for the Jade Circus. He performs for Kublai Khan where several twists of fate determine Haoyou's destiny. A young boy takes on adult responsibilities all the while obeying his elder's demands. *2001 Nestle Smarties Book Prize, Bronze Medal.   ls*
Author from England

Namioka, Lensey. **The Hungriest Boy in the World**. Illustrated by Aki Sogabe. New York: Holiday House, 2001. ISBN 0-8234-1542-2. 32 p. (4–8). Picture book.

Jiro is a curious boy who puts everything he sees into his mouth—seaweed, seashells, stones. When he detects a purple blob one day, of course, he gulps it down. Unfortunately, Jiro has just swallowed *The Hunger Monster*! After Jiro's parents discover he has digested a fishing net, his quilt, a bucket of fish guts, and a cushion, they recognize his situation is desperate. Aki Sogabe's cut paper, watercolor, and airbrush illustrations provide an appropriately humorous view of a fictional Japanese fishing village. And the monster with a huge appetite ironically is the smallest creature in the book.   *lmp*
Author lives in United States

Ray, Deborah Kogan. **Hokusai: The Man Who Painted a Mountain**. Frances Foster books. New York: Farrar, Straus and Giroux, 2001. ISBN 0-374-33263-0. 36 p. (7–10). Biography.

Long ago in Japan, there was a man who made more than thirty thousand works of art. This picture book biography tells the story of passion for drawing from his childhood life of poverty to apprenticeship with a great master. The endpapers contain drawings from his sketchbooks and some of his works, including *The Great Wave off Kanagawa*, are illustrated in glowing paintings. Additional information, a chronology, and a bibliography are appended. *Starred review in Kirkus. djg*
Author/illustrator from United States

Tada, Satoshi. **Mr. Beetle**. Translated by Cathy Hirano. Minneapolis: Carolrhoda Books, 2001. First published in Japan in 1999 under the title *Kabuto-Kun* by Koguma Publishing. ISBN 1-5750-5561-9. 48 p. (5–8). Picture book.

Yoshi loves bugs, especially beetles and so when Yoshi finds some rhinoceros beetle grubs in the forest, he decides to bring them home. The grub grows, forms a chrysalis, and emerges into a huge beetle. They become friends, but Yoshi can see that the beetle longs for his forest home. Yoshi returns the creature to its habitat, but they promise to visit each other. Two pages of beetle facts are appended. *djg*
Author from Tokyo. Translator from Canada and has lived in Japan since 1978.

Tezuka, Osamu. **Astro Boy**. Translated by Frederik L. Schodt. Milwaukie, OR: Dark Horse, 2002. ISBN 1569716765. 222 p. (12 up). Graphic Novel.

Astro Boy was created for a television cartoon series in 1963 and tells the story of a character created by Dr. Tenma of the Ministry of Science as a replacement for his beloved son, Tobio, who was killed in an accident, combats evil where he finds it. Osamu Tezuka is recognized worldwide for the skill, range, and emotional power of his storytelling, placing him among the giants of graphic fiction and animation. Other graphic novel serials by him include *Metropolis, Nextworld, and Adolf. djg*

Turner, Pamela S. **Hachiko: The True Story of a Loyal Dog**. Illustrated by Yan Nascimbene. Boston: Houghton Mifflin, 2004. ISBN 0-6181-4094-8. unpaged. (8–10). Biography.

Hachiko, a pale, furry puppy, was born in 1923 in northern Japan. He lived with Dr. Ueno, a professor at Tokyo Imperial University. Each morning he walked to the Shibuya Train Station with his master and returned each evening to greet Dr. Ueno. A year after Hachiko's arrival in Tokyo, Dr. Ueno died unexpectedly. Hachiko never left the train station that day, and faithfully returned to Shibuya Station morning and afternoon, until he also died. People who had observed his

vigilance erected a statue in his honor. Today, the bronze likeness of Hachiko is one of the best-known meeting spots in Tokyo. *lmp*
Author and illustrator live in United States

Whitesel, Cheryl Aylward. **Blue Fingers: A Ninja's Tale**. New York: Harper Collins, 2004. ISBN 0-618-38139-2. 252 p. (12 up). Novel.
In fourteenth-century Japan, young boys like Koji and his twin brother, Taro, admired the samurai warrior class. When Taro saves the life of the dye maker, Koji is sent to work for the dye maker instead of Taro. When Koji displeases the dye maker, he is sent home in disgrace. Rather than face his family, Koji runs away into the forest where he is abducted to join the ninja. The time comes when Koji can use his ninja skills to defeat the local daimyo's plan to obtain muskets for his troops. Anyone interested in medieval Japan and the ninja culture will find this story fascinating. *ls*
Author from United States

Yumoto, Kazumi. **The Letters**. Translated by Cathy Hirano. New York: Farrar, Straus and Giroux, 2002. Originally published as *Papura no aki* by Shinchosha, 1997. ISBN 0-374-34383-7. 165 p. (11 up). Novel.
When six-year-old Chiaki's father died in a car accident she and her mother moved into Poplar House a place whose forbidding looking landlady and whose protective poplar proved to be Chiaki's bridge back to life and love. Mrs. Yanagi involved Chiaki in daily activities, such as raking the yard. She encouraged Chiaki to write letters to her father over the course of the year, with a promise to deliver them to her father when the landlady died. When Chiaki, in her late twenties, returns for the landlady's funeral, she discovers more healing secrets in the drawer where the letters had been kept. This wistful book ends hopefully as Chiaki comes to have a new appreciation for her mother. *Publisher's Weekly Starred Review. jvl*
Author from Japan and won the Mildred Batchelder Award for her The Friends.

Related Information

Awards

Nihon Ehon Award/Japan Picture Book Award
This award for the most outstanding Japanese picture book published in the previous year was established to popularize picture-book art, to promote book reading, and to contribute to the development of picture-book publications.

Bookfairs

Tokyo International Book Fair
http://www.bookfair.jp/english/

MY EXPERIENCE TRANSLATING JAPANESE INTO ENGLISH
BY CATHY HIRANO

As a language, Japanese is very different from English. Word order in the sentence is reversed and the style is indirect and subtle, which means that much of the information is only implied. If I literally translated only the words that exist in the Japanese text and failed to bring out the hidden meanings or to supply information about the cultural context without which a foreign reader would be lost, the result would be almost unintelligible not to mention boring. At the same time, however, I must be careful not to get carried away and add too much.

With literature, my goal in translation is to make the English as fluent and as moving as the original. To do that, I produce a rough draft that remains true to the Japanese, let it sit for a few days, and then look at it again. This time I immerse myself completely in the story, reliving it in my mind, waiting for the English words that evoke the same image or feeling. Sometimes, I have to change or add something to achieve this goal.

In *The Letters*, the most drastic change was giving the landlady a name! In the Japanese, she is called *obahsan* throughout. This is a neutral title used for all elderly women and is usually translated as "grandmother," but I felt that the English meaning and the image it inspires were incompatible with the landlady's formidable character. The main character, a child of seven, finds her highly intimidating and would be more likely to use the title of Mrs. in English. In the end, we used Mrs. "Yanagi," or "willow," as a subtle reference to the poplar tree in the story.

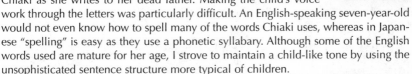

Another major hurdle in translating *The Letters* was the fact that it is written in three voices: the present voice of Chiaki, a woman in her mid-twenties, the voice of Chiaki as objective narrator relating her childhood experiences, and the voice of the seven-year-old Chiaki as she writes to her dead father. Making the child's voice work through the letters was particularly difficult. An English-speaking seven-year-old would not even know how to spell many of the words Chiaki uses, whereas in Japanese "spelling" is easy as they use a phonetic syllabary. Although some of the English words used are mature for her age, I strove to maintain a child-like tone by using the unsophisticated sentence structure more typical of children.

Japan has a very rich literature of its own, yet Japanese children read books from many other countries in translation. I think native English speakers could learn from this willingness to explore the world through the books of other cultures. Each one is a door to a fascinating journey that expands the mind and offers new ways of approaching the same theme: life.

*Farrar, Straus and Giroux was awarded the Mildred Batchelder Award for Ms. Hirano's translation of *The Friends* by Kazumi Yumoto. It also received the Boston Globe-Horn Book Award. Her work has made the IBBY Honor List for translation. She has also translated the picture book *Mr. Beetle* by Satoshi Tada. Ms. Hirano grew up in Canada and has lived in Japan since 1978. Her article "Eight Ways to Say You: The Challenges of Translation" can be found in *The Horn Book Magazine*, vol. 75.1 (1999): 34–39.

Nissan Joyful Storybook and Picture Book Exposition

In addition to displaying many outstanding storybook and picture books, creative workshops for children are also held. This exhibition is now a popular spring vacation event, attracting some 30,000 children and parents a year.
http://www.nissan-global.com/GCC/PHILANTHROPY/ACTIVITY/2000/english/2_2.html

Online Bookstore

Amazon.co—Japan site

www.amazon.co.jp

This site follows the amazon.com format but is only useful to those who can read Japanese and whose computers are set to decode Japanese.

Online Resources

Japanese Children's Books

This website is a bilingual magazine on children's books published by the Yamaneko Honyaku Club.
http://www.yamaneko.org/einfo/mgzn/index.htm

Organizations

IBBY Japan

www.jbby.org

International Institute for Children's Literature, Osaka

10-6 Banpaku-Koen, Senri Suita-Shi, 565-0826 Japan
www.iiclo.or.jp/english/english.htm

This institute houses a research collection of children's books and offers reference services and seminars; it publishes an annual bulletin and a newsletter, which is available online, in English, at its website. You can also review samples of one hundred children's books at this site.

Print Resources

Tinker Bell: Journal of JSCLE: The Japan Society for Children's Literature in English. Annual covering literature and culture of English-speaking countries. Essays in Japanese and English.
Shirayuri College (in care of Associate Professor Sumiko Shirai's Office)
1-25, Midorigaoka, Chofu-shi, Tokyo Met.
182-8525
Japan
(nijun@jcom.home.ne.jp)
Sumiko Yokokawa, Michiko Yorikoka

LAOS

Brown, Jackie. **Little Cricket**. New York: Hyperion, 2004. ISBN 0-7868-1852-2. 252 p. (8–12). Novel.

Twelve-year-old Kia, called Little Cricket by her family, tells of life in her Laotian village before the Communists take away her father and the men of her village. She escapes with her family across the Mekong River and lives for a time in a refugee camp in Thailand. Eventually, the family is separated when only her grandfather, her brother, and she are chosen to go to Minnesota. The story, simply told, makes frequent mention of Hmong culture and beliefs. The book contains a pronunciation guide for the few Hmong words used in the text as well as some suggested readings and a short history of Hmong immigration. *Paul Zindel First Novel Award.*

MICRONESIA

Schaefer, Carole Lexa. **The Biggest Soap**. Pictures by Stacey Dressen-McQueen. New York: Melanie Kroupa/Farrar, Straus and Giroux, 2004. ISBN 0-374-30690-7. 32 p. (4–8). Picture books.

It's laundry day on this South Pacific Truk Island and Mama has picked Kessy to go to Minda's Store to bring back the biggest piece of laundry soap on the shelf. Fast as a typhoon wind, he is off, but is distracted first by his brothers playing monsters in the muddy water, then by Uncle Cho, making a new window for his house, and finally by Amina, looking through a tin-can camera. He must use the soap to help each of his friends, but he returns home with soap and a good story to tell as well. The illustrator, who was inspired by Gauguin and Oceanic art, uses colored pencil, oil pastel, and acrylic and bold colors to illustrate this exuberant story. *Charlotte Zolotow Award Highly Commended 2005; Booklist starred review. djg*

NEPAL

Tenzing Norbu, Lama. **Himalaya**. Translated by Shelley Tanaka. Toronto: Douglas & McIntyre, 2002. Originally published as *Himalaya: L'Enfance d'un Chef* by Editions Milan in 2000. ISBN 0-88899-480-X. 32 p. (7–9). Picture book.

Based on a French film, this beautiful book in Nepali and English is the story of a remote Nepali community's annual trek across Tibet to collect rock salt to use in trade. On the annual trip, the leader dies and dissension and mistrust break out among the people, leading to two separate caravans across the wilderness. The large dramatic illustrations are rich in drama and cultural detail, emphasizing the remoteness of the landscape and the stoicism of the people. See also description of *Secret of the Snow Leopard* in Canada. *Parents' Choice Award. sg Author lives in Nepal*

Young, Ed. **I, Doko: The Tale of a Basket**. New York: Philomel, 2004. ISBN 0-399-23625-2. 32 p. (5–10). Picture book.

Ed Young skillfully tells this simple fable of a Nepalese basket, a doko, to illustrate a lesson in honoring your elders with masterful illustrations distinguished in gilded borders. In this simple tale, Yeh-yeh chooses a basket to give to his wife Nei-nei. It is used first to carry their child and then, in the blink of an eye, when the child grows, it is used by him to carry heavier things until it carries home the dowry of his wife. Time passes, the wife dies, and the young man, past his prime, is also past his usefulness. When the son is ready to carry his now aged father to the temple to leave him on the steps, it is the young grandson, who, with love and respect is able to convince his elders of the proper way to care for the elders. *Washington Post Best Books, 2004.*   *djg*

NORTH AND SOUTH KOREA

Holman, Sheri. **Sŏndŏk: Princess of the Moon and Stars**. New York: Scholastic, 2002. ISBN 0-439-16586-5. 187 p. (9–12). Novel.

Set in Korea in the year 595, this novel is based on the life of the Princess Sŏndŏk. This outspoken, young girl has a passion to learn about astronomy and is frustrated by the prohibition against women studying this science. As the heir to her father's throne, she struggles to understand her place in society. As in other books in "The Royal Diaries" series, this book includes an epilogue and historical notes.

Author from United States

Lee, Ho Baek. **While We Were Out**. La Jolla, CA: Kane/Miller, 2003. Originally published under the title *What on Earth Happened during that Time?* by Jaimimage Publishing, Seoul, Korea. ISBN 1-929132-44-1. 32 p. (4–8). Picture book.

The family has gone to Grandma's house and when the white rabbit discovers that the door has been left open, she hops right in. She helps herself to a snack and sits at the table to eat and then on to enjoy a movie. There's still some time to explore the dressing table, a costume from babies first birthday, and roller skates. The family will never know, or will they? Watercolor illustrations alternate with black-and-white drawings and add to the humor of the story. *New York Times Best Illustrated Book of the Year, 2003.*   *djg*
Author began the publishing company, Jaimimag, and lives in Seoul, South Korea

Liu, Jae Soo. **Yellow Umbrella**. La Jolla, CA: Kane/Miller, 2002. Originally published in Korea by Jaiminage Publishing, 2001. ISBN 1-9291-3236-0. 32 p. (4–8). Picture book.

A journey in the rain is traced through the city as the children proceed to school. First one yellow umbrella on a quiet street is joined by a blue, then orange and green as they cross a bridge. Swirls of brightly colored umbrellas liven the dull day until at last they arrive at the school. The view from the sky reveals only the colors of the umbrella, and as the author says in the statement on the jacket flap, whether "boys or girls, fat or skinny, tall or short . . . all those physical differences disappear, what remains is harmonized colors." This book contains a companion musical recording. Instructions in the book guide the reader to begin the CD and turn the pages in the brief periods of silence between the lovely piano vignettes after the initial sound of rain. The musical themes are based on the song "Underneath the Sky" and the music and English lyrics are at the back of the book. The song is recorded in Korean. A lovely book, don't wait for a rainy day to share this book with a child. *New York Times Best Illustrated Book of the Year, 2003. djg*
Author/illustrator from Choognam, Korea

Myers, Tim. **Basho and the River Stones**. Illustrations by Oki S. Han. New York: Marshall Cavendish, 2004. ISBN 0-7614-5165-X. 32 p. (5–10). Picture book.

When Japan's great Poet, Matuao Basho, came to live near the Fuka River, he discovered a cherry tree on his property and agreed to share its cherries with the local foxes. One particularly greedy fox conceives of a plan to trick Basho into giving all the cherries to the foxes. To the fox's surprise, he finds that the poet, rather than being angered by the trick, is grateful, for it has inspired him to write a beautiful haiku. Though he lived four hundred years ago, Matsuao Basho is still Japan's most famous poet and this original story, illustrated with Han's expressive watercolor, pays tribute to the poet with this final haiku: I've eaten cherries alone—but they're much sweeter when shared with a friend. *School Library Journal Book Review Stars, 2004. djg*
Illustrator lives in Seoul, South Korea

Park, Linda Sue. **The Firekeeper's Son**. Illustrated by Julie Downing. New York: Clarion Books, 2004. ISBN 0-618-13337-2. 40 p. Picture book.

Every evening Sang-hee's father climbs to the top of the mountain carrying a pair of tongs and a little brass pot filled with coals to start a signal fire. On every hill in the hump of the dragons back, all the way to the palace walls, a fire is lit until the light reachs the palace. When all the fires are lit the king knows that all is well in the land. But when his father hurts his ankle and cannot climb the mountain, it is up to the boy to light the signal fire in time. Watercolor and pastel illustrations illustrate this story of a young boy's moment of truth. An author's note includes information about the bonfire system in nineteenth-century Korea. *Children's Literature Choice List, 2005. djg*

Park, Linda Sue. **A Single Shard**. New York: Clarion, 2001. ISBN 0-395-97827-0. 152 p. (9–12). Novel.

Set in a small village on the west coast of Korea in the 12th century, this is the story of the orphan Tree-ear, who lives with his friend Crane-man. But when Tree-ear observes master potter Min at work, he knows that he wants to learn this craft and he leaves the only person who has ever cared for him to fulfill his desire. His quest leads him on a dangerous journey during which he learns more than the fine art of celedron ware. *Newbery Award, 2002.*   djg
Author from United States

Park, Linda Sue. **When My Name Was Keoko**. New York: Clarion, 2002. ISBN 0-618-13335-6. 199 p. (10–14). Novel.

Korea has been occupied by Japan for Kim Sun-hee's whole life, but in 1940 new laws are imposed requiring the people to take Japanese names. Kim's family secretly tries to keep Korean traditions alive and her uncle becomes involved in the resistance movement. When uncle becomes suspect, her brother joins the Japanese army to divert suspicion from the family. This compelling story tells of a people's struggle against a powerful occupying force during World War II. *Notable Books for a Global Society, 2003.*

Wong, Janet S. **The Trip Back Home**. Illustrated by Bo Jia. New York: Harcourt, 2000. ISBN 0-15-200784-9. 32 p. (4–8). Picture book.

A little girl returns with her mother to her rural home in the Korean countryside. She watches Haraboji as he makes charcoal to heat the air under the floor and goes with Halmoni to feed the pigs. They shop in the open air market and play games in the evening on the oiled paper floor. All too soon the visit is over and once again the family exchanges hugs in this heartwarming tale beautifully portrayed with watercolor illustrations. *Notable Books for a Global Society, 2001. ALA Lasting Connections, 2002.*
Author from United States

Related Information

Bookfairs

Seoul International Book Fair
http://www.sibf.or.kr/

PAKISTAN

D'Adamo, Francesco. **Iqbal: A Novel**. Translated by Ann Leonori. New York: Atheneum, 2003. First published as *Storia di Iqbal* by Edizioni EL in 2001. ISBN 0-689-85445-5. 120 p. (8–12). Novel.

See Europe/Italy for description.

Khan, Rukhsana. **Ruler of the Courtyard**. Illustrated by R. Gregory Christie. Viking, 2003. 34 p. ISBN 0-670-03583-1. (3–5). Picture book.

Saba is terrified of the chickens in her courtyard until she gets to the bathhouse and finds a snake coiled in the corner. She summons the courage to overcome her fears of the dangerous snake, only to realize that the dark form is not a snake, but Nani's nala. Triumphant, Saba emerges from the bathhouse scattering the chickens, laughing and confident as the new "Ruler of the Courtyard." *Children's Literature Choice List, 2004.*   djg

Author from Lahore, Pakistan, immigrated to Canada at the age of three, and is the author of The Roses in My Caretes *(Stan) and* Muslim Child: Understanding Islam through Stories and Poems.

Shea, Pegi Deitz. **The Carpet Boy's Gift**. Illustrated by Leane Morin. Gardiner, ME: Tilbury House, 2003. ISBN 0-88448-248-0. 40 p. (7–12). Picture book.

Nadeem, a young boy sold to a carpet maker for a loan of 1,000 rupees works in the factory from dawn to sundown seven days a week. Each time he comes close to paying back the peshgi, master fines him for some indiscretion. He works hard for the honor of his family until one day when he meets Iqbal Masih, a boy who escaped from a factory, was educated, and is teaching other child laborers about the laws that are supposed to protect them. This fictional account honors the legacy of Iqbal Masih and includes resources at the end of the book to inform children about child labor issues and encourage them to support companies that honor the United Nations "Rights of the Child." *Notable Social Studies Trade Books for Young People, 2004.*

PHILIPPINES

Arcellana, Fracisco. **The Mats**. Illustrated by Hermès Alègrè. La Jolla, CA: Kane/Miller, 1999. Originally published in book form in the Philippines in 1995. First appeared in *Philippine Magazine* in 1938. ISBN 0-91629-86-3. 26 p. (5–10). Picture book.

Marcelina's father returns from a trip to the southern provinces with a bundle of sleeping mats for his family. The children are delighted with the beautiful mats, an image representing something special about each of them woven into the mats. But after everyone opens their gift, three remain. Papa said he would bring one home for everyone, reminding them of the three little sisters who had died when they were still young. This bittersweet story is illustrated with bright colors that reflect the cultural setting. *Notable Social Studies Trade Books for Young People, 2000.*

Robles, Anthony. **Lakas and the Manilatown Fish**. Illustration by Carl Angel. Translation by Eloisa D. de Jesus and Magdalena de Guzman. ISBN 0-89239-182-0. 32 p. (5–10). Picture book.

In this bilingual English-Tagalog story set in the United States, a boy of Filipino descent begins some musings among the elders about a fish who takes them on a fanciful romp through a fantastic neighborhood. The Manilatown residents chase a fish who won't stay put in his tank, run down Kearney Street, past the International Hotel, right down to the Bay.   *djg*

SINGAPORE

National Book Development Council of Singapore Book Awards
The aim of the award is to encourage and develop local literary talent. Only original work by Singapore citizens or permanent residents of Singapore are eligible for the awards. Literary Prize for Sinhala Literature.

TAIWAN

Chen, Chih-Yuan. **On My Way to Buy Eggs**. La Jolla, CA: Kane/Miller, 2003. First published in Taiwan in 2001 by Hsin Yi Publications, Taipei, Taiwan, R.O.C. ISBN 1-929132-49-2. 40 p. (4–7). Picture book.
Shau-yu goes to the store to buy eggs for making fried rice and her ordinary journey to the store becomes an adventure when she follows the cat's shadow, peeks around the wall to see Harry the dog, and finds a blue marble that can tint the world and a pair of glasses that makes the world blurry. Delightful illustrations of kraft and corrugated paper collage and line drawings enhance this simple story. *Publisher's Weekly Best Children's Books, 2003.*   *djg*

Hao, K.T. **One Pizza, One Penny**. Translated by Roxanne Feldman. Illustrated by Guiliano Ferri. Chicago: Cricket Books, 2003. First published in Chinese in 1998. ISBN 0-812627-02-4 32 p. (4–8). Picture book.
Chris Croc lives across the street from Ben Bear and they are not only best of friends, but they are the most excellent bakers. Chris Croc makes the best cakes and Ben the best pizzas. When Peerless Zhu, a publishing tycoon, sniffs out the delicious cakes and pays in gold, their friendship is threatened as they set up rival vending carts. But by the afternoon they are starving and Chris decides to spend his gold coin on a slice of pizza. The coin exchanges hands until the friends are full. It is amazing what one gold coin can do. Beautiful paintings illustrate this oversized picture book.   *djg*
Author from Taiwan. Illustrator from Italy.

THAILAND

Ho, Minfong. **Peek! A Thai Hide-and-Seek**. Illustrated by Holly Meade. Cambridge, MA: Candlewick Press, 2004. ISBN 0-7636-2041-6. unpaged. (2–4). Picture book.

The onomatopoetic verse and repetitive phrase "Jut-Ay, peek-a-boo . . ." encourage youthful listeners to join in a loving, father-daughter game of peek-a-boo. The author informs readers that "Jut-Ay," which is the phrase children in Thailand use when they play "peek-a-boo," is pronounced "Shut-A." Bright orange endpapers, covered with a scholarly script used in northern Thailand several hundred years ago, provide a welcoming invitation into this companion to Mingfong Ho and Holly Meade's 1997 Caldecott honor book, *Hush! A Thai Lullaby* (Orchard, 1996). This book opens a window on a small but enchanting segment of Thai culture. *Children's Literature Choice List.*   lmp
Author from Thailand, lives in United States

Krudop, Walter Lyon. **The Man Who Caught Fish**. New York: Farrar, Straus & Giroux, 2000. ISBN 0-374-34786-7. 28 p. (5–10). Picture book.
    Identified only on the jacket flap as Thailand, this original fairy tale tells the story of a humble fisherman's encounter with a proud king. One day a stranger comes to a village carrying only a fishing pole. He stops by the river and begins to catch fish, giving them away with the statement "one person, one fish." All the people are pleased to receive their gift except the rich king who demands a full basket. Though commanded and ultimately punished the humble man persists, one person, one fish. Ultimately, the king learns a hard lesson about the consequences of his greed. Acrylic paintings in subdued tones convey the feel of the Southeast Asian village and the lush palace of the king.   djg

Marsden, Carolyn. **Silk Umbrellas**. Cambridge, MA: Candlewick Press, 2004. ISBN 0-7636-2257-5. 134 p. Novel.
    Eleven-year-old Noi sits at her grandmother's feet and learns to paint beautiful illustrations on silk umbrellas that the family sells in the local market. Unsure of her natural talent, humble Noi is hesitant about the value of her work and understands the importance of this income to the family. When grandmother falls ill and can no longer paint, Noi fears that she will have to join her older sister, working long hours in the local radio factory to supplement the family's income. Customs and language of Thailand are woven into this poignant coming-of-age story. *ALA Top 10 Art Books for Youth, 2004; Starred reviews.*   djg
Author lives in United States

Sobol, Richard. **An Elephant in the Backyard**. New York: Dutton Children's Books, 2004. ISBN 0-525-47288-6. 32 p. (7–10). Informational book.
    This beautiful photo-essay depicts life in the small Thai village of Tha Klang, a village where domesticated elephants roam free. The reader gets a glimpse of a day in the life of nine-year-old Jak and seven-year-old Muay and their four-year-old elephant, viewing adults in their work as teachers, farmers, and silk wavers. Children are shown doing chores and at play or in school and, of course, caring for the elephants who live in and around their village. Combine this book with *The Elephant Hospital* by Kathy Darling (Millbrook Press, 2002).   djg

TIBET

Berger, Barbara Helen. **All the Way to Lhasa: A Tale from Tibet**. New York: Philomel Books, 2002. ISBN 0-399-23387-3. (3–9). Picture book. Folktale.

Two travelers begin their pilgrimage to the holy city but who will arrive first? The rider and his horse gallop up sloping mountains while the young boy gently leads his yak up the path, across the river, and through the blinding snow. "One foot in front of the other" brings the boy and his yak to the gates of Lhasa just before the sun goes down! Where is the rider? Sleeping beside his horse along the trail. The text is exquisitely simple with poetic flair. Berger's illustrations gently propel the nameless child toward his goal. Colors are subtly rich with burgundy, brown, and orange. Every illustration portrays a unique element of Tibetan culture. The author's note at the end of the book explains why she included prayer flags, mani stones, and stupas. *Parents' Choice Recommended Award; Junior Library Guild Selection.   nrn*
Author from United States

Soros, Barbara. **Tenzin's Deer: A Tibetan Tale**. Illustrated by Danuta Maya. Cambridge: Barefoot Books, 2003. ISBN 1-84148-811-9. 32 p. (6 up). Folktale.

Deep in the Himalayas, Tenzin finds a wounded deer. He carries the deer home and names it Jampa. Through his dreams Tenzin learns how to heal the deer. During Jampa's recovery, Tenzin and the villagers chant prayers for healing and well-being. When Jampa is healed, Tenzin dreams that it is time for Jampa to return to the wild. The separation is difficult but Tenzin accepts it as part of life. *Nautilus Award, 2004; Notable Social Studies Trade Books, 2004.   ls*
Author from United States

Whitesel, Cheryl Aylward. **Rebel: Tibetan Odyssey**. New York: HarperCollins, 2000. ISBN 0-688-16735-7. 184 p. (12 up). Novel.

When he accepts medicine from a *fringie* (foreigner), fourteen-year-old Thunder is sent to live at a Buddhist monastery with his Uncle. He is rebellious and tormented by both fellow novices and his own self-doubt until an unexpected series of events makes him the companion of the newly named five-year-old Dalai Lama. Rich in cultural and religious details of turn-of-the-century Tibet, this novel also offers a suspenseful unfolding mystery and a satisfying coming-of-age tale. The author lived for 12 years in Asia, including two years in Hong Kong where she researched Tibetan history and culture. *Bank Street Best Book of the Year, 2001; Notable Social Studies Trade Book.*

VIETNAM

Shea, Pegi Deitz, and Cynthia Weill. **Ten Mice for Tet**. Illustrations by Tô Ngọc Trang. Embroidery by Phạm Viết Đinh. San Francisco: Chronicle Books, 2003. ISBN 0-8118-3496-4. 28 p. (4–8). Picture book.

This colorful counting book introduces children to the rich traditions of the Vietnamese New Year. Playful mice create scenes of preparation, gift giving, feasting, music making, dancing, and firework displays. The simple text is lavishly illustrated with vivid cotton thread embroidery reminiscent of the Hmong story cloth tradition. An informative afterword is appended. *djg*
Author from United States

Tran, Truong. **Going Home, Coming Home** = Về nhà, Thăm quê Hương. Illustrated by Ann Phong. Children's Book Press, 2003. ISBN 0-89239-179-0. 32 p. (5–8). Picture book.

Ami Chi is taking a trip to Vietnam, the country her parents left when they were children. All the talk of going back home leaves Ami Chi confused; how could this strange country be their home? She meets her uncle and grandmother and wonders how she will communicate. Getting used to the sound of the new language, foods, and customs is hard at first, but before long she discovers that home can be in two different places, on the left and right sides of her heart. In an introduction the author explains that he left Vietnam for America when he was five. It took twenty-five years to return to Vietnam to discover his heritage. *djg*

Tran-Khanh-Tuyet. **The Little Weaver of Thái-Yên Village** = Gô Bé Thợ-Dệt Làng Thái-Yên. Translated into English by Christopher N.H. Jenkins and Trấn-Khánh-Tuyết. San Francisco: Children's Book Press, 1987. ISBN 0-89239-030-1. 24 p. (7–10). Picture book.

When Hien's mother asks her to journey to a nearby village to bring rice to the people, hungry since the bombings, she is happy to go on this errand. Upon her return later that night, the fighting has come to her village, killing her mother and grandmother. Hien is so seriously wounded, she is sent to the United States for a life-saving surgery. Though she is desperately frightened, she is cared for by a family who understands her need to help her countrymen and supports her in her work to send packages to her home. Hien works at the craft she loves, weaving and embroidering the image of Me-Linh, the spirit bird of Viet-Nam into the center of each blanket. *djg*

Related Information

Awards

The Kiriyama Pacific Rim Book Prize

This award promotes books that will contribute to greater understanding and cooperation among the peoples and nations of the Pacific Rim and South Asia and has been given every year since 1996. The Prize is worth US$30,000. Half of the cash award is given to the author of the winning fiction title, and half is given to the author of the winning nonfiction title.
http://www.kiriyamaprize.org/index.shtml

Noma Concours for Children's Picture Book Illustrations
The biennial award is given to illustrators in Asia, Africa, Arab States, Oceana, Latin America, and the Caribbean to encourage them to show their works more widely. Sankei Award for Children's Books. Est. 1954.

National Book Development Council of Singapore Book Awards
The aim of the award is to encourage and develop local literary talent. Only original works by Singapore citizens or permanent residents of Singapore are eligible for the awards. Literary Prize for Sinhala Literature.

Bookfairs

Asia International Bookfair
Hong Kong Book Fair

Booksellers

Asia for Kids reviews thousands of products. Their mission is to be the best global resource for teaching Asian languages and cultures.

Pan Asian Publications
Founded in 1982, Pan Asian Publications has become a leading supplier and library service provider of Asian language materials to libraries across the world.

Southeast Asian Children's Books and Software
http://www.umiacs.umd.edu/users/sawweb/sawnet/kidsbooks.html

Online Resources

Passport: Asia
www.passport.imaginarylands
This excellent website links to Asian Awards, Bookfairs, Booksellers, Journals, and Organizations.

Organizations

Paper Tigers: a Pacific Rim Voices Project
This organization is for librarians, teachers, publishers, and all those interested in books from and about the Pacific Rim and South Asia.
http://www.papertigers.org

IBBY Kazakhstan
www.cde.kz

Chapter 6

North Africa and the Middle East

EGYPT

Eldash, Khaled, and Khattab, Dalia. **In an Egyptian City**. (*A Child's Day* series). New York: Benchmark Books (Marshall Cavendish), 2002. ISBN 0-7614-1410-X. 32 p. (6–11). Informational book.

Text and photographs portray a typical day in the life of Boushra, a seven-year-old girl who lives with her family in Cairo. She prays, goes to school, helps her mother buy vegetables at the market, visits her father at his tourist shop, plays with friends, welcomes *Ramadan* with her cousins, and talks with her grandmother. Information about Egypt, the pillars of Islam, and the Arabic language are included at the end.   *hk*

Hofmeyr, Dianne, and Jude Daly. **Star-Bearer: A Creation Myth from Ancient Egypt**. New York: Farrar, Straus and Giroux, 2001. First published in Great Britain by Frances Lincoln Ltd, 2001, by arrangement with The Inkman, Cape Town, South Africa. ISBN 0-374-37181-4. 28 p. (7–12). Myth.

This story is based on the Helioplis creation myth and tells of Atum's lonliness in the darkness. He creates Shu and Tefnut, but when their son Geb, the god of earth, and their daughter Nut, the goddess of the sky, grew so close that Atum could not complete his creation a solution must be found. With simple telling and lustrous paintings, the birth of Osiris, Horus, Set, and Isis is described. *Bank Street Best Book of the Year, 2002.*   *djg*
Author and illustrator from South Africa

Lester, Julius. **Pharaoh's Daughter: A Novel of Ancient Egypt**. San Diego: Silver Whistle, 2000. (Paperback: HarperTrophy, 2002). ISBN 0-15-201826-3. 182 p. (12 up). Novel.

Based on the biblical story of Moses and rich in detail, historical research, and imagination, this novel is divided into two parts. Part 1 is narrated by Almah, twelve, the older sister of Moses who hides him in a basket in the bulrushes and then follows the princess who finds him back to Pi-Ramesses to help raise him. Part 2 is narrated by Moses, now a confused young man torn between two identities: he is Hebrew but has been raised Egyptian. Although in great favor with the Pharoah Ramesses II, Moses watches in dismay as the Hebrews are forced to work as slaves building a temple to honor one of the Egyptian gods. After killing the Pharaoh's future son-in-law to protect Almah, he is forced to flee Khemet to the land of Midian, an act having lasting consequences on the world. An introduction, a fascinating author's note, a glossary, and a bibliography contribute to the reader's understanding of ancient Egypt and its people. *Best of the Bunch; Bank Street Best Book of the Year.   kk*
Author from United States

Marston, Elsa. **The Ugly Goddess**. Chicago: Cricket Books, 2002. ISBN 0-8126-2667-2. 218 p. (10–14). Novel.

Fourteen-year-old Princess Meret, Hector (son of the Greek commander of mercenaries serving in the royal Egyptian city of Sais), and Bata, an Egyptian orphan, comprise the trio of teens starring in this historical, action-packed adventure set in ancient Egypt. Political intrigue abounds for the princess has been kidnapped on her way to be trained as a Divine Wife. Hector is in love with her and impulsively plans to rescue her with Bata's help. Bata has his own mission of delivering the statue of the goddess Taweret to Meret's father, the reigning Pharoah. There are many challenges as these three engaging teens work together toward a just and satisfactory ending. A simple map and a 5-page informative Author's Note are included.   *bjk*
The author has lived in Egypt and now lives in United States

McCaughrean, Geraldine. **Casting the Gods Adrift**. Illustrated by Patricia D. Ludlow. Chicago: Cricket Books, 2002. Originally published by A & C Black in 1998. ISBN 0-8126-2684-2. 103 p. (10 up). Novel.

See Europe/UK for description.

Morris, Ann. **Grandma Hekmatt Remembers**. Illustrated and photographed by Peter Linenthal. Brookfield, CT: The Millbrook Press, 2003. ISBN 0-7613-2864-5. 32 p. Photographic essay.

This is the seventh title in the "What Was it Like, Grandma?" series by this author and photographer. This book provides a warm and realistic bridge between cultures based on universal bonds between grandchildren and grandparents. Candid photographs of the grandparents, their daughter and husband, and their three daughters with a lively text showing the family participating in family activities (cooking, baking, belly dancing, attending the mosque, celebrating the end of Ra-

madan) are alongside of older photographs provided by Grandma Hekmatt, inviting the reader into the pages of a family's intimate history. The richness and depth of experiences as these three girls learn about Egypt while living in the United States as Arab-Americans is clear. *bjk*
Author lives in United States

Winters, Kay. **Voices of Ancient Egypt**. Illustrated by Barry Moser. Washington, DC: National Geographic Society, 2003. ISBN 0-7922-7560-8. 32 p. (8 up). Novel.

Thirteen citizens of ancient Egypt, including scribe, birdnetter, embalmer, and marshman, explain their responsibility to Pharaoh in brief poetic form. Barry Moser's watercolor illustrations help readers to imagine the tools, clothing, and appearance of these voices. Each page's title, represented in English and ancient Egyptian hieroglyphics, establishes a connection between the illustration and the hieroglyphs. This book includes acknowledgements that substantiate the accuracy of the book's art and text. The end-matter includes two pages of detailed information about each voice as well as an adult bibliography. *Notable Social Studies Trade Books for Young People, 2004.* *lmp*
Author lives in United States

IRAN

Satrapi, Marjane. **Persepolis: The Story of a Childhood**. Translated and illustrated by the author. New York: Pantheon Books/Random House, 2003. Originally published in two volumes as *Persepolis 1* and *Persepolis 2* in Paris, France, by L'Association in 2000 and 2001. ISBN 0-375-42230-7. 153 p. (12 up). Graphic novel.

Satrapi, Marjane. **Persepolis 2: The Story of a Return**. Translated and illustrated by the author. New York: Pantheon Books/Random House, 2003. Originally published in two volumes as *Persepolis 1* and *Persepolis 2* in Paris, France, by L'Association in 2000 and 2001. ISBN 0-375-42288-9. 192 p. (YA). Graphic novel.

In 1979, when the Islamic Revolution toppled the Shah, Marjane was nine. Overnight, Iran was transformed from a modern, westernized dictatorship to a theocracy. Marjane, like her peers, didn't understand the changes. "We didn't really like to wear the veil, especially since we didn't understand why we had to." In simple black-and-white graphic format, Satrapi explains life in Iran, first from a child's point of view, then as a young adult. In *Persepolis 2*, Marjane's parents send her to Austria for high school. Sex and drugs permeate Marjane's years away from her family. The graphic format clarifies and personalizes life in Iran during the past 25 years. *2003 Fernando Buesa Peace Prize (Spain).* *lmp*
Author lives in Paris

Related Information

Online Resources

The History of Children's Literature in Iran
   The History of Children's Literature in Iran (HCLI) is a research project undertaken by the Foundation for Research on the History of Children's Literature in Iran (a non-governmental organization). Started in 1997, the project will be spread over 7 volumes.
http://www.payvand.com/news/03/jan/1108.html

Organizations

IBBY Iran
www.cbc.ir

IRAQ

Stamaty, Mark Alan. **Alia's Mission: Saving the Books of Iraq; Inspired by a True Story**. New York: Alfred A. Knopf, 2004. ISBN 0-3758-3217-3. unpaged. (8 up). Biography.
   In 2003, as bombs exploded over Basra, Alia Muhammad Baker attempted to preserve the collective history of Iraq. Alia was the chief librarian of the Central Library and as she watched her city prepare for war, she recalled her childhood history lessons—stories of the great library of Baghdad's destruction in 1258. Alia begged local officials to help but instead, as the war drew nearer, government officials commandeered her building and positioned anti-aircraft weapons and soldiers on the roof. Secretly and heroically, Alia and her friends transported 30,000 volumes to safety before the library burned to the ground. *Alia's Mission* is presented graphically in shades of sepia on cream paper, a true biography in graphic novel format that will appeal to intermediate and middle grade students. *Booklist Starred Review, Top 10 Graphic Novels for Youth, 2005.   lmp*
Author lives in United States.

Winter, Jeanette. **The Librarian of Basra: A True Story from Iraq**. Orlando: Harcourt, 2004. ISBN 0-15-205445-6. 32 p. (8–10). Picture book.
   Books are "more precious than mountains of gold" to Alia Muhammad Baker, the librarian of Basra. She and her friends remove more than 30,000 volumes from the library and store them in their homes to prevent their destruction when a bomb hits the building. This moving true story about a real librarian's brave struggle to save her war-stricken community's priceless collection of books is a powerful reminder that the love of literature and the passion for knowledge know no boundaries. Winter tells this story in simple sentences. Her beautiful acrylic-

and-pen, folk-art style illustrations soften the terrible realities of war. *School Library Journal Book Review Stars.* djg
Author from United States

ISRAEL AND PALESTINE

Bergman, Tamar. **Where Is?** Illustrated by Rutu Modan. Boston: Houghton Mifflin, 2002. ISBN 061809539X. Originally published in Israel by Sifriat Poalim Publishing, 1998. 24 p. (4–8). Picture book.

Mommy leaves Noni at Grandma and Grandpa's and he wonders where Mommy is. Is she at work, at the gym, or having a glass of lemonade with Uncle Yirmi? But when she comes to get Noni, the tables are turned and she must discover where Noni is hiding. The comforting day ends on a happy note when Daddy comes home and finds everyone just where they belong. Illustrations by a well-known comics artist won this book the Best Illustrated Children's Book Award from the Israel Museum in 2000. His book *The Shell of Secrets* won in 1998.

Clinton, Catheryn. **A Stone in My Hand**. Cambridge, MA: Candlewick Press, 2002. ISBN 0-7636-1388-6. 191 p. (8–12). Novel.

Set during the time of the 1988 Intifada, this is the story of a young girl living in the Gaza Strip, who finds the courage to move beyond the violence that surrounds her. Malaak's father disappeared weeks ago while traveling to Israel to find work. Malaak waits in a fantasy world on her roof top, but her older brother, Hamid, and his friend, Tariq, secretly become shabab, "youth activists," throwing stones at Israeli soldiers and even joining in terrorist activities. This harsh portrayal of the Israeli occupation will be painful for many readers. Combine with other books about what it is like to be young there now such as Danielle Carmi's *Samir and Yonatan* (2000), translated from the Hebrew. There is a glossary of Arabic words appended. *Children's Book Award Notable Book 2003 Young Adult Fiction; Notable Books for a Global Society, 2003; Publisher's Weekly Starred Review.*

Ellis, Deborah. **Three Wishes: Palestinian and Israeli Children Speak**. Toronto: Groundwood/Douglas & McIntyre, 2004. ISBN 0-88899-554-7. 112 p. (8 up). Informational.

See Canada for description.

Grossman, David. **Duel**. Translated from the original Hebrew by Betsy Rosenberg in 1998 when first published in Great Britain in 1999. New York: Bloomsbury Children's Books, 2004. Originally published as *Du-Kerav* by Massada in 1982. ISBN 1-58234-930-4. 112 p. (8–12). Novel.

Twelve-year-old David is hiding under the bed of his best friend, seventy-year-old Heinrich Rosenthal, awaiting to discover how the "bully of Heidelberg," Rudy Schwartz, intends to carry out his written threat of "honour or death." A priceless painting has been stolen from Schwartz and he is convinced that his old enemy (and past love of the artist), Rosenthal, is the culprit. When Rosenthal denies the accusation, Schwartz challenges him to a duel to settle their disagreement the way it was done in the old country. David makes it his mission to stop the duel before someone gets killed by solving the mystery of how these three people's lives intertwined and finding out who really stole the painting. *Notable Books of Jewish Content; 2000 Marsh Award.   kmc*
Author lives in Jerusalem, Israel

Grossman, Laurie. **Children of Israel**. Minneapolis: Carolrhoda, 2001. ISBN 1-57505-448-5. 48 p. (9–12). Informational book.
   In a series of vignettes about children, the author gives a quick look at the geography, history, and culture of groups, both Jewish and Arab, who live there. Political difficulties are addressed but only briefly and simply. Color photographs lend authenticity to the descriptions. *Children's Catalog.   jig*
Author lives in Israel

Harel, Nira. **The Key to My Heart**. Illustrated by Yossi Abulafia. La Jolla, CA: Kane/Miller, 2003. Published by arrangement with the Institute for the Translation of Hebrew Literarture. ISBN 1-929132-40-9. 24 p. (4–7). Picture book.
   When his Dad loses the keys, Jonathan helps him retrace his steps. Not at the Post Office, where he gets a stamp, or at the barber, where he gets a haircut, or at the pizza parlor, where they have a slice of pizza. Eventually, its Jonathan's picture on the key ring that aids in their return, and why not, after all it's the key to Dad's heart. This gentle story is illustrated in watercolor.   *djg*
Author lives in Israel and has won many awards including the Anderson citation in 1994, the Prix International du Livre Espace Enfants, an Une Mention d'Honneur in 2000, and a Bergstein Prize in 2002.
Illustrator from Tiberias, lives in Har Adar, and has won an Andersen Citation, the Ben-Zvi Prize, and the Nahum Gutman Prize for Illustration.

Holliday, Laurel. **Children of Israel, Children of Palestine: Our Own True Stories**. New York: Washington Square Press, 1998. ISBN 0-671-00804-8. xxi, 358 p. (11 up). Anthology.
   A compilation of 36 autobiographical stories by Palestinians and Jews who grew up in a land claimed by people of two different cultures. These reminiscences are written by adults but provide a personal touch on the problems that affected them as children, the impact that violence has had on their young lives, how it affected their outlook on life as adults, and their dreams of peace. While both sides have inflicted harm and pain, and neither side is blameless, these stories can serve as a basis for understanding each other's feelings and create a fo-

rum for an exchange of personal histories. Some of the stories are written under a pseudonym because the authors felt a need of protection against retaliation. *ok*
Compiler lives in United States

Keret, Etgar. **Dad Runs Away with the Circus**. Illustrated by Rutu Modan. Original Hebrew text translated by Noah Stollman. Cambridge, MA: Candlewick, 2004. ISBN 0-7636-2247-8. unpaged. (4–9). Picture book.
   "The circus is coming to town," yells Dad, waking everyone in the house. Dad was so happy his children didn't want to disappoint him and so the family gets ready and goes off to the circus. But at the end of the performances, Dad decides not to come home and off he goes. He writes to tell the family about his circus training and adventures, but most of all how much he misses them. It's a long year, but at last Dad comes home and everything goes back to normal . . . well almost! The illustrations, done in pencil and digitally colored add humor, and a four page spread provides a panoramic of all of Dad's performances. *Starred reviews.*

Levine, Anna. **Running on Eggs**. Chicago: Front Street/Cricket Books, 1999. ISBN 0-8126-2875-6. 128 p. (10–14). Novel.
   Karen's kibbutz and Yasmine's Arab village are separated by a vacant overgrown field, but it is distrust and fear that keep the girls apart, in spite of their common love of track. The girls overcome their fears and begin a secret friendship, training together in the field that Karen's father had hoped would become a racecourse for runners. This novel captures the tension that surrounds everyday life in contemporary Israel. *AJL Best of the Bunch, 1999.*
Author has lived in Israel for twenty years.

Orlev, Uri. **Run, Boy, Run**. Translated by Hillel Halkin. Boston: Houghton Mifflin, 2003. Originally published as *Ruts, yeled, ruts* in Hebrew by Keter in 2001. ISBN 0-618-16465-0. 186 p. (10 up). Novel.
   Escaping from the Warsaw Ghetto at the height of the Holocaust, eight-year-old Srulik Freydman heeds his father's warning and takes on the identity of a Christian orphan, changing his name to Jurek Staniak. Amid the personal hardships and perils, the resourceful Jurek survives the mean and spiteful people but also is helped by kind ones who protect him as he wanders through the Polish countryside. He changes his name and learns to act Catholic—wearing medals and saying prayers that are convincing only because of his fair complexion. His bravery and perseverance is compelling in the face of horrors modern readers can't begin to comprehend. The hope of finding his family reinforces Srulik's determination to stay alive in the Nazi-occupied Poland. The book is based on a true story. *2004 Mildred Batchelder Award winner.   lmp*
Author was the 1996 Hans Christian Andersen Author Award winner and lives in Israel.

Piven, Hanoch. **The Perfect Purple Feather**. English text by Rachel Tzvia Back. Silhouettes by Janet Stein. Photography by Adi Gilad. Boston: Little, Brown and

Company, 2002. Originally published in Hebrew in Tel Aviv by Am Oved Publishers Ltd. in 2000. ISBN 0-316-76657-7. 1 vol. 33 p. (4–8). Picture book.

The prickling feeling on the back of Jacob's neck as he tries to sleep turns out to be a feather from his pillow. He pulls the prickly feather free and his imagination takes over as bright rhyming text lead him through a series of animal adventures. All sorts of animals, made up of unusual objects, parade before him, and each one is enhanced by that purple feather. An unexpected surprise at the end of the book is a purple feather in a see-through purple envelope. The three-dimensional collage illustrations show animals ingeniously created of cleverly appropriate found objects: the elephant's trunk is a series of heavy iron elbow pipes; the wise owl's body is made of motherboards, its nose a light bulb. The illustrations are photographs of three-dimensional collages glued on watercolor paper painted with gouache. *Child Magazine Honorable Mention, 2002.   cd and ok*
Author from Uruguay, spent teen years in Israel, art education in New York, lives in Barcelona, Spain.

Rouss, Sylvia. **Tali's Jerusalem Scrapbook**. Illustrated by Nancy Oppenheimer. New York: Pitspopany, 2003. ISBN 1930143680. 32 p. (6–9). Picture book.

Tali has lived in Jerusalem all her life and she is looking forward to her tenth birthday when her American relatives will come to visit. But she is saddened when they cancel their plans because it is too dangerous in the city she loves. One by one, she adds pictures to her scrapbook in an effort to understand the complexities of life in modern day Jerusalem. This didactic picture book may help a young child understand the daily tensions of life in Israel. *AJL Best of the Bunch, 2003.   djg*
Author lives in United States

Related Information

Organizations

Israeli Section of IBBY
c/o Levin Kipnis Center for Children's Literature
Levinsky Teachers College
PO Box 48130
IL-61480 Tel-Aviv
e-mail: kipnisl@macam.ac.il

Palestinian Section of IBBY
c/o Tamer Institute for Community Education
Ms. Jehan Helou
PO Box 1973
Ramallah
e-mail tamer@palnet.com
www.tamerinst.org/

TURKEY

Bagdasarian, Adam. **The Forgotten Fire**. New York: DK, Inc, 2000. ISBN 0-7894-2627-7. 273 p. (14 up). Novel.

Few lived as privileged a life as twelve-year-old Vahan Kenderian, and so, it is with total incredulity that he witnesses the horrific butchering of his family by Turkish police. Surviving situation after situation, he manages to retain his humanity while he becomes stronger with each encounter. Told in the first-person and based on his great-uncle's experiences during the 1915 Armenian massacre by the Turks, the author makes immediate this sometimes forgotten attempt at the extermination of a people. A foreword and epilogue give historical background. Like David Kherdian's *The Road from Home*, this book describes a dark day in history. *Best Books for Young Adults, 2001 Top Ten; Benjamin Franklin Award Winner 2001; Young Adult Fiction United States; Los Angeles Times Book Prize Finalist 2000; Notable Books for a Global Society, 2001; The Best Children's Books of the Year, 2001; Bulletin Blue Ribbons, 2000.* mln

Croutier, Alev Lytle. **Leyla: The Black Tulip**. Middleton, WI: Pleasant Company, 2003. ISBN 1-58485-831-1. 198 p. (10–14). Novel.

Set in Turkey in the early 1700s during the Ottoman Empire, the author draws on her research from the adult title *Harem: The World behind the Veil* (1989), to write her first novel for young people. To support her impoverished family, Leyla sells herself to Ottoman marriage brokers, but quickly learns that she has not been purchased as a bride, but rather a slave. She is sold to the Sultan's harem in Istambul's Tokapi Palace where she works in the gardens. The reader becomes familiar with court manners, customs, and the history of the Tulip Era, a time in which Turkey opened up to new ideas and women had more freedom. As with other books in the "Girls of Many Lands" series, this book contains a glossary, an afterword with information about the country's history at the time of the narrative, photographs, and a description of modern life for girls in that nation. *Author was born and raised in Turkey and is the author of the internationally acclaimed nonfiction book* Harem: The World behind the Veil *and* Taking the Waters.

Macaulay, David. **Mosque**. New York: Houghton Mifflin, 2003. ISBN 0-618-24034-9. 96 p. (10 up). Informational book.

Using the fictional device of a 16th-century retired Turkish admiral who decides to dedicate his wealth to a lasting monument to God, Macaulay describes both in words and with detailed line and watercolor illustrations the building of a large mosque and other buildings associated with the mosque's educational and social functions, including a college for religious education, a bath, a public fountain, a soup kitchen, and a tomb. Macaulay explains the religious functions and symbolism of the different buildings and parts of buildings, as well as the

religious and secular life surrounding the mosque. *Booklist Starred Review; ALA Notable Children's Book 2004.* *jvl*
Author from United States

Ural, Serpil. **Candles at Dawn**. Translated by Betty Toker. Ankara, Turkey: Güldikeni Yayinlari, 2000. Originally published as *Safakta Yanan Mumlar Sev-Say* in 1998. ISBN 975-67731-03-6. 152 p. (10–13). Novel.

Peggy has heard many stories about the Battle of Galipoli in far away Turkey where her great-grandfather had been one of the ANZACs, the Australian troops fighting in World War I on the Allies' side. Now she is going to Turkey with her mother to see Gallipoli for herself. In Turkey she meets Zeynep who is her age and whose great-grandfather was wounded in the same battle. Through these girls' eyes readers are introduced to the Battle of Galipoli, the tragedy of war, and hopes for peace. Black-and-white photographs from WWI are included. The author has written numerous children's books. Publisher's address: Bayindir Sok. No: 14/17 / Yensisehir / Ankara   *jvl*
Author from Turkey

NORTH AFRICA—REGIONAL

Marchant, Kerena. **Muslim Festival Tales**. Illustrated by Tina Barber. Series: Festival Tales. Austin, TX: Raintree/Steck-Vaughn, 2001. ISBN 0739827359. 32 p. (7–9). Informational book.

Attractive, includes six or seven stories, plays, traditional songs, poems, and recipes. Information material about festivals is for older readers, thus needing an adult interpreter.

Nye, Naomi Shihab. **19 Varieties of Gazelle: Poems of the Middle East**. New York: Greenwillow Books, 2002. ISBN 0-06-009765-5. 142 p. (10 up). Poetry.

"September 11 cast a huge shadow across the lives of so many innocent people and an ancient culture's pride," Nye tells the reader in the introduction of these sixty poems that tell about being Arab-American, about Jerusalem, the West bank, and her family. The poet encourages us to think and understand what it is to be Arabic, and to leap like the gazelle toward the horizon with the hope of peace spinning inside us.   *djg*

Nye, Shihab. **The Space between Our Footsteps: Poems and Paintings from the Middle East**. New York: Simon & Schuster, 1998. ISBN 0-689-81233-7. 144 p. (9 up). Poetry.

More than a hundred poets and artists from nineteen Middle Eastern countries explore themes of homeland, exile, childhood, love, and war in this brilliant anthology. Full-color paintings in a range of styles and poetry, some written in

English, many in translation, are included. Information about each of the contributors, a map, and an informative introduction by the collector are included. *Starred reviews; Notable Books for a Global Society, 1999. djg*

Young, Ed. **What About Me?** New York: Philomel, 2002. ISBN 0-399-23624-4. 32 p. (4–8). Folklore.

This teaching tale, rooted in the Sufi tradition of the Middle East provides subtle wisdom for young and old. Beautifully illustrated with textured collage on painted backgrounds, this simple cumulative of a young boy's desire to acquire wisdom from the Grand Master leads him on a journey. First, he must get a carpet, but the carpet maker asks "what about me?" I need some thread and next he goes to the spinner and so on in this tale as old as Aesop. The ultimate conclusion is that he learns that wisdom comes to us when we are giving in this timely tale. *The Children's Literature Choice List, 2002; Choices, 2003; Cooperative Children's Book Center, United States. djg*

Related Information

Organizations

Egyptian Section of IBBY
Kuwaiti Section of IBBY (KUBBY)
Lebanese Section of IBBY (LBBY)
   Contact information may be found on the IBBY website

Chapter 7

Africa South of the Sahara

ANGOLA

McKissack, Patricia. **Nzingha, Warrior Queen of Matamba**. New York: Scholastic, 2000. ISBN 0-439-11210-9. 136 p. (10 up). Novel.

Set in the West African country of present-day Angola, this novel in diary format records a year (July, 1595 to September, 1596) in the life of 13-year-old Nzingha, an Angolan princess who later became the Ngola of Ndongo and Queen of Matamba. Nzingha was a proud, intelligent leader and a warrior who was guided by principles of honor and determination not to participate in slave trade as pressured by the Portuguese colonizers. It is the sixth of "The Royal Diary" series, a series based on real royal figures and actual historical events. In the extensive historical notes that include maps, photos, glossaries, illustrations, and a family tree, Patricia McKissack provides a historical context. In tracing Nzingha's legacy McKissack explores the American connection to this area.   *ok*
Author from United States

BENIN

Gershator, Phillis. **Only One Cowry: A Dahomean Tale**. Illustrated by David Soman. New York: Orchard, 2000. ISBN 0-531-30288-1. 32 p. (4–7). Folktale.

The stingy king of Dahomey (now Benin) is ready to marry, but is only willing to pay one cowry for a bride. A clever young man offers to find a wife and begins a journey on which he trades the shell for a bride price worthy of an equally clever young woman. Rich colors in the collage illustrations adapted from a Dahomean appliqué motif convey the rural setting and humor of this 19th-century trickster tale. *The Best Children's Books of the Year; Bank Street Best*

Book of the Year, 2001; Children's Literature Choice List, 2001; Notable Social Studies Trade Books for Young People, 2001.   djg
Author lives in St. Thomas

BOTSWANA

Robson, Jenny. **Because Pula Means Rain**. Cape Town, South Africa: Tafelberg, 2002. First published in South Africa in 2000 by Tafelberg. ISBN 0-624-03925-0. 133 p. (12 up). Novel.

Emmanual, a young albino living in a small village in northern Botswana, longs for dark skin and a sense of acceptance. Against his grandmother's wishes he travels with his friend Sindiso to Gaborone, along the way describing the landscape and history of the area. He contrasts his grandmother's Christianity with Mma Zacharius's African customs, accepting bits of both himself as he listens to and thinks of these two old women, friends, arguing with one another. Ultimately he must seek answers within himself. *Sanlam Silver Prize for Youth Literature; IBBY Honor Book.*   jig
Author from South Africa, lives in Botswana

DEMOCRATIC REPUBLIC OF CONGO

Stanley, Sanna. **Monkey for Sale**. Illustrated by the author. New York: Farrar, Straus and Giroux, 2002. ISBN 0-374-35017-5. 32 p. (4–9). Picture book.

Young Luzolo is off to village market day with a five-franc coin and her parents' advice to choose wisely and to bargain fairly. After two successful purchases, Luzolo sees her best friend and they settle down to do what best friends do, to admire and share in each other's bounty. When they hear that a market vendor is offering a wild monkey for sale, the two are spurred into rescue mode and arise to the lofty goal of purchasing the monkey (through a series of time-honored, fast-moving bargains and trades) in order to set it free in the jungle. The vibrant illustrations portray not only the children's cozy comfort in their market day but also the excitement of two friends working hard to save a monkey from captivity. This is Stanley's third picture book based on her childhood in the Congo.   bjk
Author from United States

ETHIOPIA

Bulion, Leslie. **Fatuma's New Cloth**. Illustrated by Nicole Tadgell. North Kingston, RI: Moon Mountain, 2002. ISBN 0-9677929-7-5. Unpaged. (5–9). Picture book.

Fatuma, a young girl in East Africa, walks with her mother to market where they pick out kanga cloth and hear advice about how to make the best chai (tea). In the process they also discuss some of the Swahili sayings printed on the cloths. The saying on Fatuma's cloth (translated as "Don't be fooled by the color. The good flavor of chai comes from the sugar.") is applied to the goodness inside people as well as the sweetness inside chai. This is a tender mother-daughter story with kanga patterns decorating each page and a recipe for chai at the end. *2003 Children's Africana Book Award.   hk*
Author from United States

Janisch, Heinz. **The Fire: An Ethiopian Folk Tale**. Illustrated by Fabricio VandenBroeck. Toronto: Groundwood, 2002. ISBN 0-8889-9450-8. 24 p. (5–10). Folktale.
See Canada for description.

Kurtz, Jane. **Faraway Home**. Illustrated by E.B. Lewis. New York: Harcourt, 2000. ISBN 0-15-200036-4. 32 p. (4–8). Picture book.
Desta worries when her father tells her that he must go back to Ethiopia for a visit because his mother is ill. She fears that he will not return. Gradually, as he describes his childhood in Ethiopia and compares it with Desta's life, she comes to accept his love for his mother and his homeland, and asks him to tell her more about his life in Ethiopia.
Author grew up in Ethiopia, lives in United States

Kurtz, Jane. **Saba: Under the Hyena's Foot**. Middleton, WI: Pleasant Company Publications, 2003. ISBN 1-58485-829-X. 210 p. (10–14). Novel.
Set in Ethiopia in 1846, this historical adventure story is told in the first person by Saba, a young girl, who with her young brother is kidnapped from their rural home and taken to the royal palace at Gondar. Saba eventually learns about her own royal ancestor, the biblical Queen of Sheba. Kurtz creates a powerful sense of place with cultural and historic details woven into the story. As with other books in the "Girls of Many Lands" series, this book contains a glossary and an afterword with information about the country's history at the time of the narrative, photographs, and a description of modern life for girls in that nation. *2004 Children's Africana Book Award. Reviewed in Sankofa 2004.   djg*
Author moved with her family to Ethiopia and spent most of her childhood there.

Laird, Elizabeth. **The Garbage King**. Hauppauge: Barron's Educational Series, 2003. ISBN 0-7641-2626-1. Originally published by Macmillan Children's Books in 2003. ISBN 0-7641-5679-9. 329 p. (12 up). Novel.
See Europe/UK for description.

Yohannes, Gebregeorgis. **Silly Mammo: An Ethiopian Tale**. Illustrated by Bogale Belachew. Oakland, CA: African Sun Publishing, 2002. ISBN 1-883701-04-X. 32 p. (5–8). Picture book.

A long time ago there lived a boy called Mammo. The popular tale of *Kilu Mammo,* a foolish young man, who loses his wages when he can't seem to figure out how to bring them home is told in English and Amharic. First he loses his coins and his mother tells him he should put his wages in his pocket, but the next day, when he is paid in milk—disaster! This tale, similar to *Obedient Jack* is set in the rural Ethiopian countryside and is colorfully illustrated. *Children's Africana Book Honor. djg*
Author from United States, works for African Sun Publishing, San Francisco

GHANA

Ahiagble, Gilbert "Bobbo," and Louise Meyer. **Master Weaver from Ghana**. Photographs by Nestor Hernandez. Seattle, WA: Open Hand Publishing, 1998. ISBN 0-940880-61-X. 32 p. (5–10). Informational book.

Weaving together has been the family tradition of hundreds of years. In this beautiful photo essay the reader gets a glimpse of village life in Denu, Ghana, and meets the master weaver, Bobbo. Daily village life and the work of the weaver are portrayed. Every detail of creating the woven fabrics is shown, from his little sons helping with the dying of the thread to the men at work on their traditional looms in this beautiful and informative book. *djg*
Author from the Volta region of Ghana

Asare, Meshack. **Sosu's Call**. La Jolla, CA: Kane/Miller, 2001. Originally published in Ghana in 1997 by Sub-Saharan Publishers, Legon, Accra. ISBN 1-9291-3221-2. 37 p. (4–8). Picture book.

Sosu lives in a small village between the sea and the lagoon with his family. Though Sosu can't walk, his family teach him the things he will need to know. Suspertitious villagers aren't so understanding and do not want Sosu around them when are working. But it is Sosu who becomes the hero when a flood threatens to destroy the village and Sosu uses the drums to call everyone to the rescue. *1999 UNESCO Prize for Children's and Young People's Literature in the Service of Tolerance; 2001 IBBY Outstanding Books for Young People with Disabilities Award, 2002; Children's Africana Book Award 2003. djg*

Badoe, Adwoa. **The Pot of Wisdom: Ananse Stories**. Pictures by Baba Wagué Diakité. Toronto: Groundwood, 2001. ISBN 0-88899-429-X. 64 p. (7–12). Folktales.

These ten tales deal with the themes of justice, vanity, self-respect, as well as other important issues like money, food, and marriage. Ghanaian author explains

that many of these witty stories were told to him growing up in Ghana and the elements are common in other trickster tales of African origin. Colorful folk illustrations are framed with detailed pen-and-ink borders of Ananse. *djg*
Author from Ghana. Illustrator from Mali.

Provencal, Francis, and McNamara, Catherine. **In a Ghanaian City**. (*A Child's Day* series). New York: Benchmark Books (Marshall Cavendish), 2001. ISBN 0-7614-1223-9. 32 p. (6–11). Informational book.
　　Nii Kwei is a seven-year-old Ga boy living in Accra, Ghana, with his family. Their home, compound, and daily life are described in words and photographs. School, foods, games, and shopping are also portrayed. More information about Ghana and the different peoples and language groups that make up the country is included after Nii Kwei's story. This book, like others in the series, portrays a happy modern child in a caring family, though mention is made that many children in rural areas need to spend much of their time gathering water. *hk*

Related Information

Ghana Section of IBBY
c/o Ghana Library Board
PO Box 663
Accra

KENYA

Kessler, Cristina. **Our Secret, Siri Aang**. New York: Philomel, 2004. ISBN 0-399-23985-5. 218 p. (12 up). Novel.
　　The conflicts and tensions of the changes facing the Maasai people are powerfully conveyed in this gripping story of a girl and her family who have recently been forced to relocate their *enkang* to an area of better grazing for their cattle, putting them in close proximity to the Kenya National Park, a store, and a school. Twelve-year-old Namelok witnesses the birth of a baby black rhino while gathering wood. Naming the baby Siri Aang, our secret, she pledges to keep the mother and baby safe from the poachers. But this proves to be a difficult promise to keep. The change from a nomadic to a sedentary lifestyle, imposed by modern society makes Namelok aware of the need to learn to read and she wants to go to school, another secret. But finally, the time for the *emurature* ceremony (female circumcision, referred to as surgery without anesthetic in the text) has come. Knowing this means she will not be able to go out into the countryside to visit the rhinos nor attend school, she tries to keep this secret as well. A devastating event catapults Namelok on a dangerous journey that ends in a climactic meeting with her father. With courage and respect, this young girl confronts the difficult times before her people. *djg*

Author from United States and has spent nineteen years in Africa where all of her children's books are set

Lekuton, Joseph Lemasolai. **Facing the Lion: Growing Up Maasai on the African Savanna**. Washington, DC: National Geographic, 2003. ISBN 0-7922-5125-3. 127 p. (12 up). Informational book.

The author describes his life growing up with his nomadic Maasai family in northern Kenya, being the only member of his family to attend school, and finally receiving a college education in the United States. He has struggled to honor both cultures by which he has been formed. The bulk of the story describes his years in Kenya, including the ritual circumcision that signaled his exit from childhood. He then briefly describes some experiences of crossing cultures. This is an encouraging look by someone who lives in both cultures at the life of a tribal people in the midst of the modern world.   *hk*

Author from Kenya, living in United States and Kenya

LIBERIA

Paye, Won-Ldy, and Margaret H. Lippert. **Head, Body, Legs: A Story from Liberia**. Illustrated by Julie Paschkis. New York: Henry Holt, 2002. ISBN 0-8050-6570-9. 32 p. (4–8). Picture book.

Long ago, head was all by himself. He had no legs, no arms, no body. He rolled everywhere, but he could not reach good things to eat until he meets arms. But head and arms cannot find as much good food as they can with the help of body. . . . and so on. This is a traditional story from the Dan people of Northern Liberia retold by a storyteller with simple humorous illustrations in bold colors that tell of the importance of cooperation.   *djg*

Author from Liberia

LIBYA

Stolz, Joëlle. **The Shadows of Ghadames**. Translated from the French by Catherine Temerson. New York: Delacorte Press, 2004. Originally published in France as *Les Ombres de Ghadamès* in 1999 by Bayard Editions Jeunesse. ISBN 0-385-73104-3. 119 p. (10 up). Novel.

See Europe/France for description.

MALAWI

Ellis, Deborah. **The Heaven Shop**. Markham, ON: Fitzhenry & Whiteside, 2004. ISBN 1-55041-908-0. 186 p. (12 up). Novel.

See Canada for description.

MALI

Diakité, Baba Wagué. **The Magic Gourd**. New York: Scholastic Press, 2003. ISBN 0-439-43960-4. 32 p. (4–8). Folktale.

The rains have not come and everyone is hungry and Brother Rabbit goes out into the parched countryside to look for food. Instead, he finds and rescues Chameleon stuck in a thorny bush. His act of kindness is rewarded tenfold with a most amazing gift: a magic gourd. This gourd, a beautiful bowl decorated in the designs of mud cloth, fills itself with anything the owner desires. Mansa Juga, the greedy king hears of the gourd and takes it away. In extensive notes at the end of the story, the author explains that of the stories he learned around the fire after the evening meal, the Rabbit stories were his favorite. Both the tale and the lush illustrations reflect the rich heritage of his native Mali. *The 2004 Children's Africana Book Award.*   *djg*

Winter, Jeanette. **My Baby**. New York: Frances Foster Books/Farrar, Straus and Giroux, 2001. ISBN 0374351031. 32 p. (4–7). Picture book.

This is the story of the girl Nakunte, who learns to make the bògòlan cloth. Her mother teaches her to carefully select the leaves and sticks and clothes to make the traditional cloth and she paints it with black mud in the traditional techniques practiced for centuries by the women of Mali. She grows into a young woman and an artist; she lovingly prepares for her baby's arrival. Folk style of the art perfectly compliments the lyrical text.   *djg*
Author from United States

MOZAMBIQUE

Mankell, Henning. **Secrets in the Fire**. Translated by Anne Connie Struksrud. Toronto: Annick, 2003. First published as *Eldens Hemlighet* by Rabén & Sjörgen in 1995. (Paperback: Annick, 2003). ISBN 1-55037-801-5. 176 p. (10–14). Novel.

See Europe/Sweden for description.

NIGERIA

Alakiya, Polly. **Catch That Goat!** Cambridge: Barefoot Books, 2002. ISBN 1-84148-908-5. 32 p. (3–6). Picture book.

Ayoka is left in charge of her goat. The goat escapes from the family compound and runs through the street market. Ayoka asks everyone if they had seen her goat.

They reply that they had not, as the goat scampers off the page, but they find that they are missing an item of merchandise. When Ayoka returns home, her Mama shows her the goat all decked out in the missing merchandise. Bright, dynamic, busy illustrations support this simple counting story. *ls*
Author from Nigeria

Olaleye, Isaac. **Bikes for Rent!** Illustrated by Chris Demarest. New York: Orchard, 2001. ISBN 0-531-30290-3. 32 p. (5–8). Picture book.

Lateef passes by the bicycle shop in his village in western Nigeria nearly every day, and wants very much to rent a bike. He collects and sells mushrooms and firewood in order to earn money. First he rents a small blue bike, learns to ride it, then rents a larger one. When friends dare him to ride no-handed, he does, but falls and damages the bike. This time he works at the bicycle shop to earn the money for the repairs, eventually earning enough to purchase a used bike. *jig*
Author from Nigeria, lives in California

Onyefulu, Ifeoma. **Here Comes Our Bride: An African Wedding Story**. London: Frances Lincoln Children's Books, 2004. First published in Great Britain in 2004. ISBN 1-84507-047-X. 26 p. (4–8). Informational book.

When will Uncle Osaere and Aunt Efosa get married; Ekinadose cannot wait! But the joining of two families is serious and governed by many customs in Nigeria. First the groom's family is given a lists of things to do and a time limit to complete the tasks. To cement the new friendship, the families often tease each other; eventually the bride is officially introduced to her new family and an elder joins the couple in a traditional way. This is followed by a wedding ceremony in a church, mosque, or registry. Stunning photographs, so typical of Onyfulu's books, illustrate this third book in a trilogy on African ceremonies. Raised in Nigeria her recent books include: *My Grandfather Is a Magician, Ebele's Favourite,* and *A Triangle for Adaora*. *djg*

Onyefulu, Ifeoma. **Saying Good-bye: A Special Farewell to Mama Nkwelle**. Brookfield, CT: Millbrook Press, 2001. ISBN 0-7613-1965-4. 28 p. (5–10). Informational book.

Narrated through the eyes of the young great-grandson of Mama Nkwelle, this photo-essay simply tells about the traditional funeral customs in this small Nigerian village. Preparations by the family and friends take many days and the life of this skilled dancer and community leader is memorialized by those who loved and respected her. Colorful photographs of the family, homes, and village show with integrity the customs of this eastern Nigerian community. *Welcome Dede!* is the second book in this trilogy of African ceremonies. *djg*
Author is a member of the Igbo tribe of East Nigeria, now lives in England

Related Information

Bookfairs

Nigerian International Book Fair
http://www.nibf.org/

SOMALIA

Hoffman, Mary. **The Color of Home**. Illustrated by Karen Littlewood. New York: Phyllis Fogelman Books (Penguin Putnam Books for Young Readers imprint), 2002. ISBN 8-8037-2841-7. Unpaged. (5–9). Picture book.

When a young boy from Somalia begins school in the United States, he paints a picture of the home he left and the trauma that surrounded his leaving. A translator helps him tell his story to his new teacher, and afterwards the boy is able to paint a new picture to take home to his family, a picture that shows the beauty of his former home without the horrors that he experienced in being forced to relocate. This effectively shows a young audience both how trauma can deeply affect one's countenance and also how it can be eased by expressing what has happened in words and pictures.   *hk*
Author from England

SOUTH AFRICA

Cave, Kathryn. **One Child, One Seed**. Photographed by Gisele Wulfsohn. New York: Henry Holt and Company, 2002. ISBN 0-8050-7204-7. 32 p. (4–8). Picture book.

Definitely not your average counting book . . . this one is valuable beyond measure as the left hand spreads take care of the counting of pumpkin seeds with large photographs complementing the simple captions that highlight each successive numeral; the right hand spreads offer two smaller photographs with sidebar information about Nothando (the main character) and her extended family and friends as they move through the cycle of planting, growing, harvesting, food preparation, and even the family dinner. There is a common thread of family working and enjoying life together throughout this revealing and realistic book about the culture of rural South Africa. Near the end, "Ten dinner plates piled high. It's dinnertime at last. And there's plenty for everyone!" Pride in the bounty of hard work is evident. At the very end, Nothando holds one pumpkin seed that was saved from the pumpkin stew. From the caption "One child, one seed to plant next time," it is clear Nothando senses the comfort in the cycle and structure of

her daily life. Endnotes include a recipe for the traditional pumpkin stew, basic geographic facts, and a simple map. A portion of the book's profits goes to the global charity, Oxfam.   *bjk*
Author lives in England. Photographer lives in South Africa.

Daly, Niki. **Old Bob's Brown Bear**. New York: Farrar, Straus and Giroux, 2002. Originally published by Bloomsbury Children's Books, 2001. ISBN 0-374-35612-2. 32 p. (4–8). Picture book.

Old Bob has always wanted a teddy bear. When he receives one for his birthday, he thinks it is very nice but he does not love it. His granddaughter, Emma, does love the teddy bear. She takes it home and plays with it for a long time. Then Emma begins going to school and she does not have time to take care of the bear. One day, Old Bob is visiting and sees his teddy bear, worn and neglected laying in Emma's toy box. Old Bob falls in love with his fuzzy-wuzzy teddy bear and begs to take it home. A spirited, warm intergenerational story about the young who treasure new things and experiences and the elderly who treasure older things filled with memories.   *ls*
Author from South Africa

Daly, Niki. **Once Upon a Time**. New York: Farrar, Straus and Giroux, 2003. Orginally published in Great Britain by Francis Lincoln Limited in 2003. ISBN 0-374-35633-5. 26 p. (5–12). Picture book.

Reading aloud is scary and difficult for Sarie to do. Except for Emile, the children in her South African classroom tease her. With the help of her older neighbor Auntie Anna and the rusted old car where Sarie and Auntie Anna swap stories and secrets, Sarie overcomes her fears. Sarie, Auntie Anna, and Emile celebrate by taking a pretend drive in the car to far, far away. This universal story is provided its distinct location via the warm, expressive, and detailed illustrations. *2004 Children's Africana Book Award.   js*
Author/illustrator lives in Cape Town, South Africa

Daly, Niki. **What's Cooking, Jamela?** New York: Farrar, Straus and Giroux, 2001. Originally published in Great Britain by Francis Lincoln Limited in 2001. ISBN 0-374-35602-5. 32 p. (4–10). Picture Book.

Christmas preparations have begun in Jamela's South African home and she is given the responsibility of fattening up the chicken for Christmas dinner. It doesn't take long for the chicken intended for Christmas dinner to become Christmas, the pet chicken. To save her friend, Jamela takes Christmas with her when sent on an errand. Christmas escapes from Jamela's arms and havoc ensues. All ends with everyone having a happy Christmas, especially the chicken. A glossary of the African terms interspersed throughout the story is provided. The colorful, expressive illustrations that accompany the text make this story distinctively

South African. Jamela's adventures continue in *Where's Jamela*, 2004. *2002 Children's Africana Book Award.   js*
Author/illustrator lives in Cape Town, South Africa

Ferreira, Anton. **Zulu Dog**. New York: Farrar, Straus and Giroux, 2002. ISBN 0-374-39223-4. 195 p. (10–14). Novel.

This boy/dog story is set in post-apartheid South Africa and focuses on the relationships between Zulus and Afrikaners. Eleven-year-old Vusi and Shirley, the daughter of a white farmer, meet quite by accident and keep their friendship a secret. Vusi has another secret—she has nursed back to health a 3-legged dog even though his mother has said there is no spare food for a pet. Vusi's first hunt provides an important rite of passage element to the story, but it is Shirley's decision to run away to escape boarding school and the fact that black and white neighbors work together to search for her that provides the metaphor for a hopeful and peaceful future for all the citizens of South Africa. Cheryl-Ann Michael at the University of the Western-Cape, South Africa, in a review published by H-AfriTeach (June, 2003) says, "the solution itself is problematic, glossing over . . . very real difficulties . . . [and] in attempting to create an ending that symbolizes reconciliation, Ferreira's novel veers dangerously towards the suggestion that white patronage provides an adequate answer." Brenda Rudolph in an article that appears in November 2005 edition of *Sankofa* cautions that "the author fails to give readers any real ammunition to refute the negative [stereotypes] that characters bandy about." She warns "that the Author's Note reads like a page from an Apartheid textbook." *Smithsonian Notable Children's Book, 2003; Notable Social Studies Trade Book, 2003.   bjk*
Author, a former resident of Zambia and South Africa, now lives in United States

Gregorowski, Christopher. **Fly, Eagle, Fly! An African Tale**. Pictures by Niki Daly. New York: Margaret K. McElderry, 2000. First published in South Africa in 1982 as a two-color picture book. ISBN 0-6898-239-3. 32 p. (5–10). Picture book.

A farmer sets out one day to find his lost calf and instead finds an eagle chick blown from its nest in a terrible storm. He takes the chick home and shelters it among his chickens. The eagle comes to eat like the chickens and act like the chickens and forgets its heritage. A friend, determined to help the eagle remember its heritage, helps the eagle remember it belongs to the sky, not to the earth. The author discovered this powerful parable in the biography of Ghanaian James Kwegyir Aggrey and sets his retelling in the South African Transkei. Niki Daly dedicates this new full-color edition to the children of South Africa. An inspiring foreword by Archbishop Desmond Tutu sets the stage for this dramatic story.   *djg*

Grobler, Piet. **Hey, Frog**. Asheville, NC: Front Street, 2002. ISBN 1886910847. Originally published by Lemniscaat b.v. Rotterdam under the title *Een slokje, kicker!* 28 p. (4–7). Picture book.

One very hot day on the savannah all the animals were playing in the water and resting in the shade, until Frog took a sip from a puddle, then another and another until he gulped all the water from the puddle, the pond, the river, the well, and finally the lake. "Hey, Frog, unzip those lips before you pop!" All the animals try to get the water back, but it is the clever eels who figure it out. Now, when Frog looks thirsty, all the animals shout, "Hey Frog, just one sip!" This delightful story is illustrated by the author with humorous, stylized pen and watercolor.   *djg*
Author has won national and international awards for his children's book illustrations. He lives in Cape Town, South Africa.

Naidoo, Beverley. **The Other Side of Truth**. New York: HarperCollins, 2001. First published in 2000 by Puffin Books in London, England. ISBN 0-06-029628-3. 248 p. (12 up). Novel.
See Europe/UK for description.

Naidoo, Beverley. **Out of Bounds: Seven Stories of Conflict and Hope**. New York: HarperCollins, 2003. Originally published in 2001 by Puffin Books, England. ISBN 0-0605-0799-3. 176 p. (12 up). Short stories.
See Eurupe/UK for description.

Rankin, Joan. **First Day**. New York: Margaret K. McElderry, 2002. First published in 2002 in the United Kingdom by the Bodley Head as *Oh, Mum, I Don't Want to Go to School!* By arrangement with the Bodley Head, the Random House Group, and the Inkman, Cape Town, South Africa. ISBN 0-689-84563-4. 32 p. (4–7). Picture book.
It was Haybillybun's first day of school at the Yappy Puppy Play School and he is not sure he wants to go. But Bun makes friends and settles right into the fun. It is mom who finds she misses her little boy more than she thought she would. Whimsical, watercolor illustrations add humor to the story.   *djg*
Author lives in Johannesburg, South Africa. Other books illustrated by Rankin include A Frog in the Bog *by Karma Wilson McElderry, 2003 and* Mrs. McTats and Her Houseful of Cats.

Winter, Jeanette. **Elsina's Clouds**. New York: Farrar, Straus and Giroux, 2004. ISBN 0-374-32111-3. 40 p. (3–7). Picture book.
Based on a Basotho custom where women paint their houses in designs that are a prayer to their ancestors for rain, the little girl in this story looks for an opportunity to paint designs on their house. She dreams of rain clouds during the sunny winter season, wanting to paint designs on her family's house with her own designs as a prayer to the ancestors for rain. When the rains come and wash away her mama's designs, Elsina gets her chance. Thus begins the pattern where Elsina covers the walls with bright designs, the rains come and wash the walls clean, and once again she decorates the exterior of her home.   *jig and bn*
Author lives in New York

Related Information

Awards

Vivian Wilkes Award goes to "an outstanding illustrated South African children's book." Text may be written in any South African language.
http://www.childlit.org.za/vwilkesaward.html

Print and Online Resources

MacCann, Donnarae, and Yluissa Amandu Maddy. **Apartheid and Racism: In South African Children's Literature 1985–1995**. New York: Taylor & Francis, 2001.

Maddy, Yluissa Amadu, and Donnarae MacCann. "Ambivalent Signals in South African Young Adult Novels," **Bookbird**, Spring 1998.

South African Children's Literature
This website describes the history of children's literature in South Africa.
http://www.childlit.org.za/history.html

Organizations

FNB Vita Sibikwa Storytelling Festival
Capetown, South Africa
phone: 011 422 4359, e-mail: sibikwa@iafrica.com
http://www.sibikwa.co.za/festivals.htm
October

IBBY South Africa
http://www.ibby.org/index.php?id=454
    The 29th IBBY Congress was held in Cape Town, South Africa, in September 2004. Many of the papers presented at the Congress may be accessed at this website.
http://www.sacbf.org.za/

SUDAN

Kessler, Cristina. **My Great-Grandmother's Gourd**. Illustrated by Walter Lyon Krudop. New York: Orchard, 2000. ISBN 0-531-30284-9. 32 p. (5–8). Picture book.
    Fatima is delighted when her Sudanese village gets a new water pump, but her grandmother insists that they fill the trunk of the baobab tree with water, the traditional method of storing water for the dry season. When the pump breaks down,

grandmother shares her water with her neighbors, and the following year all the villagers use the traditional method as a back up for the pump. A glossary of Arabic words used in the text is included.
Author from United States and has lived in Mali

Levitin, Sonia. **Dream Freedom**. San Diego: Silver Whistle, 2000. ISBN 0-15-202404-2. 178 p. (10 up). Novel.

This novel was inspired by a fifth-grade class of American students who launched a campaign in 1997 to raise money to free Sudanese slaves and to encourage other students across the country to do the same. In alternating chapters the story of Marcus, a student struggling in school and at home but deeply involved in the campaign, and the stories of the enslaved and oppressed Dinka and Nuba people in Sudan reveal the positive and lasting impact each has had on the other. Included are a bibliography, a brief history of Sudan, names of organizations engaged in helping still today, details of the true-life events on which this is based, and an afterword by Barbara Vogel, the teacher who founded S.T.O.P. (Slavery That Oppresses People). *kk*
Author from United States and has won ALA Notable Books, Sydney Taylor, PEN Award for Young Adult fiction, and the National Jewish Book Award.

Mead, Alice. **Year of No Rain**. New York: Farrar, Straus and Giroux, 2003. ISBN 0-374-37288-8. 130 p. (10–14). Novel.

Eleven-year-old Stephen loves his home, his mother and sister (father is missing), and his books, but life is complicated in southern Sudan because of a 3-year drought and also the civil war. Suddenly it gets worse when bombs explode nearby and his mother orders him to hide in the forest with his friends. Thus begins a period of time when these young boys are truly on their own, searching for water, food, and safety without the luxury of a well-thought-out plan for survival. Throughout all their hardships, Stephen continues to yearn for home and family. He becomes a leader of sorts, persuading the others to return to their village where he finds that his sister survived the northern government soldiers' attack. Stephen himself has not only survived the "walk," but also has matured and knows that the next flight for freedom will require planning and foresight. Author's notes and map. *bjk*
Author lives in United States

TANZANIA

Mollel, Tololwa. **My Rows and Piles of Coins**. Illustrated by E.B. Lewis. New York: Clarion Books, 1999. ISBN 0-395-75186-1. 30 p. (6–9). Picture book.

Every Saturday Saruni earns five ten-cent coins for helping his mother take her produce to market. Though he could spend his coins on chapattis, rice cakes, or

toys in the market, he has his eye set on a new bicycle with which he could better help his mother. Saruni saves his ten-cent pieces until he has 305 of them. When his dream is punctured by the reality of the cost of a bicycle, his disappointment is turned to happiness as his father gives him his own grown-up bicycle. Mollel provides an author note explaining that the coins depicted were in use in northern Tanzania in the 1960s, the time of his childhood there, and gives a glossary of the Swahili and Maasai words used in the text. Lewis's illustrations vividly portray the clothing, homes, and market scenes of rural Tanzania. *Children's Africana Book Award; 2000 Coretta Scott King Honor. jvl and jig*
Author grew up in Tanzania, lives in Canada

Mollel, Tolowla. **Subira Subira**. Illustrated by Linda Saport. New York: Clarion, 2000. ISBN 0-395-91809-X. 32 p. (5–8). Picture book.

The author retells a traditional folktale, giving it a child protagonist and setting it in contemporary Tanzania. Tatu must care for her recalcitrant brother Maulidi. When she goes to an old spirit woman for help, she is told she must obtain three whiskers from a lion. She does, and is told that to change her brother, she should remember how she got the whiskers. Her patience and her singing are what is needed. The music and words of the Swahili song she sings are included. *Children's Africana Book Award 2001. jig*
Author grew up in Tanzania, lives in Canada

Stuve-Bodeen, Stephanie. **Babu's Song**. Illustrated by Aaron Boyd. New York: Lee & Low, 2003. ISBN 1-58430-058-2. 32 p. (5–8). Picture book.

Bernardi lives with his mute grandfather, Babu, and together they make enough money selling the toys Babu makes to live on. There is not enough money to pay for school, or for the new soccer ball Bernardi admires in the shop window. When he realizes he can sell a precious music box his grandfather made especially for him and buy the soccer ball, Bernardi makes a difficult decision. Watercolor illustrations portray the rural Tanzanian countryside. *2004 Children's Africana Book Award. djg*

Stuve-Bodeen, Stephanie. **Elizabeti's Doll**. Illustrated by Christy Hale. New York: Lee & Low Books Inc., 1998. ISBN 1-880000-70-9. 32 p. (4–7). Picture book.

When Elizabeti's mother has a new baby, Elizabeti finds a rock just the right size and names it Eva. She bathes, burps, and changes Eva's diaper, just like her mother does Obedi. She even carries it on her back wrapped in a kanga. It becomes obvious what a good mother Elizabeti is going to be. When Eva disappears, the whole family tries to substitute another rock, but the real Eva must be found. *jm*
Author has written several Elizabeti books inspired by her service in Tanzania, Africa, as a Peace Corp volunteer. Elizabeti's Doll won the Ezra Jack Keats award.

Stuve-Bodeen, Stephanie. **Elizabeti's School**. Illustrated by Christy Hale. New York: Lee & Low, 2002. ISBN 1-58430-043-4. 32 p. (4–7). Picture book.

Elizabeti is excited about her first day of school as she dresses in her new school uniform and puts on her new shoes. With help from her older sister and her friend Rahaili she overcomes her shyness and learns, among other things, to count to five. Yet she misses her home and family and decides that she will not go back. However, when her parents praise her for what she has learned, and when her mother plays *machaura* (like jacks with pebbles in a shallow hole), which she has learned at school, she changes her mind, though still thinks that home is the best place to be. Many facets of life in Tanzania are interwoven into both text and illustrations. *jig*
Author lives in United States

Stuve-Bodeen, Stephanie. **Mama Elizabeti**. Illustrated by Christy Hale. New York: Lee & Low, 2000. ISBN 1-58430-002-1. 32 p. (4–7). Picture book.

Elizabeti has taken care of her rock doll, but when her mother has a baby, she must take care of her toddler brother Obedi. This proves somewhat difficult. Obedi doesn't stay quietly on her back tied in the kanga as her doll had done. When she puts him down, he wanders off, but she solves the problem by tying one end of the kanga around his waist and the other around hers. The story is set in a Tanzanian village. *jig*
Author lives in United States

UGANDA

McBrier, Page. **Beatrice's Goat**. Illustrated by Lori Lohstoeter. New York: Anne Schwartz/Atheneum, 2001. ISBN 0-689-82460-2. 32 p. (4–8). Picture book.

If you were to visit the small village of Kisinga in the rolling hills of Uganda, you might meet Beatrice, a little girl who longs to attend school. Her hard working family does not have enough money, but this changes when her family receives the gift of a goat. It is her job to care for the goat and sell the milk. Soon she has saved enough money to pay for school and eventually the family is able to build a house with a shiny steel roof to keep out the rain. Bright acrylic paintings compliment the straightforward narrative. Based on a true story, the author and illustrator have created a book that explains the work of the Heifer Project—a charitable organization that donates livestock to communities around the world. A portion of the publishers proceeds will be donated to this charity.

ZAMBIA

Bryan, Ashley. **Beautiful Blackbird**. New York: Atheneum, 2003. ISBN 0-6898-4731-9. 40 p. (3–7). Picture book.

USBBY members attending the Regional Conference in Chautauqua in 2003 will have fond memories of the great Ashley Bryan reading this story of the Ila people. The colorful birds of Africa ask Blackbird, whom they think is the most beautiful of birds, to decorate them with some of his blackening brew, but he reminds them that real beauty comes from inside. Striking cut paper collages perfectly complement the simple text. *Coretta Scott King Award winner in Illustration in 2004; Best Children's Books of the Year, 2004; Notable Children's Books in the Language Arts, 2004; Notable Social Studies Trade Books for Young People, 2004.* djg

ZIMBABWE

Stock, Catherine. **Gugu's House**. New York: Clarion, 2001. ISBN 0-618-00389-4. 32 p. (5–9). Picture book.

Kukamba loves to visit Gugu (grandmother) who has the most beautifully decorated house and yard in the entire village. While the men and women are working in the field, Gugu and Kukamba paint the walls and the mud animals Gugu had fashioned. Kukamba is especially proud of a zebra she had painted. But the fields are dry and people are desperate for rain. Though Gugu gives people hope through her stories it is not until the rains, which turn Gugu's and Kukamba's beautiful paintings and animals into mud, that the villagers are relieved. Soft watercolors depict a Zimbabwean village and the arid country surrounding it. Stock provides details of north Zimbabwean life and the artist who inspired her, in an afterword. *jvl*
Author from United States

Related Information

Zimbabwe International Book Fair
http://www.zibf.org.zw/

AFRICA—REGIONAL

Bynum, Eboni, and Roland Jackson. **Jamari's Drum**. Pictures by Baba Wagué Diakité. Toronto: Groundwood, 2004. ISBN 0-88800-531-8. 32 p. (5–8). Picture book.
See Canada for description.

Diouf, Sylviane A. **Bintou's Braids**. Illustrated by Shane W. Evans. San Francisco: Chronicle Books, 2001. ISBN 0-8118-2514-0. 32 p. (5–8). Picture book.
Bintou has four little tufts of hair. She wants braids, like the older girls, more than anything else. At her baby brother's baptism, Bintou admires the many styles

of braids she sees. Feeling left out, Bintou seeks the solitude of the beach. When she sees two boys drowning, she runs to get help and the boys are saved. As a reward, Bintou gets something special that makes her proud of her black, shiny hair. A little girl who wants to grow up too fast is given a reward that makes her feel special. *ls*
Author from United States

Grifalconi, Ann. **The Village That Vanished**. Illustrated by Kadir Nelson. New York: Dial Books for Young Readers, 2002. ISBN 0-8037-2623-6. 32 p. (5–10). Picture book.

Slavers are roaming the African countryside. Life in a small village becomes unsettled. The villagers come together and decide to outwit the slavers. They dismantle their village and fields and hide in the forest until the danger has passed. The story is accompanied by Nelson's beautiful oil painting illustrations. Ned Alpers in a review appearing in the journal, *Sankofa* (Nov. 2004), states that "although the story is clearly set in the era of the slave trade in Africa, it assumes a timelessness that borders on the ahistorical because the author specifies neither a time nor a place where the village is located. . . . Despite these problems of omission with respect to the global context of the slave trade in Africa, *The Village That Vanished* remains an appealing book." *Starred reviews; White Ravens, 2003; Jane Addams Children's Book Award, 2003; Notable Books for a Global Society. djg*
Author from United States

Knight, Margy Burns, and Mark Melnicove. **Africa Is Not a Country**. Illustrated by Anne Sibley O'Brien. Brookfield, CT: Millbrook Press, 2000. ISBN 0-7613-1266-8. 39 p. (5–9). Informational book.

The author demonstrates the diversity of the African continent by describing daily life in some of its fifty-three nations. On each page realistic illustrations portray an aspect of cultural, recreational, or environmental aspects of children's lives. Cuisine, transportation, play, and school are shown in country and city. The lives of refugee children and the effects of war are shown. Every effort was made to make this book as accurate as possible. Some facts are in dispute, even by experts, although countries are not immediately identified and an alphabetic list of countries appears at the end of the book. *Children's Africana Book Award 2001. jm*

Kurtz, Jane, ed. **Memories of Sun: Stories of Africa and America**. Amistad: Greenwillow Books, 2004. ISBN 0-06-051050-1. 263 p. (10–14). Short stories.

Jane Kurtz has edited a collection of twelve stories and three poems. Kurtz says of this work: "This anthology offers glimpses into contemporary Africa . . . exploring questions about borders: what happens in those interesting places where cultures meet." Authors who live in South Africa, Tanzania, Sierra Leone,

Uganda, Ghana, as well as some American, third-culture authors struggle to find out just where they belong. In a lengthy critical review that was published by Africa Access for H-List Book Reviews (H-AfriTeach@h-net.msu.edu) titled "Racism, Pretense, Mock-Pluralism," Donnarae MacCann carefully evaluates each story and finds that many of them reflect stereotypes that present misleading portraits of African society. "Notwithstanding the few exceptional stories [and] the poems [that] are creatively expressive" she does not recommend the book. *djg*
Editor from United States

Lester, Julius. **Shining**. Illustrated by John Clapp. Orlando: Silver Whistle, 2003. ISBN 0-15-290773-3. 32 p. (10 up). Picture book.
   Long, long ago in a mountain village, a girl as black as wisdom and as quiet as the night was born. She was called Shining. Although her family loves and cares for her, her continued silence bothers and puzzles them. Then one day The One arrives and claims Shining as The One To Be. This powerful yet disquieting story has been likened to The Ugly Duckling. The illustrations give the story a dreamy quality depicting events that happened in the distant past. *Parents' Choice Award, Silver 2003; Skipping Stones Honor Awards, 2004; Society of School Librarians International Book Awards. ls*
Author from United States

Middleton, John, ed. **Africa: An Encyclopedia for Students**. New York: Charles Scribner's Sons of Gale Group, 2002. ISBN 0-684-80650-9. 4 vols.
   "Based on the scholarship in the acclaimed academic *Encyclopedia of Africa*, which is aimed at college and graduate students, this work presents Africa, from Egypt to Cape Town and from prehistoric times to the present day, in a format that is inviting to high school students. The 4-volume set spans many disciplines with its articles on animals, foods, holidays and festivals, tribal groups, ecology, music and art, trade and the economy, geography, religion, folklore, and fossil and skeletal discoveries." Booklist/ Reference Books Bulletin 20 Best Bets for Student Research, 2002.

Rumford, James. **Traveling Man, the Journey of Ibn Battuta 1325–1354**. Boston: Houghton Mifflin Company, 2001. ISBN 0-618-08366-9. 32 p. (10 up). Picture book.
   Ibn Battuta spent thirty years traveling the known world in the fourteenth century. He began his travels in Morocco, journeyed as far as Beijing, China, and returned to Morocco. Battuta's story is told as a meandering path with boxed text exploring the details of his journey. Maps, lush illustrations, and Arabic and Chinese calligraphy combine to make this book a joy to explore. *ls*
Author from United States

Stratton, Allan. **Chanda's Secrets**. Toronto: Annick Press, 2004. ISBN 1-55037-835-X. 193 p. (12 up). Novel.
   See Canada for description.

Tadjo, Véronique, ed. **Talking Drums: A Selection of Poems from Africa South of the Sahara**. New York: Bloomsbury, 2004. Originally published in Great Britain by A & C Black Publishers Ltd, 2000. ISBN 1-5823-4813-8. 96 p. (8–12). Poetry.
   This collection of 75 poems is divided into seven parts. The universe, animal kingdom, and people are described by some of Africa's very best poets. A section entitled "Love and Celebrations" describe this most important thing in life, without which there is no happiness. "Pride and Defiance" is dedicated to the Négritude movement: the struggle for independence from colonial rule. "Changing Times" describes the period of hardship, dictatorial governments, and military regimes that followed the euphoria of the Independence. Happiness and sorrow, life and death, anger and humor, disillusion and hope, the author includes all of these emotions. Tadjo correctly notes that "the themes [the poets] choose to write on are as diverse are they are universal." A glossary, a map of Africa, and an index of the poets by country, make this an enriching and valuable anthology.   *ls and lmp*
Author lives in Johannesburg

Williams, Sheron. **Imani's Music**. NY: Atheneum, 2002. ISBN 0-689-82254-5. 32 p. (5–10). Picture book.
   In the time of "Used-to-Be" when African slaves were captured and taken to the faraway land of "Here-and-Now," they brought the lilting music and stories of Imani, the grasshopper from the Serengeti. Booklist reviewer Hazel Rochman says: "the strong blend of fantasy and history is beautifully extended in Daly's bright narrative watercolors in folk-art style."   *djg*

Related Information

Awards

The Children's Africana Book Awards were established in 1991 by the Outreach Council of the African Studies Association to encourage the publication and use of accurate, balanced children's books on Africa. The awards focus specifically on books published in the United States about Africa.
http://www.africanstudies.org/asa_childbook.html

Noma Award
   Established in 1979 this award rewards African writers and scholars whose work is published in Africa. There are three categories for this award, one of which is children's literature.
http://www.nomaaward.org/

The Percy FitzPatrick Award was initiated in 1970 by the erstwhile South African Library Association (SALA) for the best South African children's book in English.

Organizations and Institutions

The Children's Literature Research Unit was established in 1996. It functions as a Unit of the Department of Information Science of the University of South Africa. The mission of the Unit is to promote children's literature and reading through study, research, community programs, and other promotional activities. Department of Information Science, University of South Africa
PO Box 392, 0003 Pretoria, South Africa   Fax: +27 12 4293221
http://www.childlit.org.za/
vdwaltb@alpha.unisa.ac.za

International Research Society for Children's Literature
http://www.childlit.org.za/irsclconf.html

Print and Online Resources

Africa Access
    Founded in 1989 to help schools, public libraries, and parents improve the quality of their children's collections on Africa, Africa Access has expanded to include research and reading projects. The online database, Africa Access Review, contains over 1000 authoritative reviews and annotations of books for children.
http://www.africaaccessreview.org/

Khorana, Meena. **Africa in Literature for Children and Young Adults: An Annotated Bibliography of English-Language Books**. Westport: Greenwood Press, 1994.

African Children's Literature.
    This website created by Lillian Temu Osaki and maintained on the University of Florida has links to several African children's authors and illustrators. Provides information about selected authors with extensive annotations.
http://web.uflib.ufl.edu/cm/africana/children.htm

Sankofa
    This annual journal first published in 2002 is written for professionals interested in children's literature. Edited by Meena G. Khorana, its objectives are to disseminate information on African children's and young adult literature; recognize common inaccuracies, stereotypes, and biases in books set in Africa; provide

in-depth book reviews and scholarly articles on emerging trends in African literatures; and stimulate a global conversation on the comparative patterns in the representation of children in literature.

The Children's Africana Book Awards section provides reviews of all the books submitted for the award each year, essays on the winners, and an analysis of publishing trends.

http://jewel.morgan.edu/~english/sankofa/index.html

Chapter 8

Australia and New Zealand

AUSTRALIA

Baker, Jeannie. **Home**. New York: Greenwillow, 2004. Published as *Belonging* by Walker, 2004. ISBN 0-06-623935-4. 30 p. (5–9). Picture book.

The view from the same window of a family's home in the double spread collage illustrations of this wordless book shows the changes in an urban neighborhood, from decaying to renewal, and the changes in the family, from the birth of a girl, Tracy, to the time when she becomes a mother. The illustrations, photographs of Baker's collage constructions using natural materials, are meticulously detailed. Reading the pictorial text reveals not only the story of Tracy's family and their neighborhood but also many mini-stories. In an afterword, Baker addresses the issue of caring for our neighborhoods, of "belonging to a living home." A companion book to *Baker's Window*. ALA Notable Book, 2005. *Horn Book Fan Fare, 2004.*   ca
Author from England, lives in Australia

Base, Graeme. **Jungle Drums**. New York: Henry N. Abrams, Inc., 2004. ISBN 0-8109-5044-8. 38 p. (5–8). Picture book.

Ngiri Mdogo is tired of being teased because he is the smallest warthog. The bigger warthogs are jealous of the other animals because they have beautiful spots, stripes, and plumage. A wildebeest gives Ngiri Mdogo magic bongo drums, which will grant wishes. The first two times Ngiri Mdogo plays the bongos with unfortunate results. The third time he plays the drums, all the animals are changed back as they were physically but they have changed in their behavior toward each other. Finding the animals hidden in the illustrations adds an element of fun.   *ls*
Author from Australia

Base, Graeme. **Truckdogs**. New York: Amulet Books, 2004. ISBN 0-8109-5031-6. 145 p. (10 up). Novel.

Creatures that are half animal and half vehicle will inhabit the futuristic desert. The young truckdogs are evicted from the town of Hubcap because they are too noisy and mischievous. Sparky, a young Jack Russell/Ute truckdog has befriended Rex, a Red Setter/Tractor and together they help save Hubcap when Mr. Big's Chihuahua/BMW Isetta group comes to tear up the town and steal all of the gasoline. This futuristic, action tale is accompanied by color plates of the various truckdogs—their specifications and other information. An added bonus is the truckbugs, which can be found in the color plates. *CBC Book of the Year for Younger Readers, 2004; KOALA winner, 2004.* ls
Author from Australia

Base, Graeme. **The Water Hole**. New York: Harry Abrams. 2004. Originally published in Australia by Penguin Puffin, 2001. ISBN 0-8109-4568-1, Paperback. 32 p. (4 up). Picture book.

This is a two-way counting book, an environmental book, a book about the world's animals, and a puzzle book for older children. Animals in increasing numbers, from one to ten arrive at the waterhole, e.g., three toucans, four snow leopard, five pandas, etc., but with each new set of arrivals the hole gets smaller, and the amusing frogs surrounding the pond diminish in numbers from ten to none and each group of animals becomes more and more concerned. Just when all the water disappears, the drought ends and life-giving rain replenishes the waterhole. While each page focuses on only one type of animal that is featured in detailed watercolor and pencil illustration, the borders show, in silhouette and with labels, other animals from around the world, which are also hidden throughout the pictures for discerning eyes to discover. *ABC Children's Booksellers' Choices Award, 2002; Young Australians' Best Book Award (YABBA) 2003; Kids' Own Australia Award, 2003, 2004; Young Australian Readers' Award, 2001.* jvl and ls
Author from Australia

Bateson, Catherine. **Rain May and Captain Daniel**. Australia: University of Queensland Press, 2002. ISBN 0-7022-3337-4. 138 p. (9–12). Novel.

Rain May and her mom, Maggie, escape to the country to live in their dream house after Rain May's parents separate. Reluctant at first, Rain May soon appreciates all that living in the country has to offer—possums in the attic, platypus hunting, and her next door neighbor Captain Daniel. Communicating about the serious issues in their lives through fridge poetry Rain May and Maggie adjust to Dad's new girlfriend Julia, making new friends and helping with Daniel's illness. This is a light-hearted look at life in the Australian country and what it means to be a real friend. *Winner CBC Book of the Year: Younger Readers, 2003 shortlisted; NSW Premiers Prize 2003.* kmc
Author lives in Melbourne, Australia

Brian, Janeen. **Where Does Thursday Go?** Pictures by Stephen Michael King. New York: Clarion, 2001. First published in Australia in 2001 by Margaret Hamilton Books. ISBN 0-618-21264-7. 32 p. (4–8). Picture book.
Thursday was Bruno the Bear's birthday and he doesn't want it to end. Bruno and his friend Bert set out on a night time adventure to find out where Thursday goes before it becomes Friday. Watercolor pictures illustrate this gentle journey.
2002 Honour Book of the Year for Early Childhood. djg
Author and illustrator live in Australia

Broome, Errol. **Drusilla the Lucky Duck**. Illustrated by Sharon Thompson. New York: Annick Press, 2003. Originally published as *Tough Luck* by Freemantle Arts Centre Press in 1998. ISBN 1-55037-799-X. 72 p. (8 up). Novel.
Carrie brings home a baby duck as her new pet. She names the duck Drusilla and teaches the duck to follow her. Carrie becomes very attached to her pet, whereas her brother, Mungo, is not. When it is time to plan the family vacation, Carrie needs to find someone to care for Drusilla. Derek, who works at the family's garden center, volunteers to look after the duck. The family vacation in the mountains is quite enjoyable. When Carrie and her parents arrive at Derek's home to take Drusilla home they find that she is not there. It seems that because of the noise and the mess that Drusilla makes, she has been handed over to several families until she ends up in the hands of a man who wants to fatten her up. Carrie rescues Drusilla from becoming Duck L'Orange. When Carrie arrives home, she finds that Mungo and his friend have made a pond for Drusilla. A light read about caring for and loving an uncommon pet. *ls*
Author from Australia

Broome, Errol. **The Judas Donkey**. Illustrated by Sharon Thompson. Freemantle, Western Australia: Freemantle Arts Centre Press, 2003. ISBN 1-92073-118-0. 108 p. (8–12). Novel.
Francesca, who lives in a very small town not far from Perth, has always wanted a horse, but Gramps brings home a Judas donkey, a marked donkey who unwittingly leads helicopter hunters to tribes of wild donkeys who are then destroyed for the damage they do to the land. Francesca and her aboriginal friend, Tula, learn to appreciate Judy's good qualities and fear for the donkey's future at the same time as Francesca must deal with her beloved grandmother's senility and her grandparents' impending move. Judy earns a new home when she patiently rescues a horse that is entangled in barbed wire. A graphic picture of the life in a small town on the edge of the outback, its flora, fauna, and lifestyle, emerges in this very appealing story of family relationships and dealing with change. *sg*
Author lives in Australia

Broome, Errol. **Missing Mem**. Illustrated by Ann James. New York: Aladdin Paperbacks, 2003. Originally published by Allen & Unwin in 2000. ISBN 0-7434-3797-7. 135 p. (10–12). Novel.

A colony of mice lives in a stable's hayloft in this sequel to *Magnus Maybe*. They are discovered by the farmer when the moldy hay must be removed. Magnus, a young mouse, is made the leader of the colony. When a kitten is brought to the stable to be a mouser, Magnus tries to befriend it but it is his daughter, Mem, who removes a thorn from the kitten's paw, who truly befriends the kitten. One day the circus comes to town. Some of the mice go to see the excitement. Mem explores the circus on her own and finds herself in the elephant's ear and performing under the Big Top. In the end, Magnus finds Mem and with the other mice convinces her that the stable is home.   *ls*
Author from Australia

Brugman, Alyssa. **Finding Grace**. New York: Delacorte, 2001. ISBN 0-385-73116-7. 229 p. (12 up). First published in Australia by Allen and Unwin, 2001. Novel.

As she begins college, Rachel takes a part-time live-in job caring for Grace, a brain-damaged adult who lives close to campus. She blunders a bit before getting the knack of the job (with sometime humorous results), but when she discovers a box of some notes written by Grace, she begins to piece together the life Grace lived before her accident. In the end, she not only has gained insight into her patient, but into herself as well. The use of Australian slang and colloquialisms may confuse young readers but Rachel's difficulties and reactions are universal. *Children's Book of the Year shortlist, Australia.   mln*

Brugman, Alyssa. **Walking Naked**. New York: Delacorte Press, 2004. First published in Australia by Allen & Unwin in 2002. ISBN 0-385-73115-9. 186 p. (14 up). Novel.

Megan Tuw is the leader of the school's most cliquish group and ridicules all who don't fit in. Perdita Wiguiggan becomes the main focus for their bullying derision. But when Megan begins to get to know Perdita, she must make a choice. In an author's note Brugman tells the reader that "this is a novel about school politics and personal responsibility." This gritty portrayal of cruelty ends in Perdita's suicide. *Children's Book Council of Australia as a 2003 Honor Book for older readers.   djg*
Author from Australia

Clarke, Judith. **Starry Nights**. Asheville, NC: Front Street, 2003. First published in Australia in 2001. ISBN 1-886910-82-0. 148 p. (12 up). Novel.

Like Clarke's earlier books, *Nighttrain*, 2000, and *The Heroic Life of Al Capsella*, 1997, this book deals with the themes of teens coping with crisis in family situations. Jess's family has just moved into a house in the suburbs, but her sisters increasingly wild behavior seems out of proportion to their problems of coping with the grief of their brother's drowning death and mother's subsequent breakdown. Jess becomes convinced that someone is watching and begins to catch glimpses of a specter in this haunting ghost story. *CBC Choices, 2004.   djg*
Author from Australia

Clarke, Judith. **Wolf on the Fold**. Asheville, NC: Front Street, 2002. First published by Silverfish/Duffy & Snellgrove in 2000. ISBN 1-886910-79-0. 169 p. (10 up). Novel.

This collection of six stories spans three generations and features a defining moment in each of the characters adolescent lives. Beginning with Kenny, fourteen at the time of his father's death during the depression, we read about each character facing a crisis. Kenny's bravery is evident in different ways in the lives of his daughters. Kenny's relationship with the neighbors, immigrants from war-stricken Uganda gives insight into the horror of conflicts in Uganda during the 1970s. The younger daughter emigrates to Israel and that story gives a glimpse of the conflict in the 1990s. The final story is about Kenny's great grandson who is inspired by stories of his courage to cope with his parent's disintegrating marriage. *2001 CBC Best Book of the Year.   djg*
Author from Australia

Cohen, Bernard. **Paul Needs Specs**. Illustrated by Geoff Kelly. La Jolla, CA: Kane/Miller, 2004. First published by Penguin Books Australia, 2002. ISBN 1-929132-61-1. 32 p. (4–8). Picture book.

Slowly, slowly, over a very long time, about a year or even more, Paul began to notice something strange. Everything has gotten fuzzy and blurry. Fortunately, he has Sal, his big sister, who realizes Paul needs glasses and takes him to the eye doctor. Bold, colorful illustrations add humor to this adventure and the discerning reader will want to follow the instructions on the end paper eye chart to find twenty frogs in this book.   *djg*
Author has written several adult novels and lives in Australia. Illustrator lives in Australia and is a commercial artist who is just turning his talents to illustrating children's books.

Cohn, Rachel. **The Steps**. New York: Simon & Schuster, 2003. ISBN 0-689-84549-9. 137 p. (8–12). Novel.

Annabel is spending her Christmas vacation in Australia with her dad and her new step family. She's hoping to win him back to New York and is prepared to dislike this family, with their "weird accent, food that doesn't taste right and television programs that looked all wrong." But she is eventually won over by the warmth of this funny and caring family. Annabel finds that she has a lot in common with her new step sister Lucy and realizes how much happier her father is with this new family in Australia. *Teens Top Ten List, 2003.   djg*
Author lives in United States

Collins, Paul. **The Earthborn**. New York: Tor, 2003 (paperback ISBN 0-7653-4199-9). ISBN 0-765-30307-8. 240 p. (12 up). Novel.

Approximately fifty years after the global war, skyworld *Colony* returns from its journey to the stars and lands in Melbourne, Australia. Unsure of Earth's at-

mosphere, the Elders of *Colony* release a few of their genetically engineered members to test earth's sustainability of life. As 14-year-old Ensign Welkin Quinn makes his way through the desolate and dangerous landscape, surviving grueling ordeals, he begins questioning the Skyborn's theory of superiority. It is after being rescued by Sarah and her family unit that Welkin undergoes a change as he joins the family in its struggle for survival. Unrelenting action and suspense propel the plot through an apocryphal landscape. At the end, the family unit feels a glimmer of hope with the affirmation that family represents unity as opposed to anarchy. *ok*
Author from England, lives in Australia

Crew, Gary. **Mama's Babies**. Toronto, New York: Annick Press, 2002. Originally published by Lothian Books in 1998. ISBN 1-55037-724-8. 160 p. (9–13). Novel.
  Sarah Pratchett at nine years old gradually comes to realize that her household is not a normal one and her mother is not her mother. Through her eyes we come to understand the practice of "baby farming" prevalent in the 19th century when poverty and shame forced unwed mothers to farm out their babies to questionable adoptive mothers. Sarah's "mother" is a composite of such women, some of whom were kind, others merely greedy, and others, as in this case, murderous. Despite the extreme poverty, lack of love, and unfolding horrors she endures, Sarah presents a hopeful face to the world and prevails. *Children's Book Council of Australia Notable Books for 1999.* *cd*
Author from Australia

Crew, Gary. **The Viewer**. Illustrated by Shaun Tan. Vancouver: Simply Read Books, 2003. Originally published by Thomas C. Lothian Pty., Ltd. in 1997. ISBN 1-894965-02-7. 31 p. (12 up). Picture book.
  An eerie, dark tale about a boy named Tristan. From infancy, Tristan loves to observe things for long periods of time. His favorite place is the junkyard where he finds things that fascinate him. One day, Tristan finds an odd-looking wooden box. Tristan takes it home, unlocks it, and finds that it contains an object reminiscent of his old Viewmaster and three disks. The Viewer allows Tristan to see and hear strange and wondrous sights from the history of the world. The Viewer seems to cast a spell on Tristan. He finds himself drawn to the Viewer until it absorbs him. When Tristan's mother goes to his room, she finds that it is empty and that a locked wooden box is sitting on Tristan's desk. This unusual story with intricate illustrations is extremely thought provoking and would lead to interesting discussions. *Publisher's Weekly Starred Review.* *ls*
Author from Australia

Disher, Garry. **The Divine Wind: A Love Story**. New York: Arthur A. Levine Books, 1998. ISBN 0-439-36915-0. 153 p. (14 up). Novel.

In 1946, Hart Penrose is recounting the events, which took place in Broome, Australia, in the early days of World War II. Hart's sister, Alice, has a best friend, Mitzy Sennosuke, with whom Hart is in love. Hart tells of a harrowing trip on his father's pearl lugger where Hart survives but is crippled and Mitzy's father drowns. The threat of a Japanese invasion seems imminent. Hart's father digs an air raid shelter. Alice leaves to become an Army nurse. When the Japanese population is interned, Mitzy and her mother, Sadako, are taken in by the Penrose's until they are also interned. In 1946, life is slowly returning to normal. Hart is managing his father's chandlery and waiting for Mitzy to return to Broome. *Winner of the 1999 New South Wales Premier's Literary Award.   ls*
Author from Australia

Earls, Nick. **48 Shades of Brown**. Boston: Graphia/Houghton Mifflin, 2004 (Paperback). Originally published by Penguin Books, Australia, in 1999. ISBN 0-618-45295-8. 274 p. (14 up). Novel.

When Dan's parents go to Geneva for a year, he stays in Australia and moves into a house with his twenty-two-year-old, bass-playing aunt Jacq and her friend, Naomi. It's his last year at school and he's struggling with calculus. When he falls for Naomi, however, math becomes the least of his problems; beer, sex, laundry, and attitude don't come with textbook instructions. This is a very funny book about coming of age. Dan's anxiety and inner dialogue reflect a commonality among all teens, whether Australian or American, and the book's wit, while very Australian in voice, is strikingly similar to that in current American mass media. *Australia's Children's Book Council 2000 Book of the Year for Older Readers.   mk*

Fienberg, Anna, and Barbara Fienberg. **The Big, Big, Big Book of Tashi**. Illustrated by Kim Gamble. Crows Nest: Allen and Unwin, 2001. ISBN 1-86508-563-4. various pagings. (8–10). Picture book.

Tashi is Jack's new friend. Bold, clever Tashi tells Jack about his daring adventures where he defeats giants, extinguishes dragons, tricks ghosts, and outsmarts evil Barons. These short, fun, fast-paced, exciting adventures only leave the reader wanting more. This collection includes six Tashi adventures: *Tashi, Tashi and the Giants, Tashi and the Ghosts, Tashi and the Genie, Tashi and the Big Stinker*. These titles, as well as *Tashi and the Dancing Shoes*, are also available as individual books. *Starred reviews.   ls*
Authors from Australia

Fienberg, Anna. **Horrendo's Curse**. Illustrated by Kim Gamble. Toronto: Annick Press, 2002. ISBN 1-55037-773-6. 158 p. (10 up). Novel.

Horrendo was born cursed. Gretel, a local witch, cursed anyone born on Horrendo's birthday so that they could never say a rude word. This causes great difficulty for Horrendo but it proves to be a great strength later on. The inhabitants of the village lived in fear of the pirates. The pirates sail to the village and capture all the twelve-year-old boys. The boys are put to work on the pirate ship and must endure hardship and cruelty. Amid the hardship, there is humor and cunning when the boys realize the power they wield together. Line drawings add humor to this swashbuckling tale. *Nominated for the 2004 Young Australian Best Book Award; 2003 Children's Book Council of Australia Honour Book.* nrn and ls *Author from Canada, lives in Sydney, Australia*

Fienberg, Anna. **Joseph**. Illustrated by Kim Gamble. Crows Nest: Allen & Unwin, 2001. ISBN 1-86448-17-3. 32 p. (8 up). Bible story.

Joseph is the youngest brother of twelve and his father's favorite. The eleven older brothers are jealous of Joseph's dreams, his winning ways, and his many-colored coat. They sell their brother to a caravan bound for Egypt. In Egypt, Joseph interprets the Pharaoh's dreams and is placed in charge of storing the grain for the coming famine. During the famine, Joseph's brothers come to Egypt for grain. Joseph recognizes them and eventually has his brothers and father come to live in Egypt. A fine retelling of the Old Testament story of Joseph accompanied by beautiful, muted oil illustrations. *Children's Book of the Year Shortlist, Australia.* ls
Author from Australia

Fox, Mem. **The Magic Hat**. Tricia Tusa, illustrator. San Diego: Harcourt, 2002. ISBN 0-15-201025-4. 32 p. (4–7). Picture book.

A wizard's magic hat blows into town turning the adults whose head it lands on into a variety of animals. This continues to the great amusement of the children until the wizard arrives, catches his hat, and returns everyone to their usual selves. The ink and watercolor illustrations effectively reflect the whimsy and humor of the story. This is a very pleasant and enjoyable trip for the imagination. *js*
This award-winning author lives in Adelaide, South Australia, and is the author of Reading Magic *(Harcourt, 2001)*

Fox, Mem. **Where Is the Green Sheep?** Judy Horacek, illustrator. Orlando: Harcourt, 2004. ISBN 0-15-204907-X. 32 p. (2–5). Picture book.

Presented with a rollicking text and clean, uncluttered illustrations, this delightful story is sure to appeal to preschoolers and beginning readers. During the quest to find the missing green sheep, readers come in contact with a variety of other concept-driven sheep. There are up and down sheep, sun and rain sheep, and near and far sheep to name a few. Every few pages the reader is reminded of their quest with the refrain, "but where is the green sheep?" The quest is successfully completed at book's end when green sheep is found sleeping and obviously unaware that he was missing. *js*
Author and Illustrator live in Australia

Fox, Mem. **Whoever You Are**. Illustrated by Leslie Staub. San Diego: Voyager Books/Harcourt, Inc. 1997. ISBN 0-15-200787-3, Hardcover; ISBN 0-150216406-5, Paperback. 30 p. (3–6). Picture book.

This celebration of the interconnectedness of all people begins with "Little one, whoever you are / wherever you are / there are little ones just like you all over the world." Each page shows a child or children of different ethnicity, wearing clothes representative of their culture, but with unifying, somewhat abstracts backgrounds of blue skies and green fields. The focus of the book is more on similarities of feelings than differences in experiences. *Included in best books lists: Adventuring With Books, NCTE, 1999; Books About Relationships, Children's Book Council.   jvl*
Author from Australia. She has won numerous awards for her work, including the Advance Australia Award for an Outstanding Contribution to Australian Literature, 1991.

French, Jackie. **Diary of a Wombat**. Illustrated by Bruce Whatley. New York: Clarion Books, 2003. First published in Australia by Angus & Robertson in 2002. ISBN 0-618-38136-8. 32 p. (4–7). Picture book.

The languid, if adorable, wombat who tells us he looks "a little like a bear, but smaller," presents his tongue-in-cheek diary of sleeping, digging, eating, and training his new human neighbors to provide him with carrots. The determined animal, who is energetic when it comes to his carrots, details all his ploys to get closer to his new human "pets." Children will enjoy the expressive, sequential pictures of the creature that show what is really happening as opposed to the wombat's interpretation. *ALA Notable Book, 2004.   sg*
Author and illustrator live in Australia

French, Jackie. **Hitler's Daughter**. New York: HarperCollins, 2003. Originally published by Angus & Robertson in 1999. ISBN 0-06-008652-1. 121 p. (9–12). Novel.

Anna, a contemporary Australian schoolgirl who entertains her friends with stories while they wait for the school bus, tells a detailed story about Heidi, Hitler's daughter, who he keeps hidden away under the care of a governess because she is lame and has a large birthmark on her face. Ten-year-old Mark becomes so engrossed in the story that he begins to wonder what it would be like to have been Hitler's child. At the same time, he starts questioning his own family's prejudices. This thought-provoking work of fiction can lead to some lively discussions. *Australian Children's Book of the Year for Younger Readers Award, 2000.   ca*
Author from Australia

French, Jackie, and Whatley, Bruce. **Too Many Pears!** New York: Star Bright Books, 2003. ISBN 1-932065-47-4. 32 p. (4–8). Picture book.

Pamela the cow loves pears and will overcome any obstacles to get them. Amy decides to give Pamela all the pears she can eat. After 600 pears, Pamela has

stopped smiling. Pamela is not interested in pears anymore but apples are looking very appealing. A clever story about too much of a good thing is just too much. *Bank Street Best Book of the Year, 2004.* ls
Author from Australia

French, Simon. **Guess the Baby**. Illustrated by Donna Rawlins. New York: Clarion Books, 2002. Originally published by ABC Books in 2002. ISBN 0-618-25989-9. 32 p. (5–8). Picture book.

When Sam brings his baby brother, Jake, to school for Show and Tell, the whole class has a lesson in learning how to take care of a baby. Mr. Judd, their teacher, tells them that everyone was once a baby. To have some fun, Mr. Judd asks the class to bring in their baby picture. The baby pictures are posted in the classroom and the students try to match their classmates to their baby pictures. The last picture is a real puzzle. It turns out to be Mr. Judd's baby picture. Thinking of their teacher as a baby amuses the students. Mr. Judd says that babies grow to be adults. Then, he asks the class how many of them are happy just being kids. The entire class raises their hands. *CBC Choices, 2002.* ls
Author from Australia

French, Simon. **Where in the World**. Atlanta: Peachtree, 2003. ISBN 1-56145-292-0. 174 p. (12–14). Novel.

Eleven-year-old Ari, a gifted musician who lives in Australia with his mother and step-father, struggles to adjust to his new home and the fear that his friends will think he is "weird" because he plays the violin. The holidays he took with his mother and his vague memories of his father, who died when Ari was three, are revealed through a sequence of flashbacks. Interspersed throughout the book are the e-mails Ari has written to his grandfather, a retired concert violinist who still lives in Germany and continues to nourish Ari's talent. When Ari surprises his mother by playing her favorite song on stage for her birthday, he realizes that through his music he has finally discovered "where in the world" he belongs. *2003 Patricia Wrightson Award; nominated for the Children's Book Council of Australia's Book of the Year Award and the Guardian Children's Fiction Prize 2003.* kk
Author from Australia

Gleeson, Libby. **Cuddle Time**. Illustrated by Julie Vivas. Cambridge, MA: Candlewick, 2004. Published in Australia by Walker Books, 2004. ISBN 0-7636-2320-2. 28 p. (3–6). Picture book.

The sun slips into their quiet room and big sister wakes up brother and they jump and roll and crawl down the hall to the monster's cave. Bravely, they creep past the heap on the chair to the lair and tumble and tickle until, all mingled and mangled, the monsters rise up and its "Cuddle Time!" Charming watercolor illustrations add bounce and giggle to a warm family story. *djg*
Author and illustrator from Australia

Gleitzman, Morris. **Toad Rage**. New York and Canada: Random House Children's Books, 2004. (Paperback, Puffin, 2000). Originally published in Australia by Penguin in 1999. ISBN 0-375-82762-5. 165 p. (8–11). Novel.

Australia's cane toads have wart-covered skin and poison-filled glands. The mud worms they eat alive crawl out from their nether ends still wiggling. Yet Limpy can't understand why humans find his species revolting and go out of their way to flatten them on Australia's highways and byways. He sets out to change his species' image with humans. Inter-species communication proves problematic, but despite failure after failure, this intrepid toad keeps trying new ideas. Many adventures and heroics later, his mission takes him to the Olympic Games where he discovers an unexpected solution. Informative and funny, this story should bolster the stick-to-it-iveness in all of us. *Winner, Dymock's Children's Choice Awards, Older Readers, 2000; Winner, Young Australian Best Book Award, Older Readers, 2000; Shortlisted, Queensland Premier's Literary Award, 2000.* cd *Author from England and Australia*

Graham, Bob. **Jethro Byrd, Fairy Child**. Cambridge, MA: Candlewick Press, 2002. ISBN 0-7636-0359-7. 32 p. (4–7). Picture book.

In this gentle story, Annabelle, a city child, persists in her search for fairies despite her father's discouragement. One day she does meet a tiny fairy child and his family, whose ice cream truck has fallen from the sky. To Annabelle's delight, the family agrees to stay for refreshments that her parents kindly agree to serve although they cannot see the fairies. A message about the things children take the time to notice that adults do not is subtly woven into the story. Graham's watercolor and ink artwork on oversize pages makes wonderful use of the difference in scale between the humans, even little Annabelle, and the truly tiny fairy family. This is a satisfying story to read and think about. *Kate Greenaway Medal, CBC Choices.* sg *Author lives in Australia*

Graham, Bob. **"Let's Get a Pup!" Said Kate**. Cambridge, MA: Candlewick Press, 2001. Concurrently published as *"Let's Get a Pup!"* by Walker (UK) in 2001. (Paperback: Candlewick, 2003; Walker, 2003). ISBN 0-7636-1452-1. unpaged. (4–8). Picture book.

Kate awoke to the summer sun streaming into her lonely bedroom. Running down the hall she exclaimed, "Let's get a pup!" Tiger the cat had died last winter and now, months later, Kate was ready for another pet. Even before breakfast, she and her parents set off for the animal rescue center where they examined "big dogs, small dogs, sniffers and sleepers, wire-haireds, short-haireds, scratchers, and leapers . . ." Humorous and animated, this jaunty text relives an experience that's all-too-familiar to families that have adopted pets. Graham's cheery watercolor cartoon illustrations offer a warm and cozy glimpse into a loving—although off-beat—family. *2002 Children's Book Council of Australia*

(CBCA) Early Childhood Book of the Year and 2002 Boston Globe—Horn Book Award for Picture Book. lmp
Author lives in Australia

Graham, Bob. **Max**. Cambridge: Candlewick Press, 2000. ISBN 0-7636-1138-7. 32 p. (4–8). Picture book.

Max's parents are superheroes and they have high expectations. When Max's superhero powers fail to materialize, his family tries to be understanding, but the children at school think Max dresses strangely. Max finds out it's hard being different. One morning, Max sees a baby bird fall out of its nest. He zips down the stairs, rushes outside, and flies up to catch the bird and returns it to its nest. Max is a superhero with gentle powers for doing quiet deeds. *ls*
Author from England, lives in Australia

Graham, Bob. **Queenie, One of the Family**. Cambridge, MA: Candlewick Press, 1997. ISBN 0-7636-0359-7. 32 p. (3–7). Picture book.

The father of a family out for a walk sees a hen struggling in the water and dives in to rescue her. The family names her Queenie, nurtures her back to health, and accepts her as part of the family. Mom realizes she must belong on a nearby farm and they return her only to find that the bantam returns each day to lay an egg in the dog's basket. Eventually, Mom has a baby and the family forgets to collects the eggs, which the dog sits on and hatches. All the chicks are returned to the farm except one that does become part of the family. An involving plot with watercolor and ink illustrations, both large and small and all full of humorous expressive details, add up to genial story about a caring family any hen (or child) would be happy to belong to. *Bank Street Best Book of the Year.* sg
Author lives in Australia

Heiman, Sarah. **Australia ABCs: A Book About the People and Places of Australia**. Illustrated by Arturo Avila. Minneapolis: Picture Window Books, 2003. ISBN 1-4048-0018-2. 32 p. (7–10). Informational book.

Presented in an alphabet book format, this title provides brief facts about Australia. Almost every letter of the alphabet has a one-page spread that includes a paragraph of text, a digitally prepared illustration, and pronunciation assistance. Some of the information is obscure and would not be found in a typical country book, such as how a lyrebird can copy the sounds of ringing telephones and honking horns. Although the format is attractive and accessible, photographs would have been preferable to the simple and blurred style of the digital illustrations. Extensive endpapers include a rock painting activity, "Fast and Fun Facts," a glossary, further reading, Internet resources, and an index. *aao*

Herrick, Steven. **Love, Ghosts, and Facial Hair**. New York: Simon Pulse, 2004. Originally published in Australia in 1996 by University of Queensland Press. ISBN 0-689-86710-7 (pbk). 115 p. (14 up). Novel.

Herrick, Steven. **A Place Like This**. New York: Simon Pulse, 2004. Originally published in 1998 by University of Queensland Press. ISBN 0-689-86711-5. 140 p. (12 up). Novel.

Herrick, Steven. **The Simple Gift**. New York: Simon Pulse, 2004. Originally published in 2000 by University of Queensland Press. ISBN 0-689-86867-7 (pbk). 188 p. (12 up). Novel.

Packaged as companions, these three free-verse books tell of Jack's coming of age in western Australia from three perspectives. Jack, an aspiring writer tells of his long-dead mother, alcoholic father and sister dying of cancer, first love, and running away. These are dramatic and compelling stories for older readers.   *djg*

Hirsch, Odo. **Bartlett and the City of Flames**. Illustrated by Andrew McLean. New York: Bloomsbury USA Children's Books, 2003. Originally published by Bloomsbury in 1999. ISBN 1-58234-831-6. 201 p. (10 up). Novel.

See Europe/UK for description.

Hirsch, Odo. **Hazel Green**. New York: Bloomsbury, 2003. (Paperback: Bloomsbury, 2005). ISBN 1-58234-820-0. 190 p. (8–12). Novel.

Hazel Green is keen to right an injustice: children are banned from participating in the annual Frogg Day parade. Hazel convinces parade planners to change the rules and, not without a few setbacks, organizes the entry of a float by the kids from the Moodey Building apartments. Hirsch introduces readers to a spunky, observant, and enterprising young heroine and to an interesting city neighborhood in this fresh, funny, and highly entertaining middle grade novel. Hazel's adventures continue in *Have Courage, Hazel Green* (Allen & Unwin, 2004), and *Something's Fishy, Hazel Green* (Bloomsbury, 2005). *Shortlisted for the 2000 Children's Book Council of Australia Book of the Year Awards and for the 2000 Australian Publishers' Association Design Award.*   *ca*
Author from Australia, lives in England

Hirsh, Odo. **Yoss**. New York: Delacorte, 2004. First published in Australia by Allen and Unwin, 2001. ISBN 0-385-73187-6. 252 p. (12 up). Novel.

Fourteen-year-old Yoss leaves his remote village, hoping to see the outside world and all its wonders. The town he comes to is inhabited by greedy, heartless, conniving citizens who involve the unsuspecting youth in their evil and ruthless escapades. When Yoss is finally able to escape and return home, those he leaves behind are changed forever. Though set in a medieval town, the contrast of good and evil seems to be a commentary on today's values. *YA books shortlist for Children's Book Council of Australia.*   *mln*

Hobbs, Leigh. **Old Tom's Holiday**. Atlanta: Peachtree, 2004. First published in Australia by ABC Books, 2002. ISBN 1-56145-316-1. (unpaged). (6–9). Picture book.

In this latest "Old Tom" book, that outrageously feisty cat secretly follows his mistress on her fabulous vacation trip (he's a stowaway in her suitcase). She begins to miss him right away, though the reader has the fun of spotting him on each page. When she finally admits to it aloud, that rascally Tom slips right into her lap. The matter of fact prose is a perfect foil for the bold gouache, acrylic and ink full-color illustrations. *mln*

Honey, Elizabeth. **Don't Pat the Wombat**. Illustrated by William Clarke. New York: Alfred A. Knopf, 2000. Originally published in Australia by Allen & Unwin, 1996. ISBN 0-375-80578-8. 144 p. (8–12). Novel.

Life at school is zany enough, but now, Jonah, Wormz, Nicko, Mitch, and Azza are off to summer camp. It's a pioneer camp, wildlife refuge complete with a wallaby and two wombats. Quirky and full of slang, this illustrated novel includes lots of hand-drawings and photographs to document the fun. *1997 Children's Book Council Honour Book, Children's Catalog. djg*
Author lives in Melbourne, Australia

Honey, Elizabeth. **Remote Man**. New York: Alfred A. Knopf, 2002. ISBN 0-375-81413-2. 260 p. (11–14). Novel.

Ned finds his screen name "Remote Man" fitting because of his ability to affect things from afar with his Internet skills, and also because of his estrangement from other kids his age in Melbourne, Australia. When his mother hits a new low in her battle against depression, Ned is sent off to northern Australia to visit his quirky cousin, Kate. When a rare python turns up missing near Kate's home, Ned and Kate, joined via email and online chat by Cleverton in Jamaica and Yvette in France, begin their search for the dangerous wildlife smuggler who is responsible. The chase ends in Concord, Massachusetts, where Ned sheds his erroneous self-perceptions by befriending his new neighbor, Rocky, and collaborating with an international friendship ring to save wildlife from the threat of poachers. The author's collection of poetry, *Honey Sandwich,* included more than fifty poems about everyday life and was shortlisted by the Children's Book Council of Australia as a best book. *aao*
Author lives in Australia

Jeans, Peter. **Bodger**. Crawley, Western Australia: University of Western Australia Press, 2002. ISBN 1-876268-65-4. 279 p. (9 up). Novel.

Angus McCrea desires only two things in this world—a bike and a dog. When a friendly farmer gives Angus one of his best pups as a birthday gift, the youngster knows he has found a forever friend. Bodger joins Angus and his mates on merry adventures in the Australian bush. As both dog and boy mature into adulthood, they are called upon to defend the small town from unexpected danger. Written from the perspective of an Australian boy during the early 1940s. Rhythmic language with authentic idioms from that time and place mark this reflective work filled with humor and adventure. *nrn*
Author from Australia

Jennings, Paul. **Listen Ear: And Other Stories to Shock You Silly**! New York: Puffin Books, 1998. Originally published as *Uncovered!* by Penguin Books, Australia, 1995. ISBN 0-14-038961-X. 12 p. (9–12). Short stories.

This is a collection of eight amusing, sometimes grotesque, sometimes weird short stories that are sure to make readers scared while they laugh out loud. From time travel to tricks with pretend cat poo, these stories will delight many reluctant readers, especially the boys. *Kids Own Australian Literature Award (KOALA) Winner 1996; Young Australian Best Book Award (YABBA) shortlist 1997.   kmc Author lives in Australia*

Jorgensen, Norman. **In Flanders Fields**. Illustrated by Brian Harrison-Lever. Vancouver: Simply Read Books, 2003. ISBN 1-8949965-01-9. 32 p. (9 up). Picture book.

It is early morning on Christmas day in the trenches of World War I. The firing has stopped in observance of the holiday. Soldiers warm themselves by the fire and read their mail and open their parcels. Many packages must be returned, as their recipients are no longer with them. One soldier keeps watch over "no man's land," a desolate landscape strewn with barbed wire and fallen soldiers. The young man spots a red-chested robin trapped on the barbed wire. Wrapping his white Christmas scarf around his rifle as a flag of truce, the soldier risks attracting enemy fire, in order to rescue the tiny bird. Enemy troops lower their guns and watch as the soldier frees the tiny bird. Harrison-Lever's pencil and watercolor illustrations are in perfect harmony with the beautifully written text. Inspired by the poem "In Flanders Fields" by John McCrae, this picture book is a touching and universal story of human compassion.   *aao Author lives in Australia. Illustrator from England, lives in Australia.*

King, Stephen Michael. **Milli, Jack, and the Dancing Cat**. New York: Penguin (Philomel), 2004. Originally published in Australia by Allen & Unwin in 2003. ISBN 0-399-24240-6. 29 p. (4 up). Picture book.

Shoemaker Milli loves to "take a thing that was nothing . . . and make it . . . a something!" but is too shy to share her creations. Her days are filled with the monotony of "Brown shoes, black shoes, and plain, ordinary work boots" until a dancing minstrel comes to town. He and his cat teach Milli to dance in exchange for her creations: fanciful shoes and clothes and musical instruments and ingenious, whimsical inventions. Both Milli and Jack find joy in her colorful creations. Milli finds that freedom requires bravery but is worth the risk. The illustrations are sure to inspire some young artists or inventors. *Children's Book Council of Australia, Picture Book of the Year: Notable Book, 2004; Shortlisted, Children's Book Council of Australia Book of the Year: Picture Book, 2004.   cd Author/illustrator from Australia*

Laguna, Sofie. **Too Loud Lily**. Kerry Argent, illustrator. New York: Scholastic, 2004. First published by Omnibus Books, an imprint of Scholastic Australia, in 2002. ISBN 0-439-57913-9. 32 p. (4–7). Picture book.

Lily, the hippo, has a very difficult time doing things quietly. She wakes the baby when she's at home and gets her friends in trouble at school because she's so loud. When Miss Loopiola comes to school to teach music and drama, Lily immediately bonds with this teacher who encourages her to sing and dance as loudly as possible. The colorful illustrations of the animal characters are delightfully expressive and reflect the lighthearted tone of the story. *2003 Book of the Year, Early Childhood shortlist. js*
Author and illustrator live in Australia

Lester, Alison. **Ernie Dances to the Didgeridoo**. Boston: Houghton Mifflin, 2001. First published in Australia by Hodder Headline Australia Pty Ltd, 2001. ISBN 0-618-10442-9. 32 p. (4–7). Picture book.
   Young Ernie goes to live in Arnhem Land, an aboriginal territory in Australia, for a year and sends his friends postcards explaining what he and his friends are doing for each of the six Aboriginal seasons. The vivid watercolor illustrations of children's activities add much to the simple text. A front note explains the origin of the book and the six aboriginal seasons and there is a page of "meanings and explanations" at the end. *Children's Best Book, Australia. sg*
Author lives in Australia

Lester, Alison. **The Snow Pony**. Boston: Houghton Mifflin Company, 2003. ISBN 0-618-25404-8. 194 p. (8–12). Novel.
   Three years of drought have reduced the Rileys' farm to a dirt patch and strained the family to the breaking point. Dusty's whole life seems to be unraveling and her only consolation is her wild horse, the Snow Pony. Setting the action in rural Australia's rugged terrain, this is a story of family, courage, adventure, and a young girl's passion for her horse. *djg*
Author grew up on a farm in Gippsland, southeastern Victora. She is the author of picture books and The Quicksand Pony.

Lindsay, Norman. **The Magic Pudding**. Illustrated by Norman Lindsay. Sydney: HarperCollins Publishers, 2004. Introduction published in New York: Philip Pullman, 2004. (Paperback: IndyPublish, 2004). Originally published as *The Magic Pudding: Being the Adventures of Bunyip Bluegum and His Friends Bill Barnacle & Sam Sawnoff*, by Angus & Robertson Publishers in 1918. ISBN 1-59017-101-2. 169 p. (9–12). Novel.
   A bottomless basin of magic puddin', which changes flavors with a whistle three and a turn of the pot, is a secret quite taxing to protect, especially with shrewd professional puddin'-thieves on the prowl. Despite the Puddin's crafty, disagreeable nature, the eclectic trio that makes up the Noble Order of Puddin'-Owners — Bunyip Bluegum, a highly refined koala, Bill Barnacle, the salty sailor, and Sam Sawnoff, the penguin bold — gladly undertake this arduous yet delightful task. With colorful prose, inventive language, spirited song and rhyme, and a good deal of nose-bending violence, these three comrades fight to retain their

rightful ownership of the ornery pudding and put a stop to puddin'-thievery for good. The original artwork of Norman Lindsay accentuates the fury and triumph of the Puddin'-Thieves persistence, Puddin's obstinacy, and Puddin'-Owners plight. *New York Review Children's Collection.*   ank
Author from Australia

Marchetta, Melina. **Looking for Alibrandi**. New York: Orchard Books, 1999. Originally published by Penguin Books Australia in 1992. Screenplay published by Currency Press in 2000. ISBN 0-531-30142-7. 250 p. (14 up). Novel.

Josephine Alibrandi is a feisty 17-year-old scholarship student in a Catholic high school in Sydney, Australia. Josie's senior year is filled with many new experiences and she finds herself in constant confrontation, whether it's with the nuns in school, her bigoted classmates, or her Italian-Australian family. Her biological father's move to Sydney disrupts Josie's world, and to complicate matters, she falls in love with two boys, each from a different background. As family secrets come to light, Josie finally begins to understand her strict single mother and her even more strict grandmother. At the end Josie feels that although life is not perfect, she will be able to cope with any future obstacles. Winner of 1993 *Children's Book Council of Australia Book of the Year Award; Multicultural Book of the Year Award; Kids Own Australian Literature Award (KOALA); and the Variety Club Young People's category of the 3M Talking Book of the Year Award.* Has been made into a movie.   ok
Author lives in Sydney, Australia

Marchetta, Melina. **Saving Francesca**. New York: Knopf, 2004. (First published by Penguin Books Australia in 2003.) ISBN 0-375-82982-2. 213 p. (14 up). Novel.

Sixteen-year-old Francesca Spinelli tries to make sense of her life at home, where her always difficult mother-daughter relationship is complicated by her mother's sudden bout of debilitating depression, and at St. Sebastian's, where she is one of 30 girls in this formerly all boys Sydney school. The first person narration is an engaging, humor-touched, coming-of-age story. Francesca is a quirky, confused, stronger-than-she-knows individual dealing with a complexity of relationship with family and friends as she goes about "saving Francesca." *YALSA BBYA, 2005; starred reviews; Capitol Choices.*   ca
Author lives in Australia

Marillier, Juliet. **Child of the Prophecy, Book Three of the Seven Waters Trilogy**. New York: Tor, 2002. ISBN 0-312-84881-1. 528 p. (14 up). Novel.

Fianne, grandaughter of Sorcha has been hidden from the evil that threatens her and as a result thinks her life no-account. However, as a new order begins to replace paganism, she is thrust into the conflict and the role of unlikely heroine. *Locus Poll Award.*   mln
Author from Australia

Marillier, Juliet. **Daughter of the Forest, Book One of the Seven Waters Trilogy**. New York: Tor, 2000. ISBN 0-312-84879-X. 400 p. (14 up). Novel.

Steeped in Celtic druid lore, the tale of Sorcha and her brothers mirrors *The Children of Lyrr* at the same time portrays the 10th century arrival of Britons on Irish soil. *1999 Aurelis Award; Young Adult Choices, IRA.*   mln
Author from Australia

Marillier, Juliet. **Foxmask**. New York: Tor, 2004. ISBN 0-765-30674-3. 464 p. (14 up). Novel. *ALA Editor's Choice, 2004.*

Marillier, Juliet. **Wolfskin**. New York: Tor, 2003. ISBN 0-765-30672-7. 464 p. (14 up). Novel.

Ulf begins his new Viking settlement in harmony with the native inhabitants but the peace is undermined by the jealous and dishonor of one of his men. As an uneasy peace is restored, two cultures begin to merge in *Foxmask*. In *Wolfskin*, the second volume of the author's Saga of the Light Isles, his daughter Creidhe secretly accompanies her friend Thorvald, who has set sail westward in search of his true father. They find islands that closely resemble the Faroes, and on them, three separate groups: Vikings called the Long Knife people, Irish monks, and two separate indigenous groups. The two young people find their destinies in most unlikely roles. Replete with arcane and ancient tales and mythology, 10th century life of Orkney and the Faroes is richly portrayed.   mln
Author from Australia

Marillier, Juliet. **Son of the Shadows, Book Two of the Seven Waters Trilogy**. New York: Tor, 2001. ISBN 0-312-84880-3. 462 p. (14 up). Novel.

Amid Briton treachery in a time of conflict and crisis, the two daughters of Sorcha and Iabdan are put to the test. *2000 Aurelis Award; 2001 Alex award.*   mln
Author from Australia

Marsden, John. **The Rabbits**. Illustrated by Shaun Tan. Vancouver: Simply Read Books, 2003. Originally published by Thomas C Lothian Pty. Ltd. in 1998. ISBN 0-9688768-8-9. 32 p. (9–12). Picture book.

The introduction and spread of rabbits across Australia serves as a metaphor for the advance of colonial power there. The opening line, "The rabbits came many grandparents ago," sets the mournful tone of the story, told from the point of view of the original inhabitants. The resulting culture clash is chronicled in stark text and outstanding graphic illustrations. Upright, clothed, armed rabbits advance relentlessly, spreading their military might and industrial power with devastating effects on the indigenous population and the natural environment. The sharp angles and harsh colors within the story contrast with the life-filled, blue wetland scene of the endpapers. *Winner, Children's Book Council of Australia Picture Book of the Year, 1999.*   cd
Author and illustrator from Australia

Marsden, John. **Tomorrow series: Tomorrow, When the War Began** (1995), ISBN 0395706734; **The Dead of Night** (1997), ISBN 0395837340; **A Killing Frost** (1998), ISBN 0732908183; **Darkness Be My Friend** (1999), ISBN 0395922747; **Burning for Revenge** (2000), ISBN 0395960541; **The Night Is for Hunting** (2001), ISBN 0618070265; and **The Other Side of Dawn** (2002), ISBN 0618070281. Boston: Houghton Mifflin Company. Originally published by Pan Macmillan Australia. (13–19). Novel.

Seven teenagers return from a camping trip to discover that Australia has been invaded and their country is at war. With their families gone and many of their homes occupied by soldiers, Ellie and her friends create a hidden garrison in the outback. The determined teens respond with cunning and bravery as they doggedly sabotage the enemy. Each book depicts with vivid realism, Ellie's narratives, as she candidly explores the group's shifting relationships and their responses to the realities thrust upon them by war. Books from this highly-acclaimed series have been translated into five languages and have won several awards, including the *Young Australian Best Book Award; Australian Bookseller's Book of the Year; Bilby Award for Older Readers; the CYBER Award; the WAYBRA award for Older Readers; and the Children's Choice Award.* nrn
Author from Australia

Marsden, John. **Winter**. New York: Scholastic, 2002. (Paperback: Scholastic, 2004). ISBN 0-439-36849-9. 147 p. (12 up). Novel.

After living with the Robinsons for twelve years following the deaths of her parents, sixteen-year-old Winter finally returns to her childhood home haunted by her unresolved past. Strong-willed and persistent, Winter eventually discovers the shocking truth about her mother's death, and with the support of neighbors and new friends she begins to rebuild her life and restore her family home. kk
Author from Australia

Moriarty, Jaclyn. **The Year of Secret Assignments**. New York: Arthur A. Levine, an imprint of Scholastic Inc., 2004. Originally published as *Finding Cassie Crazy* by Pan McMillan Australia in 2003. ISBN 0-439-49881-3. 340 p. (12 up). Novel.

This epistolary novel explores the friendships and secret lives of three high school girls when their tenth grade English teacher assigns them a Pen Pal project with rival Brookfield Public School. Reluctant to write at first, Emily, Lydia, and Cassie make the best of it as the letter writing leads to secret spy missions, cutting classes, and new boyfriends. When Cassie's Pen Pal uses the assignment as a way to hurt her, an all out war breaks out between Ashbury Private School and Brookfield. *YALSA BBYA, 2005; Horn Book Fanfare.* kmc
Author from Sydney, Australia

Murray, Martine. **The Slightly True Story of Cedar B. Hartley**. New York: Levine, 2002. (Paperback: Scholastic, 2004). ISBN 0-439-48622-X. 233 p. (10–14). Novel.

At thirteen, Cedar, "who planned to live an unusual life," is full of questions: Why did her father die? Why did her brother run away? Where is he now? With the support of her hard-working mother; her dog, Stinky; and her diverse group of friends including Caramella from Italy; Rucci from Yugoslavia; Oscar who suffers brain damage; and Kite, the son of circus acrobats, she begins her transition into adolescence. While enriching the lives of all those she loves, she discovers the answers to her questions. This delightfully humorous yet touching story is peppered throughout with childlike line drawings and includes a glossary of Aussie slang. *2003 shortlisted for the Patricia Wrightson Prize for Children's Book and for Children's Book of the Year Awards. Her book* How to Make a Bird, *won the Ethel Turner Prize, 2004.   kk*
Author from Australia

Nix, Garth. **Keys to the Kingdom: Mister Monday (Book 1)**. New York: Scholastic, Inc., 2003. ISBN 0-439-55123-4 (paperback). 361 p. (9–12). Novel.

When a strange key saves Arthur's life, the asthma-ridden seventh grader must enter an unknown realm in a desperate attempt to protect his world from a deadly pandemic. Arthur hopes that finding the key's counterpart will prove powerful enough to thwart Mister Monday's plans of tyranny and destruction. Interested readers can experience the next day of Arthur's adventure in *Book 2: Grim Tuesday*. The Keys to the Kingdom series won the *2004 APA Book Design Award* for best-designed children's series. *Mister Monday* is a *2004 Children's Book Council Book of the Year* winner.   *nrn*
Award-winning author lives in Sydney, Australia

Orr, Wendy. **Nim's Island**. Illustrated by Kerry Millard. New York: Alfred A. Knopf, 2001. Originally published by Allen & Unwin in Australia in 1999. ISBN 0-375-81123-0. 126 p. (8–12). Novel.

Nim and her scientist dad, Jack, have chosen to live on a beautiful little tropical island and she is totally content with her animal friends and scientific experiments. Then one day her father sails off for a few days to conduct experiments and his boat is disabled by a storm. At the same time, Nim gets a series of email questions from a writer whose adventure stories she and her dad admire. A volcano, a storm, and other threats surface and she is aided by her new email friend. Delightful adventure and fantasy are enlivened by humorous pen-and-ink sketches. A happy ending will ensure happy sighs of relief from readers. *Publisher's Weekly Starred Review.   sg*
Author lives in Australia

Prior, Natalie Jane. **Lily Quench and the Black Mountains**. Illustrated by Janine Dawson. New York: Puffin Books, 2004. Originally published by Hodder Headline Australia Pty Limited in 2001. ISBN 0-14-240021-1. 153 p. (10 up). Novel.

Ashby Water is slowly recovering from its years of occupation by the Black Count's troops. The Black Count is preparing to retake Ashby Water and has invented some clever flying machines called dragonets. Lily Quench and her dragon, Queen Dragon, embark on a dangerous quest to the Black Mountains to find the rare blue lily, which is used as a major ingredient in Quenching Drops, a defense weapons against anything metal. Another fast-paced adventure filled with twists and turns and suspicious characters.   *ls*
Author from Australia

Prior, Natalie Jane. **Lily Quench and the Dragon of Ashby**. Illustrated by Janine Dawson. New York: Puffin Books, 2004. Originally published by Hodder Headline Australia Pty Limited in 1999. ISBN 0-14-240020-3. 151 p. (10 up). Novel.

The evil Black Count has invaded and conquered Ashby Water. The king was killed and the prince is missing. Lily Quench is the last of the Quenches, a family whose existence is necessary for crowning and protecting the king. A dragon arrives at Ashby Water and settles on the grommet factory, which is built on the grounds of the Botanic Gardens. Lily is dragged out to slay the dragon, but instead, is carried away by the dragon. Lily discovers that rather than killing dragons, she must crown the prince and rid Ashby Water of the Black Count's Black Squads. A fast-paced, exciting adventure with a strong heroine, which is sure to capture the reader.   *ls*
Author from Australia

Regan, Dian Curtis. **Chance**. Illustrated by Dee Huxley. New York and Canada: Penguin (Philomel), 2003. ISBN 0-399-23592-2. 32 p. (4–8). Picture book.

Chance is a diaper-clad baby boy dissatisfied with the hot and itchy conditions at home so he takes off on his own to try a bear's life further north, monkey habitat in a zoo, sea lions' lifestyle on a beach, and finally lizard life in desert conditions before he misses home enough to return. This plucky character loves his freedom but comes to realize that every environment has its drawbacks and that his homely parents and simple country life have greater charms. Baby roundness is echoed in the rolling, expansive landscapes and plump animals of the illustrations.   *cd*
Author from United States. Illustrator from Australia.

Riddle, Tohby. **The Singing Hat**. New York: Farrar, Straus and Giroux, 2001. First published in Australia by Penguin Books Australia Ltd. in 2000. ISBN 0-374-36934-8. 32 p. (5–9). Picture book.

In this contemporary fable, a sober businessman wakes up with a bird's nest, complete with bird, on his head. His life changes when he refuses to disturb it. He loses his job, while other people appreciate his stance. Finally, the birds hatch, the fledglings fly away, the nest comes off his head, and he continues to look for the

rare and the beautiful in life. The mixed-media illustrations combine photos with line drawings that illustrate the quandaries and inconveniences of his chosen path. This is a very discussable book for the picture book age and up. *Children's Book of the Year, Australia.* sg
Author lives in Australia

Rodda, Emily. **Rowan of Rin series: Rowan of Rin** (2001); **Rowan and the Travelers** (2001), ISBN 0060297751; **Rowan and the Keeper of the Crystal** (2002), ISBN 006029776X; **Rowan and the Zebak** (2002), ISBN 0060297786; and **Rowan and the Ice Creepers** (2003), ISBN 0060297808. New York: Greenwillow Books. Originally published by Omnibus Books (Australia) from 1993–2003. (8 up). Novel.

In the ancient village of Rin, Rowan performs the lowly task of caring for the town's flock of bukshah. He is not strong enough to work in the fields and his shy, fearful nature sets him apart from other youngsters his age. In the first book of this award-winning series, Rin's water source disappears. The village witch chooses Rowan to join the team of heroes destined to challenge the dragon atop a nearby mountain. In each book, Rowan of Rin shows that strength of heart proves more valuable than brute force as he engages the people around him to unravel Rodda's poetic clues. The series continues as Rowan teams with unlikely characters to save his people from the Zebak, historic enemies who once enslaved his ancestors. Rodda is author of the award-winning series, Deltora Quest. The Rowan of Rin series was shortlisted for 2003 Books I Love Best Yearly Awards (BILBY). Books in this series have won a variety of awards, including *Young Australian's Best Book Award (YABBA); Children's Book Council of Australia Book of the Year Award; Children's Book Council Notable Australian Children's Books;* and *Dymock's Children's Choice Award.* Several titles have also been shortlisted for *YABBA, KOALA, and Bilby awards. Children's Books of the Year Awards Winner 1994, Australia, Young Australians' Best Book Awards (YABBA) Winner 1994 Older Australia.* nrn
Author lives in Australia

Rogers, Gregory. **The Boy, the Bear, the Baron, the Bard**. A Neal Porter Book. Brookfield, CT: Roaring Brook Press, 2004. First published in Australia in 2004 by Allen & Unwin. ISBN 1-59641-009-5. 32 p. (5–10). Picture book.

A little boy kicks his soccer ball through the window of an abandoned theater and begins a time travel adventure that takes him back to the Globe Theater in this wordless picture book illustrated in comic strip vignettes. After appearing on the bard's stage and disrupting a performance the boy is chased through London where he frees a captive bear. They dash through the streets, markets, and the Tower of London where he liberates a baron. Out onto the Thames they go rowing out to a Lady's pleasure boat. But the angry bard catches up to the unlikely trio. Will they escape? Will the boy return to his proper time? The curious reader will fly through this action packed picture book to find out. *ALA Notable Book, 2005; starred reviews.* *djg*

Rowe, John A. **Tommy DoLittle**. New York: North-South Books, 2002. Simultaneously published in the United States, Great Britain, Canada, Australia, and New Zealand. ISBN 0-7358-1718-9 (tr.), 0-7358-1719-7 (lib. ed.). 32 p. (5–8). Picture book.

Lazy Tommy, who always wears pajamas and whose dog walks him, somehow gets sucked into the book he is hiding behind in class and has wild adventures in Australia and with aliens before returning to his none-too-sympathetic mother in this over the top tale. Rowe's illustrations are raucous and innovative, incorporating a comic strip, graphic style art, wonderful black-and-white drawings, wild perspectives, and bold colors. There is even a "secret" message, to be read in a "magic mirror" (the opposite foil page). A truly different, galloping good read. *sg* *Author lives in Australia*

Southall, Ivan. **Ash Road**. New York: Morrow, 1978. Originally published by Angus Robertson in 1966. (Paperback: Front Street, 2004. ISBN 1-932425-11-X). 160 p. (10–14). Novel.

A twenty-four-hour nightmare is caused when three teenaged campers carelessly start a bushfire in the foothills around Tinley, Australia. Trying to escape the fire and the blame for having started it, the boys come to Tinley and see what havoc they have wrought, as children whose parents have gone to fight the fire narrowly avoid death. The courage and cowardice that lies in everyone, as well as the power of cooperation, are explored during this wild narrative of emergency. *Australia's Children's Book of the Year for Older Readers Award.* *cmt*

Southall, Ivan. **Josh**. New York: Macmillan, 1971. Originally published by Angus & Robertson in 1971. (Paperback: Front Street, 2005. ISBN 1-932425-36-5). 160 p. (12–14). Novel.

Fourteen-year-old Josh Plowman from Melbourne visits his great-aunt Clara at Ryan's Creek, the sleepy town founded by Great Grandfather Plowman. A sensitive boy, more interested in writing poetry than in playing cricket, Josh is half curious, half apprehensive about his redoubtable relative. What he does not expect is the hostility and prejudice of the young people in the town who see him as just another spoiled and selfish Plowman come to sponge off his aunt. An internal, psychological novel, this book vividly describes life in a rural Australian town. *IBBY Honour List; Carnegie Medal.* *jvl*

Stanley, Elizabeth. **The Deliverance of Dancing Bears**. La Jolla, CA: Kane/Miller Book Publishers, 2003. Originally published under the same title by University of Western Australia Press, under Cynet Books Imprint in 1994. ISBN 1-92932-41-7. 40 p. (5–9). Picture book.

This tenderly poignant picture book begins with a bear dreaming of a better life in the forest fishing in streams. Instead, she is locked and chained in a cage, claws blunted and teeth filed down, made to dance in the streets of a Turkish marketplace, humiliated. Yusuf, an old peasant man, witnesses this degrading act and dreams of freeing her to live out her days in the woods. In this beautifully illustrated modern fable, Yusuf sacrifices his life's savings to purchase the freedom of the bear but not before reminding the onlookers that the price of freedom and dignity for any living creature can never be too high. Postscript explains author's experience with real dancing bears in Turkey and Greece. *The Australian Children's Picture Book of the Year Award, 1995; Wilderness Society Environment Award for Children's Literature shortlist, 1994; West Australian Premier's Book Awards shortlist, 1995; Young Australian Best Book Award shortlist, 1996; 2003 ASPCA Henry Bergh Chidren's Book Award for writing and illustration.   kmc Author lives in Sydney, Australia*

Tan, Shaun. **The Red Tree**. Vancouver, Canada: Simply Read Books, 2003. ISBN 0968876838. First published in Australia, 2001 by Thomas C. Lothian. 32 p. (7–12). Picture book.

Sometimes the day begins with nothing to look forward to, darkness overcomes you and nobody understands. Everything seems hopeless to the little girl as she travels through intense imaginary landscapes in this powerfully overwhelming tale of isolation and despair. The detailed illustrations created in a mix of media set the mood that eventually leads the girl to a small light, vivid and bright, and finally to the Red Tree, just as you imagined it would be. The author illustrator lives in Perth, Australia, and has won numerous awards. *2002 Picture Book of the Year Honour book. In 2001 he was named Best Artist at the World Fantasy Awards in Montreal.   djg*

Wheatley, Nadia. **Luke's Way of Looking**. Illustrated by Matt Ottley. La Jolla, CA: Kane/Miller, 2001. First published in Australia in 1999 by Hodder Headline Australia. ISBN 1-929132-18-2. 32 p. (5–10). Picture book.

Luke looks at things differently. Mr. Barraclough screams at him when he paints with imagination. The sepia tones of the classroom and the ogre-like teacher are sharply contrasted with Luke's colorful and imaginative art. When Luke takes a wrong turn and spends the day in a museum of modern art, colorful art representing the works of Dali and Pollack affirm Luke's way of seeing things.   *djg*

Wild, Margaret, and Ron Brooks. **Fox**. La Jolla, CA: Kane/Miller, 2001. Originally published in Australia in 2000 by Allen & Unwin. ISBN 1-929132-16-6. 32 p. (7 up). Picture book.

A dog finds a wounded magpie in the burnt forest and coaxes the bird out of despair by offering a home and true friendship in this compelling story of loyalty and betrayal. Though the magpie has no hope of flying again, the dog, who himself is missing an eye, encourages the bird. Together, they make a new life, the bird is the dog's eye and the bird on the back of the dog is the bird's wing. Fox returns and convinces magpie to abandon dog. When magpie realized what she has lost, she understands that she must find her way back to dog. The large format picture book is illustrated with mixed media and collage, and the text is hand-lettered by Ron Brooks. *New South Wales Premier Award.* djg

Wild, Margaret. **Midnight Babies**. Illustrated by Ann James. New York: Clarion Books. 1999. ISBN 0-618-10412-7. 32 p. (3–5). Picture book.
   Baby Brenda bounced out of bed at midnight, wiggled through the cat door, and found her friends waiting for her. Reminiscent of *The Wild Ones*, they danced and feasted at the Midnight Cafe, then used the food on themselves to play dress-up. When morning is near, they run home through the sprinklers. The next morning Baby Brenda, too sleepy to eat, just tips her cereal bowl over her head and burps. Ann James has done full-page illustrations on a midnight blue paper background, using chalk pastels. *ALA Editor's Choice, 2002.* jm
Author lives in Australia and is an award-winning author of more than thirty books for children published throughout the world.

Wild, Margaret. **Nighty Night!** Illustrated by Kerry Argent. Atlanta: Peachtree Publishers, 2000. ISBN 1-56145-246-7. 33 p. (2–5). Picture book.
   At bedtime the farm animal parents encounter tricks. Piglets and ducklings have traded places. Then the baby animals use delaying tactics to postpone bedtime— kisses, drinks, go wee. Everyone finally settles down and says *Nighty Night*. Margaret Wild has used alliteration (lovely lambs, chicky chicks) and pleasing rhythms to lull less than sleepy children to dreamland. Kerry Argent's double page pictures of pigs and clucking hens will make this a story to rival *Goodnight Moon.* jm
Author lives in Australia. Illustrator from Australia.

Wild, Margaret. **One Night**. New York: Alfred Knopf, 2004. ISBN 0-375-82920-2. 236 p. Originally published by Allen & Unwin, Australia, 2003. (14 up). Novel.
   Told in free verse through three perspectives, Gabe's, Helen's, and a narrator's, kaleidoscopic images of five troubled teenagers unfold as we see them "enjoy" parties where drinking and fast sex prevail in wealthy homes commandeered by them for the night from friends whose parents are out for the evening. To Gabe, Helen was just another one night stand, but baby Raphael is the result and ultimately the means for mending the many frayed and broken ties in all the lives surrounding him. Both Helen and Gabe are strong characters who would appeal to young people in search of their own identities. *Ethel Turner Prize, 2004; Selected for Senior High School Library Catalog.* jvl
Author from South Africa, lives in Sydney, Australia

Wild, Margaret. **The Pocket Dogs**. Illustrated by Stephen Michael King. New York: Scholastic Press, 2001. Published by arrangement with Omnibus Books, an imprint of Scholastic Australia, 2000. ISBN 0-439-23973. 32 p. (3–5). Picture book.

Mr. Pockets carries his two small dogs, Biff and Buff, in the very big pockets of his coat. One day, there appears a small hole in Biff's pocket. He worries that he will fall out and get lost and so it happens that one day Biff falls out in the grocery store. Kindly people pick Biff up and try to find his home, but he is a pocket dog, not a shopping cart dog. Eventually, he is happily reunited with his master and friend. *Children's Book of the Year shortlist, Australia.* *djg*

Williams, Sue. **Let's Go Visiting**. Illustrated by Julie Vivas. New York: Harcourt, 1998. First published by Scholastic Australia in 1998. ISBN 0-15-201823-9. 32 p. (3–5). Picture book.

This rhyming counting book goes from one to six animals as a young child visits a farm. The repetition gives sound to the bouncy and action-packed illustrations. At the end the child snuggles down in the hay with the animals. *Author and illustrator live in Australia*

Winch, John. **Keeping Up with Grandma**. New York: Holiday House, 2000. First published by Scholastic Australia in 2000. ISBN 0-8234-1563-5. 32 p. (4–8). Picture book.

Grandma baked and Grandpa painted until Grandma decided that they should get outside and do more things together. She leads Grandpa into mountain climbing, sledding, sailing, exploring caves, and other activities, all of which leave Grandpa hanging on for dear life. Finally, extremely tired, he asks why they can't just stay home, and so they do—she baking and he painting. *Author lives in Australia*

Winch, John. **Two by Two**. New York: Holiday House, 2004. ISBN 0-8234-1840-5. 31 p. (4–8). Picture book.

Stunning double spread oil paintings and a brief lyrical text tell the story of the great flood, keeping the focus on the animals of the world rather than Noah (who is never named). In an author's note, Winch points out that over 300 cultures throughout the world have stories of a great flood in the distant past, all sharing a common theme of "the earth being cleansed of man's evil and the rebirth of goodness." *ca* *Author from Australia*

Zusak, Markus. **Fighting Ruben Wolfe**. New York: Scholastic, 2001. First published by Scholastic Australia in 2000. ISBN 0-439-24188-X. 219 p. (12 up). Novel.

Cameron and Ruben Wolfe, brothers, live in a working-class neighborhood with their parents and sister Sarah. They've boxed with each other, each using just one glove, but get serious about fighting when a promoter recruits them. Ruben is the good fighter, getting winnings regularly, and Cameron, the younger, less adept and more vulnerable brother, getting tips for simply showing "heart" and staying in the ring. The book gives a strong portrayal of a family scraping by financially and the strong ties within it. *YALSA BBYA, 2002. jig*

Zusak, Markus. **Getting the Girl**. New York: Scholastic, 2003. Originally published as *When Dogs Cry* by Pan Macmillan, Australia, 2001. ISBN 0-439-38949-6. 261 p. (12 up). Novel.

In this sequel to *Fighting Ruben Wolfe,* Cameron watches his popular older brother Ruben get girl after girl, while he doesn't seem to know how and lacks Rube's instant charm. Finally his opportunity comes as he begins to date Octavia, one of Rube's discarded girlfriends. As Cam develops respect for himself he comes to better understand not just Rube but the rest of his family as well. Cam's poetic and insightful writing ends each chapter. *2001 Book of the Year Honour for Older Readers.* His book *Messenger* was published in the United States as *I Am the Messenger* in 2005 and received the *2003 Book of the Year Award. CBC Choices, 2004. jig*
Author lives in Australia

Related Information

Awards

Australian Children's Choice Awards are organized by territory and administered by local bodies; these include BILBY (Queensland), COOL (Australian Capital Territory), CROW (South Australia), CYBER (Tasmania), KOALA (New South Wales), KROC (Northern Territory), YABBA (Victoria), WAYRBA (West Australia), and Dymocks (national).

Children's Book of the Year Award

First awarded in 1946 by the Australian Children's Book Council, this award bestows honors in five categories: early childhood, younger readers, older readers, picture book, and nonfiction.

Crichton Award recognizes new talent in the field of Australian children's book illustration.

Nan Chauncy Award is a biennial award named after the noted Tasmanian author of children's books and created to honor people who have made an outstanding contribution to the field of Australian children's literature. The recipient must be an Australian citizen, no matter where residing, or a person who has been resident in Australia for at least five years. This award and the two listed above it are administered by the Children's Book Council of Australia.

Young Australian Readers' Award, the first national, online students choice award in Australia, allows students to review the latest titles from the best Australian authors. After reading the books children can log on and vote for their favorites in October of each year.

Online Bookstores

Gleebooks Children's Bookshop is a virtual site of an independent bookstore in Sydney where you can browse, read the newsletter, view books by age group, and order online or by fax or e-mail.
www.gleebooks.com.au

Organizations

Austral Ed is an Australian book supplier from Adelaide, Australia, specializing in the supply of books to overseas International Schools and Universities, especially in Asia, the Middle East, and Europe with an emphasis on international and multicultural children's books.
http://www.australed.iinet.net.au

Australia Centre for Youth Literature, State Library of Victoria, has put together a commented list of young adult books that "explore the lives and experiences of young people from many cultures and countries."
http://www.statelibrary.vic.gov.au/acyl

The Children's Book Council of Australia manages the Children's Book of the Year Awards and links to information about children's book author's and illustrators.
www.cbc.org.au

Society of Children's Book Writers and Illustrators (SCBWI)
SCBWI Australia provides information, support, and encouragement to writers and illustrators of children's books. Founded in 1971, the Society of Children's Book Writers and Illustrators (SCBWI) is an international organization with over 20,000 members and chapters in 17 countries.
http://scbwi.ampl.com.au/

Print Resources

Barley, Janet Crane. **Winter In July: Visits with Children's Authors Down Under**. Lanham, MD: Scarecrow Press, 1995. ISBN 0-8108-2945-2. 227 p.
Dozens of well-known New Zealand and Australian authors of literature for children share the stories behind their books. Experts give an overview of the development of children's literature.

Australian Children's Books: Writers and Illustrators is the name of a website article describing children's literature in Australia with additional links. http://www.cultureandrecreation.gov.au/articles/childrensbooks/

NEW ZEALAND

Allen, Pamela. **Who Sank the Boat?** New York: PaperStar, 1996. ISBN 0-6981-1373-X (pbk). 32 p. (3–6). Picture book.

A rowboat is tied to the dock. Who sank the boat? Was it the cow, the donkey, the sheep, the pig, or the mouse? The reader is invited to guess who is responsible for this wet calamity. The bright, humorous watercolor and ink illustrations and the simple bold text are very inviting for young readers. A lot of fun in a simple, brief story. *1983 CBC Picture Book of the Year*. She is the only author to win the award in two consecutive years. In 1984 *Bertie and the Bear* received that honor.   *ls*
Author from New Zealand

Batt, Tanya Robyn. **The Princess and the White Bear King**. Illustrated by Nicoletta Ceccoli. ISBN 1-84148-339-7. 38 p. (5–10). Picture book.

Storyteller Batt seamlessly weaves together three classic wonder tales: *East of the Sun, West of the Moon, The Black Bull of Norraway*, and *The White Bear King*. She says, "the story begins with a dream, as do so many of our adventures in life, and ends as all fairy tales should, with laughter, love and happiness." Luminous, watercolor pictures illustrate this tale of courage and compassion. *Notable Children's and YA Books of 2005.   djg*
Author from New Zealand. Illustrator from San Marino and has won the Italian Andersen Prize for Best Illustrator of the Year, 2001.

Beale, Fleur. **I Am Not Esther**. New York: Hyperion, 2002. First published by Longracre Press in 1998. ISBN 0-7868-0845-4. 250 p. (12 up). Novel.

When Kirby's mother suddenly decides to work with the refugees in Africa, she leaves fourteen-year-old Kirby with relatives who are members of the Children of Faith, a strict religious sect. In this repressive, male-dominated community, Kirby's name is changed to the biblical name Esther, and she must conform to a strict dress code and language restrictions and participate in long hours of prayer and Bible reading. Although she quickly becomes attached to the children of the family, she desperately wants to find her mother and escape the confines of the community. Finally, she confides in a school counselor who begins the search for her mother. By this time, however, she is struggling with her own identity: is she Kirby or is she Esther? *1999 New Zealand Post Children's Book Award.   kk*
Author lives in New Zealand

Bishop, Gavin. **Stay Awake, Bear!** New York: Orchard Books, 2000. ISBN 0-531-3249-0. 32 p. (4–8). Picture book.

Bear decides that sleeping is a waste of time and determines to stay awake. As the snow falls and the neighborhood grows quiet bear is busy reading books, baking tarts, and playing the banjo. When Brown Bear can't sleep, he comes over for a visit and the friends play scrabble and plan their summer vacation. When at last the summer arrives the two friends sleep on the train, snooze on the beach, and slumber in the mountains, but what memories! The author of over twenty books, *Little Rabbit and the Sea* (2000) and *Maui and the Sun* (1996) have been published in the United States. *djg*
Author lives in New Zealand

Cowley, Joy. **Hunter**. New York: Philomel, 2004. ISBN 0-399-24227-9. 153 p. (9–12). Novel.

Jordon, at fourteen, has been very interested in her Maori heritage. When the small plane carrying her and her two younger brothers crashes, killing the pilot and leaving them to fend for themselves in the wilderness, she seems to hear a voice telling her how to survive. Two hundred years earlier, Hunter, a Maori slave guiding three warriors in search of the moa bird has visions of a silvery canoe with wings crashing into the water and a young girl with light hair and endangers himself as he attempts to communicate with her. Maori words and customs are included as the stories of Hunter and Jordon are told in alternating chapters. *jig*
Author is one of New Zealand's most prolific writers with over 600 titles published including the popular Mrs. Wishy-Washy series.

Cowley, Joy. **The Wishing of Biddy Malone**. Illustrated by Christopher Denise. New York: Philomel Books, 2004. ISBN 0-399-23404-7. 34 p. (5–8). Picture book.

To be sure Biddy loved to sing and dance, but she has no talent for it and she has a temper as hot as a baker's oven. But when Biddy storms out of her home and into a faerie village the music fills her heart. Granted three wishes by the most beautiful boy, she wishes to sing as sweet as a thrush, to dance as lightly as a deer, and for a loving heart. When she returns home it is without the abilities, but she works hard to acquire the talents and learns that something gained for nothing has no value. Beautiful paintings illustrate this tale. *New Zealand Notable Picture Book, 2005. djg*

Dodd, Lynley. **Hairy Maclary and Zachary Quack**. Milwaukee, WI: Gareth Stevens, 2000. First published in Jew Zealand by Mallinson Rendel, 1999. ISBN 0-8368-2676-0. 32 p. (4–8). Picture book.

The playful pup Hairy Maclary made his debut in New Zealand in 1983 and the jaunty alliterative rhymes keep his adventures in print in many countries. Many of the books in the series are imprints in the United States including this title in which Zachary Quack scampers after his friend on a romp through field, forest, and stream until they find a cozy place to tuck up together to dozily dream the afternoon away. *2000 New Zealand Post Children's Choice Award. djg*

Hill, David. **See Ya, Simon**. New York: Dutton, 1994. Originally published in New Zealand in 1992 by Mallinson Rendel Publishers. ISBN 0-525-45247-8. 153 p. (12 up). Novel.

  From the opening of this book, when Simon, aged fourteen, has a new electric wheelchair because his muscles have become too weak for him to continue to push his old chair with his hands, the reader knows that Simon is going to die from muscular dystrophy. His friend Nathan tells about Simon, enjoying his humor and wisecracking, going with him on some of his trips to the hospital, and finally going to his home to say his final good-bye to his friend's body. This story of friendship and family relationships is strong in characterization and in its picture of teens dealing with what life has given them. *jig*
Author lives in New Zealand

Hill, David. **The Sleeper Wakes**. New York: Penguin, 2001. First published by Penguin New Zealand, 2001. ISBN 0-14-131324-2. 132 p. (9–12). Novel.

  Corey is fascinated by Mt. Taranaki, the volcano called "the sleeper" because it has not erupted in over 250 years. He endures the scorn of his classmates about this interest, sharing his enthusiasm with his father, a field officer for the department of conservation and an expert on volcanoes. When the sleeper does begin first to rumble and then finally to erupt, Corey is able to aid in the rescue of his father who has become trapped on the mountain. *Esther Glen Award, shortlist. jig*
Author lives in New Zealand

Jordan, Sherryl. **The Hunting of the Last Dragon**. New York: HarperCollins Publisher, 2002. ISBN 0-06-028902-3. 186 p. (12 up). Novel.

  Jude, who is no hero, tells the story to a monk in 1356 who records it in an effort to provide books for ordinary people. When Jude's village is destroyed by a fire-breathing dragon he suffers the guilt of still being alive, wondering what he was spared for. Jing wei, a Chinese girl, uses knowledge from an old Chinese crone about inventions from China that have not yet come to England to help him kill the last dragon. *ALA Top 10 Fantasy Books for Youth, 2003. jm*
Author lives in New Zealand

Jordan, Sherryl. **The Raging Quiet**. New York: Simon & Schuster, 1999. ISBN 0-689-82140-9. 266 p. (12 up). Novel.

  Set in a time when magic was a force to be reckoned with, this epic saga tells of a remarkable woman, Marnie, forced to marry the noble's son, who lives alone in the tiny fishing hamlet of Torcurra. When her husband Isake falls to his death within days, the superstitious people of the country rumor "witchcraft." When Marnie befriends a wild young deaf boy and develops a system of hand-signs that seem to "tame" the youth the people force her only friend, the local priest to make

her submit to ordeal to prove her innocence. A compelling tense story of human emotion. *2001 Margaret Mahy Medal and Hans Christian Andersen nominee in 2002.* djg
Author lives in New Zealand

Mahy, Margaret. **Alchemy**. New York: Margaret K. McElderry Books, 2003. ISBN 0-689-85053-0. 207 p. (14 up). Novel.

Seventeen-year-old Roland Fairchild, school prefect, is haunted by a reoccurring, terrifying dream and is puzzled by an inner voice that advises him in ambiguous situations. When a teacher blackmails Roland into befriending Jess Ferrett, a quiet, solitary girl, the strangeness in Roland's life increases to a fever pitch, especially with the reappearance of an odd magician who eagerly wants Roland to divulge his secrets. Roland discovers he possesses talents and abilities that go beyond ordinary magic. The action slowly builds to an intense climax and a hopeful ending. *2003 Esther Glen Award shortlist.* ls
Author from New Zealand

Mahy, Margaret. **Dashing Dog**. New York: Greenwillow Books, 2002. ISBN 0-06-000457-6. 32 p. (4–8). Picture book.

A family takes their newly groomed dog strolling along the seaside. Their wonderful dog has a grand time catching frisbees and chasing gulls and cats. When baby Betty falls off the jetty, their dog rescues her and becomes a hero. A lilting rhyme and splashy, dynamic illustrations extol a family's love for their exuberant dog. *Children's Catalog.* ls
Author from New Zealand

Mahy, Margaret. **Down the Dragon's Tongue**. Illustrated by Patricia MacCarthy. New York: Orchard Books, 2000. ISBN 0-531-30272-5. 32 p. (4–8). Picture book.

The Prospero twins talk their buttoned-down father into taking them to the playground to slide down the dragon's tongue, an enormous slide. Mr. Prospero eats his tie, loses his buttons, and has an absolutely wonderful time sliding down the dragon's tongue. This clever story encourages parents to loosen up and enjoy activities with their children. ls
Author from New Zealand

Mahy, Margaret. **24 Hours**. New York: Margaret McElderry Books, 2000. ISBN 0-689-83884-0. 200 p. (14–17). Novel.

Ellis has just returned home from finishing prep school and immediately lands in a day-and-night-long adventure in an inner city neighborhood that changes his life and increases his sense of who he really is. Complex characters, gripping plot, and wonderful writing will attract mature teens. *Horn Book Fanfare Honor List, 2000.* sg
Author lives in New Zealand

Related Information

Awards

Esther Glen Award, given to the New Zealand author of the book considered the most distinguished contribution to literature for children in the preceding year.

Russell Clark Award, given to a New Zealand illustrator responsible for the most distinguished illustrations for children's or young adult's book. Non-fiction as well as fiction titles are eligible.

NZLIA Young People's Non-Fiction Award, given to the New Zealand author of the book that is considered to be the most distinguished contribution to non-fiction for young people. The above three annual awards, as well as several others, are administered by the Library and Information Association of New Zealand Aotearoa.

The New Zealand Post Children's Book Awards, sponsored by the newspaper firm, recognize the best in New Zealand children's books in four categories: junior fiction, senior fiction, picture book, and nonfiction.

Organizations

New Zealand Children's Book Council promotes books and reading by bringing readers, writers, publishers, editors, and schools together. The Book Council also welcomes international visitors to literary New Zealand and presents a literary map of New Zealand.
www.bookcouncil.org.nz/index.html

Storylines is the National Section of IBBY, a non-profit organization that represents an international network of people from all over the world who are committed to bringing books and children together.
www.storylines.org.nz

Print and Online Resources

Mills, Wayne. "New Zealand Children's Literature (1970–2001)." **Bookbird**, 2001.

New Zealand Children's Book Awards provides information on a variety of awards for children and includes listings of winners and books shortlisted since 1988. The site also contains information about all major awards.
http://lib.cce.ac.nz/nzcba/

Chapter 9

Europe

AUSTRIA

Denenberg, Barry. **One Eye Laughing, the Other Weeping: The Diary of Julie Weiss**. New York: Scholastic Inc., 2000. ISBN 0-439-09518-2. 250 p. (12 up). Novel.

Through her diary, Julie Weiss, 12, records the events of her life beginning in January 1938 in Vienna, Austria, and ending in December 1938 in New York City. Julie lives a quiet, pampered life in Vienna as the daughter of a physician. Rumors about Hitler and the Nazis abound but it is not until the Anschluss in the spring that the rumors become reality. Jews in Vienna are ostracized from society. Life becomes very difficult, cruel, and unpredictable. After Julie's mother dies and her brother leaves for Palestine, Julie is sent to live with her Aunt Clara and Uncle Martin in New York City. It takes time for Julie to adjust to her new surroundings and much to her surprise and delight, Julie becomes an actress. A story highlights the differences between the two cities in 1938. One city is suffering terrible oppression and persecution, while the other city is bustling with commerce and culture. *ls*
Author from United States

Havill, Juanita. **Eyes Like Willy's**. New York: HarperCollins Children's Books, 2004. ISBN 0-688-13672-9. 135 p. (12 up). Novel.

In 1906, Guy and his sister, Sarah, travel with their parents from Paris for a summer vacation at Bregenz, an Austrian village on Lake Constance. Soon after arriving at the village, Guy and Sarah meet Willy. Almost every summer thereafter, Guy, Sarah, and Willy share a summer vacation at Bregenz until the summer of 1914. Guy eventually enlists in the French Army. In 1915, he is wounded

and discharged from the army. While recovering from his injuries and trying to decide what he should do with his life, Guy's friend, Willy, reenters his life. They've been changed by the war but their friendship is as strong as ever.   *ls*
Author from United States

Krischanitz, Raoul. **Molto's Dream**. Translated by J. Alison James. New York: North-South Books, 2001. First published in Switzerland under the title *Molto*. ISBN 0-7358-1507-0. 30 p. (4–8). Picture book.

Molto the tiger cat has a backyard full of toys but still isn't happy. When he sees two kittens, Felix and Luna, playing with one of his many balls he scolds them. "I don't want to share," Molto whines. What he wants is to see the world from above, so Felix and Luna spend days constructing a hot air balloon for Molto. When the balloon is ready, Molto thoughtlessly hops in and leaves Felix and Luna behind. At first, Molto loves to fly, but he soon feels lonely and re-members that Luna and Felix wanted to fly, too. Upon landing, Molto crashes the balloon, but he works on a bigger and better balloon to surprise his new friends. The three cats go soaring in the beautiful new balloon. Flying is much better, Molto discovers, "when you share it with your friends."   *aao*
Author was born and lives in Vienna, Austria

Weninger, Brigitte. **A Child Is a Child**. Translated by Charise Myngheer. Illus-trated by Eve Tharlet. New York: Michael Neugebauer/Minedition/Penguin Put-nam, 2004. ISBN 0-698-40006-2. 28 p. (4–8). Picture book.

When something terrible happens to mama and papa frog the animals all won-der who will take care of the babies. They can't live in Blackbird's nest, or Mole's hole and Hedgehog is always on the move. Nonsense, exclaims Mama Mouse, a child is a child and she finds the happy solution. Collages in textured, mixed me-dia illustrate this satisfying story of love, acceptance, and community.   *djg*
Author from Kufstein, Austria. Illustator lives in France.

Weninger, Brigitte. **Happy Birthday, Davy!** Translated by Rosemary Lanning. Illustrated by Eve Tharlet. New York: A Michael Neugebauer Book/North South, 2000. First published in Switzerland under the title *Herzlichen Glückwunsch, Pauli*. ISBN 0-7358-1345-0. 28 p. (4–8). Picture book.

Davy is eagerly anticipating his birthday, but everyone is too busy to pay him any attention. He wishes for someone to spend time with him, tell him stories, and teach him new games. Davy receives his wishes when an extra large package ar-rives. Inside the package are his grandparents, who have the time to spend with him, teaching him the games of their childhood. Turn about is fair play and Davy proposes to give himself to them for their birthday present. Other titles include: *Why Are You Fighting, Davy? Davy in the Middle* (2004).   *mw*

Weninger, Brigitte. **It's Bedtime!** Translated by Kathryn Grell. Illustrated by Alan Marka. New York: North-South Books, 2002. First published in Gorrau

Zürich Switzerland by Nord-Süd Verlag AG under the title *Ich will nicht allein schlafen*. ISBN 0-7358-1602-6. 26 p. (3–8). Picture book.

It's time for bed, so Ben says good night to Daddy, Grandmother, Kitty, and the television. "But I don't want to sleep alone!" Ben tells his mother. Mother tries to comfort Ben with all the soft fuzzy toys he has in his room, including the stuffed rabbit, Davy, a character from the author's popular series. But Ben refuses each in turn until he chooses a mean, scary-looking monster doll. "He will scare away the ghosts and monsters and keep me safe," Ben explains, and then he falls asleep. Soft and playful illustrations add to the appeal of this humorous bedtime story.   *aao and nrn*
Author lives in Austria. Illustrator lives in England.

Weninger, Brigitte. **The Magic Crystal**. Translated by Harold D. Morgan. Illustrated by Robert Ingpen. New York: Minedtion/Penguin Putnam, 2004. Originally published in German in 2003 by Michael Neugebauer Verlag AG, Grossau, Switzerland, 2003. ISBN 0-698-40007-0. 28 p. (5–8). Picture book.

Kind-hearted Pico lives all alone in a small cave, ashamed of how he looks, his only friend an ugly old troll. One night, he meets a group of crystal dwarves, who are charmed by his poetry. He is taken deep into the mountain, illumined by the holographic sparkles of the crystals along the way. Pico meets the crystal king who rewards the generous soul with a piece of crystal that reflects his inner beauty. True to the fairy tale nature of the story, the old troll, made ugly by his greed, gets his true reward as well. Glittery holographs highlight the watercolor illustrations of the 1986 Hans Christian Andersen Award winning illustrator.   *djg*

Weninger, Brigette. **Precious Water: A Book of Thanks**. Illustrated by Anne Möller. New York: Michael Neugebauer/North-South, 2002. First published in Switzerland under the title *Danke, reines Wasser!* ISBN 0-7358-153-5. 28 p. (4–7). Picture book.

A young girl looks at a glass of clear water and reflects on its value for all living things. Large watercolor paintings illustrate the simple text that ends with her hope that we will always have enough water for the plants and animals and people on earth. This book is a companion to *Little Apple: A Book of Thanks* (2001).   *djg*

Weninger, Brigitte. **Zara Zebra Gets Dressed**. Illustrated by Anna Laura Cantone. New York: North-South Books, 2002. Originally published as *Zara Zebra zieht sich an* by Nord-Sud Verlag AG in 2002. ISBN 0-7358-1730-8. 12 p. (1–3). Picture book.

This smallish square book with a lightly padded cover features a zebra getting dressed in its yellow, red, blue, green, and black and white clothes. The illustrations are blocky, brightly colored, and outlined with thick black lines. Each page features some crinkly textured surfaces to add to the simple, bold appeal. Others in the series are: *Zara Zebra's Busy Day, Zara Zebra Counts,* and *Zara Zebra Draws.*   *sg*

SPOTLIGHT ON CHRISTINE NÖSTLINGER

Christine Nöstlinger is an influential and popular German language author of books for children. In 2002 her work was recognized by the Swedish government when she shared the first Astrid Lindgren Memorial Award with Maurice Sendak. Her books have been translated into numerous languages.

Vienna is the setting for most of her books including the autobiographical novel, *Fly Away Home*. While the war-time setting is realistically portrayed, the book is not about war or politics, but about childhood and the difficult business of growing up.

Konrad, winner of the 1979 Mildred Batchelder Award, is the humorous story about a woman who receives a factory-made seven-year-old boy in the mail, This humorous story about the transformation of a perfect child has a lot to say about family life.

The language of the books also betrays their origin. Nostlinger's literary language has a distinctly Viennese and Austrian quality. It is sufficiently different from the German spoken in Germany that her German publishers felt compelled to add short word lists at the end of her books (Metcalf, 2003).

Nöstlinger is the winner of many international and national awards, Hans Christian Andersen Award (1984), the Friedrich-Bödecker Prize for her Contribution to Literature (1972), and the German State Children's Book Prize (1973). Sadly, her books are out of print in the United States, but the following books are available through Random House, Canada.

But Jasper Came Instead. Anderson Press/Random House, Canada, 2000. ISBN 0-86264-987-0.

Conrad. Anderson Press/Random House, Canada, 1999. ISBN 0-86264-936-6.

Fly Away Home. Anderson Press/Random House, Canada, 2003. ISBN 1-84270-227-0.

Other titles include: *The Cucumber King,* 1975; *Fiery Frederica,* 1975; *Girl Missing,* 1976; *Luke and Angela,* 1981; *Marrying Off Mother,* 1982.

Fuchs, Sabine. Christine Nostlinger-Werkmonographie (Chr. N.: Oeuvre). Vienna: Dachs, 2001. 239 p. ISBN 3851912438., EUR 18.80 (OS 259).

Garrett, Jeffrey. "Christine Nostlinger Celebrates her 65th birthday," Bookbird, Apr 2002.

Metcalf, Eva-Maria. "First Astrid Lindgren Memorial Award for Christine Nöstlinger and Maurice Sendak." Bookbird, Oct 2003.

Silvey, Anita. *Children's Books and their Creators.* Houghton-Mifflin, 1995.

Stories from the Bible. Illustrated by Lisbeth Zwerger. New York: A Michael Neugebauer Book/North-South Books, 2000. First published in Germany under the title *Die Bibel.* ISBN 0-7358-1413-9. 160 p. (7–10). Bible stories.

Hans Christian Andersen Medal winner Lisbeth Zwerger illustrates selected stories from the Old King James version of Old and New Testament. From the creation, flood, and tower of Babel, King David and the Psalms to the birth of Jesus, His teachings, Last Supper, and the Passion, the one hundred fifty-six passages with scripture references cited in the index are enhanced with Zwerger's masterful watercolor illustrations.

Illustrator lives in Vienna, Austria

Related Information

Awards

Österreichische Kinder-und Jugenbuchpreise/Austrian National Children's and Youth Book Award

Sponsored by Federal Chancellery Department of the Arts, these awards are given in three categories: fiction, illustration, and translation.

Organizations

IBBY Austria
www.jugendliteratur.net

Österreichische Gesellschaft für Kinder- und Jugendliteraturforschung
/Austrian Research Society for Children's Literature (in German only)
http://www.biblio.at/oegkjlf

Print and Online Resources

"History of Austrian Children's Literature from 1800 to the Present." **Bookbird**, Summer 1998 issue.

The twenty-three prominent contributors represented in this volume consider the themes, genres, authors, and artists that have made Austrian children's literature one of the world's most interesting and diverse traditions. A wealth of illustrations, many in color, and extensive bibliographic references enhance the value of this first-ever history of Austrian children's books. The essays are based on papers presented at a conference that took place at Schloss Rauischholzhausen, October 8–11, 1995.

BELGIUM

Ashbé, Jeanne. **And After That**. La Jolla, CA: Kane/Miller, 2002. Originally published in Belgium under the title *et après il y aura . . .* by L'Ecole Des Loisirs, Paris, 2000. ISBN 1-9291-3224-7 (pbk). 14 p. (2–5). Picture book.

A delightful, miniature lift-the-flap book perfect for conveying the concept of sequencing for little ones. After daytime, lift the flap, it's nighttime, after socks, you put on your shoes and so on. Sturdy pages and simple watercolor illustrations portray everyday items and events in the life of a toddler.   *djg*

Bosschaert, Greet. **Teenie Bird and How She Learned to Fly**. New York: Harry N. Abrams, 2001. Copyright in 2000 Uitgeverij Clavis, Hasselt. ISBN 0-8109-3586-4. 26 p. (4–7). Picture book.

Teenie Bird is smaller and different in color than her brothers. She is afraid of everything and wishes she were in her egg again, where no one could see how different she looks and acts. But as she grows and her mother urges her to fly, she slowly gains courage and confidence. This simple story, illustrated with large acrylic paintings will encourage the little ones among us.   *djg*

Cneut, Carll. **The Amazing Love Story of Mr. Morf**. Illustrated by author. New York: Clarion Books, 2003. Originally published in the United Kingdom by Macmillan Children's Books in 2002. ISBN 0-6183-3170-0. 32 p. (4–8). Picture book.

Mr. Morf takes a leave of absence from his job as a circus dog to search for true love. He meets the most unlikely creatures along the way, but returns to the circus alone. While practicing for his circus act, the kindly canine finds the most uncanny partner of all! Text font and illustrative style clue the reader to a unique and thoroughly remarkable reading experience. Vivid acrylic paintings with a collage motif.   *nrn*
Author/illustrator lives in Belgium

Genechten, Guido van. **The Cuddle Book**. New York: HarperCollins, 2003. First published in the Netherlands by Clavis Editions, 2003. ISBN 0-06-075306-4. 28 p. (3–7). Picture book.

Everybody likes a good cuddle. Simple text and bright, bold illustrations show playful monkey cuddles and slow turtle cuddles. Kangaroos find cuddling easy, but for crabs, cuddling is hard. The best cuddles are, of course, from mommy.   *djg*

Genechten, Guido van. **Potty Time**. New York: Simon & Schuster, 2001. First published in Belgium in 2000 by Uitgeverij Clavis, Hasselt, 2000. ISBN 0-689-84698-3. 28 p. (2–5). Picture book.

"It's Potty Time!" said Joe. And one by one all the animals take a turn putting their bottoms on the potty. Nellie Elephant puts her great big bottom down with a thump; giraffe, pig, zebra, dog, hen mouse, polar bear, frog, and finally Joe take a turn. No matter the size or shape—everyone uses the potty. Colorful paints on newsprint illustrate this simple story for toddlers.   *djg*
Author/illustrator lives in Belgium and has won numerous awards.

Guettier, Bénédicte. **In the Jungle**. La Jolla, CA: Kane/Miller, 2002. Originally published as *Dans la jungle*. ISBN 1-9291-3238-7. 14 p. (3–6). Picture book.
Another book in the Petit théâtre this book contains illustrations of various jungle creatures, with a cutout where the face should be. Bright colors on cardboard pages make this attractive for the youngest readers.

Kanefield, Teri. **Rivka's Way**. Chicago: Front Street Books, 2001. ISBN 0-8126-2870-5. 137 p. (12 up). Novel.
In 1778, the Jews of Prague lived a restricted life in a walled ghetto. Fifteen-year-old Rivka Liebermann's parents have arranged a marriage for her to Oskar Kara, a medical student. Rivka's stomach aches anticipating the announcement of the engagement. Before she is married, Rivka longs to see what is outside the ghetto walls. A short excursion with her father only whets her appetite to see and learn more about life outside the ghetto. Rivka endangers herself and her future by disguising herself as a boy, stealing out of the ghetto, and befriending a Christian boy. An interesting view of Jewish life in 18th-century Bohemia. *ls*
Author from United States

Robberecht, Thierry. **Angry Dragon**. Illustrated by Philippe Goosens. New York: Clarion, 2004. First published as *Boze Draak* in Belgium by Clavis Uitgeverij Amsterdam-Hasselt, 2003. ISBN 0-618-47430-7. 26 p. (4–8). Picture book.
"The answer is NO!" says mom and that makes the little boy mad, so mad that he feels trapped inside a stone. Hands clenched, anger leaping inside like flames, this boy is so angry that he turns into a dragon that destroys everything in its path. Finally, alone in his room he begins to feel ashamed, then sad and his tears put out the angry dragon fire. Oil paintings convey the anger and its resolution in the context of an understanding mother and father who patiently wait for the dragon to disappear and turn back into their little boy. *djg*
Author and illustrator live in Brussels

Simoen, Jan. **What About Anna?** Translated by John Nieuwenhuizen. New York: Walker & Company, 2002. Originally published as *En met Anna?* by Querido in 1999. ISBN 0-8027-8808-4. 254 p. (12 up). Novel.
See Europe/Netherlands for description.
Flemish author is a French teacher living in Louvain, Belgium.

Slegers, Liesbet. **Kevin Goes to School**. La Jolla, CA: Kane/Miller Book Publishers, 2002. Originally published under the title *Karel gaat naar school* by Uitgeverij Clavis, Hasselt, Belgium. ISBN 1-929132-31-X. 26 p. (2–5). Picture book.
Kevin is on his way to school for the first time. He describes the events of his first day: crying as his mom leaves, his teacher cheering up the class with a

puppet show, making paper hats (simple instructions are included), and meeting his new friend, Ali. When Kevin's mother arrives to take him home, Kevin is ready to go but is looking forward to returning the next day to his new classroom and his new friend. The simple text and colorful pictures on sturdy pages make this a good title to use for introducing young children to the experience of going to preschool or kindergarten. His misadventures continue in *Kevin Goes to the Hospital* (2002).   *aao*

Additional Resources

IBBY Belgium (French Branch)
www.ibby.be
IBBY Belgium (Flemish Branch)
www.villakakelbont.be
    The Belgian section of IBBY consists of two departments: a Flemish and a Walloon (French-speaking). The Flemish department nominated candidates for the Hans Christian Anderson prizes and the biennial honour List. It also recommends candidates for the Biennale of Illustrations in Bratislava.

Nationaal Centrum voor Jeugdliteratatuur/NCJ (National Centre for Children's Literature) Minderbroedersstraat 22, B – 2000 Antwerpen/Belgium.
    Documentation and information center for Flemish literature for children and young adults. Organizer of the annual children's book week in Flanders, which is the first week of March.

BOSNIA-HERZEGOVINA

Bunting, Eve. **Gleam and Glow**. Illustrated by Peter Sylvada. San Diego: Harcourt, 2001. ISBN 0-15-202596-0. 32 p. (6–10). Picture book.
    Based on an incident reported by a villager in Bosnia-Herzegovina, this is a story of hope in the face of war. Papa has left home to join the Liberation Army and the war is coming closer. Mama, Viktor, and Marina must flee. They leave two gold fish in the small pond near their house and travel to safety. When the war is over, they are happily reunited with Papa and return to the ruins of their home, but find the pond teaming with life. Beautiful oil paintings capture the emotion of the story.   *djg*
Author and illustrator from United States

Dorros, Arthur. **Under the Sun**. New York: Harry N. Abrams, 2004. ISBN 0-8109-4933-4. 211 p. (12 up). Novel.
    Thirteen-year-old Ehmet's father is Muslim and mother is a Catholic Croat living in war-torn Sarajevo. When a sniper shoots at his mother they flee to his

grandparent's village in the Croatian mountains, a village rumored to be a place where Croat, Serb, and Muslim people, mostly orphans and refugees work together to rebuild a peaceful life. Harrowing and deadly encounters with rebels, snipers, and landmines and struggles to find food make this a compelling story of survival and hope during war. In a note at the end of the book Doros explains that there is a real "Children's Village"; it is Nadomak Sunca, in Oprtalj, Croatia.

BULGARIA

Kyuchukov, Hristo. **My Name Was Hussein**. Honesdale, PA: Boyds Mills, 2004. ISBN 1-5639-7964-0. 32 p. (7–10). Picture book.

A Muslim boy describes his quiet Roma life in a small village in Bulgaria. Ramadan is observed, some customs are simply explained or shown in the watercolor illustrations. But peaceful family life is abruptly ended when the soldiers come into the village and the Roma people are persecuted. His name, passed down in the family, must be changed to a Christian name. The author's note explains that he was a Roma forced to change his name under the communist government of Bulgaria in the 1980s.

CROATIA

Shields, Carol. **Music**. Paintings by Svjetlan Junaković. New York: Handprint Books, 1999. Originally published in Switzerland by Bohem Press. ISBN 1-929766-05-X. 24 p. (4–8). Picture book.

Carol Sheild's fresh poetry is cleverly illustrated in this book of riddles. Stiff fold out pages transform musical instruments into the animals who play them. "I plod thrugh the desert ba-rumpity-bump. My drums keeping time, ka-thumpity-thump. Bumpity, thumpity, rumpity, thump, I am a . . . camel with a drum on each hump." Other titles in the Animagicals series include: *Homes* (2001), *Sports* (2001), *On the Go, Patterns and Colors* (2000). *djg*
Author from United States. Illustrator from Zagreb, has won numerous awards including prizes at the BIB in Bratislava, 2002. His books have been translated in twenty languages.

CZECH REPUBLIC

Bitton-Jackson, Livia. **My Bridges of Hope: Searching for Life and Love after Auschwitz**. New York: Simon & Schuster, 1999. ISBN 0689848986. 258 p. (12 up). Biography.

In this sequel to *I Have Lived a Thousand Years*, fourteen-year-old Elli tells of her attempt to rebuild her life in Czechoslovakia with her brother and mother. Her struggles against the continued anti-Semitism force them to immigrate to America. The Kirkus reviewer said: "Interesting and inspiring, this story makes painfully clear how the fight to survive extended well beyond the war years." *djg*

Horáček, Petr. **Flip's Day**. Cambridge, MA: Candlewick, 2002. First published by Walker. ISBN 0-7636-1798-9. 18 p. (3–7). Picture book.

Stiff, die-cut pages illustrate Flip the penguin's day in this colorful book for young children. He gets dressed, plays soccer, has lunch, walks in the rain, colors a drawing, and takes a bath before bedtime. The final page includes a pull-tab making bright yellow stars appear in the night sky. *djg*

Horáček, Petr. **A New House for Mouse**. Cambridge, MA: Candlewick, 2004. First published by Walker. ISBN 0-7636-2517-5. 28 p. (4–8). Picture book.

Mouse looks out of the tiny hole where she lives and sees a juicy red apple. But when it won't fit into her house, she journeys around to find a bigger house. No one has room for her, but she works up an appetite and bites into her apple. At the end of the day, she doesn't have a bigger house, but rather a smaller apple. Bold acrylic paints and mixed media, combined with the author/illustrators trademark die-cut pages will make this book a winner with the picture book crowd. *djg*
Author/illustrator from Czech Republic, lives in England

Levine, Karen. **Hana's Suitcase: A True Story**. Morton Grove, IL: Albert Whitman, 2002. ISBN 0-8075-3148-0. 112 p. (9–12). Biography.

When a battered suitcase bearing the words *Hana Brady 1931* and the German word for *orphan* arrives with a group of artifacts at a Holocaust Education Center for young people in Tokyo, the children ask the curator, Fumiko Ishioka, to discover Hana's identity. The story of the Czech girl who perished at Auschwitz is told in alternating chapters with Ishioka's search for information about her, leading her across Europe to Canada. Ishioka eventually finds Hana's brother, the only one of the family to survive, and he travels to Japan to meet the young members of the peace club. Based on a Canadian radio documentary and illustrated with photos and documents of Hana and her family, Ishioka, and her peace club, this is both a sad Holocaust story and an uplifting picture of today's children who long to help establish a peaceful world. *sg*
Author lives in Canada

Melnikoff, Pamela. **Prisoner in Time: A Child of the Holocaust**. Philadelphia: The Jewish Publication Society, 2001. Originally published by the Penguin Group in 1992. ISBN 0-8276-0735-0. 142 p. (12 up). Novel.

World War II
See England for description.

Sendak, Maruice. **Brundibar**. Illustrated by Tony Kushner. After the opera by Hans Krása and Adolf Hoffmeister. New York: Michael DiCapua Books/Hyperion,

2003. *The Opera Brundibár* by Hans Krása and Adolf Hoffmeister is published by Tempo Praha. ISBN 0-7868-0904-3. 56 p. (7 up).

Their mother is sick and the doctor sends them to town to get milk, but the milkman won't give them milk unless they have the money. Aninku and Pepicek's efforts to earn the money are thwarted by the bully Brundibar who tyrannizes the town. With the assistance of the animals and a cast of characters from the village, the children eventually earn the money to buy the milk. The towns people sing the exhuberant finale "The wicked never win!" but Brundibar's hand-written note on the last page leaves the reader with the ominous warning—bullies don't give up—as soon as one departs, the next appears. Based on an opera that completed in 1938 and was performed fifty-five times by the children of Terezin, the Nazi concentration camp. *djg*

Related Information

Awards

Golden Strip Award/Zlatá stuha

Since 1992, this annual Award of the Albatros Publishing House (Vý-roc ní cena nakladatelství Albatros) has been the only national award devoted to new production of Czech publishing houses for children and youth.

Book Fair

Book World Prague International Book Fair
Prague, Czech Republic
http://bookworld.cz
April

DENMARK

Andersen, Hans Christian. **The Little Mermaid**. With pictures by Lisbeth Zwerger. Translated from the Danish by Anthea Bell. New York: Minedition/Penguin, 2004. Jubilee Edition: 200 years Hans Christian Andersen/50 years Lisbeth Zwerger. ISBN 0-698-40001-1. 44 p. (7 up). Picture book.

This faithful translation of the classic tale is illustrated in Zwerger's classic style of luminous watercolor paintings. Zwerger has won the Hans Christian Andersen Medallion 1990 in recognition of her lifetime achievement and contribution to children's literature.

Bodecker, N.M. **Hurry, Hurry, Mary Dear!** Illustrated by Erik Blegvad. New York: Margaret K. McElderry, 1998. ISBN 0689817703. First published by McElderry, 1976. 32 p. (5 up). Picture book.

Erik Blegvad illustrates his friend's witty poem as a picture book and bases his watercolor paintings on Bodecker's original pen sketches. Mary hurries at her husband's every command until, frazzled and exhausted, she lets him know just how she feels. The complete collection of Bodecker's nonsense verse has been out of print for some time, but this fresh edition will send you to the library stacks looking for more. *Starred reviews in Kirkus and Publisher's Weekly. Original edition received the Christopher Award in 1977.* djg

Bredsdorff, Bodil. **The Crow-Girl**. Translated by Faith Ingwersen. New York: Farrar, Straus and Giroux, 2004. ISBN 0-374-31247-8. 155 p. (10–12). Novel.

Growing up in a small house on a cove with only her grandmother, a young girl learns to be proficient in providing food. After her grandmother's death she follows two crows on a journey where she learns to appreciate her grandmother's wisdom as she encounters a variety of people. In the end she returns home bringing with her friends she has made along the way. *bn*
Author from Denmark

Holm, Anne. **I Am David**. New York: Harcourt, 2004. First published as *David* by Gyldendal in Copenhagen in 1963. Translated from the Danish by L.W. Kingsland and published as *North to Freedom* by Harcourt, 1965. Copyright renewed by Harcourt 1993. ISBN 0-15-205161-9 hardcover; 0-15-205160-0 pb. 239 p. (12 up). Novel.

Twelve-year-old David has lived his entire life in a concentration camp somewhere in eastern Europe. When a guard arranges for him to escape, he follows the directions he is given, to head south, stow away on a ship to Italy, and then walk north until he reaches Denmark. All his judgments about other people are based on his experiences and his own very high standards and it is not easy for him to trust anyone. He experiences for the first time both physical pleasure—sunshine and warmth, food that tastes good, the feel of being clean—and psychological pleasure—freedom to make decisions, decide his own fate. The book can lead to discussions of how and why people think about particular issues. *Lewis Carroll Shelf Award; American Librarian Association Notable Book; Gyldendal Prise for Best Scandinavian Children's Book.*
Author from Denmark

Kaaberbol, Lena. **The Shamer's Daughter**; book 1: The Shamer's Chronicles. Translated by Lena Kaaberbol. New York: Henry Holt, 2004. First published as *Shammerens Datter* by Forum, 2000. ISBN 0-805-07541-0. 240 p. (10–14). Novel.

In this first volume of a promising new fantasy series, Dina learns to use her truth-telling abilities to unmask a triple murder and rescue her mother. At the conclusion, Dina's small group goes into hiding, destined to confront the same evil forces another day. Action is brisk, though sometimes gory, and dialog is lively, though sometimes earthy. *mln*

Levitin, Sonia. **Room in the Heart**. New York: Dutton Books, 2003. ISBN 0-525-46871-4. 285 p. (12 up). Novel.

In April 1940, the German's occupied Denmark, but they could not rule the country. Niels, Julie, Fredericka, and Emil find themselves involved in surviving the Nazi oppression. Everywhere in Denmark ordinary people, like Niels, are involved in sabotaging the Germans efforts to gain supplies and destroy German military property. Emil is caught up in the false promises of the Danish Nazis. Julie's family is Jewish. Fredericka observes what is happening and tries to help defeat the Nazis. In the fall of 1943, the Germans have a secret plan to round up Denmark's seven thousand Jews on Rosh Hashanah eve. Word gets out, the Danes quickly contact their Jewish compatriots and assist in getting them to Sweden. At the end of the war, the Danish Jews returned to their homes and businesses that were preserved for them waiting their return. A story of a nation's courage and heroism to quietly stand up for what is right for its citizens in the face of great danger. *ls*
Author from United States

Reuter, Bjarne. **The Ring of the Slave Prince**. Translated from the Danish by Tiina Nunnally. New York: Dutton, 2003. First published by Gyldenhal, Copenhagen, Denmark under the title *Prins Faisal's Ring*. ISBN 0-525-47146-4. 373 p. (12 up). Novel.

On both the high seas and colonial plantations fo the Caribbean, the adventures of Tom O'Connor spin out in bold humor, grandiose schemes, and incredulous coincidences. The language is colorful, if sometimes crude, but the author makes his point effectively; slavery is brutal, immoral, and unacceptable, even to his 17th-century hero (a hero who leads with his heart and bonds deeply with the black prince of the title). *The author has won the Silas Award from the Danish Academy, the Mildred Batchelder Award in 1994, and twice honorably mentioned by the Hans Christian Andersen Medal Jury. Also an ALA notable book.* *mln*

Related Information

Collections

The National Library of Education contains one of the largest collections of children's literature in Europe. Librarian Vibeke Stybe started the collection in 1954 and today it consists of approximately 80,000 volumes: Danish children's literature, a certain amount of non-Danish (especially Nordic) children's literature, cartoons and children's magazines, Danish and non-Danish scholarly literature, and other literature about children's books and Danish and non-Danish journals. http://www.cfb.dk

Organizations

IBBY Denmark
www.ibby.dk

FINLAND

Jansson, Tove. **Moominvalley in November**. New York: Farrar, Straus and Giroux, 2003. 176 p. (8-12). Novel.

This whimsical fantasy is set in the house of the Moomin family, which is the meeting place for all the familiar characters, yet none of the members of the Finn Family appear in this final book of the series.

SPOTLIGHT ON THE MOOMINTROLLS

Moomintrolls and a cast of fantastic Scandinavian creatures people the thirteen books including eight novels, one collection of short stories, and four picture books about the Moomins. The books were written in Swedish by native Finlander, Tove Jansson (1914–2001). The *Finn Family Moomintroll* was first published in 1948. *The Book about Moomin, Mymble and Little My* won the Selma Lager-loef Medal in 1953. Books about the Moomin family have enjoyed immense popularity and have been translated into thirty-four languages.

"As children's stories, the Moomin novels are funny, and beautifully drawn with strong narratives. But there is also a deeper resonance for adults. Moominland is strongly evocative of real Nordic landscapes, especially the dense forests and tiny coastal archipelagos" (Coward).

Further information about Tove Jansson and the Moomin books may be found at the Moominvalley site that is maintained in five languages by the The Tampere Art Museum in Finland: http://www.tampere.fi/muumi/english/

Moominworld is a theme park located on the island of Kailo and inhabited by the ceatures from the Moominvalley stories. A five story replica of Moominhouse, Groke's hut, and Humulen's House are some of the attractions. http://www.muumimaailma.fi/englanti/puisto.html

Coward, Ros. "Tove Jansson. The Guardian, June 30, 2001.
    http://books.guardian.co.uk/news/articles/0,6109,514869,00.html
Galenet. *Literature Resource Center.* www.galenet.com
Hüriliman, Bettina. **Three Centuries of Children's Books in Europe**. Translated and edited by Brian W. Alderson. Cleveland, OH: World Publishing, 1968.
Silvey, Anita. **Children's Books and Their Creators**. Boston: Houghton Mifflin, 1995.

Additional Resources

IBBY Finland
www.ibbyfinland.fi

FRANCE

Banks, Kate. **The Cat Who Walked across France**. Illustrated by Georg Hallensleben. New York: Frances Foster Books; Farrar Straus and Giroux, 2004. ISBN 0-374-39968-9. 32 p. (5–7). Picture book.

A cat, shipped off to the north of France with his late owner's possessions to an heir, is forgotten and begins the long, arduous journey back to his former home by the edge of the sea. Finally, frail and exhausted, he completes his journey and is happily adopted by the children who now live in the house. This satisfying understated story is accompanied by glorious, richly-colored and applied paintings of French city, towns, and countryside that evoke a strong sense of place. A map of the cat's route is on the back cover, allowing readers to follow the cat's courageous trek. *sg and js*
Author from United States, living in France. Illustrator lives in France.

Banks, Kate. **A Gift from the Sea**. Pictures by Georg Hallensleben. New York: Frances Foster/Farrar, Straus and Giroux, 2001. Originally published in France under the title *Un don de la mer* by Gallimard Jeunesse, 1999. ISBN 0-374-32566-9. 36 p. (4–8). Picture book.

The boy crouched low on the beach and picked up a rock hidden in the cool wet sand. He didn't know that the rock had been spewed from a fiery volcano thousands of years before. The journey of the rock through time is imagined by the boy as he turns the rock over in his hand and studies its etchings and curves. He knows as he holds it in his hands that it is a gift from the sea. Bold acrylic paintings fill each double page spread. *Close Your Eyes* (2002) is another title by the popular author/illustrator team. *djg*

Banks, Kate. **Mama's Coming Home**. Pictures by Tomek Bogacki. New York: Frances Foster/Farrar, Straus and Giroux, 2003. ISBN 0-374-34747-6. 28 p. (3–7). Picture book.

Papa turns the oven on. Ties an apron round his waist. Horns are blaring. Whistles blowing. Mama's coming home. Young readers will delight as they turn each watercolor page to see the activities of Papa and the boys on the left as they prepare dinner and put away their toys and see Mama on the right eagerly hurrying home through the crowds on the subway and, at last, arriving home just in time for dinner. *djg*
Author lives in southern France

Read an interview with Kate Banks at:
http://www.soemadison.wisc.edu/ccbc/authors/experts/banks.asp

Barbero, Maria. **The Bravest Mouse**. Translated by Sibylle Kazeroid. New York: North-South, 2002. First published in France by Éditions Nord-Sud under the title *Stanislas et le grelot*. ISBN 0-7358-1708-1. 28 p. (4–8). Picture book.

Sasha the mouse lived in an old house with his family. He is happy until he realizes that he is different from the other mice—he has a dark circle around one eye. But Sasha is different in another way. He has a brave plan to bell the cat and keep the mice safe from Barnabas the cat. When his plan succeeds all the young mice paint circles around their eyes to be like Sasha, the bravest mouse.   *djg*

Brami, Élisbeth. **Mommy Time!** Illustrated by Anne-Sophie Tschiegg. La Jolla, CA: Kane/Miller, 2002. Originally published under the title *Drôde Maman* by Editions de Seuil, Paris, 2000. ISBN 1-9291-3222-0. 44 p. (4–8). Picture book.

What is Mommy doing while I'm at school? the child wonders. Is she fixing things, washing dishes or having a wild time? Is she kissing Daddy, going for a walk, or reading in the bathroom? Does she know I worry about her, will she forget to pick me up? So many questions, until at last it is Mommy time! Stylized illustrations in mixed media, collage, and paintings add interest to this small format picture book.

Brun-Cosme, Nadine. **No, I Want Daddy!** Illustrated by Michel Backès. New York: Clarion, 2004. Published in France in 2002 as *C'est mon papa!* ISBN 0-618-38157-0. 26 p. (4–7). Picture book.

Anna comes home from school happy and full of plans, but Mama is tired and says no to everything. Anna doesn't understand why mama is cross and it makes her cross too. When Daddy comes home, Anna only wants him to help her cut her meat, or read her bedtime stories. This story told in a simple and straightforward manner, conveys a family dynamic familiar to most households. The heavy black line drawings with acrylic paintings portray the emotions.   *djg*
Author and illustrator live in France

Bujor, Flavia. **The Prophecy of the Stones**. New York: Hyperion, 2004. Translated from the French by Linda Coverdale. Originally published in France as *La prophétie des pierres* by Editions Anne Carrière, 2002. ISBN 0-7868-1835-2. 386 p. (11–14). Novel.

On their fourteenth birthday three girls are each given the stone that matches their name and are told that although they are strangers now, they must fight their enemies together trusting no one. Jade, Opal, and Amber are made to flee the only homes they have known to go on a dangerous journey to the magical land of Fairytale with nothing but their stones for protection to fulfill an ancient prophecy that will save the land from the evil Council of Twelve. In a parallel world, pres-

ent day Paris, Joa is deliriously fighting for her life in a hospital bed. The survival of all involved is dependant upon the success of Jade, Opal, and Amber in Fairytale and the fulfillment of the prophecy. Bujor was only thirteen years old when she began writing this spellbinding fantasy. *kmc*
Author lives in France

Clavel, Bernard. **Castle of Books**. Translated from the French. Illustrated by Yan Nascimbene. San Francisco: Chronicle Books LLC, 2002. Originally published as *Le Château de papier* by Albin Michele Jeunesse in 2001. ISBN 0-8118-3501-4. 30 p. (5–9). Picture book.

Benjamin's house is so filled with books that he decides to use them as blocks for building a castle. As he empties the house and his castle grows, his father is busy writing the perfect poem, now 4,512 verses long. Dissatisfied with it, his father throws it out, only to have some mice nibble away many of the words. As the mice recite the new version, the poem now sounds perfect to both father and son and each wants to learn the other's craft. *ok*
Author from France, lives in Switzerland. His more that 80 books have been translated into many languages. In 1968 he was the winner of the Goncourt prize for his Les Fruit de l'Hiver.

Dahan, Andre. **Squiggle's Tale**. Originally published in French as *Au Jardin du Luxembourg*. San Francisco: Chronicle Books, 2000. ISBN 0-8118-2664-3. (4–7). Picture book.

Squiggle the piglet goes to Paris to spend the summer with his aunt and cousins, Snook and Puddin. He relates his adventures to his parents through a letter. Typical of a child, the letter makes Squiggle sound like the perfectly behaved piglet. The illustrations, oil painting in Impressionist colorations, humorously tell the real story of the mischievous little pigs. For example, when Squiggle says that they barely dipped their toes in the fountain at the park, the artwork shows the piglets sitting on chairs in the large fountain having a gloriously splashy time. A visual delight. *sl*

D'Allance, Mirreille. **Bear's Christmas Star**. Originally published in French. New York: Margaret K. McElderry Books, 2000. ISBN 0-6898-3826-3. (5–7). Picture book.

Little Bear wants to help Papa Bear decorate the Christmas tree, but he is too small and everything he touches turns into a disaster. Brokenhearted, Bear goes to his room. Papa discovers that he alone is not tall enough to place the star atop the tree and garners Little Bear's help. Delighted, he sits on Papa's shoulders and places the star perfectly. Expressive pastel illustrations lend emotion to the story. *sl*

Desmoinaux, Christel. **"Hallo-What?"** New York: Margaret K. McElderry, 2003. Originally published in France in 1998 as *Dis-moi, qu'est-ce que c'est Halloween?* ISBN 0-689-84795-5. 28 p. (4–8). Picture book.

Little Marceline the witch doesn't understand why all the witches are gathering pumpkins and don't have time to talk to her until Grandma witch pulls her onto her lap and explains the Halloween customs. Bright watercolor illustrations add humor to the story.   *djg*
Author lives in France

Desmoinaux, Christel. **Mrs. Hen's Big Surprise**. New York: Margaret K. MeElderry Books. First published in 1998 by Hachette Livre, S.A., Paris. ISBN 0-689-83403-9. 32 p. (4–8). Picture book.

Mrs. Hen is in for a surprise when the giant polka-dotted egg she brings home begins to hatch. All the barnyard animals have been talking behind her back, but they are amazed when a reptile emerges from the cracked shell and Mrs. Hen begins to live the life about which she has always dreamed.   *djg*
Author lives in France, this is her first book to be published in United States

Dieterlé, Nathalie. **I Am the King!** Translated from the French. New York: Orchard, 2001. First published in Franch in 1999 by Kaléidosciope under the title *C'est Moi le Roi!* ISBN 0-531-30324-1. 28 p. (4–8). Picture book.

One day Little Louis's mom gave him a beautiful golden crown. "For my little king!" Little Louis proudly goes to his room to practice making proclamations. The little king quickly becomes a little tyrant and nobody wants a king like that. So the little king decides he won't be a king—he'll be a big bad wolf!   *djg*
Author from Ghana, lives in Paris

Doray, Malika. **One More Wednesday**. Translated from the French by Suzanne Freeman. Illustrated by the author. New York: Greenwillow, 2001. ISBN 0-06-029590-2. (4–6). Picture book.

A young rabbit loves his Granny and the special times they spend together each Wednesday. When Granny dies, he is devastated. He does not understand her death or the funeral, and asks his Mama about what happened. Questions about an afterlife or returning to the earth in some other form are mentioned, but not answered. However, Mama lets him know, "In some way she'll always be here because you love her so much." Simple black-line illustrations with touches of a single color are just the right touch for this simple story that is perfect for those who try to answer questions about death and grief.   *mw and ls*
Author from France

Eduar, Gilles. **Gigi and Zachary's around-the-World Adventure**: A Seek-and-Find Game. Translated from the French. San Francisco: Chronicle Books, 2003. ISBN 0-8118-3909-5. 56 p. (7–10).

Travel the world with a giraffe and zebra from Australia to Alaska, Chicago to China, and points beyond. The double-page spreads rendered in gouache on craft

paper are visual seek-and-find illustrations of the vocabulary words listed at the bottom of the page. A line of text on the left identifies the location. Humor and detail abide with the appended page-bypage identification charts. Maps on the endpapers indicate the route taken. *sl*
Author owns a design studio in Brazil

Gavalda, Anna. **95 Pounds of Hope**. Translation by Gill Rosner. New York: Viking, 2003. First published in France by Bayard Éditions Jeunesse, 2002. ISBN 0-670-03672-2. 90 p. (10 up). Novel.

Gregory hates school and every day has been a struggle. He has been left back twice and now at thirteen things couldn't be worse. Grandpa Leon has always been the one to stand up for him, but even he seems to abandon Gregory. And to make matters worse his parents decide to send him to boarding school. But maybe this fresh start is just what Gregory needs. In his admission letter to the school he confesses that he is small for his age, just 95 pounds . . . 95 pounds of hope. A remarkable and inspirational story. *djg*

Gay, Michel. **Zee Is Not Scared**. Illustrated by the author. Translated by Marie Mianowski from the French. New York: Clarion Books, 2004. Originally published in France under the titles *Zou n'a pas peur*. ISBN 0-618-43931. (4–7).

Zee is back in this sequel to *Zee* (2003). This time he is furious that his parents can watch a scary movie, but he is not allowed, Zee decides to don a bed sheet and sneak up on his parents. His ghostly trick works, and is predictable enough to entertain preschoolers and kindergartners especially when roles are reversed and Zee promises to keep his parents safe through the night. Simple line drawings with gray-beige wash evoke just the right amount of spooky ambience for the young set. The characters' movement and emotions are portrayed through their body language and facial expressions. Ample white space around the borders balances the subdued palette. *sl*

Gutman, Anne. **Gaspard and Lisa at the Museum**. Illustrated by Georg Hallensleben. New York: A. Knopf, 2001. Originally published as *Gaspard et Lisa au musee* by Hacette Jeunesse in 1999. ISBN 0-375-81117-6. 32 p. (5–8). Picture book.

On a class trip to the museum, Gaspard and Lisa's teacher cautions them to stay out of trouble. Gaspard and Lisa enjoy looking as the exhibits. Then they get a clever idea to trick their classmates. Lisa and Gaspard pose as part of an exhibit. They enjoy tricking their friends but they do not enjoy being locked in the museum. Much to everyone's relief, Gaspard and Lisa are found. Everyone is happy to be reunited. Thick lined paintings in vibrant acrylic colors illustrate the little dogs' misadventures that continue in the entertaining series "The Misadventures of Gaspard and Lisa" *Gaspard In The Hospital* (2001), *Gaspard On Vacation*

(2001), *Gaspard At The Seashore* (2002*), Gaspard and Lisa's Rainy Day* (2003), and *Gaspard and Lisa, Friends Forever* (2003). *ls*
Author from France

Gutman, Anne. **Lisa's Airplane Trip**. Illustrated by Georg Hallensleben. New York: A. Knopf, 2001. Originally published as *Lisa Prend L'Avion* by Hacette Jeunesse in 1999. ISBN 0-375-81114-1. 32 p. (5–8). Picture book.

Lisa, a little white rabbit-eared dog with a red bow, is taking her first airplane trip alone from Paris to New York. Lisa finds it difficult to sit still and when the movie is playing, Lisa finds a creative solution to watch it. Disaster ensues when Lisa spills orange juice all over herself. The flight attendant gives her a bath with nice smelling soap. When Lisa arrives in New York, she is met by her uncle and they both call Lisa's parents to tell them that Lisa arrived safely. Delightful story with rich, attractive illustrations will be a favorite with children and especially useful helping children who are going on their first plane ride. In the sequel, *Lisa in New York* (2000), she visits her uncle and sees the sights. *ls*
Author from France

Ichikawa, Satomi. **The First Bear in Africa!** New York: Philomel Books, 2001. First published in France by l'ecole des loisirs, Paris. ISBN 0-399-23485-3. 32 p. Picture book.

Meto lives with her family and their animals in a very small village in the middle of the African savanna. One morning a motorcar arrives with tourists who come to take pictures and the little girl leaves behind an unusual stuffed animal. Meto races through the countryside past the animals of the savanna and at last catches up to the visitors and returns the little girl's toy bear, the first bear in Africa. Five Swahili words are appended in a glossary.
Author from Japan and has lived in Paris for over thirty years.

Ichikawa, Satomi. **La La Rose**. New York: Philomel, 2004. ISBN 0-399-24029-2. unpaged. (4–7). Picture book.

La La Rose, a pink stuffed rabbit is the favorite toy of Clementine, a young French girl. While on a grand outing in the beautiful Luxembourg Gardens they inadvertently become separated, and the rabbit careens through a series of misadventures and rescues until she is finally reunited with Clementine. Charming watercolor paintings focus on the rabbit's odyssey, but also provide a memorable tour of the beauty of one of Paris's most famous parks.
Author from Japan and has lived in Paris for over 30 years.

Ichikawa, Satomi. **My Pig Amarillo**. New York: Philomel Books, 2003. First published in France as *Mon Cochon Amarillo* in 2002 by l'école des loisirs, Paris. ISBN 0-399-23768-2. 32 p. (3–5). Picture book.

Pablito, a Guatemalan boy, is excited when Grandpa arrives home with a pet pig on a leash. He builds a hut for him and names the pig Amarillo because of his color. But one day, Pablito arrives home from school to find his pet missing. Searching his neighborhood for days, it becomes evident that the pig will not be coming back. Grandpa wisely helps his grandson adjust to the loss. *djg*
Author lives in Paris, France

Judes, Marie-Odile. **Max, the Stubborn Little Wolf**. Translated by Joan Robins. Illustrated by Martine Bourre. New York: HarperCollins, 2001. Originally published in French as *Maxime Loupiot* by Flammarion, 1996. ISBN 0-06-029417-5. 32 p. (4–7). Picture book.
When Max the Wolf tells his father that he wants to be a florist, his father furiously twitches his tail and cries, "Wolf fathers and sons are hunters." Max stubbornly stands his ground, and though father insists that Max will hunt or "he will eat his hat," he does not become a hunter. Poor father wolf keeps his word while Max enjoys the smell of flowers. *djg*
Author lives in France

Kositsky, Lynne. **The Thought of High Windows**. Toronto: Kids Can Press, 2004. ISBN 1-55337-621-8. 175 p. (12 up). Novel.
See Canada for description.

Leonard, Marie. **Tibili, the Little Boy Who Didn't Want to Go to School**. Illustrated by Andree Prigent. La Jolla, CA: Kane/Miller Book Publishers, 2002. Originally published as *Tibili, le petit garcon qui ne voulait pas aller a l'ecole* by Editions Magnard in 1996. ISBN 1-929132-20-4. 32 p. (4–6). Picture book.
Tibili does not want to go to school because he thinks it will be boring. He would rather read the signs in the sky like his grandfather, so he asks the animals for advice. When he asks the spider how he can avoid going to school, the spider tells him to look for the box of knowledge. After digging up the box, Tibili discovers he needs to read the instructions on the bottom of the box. He does not know how to read. Now, Tibili is anxious to go to school. Bright, naive illustrations using African motifs bring this story to life. *ls*
Author from France

Le Rochais, Marie-Ange. **Desert Trek: An Eye-Opening Journey through the World's Driest Places**. Translated from the French by George L. Newman. New York: Walker & Company, 2001. Originally published in France in 1999 under the title *Vide, le Désert*. ISBN 0-8027-8765-7. 38 p. (6–12). Informational book.
People often think of the desert as a vast wasteland, not so, as aptly demonstrated in this beautiful picture book. The journey takes the reader to deserts on all the continents and shows the rich cultures and ecology of these arid places.

Herders in Ethiopia, hunters in the Kalahari, nomads in the Sahara are painted in fine detail. Front endpapers are illustrated with animals and insects and the backs contain illustrations of paintings found in dried clay and rock. A map and end-notes identify the location of each desert.   *djg*

L'Homme, Erik. **Quadehar the Sorcerer**. Translation of *Quadehar le sorcier.* Il-lustrated by David Wyatt. New York: Scholastic, 2003. Originally published by Chicken House in 2003. ISBN 0-439-53643-X. 275 p. (12 up). Novel.

Twelve-year-old Robin Penmarch lives a happy normal life with his four friends on the Lost Isle. When a fight breaks out at his Uncle Urian's birthday cel-ebration, Quadehar the sorcerer breaks it up. Robin's proximity to the powerful magic awakens the magic he possesses. Robin becomes an apprentice sorcerer. With his four friends he embarks on a journey to the Uncertain World that is in-habited by bizarre creatures to rescue Agatha Balangru, a girl who has been bul-lying Robin.   *ls*
Author from France

Lisle, Janet Taylor. **Siren and Spies**. New York: Bradbury Press, 1985. ISBN 0-02-759150-6. 169 p. (10–14). Novel.

No one in the large, chaotic Potter household can understand why independent Elsie has turned against her beloved violin teacher, Miss Fitch. Elsie's less tal-ented but kinder older sister Mary refuses to believe Elsie's claim that Miss Fitch is an "old fraud," and is shocked by Elsie's refusal to visit Miss Fitch in the hos-pital after the elderly teacher is assaulted in her own home. In a moment of con-fidence that has become rare between the estranged sisters, Elsie shows Mary a photograph in a book of Nazi collaborators in France—a picture that includes a young Miss Fitch. When the girls confront their teacher about the photo, Miss Fitch's story about her tragic love affair with a German soldier in Nazi-occupied France makes the sisters question their ability to judge.   *aao*
Author lives in United States

Luciani, Brigitte. **Those Messy Hempels**. Illustrated by Vanessa Hié. New York: North-South Books, 2004. Translated by J. Alison James. Originally published in Gossau Zurich, Switzerland as *Die Hempels räumen auf* by Michael Neugebauer Verlag, an imprint of Nord-Süd Verlag AG, 2004. ISBN 0-7358-1910-6. 32 p. (4–6). Picture book.

The Hempel family wants to bake a cake, but they are unable to find the whisk because their kitchen is in such disarray. They find a pillow that belongs in the bedroom and that room is as messy as the kitchen so they decide to clean the bed-room where they find an object that belongs in yet another room. This pattern continues until the house and the yard are completely cleaned up and the Hempels are finally ready to make their cake. Children will enjoy searching for the out-of-

place items in the colorful collage illustrations and naming the proper room for each object before turning the page. *kmc*
Author and Illustrator live in France

Magnier, Thierry. **Isabelle and the Angel**. Illustrated by Georg Hallensleben. English text by Kristine Brogno. San Francisco: Chronicle Books, 2000. Originally published in France as *Solange et l'ange* by Éditions Gallimard Jeunesse, 1997. ISBN 0-8118-2526-4. 32 p. (4–6). Picture book.

Isabelle the pig lives alone and is bored. She loves to eat and to paint with pink cake and strawberry jam. Her favorite place to visit every day is the museum where the little Angel lives in Isabelle's favorite painting. One day the Angel, who resembles Cupid, speaks to her and Isabelle finds what she was longing for: a friend. Since her new friend is unable to leave the museum, Isabelle finds a reason to be near the Angel everyday. The heavy brush strokes and solid lines give strong expression to Isabelle in this slight but fanciful story. *kmc*

Morgenstern, Susie. **A Book of Coupons**. Translated by Gill Rosner. Illustrated by Serge Bloch. New York: Viking, 2001. Originally published as *The Joker* by l'école des loisirs, 1999. ISBN 0-670-89970-4. 62 p. (8–12). Novel.

Hubert Noel gives each student in his class a gift, a book of coupons. The extraordinary coupons can be used for a variety of activities including losing your homework, clowning around, and eating in class. However, Madame Incarnation Perez, the principal, takes an extremely dim view of Monsieur Noel's teaching methods and forces him into retirement. A poignant and amusing story of an unconventional teacher whose lessons impart a love of learning and living. *2002 Mildred Batchelder Honor. ls*

Morgenstern, Susie. **Princesses Are People, Too: Two Modern Fairy Tales**. Translated by Bill May. Illustrated by Serge Bloch. New York: Viking, 2002. Originally published as *Même les princesses doivent aller à l'école,* 1991, and *Un jour mon prince grattera*, 1992, by l'école des loisirs. ISBN 0-670-03567-X. 52 p. (8–12). Novel.

Two delightful stories, *Even Princesses Have to Go to School* and *Someday My Prince Will Scratch*, suggest that the storybook life of a princess is really quite tedious. After a very bored Princess Yona follows a group of children one morning, she is informed that "even princesses have to go to school." This revelation propels Yona to cast aside the storybook expectations of a princess's life and immerse herself into everyday reality. In the second story, Princess Emma decides that she has no interest in the perfect storybook prince. Emma sets her own standards. She will know her prince when he scratches the itch in her back in just the right way. Both stories are enhanced with whimsical line drawings. *js*
Author from New Jersey, lives in France

SUSIE MORGENSTERN IN TRANSLATION
BY JILL DAVIS

Do French kids know that their favorite author, Susie Morgenstern, is American? They must. After all, her name is not *Francoise* or *Genevieve*—it's *Susie*. What could be more American? And what about Susie's American readers? They must know that Susie lives in France since her characters are often called Madame or Monsieur and they live in Paris or in other French towns . . . and eat croissants.

In the world of translations in children's literature, Morgenstern is somewhat unique. Born American, she began her writing career in France after she became a mother of two daughters. Susie writes in French, and is then translated into English by a British translator. The translator is a close friend and collaborator, Gill Rosner, about whom Susie has said: "She makes me sound like Shakespeare." And as far as explaining why she needs to be translated back into her native language, Susie said: "My editor told me never to translate myself. He said I'm lousy at it."

I have explained this scenario to a lot of Susie's fans, and to them it seems surprising that Susie cannot translate herself back into American English. But the truth is that Susie *can* translate herself, if she wants to. But I suspect that when she reads herself translated with the elegant vocabulary of her British colleague, Gill, she sees her writing turn into something perhaps more elevated than she could have imagined herself doing. And she loves it.

As for the journey of a Morgenstern book, the translation makes its way to New York from Nice, and that's when I begin the process of taking some of the French concepts and British expressions and changing them into ones I think American kids will understand. Susie gets a new version from me, makes the changes she wants made, and then only after Viking copyeditor, Janet Pascal, makes her opinions known, voila! We have another international hybrid. . . .

Here is one example of what I have described: *A Book of Coupons*, originally called *Joker* in France was based on the jokers (or wild cards) in card games. I chose "coupons" because this is how I thought Susie really meant to describe something that gives the recipient something for free. I didn't see how "joker" could work. So changes were made accordingly, and what follows is a sentence from Gill's translation where the word joker was originally used: *"Don't tell me we're going to spend the year playing cards," cried Barbara, thinking of her grandpa who spent his life in front of a card table.* And here is the U.S. version after we decided to substitute "joker" with "coupon": *"Don't tell me we're going to spend the year tearing out coupons," cried Benedicte, thinking of her grandpa who spent his life sticking in green stamps.* The irony here is that Susie took the concept of the joker in an American card deck and put it into a French story. And without interpretation, it didn't quite translate. Translation is a serious group effort, especially if children are going to benefit from, understand, and enjoy the end result.

Morgenstern, Susie. **Sixth Grade**. Translated by Gill Rosner. New York: Viking, 2004. ISBN 0-670-03680-3. 137 p. (9–12). Novel.

Margo Melo finally receives the letter notifying her that she has been accepted to Pine Tree Junior High and anxiously begins preparing for sixth grade. Although disappointed when she is placed in a class without any of her old friends, she is determined to be a conscientious student and volunteers to be the class representative. However, her attempts to motivate and organize her classmates are greeted with apathy and disdain. Even the class trip to Rome is a disappointment. Although sixth grade is not what she expected, she manages to maneuver successfully, and humorously, through the difficult transition between elementary school and junior high. *kk*
Author from United States, lives in southern France

Morgenstern, Susie. **3 Days Off**. Translated by Gill Rosner. New York: Viking, 2001. Originally published as *Trois Jours Sans* by L'École des Loisirs in 1998. ISBN 0-670-03511-4. 89 p. (14 up). Novel.

Good-looking, fifteen-year-old William apathetically shuffles through his daily routine until, one day, when his young, dedicated, but frustrated teacher demands that he reveal what is on his mind, he shocks even himself with his response. His inappropriate comment earns him a three-day suspension. As he wanders through the suburbs of his Northern France community for three days, he encounters an unemployed American, two older laborers, and a female art history student and begins to realize that "Life is worth the effort." This short, humorous book gives the reader a glimpse into the reality of a teenager who struggles with the abandonment of his father, the fatigue and sadness of his mother, his own awakening sexuality, and the importance of an education. *kk*
Author from United States, lives in southern France

Mosher, Richard. **Zazoo**. New York: Clarion, 2001. ISBN 0-6181-3534-0. 248 p. (12 up). Novel.

Thirteen-year-old Vietnamese Zazoo, adopted at the age of two, lives with Grand-Pierre on the bank of a French canal, where they work as lockkeepers. When she meets a young man who asks questions she cannot answer, she realizes how much she does not know about the man who has raised her. This lyrical story, rich in imagery, portrays a loving, if changing, relationship between father and daughter. *Notable Books for a Global Society, 2002; Society of School Librarians International Book Awards; Best Books for Young Adults, 2002 Top Ten.* *djg*

Norac, Carl. **Hello, Sweetie Pie**. Illustrated by Claude K. Dubois. Originally published in French. New York: A Doubleday Book for Young Readers, 2000. ISBN 0-3853-2733-1. (3–6). Picture book.

Lola the hamster is teased about her family nicknames, "babycake, sweetie pie, and fairy princess," by her friend Lulu and classmates. Crushed and angry, Lola surveys adults on the walk home about their childhood nicknames. Lulu apologizes the next day, and the two friends realize that family nicknames can be used by anyone. The ups and downs of friendship and lightning-quick emotional redirection of the very young are well portrayed. Watercolor illustrations, full of action and emotion, lend strength to the identifiable story.   *sl*

Pennac, Daniel. **Dog**. Translated by Sarah Adams. Illustrated by Britta Teckentrup. Cambridge: Candlewick Press, 2004. Originally published as *Cabot Caboche* by Editions Nathan in 1982. ISBN 0-7636-2421-7. 181 p. (10 up). Novel.

Dog is an ugly, scruffy stray puppy that survives being drowned to eventually becoming the pet of a fickle, demanding girl. Dog's life is a series of misadventures: learning survival skills in the city dump, roaming the city, getting caught by the dog catcher and rescued in the eleventh hour by the little girl, whom Dog calls Plum. When Plum loses interest in Dog, he runs away from his miserable existence in a city apartment. Dog meets another dog, named Hyena who completes Dog's survival training and introduces Dog to some very special feline friends. When Dog meets Plum again, he makes sure that Plum wants him back. Life with Plum is very good but her parents scheme to get rid of Dog on their vacation. Dog foils their plans and with the help of his friends, Dog makes a definite place for himself in Plum's life. A great story full of humor and tension.   *ls*
Author from France

Pennac, Daniel. **Eye of the Wolf**. Translated by Sarah Adams. Illustrated by Max Grafe. Cambridge: Candlewick Press, 2002. Originally published by Editions Nathan in 1982. ISBN 0-7636-1896-9. 111 p. (10 up). Novel.

A one-eyed Alaskan wolf pacing in his cage at the zoo makes eye contact with a boy who is staring into his cage. Through their eyes, the wolf and the boy exchange the stories of their lives and how they came to be at the zoo. A quick-paced, unusual story concerning the fellowship between living things. *Marsh Award for Children's Literature in Translation, 2005*; *Choices, 2004*.   *ls*
Author from France

Pietri, Annie. **The Orange Trees of Versailles**. Translated by Catherine Temerson. New York: Delacorte Press, 2004. First published as *Orangers de Versailles* by Bayard Editions Jeunesse in 2000. ISBN 0-385-73103-5. 137 p. (9–12). Novel.

Marion Dutilleul, 14-year-old daughter of the gardener at Versailles during the reign of the King Louis XIV, is sent to be a servant to the king's favorite mistress Marquise de Montespan. Marion has a special gift for identifying scents and making perfumes, which is noticed by the marquise, and Marion is put to work mak-

ing exotic perfumes with the credit going to someone else when the scents are admired. While spending long nights catering to the marquise, Marion opens her eyes as well as her nose and learns of mystery, intrigue, and a plot to murder the Queen. When her high-quality sense of smell alerts others to the danger and ultimately saves the King and Queen, Marion is given a new post in the King's court: perfumer to the Queen. An author's note discussing the history of perfumes, the profession of a "Nose" in seventeenth-century France, and perfume manufacturing today give this story historical context. *kmc*
Author lives in France

Ponti, Claude. **DeZert Isle**. Translated by Mary Martin Holliday. Boston: Godine, 2003. Originally published in France by LEcole des loisirs, 1999. ISBN 1-56792-237-6. 64 p. (7–10). Picture book.

Jules is a Zert who lives on Zert Isle. This comic-style cartoon land is peopled with his best friend Ned the Nail and other unusual characters. They must be on guard against their enemy, SledgeHead, who loves to hammer the nails into the ground and the Big Mouth who lies in wait ready to swallow them up. Jules, a cube, loves to play with the other cubes Pyth and Goras. Simple chapters tell of the adventures of these imaginative creatures. *djg*
Author from France

Sanvoisin, Éric. **Little Red Ink Drinker**. Translated by Georges Moroz. Illustrations by Martin Matje. New York: Delacorte Press, 2003. Originally published by Les Éditions Nathan, Paris, 2002. ISBN 0-385-72967-7. 40 p. (7–10). Transitional book.

The Ink Drinkers are back in this companion book to *A Straw for Two* and *The City of Ink Drinkers*. In this tasty little book Carmilla and Odilon decide to turn their straws to the tale of Little Red Riding Hood. The are vigorously sipping down the words when suddenly, à la Alice in Wonderland, they are sipped right into the story. Odilon tries to resist the temptations to wolf down his girlfriend Carmilla, but just in the nick of time, Uncle Draculink, in disguise as Grandma, helps them modify the story and return to "normal." *djg*

Sauerwein, Leigh. **Song for Eloise**. Asheville: Front Street, 2003. ISBN 1-886910-90-1. 133 p. (15 up). Novel.

Fifteen-year-old Eloise's joyful childhood ends when she is married to a gruff man who is her father's best friend and is twice her age. Eloise moves away from her home and familiar surroundings to her husband's mountain castle. She endures her married state performing her duties but finding no joy in her lonely, restricted life. In an effort to cheer his wife, Robert de Rochefort has a troubadour come to the castle to entertain Eloise. The troubadour turns out to be a former kitchen boy whom Eloise knew in her childhood. An illicit romance ensues with

Eloise sneaking off to the woods for trysts with the troubadour. Eloise's life takes a sudden turn when her husband is killed. She goes on a pilgrimage to the Holy Land and then retires to a convent. A sad tale recounting how a woman is seen merely as a pawn in alliances and power.   *ls*
Author from France

Schoch, Irene. **The Cat's Vacation**. San Francisco: Chronicle Books, 2004. Originally published as *Hotel d'Ete* by Editions de Seuil in 2003. ISBN 2-02-061884-2. 32 p. (4–8). Picture book.

When the family is away, the cat will play. He invites several friends to spend their vacation with him—the crocodiles, the penguins, the tigers, and his best friend, moose. Together they enjoy sunbathing, singing songs, eating ice cream, and playing board games. A festive cookout on the last evening sets the friends off on their homeward journeys. Then moose and cat must clean up the house before the family returns. A bright palette and busy patterns warm up the stylized illustrations. The whole feeling of the book is very French. Children will enjoy the antics of animals alone without supervision.   *ls*
Author from France

Sfar, Joann. **Little Vampire Does Kung Fu**. Translated by Mark and Alexis Siegel. Colors by Walter. New York: Simon & Schuster, 2003. ISBN 0689857691. Originally published in France in 2000 as *Petit Vampire fait du Kung-Fu!* by Guy Delcourt Productions. 32 p. (10–14). Graphic Novel.

Michael is distraught when a gang of bullies humiliate him in front of his friend Sabrina and he tells Grandfather he wants to kill them. Grandps tells him it's never right to fight, but when Gramps leaves, a cast of ghouls take him to a Rabbi/Kung Fu master so he can learn to fight. He learns a variety of fighting methods, including how to use the nunchaku, but too late, the monsters have eaten Jeffrey. What to do? The monsters spit him up and sew him back together. The comic book style of illustration with dialogue of "Hi-Ya!" "Bop," "Bonk," and "Ouch" are fitting for the gruesome, tongue-in-cheek humor. *Little Vampire Goes to School* (2003) was an IRA Children's Choices winner in 2004.   *djg*

Skurzynski, Gloria. **Spider's Voice**. New York: Atheneum, 1999. ISBN 0-689-82149-2. 234 p. (12 up). Novel.

The story of lovers Eloise and Abelard from twelfth-century France is told from the viewpoint of Aran, a young mute boy, nicknamed Spider. Rescued from his fate as a freak, he had been encased in a carapace designed to make his legs and arms grow long by Abelard. Spider serves him and is witness to the happenings in the life of this famous philosopher and teacher. He learns to read and eventually to speak and is the person designated to deliver letters between

Abelard and Eloise. Life in medieval France is presented through Aran's eyes, as is the famous romance.
Author from United States

Stock, Catherine. **A Spree in Paree**. New York: Holiday House, 2004. ISBN 0-8234-1720-4. 32 p. (4–9). Picture book.

Farmer Monmouton and his animals need a change of scene. They leave their quiet farm in the French countryside for the beauty and excitement of Paris. Farmer Monmouton and the livestock see the sights—a cruise on the Seine, a visit to the Louvre, and climbing the steps of the Eiffel Tower. When they return to the farm, Farmer Monmouton vows "Never again," while his animals have other ideas. A wonderful glimpse of French life, countryside and city, that is sure to entertain young travelers. *ls and jig*
Author from United States

Stolz, Joëlle. **The Shadows of Ghadames**. Translated from the French by Catherine Temerson. New York: Delacorte Press, 2004. Originally published in France as *Les Ombres de Ghadamès* in 1999 by Bayard Editions Jeunesse. ISBN 0-385-73104-3. 119 p. (10 up). Novel.

Eleven-year-old Malika resents the restrictions placed upon her by her father in the 19th-century Libyan city of Ghadames. But when he leaves on a trading trip, she begins to discover the strength and learn the secrets of the women's community. Slowly, as she is introduced to the world of the rooftops, and with the help of strong women, she is able to satisfy her desires to learn and grow within the avenues available to her. She learns of powers the women posses, if in the shadows. *2005 Mildred Batchelder Award.*

Taravant, Jacques. **The Little Wing Giver**. Translated from the French by Nina Ignatowicz. Illustrated by Peter Sis. New York: Holt, 2001. ISBN 0-8050-6412-5. (2–6).

A simple child's story of how perhaps God decided to have angels. Taravant, a French diplomat, wrote the story for his son's sixth birthday. Little Wing Giver is giving out wings to all of the birds, butterflies, and windmills, expecting nothing in return. When he grows tired, he falls asleep and a storm takes all of his remaining wings. Little Wing Giver goes back to sleep never to awaken until those that he has given wings to come to his rescue. Sis's use of a palette of soft tones and gentle lines are a perfect match to this story that you will want to share with young children. *mw*

Teyssèdre, Fabienne. **Joseph Wants to Read**. Illustrated by the author. New York: Dutton Children's Books, 2001. Originally published in France by Éditions Albin Michel Jeunesse in 2001. ISBN 0-525-46692-4. 32 p. (3–8). Picture book.

The School of the Tropics is about to adjourn for the summer, but monkey pupil Joseph wants to learn more about how to read. His teacher comes up with an idea to help him practice during vacation. All the animals will wear a letter so that Joseph will learn to associate the letters with the sounds they make: E for egret, G for gorilla, etc. Joseph and his lettered friends play together and master the alphabet by the end of the summer. The author's vibrant illustrations also teach animal recognition and display a colorful habitat for young listeners to explore.   *cd*
Author/illustrator from France

Vaugelade, Anaïs. **The War**. Translated by Marie-Christine Rouffiac and Tom Streissguth. Minneapolis, MN: Carolrhoda, 2001. Originally published by l'école des loisirs under the title *La Guerre*. ISBN 1-57505-562-7. 32 p. (5–10). Picture book.

The Reds and the Blues were at war and the war had lasted for so long that no one could remember why it had started. With only eighty men left the kings realize they can no longer continue the war. Prince Julius of the Reds challenges Prince Fabien to a duel to settle the war, but Fabien is not a warrior and his apathy results in a tragedy that enrages the kings. Fabien is forced into exile. Ah, but he is clever and becomes wise enough to find a way to end the war. Bold watercolors illustrate this fable that has been translated into six languages.   *djg*
Author lives in Paris

Weil, Sylvie. **My Guardian Angel**. Translated by Gillian Rosner. New York: Arthur A. Levine Books/Scholastic, 2004. Originally published in France in 2001 by L'école des loisirs, Scholastic and the Lantern Logo. ISBN 0-439-57681-4. 203 p. (10–14). Novel.

Elvina, age twelve, is the feisty granddaughter of the great teacher Solomon ben Isaac and lives in Troyes, 1096, at a time when the Crusaders, led by Peter the Hermit are moving through the town on their way to the Holy Land. Told in the first person, as Elvina confides in her guardian angel, we learn that this outspoken young lady, taught to read and write, helps a wounded Crusader and later smuggles food to a young runaway soldier. These bold actions seemingly put her community at risk, for it is not uncommon for the Crusaders to break down doors and burn down the houses of Jews. This story of compassion and tolerance is told in a witty, fresh voice and the message is Winner of the *Prix Sorcières*.   *djg*

Wellington, Monica. **Crepes by Suzette**. New York: Dutton, 2004. ISBN 0-525-46934-6. 32 p. (5–7). Picture book.

Readers get a fun tour of Paris as they accompany Suzette selling her crepes from a cart at stops all over the city. Clever mixed-media collages of marker and colored pencil artwork superimposed on artfully arranged color photographs are enhanced with decorations such as postcards, tickets, and wrappers. A map of

Suzette's stops, as well as a crepe recipe and a glossary add to the French feel. Suzette's customers are based on artworks by French artists that are also described in the end matter. *sg*
Author from United States

Related Information

Awards

Prix Sorcières

IBBY France
www.lajoieparleslivres.com

Ricochet—Centre International/d'Etudesen Litterature de Jeunesse/ Inter-national Center of Studies in Youth Literature (Charleville-Mezieres, Ardennes-France)
The site, available in French, German, and English, offers the reader a series of identification sheets about books, authors, illustrators, and film adaptations of children's and young people's literature. It provides comments and links to authors' works and to some excerpts of the original writing. It also provides a nationality index.

GERMANY

Bauer, Jutta. **Selma**. La Jolla, CA: Kane/Miller, 2003. Original title: *Selma*. Published by Verlag GmbH, D-26121 Oldenburg, Germany. ISBN 1-929132-50-6. 50 p. (5–8). Picture book.
When the old ram is asked the question, "what is happiness?" he tells the tale of Selma, who is content with her life of eating a little grass, playing with her children in the morning, exercising in the afternoon, eating some more grass, and chatting with Mrs. Miller. What would she do if she won a million dollars? She would eat a little grass . . . *djg*

Chotjewitz, David. **Daniel Half Human and the Good Nazi**. Translated by Doris Orgel. New York: Richard Jackson/Atheneum, 2004. ISBN 0-689-85747-0. First published in Germany under the title *Daniel Halber Mensch* by Carlsen Verlag, 2000. 298 p. (12 up). Novel.
Daniel returns to the German town in which he was raised after World War II and remembers his adolescent years growing up during the pre-Hitler years. School days were filled with soccer, challenging academics, and pranks with his best friend Armin. Like many of his peers, he is swept up in the frenzy to join the HJ and it is in preparing his family tree that he learns that his mother is Jewish

ABOUT TRANSLATING CHILDREN'S BOOKS BY DORIS ORGEL

A lucky thing happened for English-speaking children back in 1823: The first translation of Grimm tales into English appeared. The translator was Edgar Taylor. His breakthrough volume consisted of some fifty tales. By choosing them "with the amusement of young friends principally in view," he made Grimm a vibrant part of children's literature in English.

Countless translations and retellings followed. Mine, **The Bremen Town Musicians and Other Animal Tales from Grimm** (as far as I know, the only *animal*-tale collection) is a retelling in that I changed things around a bit to keep the tales as fresh to children now as once upon a time they were to me (but took care to keep the "oldness" in, because that's where the magic lies). It's also a translation in that I worked directly from the German, the language of my childhood. This allowed me to relive my pleasure on first hearing the tales read aloud, and—I hope!—enabled me to render them in English with their fun and wonders undiminished.

Lucky as it was that Grimm came early into English, it's *un*lucky and sad how little access today's English-speaking children have to books from other cultures. Almost everywhere in Europe there's a plentiful supply of young readers' literature from the U.S. and UK; whereas a mere handful of foreign books get translated and published over here.

One explanation, that kids here just aren't interested or don't care about what happens someplace far away, is effectively refuted when a novel like David Chotjewitz's **Daniel Half Human and the Good Nazi** (Batchelder Honor, Sydney Taylor Honor, ALA Notable) comes along. It grabs you by the collar (by "you" I mean young readers, older ones, too), and makes indifference not an option. It transplants you into Hamburg, Germany, a place you might never have heard of. But you get to know it, neighborhood by neighborhood. It feels as though you're living there, through the Nazi years, then trudging through the rubble, all that's left of this once bustling city when Daniel returns to it in 1945.

Chotjewitz writes urgently. He pulls you in. You can't *not* care when Daniel finds out that he's half Jewish, therefore scum in Nazi eyes; or when Armin, member of the Hitler Youth, sticks by Daniel out of friendship; or when this Aryan boy imperils his future in the Reich by loving Miriam who's wholly Jewish; or when Miriam risks her life by loving Armin back. Everything that happens in this book feels like it's happening to you.

Average U.S. teenagers know little about Hitler's rise to power, life under Nazi rule, and what World War II was about. **Daniel Half Human**, which I'm happy I translated, not only tells a riveting story, it brings these subjects more alive than cursory high-school history can, and makes readers recognize their relevance to our here-and-now.

and that he, in the eyes of the Ayran's, is half human. Daniel's father refuses to acknowledge their new status and he clings to the strength of his war record in WWI to save his family from the inevitable tragedy. The reader is overwhelmed with the increasing intensity of the chilling events of Crystal Night and the persecution of the Jews that are powerfully revealed in this compelling narrative. *djg*

Friedrich, Joachim. **4½ Friends and the Secret Cave**. Translated from the German by Elizabeth D. Crawford. New York: Hyperion Books for Children, 2001. Originally *4½ Freunde* by K. Thienemanns Verlag, Stuttgart-Wien., 1992. ISBN 0-7868-0648-6. 154 p. (7–10). Novel.

Steffi, Collin, and Norbert have formed a detective club. They reluctantly let Steffi's twin brother Austin "Radish" into the club when he discovers a cave containing a toy bear, a doll, and treasure map in the woods near their house. The children are off on a treasure hunt when the toys disappear and they find a mysterious coin in their place. Misadventure abounds in this funny story that is followed by another book in the series, *4½ Friends and the Disappearing Bio Teacher. djg*

Funke, Cornelia. **Dragon Rider**. Translated by Anthea Bell. Illustrations by author. New York: Scholastic/Chicken House: 2004. Originally published as *Drachenreiter* (Hamburg, Germany) by Cecilie Dressler Verlag in 1997. ISBN 0-439-45695-9. 523 p. (8–12). Novel.

Firedrake and his brownie friend, Sorrel, embark on a quest to find a safe home for the world's remaining dragons. As they journey to the Rim of Heaven, they collect an odd assortment of comrades—a homunculus, an ace-pilot who happens to be a rat, an archeologist, a dracologist, several Buddhist monks, and an orphan who is destined to become the next rider of dragons. Anticipation mounts as this band of companions outwit the horrific dragon-killer, Nettlebrand, and unlock secrets that have lain dormant for centuries. Written with sensitivity and wit. Detailed illustrations introduce each chapter. Award-winning author lives in Germany. *nrn*

Funke, Cornelia. **Inkheart**. Translated by Anthea Bell. Illustrated by Cornelia Funke. New York: Scholastic, Inc. First published as *Tintenherz* by Cecilie Dressler Verlag in 2003 and in the United Kingdom by The Chicken House in 2003. ISBN 0-439-53164-0. 534 p. (9 up). Novel.

Meggie wonders why her father refuses to read aloud until she meets the characters that he unwittingly summoned into the world with his voice. After encountering Capricorn and Dustfinger, Meggie, her aunt, and her father embark on a dangerous quest to change the bizarre tale. Their goals? Find Meggie's mother who is lost in the book and return the treacherous Capricorn and his henchman to their rightful places among the pages. While searching for her mother, Meggie discovers that she, too, has the gift of conjuring life from the written word. Each chapter begins with an excerpt from great literary works with full citations at the book's end. All chapters conclude with an illustration by the author. Cornelia

Funke is a well-known children's author and illustrator in Germany. She has written over 40 books, including award-winning *The Thief Lord*. *ALA Notable Children's Book, 2004.* nrm
Author lives in Hamburg, Germany

Funke, Cornelia. **The Princess Knight**. Translated by Anthea Bell. Illustrated by Kerstin Meyer. New York: Scholastic, 2004. Originally published in Germany by Fischer Taschenbuch Verlag GmbH in 2001. United Kingdom: Chicken House, 2003. ISBN 0-439-53630-8. 32 p. (4–8). Picture book.
Princess Violetta's brothers tease her when she tries to do all the things that young knights do. They laugh and taunt: "Itsy-Bitsy Vi—little girl can't hurt a fly!" Violetta has the last laugh when she secretly masters knightly skills to reign victorious at her father's jousting tournament. Playfully written and delightfully illustrated, this is Funke's first picture book published in the United States. nrn
Award-winning author lives in Hamburg, Germany

Funke, Cornelia. **The Thief Lord**. Translated by Oliver Latsch. New York: Chicken House, 2002. Originally published as *Herr der Diebe* by Hamburg: Cecile Dressler, 2000. ISBN 0-439-40437-1. 349 p. (11 up). Novel.
After running away from their aunt and uncle in Hamburg, Prosper and his brother Bo arrive in Venice and are befriended by a gang of street urchins whose leader calls himself the Thief Lord. When the gang agrees to commit a theft for a great reward, they set in motion a chain of events that will change their lives. This great adventure story involves love, loyalty, and danger. *2000 Zurich Children's Book Award; 2001 Children's Book Award from the Vienna House of Literature; 2003 Mildred Batchelder Award.* ls
Author from Germany

Futterer, Kurt. **Emile**. Translated by Ingrid MacGillis. Illustrated by Ralf Futterer. San Francisco: MacAdam/Cage, 2004. Originally published as *Emile-Ene bunte Katzengeschichte* by Futterer Eigenverlag, Germany, 1999. ISBN 3-00-004438-8. 28 p. (4–8). Picture book.
Once upon a time there lived a snow-white cat named Emile who belonged to a man and a woman. They lived quietly together in a grey environment until Emile's eyes are opened to the colorful world outside his insulated home. He sets out to see the world and finds his way to the studio of a painter, Vincent. Splashed with the colors of the outside world, Emile returns home to open the eyes of his owners. Bold paintings illustrate this book and pay homage to Vincent van Gogh. *Troisdorfer Bilderbuchpreis, 2000, the most prestigious prize for picture books in Germany.* djg

Gebhard, Wilfried. **What Eddie Can Do**. La Jolla, CA: Kane/Miller, 2004. Originally published in Germany under the title *Was Benni alles kann*. ISBN 1-929132-60-3. 28 p. (3–6). Picture book.

Eddie's mother wants to teach him how to tie his shoes, but Eddie has no time. He has to dive down to a sunken ship, discover secrets in a dark cave, travel to outer space, explore the rain forest, tame tigers, and fly with the birds. It is only when he needs to rescue his friend Clara from the double-tailed monster, that he decides to rush back home for a quick lesson in tying. *djg*
Born in Germany, the author has illustrated numerous books for children.

Glitz, Angelika. **A Monster under Alex's Bed**. Illustrated by Imke Sönnichsen. Wilton, CT: Tiger Tales, 2002. First published in Germany in 2000 by K. Thienemanns Verlag, Stuttgart. 28 p. (4–8). Picture book.

When Alex hears strange noises under his bed he calls for Mommy who reassures him that there couldn't possibly be a monster under his bed. In order to reassure her son, she turns on the flashlight and peeks under the bed—what a mess! Tomorrow Alex will have to clean—but what's this . . . two glowing eyes? Alex will have to spend the night in mommy's room after all and tomorrow they will have to catch that-mouse! Large full-color illustrations depict a loving relationship between mother and son. *djg*

Grégoire, Caroline. **Counting with Apollo**. La Jolla, CA: Kane/Miller, 2004. Originally published in 1999 under the title *Apollo, rundrum schön gezählt!* by Baumhaus Buchverlag GmbH, Frankfurt am Main, Germany. ISBN 1-929132-58-1. 28 p. (4–8). Picture book.

Apollo the dachshund is not only adorable, but he is amusing, kind, and clever. He can count to ten by twisting and turning and eating 5 bones, 6 bones, 7 bones, oh no, that's too many and now he demonstrates the colors when he gets sick from eating too many bones. Soon enough he is back to himself and reviews the numbers with his flexible body. Humorous, cartoon style watercolor pictures will make this an enjoyable review for young children. *djg*

Gündisch, Karin. **How I Became an American**. Translated by James Skofield. Chicago: Cricket Books, 2000. First published as *Paradies liegt in Amerika* by Beltz Verlag, 2000. ISBN 0-8126-4875-7. 120 p. (10–12). Novel.

This episodic historical fiction tells of a family's experiences in 1902 Youngstown, Ohio, through the eyes of twelve-year-old Johnny, who is asked by his teacher to record the family's adventures from the time they began to emigrate from Siebenbergen in Romania. Life's vicissitudes are well told from tragedies, such as baby Elissa's death upon the family's arrival in America to light-hearted episodes such as Johnny's being stuck on the dance hall roof where he had been spying on his older sister. *Mildred Batchelder Award.* *jvl*

Hänel, Wolfram. **Weekend with Grandmother**. Translated by Martina Rasdeuschek-Simmons. Illustrated by Christina Unzer. New York: North-South Books, 2002. ISBN 0735816301. Originally published as *Ferien mit Oma* by Nord-Sud Books, in 2002. ISBN 0-7358-1630-1. 62 p. (7–9). Transitional book.

Tony's busy parents never take him to see his grandmother, who lives in another part of the country. Finally, grandmother sends a note that she will be picking up her grandson for a short trip, and what a trip it is in her BMW V-8 classic convertible! This independent, spunky woman shares adventures and quiet times with Tony as they get to know and appreciate each other. After a wonderful weekend, Tony's parents say that next time they will go along too. Lots of white space, expressive illustrations, and a fun story will encourage newly independent readers. *sg*
Author lives in Germany and Ireland

Igel, E.T.W. **Mole's Journey**. Translated by Sibylle Kazeroid. Illustrated by Jakob Kirchmayr. New York: North-South Books, 2004. Originally published as *Maulwurfs Weltreise* by Nord-Sud Verlag AG, in 2003. ISBN 0-7358-1879-7. 24 p. (3–6). Picture book.

Poor mole, sick with a cold and envious of friend Owl's trip, starts digging in his underground home and has adventures at the North Pole, the desert, the mountains, and the jungle before he gets home, the place that's just right for him. He finds his good friends gathered around nursing him through a high fever. Was his trip just a dream? Richly saturated color paintings are full of humor and a magical sense of place. *sg*
Author from Germany

Jandl, Ernst. **Next, Please**! Translated from the German. Illustrated by Norman Junge. New York: Putnam's Son, 2003. ISBN 0-399-23758-5. 32 p. (3–6). Picture book.

Five injured toys sit in chairs in the "doctor's" waiting room. Each toy has a missing appendage or is obviously hurt in some way: the penguin has a missing wing, the duck a missing wheel, the bear a hurt eye and arm, the frog has a large bandage on his back, and lastly, a Pinocchio-looking doll has a broken nose. Each one enters the doctor's office and leaves whole again. The crosshatch illustrations, use of minimal text on one page, and a full-page illustration on the other, works beautifully. Junge, the illustrator, won the *Premio Bologna Ragazzi Award for the German edition of the book in 1997.   mw*

Johansen, Hanna. **Henrietta and the Golden Eggs**. Translated by John S. Barrett. Pictures by Käthi Bhend. Jaffrey, NH: Godine, 2002. Originally published in German as *Von Hühnchen das goldene Eier legen wolte* by Verlag Nagel & Kimche AG, Zürich/Frauenfeld. ISBN 1-56792-210-4. 64 p. (5–10). Transitional reader.

Henrietta lives in a great big chicken house with three thousand three hundred and thirty-three chickens. The heat and the smell create a dreary environment for the chickens. But Henrietta has big dreams for a little chicken: learning to sing, to swim, to fly, and most important of all, to lay golden eggs. The others mock her, but our heroine is no fool; she knows her limitations, but doesn't let them destroy her ambitions. *2003 Mildred Batchelder Award.   djg*

Jung, Reinhardt. **Bambert's Book of Missing Stories**. Translated by Anthea Bell. New York: Knopf, 2004. First published in Austria in 1998 by Jungbrunnen. Under the title *Bamberts Buch der verschollenen Geschichten*. Originally published in translation: London: Egmont Books Ltd., 2002. ISBN 0-375-82997-0. 124 p. (10 up). Novel.

   Bambert is a lonely man with only his stories to keep him company. A dwarf, he lives alone in a second story apartment with only the grocer, Mr. Bloom ground floor tenant to care about him. But Bambert is a writer and when he completes his book, "A Book of Wishes," a collection of 10 stories with room enough for just one more, he realizes that he must send the stories out into the world, that they might find their setting and true characters. He rips the stories from the cover and sets them on their way in miniature balloons. Eventually they do come back, all but one last story. The transformation of the stories include Bambert's reflection on his life and the world around him.   *djg*

Jung, Reinhardt. **Dreaming in Black & White**. Translated by Anthea Bell. New York: Phyllis Fogelman Books, 2003. Originally published as *Auszeit oder Der Lowe von Kauba* in 1996. ISBN 0-8037-2811-5. 112 p. (10–14). Novel.

   A boy with physical disabilities living in Germany finds that studying the Third Reich in school leads to vivid black and white dreams of living in the 1930s as a boy named Hannes. In his dreams, the narrator becomes Hannes, but he also becomes an omniscient observer of the frightening events taking place in his town. Hannes cannot speak clearly or walk without a crutch, and he is soon betrayed when his own father signs papers to have him institutionalized as part of the Nazi extermination of "lives not worth living." Hannes's experiences mirror the narrator's own, and the boy draws a chilling connection between the Holocaust and the practice of preventing births of children with disabilities through genetic engineering. Historical information and the author's sources are included in the appendix.   *aao*
Author lived in Germany

Lewin, Waldtraut. **Freedom beyond the Sea**. Translated by Elizabeth D. Crawford. New York: Delacorte Press, 2001. Originally published as "Jenseits des Meeres Freiheit" by Ravensburger Buchverlag in 1997. ISBN 0-385-32705-6. 262 p. (14 up). Novel.

   In 1492, the Spaniards are in the midst of the Inquisition. Columbus is making his voyage to the Indies. A sixteen-year-old Jewish girl, Esther, disguises herself as a boy named Pedro and joins Columbus's crew on the Santa Maria. Life on board ship is brutal and full of deception. Pedro must keep his secrets well-hidden and finds himself employed as scribe to Columbus. Pedro finds himself without protectors and fears for his life. He cannot complete the voyage and leaves the ship at the Canary Islands, where he can resume his life as Esther. Full of political intrigue and action this is an unusual story about Columbus's voyage.   *ls*
Author from Germany

Liersch, Anne. **Nell & Fluffy**. Illustrated by Christa Unzner. New York: North-South Books, 2001. Translated by J. Alison James. Originally published in Gossau Zurich, Switzerland as *Nele & Wuschel* by Nord-Sud Verlag, 2001. ISBN 0-7358-1425-2. 32 p. (3–6). Picture book.

Nell, who loves animals, has an array of toy animals that fills up her bedroom but most of all she would like to have a live animal of her own. When she gets a guinea pig for her sixth birthday, they become best friends as she holds him in her lap feeding him fresh carrots and sharing her thoughts. Right before her seventh birthday Nell's schoolmates tell her that guinea pigs are boring and for babies. Nell, embarrassed, succumbs to peer pressure and hides her guinea pig in a box in the bushes so she can ask her parents for a more respectable pet. Racked with guilt about what she has done she goes to look for Fluffy only to find him missing. Nell's parents, although angry with her actions, help Nell to make signs, hoping that someone has found the box. A happy reunion ensues and Nell presumably learns her lesson. A didactic story saved by the pen, ink, and watercolor paintings that capture Nell's love and anguish.   *kmc*
Author lives in Germany

McCann, Michelle Roehm. **Luba: The Angel of Bergen-Belsen**. As told to Michelle R. McCann by Luba Tryszynska-Frederick. Illustrations by Ann Marshall. Berkeley, CA: Tricycle Press, 2003. ISBN 1-58246-098-1. 48 p. (8 up). Picture book biography.

This biographical story is based on the actual events that occurred in the Bergen-Belsen concentration camp. Luba, unable to sleep, goes out into a frozen night in December of 1944 and finds fifty-four children huddled together in a field. She brings all of them into her barrack and despite all the dangers, gives shelter and finds food enough to keep the children alive until the liberation in April 1945. A quote at the beginning of the book by the youngest child rescued says "my mother always told me that she gave birth to me, but that Luba gave me life." An epilogue, notes on WWII and the Holocaust, and an extensive bibliography are appended in this story of courage and bravery.   *djg*

Monnier, Miriam. **Just Right!** Translated by J. Alison James. New York: North-South Books, 2001. First published in Switzerland under the title *Ich bin ich*. ISBN 0-7358-1521-6. 26 p. (3–6). Picture book.

"I don't know if I'm too big or too little!" a young girl tells her mother. She constantly hears she is too big too be carried up the stairs or to eat with her fingers, but too small to chew gum or play with the older boy downstairs. So the little girl wonders which is right: is she too big or too little? As she explores this familiar childhood issue, pastel paintings portray the little girl shrinking or growing in her environment. When her mother assures her she is just the right size and loved more than anything in the world, the little girl begins to feel com-

fortable with her size. This story is sure to be enjoyed by parents and preschoolers alike. *aao and ls*
Author lives in Hamburg, Germany

Pressler, Mirjam. **Malka**. Translated by Brian Murdoch. New York: Philomel/
Penguin Putnam, 2003. Originally published as *Malka Mai* by Beltz Verlag, 2001.
ISBN 0-399-23984-7. 280 p. (11 up). Novel.
  Seven-year-old Malka is separated from her mother and older sister during their escape from Nazi-occupied Poland to Hungary. Tortured by her decision to go on without the child, the mother cannot rest in the relative safety of Hungary until she returns to Poland to fetch her. Most of the story, however, is told by Malka, who survives through her will to go on living, hiding in a coal shoot, in abandoned buildings, and in the streets, as well as through some help from kind strangers. The reunion with the mother, who she feels had abandoned her, is poignant. *International Reading Association Notable Book for a Global Society; Kirkus Book Review Stars. jvl*
Author from Germany

Pressler, Mirjam. **Shylock's Daughter**. Translated by Brian Murdoch. New York:
Dial, 2001. First published as *Shylocks Tochter* by Alibaba Verlag GmbH in 1999.
(Paperback: Pan Macmillan, 2001). ISBN 0-8037-2667-8. 266 p. (12 up). Novel.
  Inspired by William Shakespeare's play *The Merchant of Venice*, this novel is the story of Shylock, a Jewish money-lender, and Jessica, his sixteen-year-old daughter. In sixteenth-century Venice, Jews were segregated from Christians and restricted to their own communities called "ghettos." Jessica rejects this austere lifestyle, her miserly father, and her religion by falling in love with and marrying an aristocrat. In an act of revenge against all Christians, grief-stricken Shylock demands "a pound of flesh" from a merchant who is unable to pay his debt, even though others agree to repay double what is owed. This novel delivers a sobering perspective of anti-Semitism during the Middle Ages. An insightful afterword by the translator includes a historical perspective and clarifies the relationship between the play and the novel. *Top 10 Historical Fiction for Youth, 2002, starred reviews. kk*
Author from Germany

Reiche, Dietlof. **Freddy in Peril: Book Two in the Golden Hamster Saga**.
Translated by John Brownjohn. Illustrated by Joe Cepeda. New York: Scholastic,
2004. Originally published as *Freddy: Ein Hamster Lebt Gefahrlich* in German by Program Anrich, an imprint of Beltz Verlag, in 1999. ISBN 0-439-53155-1.
204 p. (10 up). Novel.
  Freddy's back, along with human friends Mr. John and Sophie, Sir William the cat, and the nettlesome guinea pigs, Enrico and Caruso, whom readers encountered in the first book of this fun-loving fantasy duo. This time, Freddy's life is jeopardized by Professor Fleischkopf, a malevolent scientist who is determined

to prove that golden hamsters are the world's smartest non-humans. Of course, Freddy's reading and writing skills—not to mention his facility with computers— are at the heart of his problems. Sewer rats and a beautiful lady reporter add to the frivolity of Reiche's second book in the golden hamster saga. *lmp*
Author lives in Germany

Reiche, Dietlof. **I, Freddy: Book One in the Golden Hamster Saga**. Translated by John Brownjohn. Illustrated by Joe Cepeda. New York: Scholastic, 2003. Originally published as *Freddy: Ein Wildes Hamsterleben* in German by Program Anrich, an imprint of Beltz Verlag, in 1998. ISBN 0-439-28356-6. 201 p. (10 up). Novel.

Born in jail, surrounded by noisy, jostling, uneducated siblings, but encouraged by his grandmother's tales of freedom, Freddy strives to distinguish himself from his peers. His first goal, after teaching himself to read, is to escape his crowded prison. He devises a plan that, surprisingly, succeeds and he is sold as a pet. It's probably wise to mention here that Freddy is (strictly speaking) classified as *mesocricetus auratus*—a golden hamster. This hilarious autobiography of a rodent, struggling to cope with less intelligent—not to mention odiferous—creatures, chronicles the hardships and dangers as Freddy achieves literacy and freedom. *lmp*

Ruepp, Krista. **The Sea Pony**. Translated by J. Alison James. Illustrated by Ulrike Heyne. New York: North-South, 2001. First published as *Meerpony* by Nord-Süd in 2001. ISBN 0-7358-1534-8. 62 p. (7–10). Novel.

Nine-year-old Philip and his family have moved to Outhorn Island. Both Philip and his Icelandic pony, Goblin, miss their previous home. His friendship with Charlie and her stallion, Starbright, help to ease the pain, especially when she rescues Philip after Goblin plunges into the ocean and begins to swim northward. Textual descriptions and the illustrations give a feel for the dune-covered island. *jig*
Author and illustrator live in Germany

Scheffler, Ursel. **The Man with the Black Glove**. Translated by Rosemary Lanning. Illustrated by Christa Unzner. Originally published as *Der Mann mit dem schwarzen Handschuh* by Nord-Sud Verlag AG in 1999. ISBN 0-7358-1178-4. 62 p. (6–10). Novel.

Martin and Pauline see a man wearing black gloves leave a silver suitcase in a shed. The children report the man's suspicious behavior to the police. Martin and Pauline are given IDs permitting them to check clues and investigate the case. The children have also found a wallet. Does it belong to the man with the black glove? This mystery is full of action and suspense and is sure to please the young reader. *ls*
Author from Germany

Schneider, Antoinie. **Come Back, Pigeon!** Translated by J. Alison James. Illustrated by Uli Waas. New York: North-South, 1999. ISBN 0735811415. First published in Switzerland under the title *Eine Taube Für Bollibar* by Nord-Süd, 1999. 48 p. (6–9). Transitional reader.

Flora and Barnaby have just moved to the country and love the birds, especially the pigeons kept by their neighbor Gabriel. But when Barnaby buys his own pigeon and it flies away, their only comfort is helping Gabriel care for his birds. The children form a fast friendship and when spring arrives, so does their pigeon, because Pigeons always come back. This easy to read book is colorfully illustrated in watercolors. *djg*

Schwab, Eva. **Robert and the Robot**. Ashville, NC: Front Street, 2001. Originally published in Germany under the title *Robert und der Roboter*. Copyright in 2000 Moritz Verlag Frankfurt/Main. ISBN 1-8869-1059-6. 32 p. (4–8). Picture book.

Robert must clean his room before tomorrow morning, but it is such a mess he decides to finish the next day. He is startled out of bed by a loud bang and finds a robot has crashed through the roof of his tool shed. A few adjustments and some new batteries and Robert has Hugo 2 whirling around his room like a tornado, cleaning it up, just in time. Large, bright, acrylic paintings liven up the text. *djg*
Author lives in Germany

Stiekel, Bettina, ed. **Nobel Book of Answers**. Translated by Paul de Angelis and Elisabeth Kaestner. New York: Atheneum, 2003. Originally published in Germany in 2001 as *Kinder fragen, Nobelpreisträger antworten* by Wilhelm Heyne Verlag, Munich. ISBN 0-689-863101. 256 p. (8–12). Informational book.

Questions posed by children are presented to twenty-one Nobel Prize winners in the fields of medicine, physics, chemistry, mathematics, literature, and peace. The answers are given in clear and insightful essays that will satisfy a child's curiosity and intrigue adults as well. Questions explore such topics such as "Why do we feel pain?" and "Why are some people rich and others poor?" With an introduction about the Peace prize by Jimmy Carter and the question "Why is there war?" addressed by Desmond Tutu, this collection of essays is as timely as it is fascinating. *djg*

Related Information

Awards

Deutscher Jugendliteraturpreis/The German Children's Literature Prize

Given to a book written by a German author or translated into the German language, this is the premier prize for children's literature in Germany and is presented annually at the Frankfurt Book Fair in October. Awards are made in four categories: picture book, children's book, young adult book, and non-fiction.

Literary awards in Austria, Germany, and Switzerland

Marilen Daum lists the major awards and what they are given for from all three countries since 1995. This selection focuses on the most important prizes awarded for fiction and poetry written in German. It covers awards in all literary genres, including children's and teenage literature. Each description lists the purpose of the prize, the award criteria and procedure, and the winners of recent years. http://www.new-books-in-german.com/info5.htm

Library Collections

Internationale Jugendbibliothek/International Youth Library
www.ijb.de (in German only)
   This is a noncirculating collection of post-World War II children's books from all over the world. Schloss Blutenburg, D – 81247 Munich, Germany; e-mail bib@ijb.de.

Institut für Jugendbuchforschung/Institute for Youth Book Research
www.uni-frankfurt.de/fb10/jubufo (in German only)
   Collected here are historical and contemporary children's books, primarily German-language. Johann Wofgang Goethe-Universität, Grüneburgplatz 1, 60323 Frankfurt am Main; e-mail jubufo@rz.uni-frankfurt.de.

Frankfurt Book Fair
Frankfurt, Germany
http://www.frankfurt-book-fair.com
2004—Oct. 6-11, 2005—Oct. 19-24, 2006—Oct. 4-9

Online Bookstores

Amazon.de
www.amazon.de

Adoris
www.adorishop.de

Bol.com
www.bol.de

Organizations

IBBY Germany
http://www.jugendliteratur.org/

German Book Office
   The German Book Office New York, Inc. (GBO) serves as a bridge between the German and American publishing industries. Although not specific to works

for children, their website includes links to sites about German authors, literary journals, and organizations.
www.gbo.org

Print Resources

Garrett, Jeffrey. "German Children's and Youth Literature in Exile 1933–1950: Biographies and Bibliographies." Bookbird, July 2002.

GREECE

Galloway, Priscilla. **The Courtesan's Daughter**. New York: Delacorte, 2002. ISBN 0-385-72907-3. 254 p. (12–16). Novel.
  See Canada for description.

Rousaki, Maria. **Unique Monique**. Illustrated by Polina Papanikolaou. La Jolla, CA: Kane/Miller, 2003. First published as *Melpo the Unique* by Papadopoulos Publishing, 2001. ISBN 1-929132-51-4. 28 p. (5–8). Picture book.
  At Monique's school all the children had to wear brown and blue uniforms. More than anything, she wants to be different and when she finds an old trunk full of wild accessories in the attic, Monique becomes unique! Big hats, wild glasses, and beaded headband cause quite a stir and the teachers don't appreciate it one bit. Humorous, cartoon-style watercolor illustrations will have you laughing out loud at her indomitable spirit. *djg*

Related Information

Circle of Greek Children's Books (IBBY Greece)
This group administers several annual awards, funded by cultural institutions or private donors. Awards are given for books published the previous year in the following categories: for younger children; for intermediate readers; and for older children and young adults. A fourth award is given to a Greek children's book for its illustrations. The Penelope Delta Award is given for the body of work.
www.greekibby.gr

State Prize for Children's Literature
This annual prize, given to a book published in the previous year, is awarded in December and consists of a diploma and a sum of Drs. 5,000,000.

Online Resources

Greek Children's Literature Page
This comprehensive resource for both Greek and foreign scholars interested in Greek children's literature and its research gives an historical overview of Greek

children's literature, links to conferences, descriptions of the journals, and information about Greek authors and illustrators.
http://www.angelfire.com/pe/GrChildLit/

HUNGARY

Cheng, Andrea. **Marika**. Asheville, NC: Front Street Books, 2002. ISBN
1-886910-78-2. 163 p. (11–14). Novel.

The book, which begins in 1939 with Marika forging Catholic birth certifi-
cates for her Jewish family, provides an accurate picture of Nazi-era Budapest,
where the war and the worst aspects of the Holocaust were held off for a while
due to the government's collaboration with Germany. As a sheltered child,
Marika finds it hard to understand her father's continual efforts in the next five
years to ensure her family's safety. Her more immediate concern is her father's
infidelity, her mother's self-absorption, and her friendships. When the Nazis invade Hungary, however, she has no further illusions left. The story is based on
her mother's experiences. *jvl*
Author from United States

Dillon, Eilís. **Children of Bach**. New York: Charles Scribner, 1992. ISBN 0-684-
19440-6. 164 p. (10–13). Novel.

A family of Jewish musicians seems to be living a charmed life in Nazi-era
Budapest—they do not even have to wear a yellow star. All this ends when the
three children and a friend come home from school one day to find their parents
and great aunt Eva gone. Fears of neighbors and the need to trust some of them
dominate the children's days until their resourceful aunt, who had escaped, returns. With the help of a kind neighbor, a truck driver, and an Austrian priest
they are smuggled out in a truck to the isolated, and therefore fairly safe, Italian
Alps. *jvl*
Author was prolific Irish writer of historical fiction for children

Strom, Yale. **Uncertain Roads: Searching for the Gypsies**. New York: Four
Winds Press, 1993. ISBN 0-0278-8531-3. o.p. 112 p. (12 up). Informational book.

Strom, an American musician, film maker, and photographer, interviewed Rom
(Gypsies) in Romania, Hungary, Ukraine, and Sweden. Through his own commentary, photographs, and first-person narratives by various individuals, often
12–18-year-olds, the author builds vivid impressions for the reader about the
Rom's lifestyles, hopes and aspirations, as well as their history and fears of in-
creased anti-Rom sentiment from the larger societies in which they live. One
gains a rounded picture of the warmth, family and community cohesiveness, and
diverse ways of life of the Rom people. Musical scores and lyrics for Rom
melodies are included at the conclusion of each chapter. *jvl*
Author from United States

Szablye, Helen, and Peggy King Anderson. **The Fall of the Red Star.** Hoensdale, PA: Boyds Mill Press, 1996. ISBN 1-56394-419-3. 166 p. (10–14). Novel.

On October 23, 1956, the world changed for fourteen-year-old Stephan and his Scout friends. The Hungarian Revolution had begun; Stephen and his friends would no longer have to hide from the AVO (secret police) during Scout meetings. Freedom was about to be wrested from the Soviets and even Stephen's father would return from prison where, as Scout leader, he had been incarcerated for eight years. The next ten days of fighting, fear, death, hope, and bitter disappointment as the brief moment of freedom was extinguished by the Soviets are all vividly and accurately described. *Notable Children's Trade Books in the Field of Social Studies, 1996.* jvl
Szablye from Hungary, escaped in 1956, and lives in United States. Anderson from United States

Related Information

Awards

Szep Magyar Konyv
Literally "The Fine Hungarian Book," this award is given out during Children's Book Week in Hungary.

IBBY Hungry
www.ibby.hu

ICELAND

McMillan, Bruce. **Days of the Ducklings**. Photographs by the author. Boston: Houghton-Mifflin, 2001. ISBN 0-618-04878-2. 32 p. (5–8). Informational book.

McMillan records the reestablishing of a colony of common eider ducks on a remote island off the coast of Iceland. Young Drifa nurtures the ducklings that hatch from the 200 eggs brought from neighboring islands. She must care for the ducklings yet keep her distance, for if they become pets they will not be able to survive in the wild. McMillan captures both the cuteness of the newly hatched ducklings and the beauty of Iceland. *jig*
Author lives in United States

Ruepp, Krista. **The Sea Pony**. Illustrated by Ulrike Heyne. Translated by J. Alison James. New York: North-South, 2001. First published as *Meerpony* by Nord-Sud in 2001. ISBN 0-7358-1534-8. 62 p. (7–10). Novel.

See Europe/Germany for description.

Related Information

IBBY Iceland
http://www.ibby.is/

REPUBLIC OF IRELAND

Bartoletti, Susan Campbell. **Black Potatoes: The Story of the Great Irish Famine, 1845–1850**. Boston: Houghton-Mifflin, 2001. ISBN 0-618-00271-5. 184 p. (10 up). Informational book.

This books tells the story of the great Irish famine, when successive potato crops were destroyed by a fungus, causing over a million people to die from starvation and disease and over two million to emigrate to the United States, Canada, and Great Britain. The author builds on stories from ordinary people who experienced the famine as well as from published histories. The illustrations are from newspapers and illustrations of the day. This book explores many sides of the problem as the author presents a thorough explication of the political and social context in which the famine occurred.
Author from United States

Brown, Don. **Across a Dark and Wild Sea**. Calligraphy by Deborah Nadel. Brookfield: Roaring Brook, 2002. ISBN 0-7613-2415-1. 32 p. (5–8). Picture book.

Columcille, born in 521 to an Irish king, loved books and reading as a child and became a scribe and monk. When he secretly copied a book of psalms without permission of the owner, he became involved in a dispute that led to a battle in which 3000 men were killed. Although Columcille's army won, he and twelve followers remorsefully fled to a remote Scottish island where they founded their first of many monasteries. They continued to create books and encourage reading and writing. The exquisite watercolor illustrations of this biography include drawings of the writing tools used during the Dark Ages and double-page spreads of the battle and their journey to the island. An author's note, the Uncial alphabet, and a bibliography are appended.   *kk*
Author from United States

Colfer, Eoin. **Artemis Fowl**. New York: Miramax, 2001. (Paperback: Miramax, 2002) ISBN 0-7868-0812-0. 277 p. (12 up). Novel.

Twelve-year-old Artemis Fowl, a child prodigy and a criminal, tries to rebuild the family fortune by masterminding a plan to steal gold from the fairies. In his attempt, he encounters sprites, trolls, a centaur, goblins, and a mud-eating dwarf. During this time all creatures except the Mud People (humans) have been forced to live underground. However, they flee to the surface when Fowl and his huge bodyguard kidnap Captain Holly Short of the LEPrecon (underground police) and hold her ransom for fairy gold. Set in Ireland during the 21st century, this first in a series of five books, is a combination of fantasy, high-tech, and action. Others in the series: *The Artic Incident, The Eternity Code, The Artemis Fowl Files*, and *Artemis Fowl: The Opal Deception.   kk*
Author from Ireland

Colfer, Eoin. **The Wish List**. New York: Hyperion Books for Children, 2003. Originally published by O'Brien Press Ltd. in 2000. ISBN 0-7868-1863-8. 252 p. (14 up). Novel.

Meg Finn backs out of robbing elderly Lowrie McCall's house with her partner in crime, Belch. When Belch fires a shotgun over Meg's head, just to scare her, the pellet hits a gas tank and the ensuing explosion sends them down the tunnel to the afterlife. Belch heads straight for the nether regions but Meg's life record is evenly balanced between good and bad. Meg is sent down to earth to help Lowrie McCall complete his Wish List, four tasks he wants to complete before he dies. Beelzebub complicates matters by sending Belch to earth to foil Meg's good works. A humorous, touching adventure where good overcomes evil—in the nick of time. *ls*
Author from Ireland

Doyle, Malachy. **Splash, Joshua, Splash!** Illustrated by Ken Wilson-Max. New York: Bloomsbury Children's Books, 2004. ISBN 1582348375. Published simultaneously in New York and London. 28 p. (3–7). Picture book.

Joshua loves to splash in the water when he feeds the ducks, while walking the dog through the puddles, or even while Granny is doing her shopping. Whether splashing down the water slide in the pool or on the bus ride home in the rain, the exuberant vibrant paintings will make you want to join in this watery romp. *djg*
Author lives in Northern Ireland. Award-winning illustrator from Zimbabwe, lives in London. His other books include The Big Yellow Taxi, Tickle Tickle, *and* The Little Red Plane.

Giff, Patricia Reilly. **Maggie's Door**. New York: Random House, 2003. ISBN 0-385-32658-0. 160 p. (8–12). Novel.

In this sequel to *Nory Ryan's Song*, Nory and some of her family and neighbors have put into action their hopes for the future by leaving their homes and the potato famine in Ireland for Galway, where they will get the boat for America. This journey by foot is fraught with difficulty, hunger, and danger as is the sea journey itself. The story unfolds in the alternative voices of Nory and her best friend, Sean (they do not know for most of the story that they are on the same boat). This device cleverly mirrors other alternating events: brutal blows are countered by strokes of luck or simple kindnesses; Nory's grief at not being able to heal Granda is balanced by knowing what to do when Sean is badly burned; Sean suffers at the hands of the cruel cook but a passenger takes an interest in him. Memories of the Great Hunger and the humiliation at the hands of the English landlords contrasts with the hope of being united with the family at 416 Smith Street in Brooklyn. The courage, determination, and strength of Nory and Sean are beacons during the brutal conditions of the long voyage; the joyful reunion is their well-deserved reward. A glossary and afterword are appended. *bjk*
Author lives in United States

Giff, Patricia Reilly. **Nory Ryan's Song**. New York: Random House, 2003. ISBN 0-385-32141-4. 148 p. (8–12). Novel.

Twelve-year-old Nory is motherless but rich in extended family, friends, and tradition and has the gift of a lovely singing voice. The beauty of the Irish countryside and coastline is the setting for the unrelenting hardships and hunger caused by the potato famine as well as the cruelties of the English landlords. When Nory's oldest sister emigrates to America with the promise of making a home for those to follow, Nory becomes a tower of spunky and spirited strength for the rest of her family (Da is working away at sea), especially her 3-year-old brother. Her friendship with an aging healer and what she learns from her is the gift she takes with her when the boat tickets arrive from her Da and she leaves for America and her new life. Glossary and Letter to the Reader. *bjk*
Author lives in United States

Hazen, Barbara Shook. **Katie's Wish**. Illustrated by Emily Arnold McCully. New York: Dial, 2002. ISBN 0-8037-2478-0. Unpaged. (5–8). Picture book.

Set in Ireland at the beginning of the potato famine, Katie is being cared for by her grandparents because her mother has died and her father has emigrated to America. Shortly after Katie complains about eating plain, boiled potatoes (she misses the way her mother made them), the potato blight arrives. Katie is sure her words caused it and she suffers untold guilt at the misery and upheaval around her caused by the blight and famine. Katie and an older cousin are sent to America, but throughout the difficult sea voyage her guilt at "causing" the famine almost exceeds her excitement at being reunited with her father. The reunion is made all the more joyous when Katie pours out her heart to her father and is reassured that the blight was caused by a fungus and not her words. Both Katie and the various settings come alive in the illustrations done in watercolor. An author's note is included. *bjk*
Author and illustrator live in United States

Marillier, Juliet. **The Seven Waters Trilogy**. New York: Tor.
See Australia for description.

McBratney, Sam. **Once There Was a Hoodie**. New York: G.P. Putnams's Sons, 1999. Illustrated by Paul Hess. Published in Great Britain 1999 by Hodder Headline, Ltd. ISBN 0-3999-23581-7. 28 p. (4–7). Picture book.

Once there was a Hoodie who lived under a hill and a very fine Hoodie he was. But he wasn't truly happy and so one day, off he goes to find what makes a Hoodie happy. Everyone he meets runs away from him, until at last, he meets what makes Hoodie happy-another Hoodie. A simple story, colorfully illustrated. *djg*
Author lives in Northern Ireland. Illustrator lives in England.

McMahon, Patricia. **One Belfast Boy**. Photographs by Alan O'Connor. New York: Houghton Mifflin, 1999. ISBN 0-395-68620-2. 54 p. (7–10). Informational book.

The author begins with the old story, an eleven-page overview of the political complexities of the region. The new story is of Liam, an eleven-year-old young Catholic boy who loves boxing. Striking photographs help the reader visualize his day filled with school, family, and his passion, boxing. Juxtaposing the activities of daily life with the soldiers and military helicopters, the author and photographer have captured the innocence of childhood lived in the shadow of violence. *djg* *Author from United States. Photographer lives in Dublin, Ireland.*

Milligan, Bryce. **Brigid's Cloak: An Ancient Irish Story**. Illustrated by Helen Cann. Grand Rapids: Eerdmans, 2002. ISBN 0-8028-5224-6. 32 p. (6–10). Picture book.

Legends of the fifth-century Irish saint revolve around the blue cloak, purported to have been given to her at birth and that came to symbolize her lifelong care for needy wayfarers. In this tale, the 10-year-old shepherdess is transported to Bethlehem, where she uses her cloak to warm Baby Jesus. The rich hued, mixed-media illustration enhance the gentle story. End matter contains the little we actually know about St. Brigid. *mln* *Author from United States. Illustrator divides her time between Germany and United States.*

Waddell, Martin. **Night Night, Cuddly Bear**. Illustrated by Penny Dale. Cambridge: Candlewick Press, 2000. ISBN 0-7636-1195-6. 32 p. (3–6). Picture book.

An imaginative bedtime game ritual involves the whole family searching for cuddly bear. As luck would have it, Mom is the best bear finder in the world. Once the bear is found, mother and son settle down with a bedtime story. A warm story for children who need a little more time to settle down for bed with their bedtime friend. *ls* *Author from Northern Ireland*

Waddell, Martin. **The Orchard Book of Ghostly Stories**. Illustrated by Sophy Williams. London: Oxford University Press, 2000. ISBN 1-8603-9421-3. 93 p. (10–14). Short Stories.

The eight original ghost stories evoke their rural Irish setting of an earlier time. The stories tend to be humorous or tender, as ghosts bring lovers together, estranged brothers become reconciled even after death, a child stolen by the fairies finds her way back to her now grandmother-aged sister, and a drunken farmer claims the donkey he bought at the fair was repossessed by its former owner, whose ghost he passed on Gallows Hill. Only one of the tales, "Hunger," is gruesome, but satisfies readers' need for justice. The lovely illustrations further enhance the setting, characterization, and dreamy tone of the stories. *2004 Hans Christian Andersen Award. jvl*

Waddell, Martin. **Snow Bears**. Cambridge, MA: Candlewick Press, 2002. ISBN 0-7636-1906-X. unpaged. (4–7). Picture book.

Mommy Bear comes out to frolic playfully one wintry day with her three snow-covered babies, and they all enjoy a game of make believe. "Where are my baby bears?" Mommy wonders, and the three clever babies each have their own playful responses—even baby: "We aren't here. Mommy bear." They slide down hills and throw snowballs, but soon baby bear is cold so they go inside to curl by the fireplace where the snow melts away and reveals the little bears. Waddell delivers a satisfying story that will delight young listeners and their caregivers, while Sarah Fox-Davies's soft watercolor and pencil drawings capture both the antics of the frigid outdoor play and the warmth of the cabin and the family relationships.

Waddell, Martin. **Tiny's Big Adventure**. Illustrated by John Lawrence. Cambridge, MA: Candlewick, 2004. First published by Walker in the UK. ISBN 0-7636-2170-6. 28 p. (4–8). Picture book.

Tiny the mouse has never been to the wheat field and so he scampers off with his big sister Katy past the stream up the knobby tree, along the top of the gate, and over to the field. This first adventure, tinged with the fear of being lost and found, is illustrated with vinyl engravings and watercolor wash. *djg*

Waddell, Martin. **Tom Rabbit**. Illustrated by Barbara Firth. Cambridge: Candlewick Press, 2001. ISBN 0-7636-1089-5. 32 p. (4–8). Picture book.

Sammy takes Tom Rabbit outside to see the real rabbits. When Sammy goes off to help with the cows, Tom Rabbit is left on the stone wall waiting for Sammy to return, which he does—just before bedtime. Children who are dealing with the fear of being left behind will find this story reassuring. The large, pastel illustrations lend a quiet, simple tone. *ls*
Author from Northern Ireland

Related Information

Awards

Bisto Book of the Year Award

Sponsored by Children's Books Ireland and supported by RHM Foods, the Book of the Year and three Merit Awards recognize books by authors and/or illustrators born or residing in Ireland.

Eilís Dillon Memorial Award

This award to the author of an outstanding first children's book is given only at the discretion of the judges of the Bisto Award.

Reading Association of Ireland Award

Established in 1985, this program now presents two awards every other year: the RAI Children's Book Award and the RAI Special Merit Award. The RAI is affiliated with the International Reading Association.

Online Bookstores

Eason.ie
www.eason.ie

Several categories of children's books make it easy to browse this website, which features ratings and reader reviews.

Organizations

IBBY Ireland
www.ibbyireland.ie

Children's Books Ireland (CBI)

Formed in 1996 Children's Books Ireland (CBI) is the national children's book organization of Ireland. CBI publishes *Inis*, a quarterly magazine of Children's Books Ireland, which contains reviews and articles on Irish and International children's books. CBI also administers the prestigious Bisto Book Awards, Ireland's only annual children's book awards.
http://www.childrensbooksireland.com/

Print Resources

Dunbar, Robert. **Enchanted Journeys: Fifty Years of Irish Writing for Children**. Dublin: O'Brien Press, 1997. ISBN 0-8627-8518-9. 192 p. Reference book.

This survey of the last fifty years of Irish writing for children, selected by an expert in children's literature includes Walter Macken, Eilís Dillon, Meta Mayne Reid, Patricia Lynch, and Marita Conlon McKenna. Compiler Robert Dunbar is a lecturer in English and children's literature and presents a weekly radio show about children's books. He is an active member of Children's Books Ireland.

Inis "is the quarterly magazine of Children's Books Ireland, edited by Siobhán Parkinson and Valerie Coghlan. *Inis* contains reviews and articles on Irish and international children's books. *Inis* takes an Irish perspective on children's literature issues and there is an emphasis on books published in Ireland or by Irish writers, but the magazine is international in its range, outlook and contributors."
http://www.childrensbooksireland.com/inis/

ITALY

Bini, Renata. **A World Treasury of Myths, Legends, and Folktales: Stories from Six Continents**. Illustrations by Mikhail Fiodorov. Translated by Alexandra Bonfante-Warren. New York: Harry N. Abrams, 2000. Originally published as *Miti e leggende di tutti i tempi* by Happy Books, Milan, 1999. ISBN 0-8109-4554-1. 126 p. (9–14). Folklore.

This beautifully illustrated book includes 33 myths and legends, some well-known, such as the "The Sword in the Stone" from Britain, others, such as "Izanagi and Izanami" from Japan, new to most readers. About one third of the stories are Native North and South American. Some of the choices of names for characters, however, such as "dragon" for a water monster Gluskap fights, are not quite accurate. An illustrated glossary gives further information and the twenty-three item "Further Reading" is well chosen.   *jvl*
Author from Italy

Bosca, Francesca. **The Apple King**. Illustrations by Guiliano Ferri. Translated from the German by J. Alison James. First Published in Switzerland under the title *Der Apfelkönig*. A Michael Neugebauer Book/North-South, 2001. ISBN 0-7358-1397-3. 28 p. (6–8). Picture book.

No one is allowed to touch the apple tree of the selfish King (portrayed as a pig dressed in robes). When the tree becomes infested with worms, the King is furious. He attempts to rid the tree of the worms by bribery, military force, and magic—nothing succeeds. When the king learns that the apple tree invited the worms to dine because it was lonely, he mends his ways and declares an Apple Festival. Everyone is invited. Playful illustrations use soft muted colors.   *djg*
Author from Pesaro, Italy, where she still lives. She has written many stories for children, which have been published in numerous languages.
Illustrator from Pesaro, Italy. He studied at the Instituto d'Arte in Urbino, where he specialized in animation.

Buzzati, Dino. **The Bears' Famous Invasion of Sicily**. Translated from the Italian by Frances Lobb. New York: New York Review of Books, 2003. First published in Italian as *La famosa invasione degli orsi* in Sicilia, 1947. ISBN 1-59017-076-8. 147 p. (9–12). Novel.

This unusual opera-like fairy tale originally published in 1947 in Italy begins during a harsh winter when the bears, living in the mountains of Sicily, decide to go down to the plains closer to the city of men in search of food and warmth. With the misguided aid of the magician Professor Ambrose, the bears engage in a bloody war against the Grand Duke eventually defeating his army and they live in peace among the humans for thirteen years with King Leander of the bears ruling the city. The bears begin to mimic the more corrupt ways of the humans by gambling, dressing in elaborate clothing, and stealing. When King Leander is be-

trayed by one of his own seeking power, he convinces the bears to go back to the mountains where life was simpler and happier. Narrated by an adult voice telling the story years into the future, Buzzatti inconsistently includes poetry interspersed throughout the text that at times disrupts the flow of the narrative. This technique may be reflective of the author's background in writing opera librettos. The references within the text to the pen and ink drawings done by the author attempt to give validity to the story. *kmc*
Author lived in Italy

Collodi, Carlo. **Pinocchio**. Compiled by Cooper Edens. San Francisco: Chronicle, 2001. ISBN 0-8118-2283-4. 173 p. (5–10). Illustrated novel.
   Since its publication in 1881, this tale has been one of the most loved children's stories. This unique edition is an abridged retelling to highlight a collection of illustrations from the late nineteenth and early twentieth centuries and includes the work of Enrico Mazzanti, Carlo Chiostri, Attilio Mussino, Frederick Richarson, and Charles Folkard.

Collodi, Carlo. **Pinocchio**. Translated by Emma Rose. Illustrated by Sara Fanelli. Cambridge, MA: Candlewick, 2003. ISBN 0-7636-2261-3. 194 p. (7–12). Novel.
   This fresh interpretation of the famous story brings the classic tale to a new audience. The quirky, tongue-in-cheek language is complimented by sophisticated, stylized illustrations in mixed media collages. The story is retold, chapter by chapter, and the plot of the original story is complete. *Best Children's Books of the Year, 2004; Bank Street Best Book of the Year.* *djg*

D'Adamo, Francesco. **Iqbal: A Novel**. Translated by Ann Leonori. New York: Atheneum, 2003. First published as *Storia di Iqbal* by Edizioni EL in 2001. ISBN 0-689-85445-5. 120 p. (9–12). Novel.
   This fictionalized account of Iqbal Masih, an actual thirteen-year-old Pakistan boy who worked to free children from servitude, is narrated by Fatima, a young co-worker whose father sold her to pay his debts. For three years, she and other children were forced by the owner of a carpet factory to work long hours in filthy conditions with the threat of inhuman punishments if they failed to meet the demands of their owner. Shortly after Iqbal is sold to the factory, he escapes and manages to free the children with the help of the Bonded Labor Liberation Front. For his efforts, he is awarded an international award and travels to Sweden and the United States. He is murdered shortly after returning to his home in April 1995. An introduction provides an overview of child labor abuses, and an epilogue explains Iqbal Masih's murder and provides a list of sources for further reading. *kk*
Author from Italy

Di Pasquale, Emanuel. **Cartwheel to the Moon: My Sicilian Childhood**. Illustrated by Kathryn Dyble Thompson. Selected and arranged by Marianne Carus. Chicago, IL: Cricket Books, 2003. ISBN 0-8126-2679-6. 64 p. (10 up). Poetry.

Cartwheel to the Moon is a bittersweet glimpse into an immigrant's heart. There is one extended recollection and 28 brief poems—divided into a prologue, epilogue, and four seasons. *Spring* explains: "The sun has a tail/that . . . tickles seeds" (p. 14). Di Pasquale employs similes and metaphors throughout that allow him to vividly portray a Sicily he fondly recalls: "Look at the hilly Sicilian villages: walls of stone houses chewed up by moon tides, sun swells/their blue or yellow faces cracked/left cracked" (p. 10). Thompson's evocative illustrations, done in midnight blue watercolors, resemble old family snapshots.   *lmp*
Author from Italy, lives in United States

Fritz, Jean. **Leonardo's Horse**. Illustrated by Hudson Talbott. New York: Putnam, 2001. ISBN 0-399-23576-0. unpaged. (10–14). Informational book.

In the fifteenth century during the Italian Renaissance, Leonardo da Vinci was making his mark in many artistic and scientific endeavors; but one project, a larger than life bronze sculpture of a horse, was never completed beyond the clay model. Leonardo died and the horse was forgotten until some 400-plus years later when the idea was resurrected by Charles Dent, an American art lover. His preparations were in vain because he too died before the horse could be cast into bronze. The American sculptor, Nina Akanu, took over the project and 500 years later, the bronze horse was home at last in Milan, Italy. Fritz's well-researched text is enhanced by Talbott's doubles-spread period watercolors. The die-cut dome shape of the book and the "bronzed" endpapers lend a final artistic touch to this book. The theme of a common dream across cultures and time is underscored by horse images throughout the book as the setting changes from Renaissance Florence to the American countryside to modern day Milan. *2002 ALA Notable Children's Books; 2002 NCTE Orbis Pictus Award Recommended Title; 2002 NCSS-CBC Notable Social Studies Trade Books For Young People; 2002 Children's Book Council Not Just For Children Anymore! Selection.   mk and bjk*
Author and illustrator live in United States

Gandolfi, Sivana. **Adalbra, or the Tortoise Who Loved Shakespeare**. Translated by Lynne Sharon Schwartz for the Italian. New York: Arthur A. Levine Books/Scholastic, 2004. ISBN 0-439-49741-8. 151 p. (12–14). Novel.

Relationships define this novel, which begins seemingly as realistic fiction and evolves into fantasy. Elisa and her grandmother, Nonna Eia, share a close relationship peppered with secrets. Why has Elisa's mother cut off all contact with Nonna Eia, yet does not restrict Elisa's visits with her? Nonna Eia shares a legend with Elisa about a "people at the far ends of the earth where the women could choose never to die." Elisa's devotion to her Shakespeare-loving grandmother surpasses all expectations as Nonna Eia slowly changes from her human form into a long-lived tortoise. Because of its literary excellence, this change is acceptable to the reader and draws one into the complex history of their familial relationships. *Italy's Andersen Prize.*

Heuston, Kimberly. **Dante's Daughter**. Asheville, NC: Front Street, 2003. ISBN 1-886910-97-9. 302 p. (14 up). Novel.

While the facts about the poet Dante are accurate, this historical fiction focuses on the imagined life of his daughter Antonia, about whom little is known. The author immerses us in the life of a young girl whose family is embroiled in the violent politics of early 14th-century Florence. Through Antonia's narrative we witness her education, which includes learning Latin from her father as they journey by horseback from Florence to the University of Paris, learning to paint murals and to prepare vellum from his artist uncle (she even has a brief encounter with the painter Giotto), and learning manuscript illumination from an independent woman artist at a women's quasi-religious community, the Beguine, in Paris. A vivid picture emerges of 14th-century options for women in Italian society and of Italian family life, as does a portrait depicting Dante's personal, political, and artistic struggles, especially in the context of the Divine Comedy. *jvl*
Author from United States

Innocenti, Roberto. **The Last Resort**. Illustrated by the author. Mankato: Creative Editions, 2002. ISBN 1-56846-172-0. 48 p. (10 up). Picture book.

A painter's imagination disappears one day. To recover it, he goes on a trip and finds himself driving to a little seaside hotel called The Last Resort. There, he meets other characters who are also searching—for wonder, for bravery, for love, and other treasures. Recognizably figures from literature or popular culture, they re-kindle the artist's fantasy and he regains the "inward eye" he thought he had lost. Mysterious, surrealistic illustrations and quickly recognizable literary figures invite the reader to journey into the imagination. A picture book for older readers. Innocenti was a finalist for 2004 Hans Christian Andersen Award for Illustration. *New York Times Best Illustrated Book of the Year*; *Newsweek Top Selection for Children*; *National Parenting Publications Award Gold Medal. mk*
Author/illustrator from Italy

McCully, Emily Arnold. **The Orphan Singer**. New York: Scholastic, 2001. ISBN 0-439-19274-9. 32 p. (8 up). Picture book.

The Dolcis are a very poor, musically gifted family that cannot provide their children the musical education they desire them to have. The parents make the difficult decision to leave their baby girl at the ospedalo (orphanage) where they know she would receive musical training and the chance at a better life than they could give her. The dreams, sacrifices, and hard work of the Dolci family are vividly expressed in the watercolor illustrations in which the Venice architecture serves as backdrop to the evolving events of the story. The author's note at the end of the book more fully explains the ospedalo, the musical education provided there, and the culture of eighteen-century Venice. *js*
Author from United States

Norris, Kathleen. **The Holy Twins: Benedict and Scholastica**. Illustrated by Tomie. New York: G. P. Putnam's Sons, 2001. ISBN 0-399-23424-1. 40 p. (5–8). Picture book.

Over one thousand years after they lived, St. Benedict's guidelines for living, or Rule, and St. Scholastica's life of prayer still inspire current generations. This tribute to the holy twins follows their spiritual growth and human obstacles from childhood to death. Children will relate to Benedict's personal challenges—competition, disagreements, jealousy—and be delighted by the mythical quality of the miracles that surrounded the twins. DePaola's illustrations highlight the twins' distinct personalities and their parallel, while separate, paths and picture the Umbrian countryside in a style modeled on medieval art. Serene, earthy Mediterranean images mirror the peace-filled lives the twins strove for. The final spread includes information and illustrated excerpts from Benedict's Rule. A short list of further reading is limited to adult titles.   *mk and sg*
Author from United States. Illustrator from United States and was the 1990 U.S. nominee for the Hans Christian Andersen Award in illustration.

Pressler, Mirjam. **Shylock's Daughter**. Translated by Brian Murdoch. New York: Dial, 2001. First published as *Shylocks Tochter* by Alibaba Verlag GmbH in 1999. (Paperback: Pan Macmillan, 2001). ISBN 0-8037-2667-8. 266 p. (12 up). Novel.
See Europe/Germany for description.

Sabuda, Robert. **The Adventures of Providence Traveler 1503: Uh-Oh, Leonardo!** New York: Atheneum Books for Young Readers, 2002. ISBN 0-689-81160-8. unpaged. (5–8). Picture book.

Providence Traveler was an extraordinary mouse. Not only was she curious about how things worked but she also was constantly studying designs and creating new inventions. Providence's hero was Leonardo da Vinci. She knew everything about him and painstakingly reproduced many of his inventions. The one design that intrigued her most turned out to be most fascinating—a time travel wooden mouse that carried her and her friends to 16th-century Renaissance Florence, Italy, where she actually met Leonardo. After numerous adventures Providence and her friends barely escape the evil clutches of Bishop Strozzi and return home.   *ok*
Author from United States

Testa, Fulvio. **The Endless Journey**. New York: North-South, 2001. First published in Switzerland under the title *Die unendliche Reise*. ISBN 0-7358-1503-8. 28 p. (4–8). Picture book.

Simple text takes the reader on a visual journey in and out of the objects in a boy's room. Detailed watercolor and pen-and-ink drawings show a toy box full of objects and paintings. The clue, "where have we seen these before," invites the

reader to examine the pages that alternate between a view of the room and the view from inside the paintings.
A delightful visual puzzle. *jig*
Author/illustrator lives in Italy

Testa, Fulvio. **Too Much Garbage**. New York: North-South Books, 2001. Originally published as *Ein kleines Wunder im Mull* by Nord-Sud Verlag AG in 2001. ISBN 0-7358-1451-1. 32 p. (5–8). Picture book.
Two boys are carrying garbage bags to the curb. They stand at the corner noticing garbage being thrown out of cars, tossed out of windows, and hanging from trees. The story ends limply when the boys see a flower growing in the dump leading them to plant more flowers and create less garbage. *ls*
Author/illustrator lives in Italy

Weston, Carol. **The Diary of Melanie Martin, or, How I Survived Matt the Brat, Michelangelo, and the Leaning Tower of Pizza**. New York: Knopf, 2000. ISBN 0-375-80509-5. 144 p. (9–12). Novel.
Fourth-grader Melanie Martin loves keeping a diary and is excited about the family trip to Italy over spring vacation. But who want to spend it with a bratty six-year-old brother? To make matters worse, because she is missing some school, Melanie has to write a poem about her family. As they travel around Italy and visit all the famous historical places her father has chosen, and the art treasures on her mother's list, Melanie discovers that she is enjoying herself and, to her amazement, that she actually likes her family. *ok*
Author from United States

Related Information

Book Fairs

Bologna Book Fair Bologna, Italy
http://www.xbf2k.bolognafiere.it/ Scroll down the page and click on *Fiera del Libro per Ragazzi*.
April

Organizations

Italian Section of IBBY
c/o Biblioteca Sala Borsa Ragazzi
Piazza del Nettuno 3
IT-40 124 Bologna
e-mail RagazziSalaBorsa@comune.bologn.i

LITHUANIA

Morris, Ann. **Grandma Esther Remembers: A Jewish-American Family Story**. (What Was It Like, Grandma? series). Photographs and illustrations by Peter Linenthal. Brookfield, CN: Millbrook Press, 2002. 32 p. (6–11). Informational book.

Two Brooklyn girls regularly visit with their grandmother who lives in Manhattan. In the course of these visits, the grandmother passes on Jewish traditions and family history. She tells them of her early life in Lithuania and the upheaval of World War II. They also sing, cook, and celebrate holidays together. As with the other books in this series, children are encouraged to explore their own family histories. This is a good combination of photographs and activities that convey a sense of ethnic uniqueness within U.S. culture.   *hk*
Author from United States

Related Information

Lithuanian Section of IBBY
Children's Literature Centre
Martynas Mazvydas National Library of Lithuania
Gedimino Ave. 51
LT-01504 Vilnius
e-mail vaikai@Inb.It
http://www.lnb.lt/clc/clc.html

THE NETHERLANDS

Arqués, Isabel M. **Ken's Cloud**. Illustrated by Angela Pelaez. First published in Holland under the title *Koen wile een wolk*. English translation by North-South Books, 2001. ISBN 0-7358-1525-9. 28 p. (4–7). Picture book.

Ken was bored with all his toys. So he climbs onto the rooftop and invites a fluffy white cloud into his bedroom. But now he wants it to rain and he paints the cloud dark. What an adventure when the rain fills the room and a shark appears. Ken has just to open the door to make it all disappear. What next? A snow storm, some sunshine? It's all in a day for an imaginative little boy.   *djg*

Attema, Martha. **Hero**. Victoria, BC: Orca Book Publishers, 2004. ISBN 1-55143-251-X. 130 p. (7–10). Novel.

As World War II draws to a close, eight-year-old Izaak must leave his mother and their hiding place in Amsterdam to assume a new identity on a farm in the northern part of the Netherlands. The farm family is kind, but the Jewish boy is sad and lonely until he gets to know Hero, a beautiful black stallion. Izaak shows resourcefulness and courage in hiding Hero from the Nazis who come to appropriate the horse for their escape from the advancing Allied troops. The Dutch author now lives in Canada; the story is based on the actual experiences of her great uncle. *Rocky Mountain Book Award, 2005 Nominee, Alberta, CA*

Borden, Louise. **The Greatest Skating Race: A World War II Story from the Netherlands**. Illustrated by Niki Daly. New York: Margaret K. McElderry Books, 2004. ISBN 0-689-84502-2. 44 p. (5–10). Picture book.

The story of a brave young Dutch boy from Sluis is simply told in this story of adventure and bravery. Piet is a young school boy from a family of skate makers in 1941 with dreams of racing in the north country's great Elfstedentocht, a 200 kilometer skate race. But when Jews are arrested and taken from their homes, his grandfather gives him the important job of skating to a town 16 kilometers away to bring two children to safety. Keeping the words of his mother in his mind "This is what it means to be Dutch, not only to love skating on our canals but also to be brave in our hearts" he braves confrontations with German soldiers and weariness to bring the children to the safety of their aunt's bookstore. Brief information about the country after the war, the Elfstentocht Race, and the history of skating are appended to this beautifully illustrated and inspiring story. *School Library Journal Book Review Stars.*   *djg*

Bos, Burny. **Alexander the Great**. Translated by J. Alison James. Illustrated by Hans de Beer. New York: North-South Books, 2000. Originally published as *Ich bin Mäus Katze nBären Stark* by Nord-Süd Verlag, 2000. ISBN 0-7358-1343-4, trade binding; ISBN 0-7358-1344-2, library binding. 26 p. (3–6). Picture book.

Alexander, a mouse, dreams of being like his comic book superhero, Mighty Bruno. When Rats, the household cat begins terrorizing the mouse family, Alexander sews a bear costume, and venturing into the kitchen, succeeds in bringing cheese to his hole. During one of his trips Rats catches him, but instead of eating him, she brings him to her kittens to play with. Thinking Rats had taken him for a bear, Alexander begins to relax, and enjoys the kittens' company, only to discover that Rats has known all along that he is a mouse. Alexander happily moves back and forth between his two loving families. De Beer's *Little Polar Bear* series is very popular and has been translated into 25 languages.   *jvl*
Illustrator from Netherlands

Bos, Burny. **Fun with the Molesons**. Translated by J. Alison James. Illustrated by Hans de Beer. New York: North-South Books, 2000. First published in Switzerland under the title *Familie Maulwurf Dicke Luft!* ISBN 0-7358-1353-1. 47 p. (5–8). Transitional book.

This is the fourth book in a series about the Mole families and contains eight short vignettes describing everyday events. When a bad dream awakens Dugless a nighttime of bed switching occurs. Grandma always has a trick up her sleeve as she wheels around in her motorized wheelchair. Homework, fitness training, and outings in the park all make for fun and de Beer's ink and watercolor illustrations add humor to this easy-to-read chapter book. Other titles include: *Meet the Molesons, Leave it to the Molesons*, and *Good Times with the Molesons.* djg

De Beer, Hans. **Little Polar Bear and the Big Balloon**. Translated by Rosemary Lanning. New York: North-South, 2002. First published in Switzerland under the title *Kleiner Eisbär hilf mir fliegen!* in 2001. ISBN 0-7358-1533-X. 28 p. (4–8). Picture book.

Little Polar Bear is back in another adventure, this time with Lars the puffin who has lost his way. He wants to get back home, but can't because his wings are covered in oil from an oil slick. Little Polar Bear takes him to the hot springs to clean his wings, but he is still too weak to fly home. But luckily, the new friends discover a hot air balloon and off they go. The full-color watercolor illustrations that have made these books favorites with children reading them in eighteen languages will delight de Beer fans. There are many other titles in the series including *Little Polar Bear and the Husky Pup (2004).* djg
Author/illustrator lives in the Netherlands

Dematons, Charlotte. **The Yellow Balloon**. Illustrated by the author. Translated from the Dutch. Asheville, NC: Front Street/Lemniscaat, 2004. ISBN 1-932425-01-2. 32 p. (5–8). Picture book.

Follow the complex trail of the yellow balloon as it travels through a landscape composed of diverse and unrelated places and times. On one page you'll find Wall of China, a volcano, snow skiing, and kayaking. Continue the chase after the yellow balloon in this oversized, wordless picture book and track a small blue van, a man on a flying carpet, an escaped convict, or a truck load of giraffes. Like her previous books *Let's Go* (2000), in which we follow an imaginative boy in a red shirt through through the village on his way to buy apples, and *Looking for Cinderella* (1992), this book has child appeal and creative storytelling possibilities and children may compose their own stories about what is really happening. *Kirkus starred review.* mw and djg

Dijkstra, Lida. **Little Mouse**. Illustrated by Piet Grobler. Asheville, NC: Front Street/Lemniscaat, 2003. Originally published by Lemniscaat b.v. Rotterdam under the title *Muisje mijn Meisje*. ISBN 1-9324-2506-3. 28 p. (3–7). Picture book.

Long ago an owl drops a mouse into the life of an old hermit, who loves it and takes care of it as he would a daughter. When the mouse becomes old enough to marry she tells him of her desire to marry the strongest being on earth. This retelling of a story that leads to the mountain and ultimately to the little mouse who is able to burrows through it, is portrayed with stylized ink and watercolor illustrations. djg
Author lives in Friesland. Illustrator lives in Cape Town, South Africa.

Haan, Linda de, and Stern Nijland. **King & King**. Berkeley, CA: Tricycle Press, 2002. Originally published under the title *Konig & Konig* by Uitgeverij J.H. Gottmer/H.J.W. Becht bv, Haarlem, The Netherlands, 2000. ISBN 1-58246-061-2. 32 p. (5–10). Picture book.

The queen had been ruling for a long time and was sick of it. She made up her mind that the prince would marry and become king by the end of the summer. But the prince had never much cared for princesses. He and the queen interview princess after princess, but it is not until Princess Madeleine and her brother Prince Lee arrive that he feels a stir in his heart. "What a wonderful prince!" and the wedding was very special. Bright cut-paper and mixed media art add a playful touch to this modern day fairy tale. *djg*

Hogeweg, Margriet. **The God of Grandma Forever**. Translated by Nancy Forest-Flier. Asheville, NC: Front Street, 2001. Originally published as *De God van oma Vanouds* by Lemnicaat b.v. in 1999. ISBN 1-886910-69-3. 111 p. (10 up). Novel.

Maria is angry when her parents turn her attic into a bedroom for Grandma Forever. Grandma Forever is very old and keeps to her bed. She is cranky and impatient but she does tell Maria stories. When Grandma Forever dies, Maria is bereft. A prickly relationship between grandmother and granddaughter hides the love that exists between them. *ls*
Author from the Netherlands

Jagtenberg, Yvonne. **Jack's Kite**. A Neal Porter Book. Brookfield, CT: Roaring Brook Press, 2004. ISBN 0761323856. First published in the Netherlands by Uigeverij Hillen, Amsterdam as *De vlieger*, 2003. 32 p. (4–8). Picture book.

It was a beautiful day at the campground. Jack is sitting in front of his tent wishing his father was there to help him fly his kite. When his mother suggests that he practice, he walks across the campground meeting the owner's family who try to help him learn to fly the kite. Little by little he improves but, alas, the kite string is dropped and the kite flies away. Not to worry, a man comes into the campground . . . not just any man, but Jack's father. Simply told with bright childlike crayon pictures, this is the third Jack tale by this award-winning author and illustrator. Other titles include *Jack's Rabbit*, winner of a 2003 Parents' Choice Silver Honor Award and *Jack and the Wolf*, which The Horn Book called "offbeat and humorously understated." *djg*
Author lives in the Netherlands

Kliphuis, Christine. **Robbie and Ronnie**. Illustrated by Charlotte Dematons. New York: North-South, 2002. First published in the Netherlands under the title *Robbie en Ronnie*. ISBN 0-7358-1626-3. 47 p. (7–10). Transitional book.

Robbie and Ronnie are friends, one is chubby and the other is thin, but they don't care, they just like each other. One day at the pool the bully Dennis and his pals torment the boys. When the boys find a bracelet in the pool and try to turn it in, Dennis starts a fight with them. The lifeguard intervenes and the boys are rewarded for their honesty. Simple to read text and colorful illustrations make this an attractive easy reader. *djg*

Lieshout, Elle van, and Erik van Os. **A Nice Party**. Illustrated by Paula Gerritsen. Asheville: Front Street, 2002. Originally published as *Fijn feestje* by Lemiscaat b.v. in 2002. ISBN 1-886910-89-8. 32 p. (4–8). Picture book.

Tomorrow is Gus's birthday but he is not happy about it. When his friend, Boris, asks why, Gus tells him how awful his family parties are. Boris suggests they get a birthday cake and spend the day fishing. The next morning, Gus posts a note saying he will not be home and goes fishing with Boris. Gus's family parties hearty at his house not noticing that Gus was absent. A different take on the typical birthday party story. Young children will be able to identify with Gus's feelings about being overwhelmed by large, noisy adults. *ls*
Authors from the Netherlands

Lieshout, Elle van, and Erik van Os. **The Nothing King**. Illustrated by Paula Gerritsen. Asheville, NC: Front Street, 2004. Simultaneously published as *Een Koning van Niks* in the Netherlands by Lemniscaat in 2004. ISBN 1-932425-14-4. unpaged. (4–8). Picture book.

Occasionally, everyone experiences the urge to jettison all responsibility. Kings are no different. When reigning becomes a burden, King Bear packs his pansy and pet rabbit then moves to a third-floor walkup. Next morning, the mayor inquires why the royal carriage is parked on a common street. The king responds by putting the horses out to pasture and selling the golden carriage. The queen shakes her head at his foolishness; the prime minister begs him to return; the neighbors laugh, calling him "the nothing king." But in his new, less complicated life, King Bear finds the secret of joy. *lmp*
Authors and illustrator live in the Netherlands

Linders, Clara, and Marijke ten Cate. **The Very Best Door of All**. Asheville, NC: Front Street, 2001. Originally published in the Netherlands as *De mooiste deur van overall* by Lemniscaat b.v. Rotterdam, 2000. ISBN 11-886910-64-2. 32 p. (3–5). Picture book.

Evan, the skunk, invites his best friend Pip, the hedgehog, to his birthday party. After knocking on the different doors of all his friends, Evan proclaims that Pip's door is the best door of all. When Pip fails to find the perfect present for his friend he decides to take down and wrap up his front door as a gift for Evan. Evan, confused when receiving his gift proclaims that Pip's was the best door of all because Pip is his best friend of all. The two friends then work together to put the door

back on Pip's house reaffirming their friendship. The full-color illustrations of this straightforward picture book include a subplot of a bird wounded from flying nails during the destruction of the door. *kmc*
Author lives in the Netherlands

Loo, Sanne te. **Little Fish**. La Jolla, Kane/Miller, 2004. Originally published by Lemniscaat b.v. Rotterdam. ISBN 1-920132-59-X. 28 p. Picture book.
　　Rosa is bored. Grandmother is making tortillas for market and there is no one to play with. So Rosa goes to the beach and, as she watches, the pelican tries to catch fish and a little fish jumps into her lap. The fun begins when Rosa brings little fish home and begins to make her favorite foods. The fish grows out of its dish, into the tub and the trough and finally Rosa and her friends carry it back to the sea and celebrate with a delicious cake Grandmother has made. Vibrant, colorful illustrations add to the magic of this unlikely fish tale reminiscent of Palmer's *Fish Out of Water* with an Hispanic setting. *djg*

Loo, Sanne te. **Ping Li's Kite**. Asheville, NC: Front Street/Lemniscaat, 2002. ISBN 1886910758. Originally published in the Netherlands under the title *Ping Li en zijn vlieger* by Lemniscaat b.v. Rotterdam, 2001. 28 p. (4–8). Picture book.
　　Ping-Li wants to make a kite that will fly higher and be bolder than any kite he has ever seen. He rides his bike into the city to visit Mr. Fo's shop for paper, sticks, and string and rushes to the temple steps to build his kite, ignoring Mr. Fo's warning to be sure to paint his kite before he flies it. But Ping-Li is impatient and does fly the kite, angering the emperor of the sky. He is taken into the emperor's dragonship, where he learns to paint his kite to make it the boldest of any other kite in the sky. *Best Children's Books of the Year, 2003. djg*

Moeyaert, Bart. **It's Love We Don't Understand**. Translated from the Dutch by Wanda Boeke. Asheville, NC: Front Street, 2002. ISBN 1-8869-1071-5. 127 p. (14 up) Novel.
　　The young narrator describes a fierce quarrel between her mother and her brother Axel about her mother's latest boyfriend who has been sexually abusing him in the opening episode of this novel about desperately troubled relationships. The next episode in the life of this unhappy family describes the arrival of an old man, curiously willed to them by their grandmother. Through imaginary conversations with her brother Axel, she tries to make sense of his leaving and understand "what love has to do with it." The innocent voice of the narrator pulls the reader through this complex novel. *Publisher's Weekly Starred Review. djg*

Piumini, Roberto. **Doctor Me Di Cin**. Pictures by Piet Grobler. Asheville, NC: Front Street /Lemniscaat, 2001. Originally published by Lemniscaat b.v. Rotterdam, 2001. ISBN 1-8869-1067-7. 26 p. (7–10). Picture book.

Prince Ma La Di has grown pale and thin but when the wise doctor advises a walk outdoors he refuses. The clever doctor appeals to the boy's curiosity and eventually lures him out to the wonders of the wide world. Delicate ink and watercolor illustrations place the setting for this fable in China. *Author lives in Italy. Award-winning illustrator lives in South Africa.*

Provoost, Anne. **In the Shadow of the Ark**. Translated by John Nieuwenhuizen. New York: Arthur A. Levine Books, 2004. Arkvaarders. Trans. Funded by the Flemish Literature Fund. www.fonsvoordeletteren.be. Text copyright 2001. ISBN 0-439-44234-6. 368 p. (12 up). Novel.

The rising waters of the marsh lands drive Re Jana's family to the desert where they find the builder, Noah, and his sons in the center of a construction project of unparallel proportions. Boat builders and laborers from all over work alongside the builder's sons but the rumor of the coming flood is dismissed by most. But as the animals begin to amass and the mists and rains slowly begin, anxiety intensifies. Re Jana, in love with the boat builder's youngest son, realizes the truth and struggles to find a way to save her family in this powerful novel.   *djg*

Roep, Nanda, and Marijke ten Cate. **Kisses**. Asheville, NC: Front Street/Lemniscaat, 2002. Originally published by Lemniscaat b.v. Rotterdam under the title *Kusje*. ISBN 1-8869-1085-5. 28 p. (3–6). Picture book.

Lissa Racoon asks her father for a kiss and Daddy wants to know if she wants a witch's kiss or a butterfly kiss, or a grandma kiss, vacation kiss, birthday kiss. . . . Who knew how many kinds of kisses there could be, but Lisa is content with a goodnight kiss and is fast asleep on the last page. Bright paintings will make little ones giggle.   *djg*
Author and illustrator live in the Netherlands

Schubert, Ingrid, and Dieter Schubert. **Hammer Soup**. Asheville, NC: Front Street, 2003. Originally published in the Netherlands as *Gekke buren* by Lemniscaat b.v. Rotterdam, 2003. ISBN 1-932425-02-0. 32 p. (3–8). Picture book.

Kate keeps a tidy house, works hard at her garden, and keeps to herself while preparing for winter. Bruce builds a monstrous drafty house next door, fishes, and plays instead of preparing for winter. His attempts at friendship are turned down and Kate's attempts to get Bruce to collect apples or to do something useful are answered with "Maybe tomorrow." When his house blows away during a storm Kate takes him in but tells him ". . . you can't eat up my food." Bruce suggests they make hammer soup. When the soup is bland, Kate adds vegetables from her garden and the two opposites become friends in this Dutch version of *Stone Soup*. The full-color, welcoming illustrations exemplify how different Kate and Bruce really are and assist in making this an enjoyable version of a well-known tale.   *kmc*
Authors live in Amsterdam

Schubert, Ingrid, and Dieter Schubert. **There's Always Room for One More**. Asheville, NC: Front Street/Lemniscaat, 2002. Originally published in the Netherlands under the title *Er Kan nog meer bij*. ISBN 1-886910-77-4. 32 p. (2–6). Picture book.

One day beaver builds a little boat just for fun. He invites all his animal friends (originally introduced in *Bear's Eggs, There's a Hole in My Bucket*, and *Beaver's Lodge*) and realizes he will need a bigger raft. The fun really begins when all his friends climb on board sinking the raft lower and lower into the water. When butterfly gently lands and capsizes the raft (a la *Mr. Gumpy's Outing*), beaver decides to go back to his original little boat. Beautiful watercolor illustrations will make this a sure hit with preschoolers.   *djg*
Authors are the creators of Amazing Animals, *winner of the National Parenting Publications Gold Award. Their first book,* There's a Crocodile under My Bed *was published in 14 countries and their books have been translated in 21 languages.*

Simoen, Jan. **What About Anna?** Translation by John Nieuwenhuizen. New York: Walker, 2002. First published in 1999 as *En met Anna?* in the Netherlands by Em Querido's Uitgeverij. First English language edition published in 2001 in Australia by Allen & Unwin. ISBN 0-8027-8808-4. 254 p. (12 up). Novel.

As sixteen-year-old Anna is about to graduate from school in Louvain, Belgium, that June of 1999, she is trying to refocus her family life. While it is the past that holds the key to her future, it is a past that this dysfunctional family finds hard to face. When an unexpected and cryptic letter arrives from Hugo, a family friend, suggesting that perhaps Anna's bother Michael is alive and did not die in a landmine explosion in Bosnia, Anna is drawn into a secret search for the truth and the fragile family relationship is tested. *Book Club Award in 1997 for Met Mij Gaat Alles Goed (Everything's Fine with Me), 1996; Flemish Youth Jury Award in 2001.*   *ok*
Author lives in Louvain, Belgium

Veldkamp, Tjibbe. **The School Trip**. Pictures by Philip Hopman. Asheville, NC: Front Street, 2001. Originally published in the Netherlands under the title *Het Schoolreisje* by Lemniscaat b.v. Rotterdam, 2000. ISBN 1-8869-1070-7. 28 p. (4–8). Picture book.

Davy's mother sends him off to school, but he heard about stern teachers and homework and bullies and didn't like the sound of it. So he heads off to build his own school. The next day, Davy adds wheels to his school so that he might "go far" and so he does, crashing right into Mr. Stern's classroom. At recess, the children are intrigued with Davy's ingenuity and put the wheels on *their* school. They all planned to go far! Watercolor illustrations add to the humor and merriment of the tale.   *djg*
Author and illustrator won the Silver Brush Award for 22 Orphans *in 1999.*

Velthuijs, Max. **Frog and the Wide World**. Kim Wood, Janice Thomson. Illustrated by author. London: Milet Publishing Ltd., 2002. ISBN 1-840-59199-4. 32 p. (3–7). Picture book.

Frog joins Rat on an expedition to explore the world. When Frog becomes homesick, he discovers that it is always possible to return home. Like other books in the Frog series, this book has been translated into Spanish and appears as a bilingual picture book in at least eight languages. Timeless elegance permeates these pithy stories about friendship and life. Other books include: *Frog and Duck, Frog Finds a Friend, Frog Is Frog*, etc. The author-illustrator lives in The Hague where he has earned the *Dutch Silver Pencil Award, German Bestlist Award, French Prix de Treize, Dutch Golden Brush Award, and the American Graphic Award of the Society of Illustrators.   nrn*

Vos, Ida. **The Key Is Lost**. Translated by Terese Edelstein. New York: Harper-Collins, 2000. First published in the Netherlands, 1996. ISBN 0-6881-6283-5. 272 p. (9–12). Novel.

Twelve-year old Eva and her sister Lisa go into hiding in Nazi-occupied Holland and must change locations and even their names to escape discovery. The sisters are separated from their parents and eventually end up with a kindly puppeteer, who keeps them safe. CCBC calls this "a unique, suspenseful novel about terror-filled experiences, filled with believable dialogue and credible responses on the parts of children and adults." Like her first book, *Dancing on the Bridge of Avignon*, Vos bases this revelatory series of vignettes on her experiences as a Jewish child in Holland during WWII. *Best Children's Books of the Year, 2001; Publishers Weekly Starred Review; Sydney Taylor Book Awards Winner 2000.   djg*

Vries, Anke de. **Bruises**. Translated by Stacey Knecht. Asheville, NC: Front Street/Lemniscaat, 2003, c1995. ISBN 1-8869-1009-X. Originally published as *Blauwe Plekken* in 1992. 176 p. (12 up). Novel.

Michael, athletic but reading disabled, and Judith, painfully withdrawn but intelligent, meet in school. They both have family secrets: Michael's overachiever father berates his every move; Judith is regularly and severely beaten by her mother. Both are scarred, but Michael is recovering with the help of his aunt and uncle. Despite obvious telltale signs, no one realizes Judith's problem until Michael sees her carefully concealed bruises and convinces Judith that she must take the first step to stop the abuse. Several violent scenes.   *cmt*

Related Information

Awards

Jenny Smelik-IBBY Prize
This award is given annually to the author/illustrator/initiator of a work of children's fiction that contributes to better understanding of ethnic minorities.

Golden Brush Award

This is given for the year's most beautiful illustrations, with up to two Silver Brush Awards given to honorable mentions.

Golden Kiss Award

Established in 1997, this is the counterpart to the Golden Pencil for young adult novels; similarly, honor books are given the Silver Kiss Award.

Golden Pencil Award

This annual prize for the best children's book is considered the most important Dutch prize; honor books are called Silver Pencils and up to six are awarded annually.

The Netherlands shares a common language with Flanders, one of the federal states of Belgium, and a group of Flemish awards corresponds to the above. They are the **Book Lion** (with honor books called Book Cubs) given for text and the **Book Peacock** given for illustrations. Several other national prizes are awarded for children's books. The website of the Dutch publisher E.M.

Querido's Uitgeverij offers an explanation at www.querido.nl/summary.html.

Organizations

Stichting IBBY sectie Nederland (Dutch section of IBBY), PO Box 17162, NL-1001 JD, Amsterdam, The Netherlands

Stichting Collectieve Propaganda van het Nederlandse Boek (CPNB)

Foundation for the Collective Promotion of the Dutch Book CPNB in Amsterdam, PO Box 10576, NL-1001 EN Amsterdam, The Netherlands.

The CPNB organizes the annual children's book week during the first week in October, in order to promote reading and sale of books. It is responsible for the Slate Pencil and Brush awards.

Print and Online Resources

Linders, Joke, and Marita de Sterck. **Behind the Story: Children's Books Authors in Flanders and the Netherlands**. With an introduction by Aidan Chambers. Translated from the Dutch by Jan Michael and Rina Vergano. Published under the auspices of Miniterie van de Vlaamse Gemeenschap Administratie Cultuur, 1996. ISBN 90-803223-1-8. 239 p. Reference.

This second companion to Dutch and Flemish children's authors is the successor to *Nice to Meet You* (1993). An overview of the literature of the low countries is followed by biographical information of prominent children's book authors and illustrators, a listing of the awards, and selected institutions and organizations and periodicals. A list of translators from the Dutch language and publishing houses in Flanders and the Netherlands is appended.

Bol.com
www.nl.bol.com
This site follows the familiar format of the online bookstore and is easy to negotiate, even for those who do not know Dutch.

NORWAY

Mette Newth presented the Dorothy Briley Memorial Lecture at the the fifth IBBY Regional Conference sponsored by USBBY and held at the Chautauqua Institute in October 2003. The text of this speech may be read in the Horn Book Magazine, March/April, 2004. Her book **The Abduction** (1989) was annotated in *Children's Books from Other Coutries* and **The Dark Light** (1998) and **The Transformation** (2000) in *The World through Children's Books*.

Ørdal, Stina Langlo. **Princess Aasta**. New York: Bloomsbury, 1999. ISBN 1-58234-783-2. 28 p. (4–8). Picture book.

Once upon a time, the princess wanted a bear to love and so she sent a letter to the newspaper. She receives responses from all over the world, but chooses a polar bear named Kvitebjørn in this original tale based on the Norwegian folktale "Kvitebjørn Kong Valemon." The typed text is cut and pasted in a collage fashion and the stylized, scribbley line drawings are filled in with dashes of color giving this tale a contemporary, fantasy feeling. *djg*

Pattou, Edith. **East**. Orlando, FL: Harcourt, 2003. ISBN 0-15-20463-5. 498 p. (12 up). Literary fairy tale.

At Rose's birth, her parents hide the portents of her wanderlust. Nevertheless, many years later Rose departs riding a white bear, headed for the frigid North. Inevitably, Rose betrays her bewitched bear/prince, condemning him to life with the trolls and herself to a heroic journey of repentance, finally breaking the Troll Queen's spell. As with Robin McKinley's *Beauty*, Pattou retains the essence of Asbjørnsen and Moe's Norwegian fairy tale, "East o' the Sun and West o' the Moon," while expanding characterization and setting. Told in alternating voices, this novelization establishes a tangible sense of Norway's terrain, heritage, and folklore. *lmp*
Author lives in United States

ALF PRØYSEN (1914–1971)

Prøysen was born in Norway and started writing when he was in his early twenties. He produced radio programs for children and wrote a weekly column in one of Norway's largest daily newspapers. His books about the amazing Mrs. Pepperpot became widely known after being read on the radio. Although many of the books are now out of print, it is fitting that two of the stories have been brought to life on an audio recording by Chivers.

Prøysen, Alf. **Little Old Mrs. Pepperpot and Mrs. Pepperpot Again**. Bath, UK: Chivers Audio Books, 2002. ISBN 0-7540-6531-6. Read by Penelope Keith. Mrs. Pepperpot is an ordinary woman who shrinks to the size of a pepperpot from time to time. The setting of the stories adds to their charm; they take place in Norway and contain traditional features of Norwegian life.

Sortland, Bjørn. **The Dream Factory Starring Anna & Henry**. Translated by Emily Virginia Christianson and Robert Hedin. Illustrated by Lars Elling. Minneapolis: Carolrhoda, 2001. First published in Norway in 1999 by Det Samlaget, Oslo, under the title *24 I sekundet*. ISBN 0-87614-009-6. 40 p. (7–12). Picture book.

Uncle Paul wraps Anna and Henry's Christmas gift in a riddle and hides it. When the children venture into the dark, creepy recesses of the attic to find the gift, they encounter sixteen actors and actresses from classic movies. The children meet up with Charlie Chaplin and Johnny Weismuller, Gene Kelly and King Kong, and even Ben Hur. Remembering uncle's advice that it is better to give than receive, they give their gift—a sled—to Orson Wells. The surrealistic art adds to the scary effect.

Author and illustrator from Norway. Their first book Anna's Art Adventure won Norway's Gold Medal for illustration.

Related Information

Norwegian Section of IBBY
Norsk Barnbokforum
c/o Ms. Vibeke Voss
Valdresgt. 13 D
NO-0557 Oslo
e-mail e-nyr@online.no

Online Resources

"Children's Literature" an informative article about Norwegian Children's Literature can be found on the website Norway: the official site in the UK.
http://www.norway.org.uk/culture/literature/children/children.htm

"Norwegian Children's Literature"
The Ministry of Foreign Affairs offers a comprehensive collection of feature articles and background information about Norway written by specialists in various fields.
http://odin.dep.no/odin/engelsk/norway/history/032001-990014/index-dok000-b-n-a.html

POLAND

Bogacki, Tomek. **Circus Girl**. New York: Farrar, Straus and Giroux, 2001. ISBN 0-3743-1291-5. 32 p. (4–7). Picture book.
When the circus comes to town, everyone is excited except Tim. But the outgoing Circus girl befriends him and when she realizes the other children make fun of him, she teaches them a lesson in tolerance. Soft, impressionistic style illustrations add to this story of friendship and compassion. *Best Children's Books of the Year, 2002; Bank Street College of Education; Notable Social Studies Trade Books for Young People, 2002; National Council for the Social Studies NCSS; Publisher's Weekly Starred Review, August 2001; Smithsonian Magazine's Notable Books for Children, 2001.* Other books illustrated by Bogacki include: *When You Visit Grandma & Grandpa (2004), Daffodil (2004), and Mama's Comin' Home (2003). djg*
Author from Poland, lives in New York

Hesse, Karen. **The Cats in Krasinski Square**. Illustrated by Wendy Watson. New York: Scholastic Press, 2004. ISBN 0-439-43540-4. 32 p. (5–10). Picture book.
A ten-year-old Jewish girl walks her Polish walk and wears her Polish look to "pass" and escapes the German soldiers to assist the resistance in smuggling food into the Warsaw ghetto during World War II. When she learns that the Germans plan to raid a train in which many resisitance workers are hiding food, she conceives of a plan to confound the Nazi search dogs with the aid of the hundreds of abandoned cats in Krasinski Square. Hesse's spare text combined with Watson's luminescent watercolor illustrations combine to bring this powerful and haunting account of bravery and courage to life. *Sydney Taylor Book Award Honor Book 2004; Notable Children's Books, 2005; Publisher's Weekly Starred Reviews; Kirkus Booklist. djg*

Korczak, Janusz. **King Matt the First**. Translated by Richard Lourie. Chapel Hill, NC: Algonquin Books, 2004. First published in Polish in 1923 as *Król Maciuâs Pierwszy*. ISBN 1-56512-442-1. 330 p. (10–13). Novel.

After the death of his father, little Matt must take over the daunting role of King. Overwhelmed at first by the power and influence of his ministers, Matt despairs he will never be able to make a proper king, and his three neighboring kings take advantage by declaring war. Matt's friendship with a common boy, Felek, leads Matt to run away to join the fight along the front lines. King Matt returns home a war hero and his new experience and wisdom allow him to embrace his role and begin making reforms to benefit his country, particularly the children. The "Reformer King" builds a zoo, creates summer camps for poor children, and establishes two parliaments—one for adults, one for children. These expensive reforms will eventually be his undoing, but King Matt establishes a reputation for being a good and kind king. An introduction by Esme Raji Codell is included, in which she explores the question: "What makes this children's book one of the greatest of all time?" *aao*
Author lived in Poland

Pieńkowski, Jan. **The Animals Went in Two by Two: A Noah's Ark Pop-up Book**. Cambridge, MA: Candlewick, 2003. ISBN 0-7636-199-4. 18 p. (4–8). Picture book.

The words to this silly song are cleverly animated in this movable book. Using vibrant colors and creative pop-ups the reader views animals two by two, three by three, and so on. They all climb onto the ark to get out of the rain. Born in Warsaw and living in England, this renowned illustrator has won two Kate Greenaway Medals. *djg*

Related Information

IBBY Poland
free.ngo.pl/ibby

PORTUGAL

Zink, Rui. **The Boy Who Did Not Like Television**. Translated by Patrick Dreher. Illustrated by Manuel Jao Ramos. San Francisco: MacAdam/Cage, 2004. First published as *Bebé que não gostava de televisão* in Portugal by Publicaçõeso Dom Quixote, Lda, 2002. ISBN 1-9311561-96-6. 24 p. (3–7). Picture book.

Once upon a time there was a very cute little boy who loved his daddy and mommy very much. So begins this picture book about a little boy who loved to eat and sleep and dream happy dreams. But to the amazement of his loving parents, the neighbors, and all the experts, he does not like TV. Could something be wrong? Not hardly! This little boy knows what is important in his life. Simply told with bright, colorful illustrations, this little story packs a big lesson. *Author from Portugal*

ROMANIA

Răscol, Sabina I. **The Impudent Rooster**. Adapted from a Romanian Story by Ion Creangă. Illustrated by Holly Berry. New York: Dutton, 2004. ISBN 0-525-47179-0. 32 p. (4–9). Picture book.

When the rooster's owner, desperate hunger, becomes angry, the rooster goes out into the world and finds a fortune. A greedy nobleman takes the fortune from him before he can return to his master, thus beginning a clever tale of justice and love. Stylized, folk illustrations in bright colors complement this traditional story. The author tells us in a note that she adapted it because all Romanian children grow up knowing this amazing rooster and she wanted English-speaking children to have that privilege, too. *djg*

Related Information

Organizations

IBBY Romania
www.aep.ro

RUSSIA

Beneduce, Ann. **Philipok** by Leo Tolstoy. Illustrated by Gennady Spirin. New York: Philomel, 2000. ISBN 0-399-23482-9. 32 p. (4–8). Picture book.

Leo Tolstoy's tale is simply told and richly illustrated. This is the story of a younger brother who wants nothing more than to go to school with his elder brother, Peter. He waits until grandmother falls asleep, takes his hat and coat off the peg, and sets out through the snow to the schoolhouse on the other side of the village. Though cold and frightened when he arrives at school, he earns the privilege of staying at school. Beneduce uses her considerable storytelling skill to produce a charming read aloud edition. Spirin, born in Russia, combines contemporary Russian technique with traditions of the Renaissance to illustrate this story. Notes about Tolstoy are appended. *djg*
Author from United States

Whelan, Gloria. **Angel on the Square**. New York: HarperCollins, 2001. ISBN 0-06-029030-7. 293 p. (10–14). Novel.

Katya, a twelve-year-old girl of privilege, is growing up in St. Petersburg and witnesses the outbreak of both the Great War and the Russian Revolution. Her friend Misha opens her eyes to life beyond her sheltered world and she becomes aware of the poverty and plight of child laborers. This novel gives a child's view of a complex period of history. A glossary of Russian terms is appended. The companion, *The Impossible Journey (2000)*, is set during Stalin's reign of terror. *Best Children's Books of the Year, 2002; Notable Social Studies Trade Books for Young Readers, 2002; Publisher's Weekly Starred Review.* *djg* *Author from United States*

Related Information

Organizations

IBBY Russia
www.rbby.ru

SPAIN

Castán, Javier Sáez. **The Three Hedgehogs: A Pantomime in Two Acts and a Colophon**. Translations from the Latin: David Wachsmuth. First published in Spanish as *Los Tres Erizos* by Ediciones Ekaré, 2003. Toronto: Groundwood Books, 2004. ISBN 0-88899-595-4. 32 p. (4–8). Picture book.
 Early one beautiful morning in the French countryside three hungry hedgehogs leave their house to look for food. They find apples in an orchard and roll around until the apples stick to their spines, go home, and have a feast. The farmers wife calls a posse to find the thieves, but alas there are no tracks. The action is portrayed in this simply told pantomime (meaning here a short, comic play) in three acts and a colophon. Visual puns abound in the soft watercolor illustrations. A glossary defines the Latin, French, and Spanish phrases integrated into the set design of each act. *djg*

Juan, Ana. **The Night Eater**. New York: Arthur A. Levine/Scholastic, 2004. ISBN 0-439-48891-5. 32 p. (4–7). Picture book.
 With his pointy red nose and flowing pink cap, the Night Eater follows the moon, snacking on stars, gobbling up the nighttime and making room for his friend the sun. But one night, when the moon looked back at his friend, he notices that Night Eater has grown a bit large. Embarrassed, he decides not to eat another bit. With no room for the sun to appear the fantastic creatures must endure the darkness. It is the children who look up and cry out for the Night Eater and set things aright. Stylized folk paintings using acrylics on wax paper add to

the simple storytelling. *Ezra Jack Keats New Illustrator Award Winner, 2005; starred reviews in Booklist and Publishers Weekly.* djg

Keselman, Gabriela, and Noemí Villamuza. **Marc Just Couldn't Sleep**. La Jolla, CA: Kane/Miller, 2004. First published in 2001 by Editorial Kókinos, Spain. ISBN 1-929132-68-9. 28 p. (4–7). Picture book.

Marc really did want to go to sleep, but he was afraid a mosquito would fly in to bite him. Clever mom fixes that by making him a special pair of mosquito proof pajamas. Next he is afraid he will fall out of bed, and mom fixes that too. Long into the night after mom fixes all the fears they learn that really only one thing is needed, in this comforting bedtime tale. Deep earth-tone watercolor and crayon drawings illustrate the story with gentle humor.   djg
Author lives in Spain and Argentina and has published over thirty books in both countries. Illustrator lives in Spain and was a finalist for the Spanish National Prize of Illustration in 2002.

Lairla, Sergio. **Abel and the Wolf**. Translated by Marianne Martens. Illustrated by Alessandra Roberti. New York: North-South, 2004. ISBN 0-7358-1903-3. 32 p. (4–7). Picture book.

When Abel leaves home his parents give him a pot, a walking stick, a knife, some seeds, and a book with golden letters. He finds the perfect place to build his house, but the wolf thinks it will be perfect too. The two become friends in this charming story illustrated with watercolor paintings.

Sepulveda, Luis. **The Story of a Seagull and the Cat Who Taught Her to Fly**. Translated by Margaret Sayers Peden. Illustrated by Chris Sheban. New York: Arthur A. Levine Books, 2003. First published under the title: *Historia de una gaviota y del gato que le enseno a volar*. ISBN 0-439-40186-0. 126 p. (8–12). Novel.

Zorba, a fat, black, lazy cat in Hamburg, Germany, gets ready to enjoy four weeks of uninterrupted peace while his owners are away on vacation. Plans change when a seagull poisoned by a nearby oil spill lands on his deck and makes a dying request. The gull, Kengah, is about to lay an egg, and she asks Zorba to take care of the egg, raise the baby gull after it's born, and teach the gull to fly. Zorba agrees, believing he will get help for the gull before she dies and therefore be free of his promise. But help arrives too late, and Zorba must be true to his word. Since "the word of one cat of the port is the word of all the cats of the port," Lucky, the baby gull, is born into a community of cats determined to fulfill their promise to Kengah. This timeless, heart-warming story about courage and the power of love over individual differences is filled with humor and memorable characters, and is sure to find readers for years to come. *Best Children's Books of the Year, 2004; Publisher's Weekly Starred Review.*   aao
Author from Chile, lived in Germany for ten years, now lives in Spain

Related Information

Bookfairs

LIBER. Feria Internacional del Libro (Barcelona)
http://www.liber.ifema.es/
October—alternates between Barcelona (even year) and Madrid (odd year)

Organizations

IBBY Spain
www.oepli.org

IBBY Spain (Basque Branch)
www.oepli.org/galtza

IBBY Spain (Catalán Branch)
www.oepli.org/cclij

IBBY Spain (Galician Branch)
www.oepli.ort/galix

Amigo del Libro Infantil y Juvenil
http://www.amigosdelibro.com/objetivos.htm (Spanish only)

SWEDEN

Ahvander, Ingmarie. **Pancake Dreams**. Translated by Elisabeth Kallick Dyssegaard. Illustrated by Mati Lepp. Stockholm: R&S Books, 2002. Originally published as *Farmors Pangkakor* by Rabén & Sjögren in 2001. ISBN 91-29-65652-4. 28 p. (3–8). Picture book.

After Stefan and his family move to Jordan, he soon misses his grandma Elsa who remained in Sweden. Stefan particularly misses his grandma's specially made pancakes. With help from his family and several kind travelers, a plan is devised that allows his grandmother to send Stefan a box of her special pancakes without worry of them being reduced to crumbs. This is a delightful portrayal of the special bond existing between grandparent and young grandchild. Colorful, cartoon-like illustrations in pen, ink, and watercolor equal the quiet humor of the text. *js*

Arro, Lena. **By Geezers and Galoshes!** Translated from the Swedish by Rabén and Sjögren Bokforlag. Illustrated by Catarina Kruusval. Stockholm: R&S

Books, 2001. Originally published in Sweden under the title *Gubbar och ga-loscher!* ISBN 91-29-65348-7. 28 p. (5–8). Picture book.

Old man Granstrom and his brother Herring August receive a surprise deliv-ery on the mail boat—their grandnephew, Bubble, with a note attached to the back of his jacket. How will they keep a little boy amused for a whole week? Bubble opens up a large box that contains a ship model kit with "close to a mil-lion pieces." The uncles build the model while Bubbles falls asleep. They finish at midnight and follow the last direction: "for full size, please place model in water." The next morning, to their surprise, the model has become a full-size sailing vessel. The three decide to sail away as pirates with hilarious results. The inviting, cozy, and very detailed watercolor illustrations will draw the reader into the imaginative storyline. Also by this author is a simple picture book, *Good Night, Animals*, translated by Joan Sandin and published in 2002 under the title *Godnatt alla djur.* *sl*

Carlsson, Janne. **Camel Bells**. Translated by Angela Barnett-Lindberg. Toronto: Groundwood, 2002, 1989. Originally published in 1987 as *Kamelklockorna* by Rabén & Sjögren. ISBN 0-88899-515-6. 120 p. (10 up). Novel.

Set in Afghanistan during the late 1970s when a left-wing group supported by the Soviet Union took over Kabul, this is the story of two young boys and their struggle to survive. Twelve-year-old Hajdar must find a way to support his fam-ily now that his father is dead. He is able to make his way to the city where he earns some money, but he longs to get back to the countryside. But when heli-copters fly over the city and bombs begin to fall, he wonders if he will ever see his family again. *djg*

Edvall, Lilian. **The Rabbit Who Didn't Want to Go to Sleep**. Translated by Elisabeth Kallick Dyssegaard. Illustrated by Sara Gimbergsson. New York: R&S, 2004. Originally published as *Kaninen Som Inte Ville Sova* in Swedish, by Rabén & Sjögren in 2003. ISBN 9-1296-6001-7. unpaged. (3–5). Picture book.

After a long and busy day the rabbit is still not ready to go to bed. He begs his parents for extra time and, as he races his cars around the apartment, he acci-dentally knocks over a vase and wakes up his sister who thinks it is morning and wants her oatmeal. The tired parents want to read the children a bedtime story, but can't find little rabbit who, despite all his protests, has fallen asleep. As mommy carefully carries him to bed, his little sister says that she's not tired and can stay awake all night. Also by the author is *The Rabbit Who Longed for Home* (2001). *ok*
Author lives outside Stockholm, Sweden

Eriksson, Eva. **Molly Goes Shopping**. Translated from the Swedish by Elisabeth Kallick, Dyssegaard. Illustrated by the author. ISBN 91-29-65819-5. New York: R&S Books, 2003. (3–7). Picture book.

Molly is finally old enough to go to the store alone, but makes three trips before it turns out almost right. The first time she is overwhelmed and lies to her grandmother about why she returns with the wrong item. On the second trip she loses grandmother's purse, and finally succeeds on try number three. Molly is a pig and grandmother is a polar bear, but it doesn't matter to the reader. Soft colored pencil drawings with lots of white space and contrast with a timeless story make this book succeed. *mw*

Höjer, Dan, and Lotta Höjer. **Heart of Mine: A Story of Adoption**. New York: R&S Books, 2001. Originally published in Sweden by Rabén & Sjögren Bokförlag, Stockholm, 2000. ISBN 91-29-65301-0. 28 p. (4–8). Picture book.

This simple story of a family who longs to adopt a child is illustrated in watercolor and crayon and tells of a mommy and daddy who long for a child to love. One day the phone rings and they are told that their daughter, Tu Thi, has been born. They journey to a faraway land and meet their little girl and bring her home where she is never farther away than their thoughts and dreams. In a note at the back of the book we learn that Dan and Lotta Höjer traveled to Vietnam to bring their daughter home to Sweden. *djg*

SPOTLIGHT ON SELMA LAGERLÖF

One of Tove Jansson's favorite activities as a child was reading, and she listed Selma Lagerlöf among her favorite writers in *Min väg till barnboken*. The most famous children's work of Sweden's greatest fiction writer and Nobel Prize winner, *The Wonderful Adventures of Nils,* first published in Stockholm, in 1906, was partly inspired by Kipling's animal stories. Nils, transformed to elf-size, jumps on the back of the farm's gander and joins a flock traveling to Lapland.

Read excerpts from the book at: http://digital.library.upenn.edu/women/lagerlof/nils/nils.html

---

Landström, Lena. **The New Hippos**. Translated from the Swedish by Joan Sandin. Stockholm: R&S Books, 2003. ISBN 91-29-65923-3. unpaged. (3–7). Picture book.

A delightful look into the way a family assimilates itself into the established neighborhood of hippos. First, they are ignored until Baby Hippo shows the other babies how to somersault off the diving board. Then, a kind Mama Hippo helps the new Mother Hippo with tools to build her hut. They seal the deal by gathering fresh fruit from the jungle to share with the neighbors. The message,

neighbors accepting and caring for each other, comes across without being didactic. Watercolor illustrations in subdued colors support the story without
overpowering the text. Sequel to *The Little Hippos' Adventure* (R & S Books,
2002). *sl*

Lindahl, Inger. **Bertil and the Bathroom Elephants**. Translated by Elisabeth
Kallick Dyssegaard. Illustrated by Eva Lindström. Stockholm: R&S Books, distributed by Farrar Straus and Giroux, 2003. Originally published as *Bertil och
Badrums-Elefanterna* in Sweden by Raben & Sjogren in 2002. ISBN 91-29-
65944-2. unpaged. (4–8). Picture book.

Bertil blames the bathroom ocean and dad's missing underwear (jammed
down the toilet) on elephants living beneath the tub. One evening the elephants
growl and grab, which triggers toilet-phobia in Bertil. This delightfully imaginative fantasy provides striking contrast between picture storybooks from Sweden and America in topic, treatment, and illustrative technique. Bertil's individ-
uality is respected, his fears never demeaned. The bathroom setting includes
toilet, underwear, and bare bottoms—things rarely included in American publications. All ends happily when the elephants move from Bertil's bathroom—into
a musical neighbor's parlor. "How lucky it is that Bengali bathroom elephants
like the saxophone!" *lmp*
Author and illustrator live in Sweden

Lindenbaum, Pija. **Bridget and the Gray Wolves**. New York: R&S Books, 2001.
ISBN 9129653959. Translated by Kjersti Board. Originally published in Sweden
as *Gittan och gråvargarna* by Rabén and Sjögren Bokförlag, 2001. 32 p. (4–7).
Picture book.

Bridget is a very careful child who won't play on the roof, pet the dog, or jump
over a muddy ditch at day care. However, when Bridget is lost in the woods
overnight she tames a wolf pack. As she invents games for them to play together,
Bridget even climbs a tree to save a scared wolf. After seeing Bridget safely to
the edge of the forest the next morning near her day care it is the wolf pack that
is too afraid to leave the safety of the woods and they beg Bridget to come back
some day. The ink and watercolor paintings show a timid Bridget at first but as
she finds her courage it is the wolves that appear apprehensive and fearful. Other
books in the series include: *Bridget and the Muttonheads* (2002) and *Bridget and
the Moose Brothers* (2003). *kmc*
Author lives in Sweden

Lindgren, Astrid. **Mirabelle**. Translated from the Swedish by Elizabeth Kallik
Dyssegaard. Pictures by Pija Lindenbaum. New York: R&S Books, 2003. ISBN
91-29-65821-7. unpaged. (4–8). Picture book.

A little country girl wishes for a doll of her own, but her parents barely make
enough from the sale of their garden bounty to feed and clothe the family. One

"strange" evening an old man passes by their lane and gives her a golden seed to plant. What grows, to her surprise, is a doll that comes to life only in her presence. Pure fantasy enhanced by watercolor illustrations that are both quirky and humorous. Story was originally published in 1949. *sl*

Lindgren, Astrid. **Most Beloved Sister**. Translated by Elisabeth Kallick Dyssegaard. Illustrations by Hans Arnold. New York: R&S Books, 2002. Originally published in Sweden by Rabén & Skögren under the title *Allrakäraste Syster*. Text copyright 1949 by Astrid Lindgren. Illustrations 1973 by Hans Arnold. ISBN 91-2965502-1. 28 p. (5–10). Picture book.

Barbara introduces us to her imaginary twin sister Lalla-Lee and tells of their magical adventures behind the rosebush where she enters the Great and Horrible Forest. There are friends and animals everywhere and the two girls gallop away on horseback. But at the end of the day, she must say good-bye to her friends and return to the nursery and her worried parents; she finds a surprise waiting for her. *djg*
Author and illustrator from Sweden

Lindgren, Barbro. **Benny and the Binky**. Translated by Elizabeth Kallick Dyssegaard. Illustrated by Olaf Landström. New York: R&S Books, 2002. Originally published as *Jamen Benny* by Raben & Sjogren in 2001. ISBN 91-29-65497-1. 28 p. (3–5). Picture book.

Benny the pig had been looking forward to the arrival of his new brother, but finds he would rather have the baby's binky (pacifier). Mother says he's too old for one so Benny puts his brother outside (unbeknownst to her) and runs away with the binky. Before long other children began to jeer at him because of the pacifier sticking out of his mouth. After a close call with some bullies, Benny ran home, and decided that he really did like his brother and that the binky is more appropriate for the baby than for himself. Cartoon style illustrations in pastel and autumnal colors portray a self-sufficient preschooler (piglet) and show lots of emotions and movement with great humor and empathy. *sg and jlv*
Author lives in Sweden

Lindgren, Barbro, and Eva Eriksson. **Julia Wants a Pet**. Translated by Elisabeth Kallick Dyssegaard. New York: R&S Books, 2003. Originally published in Sweden by Eriksson & Lindren under the title *Julia vill ha ett djur*. Rabén & Sjögren, 2002. ISBN 91-29-65940-X. 28 p. (5–9). Picture book.

Julia comes racing out of her apartment building pushing a baby carriage and she is in a big hurry! She wants to play, but even more she wants a pet. She would like a pony, but she would take a hedgehog or a swan or a dog or a rat, but she doesn't want a worm. The dog tied outside a shop doesn't work out, nor does the little boy . . . perhaps a beetle. But then, for her eighth birthday Julia gets her very own cat.

Lindgren, Barbro. **Rosa Goes to Daycare**. Translated by Maria Lundin. Illustrated by Eva Eriksson. Toronto: Groundwood Books/Douglas & McIntyre, 2000. Originally published as *Rosa pa dagis* by Eriksson & Lindgren in 1999. ISBN 0-88899-391-9. 28 p. (3–6). Picture book.

Rosa, a bull terrier, is upset by city life so her "aunt" (owner) enrolls her in a friendly doggy daycare center and Rosa makes lots of friends with the other dogs. One snowy day Rosa runs away from her caretakers, falls in the icy water, and is promptly rescued and given lots of attention. Children will identify with Rosa's experiences and be charmed by the colored pencil illustrations that express the dogs' individual natures and quirks with humor and warmth. *sg*
Author lives in Sweden

Mankell, Henning. **Secrets in the Fire**. Translated by Anne Connie Struksrud. Toronto: Annick, 2003. First published as *Eldens Hemlighet* by Rabén & Sjörgen in 1995. (Paperback: Annick, 2003). ISBN 1-55037-801-5. 176 p. (10–14). Novel.

Set in war-torn Mozambique, this story begins the night bandits attack a small village killing most of the villagers. Maria and Sophia and their mother and younger brother flee to a village in the mountains; it is in this village that Sophia steps on a landmine. With the help of many, Sophia walks again on artificial legs and learns to sew so that she can support herself. Although her story is about severe poverty and a constant struggle for survival, it is also about the strength and perseverance of the human spirit in overcoming pain and despair. The author's introduction provides an overview of the civil war in Mozambique. According to UNICEF, 30–40% of all landmine victims around the world are children, and those who survive face "physical, psychological, and economic hardship." Sofia Alface, an actual person, is one who survived after stepping on the landmine that killed her older sister Maria and robbed Sofia of both legs. Appended is a "Message from Adopt-A-Minefield." *Winner of the 2002 International Sankei Children's Publishing Culture Award; NY Public Library's Books for the Teen Age 2004 List.* *kk*
Author from Sweden but lives part of the time in Mozambique

Matthis, Nina. **The Grandma Hunt**. Pictures by Gunilla Kuarnström. Translated by Elisabeth Kallick Dyssegaard. New York: R&S Books, 2002. ISBN 9129656567. Originally published in Sweden by Rabén & Skögren Bokförlag, 2001. 26 p. (5–8). Picture book.

Every summer Jacob spends a week with Grandpa. They have lots of fun collecting things and building things until all the cousins arrive. For a time Jacob is jealous until the cousins become united in a mission . . . to find a grandma for grandpa. The fun begins and the ending intimates that the children are successful. Cartoon style, watercolor illustrations add to the humor of this charming story.

Mazetti, Katerina. **God and I Broke Up**. Translated by Maria Lundin. Toronto: Douglas & McIntyre, 2004. ISBN 0888995849. Originally published in Sweden. 127 p. (14 up). Novel.

For all of her 16 years, Linnea has been a thinker. She thinks about everything from boys to zits to why parents get divorced to whether or not God really exists and what happens when you die. When she and Pia become best friends, Linnea becomes a talker. Whether the subject is guys, school, the afterlife, or politics, Pia is someone she can talk to about everything. They're so close they're like twin souls. So why did Pia have to go and kill herself? With self-deprecating candor, Linnea recounts the year following her friend's suicide as she struggles to heal her grief. Alternately hilarious and profoundly sad, Linnea's voice illuminates both her inner and outer selves, vividly portraying the difficulty of appearing to be a smart, savvy teen while inwardly feeling crushed by the loss of her soul mate. Her dilemma, told with honesty, grace, and often-unsettling wit, is sure to resonate with young readers. Annotated by publisher.

Nilsson, Per. **Heart's Delight**. Translated by Tara Chace. Asheville, NC: Front Street-Lemniscaat, 2003. ISBN 1-886910-92-8. 155 p. (14 up). First published by Rabén & Skögren Bokförlag, 2003. Novel.

An unnamed narrator contemplates suicide as he revisits the beginning, middle, and end of his "first love" relationship with a girl who never felt as deeply as he. The depth of the turbulent feelings that he experiences is evoked by the almost lyical language of this award-winning author whose prizes include the Rabén & Skögren Bokförlag in 1992, the Deutscher Jugendliteraturepreis in 1997, and the Dutch "Silver Kiss" in 1999. *Children's Literature Choice List, 2004; four starred reviews.*   *mln*
Author from Sweden

Olofsson, Helena. **The Little Jester**. Translated by Kjersti Board. Stockholm: R&S, 2002. Originally published as *Gyclarpojken* by Rabén and Sjögren in 2002. ISBN 91-29-65499-8. 28 p. (8 up). Folktale.

One stormy night in the Middle Ages, a small jester is given shelter in a monastery. After a large dinner, the jester entertains the monks in the chapel. He juggles, tumbles, and plays tunes on his flute. The Abbot hears the commotion and when he discovers what is happening in the chapel he wants to throw the jester out. However, the monks see that a miracle has taken place. The painting of the Weeping Madonna has changed to the Smiling Madonna. The Abbot asks the jester's forgiveness and grants the jester's charitable wish.   *ls*
Author from Sweden

Olsson, Sören, and Anders Jacobsson. **In Ned's Head**. Translated from the Swedish by Kevin Read. New York: Atheneum, 2001. ISBN 0-689-83870-0. 133 p. (8–12). Novel.

Get right inside the head of this funny, quirky eleven-year-old boy through the entries in his diary. Most guys don't keep diaries but Ned, alias Treb Vladinsky, doesn't think he is like most guys. He tries to avoid the class bully, falls "in love" with the most beautiful girl in the class, and forms a spy club and a rock band with his best friends. So what makes Ned different from most guys? Read this fast-paced, laugh-out-loud novel and find out. The authors of *Ned's Diary* (*Berts Dagbok*) have written sixteen books about Ned, which have been the biggest selling book in Sweden's history and have been translated into thirteen languages. They are also the authors of the Swedish *Tosh* series and *Big Sister and Little Brother*. *Starred review in Booklist.*   *djg*
Authors live near Örebro, Sweden

Schyffert, Bea Uusma. **The Man Who Went to the Far Side of the Moon: The Story of Apollo 11 Astronaut Michael Collins**. Translated by Emi Guner. San Francisco: Chronicle Books, 2003. Originally published as *Astronauten Som Inte Fick Landa Om Michael Collins, Apollo 11 Och 9 Kilo Checklistor* in Sweden by Alfabeta in, 1999. ISBN 0-8118-4007-7. 77 p. (9–12). Informational book.

Michael Collins, unlike his two companions Buzz Aldrin and Neil Armstrong, never stepped foot on the moon. Instead he patiently circled it, waiting to link up with the lunar module. This informational text offers something for everyone: biographical charts and photos; a list of personal objects each astronaut carried to the moon; space suits and their specifications; even meal descriptions. This books answers the types of questions kids would love to ask an astronaut: "After 8 days, 3 hours, and 18 minutes in Columbia without washing, the entire body itches. . . . [The capsule] smells like wet dogs and rotten swamp" (p. 68). *Swedish Book Art award; 2004 Mildred Batchelder Award.*   *lmp*
Author lives in Sweden

Stalfelt, Pernilla. **The Death Book**. Toronto: Groundwood, 2002. First published in Sweden as *Doden Boken* by Eriksson & Lindren in 1999. ISBN 0-88899-482-6. 28 p. (7–10). Honor book for the Deutscher Jugendliteraturpreis. Picture book.

Stalfelt, Pernilla. **The Love Book**. Toronto: Groundwood, 2002. First published in Sweden as *Karlek Boken* by Eriksson & Lindgren, 2001. ISBN 0-88899-455-9. 28 p. (7–10). Picture book.

The author tackles the subject of love and death with candor and tongue-in-cheek humor attempting to answer tough questions. In *The Death Book* questions such as: where do you go when you die, do ghosts exist, and what's a funeral are tempered with statements like "some think you become a star in the sky" and "there may be those who turn into vampires." Concepts like grief, cremation, graves, and wills are all introduced. *The Love Book* deals with all aspects of this joyful but overwhelming experience, from crushes to marriage, from sex to jealousy, love of God, love of rock stars, same-sex love, love potions, and dating to love of pets, food, and siblings. It's all here with a style of writing that is as quirky

as the line drawings with casual talk-bubbles that may be more entertaining for adults than for young children. *djg*
The author's first book, The Hair Book, *received the Elsa Beskow Award, the finest honor bestowed on illustrators in Sweden.*

Related Information

Awards

Astrid Lindgren Memorial Award

The Astrid Lindgren Memorial Award (ALMA), the world's largest prize for children's and young people's literature, was established by the Swedish Government in 2002. The annual prize of SEK 5 million (equivalent to approx. USD 655,000 or 530,000 Euros) may be awarded to authors, illustrators, and promoters of reading whose work reflects the spirit of Astrid Lindgren. The aim of the award is to increase interest in children's and young people's literature, and to promote children's rights on a global level. The award is administered by The Swedish National Council for Cultural Affairs.

Bookfairs

Göteborg International Book Fair
Göteborg, Sweden
phone: +46 (0) 31 708 8400
e-mail: info@goteborg-bookfair.com
http://www.bok-bibliotek.se/indexeng.htm

Organizations

IBBY Sweden
www.ibbysverige.a.se

The Swedish Institute for Children's Books

The foundation Svenska barnboksinstitutet, SBI (The Swedish Institute for Children's Books), is a special library open to the public and an information center for children's and young people's literature. The aim is to promote this kind of literature in Sweden as well as Swedish children's and young people's literature abroad. The charter is dated December 7, 1965, and operations commenced in 1967.
http://www.sbi.kb.se/
Odengatan 61
SE-113 22 STOCKHOLM
Underground station: Odenplan
Tel +46 (0)8-54 54 20 50, Fax +46 (0)8-54 54 20 54
email: info@sbi.kb.se

SWITZERLAND

Bardill, Linard. **The Great Golden Thing**. Translated from the German by J. Alison James. Illustrated by Miriam Monnier. New York: Michael Neugebauer/ North-South, 2001. First published in Switzerland under the title *Das Gelbe Ding*. ISBN 0-7358-1593-3. 28 p. (4–8). Picture book.

Bramble Bear is frightened by a strange golden sight on the other side of the forest and enlists the help of Gimli to find out if it is dangerous. As they travel across their island home they are joined by Hopple Hare and Brindle Bear. Brindle knows just what it is and when the friends discover that the great golden thing is a giant sunflower the frightened bear is relieved. Large, colorful paintings illustrate this book. *djg*

Blaich, Ute. **The Star**. Translated by Sibylle Kazeroid. Illustrated by Julie Litty. Originally published in Switzerland. New York: North-South Books, 2001. ISBN 0-7358-1509-7. (5–9). Picture book.

It is Christmas Eve and bitterly cold in the snow-covered field. Owl and his animals friends are discussing the lack of food when he realized that they do not know what Christmas Eve and the star of Bethlehem are. In childlike terms, Owl patiently explains the birth of the Son of God, love, and also less endearing qualities of the human race. The animals are familiar with people who treat them unkindly and are pleasantly surprised by a father and child who bring them sacks of fresh vegetables. *sl*

Chen, Kerstin. **Lord of the Cranes: A Chinese Tale**. Translated by J. Alison James. Illustrated by Jian Jiang Chen. First published in Switzerland under the title *Der Herr der Kraniche-Ein chinesische Sage*. ISBN 0-7358-1192-X. 32 p. (4–8). Folktale.

Tian, whose name means "heaven," lives in the clouds with his friends the crane. One day Tian decides to go to the city to see if the people are remembering to be kind and generous. After many months, he finds one, a humble innkeeper named Wang, who shows him kindness. Tian rewards the man by painting a beautiful mural of three cranes that can come to life when the guests sing and clap. Wang soon becomes rich, but always shares with those in need. Paintings on canvas illustrate this tale of compassion and humility. *djg*
Author lives in Germany and remembers the story from his childhood in China. Illustrator from Germany and has worked in Shangai, China.

Damjan, Mischa. **Atuk**. Illustrated by Josef Wilkon. New York: North-South Books, 2002. Originally published as *Atuk, der Eskimojunge* by Nord-Sud Verlag. ISBN 0-7358-1795-2. 28 p. (7–10). Picture book.

Atuk, an Inuit boy, swears revenge when his dog is killed by a wolf. He grows up, becomes a fine hunter, and kills the wolf but learns it does not bring

his dog back. At last he learns a lesson about living in peace with the environment. This unusual, almost abstract, tale is illustrated with atmospheric and psychologically expressive illustrations in wintry blues, grays, and white. The telling is somewhat choppy, but it may lead to good discussions on issues like peace and acceptance. *sg*
Author lives in Switzerland

Damjan, Mischa. **The Clown Said No**. Translated by Anthea Bell. Illustrated by Christa Unzner. New York: North-South Books, 2002. Orignally published as *Der Clown sagte Nein* by Nord-Sud Books in 2002. ISBN 0-7358-1552-6. 28 p. (5–7). Picture book.
A circus clown, tired of his ordained role, refuses to go on, and he and five of the animals leave to find their own destinies. Although they don't have a tent, they start an open air circus doing what they enjoy "for Children and Poets," to an appreciative crowd. The illustrations in the first part of the book are shadowed by gray tones, expressing the alienation of the clown and the animals. They brighten to fresh, joyous, spring colors when the performers are free to perform as they wish, for whom they wish. *sg*
Author, whose real name was Dimitrije Sidjanski, lived in Switzerland

Elschner, Geraldine. **Moonchild, Star of the Sea**. Translated by J. Alison James. Illustrated by Lieselotte Schwarz. New York: North-South Books, 2002. Originally published as *Sternenkind* in German by Michael Neugebauer Verlag (Switzerland) in 2002. ISBN 0-7358-1664-6. unpaged. (4–8). Picture book.
As the little star looks upon the earth, he sees some dark places and some lovely blue ones. Curious as to what they are, he asks the moon, who explains that the dark places are land and the blue ones are seas. Ever-curious, the little star wants to explore them for himself, and so he descends to earth on a beam of light and travels all over the land and water learning something new every day. Eventually the little star feels that he has seen everything and returns home to his place in the sky where he is welcomed back by a smiling moon. The watercolor illustrations primarily of blues, yellows, and pinks allow the textured paper to show through. They expand the little star's journey and lend a dreamy quality to the book. *ok*
Author from France, lives in Heidelberg, Germany. Illustrator from Poland, lived in Wiesbaden, Germany. Died in 2003. Honored with a Silver Medal of the Trienale in Milan and the Grand Prize of the Biennale for Illustration in Bratislava.

Fietzek, Petra. **Sophie and the Seagull**. Illustrated by Julia Ginsbach. Milwaukee, WI: Gareth Stevens Publishing, 2002. First published as *Sofie und die Lachmöwe*, 2000 by Atlantis Kinderbücher, Verlag Pro Juventute, Zürich. ISBN 0-8368-3174-8. 32 p. (5–8). Picture book.

When Sophie looks through her telescope she sees the waves, the lighthouse, and the boats. She would rather see the world through her telescope than play with the other children, but when the children see something moving in a distant bush, Sophie uses her telescope to help them discover an injured seagull. In caring for the bird and watching him rejoin the other seagulls, Sophie forms a friendship with the other children in this heart-warming story. Vibrant watercolors are used to illustrate the text.   *djg*

Hächler, Bruno. **Pablo the Pig**. Translated by J. Alison James. Illustrated by Nina Spranger. New York: North-South Books, 2002. Originally published as *Pablo* (Gorrau Zürich, Switzerland) by Nord-Süd Verlag AG in 2002. ISBN 0-7358-1566-6. 25 p. (5–8). Picture book.

After retiring from show business, Pablo the Pig enjoys his lazy days in the meadow near town. When plans to build a housing development threaten to destroy Pablo and his hut, his young friend Vera helps him find a safe haven in a garden with blueberries and an apple tree. Soft, fluid illustrations.   *nrn*
Author lives in Switzerland

Hächler, Bruno. **Snow Ravens**. Translated by Marianne Martens. Illustrated by Birte Müller. New York: Michael Neugebauer/North-South, 2002. First published in Switzerland under the title *Der Schneerabe*. ISBN 0-7358-1689-1. 28 p. (4–8). Picture book.

Three ravens perched on the gnarly branch of an old tree. Two grumbled and complained about the cold and the snow, but the third didn't say much. He watched the children playing and making snow angels. As the sun set, the third raven flew down and in spite of the taunting of his comrades he practiced making an angel. Aren't the children surprised the next day to find a tiny angel print in the snow! Stylized, expressive paintings reflect the humor in the tale.   *djg*

Hänel, Wolfram. **Little Elephant's Song**. Translated by J. Alison James. Illustrated by Cristina Kadmon. North-South, 2000. ISBN 0-7358-1297-7. 28 p. (4–7). Picture book.

Little Elephant has learned to do a lot of things, but he has not learned how to trumpet. His father tries to teach him, but mother chides, "he will learn when he is ready. But soon enough, Little Elephant learns to trumpet and call for help when he is in need of it.   *djg*

Itaya, Satoshi. **Buttons and Bo**. Translated by Marianne Martens. Originally published as *Grosser Bar & kleiner Bar* by Michael Neubauer Verlag, an imprint of Nord-Sud Verlag AG in 2003. ISBN 0-7358-1883-5. 26 p. (3–5). Picture book.

Buttons the bear is really angry that his crybaby brother Bo gets anything he wants, including Buttons's toys. Buttons goes off to the meadow, but his brother

follows along and they get lost in the scary forest. Buttons is surprised that Bo is not afraid because his big brother is with him and he has little Bo use his lung power to howl until mother and father rescue them. The simple, charming story is extended by idyllic pictures of the two playing in the meadow and the appropriately dark and gloomy forest in which the text is printed in silver. *sg*
Author from Japan. He was twice awarded the Bologna Ragazzi Prize at the Bologna Children's Book Fair.

Johansen, Hanna. **Dinosaur with an Attitude**. Berkeley, CA: First Wetlands Press, 1994. Translated from the German by Elisabetta Maccari. First published in Switzerland as *Dinosaurier gibt es nicht* by Nagel & Kimche, Zurich, 1992. ISBN 1-5714-3018-0. 144 p. (9–12). Novel.

Still in print, this accessible and humorous novel with linoleum prints on every page will be a hit with dinosaur fans. With Compsognathus, the existential dinosaur with an attitude, this story is about a royal pain, dog-sized dino who hatches out of Zawinul's Easter egg. The young owner tries to tame the dinosaur by putting him on a leash to no avail. *Winner of the 1993 Austrian Children's Book Prize.* *djg*

Kurt, Kemal. **Mixed-up Journey to Magic Mountain**. Translated by Marianne Martens. Illustrated by Wolfgang Slawski. New York: North-South, 2002. First published in Switzerland under the title *Die verpatzten Zaubersprüche*. ISBN 0-7358-1632-8. 62 p. (7–10). Transitional reader.

Nina likes everything about the circus, especially Marco the magician who always seems to get the spells wrong. When the magician is fired from the circus, it is Nina who encourages him to try to find the Magic Master of Magic Mountain to help. They bumble their way first to the African savannah, then to the mountains of Peru, and finally to China, until he gets it right. At last the master magician is able to figure out what Marco is doing wrong. *djg*
Author from Corulu, Turkey. Illustrator from Germany.

Lachner, Dorothea. **Danny, the Angry Lion**. Illustrated by Gusti. Translated by J. Alison James. New York: North-South Books, 2000. Originally published in Gossau Zürich, Switzerland, as *Eigentlich wolte er böse sein!* By Nord-Süd Verlag, 2000. ISBN 0-7358-1387-6. 32 p. (3–6). Picture book.

Danny's lunch of green beans and potatoes doesn't satisfy him and he roars with rage that he didn't get sausages and raspberry juice. Putting on his lion suit and sharpening his claws Danny takes his fury out on his neighbors where he hunts down his lunch of choice. It's hard to stay an angry lion as he helps the man fix his bicycle, gets coffee for the newspaper lady, and makes friends with the boy playing ball whose mother finally feeds him sausages and raspberry juice. Danny

heads for home after a busy day of making friends leaving his now uncomfortable lion skin at the gate. The ink and watercolor drawings follow Danny on his
adventure as his mood changes from a grumpy lion to a happy boy having fun
with his friends. A humorous story that portrays the emotion of anger in a manner young readers will understand. *kmc*

Luciani, Brigitte. **How Will We Get to the Beach?** Translated by Rosemary Lanning. Illustrated by Eve Tharlet. New York: Michael Neugebauer/North-South,
2000. First published in Switzerland under the title *Wer Fährt mi tans Meer?*
ISBN 0-7358-1268-3. 32 p. (3–7). Picture book.

One beautiful summer day Roxanne decides to go to the beach. She wants to
bring the turtle, the umbrella, the thick book of stories, the ball, and of course, her
baby. But the car won't start. The bus, the bicycle, the kayak? But each mode of
transport means leaving something behind and that will never do. At last a farmer
and his cart solve the problem, and they have a wonderful time! Delightful watercolor paintings illustrate this guessing-game story. *djg*

Müller, Birte. **Finn Cooks**. Translated by J. Alison James. New York: North-
South Books, 2004. Originally published as *Fin Kocht* by Michael Neubauer Verlag, an imprint of Nord-Sud Verlag AG in 2004. ISBN 0-7358-1935-1. 24 p.
(4–6). Picture book.

Young Finn dislikes the healthy foods his mother cooks and offers to do the
cooking if it can be foods he likes. His mother agrees to a one day test. Candy and
donuts for breakfast followed by numerous snacks with television lead to a bad
stomachache, which is cured by a rest and playing outdoors with a friend. At dinner Finn has a rude shock when his mother hasn't cooked and he manages a left-
over spaghetti dinner to his great relief . . . with one bite of chocolate for dessert.
A didactic subject is treated with humor and lightness and goes down easily. Illustrations are bright and sunny too, except when Finn feels ill! *sg*

Neugebauer, Charise. **The Real Winner**. Illustrated by Barbara Nascimbeni.
New York: Michael Neugebauer/North-South Books, 2000. First published in
Switzerland by Nord-Süd Verlag AG,Gossau Zürich under the title *Wer Gewinnt?*
ISBN 0-7358-1252-7. 28 p. (4–8). Picture book.

Gentle Humphry the hippo is off for a quiet day of fishing when Rocky Racoon
begs to go along. No one wants to play with Rocky; he turns everything into a
contest and whines and cries if he doesn't win. But Humphry loves everyone and
so he lets Rocky come along. Rocky challenges him to contest after contest, but
Humphrey stops to help needy animals along the way. Ultimately Rocky is influenced by his kind friend and learns a valuable lesson. Bold full-color illustrations
add humor to the text. *djg*
*Author from United States and has taught in China and Austria. Illustrator from
Italy, lives in Germany. Her illustrations have been included in the International
Exhibition at the Bologna Children's Book Fair.*

Pfister, Marcus. **Just the Way You Are**. Translated by Marianne Martens. Illustrated by the author. New York: North-South Books, 2002. Originally published as *Hallo Freund!!* (Gorrau Zürich, Switzerland) by Nord-Süd Verlag AG in 2002. ISBN 0-7358-1615-8. 26 p. (4–8). Picture book.

When Lion decides not to attend tonight's party because he doesn't look spectacular enough, his friends begin wishing they looked different, too. Chameleon longs for Stork's elegance while Elephant imagines himself hopping like Kangaroo. Die-cut pages offer young readers a sneak peek at the antics of Pfister's hilarious animal combinations. Language patterns flow naturally. Theme: I like you just the way you are. Lively illustrations invite children to explore a variety of art media.   *nrn*
Award-winning author lives in Switzerland

Pfister, Marcus. **Milo and the Mysterious Island**. Translated by Marianne Martens. New York: North-South, 2000. First published in Switzerland by Nord-Süd Verlag AG, Gossau Zürich under the title *Mats und die Streifenmäuse*, 2000. ISBN 0-7358-1352-3. 28 p. (4–8). Picture book.

Milo the mouse lives on a beautiful island of magical stones, but becomes bored and decides to go exploring. The bravest mice on the island travel with him on a raft and discover the mysterious island inhabited by striped mice. The pages are split into upper and lower haves and labeled The Happy Ending and The Sad Ending and readers are invited to choose the story of their choice. In the happy story, the mice strive to understand each other and are enriched by their association. In the sad story, the mice are suspicious and greedy, resulting in disaster. Endpapers have crayoned sketches drawn in a child-like hand. The watercolor illustrations throughout the story are highlighted by shimmering foil for the magical rocks. This prolific author-illustrator lives in Switzerland and also created *The Happy Hedgehog* (2000).   *djg*

Pfister, Marcus. **Rainbow Fish and the Sea Monster's Cave**. Translated by J. Alison James. First published in Switzerland by Nord-Süd Verlag AG, Gossau Zürich under the title *Der Regenbogenfisch hat keine Angst mehr*, 2001. ISBN 0-7358-1536-4. 28 p. (4–8). Picture book.

Rainbow Fish is back in his fourth adventure. This time, in order to save the bumpy-backed fish he must travel through the dark and scary cave of the rock monster to get some red algae. It is a scary journey, but with the help of encouragement from the little blue fish, the two friends overcome their fears to save their friend. Watercolor illustrations enhanced by holographic stamped papers will entice young readers.   *djg*

Romanelli, Serena. **Little Bobo Saves the Day**. Illustrated by Hans De Beer. New York: North-South Books, 1997. Originally published as *Kleiner Dodo Lass den Drachen fliegen!* by Nord-Süd Verlag, 1997. ISBN 1-55858-786-1, trade binding; ISBN 1-5585-787X, library binding. 28 p. (3–6). Picture book.

Little Bobo, a small orangutan loves to play his violin and his uncle loves to hear him play. When Uncle Darwin becomes ill, Little Bobo goes in search of a healing medicine, taking only his violin with him. Music becomes the key to opening doors, as Little Bobo meets a young boy who is painting the scenery of their South Pacific island. Soon the two teach each other their art and the boy helps Bobo obtain the needed medicine. When he returns home, Uncle Darwin is delighted to discover that Bobo has painted their white kite multicolored. De Beer's Little Polar Bear series is very popular and has been translated into 25 languages. *jvl*
Illustrator from the Netherlands

Rühman, Karl. **Who Will Go to School Today?** Translated by J. Alison James. Illustrated by Miriam Monnier. New York: Michael Neugebauer/North-South, 2002. First published in Switzerland under the title *Wer geht in den Kindergarten?* ISBN 0-7358-1622-0. 28 p. (4–9). Picture book.

One day Sam decides to stay home from school and send his toy monkey, Timbo. He has to prepare Timbo for the day: a delicious breakfast, fun with the children at school, circle time when the teacher reads a good book, snack, and playground. On second thought maybe he will go to school and bring his toy monkey. Acrylic paintings in subdued colors portray the mood of the story. *djg*
Author from Yugoslavia, lives in Switzerland. Illustrator from Germany.

Schneider, Antonie. **Come Back, Pigeon!** Translated by J. Alison James. Illustrated by Uli Waas. New York: North-South Books, 1999. First published in Switzerland under the title *Eine Taube für Bollibar.* ISBN 0-7358-1140-7. 48 p. (5–8). Transitional book.

Flora and Barnaby move from the city and discover how different life is in the country. When Barnaby sees their neighbor, Gabriel, surrounded by pigeons, he runs off to purchase one for a pet. After just a few hours their pigeon flies away, but the children are consoled by their new friend Gabriel. They learn how to care and keep pigeons and their patience is rewarded in the spring when their pigeon Jewel returns home. Full-color illustrations make this an entertaining first reader. *djg*
Author from Mindelheim, Germany. A former schoolteacher, she is the author of picture books, Luke the Lionhearted, You Shall Be King, *and* Good-Bye, Vivi!, *and an easy-to-read book,* The Birthday Bear, *all published by North-South. Illustrator from Donauworth, Bavaria. She has illustrated many books for children, including five other easy-to-read books for North-South:* Where's Molly?, Spiny, A Mouse in the House!, The Ghost in the Classroom, *and* The Birthday Bear.

Vainio, Pirkko. **The Best of Friends**. New York: North-South Books, 2000. Translated by J. Allison James. Originally published in Gossau Zürich, Switzerland as *Freunde* by Nord-Süd Verlag, 2000. ISBN 1-7358-1151-2. 32 p. (3–5). Picture book.

Hare feels small and ordinary compared to other animals until despite their differences in size he and Bear become best friends playing in the sunny meadow and sharing food. Bear protects Hare when danger is near and Hare helps Bear find a cave to hibernate in during winter. The attractive watercolor paintings combine with simple but tender text to create a charming and memorable celebration of friendship. *kc and aao*
Author from Finland, lives in Italy

Weigelt, Udo. **Alex Did It!** Illustrated by Cristina Kadmon. Translated by J. Alison James. New York: North-South, 2002. First published in Switzerland under the title *Alex war's!* ISBN 0-7358-1578-X. 28 p. (4–7). Picture book.

When the three little hares Bouncer, Buster, and Baby get caught red handed making noise and waking up bear, Bouncer pipes up "Alex did it!" What a great idea. The three rascals make trouble for all the animals of the forest, but at the end of the day, here comes the new bunny and his name is Alex! There is only one thing to do. The bunnies must confess and so they do. Full-page watercolor illustrations depict the bunny antics. *djg*
Author lives in Germany and has written many other books for North-South including The Strongest Mouse in the World *and* Who Stole the Gold. *Illustrator from Milan, Italy, lives in Israel, and has illustrated many books including* When I Grow Up.

Weigelt, Udo. **It Wasn't Me!** Translated by J. Alison James. Illustrated by Julia Gukova. New York: North-South, 2001. First published in Switzerland under the title *Ich was nicht!* ISBN 0-7358-1523-2. 28 p. (4–8). Picture book.

In this sequel to *Who Stole the Gold,* Raven becomes the immediate suspect when Ferret's raspberries go missing. After all, he is a known thief. But some of the animals come to Raven's defense saying that last time he confessed and this time he denies the charge. The animals investigate and find the real culprits. This picture book with large format watercolor illustrations has a lot to say about prejudice and jumping to conclusions. *djg*

Weigelt, Udo. **Old Beaver**. Illustrated by Bernadette Watts. Translated by Sibylle Kazeroid. New York: North-South, 2002. First published in Switzerland under the title *Der Biber geht for.* ISBN 0-7358-1564-X. 28 p. (4–7). Picture book.

Old Beaver is tired and after many years of hard work he enjoys sunning himself on the roof of his lodge. But the other animals decide to look for a young, energetic beaver to take over the work of the pond. New Beaver comes to the pond, but without experience, he can't build a dam. The animals soon realize they need the help of the old beaver in this fable brought to life with detailed watercolor illustrations. *djg*
Author lives in Germany. Illustrator lives in England and has written and illustrated her own books.

Zullo, Germano. **Marta and the Bicycle**. Illustrated by Albertine. Originally published in Switzerland under the title *Marta et la Bicyclette* by Editions La Joie de lire SA, Genève, 2002. ISBN 1-9291-3235-2. 28 p. (4–8). Picture book.

Marta the cow loves her quiet farm, but everything around seems so noisy until one day a bicycle race passed through town—so fast, so graceful, so quiet. Marta decides she must have a bicycle of her own and since it is unlikely that Monsieur Gruyere will give her one for her birthday she goes to the dump to gather the parts. She makes a bike, learns to ride, and wins the race! But now all the other cows have bikes, Marta will have to find a new hobby . . . *djg*
Author and illustrator live in Geneva

Related Information

Organizations

IBBY Switzerland
www.sikjm.ch

UKRAINE

Gorbachev, Valeri. **Chicken Chickens Go to School**. New York: North-South, 2003. ISBN 0-7358-1600-X. 32 p. (4–7). Picture book.

Richard Scarry-like illustrations populate this simple picture book about Mother Hen who takes her chickens to school for the first time. The chicks are scared, but Mrs. Heron welcomes them to class, and with the help of new friends they have a wonderful time and learn a few things as well.
Author emigrated to the United States from his native Ukraine. While in the Ukraine he illustrated over forty books for children. Since his arrival in the United States he has continued to produce well-loved children's books including One Rainy Day *(2002) and* The Big Trip *(2004).*

UNITED KINGDOM

Agard, John, and Grace Nichols, eds. **Under the Moon and over the Sea: A Collection of Caribbean Poems**. Illustrated by Cathie Felstead, Jane Ray, Christopher Corr, Satoshi Kitamura, and Sara Fanelli. Cambridge, MA: Candlewick, 2003. ISBN 0-7636-1861-6. 77 p. (8–12). Poetry.

Fifty poems to delight the reader from thirty poets, divided into themes concerning the sea, moonlight and storytelling, the land and its creatures, food, and travels, are invitingly introduced and enhanced by Caribbean proverbs and folklore. Each section is illustrated by a different artist, who may have no connection

to the area but who use their very different styles to bring out the mood of the poems. There is an index of poets and first lines, but short biographies of the poets would have been very welcome. *White Ravens Award Winner 2003, Great Britain International; CLPE Poetry Award Winner, UK.* sg
Editors (who are also poets represented in the book) were raised in Guyana and live in England

Ahlberg, Allan. **The Cat Who Got Carried Away**. Cambridge, MA: Candlewick Press, 2003. ISBN 0-7636-2073-4. 77 p. **The Man Who Wore All His Clothes**. New York: Candlewick Press, 2001. ISBN 0-7636-1432-7. 77 p. **The Woman Who Won Things**. New York: Candlewick Press, 2003. ISBN 0-7636-1721-0. 79 p. (8–10). Novel.
The Gaskitt family's days are fun-filled and action-packed. Mrs. Gaskitt drives a taxi. Mr. Gaskitt keeps trying different jobs. Mrs. Fritter, Gus and Gloria's teacher, is accident-prone so they always have substitute teachers—an old-fashioned one, an athlete, and a kind elderly woman. Each tale involves a crime—robbery, pet napping, theft plus a great chase involving the whole Gaskitt family including their cat, Horace. A delightful, easy read for children venturing into chapter books. ls
Author from England

Ahlberg, Allan. **The Improbable Cat**. Illustrated by Peter Bailey. New York: Delacorte Press, 2004. Originally published by Penguin Books, 2002. ISBN 0-385-73186-8. 110 p. (9–12). Novel.
When the kitten showed up at Josie's party it was love at first sight for the family. Josie, Mom, and Dad couldn't stop stroking it; only Dave and Bailey, his wire-haired terrier were unmoved by the lovely kitten, who became the prince of the family in no time, taking over the living room and their entire lives. This is a spooky horror story with enough suspense to keep readers turning pages, but sufficient foreshadowing of a safe and happy ending to keep them from becoming too frightened. The brave-dog-as-hero theme adds to the enjoyment. jvl
Author lives in England and has written the award-winning Jolly Postman books.

Aiken, Joan. **Midwinter Nightingale**. New York: Delacorte, 2003. ISBN 0-3857-3081-0. 248 p. (10 up). Novel.
Feisty, sharp-witted Dido Twite returns in the eight book of the Wolves Chronicles. Dido, just returned from a trip to the Americas, discovers that her friend Simon, the Duke of Battersea and heir to the throne, is missing along with the ailing King Richard. Before Dido can begin looking for him, she is kidnapped by the notorious Baron Rudh and his unruly son Lot, pretender to the throne. Fast-paced and action packed, Dido and Simon are up to their necks in danger. *Publisher's Weekly* reviewer sums it up: "Playful, urgent and wildly inventive, Aiken's language is always potent." djg

SPOTLIGHT ON JOAN AIKEN

This prolific author of books for children and adults, daughter of poet Conrad Aiken was born in Rye, Sussex, in 1924. Aiken's first book for children was an fantastic adventure, *The Wolves of Willoughby Chase* (1962). In this book, two cousins, Bonnie and Sylvia, have their ancestral home stolen from them by their evil guardian, Miss Slighcarp. Set in the bleak north-country in an "alternate," but still recognizable, Victorian England in the reign of the Stuart King James III, the book won the 1965 Lewis  Carroll Shelf Award and was made into a successful film in 1988. Joan Aiken's prose style drew heavily on fairy tales and oral traditions in which plots are fast-moving and horror is matter-of-fact but never grotesque.

During an interview Aiken once stated, "Why do we want to have alternate worlds? It's a way of making progress . . . if you write about something, hopefully you write about something that's better or more interesting than circumstances as they now are, and that way you hope to make a step towards it" (Locus).

Joan Aiken died in 2004. She was a popular and prolific author who infused her work with a sense of wonder and justice. She wrote 92 novels—including 27 for adults—as well as plays, poems, and short stories, although she will be best known as a writer of charmingly quirky children's stories, notably *The Wolves of Willoughby Chase* (1962).

DeGrummond at www.lib.usm.edu/~degrum/html/research/findaids/aiken.htm
Locus Magazine at www.locusmag.com/1998/Issues/05/Aiken.html
Silvey, Anita. *Children's Books and Their Creators.* New York: Houghton Mifflin, 1995.
Teacher Resource File at www. falcon.jmu.edu/~ramseyil/aiken.htm

Aiken, Joan. **The Witch of Clatteringshaws**. New York: Delacorte Press, 2005. ISBN 0-385-73226-0. 132 p. (10 up). Novel.

This is the final adventure in the Wolves chronicle that began in 1962. In this book, Dido is assisting her friend Simon who has become king, but would gladly give up this confining role if another heir can be found. Dido follows clues to the hinterlands of Scotland, in the town of Clatteringshaws coming against monsters, witches, and man-eating hobyahs in this ever-satisfying conclusion to the saga.

Alexander, Cecil Frances. **All Things Bright and Beautiful**. Illustrated by Bruce Whatley. New York: HarperCollins, 2001. ISBN 0-06-026617-1. 32 p. (all ages). Informational book.

Alexander's familiar hymn is presented in this illustrated book. Whatley's realistic watercolor illustrations add interest to the lovely text. Music and lyrics are located at the end of the book. *ls*
Author from Ireland

Almond, David. **Counting Stars**. New York: Delacorte Press, 2002. Originally published in Great Britain in 2000 by Hodder Children's Books. ISBN 0-385-72946-4. 205 p. (12 up). Novel.

In a series of short stories, David Almond chronicles different events that occurred during his childhood and we gain insight into his family, his faith, and what it was like growing up in Felling, England. His vivid descriptions of Felling bring the reader home with him as we learn that Almond experienced death and loss at an early age, how he battled bullies and challenged authority, and why the telling of these stories is so important to him. Many of these childhood accounts have been developed into full-length stories and the reader can bring a sense of inside information with them when reading his other novels. *Los Angeles Times Book Review Best Children's Book of 2002.* *kmc*

Almond, David. **The Fire-Eaters**. New York: Delacourt Press, 2004. Originally published under the same title in Great Britain by Hodder Children's Books, 2003. ISBN 0-385-73170-1. 218 p. (9–12). Novel.

It's late summer, 1962, and life in Keely Bay is getting interesting—and scary—for Bobby Burns. He's about to start the school year, without his two best friends, at a new private school where the teachers don't think twice about beating with a switch and humiliating the students. Daniel, the new kid from Kent, wants to take on the school authorities by chronicling the abuse with photographs. His father has a strange illness and the doctors don't know what is wrong with him. In town Bobby meets Mr. McNulty, an old war buddy of his fathers and an escapologist living on the fringe of reality who eats fire and sticks skewers in his cheeks for money. And the black cloud hanging over all their lives is the Cuban Missile Crisis. All Bobby and everyone else in Keely Bay can do is watch as Russia and the United States send ships to sea pushing each other back and wait for the missiles to explode wondering if tomorrow will come. Bobby feeling helpless and useless cannot control the world but he and the people of Keely Bay can fight for their "tiny corner of the world" and how they live there. Almond effectively uses the local language of Keely Bay and other English dialects to define the characters and to tell their story as they face the world crisis and their personal struggles together. *Whitbread Children's Book Award, 2004; Boston Globe-Horn Book Award, 2004; 2003 Nestle Smarties Book Prize.* *kmc*

Almond, David. **Heaven Eyes**. New York: Delacorte, 2001. Originally published by Hodder in 2000. (Paperback: Laure Leaf, 2002). ISBN 0-385-32770-6. 233 p. (10–14). Novel.

Called "damaged children," Erin Law and her friends January Carr and Mouse Gullane flee their orphanage on a makeshift raft in search of freedom. After a frightening and wild river ride on a misty night, they become stuck in the putrid and debris-filled mud of the Black Middens. Wet and frozen, they crawl to safety and are greeted by Heaven Eyes, a wisp of a girl with webbed fingers and toes. Thinking the three are her long lost sister and brothers, she leads them onto the quay into an area of abandoned and dilapidated warehouses where she lives with Grandpa, the Caretaker. Although the three children are terrified and suspicious of Grandpa, they are soon won over by Heaven Eyes's unshakeable trust and joy. This haunting tale, a blend of the real and the mystical, reveals that love, friendship, and family can emerge from the most unlikely places. *kk*
Author lives in England

Anholt, Catherine, and Laurence Anholt. **Chimp and Zee**. New York: Phyllis Fogelman Books, an imprint of Penguin Putnam Books for Young Readers, 2001. First published by Frances Lincoln Limited, Great Britain, 2001. ISBN 0-8037-2671-6. 32 p. (3–6). Picture book.

Chimp and Zee, twin monkeys, begin their adventures in *Chimp and Zee* by playing hide and seek from Mumkey while shopping and ultimately getting lost in Jungletown when their latest hiding spot moves on them. They continue their mischievous ways in *Chimp and Zee and the Big Storm* (ISBN 0-8037-2700-3, 2002) when, while squabbling instead of helping Papakey bring in the laundry during a windy storm, they are almost blown out to sea. Both picture books use large, bright primary-colored illustrations and the rhyming refrains, such as "Up jumps Chimp, Up jumps Zee, Ha, ha, ha! He, he, he!" whenever Mumkey asks where her naughty monkeys have gone to, make these a delightful read aloud. The Anholts have also written two board books, *Chimp and Zee's Noisy Book* (ISBN 0-8037-2772-0, 2002) and *Monkey Around with Chimp and Zee* (ISBN 0-8037-2773-9, 2002) illustrated with the same bright watercolor pictures but with less text so younger audiences can join in the adventures of Chimp and Zee. *Chimp and Zee* was a 2001 Smarties Gold Award Winner. *kmc*
Authors live in England

Ardaugh, Philip. **A House Called Awful End: Book One in the Eddie Dickens Trilogy**. Illustrated by David Roberts. New York: Henry Holt, 2002. Originally published by Faber & Faber in 2000 under the title *Awful End*. ISBN 0-8050-6828-7. 120 p. (9–12). Novel.

This over-the-top parody of nineteenth-century British fiction begins as Eddie Dickens sets out to stay with his Mad Uncle Jack and Even Madder Aunt Maud while his parents recover from a bizarre illness that has them looking jaundiced and "crinkly around the edges." The journey is full of surprises (few of them pleasant), and Eddie, mistaken for a runaway orphan, ends up in St. Horrid's Home for Grateful Orphans before being happily reunited with his parents. A fast-paced plot, a narrator who frequently addresses the reader to define elevated words such as *languish*, and nonsensical elements worthy of *Alice's Adventures in Wonderland* all combine to create an entertaining, runaway tale. Much of the British usage has been retained and terms that will be unfamiliar to young readers (e.g., ha'penny, bobble hat) are defined in a glossary in the back. Completing the trilogy are *Dreadful Acts* (Holt, 2003) and *Terrible Times* (Holt, 2003), both written in the same zany style.   *ss*

Berkeley, Laura. **The Seeds of Peace**. Illustrated by Alison Dexter. Cambridge, MA: Barefoot Books, 1999. ISBN 1-84148-007. 36 p. (5–10). Picture book.

An old hermit and a rich young man live at opposite ends of the rainbow in this fable about the meaning of peace and true happiness. The old hermit lives simply and humbly enjoying the beauty of nature. The young man cannot contemplate life without the luxuries he possesses and invites the old man to his rainbow mansion. The old man teaches by example that "peace, like a seed comes from within you." You must give it love and freedom so that it can grow. Batik-like illustrations in rich colors add a folk quality to this fable about the universal search for happiness. *Author lives in England. Illustrator lives in Wales.*

Blake, Quentin. **Loveykins**. Atlanta: Peachtree, 2002. Originally published in Great Britain by Random House, 2002. ISBN 1-56145-282-3. 32 p. (4–8). Picture book.

One windy spring morning Angela Bowling finds a little bird who's blown out of his nest, names him Augustus, and takes him home to coddle and protect like a child. Augustus outgrows his overly cozy life and flies off to discover the life he's meant for, though he returns to visit sometimes with a few beetles or a dead mouse. Pen and watercolor illustrations full of humorous details and lively movement help make this offbeat tale a treat.   *sg*
Author lives in England and France

Blake, Quentin. **Mrs. Armitage: Queen of the Road**. Atlanta: Peachtree, 2003. Originally published in Great Britain by Jonathan Cape in 2003. ISBN 1-56145-287-4. 32 p. (4–8). Picture book.

Intrepid Mrs. Armitage and her dog immediately hit the road when her uncle gives her his old car. Through happenstance and carelessness, various parts fall off but she continues unfazed until she meets up with her uncle and his motorcycling friends who are impressed with her and her vehicle. This delightful story, with its eccentric heroine and wonderful sound effects will be a great read-aloud, and Blake's color washed sketches add large doses of silly humor and charm.   *sg*
Author lives in England and France

Blake, Quentin. **Tell Me a Picture**. Brookfield, CT: Millbrook Press, 2003. Originally published by The National Gallery (London), in 2001. ISBN 0-7613-2748-7. 129 p. (7–12). Informational book.

This engaging introduction to art appreciation originally accompanied an exhibition put together by illustrator Blake in London. A group of illustrator Blake's squiggly children introduce and later react to each full-page color reproductions of art from European illustrators and classic artists, arranged alphabetically by artists' name. The irreverent children give honest reactions to the work and make going to a gallery a joyful event. Although Blake emphasizes the value of spontaneous feelings and thoughts about the pictures, there is a section at the end with more information about each picture and artist. Although many of the artists may be unfamiliar to American children, they will enjoy the experience. *sg*
Author lives in England

Breslin, Theresa. **Remembrance**. New York: Delacourte, 2002. Originally published by Doubleday in 2002. (Paperback: Laure Leaf, 2004). ISBN 0-385-73015-2. 297 p. (12 up). Novel.

The lives of five young people, three from the working class and two from the upper class of a small village in Scotland, are changed forever by World War I. After her sweetheart John Malcolm, 18, is killed at Somme, fifteen-year-old Charlotte becomes a nurse in France. She is soon joined by Maggie, John's twin sister, who is determined to fight societal gender restrictions and stereotypes. Alex, the twin's younger brother, although underage, enlists to avenge his brother's death. Finally, Charlotte's older brother, Francis, an anti-war university graduate eventually succumbs to societal pressures and enlists. Haunted by what he sees and does, Francis struggles to maintain his sanity and courage on the frontline but finds strength in the letters he writes to and receives from Maggie. This historical novel reflects careful research and vividly portrays the initial exhilaration of going into battle followed by the reality of war's suffering, death, and waste. *ALA Best Book for Young Adults.* *kk*
Author lives in England

Browne, Anthony. **Into the Forest**. Cambridge, MA: Candlewick Press, 2004. Published under same title by Walker Books, 2004. ISBN 0-7636-2511-6. 32 p. (5–8). Picture book.

A young boy is awakened in the middle of the night by a loud noise during a storm and the next morning finds that his father is away. Not knowing where his father has gone, the young boy is depressed and misses his father terribly. His mother sends the young boy to take a basket of food to his sick grandmother and against his mother's wishes he decides to take the short way through the forest. Once in the dark, ominous forest the young boy meets a number of literary characters from fairy tales including Jack selling his cow, Goldie Locks, and Hansel and Gretel. Looking closely behind the trees in the forest you find Jack's Beanstalk, Rumpelstiltskin's spinning wheel, and Cinderella's slipper among other literary references. The young boy even finds a red cape and you see a sly wolf hiding in the background. Browne's use of color to highlight the young boy

in the harshly illustrated black-and-white forest creates an eerie atmosphere adding to the suspense. With the allusions to the *Little Red Riding Hood* complete, the reader and the young boy reach Grandma's house expecting the worst. In a reassuring twist the boy's grandmother is full of dazzling smiles when he enters and the young boy finds, not a wolf, but his dad. *kmc*
Author lives in England

Browne, Anthony. **The Shape Game**. New York: Farrar, Straus and Giroux, 2003. Originally published in Great Britain by Doubleday, an imprint of Random House Children's Books, 2003. ISBN 0-374-36764-7. 32 p. (5–12). Picture book.
   Anthony Browne, recipient of two Kate Greenaway Medals and the prestigious Hans Christian Andersen Medal for a lifetime achievement in illustration, presents a glimpse into his artistic genesis—the day that changed his life forever. As her birthday present, Browne's mother requested a family outing to the Tate Museum in London. While he and his father and brother were initially reluctant, all changed their opinion of fine art before the day was over. Browne connects this personal epiphany to his literacy work with children during his term as writer-and-illustrator-in-residence at the Tate Britain from June 2001 to March 2002. *lmp*
Author lives in England

Browne, N. M. **Basilisk**. New York: Bloomsbury USA Children's Books, 2004. ISBN 1-58234-876-6. 319 p. (12 up). Novel.
   Rej, who lives Below, and Donna, an oppidan who aspires to become a scribe, share the dream of being golden dragons flying high above the city of Lunnzia. Donna and Rej meet and find out that the Arkel is devising a machine called the Basilisk Contrivance, which he plans to use with the dragon dreams to kill all of the people Below who are exiled from Lunnzia by scaring them to death. Rej and Donna embark on a harrowing adventure to save their families. This dark, dystopian fantasy begins slowly drawing the reader into a complex, intense adventure where the winners are those who have lost the least. *ls*
Author from England

Child, Lauren. **That Pesky Rat**. Cambridge, MA: Candlewick Press, 2002. ISBN 8484880583. unpaged. (7–9). Picture book.
   British author-illustrator Lauren Child charms with a hilarious tale told in the voice of a brown street rat who longs to have a home and a name other than "that pesky rat." The determined rodent hangs a sign in the pet store ("brown rat looking for kindly owner with an interest in cheese"), and triumphs when he's taken home by an eccentric man with boundless love and limited eyesight ("I've been looking for a brown cat as nice as this one for ages"). Vibrant collages, bold watercolors, and heavy black outlines cavort with expressively placed typeface in these energetic double spreads. *Smarties Gold Award, 2002 (under 5 category)*. *dw*

Cole, Babette. **Lady Lupin's Book of Etiquette**. Atlanta, GA: Peachtree Publishers, 2002. Originally published in England by Penguin Books Ltd for Hamish Hamilton, Ltd, 2001. ISBN 1-56145-257-2. 32 p. (5–8). Picture book.

Lady Lupin, an elegant deerhound, gives etiquette lessons to her brood, whose interpretation of such lessons as "At dinner, never serve yourself first" result in humorous images, such as a chicken being lobbed with a tennis racket to Lady Lupin by one of her "obedient" daughters. Most of the advice teaches common courtesy, though perhaps English society manners are also slightly spoofed, as for instance when Lady Lupin tells her daughters not to wear too much make-up because it might attract the wrong mate, and we are shown a mongrel walking off with the oldest daughter. *jvl*
Author from UK

Collicutt, Paul. **This Truck**. New York: Farrar, Straus, and Giroux, 2004. ISBN 0-374-37496-1. 26 p. (3–6). Picture book.

Collicutt's winning formula in the series that includes *This Train* (1999), *This Plane* (2000), *This Boat* (2001), and *This Car* (2002) continues to succeed admirably, entertaining young transportation enthusiasts and broadening their scope beyond the vehicles appearing on their own streets. Each large, colorful painting, one per page, is coupled with a single line of text to both describe the vehicle and introduce concepts through judicious use of verbs or adjectives—e.g., mail trucks deliver and garbage trucks collect. Endpapers feature an array of old and new examples from several eras and countries and will no doubt interest older generations as much, if not more, than the children with whom they are sharing the books. *ss*
Author/illustrator from Britain, book originated in United States

Cooke, Trish. **Full, Full, Full of Love**. Illustrated by Paul Howard. Cambridge, MA: Candlewick Press, 2003. ISBN 0-7636-1851-9. unpaged. (4–7). Picture book.

Little Jay Jay (introduced in the earlier *So Much*) helps his grandmother as she prepares for the weekly gathering of his loving and lively African-American family. Jay Jay struggles to contain his excitement and curb his hunger, but Grannie keeps him busy setting the table, feeding the fish, and cuddling as they watch for the arrival of the others. Finally everyone arrives to savor the company and the feast ("Biscuits/gravy/collard greens/pasta salad/rice and red beans"). Howard's oversized double spreads are full of luminous color and activity and Cooke's lilting prose conveys the rhythms of the dialect while celebrating the joys of family harmony.

Cooper, Susan. **Frog**. Illustrated by Jane Browne. New York: Margaret K. McElderry Books, 2002. First published by Bodley Head in 2002. ISBN 0-689-84302-X. 26 p. (4–6). Picture book.

Little Joe cannot swim though his family can. A little frog accidentally jumps into the pool and the boy watches it swim. After the rest of the family tries without success to get it out, Little Joe goes into the pool and rescues it. He then imitates the frog and succeeds in swimming across the pool. Both the story and the realistic watercolor illustrations are clear and straightforward. *bn*
Author from UK, lives in United States

Cousins, Lucy. **Jazzy in the Jungle**. Illustrated by the author. Cambridge, MA: Candlewick, 2002. ISBN 0-7636-1903-5. 32 p. (2–4). Picture book.

Mama JoJo, a lemur, plays hide-and-seek with her baby, asking each of the animals she meets in the jungle if they have seen Jazzy. Readers can help look for Jazzy by lifting flaps and die cut pages that reveal new rainforest scenes. A part of one picture will become a different part of the next picture, with the final spread showing all the animals, who help to unite JoJo and Jazzy. *Smarties Gold Award, 2002 (6–8 category).*
Author lives in England

Cross, Gillian. **The Dark Ground**. New York: Dutton, 2004. Originally published in Great Britain by Oxford University Press, 2004. ISBN 0-525-47350-5. 264 p. (10–14). Novel.

First in a projected trilogy, this is an unnerving survival story in which Robert suddenly finds himself in a terrifying world. Returning from a vacation with his family, Robert is at one moment on a plane and the next in a damp, jungle. Days go by, when cold and hungry he finds a small gift of blankets and food. Realizing he is not alone, he searches for other people, eventually learning that he has been reduced to a size where grass is as tall as trees. Determined to find out what happened to him, he embarks on a dangerous journey. Readers will have to wait until the next installments to find out if he can succeed. Another gripping fantasy from this British author, winner of the Carnegie Medal, the Smarities Book Prize, and the Whitbread Children's Novel Award. *djg*

Crossley-Holland, Kevin. **The Seeing Stone**; Arthur Trilogy Book One. New York: Scholastic Press, 2001. First published in London: Orion Children's Books, 2000. ISBN 0-439-26326-3. 342 p. (12 up). Novel.

Crossley-Holland, Kevin. **At the Crossing-Places**; Arthur Trilogy Book Two, 2002.

Crossley-Holland, Kevin. **King of the Middle March**; Arthur Trilogy Book Three, 2003.

Here we have two Arthurs: one the legendary king of Britain, the other a squire living at the turn of the 13th century in the Marches, both with much in common including a friend called Merlin. The latter, Arthur de Caldecott, is given a special stone by Merlin, in which he can view the events of the fabled king's life, events with uncanny similarities to his own. Both Arthur's parentages are in question and as the future king begins to discover his true heritage, our Arthur gains insights into his own situation. The place and period are brought to life in one hundred highly readable chapters. In books two and three, the "seeing stone" allows our hero to become privy to the entire life of King Arthur with its conflicts, subterfuges, and ultimate tragic demise. These events continue to parallel his own life situation as he is knighted and participates in the ill-fated Fourth Crusade. Eventually they become quite different as our hero becomes an enlightened lord of his inherited manor on the border of Britain and Wales. *ALA Notable Book and recipient of the Guardian Children's Fiction Prize; shortlisted for the Whitbread Award.*   mln

Dickinson, Peter. **The Kin**. Illustrations by Ian Andrew. New York: G. P. Putnam's Sons, 2003. Originally published by Macmillan Children's Books in 1998. ISBN 0-399-24022-5. 628 p. (12 up). Novel.

The four books that comprise the Kin series are contained in this volume: *Suth's Story, Noli's Story, Ko's Story,* and *Mana's Story.* Set in prehistoric Africa, Suth and Noli, members of the Moonhawk kin, leave their clan to find the four babies, Ko, Mana, Tinu, and Otan, whom the clan had abandoned. The six children are in search of a Good Place when they are captured by another clan. The children bide their time waiting to escape. Eventually, they are reunited with their Moonhawk kin. Short pourquoi tales are between the chapters. A thought-provoking story about how early homosapiens thought, felt, and lived.   ls
Author from England

Dickinson, Peter. **The Ropemaker**. New York: Delacorte Press, 2001. ISBN 0-385-72921-9. 375 p. (12 up). Novel.

The magic that has protected the Valley from invasion has begun to break down. Tilja and her grandmother, who can whisper to the cedars along with Tahl and his grandfather who both can talk to the streams, undertake a dangerous journey to find the magician who enchanted the Valley. The land they travel through is filled with magic and where to speak the magician's name means death. Along the way, Tilja finds her own tremendous powers, which will lead her to live a life away from the Valley. A journey changes many lives in unexpected ways.   ls
Author from England

Dickinson, Peter. **Inside Grandad**. New York: Wendy Lamb Books, 2004. ISBN 0-385-74641-5. 117 p. (10 up). Novel.

Gavin's grandad has taken care of him since he was very young. They have a special, close relationship and enjoy fishing and building model boats. One Saturday, when they are home alone, Grandad has a severe stroke. Gavin is determined to rehabilitate his Grandad by reading and talking to him and by helping with Grandad's physical therapy. A touching, sympathetic story of a loving grandson who must come to terms with his grandfather's debilitating illness.   ls
Author from England

Dickinson, Peter. **The Tears of the Salamander**. New York: Wendy Lamb Books, 2003. ISBN 0-385-90125-9. 197 p. (12 up). Novel.

According to legend, the tears of the salamander heal the body and the mind. Alfredo, a twelve-year-old boy living in eighteenth-century Italy, has become a member of the church choir and is assured of a secure future. One day his father's bakery blazes into an inferno. Alfredo's entire family is killed. His mysterious Uncle Giorgio comes to take Alfredo to his home near Mount Etna. What Alfred discovers is that his uncle is an evil sorcerer whose kindness hides an ulterior motive and that his family's deaths were not an accident. Alchemy plus mythic salamanders and the volcano combine for a compelling read. *ls*
Author from England

Doherty, Berlie. **Coconut Comes to School**. Illustrated by Ivan Bates. London: HarperCollins, 2003. ISBN 0-00-710433-2. 32 p. (3–6). Picture book.

All the children love Coconut, the donkey, who comes to school each day with the cook, but Mr. Capper, the teacher, doesn't approve and tries to lure Coconut far away with carrots. When Mr. Clapper falls in the ditch and hurts his foot he is rescued by none other than Coconut who carries him back to school to the children's delight. Appealing pastel illustrations convey the humor of the tale as well as the lovely English countryside. This would make a delightful, gentle read-aloud. *sg*
Author lives in England

Doherty, Berlie. **The Famous Adventures of Jack**. New York: Greenwillow, 2001. First publisher in Great Britain by Hodder Children's Books, 2000. ISBN 0-06-623619-3. 148 p. (7–10). Folklore.

First Mother Greenwood tells a series of Jack tales to a young girl named Jill and then shows her to a beanstalk and her own "Jack" adventure. These remnants with their giants, princesses, brave deeds, and clever tricks are cleverly woven into an amusing, lively romp. Author has won Carnegie medals for *Granny Was a Buffer Girl* (1988) and *Dear Nobody* (1992); she also received the Phoenix Award in 2004 for *White Peak Farm* (1984). *mln*

Doherty, Berlie. **Holly Starcross**. New York: Greenwillow, 2002. First published in Great Britain by Hamish Hamilton in 2001. ISBN 0-06-001341-9. 186 p. (12 up). Novel.

Having been lied to about her father for all her 14 years, it's no wonder that Holly is filled with conflicting emotions when he finally presents himself to her one day after school. The little things that occur as they re-discover each other brings Holly new hope and self-understanding. Set in the Peak District of Derbyshire that the author so skillfully realized in her Phoenix award winning *White Peak Farm* (Methuen, 1984), family relationships in rural England are succinctly explored. Author had also won Carnegie medals for *Granny Was a Buffer Girl (1988)* and *Dear Nobody (1992)*.   *mln*

Doyle, Malachy. **Antonio on the Other Side of the World, Getting Smaller**. Illustrated by Carll Cneut. Cambridge, MA: Candlewick Press, 2003. ISBN 0763621730. 32 p. (4–7). Picture book.

Antonio is having a great time visiting his grandmother on a tiny island far from home. The longer he stays rowing around in Granny's boat, however, the smaller he gets. Soon he can't even see over the edge of the boat. Grandmother realizes his problem; he misses his mom and immediately sends him home before he gets any smaller. Antonio then goes on a great adventure working on a ship and a train and riding a horse like a cowboy before finally being reunited with his mother. The surreal acrylic paintings use strong line and perspective to illustrate Antonio's dilemma as the final illustration suggests that just across the river could seem to be the other side of the world to a small child.   *kmc*
Author lives in Wales

Doyle, Malachy. **Cow**. Illustrated by Angelo Rinaldi. New York: Margaret K. McElderry Books, 2002. Simon and Schuster UK, Ltd, 2002. ISBN 0-689-84462-X. 34 p. (3–8). Picture book.

In measured, poetic lines the author depicts the life of a cow on a hot summer's day, starting with early morning milking and ending with late evening grazing, chewing, and resting under the stars, and the slightly ironic words, "it's hard being a cow." The illustrator depicts idyllic scenes of meadows, streams, and sky, an old-world farmyard, and the cool spring where children splash. *2003 nominee for the Kate Greenaway Medal.*   *jvl*
Author lives in Wales

Dunbar, Polly. **Dog Blue**. Cambridge, UK: Candlewick, 2004. First published by Walker. ISBN 0-7636-2476-4. 38 p. (4–7). Picture book.

Bertie's favorite color is blue. What Bertie wants more than anything is a dog, a blue dog. But when he finds a black and white Dalmatian, he decides that naming it Blue will do the trick. Soft pencil and pastel watercolor illustrations complement the simple text.   *djg*

Dunbar, Polly. **Flyaway Katie**. Cambridge, MA: Candlewick Press, 2004. ISBN 0-7636-2366-0. 32 p. (4 up). Picture book.

It was a gray, gray day. Katie was feeling gray too. She wanted to be as happy and as colorful as the painting of birds on her wall. Katie dresses herself in a bright green hat, yellow tights, pink dress, and blue shoes. She paints her face blue, her arms orange, and her fingers purple. Being so colorful makes Katie feel all flittery and fluttery. She flutters into the painting and spends the afternoon flut-

tering with the birds until it's time for her bath. This colorful, quirky, whimsical delight is sure to brighten anyone's gray day. *Books of the Year Winner 2004 Ages 2 to 4.* *ls*
Author from England

Fine, Anne. **Bad Dreams**. New York: Random House, 2000. First published in UK by Doubleday in 2000. ISBN 0-440-41690-6. 133 p. (8–10). Novel.
　　Bookworm Melanie is asked to spend time with Imogen, a new girl in her class. It doesn't take her long to realize something is very strange about this girl who seems to know what is happening in a book by just touching it. Indeed, she actually enters into the book as though it were happening to her. When she realizes it is magic, Mel determines to find a way to free her new friend from this "gift," which she comes to feel is more of a curse. *bn*
Author from UK

Fine, Anne. **The Jamie and Angus Stories**. Illustrated by Penny Dale. Cambridge, MA: Candlewick Press, 2002. ISBN 0-7636-1862-4. 108 p. (4–8). Novel.
　　Preschooler Jamie "saw Angus staring forlornly out of the shop window. His silky coat looked smooth as bath water and white as snow" (7). Angus is a Highland Bull who, if we wish hard enough, will share our secrets, too, just as he does with Jamie. Disaster strikes when Angus's smooth, white coat gets dingy, just like the Velveteen Rabbit's. Mother calls him "scruffy" and Granny describes him as "downright unsanitary" (15). Jamie, however, cherishes Angus regardless of his appearance. These six short stories, unified by Jamie and Angus's strong personalities, will delight caregivers and lap-sitters equally. *Boston Globe-Horn Book Award.* *lmp*
Author lives in England

Fine, Anne. **Ruggles**. Pictures by Ruth Brown. London: Andersen Press, 2001. ISBN 1-8427-0212-2. First published in Great Britain. 28 p. (4–8). Picture book.
　　Ruggles is a dog with spirit and in spring, summer, autumn, and winter, he manages to find a way out of his yard and find adventure out in the neighborhood. Everyone knows him, even the dog lady, who brings him home to his mistress. But even a roughish pet with wanderlust in his blood can tire of adventuring when there is a chill in the air and a warm hearth indoors. Delightful text by Britain's new children's laureate and realistic watercolor illustrations capture Ruggle's world. *djg*

Fine, Anne. **Up on Cloud Nine**. New York: Delacorte Press, 2002. First published in UK by Doubleday in 2002. ISBN 0-385-90058-9. 151 p. (8–10). Novel.
　　Ian's best friend, Stolly, lies unconscious on a hospital bed after a suspicious accident. Stolly spends more time at Ian's house than his own while his lawyer father and fashion photographer mother are often unavailable. His grounding in

reality comes from Ian's family. While sitting with him, Ian writes his friend's bi-ography, detailing his eccentricities as well as their childhood escapades. *bn Author was named the Children's Laureate for Lifetime Contribution in Writing, 2003, taking over from Quentin Blake.*

Finney, Patricia. **I, Jack**. By Jack the Dog as told to Patricia Finney. Illustrated by Peter Bailey. New York: HarperCollins, 2004. A paperback edition was pub-lished in the UK in 2000 by Corgi Yearling Books. ISBN 0-06-052207-0. 185 p. (8–12). Novel.

Jack, a big, yellow lab introduces the reader to his family of apedogs (with a little help from the three pack cats). Jack loves his pack huge amounts. Then Pe-tra the female Samoyed moves in. "Isn't she gorgeous?" Find out how Jack be-comes friends with Petra, braves the FIERCE garage dog, and saves the Pack-leader from Huge Scary Metal Monsters. ARROOF! Cleverly told, this book is illustrated with comical line drawings. An interpreter's note and glossary of Jack-speak are appended for the doggie impaired. *djg*

Fisk, Pauline. **Midnight Blue**. New York: Bloomsbury USA Children's Books, 2003. Originally published under the same title in England by Lion Publishing, 1990. ISBN 1-58234-829-4. 217 p. (10 up). Novel.

Bonnie, a girl caught between a weak mother she hardly knows and the strong-willed grandmother who raised her, runs away from the hatred in her life to a "land beyond the sky" in a hot air balloon in this exciting fantasy tale slightly reminiscent of the *Wizard of Oz*. In this new land, Bonnie is taken in and accepted by the friendly family who lives on a farm on Highholly Hill in the hills of England. As in the *Wizard of Oz*, all of the people Bonnie meet in this new land resemble people from her own life and she is startled when the daughter, Arabella, looks and sounds just like Bonnie. This new family never asks where Bonnie came from or who she is, nor do they notice the resemblance. In this world, Bonnie finds the family and security she always wanted and doesn't think much about trying to get back to her own world until she and Arabella meet evil Grandmother Marvell at the County Fair. Grandmother Marvel looks just like the grandmother Bonnie ran away from and has a mysterious way of sucking the life out of anyone who enters her magical mirrors. Bonnie and Arabella work to-gether to try to get Grandmother Marvell out of their lives but it isn't until Ara-bella is lost to her that Bonnie finds the courage to return home saving her new family from Grandmother Marvell. *Nestle Smarties Grand Prix Book Prize, 1990; Whitbread Award shortlist. kmc Author lives in England*

Freedman, Claire. **Dilly Duckling**. Illustrated by Jane Chapman. New York: Mar-garet K. McElderry Books, 2004. Originally published by Little Tiger Press, 2004. ISBN 0-689-86772-7. 26 p. (2–4). Picture book.

When a gust of wind blows one of Dilly Duckling's fluffy, yellow feathers away, she chases after it, concerned that she had lost an important part of herself. In vain, her friends, a hedgehog and a mouse, try to catch it for her, but Mama reassures a sad Dilly that she will soon grow new white feathers and will look grown-up. Large-scale, fluffy looking ducklings and duck, warm expressions on all the animals' faces, Dilly's textured surface, and lovely acrylic backgrounds of blues and greens all make this a delightful book for young children. *jvl*
Author and illustrator live in England

Geras, Adele. **The Cats of Cuckoo Square**. Illustrated by Tony Ross. New York: Delacorte Press, 2001. ISBN 0-385-72926-X. 191 p. (7–9). Novel.

The four cats who live in Cuckoo Square share stories about their lives and owners and give one another advice. In the first of two stories, Blossom tells about the visit of six-year-old Prissy, a spoiled young girl who blames all her nasty tricks on Blossom. In the second story, Perkin's owner wants to win the prize for the best picture of a pet and thus wants him to pose. The humorous illustrations match the light touch of the text. *jig*
Author and illustrator live in England

Geras, Adele. **My Wishes for You**. Illustrated by Cliff Wright. New York: Simon & Schuster, 2002. First published in Great Britain in 2002 by Picadilly Press. ISBN 0-689-85333-5. 28 p. (3–7). Picture book.

In this illustrated lyric poem, the speaker gives good wishes for events throughout the day, from "Kisses to wake you, warm sun on your face" to "a quilt to cover you and all your dreams, warm in your bed, safe through the quiet night." The soft watercolor illustrations of rabbits and other animals extend the feeling of love that permeates this book. We could all use "arms outstretched to catch you if you if you fall." *jig*
Author from Jerusalem, lives in Manchester, England. Illustrator lives in East Sussex, England.

Geras, Adele. **Time for Ballet**. Illustrated by Shelagh McNicholas. New York: Dial, 2004. Originally published in Great Britain by Orchard Books in 2003. ISBN 0-8037-2978-2. 32 p. (3–5). Picture book.

Energetic, joyful, earnest youngsters (including a boy) enjoy their ballet lessons and preparing for a show in this simple but absorbing book. Colorful double and single page spreads of realistically disheveled children in motion give young children a real feel for the fun and work of dance lessons. Parents and siblings are realistically portrayed as well in this charming book. *sg*
Author from Great Britain

Geras, Adele. **Troy**. New York: Harcourt, 2001. (Paperback, Harcourt, 2002). First published in Great Britain by Scholastic in 2000. ISBN 0-15-216492-8. 358 p. (12 up). Novel.

The Greeks have been outside the walls of Troy for ten years, the fighting continuing on a daily basis, when this story opens. The events of *The Iliad* are retold, this time from the perspective of two young sisters: Xanthe, who cares for wounded soldiers in the Blood Room, and Marpessa, who is a handmaiden to Helen. Love finds both of them, as Aphrodite amuses herself by having both fall in love with the same man. The perspective of the women of Troy on the war makes this a unique retelling.
Author lives in England

Gliori, Debi. **Mr. Bear to the Rescue**. New York: Orchard, 2000. First published in Great Britain in 1996 by Orchard Books London. ISBN 0-531-30276-8. 32 p. (4–7). Picture book.

It was a wild and windy night in the forest and when Mr. Rabbit-Bunns's warren collapses and the Hoot-Toowits's nest blows away, they ask Mr. Bear to help fix their homes. Out he goes into the stormy night to rescue little lost Flora and help his neighbors. Everyone comes back to the Bears' house for some hot nettle soup and a good nights sleep. Full-page watercolors illustrate the story. The Bear family adventures continue in *Mr. Bear's Vacation* (2002). A separate series featuring Flora includes the titles *Flora's Blanket* (2001) and *Flora's Surprise* (2003). *djg*
Author/illustrator lives in Scotland

Gliori, Debi. **Pure Dead Brilliant**. New York: Alfred A. Knopf, 2003. First published in Great Britain by Transworld Publishers, 2003. ISBN 0-3758-1412-4. 262 p. Novel.

Her third book in so many years, this latest entry in the Pure Dead saga is as action-packed as *Pure Dead Magic* (2001) and *Pure Dead Wicked* (2002). Here Titus Strega-Borgia is about to inherit a fortune, sorcery students from his mother's witchcraft classes come to stay at their Scottish castle, and his two-year-old sister becomes quite adept at casting spells. Filled with eccentric characters and gross humor this wild tale is described by the publisher as a "cyber-gothic-gangster fantasy" and is quite a departure from her picture books. *Pure Dead Magic* has won several Children's Choice awards, Best Books of the Year, and starred reviews. *Pure Dead Wicked—Smithsonian's Notable Books for Children.* *djg*
Author lives in Scotland

Godden, Rumer. **Gypsy Girl**. New York: Harper Collins, 2002. ISBN 0-06-029192-3. (New York: HarperTrophy, 2002). Originally published as *Diddakoi* in 1972. 169 p. (10 up). Novel.

Seven-year-old Kizzy, a gypsy girl, is having a very difficult time adjusting to the village school. The children laugh at her and bully her. She lives with her

grandmother in a wagon in Admiral Twiss's orchard. After her grandmother dies, Kizzy is taken in by Admiral Twiss because her gypsy relatives do not want her. Her adjustment to village life begins when Miss Olivia Brooke becomes her foster parent. When Kizzy accidentally sets fire to Miss Brooke's cottage, the girl who is the biggest bully saves her. This is a touching story about change, adjustment, and acceptance. Sometimes it is slow and difficult and needs a gentle hand. *ls*
Author from England

Godden, Rumer. **Miss Happiness and Miss Flower**. New York: HarperCollins Publishers, 2002. Originally published with drawings by Jean Primrose by Viking Press in 1961. ISBN 0-06-029193-1. 119 p. (8 up). Novel.
Nona Fells is sent from her father's tea plantation in India to live with her aunt's family in England. Nona is very unhappy until the day a belated Christmas gift of two tiny Japanese dolls arrive. Nona is determined that the dolls should have a proper Japanese house. It is this kinship with the two dolls and the involvement of building a house for them that draws Nona out and establishes a connection between her and her new surroundings. She explores a bookshop and meets people who want to help her complete the dollhouse. Plans for building a Japanese dollhouse are included at the end of the book. English author who lived in India a number of years. Died in Scotland in 1998. In 1972 won Whitberad Award for *The Diddakoi*. In 1993 appointed OBE. *ok and ls*

Graham, Bob. **Jethro Byrd, Fairy Child**. Cambridge, MA: Candlewick Press, 2002. ISBN 0-7636-1772-5. 32 p. (4–10). Picture book.
See Australia for description.

Graham, Bob. **"Let's Get a Pup!" Said Kate**. Cambridge, MA: Candlewick Press, 2001. ISBN 0-7636-1452-1. 32 p. (4–8). Picture book.
See Australia for description.

Graham, Bob. **Max**. Cambridge, MA: Candlewick Press, 2000. ISBN 0-7636-1138-7. 32 p. (4–8). Picture book.
See Australia for description.

Gray, Kes. **Baby on Board**. Conceived by Kes Gray. Illustarted by Sarah Naylor. New York: Simon & Schuster, 2003. First published in London by Hodder Children's Books, 2003. ISBN 0-689-86572-4. 26 p. (4–8). Picture book.
There's a baby growing in Mom's tummy and big sister is going to keep us informed. The left hand page gives a simple month by month guide to how the baby is growing while the right hand page, in clever cut pages tells anecdotes about

how mom is doing—eating pickled onions, buying bigger bras. Dad is busy picking out boys names. Finally, the day arrives and the baby is born, the midwife
washes up the baby and here's Susan! Cartoon style, watercolor illustrations add
humor to the text.   *djg*

Gray, Kes. **Our Twitchy**. Illustrated by Mary McQuillan. New York: Henry Holt,
2003. Originally published in Great Britain by the Bodley Head, 2003. ISBN
0-8050-7454-6. 28 p. (4–7). Picture book.
    When Twitchy wonders why Mom and Pop don't bunny hop like he does, Mil-
foil and Sedge have to tell him that they aren't his Bunnymom and Bunnypop. In
fact, Milfoil is a cow and Sedge is a horse. Confused, Twitchy runs away and
when they find him back in their train tunnel burrow, he has covered his white fur
brown like the cow and tied a stick to his short bunny tail to look like a horse.
Twitchy's loving parents assure him that they are his *real* parents; looks aren't
everything. This is a reassuring story about what it means to be a real family. The
author and illustrator also published *Cluck O'Clock* in 2003. Nick Sharratt illustrated Gray's *Eat Your Peas* in 2000.
Author lives in England and was voted one of the top ten children's authors by
The Independent, *the prestigious British newspaper.*
Illustrator lives in England

Grindley, Sally. **Mucky Duck**. Illustrations by Neal Layton. New York and London: Bloomsbury, 2003. ISBN 1-58234-821-9. 28 p. (3–7). Picture book.
    Mucky Duck lives in a pond in Oliver Dunkley's backyard. He is supposed to
be white, but she mostly wasn't and here is why: Mucky Duck likes to cook and
play soccer in the mud, and likes to paint and garden. She simply must have a
bath once a week, but doesn't stay clean for long! Other picture books by this
popular author include: *A New Room for William* (2000), *No Trouble At All*
(2002), and *The Big What are Friends For? Storybook* (2003).   *djg*
Author and illustrator live in England

Grindley, Sally. **Spilled Water**. New York: Bloomsbury, 2004. ISBN 1-58234-
937-1. 224 p. (10–14). Novel.
    Eleven-year-old Lu Si-yan finds she is worth no more than "spilled water"
when her father dies and her uncle sells her into indentured servitude to pay the
family debts. Cruelty and deprivation drive her to run away and she finds herself
working in horrific conditions in a toy factory. She eventually falls ill. Set in contemporary China, this book portrays the grim position of poor women.   *djg*

Heap, Sue. **Four Friends Together**. Illustrated by the author. Cambridge, MA:
Candlewick, 2003. ISBN 0-7636-2111-0. 32 p. (3–5). Picture book.
    Seymour the sheep, Rachel the rabbit, and Florentine the bear all wait until
Mary Clare wakes up so that she can read to them. However, it is only after sev-

eral difficulties with seating and with being able to see the pictures that the story reading is successfully begun. The problem solving will be recognized by children and adults alike who have participated in story hours. *jig*
Author lives in England

Heap, Sue. **What Shall We Play?** Illustrated by the author. Cambridge, MA: Candlewick, 2002. ISBN 0-7636-1685-0. 32 p. (3–5). Picture book.

Lily May's announcement that she and Matt and Martha should play fairies is ignored time after time, as one of her two friends suggests another idea. Lily May goes along. Finally she declares that she had a magic wand and then all three play fairies—and it's fun. The book gives a feel for the joy in imaginative play. *jig*
Author lives in England

Henderson, Katherine. **And the Good Brown Earth**. Cambridge, MA: Candlewick Press, 2003. ISBN 0-7636-2301-6. 34 p. (3–5). Picture book.

Soft illustrations show Gram and Joe's year as they prepare the good brown earth in the spring, sow flowers and vegetables, watch and wait, and finally reap their abundant harvest. This book celebrates love between grandchild and grandmother and the joy of seeing things grow through the bounty of nature. *jvl*
Author lives in England

Hendry, Diana. **Harvey Angell**. New York: Puffin Books, 2001. First published in 1991 by Julia MacRae in Great Britain. ISBN 0-7434-2828-5. 143 p. (8–11). Novel.

A "room to let" sign in front of dusty, rundown 131 Ballentyre Road lets orphan Henry know that his stingy Aunt Agatha is interviewing prospective boarders. She selects Harvey Angell as the new boarder because he does not eat breakfast. When Harvey Angell flashes his 500-kilowatt smile, he brightens up Henry's life. Harvey tells Henry that he is an electrician looking for connections, circuits, watts, bolts, and thunderbolts. Harvey and Henry work together to make the connections, which will turn 131 Ballentyre Road into a proper home. Readers will empathize with each the sorrows of each character and will cheer when Harvey Angell accomplishes his mission. A poignant story filled with mystery and fantasy. *Whitbread Children's Book of the Year Award, 1991.* *ls and jig*
Author lives in Scotland

Hendry, Diana. **Harvey Angell and the Ghost Child**. New York: Aladdin Paperbacks, 2001. Originally published by Random House U.K., Ltd., in 1997. ISBN 0-7434-2829-3. (10 up). Novel.

Aunt Agatha has made enough money to take everyone at 131 Ballentyre Road to Scotland for a two-week seaside vacation. While exploring the house, Henry finds out that it is haunted. The unhappy ghost is looking for her Lucky. Henry

wants to help her so he sends a message to Harvey Angell to come help Henry make the connection. With a bit of good luck, Henry finds the Lucky and the connection is mended. This ghostly tale is full of mystery and fun. *ls*
Author from Scotland

Hendry, Diana. **Harvey Angell Beats Time**. New York: Aladdin Paperbacks, 2002. Originally published by Red Fox in 2000. ISBN 0-7434-2830-7. 150 p. (10 up). Novel.

Henry finds a baby amid the hollyhocks on 131 Ballantyre Road. He discovers this baby, whom he names Sweetheart, is just a little bit different. She bleeps and has feelers and buttercup ears. Then, sorrowful women dressed in black come to visit Sweetheart, plunging the household into gloom. Henry knows they need Harvey Angell. Harvey Angell arrives by balloon and tells Henry that Sweetheart has slipped through a crack in time and must be returned to her mother in the 23rd century. Harvey Angell uses his 500-watt smile, flute, and amazing clocks putting himself in grave danger to reunite Sweetheart and her mother. *ls*
Author from England

Hendry, Diana. **The Very Busy Day**. Illustrated by Jane Chapman. New York: Dutton Children's Books, 2002. First published by Little Tiger Press, an imprint of Magi Publications, London, in 2001. ISBN 0-525-46825-0. 32 p. (3–6). Picture book.

Big Mouse and Little Mouse have different ideas of what constitutes a very busy day in this brightly colored and boldly illustrated picture book. Reminiscent of *The Little Red Hen*, but with a twist, Big Mouse would like help from Little Mouse working in his garden. Each time Big Mouse asks Little Mouse to help with the digging, planting seeds, or the weeding, Little Mouse answers that he is "too busy to help" as he is "dreaming up something." Finally Big Mouse begins to get a bit grumpy. Little Mouse wins him over with his suggestion that they have a picnic and his gift of a hat, with daisies and feathers, that he has made. Together they find time to eat strawberries, wear their sun hats, and take a nap. Illustrations show clever use of materials by the mice—a wheelbarrow constructed with a clothespin, spool of thread, and small box. *kmc and jig*
Author and Illustrator live in England

Hendry, Diana. **The Very Noisy Night**. Illustrated by Jane Chapman. New York: Dutton, 1999. First published in the United Kingdom by Little Tiger Press, 1999. ISBN 0-525-46261-9. 28 p. (3–6). Picture book.

Little Mouse and Big Mouse have gone to bed but Little Mouse is having trouble sleeping. He hears huffing and puffing, a branch tapping, an owl calling. His entreaties to Big Mouse to let him sleep with him are met with rejection until he awakens Big Mouse once again and declares that he is lonely. This time Big

Mouse lets Little Mouse join him in bed, where both snuggle down and go to sleep—even sleeping through the alarm clock. Illustrations show toys, playing cards, all used in the bedroom of the mice. *jig*
Author and illustrator live in England

Hirsch, Odo. **Bartlett and the City of Flames**. Illustrated by Andrew McLean. New York: Bloomsbury USA Children's Books, 2003. Originally published by Bloomsbury in 1999. ISBN 1-58234-831-6. 201 p. (10 up). Novel.

Bartlett the explorer, his partner Jacques Le Grand, and young Gozo have just come to the end of the Margoulis Caverns thus ending their mapping of the caverns. They are suddenly captured and taken to the City of the Sun. Te Pasha, the ruler of the city, believes Gozo is his son but others believe the Pasha's son has been kidnapped by the elusive Underground people. Bartlett needs to create a plan to rescue the Pasha's son using "Ingenuity, Perseverance and Desperation." This exciting adventure full of twists and turns is the sequel to *Bartlett and the Ice Voyage* that won the Blue Peter Award and is followed by *Bartlett and the Forest of Plenty* (Bloomsbury, 2004). He is also the author of *Hazel Green* (Bloomsbury, 2003). *ls*
Author born and educated in Australia, lives in England

Hoffman, Mary. **Stravaganza: City of Masks**. New York: Bloomsbury USA Children's Books, 2002. ISBN 1-58234-791-3. 344 p. (14 up). Novel.

Fifteen-year-old Lucien is so weakened by chemotherapy that his father gives him a small, elegant notebook to save Lucien's voice. The notebook proves to be a talisman, which transports Lucien to a Venice-like parallel universe, Bellezza in the country of Talia. Each night Lucien travels to Bellezza where he meets Arianna, a spirited girl who wants to become a mandolier. Lucien's forays to Bellezza involve him in the intrigues surrounding the Duchesse, the ruler of the city. An imaginative, fascinating, and complex story that is at once foreign and familiar. *ls*
Author from England

Hoffman, Mary. **Stravaganza: City of Stars**. New York: Bloomsbury USA Children's Books, 2003. ISBN 1-58234-839-1. 452 p. (14 up). Novel.

Georgia O'Grady loves riding horses. She saves her money to buy a figurine of a flying horse, which she sees in an antique store. That night, Georgia locks her bedroom door against her bullying stepbrother and as she falls asleep holding her flying horse, Georgia finds herself transported to the city of Remora in the country of Talia. Georgia is in the midst of a great secret, the birth of a flying horse, and the city's preparations for the Stellata, a horse where the riders ride bareback with whips around the city center. The race is similar to the Palio, which is held in Sienna. This sequel to *Stravaganza: City of Masks* continues the

adventures and intrigue with the characters from the first book very much involved with Georgia and the reason why she has stravagated, or time traveled, to Remora.   *ls*
Author from England

Horowitz, Anthony. **Point Blank: An Alex Rider Adventure**. New York: Philomel, 2002. Originally published by Walker (UK) in 2001. (Paperback: Penguin, 2003). ISBN 0-399-23621-X. 215 p. (10 up). Novel.

Fourteen-year-old Alex Rider, in his second adventure as a spy for MI6, is recruited to infiltrate the Academy at Point Blanc, a school located high in the French Alps for the delinquent sons of the world's richest and most powerful. Alex, posing as the son of a wealthy English businessman, soon discovers that the deranged principal and former Russian KGB General Major, Dr. Hugo Grief, has cloned himself sixteen times as he prepares to take over the world. Now these clones are fourteen years old and are being surgically altered to replace the students at the academy. Alex attempts to save the boys, and in 007-style his thrilling adventures include surviving a treacherous ride on a snowboard fashioned from an ironing board, blasting machine guns mounted on high-power snowmobiles, a fall from the top of a speeding train, and a face-to-face battle with his own clone. Other books in this series that may also entice reluctant readers include *Stormbreaker, Skeleton Key,* and *Eagle Strike.*   *kk*
Author lives in England

Horsbrugh, Wilma. **The Train to Glasgow**. Illustrated by Paul Cox. New York: Clarion, 2004. Published in the United States by arrangement with the Albion Press. Oxfordshire, England. ISBN 0-618-38143-0. 28 p. (4–8). Picture book.

Donald MacBrain caught the train, just as the guard from Donibristle blew his whistle and the driver, Mr. MacIver pulled out of the station at Glasgow. Ah, but that is just the beginning of this cumulative rhyme that was first collected in the book *Clinkerdump and Other Stories in Rhyme* (Methuen, 1954). It is easy to see why this boy, so quick and clever, has remained a favorite in England.   *djg*
Illustrator is one of Britain's foremost illustrators

Hughes, Shirley. **Ella's Big Chance: A Jazz Age Cinderella**. New York: Simon & Schuster, 2004. Originally published as *Ella's Big Chance: A Fairy Tale Retold* by The Bodley Head, 2003. ISBN 0-689-87399-9. 32 p. (5–8). Picture book.

Celebrated author and illustrator Shirley Hughes studied old movies and 1920s fashions before creating this version of the Cinderella story. Ella Cinders is a plump dressmaker who makes the most marvelous gowns. Along comes a domineering stepmother and lazy stepsisters, but Ella's design skills save the day. Hughes' fluid, gouache and pen illustrations, inspired by the great French couturiers of the 1920s, are glamorous and colorful, as are the ball sequences. A surprise ending adds up to total contentment with a story that will be enjoyed over and over. *2003 Kate Greenaway Medal for Children's Illustration.* sg and plb *Author lives in England*

Hughes, Ted. **The Cat and the Cuckoo**. Illustrated by Flora McDonnell. Brookfield, CT: Roaring Brook Press, 2003. First published in 1987 by Sunstone Press, London. ISBN 0-7613-1548-9. 64 p. (8–12). Poetry.

This collection of poems about animals has clear descriptions, insightful humor, and the occasional surprise ending. Some are told from a third person perspective, some from first, but all capture an essential attribute of the animal, from the goat ("I'm as happy with the Thorn As I am with the rose") to the peacock ("A perfect peacock on the lawn Pranced proudly through his paces). *Author lived in England. Illustrator lives in England.*

Hutchins, Pat. **There's Only One of Me!** New York: Greenwillow, 2003. ISBN 0-06-029819-7 trade, ISBN 0-06-029820-0 library bdg. 24 p. (5–7). Picture book.

For her fifth birthday party the narrator's blended family celebrate with her. As she gets ready for the party and the guests arrive, she recounts her relationship to each member of the family, from mother and sister through half brother, stepfather, step-brother, aunt and uncle, cousin, and grandparents. This cumulative book ends with the little girl exclaiming "it's nice to be so many things when . . . there's only one of me!" *jvl* *Author lives in London, and is internationally known for her over 30 books for young children, starting with* Rosie's Walk *in 1968. Won the Kate Greenaway Medal in 1975 for* The Wind Blew.

Ibbotson, Eva. **Dial-A-Ghost**. Illustrated by Kevin Hawkes. New York: Dutton Children's Books, 2001. Originally published by Macmillan's Children's Books in 1996. ISBN 0-525-46693-2. 195 p. (10 up). Novel.

Oliver Smith, an orphan, inherits an estate, Helton Hall. Fulton Snodde-Brittle and his sister Frieda want to reclaim their inheritance. They go to the Dial-A-Ghost agency to adopt terrifying ghosts to scare Oliver to death. However, a mix-up occurs and the kindly ghosts of the Wilkerson family arrive at Helton Hall. Oliver loves his ghosts and wants to establish a Laboratory for the Study of Ghostliness. A wonderful story with twists and turns, ghost, villains, and mistakes that manages to end happily ever after. *ls* *Author from England*

Ibbotson, Eva. **The Great Ghost Rescue**. Illustrated Kevin Hawkes. New York: Dutton Children's Books, 2002. (New York, Puffin Books, 2003). Originally published by Macmillan in 1975. ISBN 0-525-46769-6. 167 p. (10 up). Novel.

Urban development and pollution is taking its toll on the ghosts of Britain. When the Craggyford ghosts' castle is renovated into a tourist resort, they must find a new home. During their search, the ghosts meet Rick, a politically-involved student at Norton Castle School. Together they decide that a ghost sanctuary is needed. Rick and the ghosts travel to London to see the Prime Minister. When it seems that their problems are solved, the ghosts find they are just beginning. This ghastly and amusing ghost story is full of ghosts and vampire bats. *ls*
Author from England

Ibbotson, Eva. **Island of the Aunts**. Illustrated by Kevin Hawkes. New York: Dutton Books, 2000. (New York, Puffin Books, 2001). Originally published by Macmillan Children's Books in 1999. ISBN 0-525-46484-0. 281 p. (10 up). Novel.

Kidnapping is never a good idea but sometimes it must be done. Three aunts are getting old and want to find children who take over their island and the care of their vast assortment of unusual creatures. Minette and Fabio, two of the kidnapped children, come to love the island and its animals. They save it from the hands of a greedy millionaire who wants to turn it into a theme park. A fantastic adventure filled with humor. *ls*
Author from England

Ibbotson, Eva. **Journey to the River Sea**. Illustrated by Kevin Hawkes. New York: Dutton Children's Books, 2001. (New York: Puffin Books, 2003). Originally published by Macmillan Children's Books in 2001. ISBN 0-52546739-4. 298 p. (10 up). Novel.

Accompanied by Miss Minton, the new governess, Maia journeys to Brazil to live with distant relatives, the Carters, on their rubber plantation. Life with the Carters, who are cruel, petty, and prejudiced, is stifling. When Maia escapes the house, she explores the rainforest and makes friends with the Indian servants. She falls in love with Brazil and the rainforest. Maia befriends two orphans, Clovis King, a child actor whose voice is breaking, and a mysterious Indian boy, whom she assists in changing their destinies. Readers of *The Secret Garden* and *The Little Princess* would enjoy this rich, suspenseful adventure. *2001 Smarties Book Prize Gold Award, Ages 9–11.* *ls*
Author from England

Ibbotson, Eva. **Not Just a Witch**. Illustrated by Kevin Hawkes. New York: Dutton Children's Books, 2003. Originally published by Macmillan Children's Books in 1989. ISBN 0-525-47101-4. 185 p. (10 up). Novel.

Heckie Tenbury-Smith is an animal witch who means to make the world a better place. She owns a pet shop and befriends a lonely, neglected boy, Daniel. Heckie's plan is to turn wicked people into animals. Then they would just be animals and no longer wicked. The scheme works well until Heckie meets the con-

niving and unscrupulous Lionel Knacksap, a furrier who deals in exotic pelts and who proceeds to sweep Heckie off her feet. Daniel and his friends foil Knacksap's fiendish plot before he breaks Heckie's heart. Crime simply does not pay in this imaginative and humorous tale.   *ls*
Author from England

Ibbotson, Eva. **The Secret of Platform 13**. Illustrated by Sue Porter. New York: Dutton Children's Books, 1994. (New York, Puffin Books, 1998). Originally published by Macmillan's Children's Books, 1994. ISBN 0-5254-5929-4. 231 p. (12 up). Novel.
    Platform 13 at King's Cross Station is the portal to another world, an island filled with fantastic and mythical creatures living in harmony. The portal opens every nine years for nine days. During one opening, the infant Prince is taken by his nurses Up There where he is kidnapped by beastly Mrs. Trottle. Nine years later, a wizard, a fairy, an ogre, and Odge, a little hag, are sent to rescue the Prince. They meet Ben who is a kind kitchen boy and Raymond who is a spoiled brat and supposedly the Prince. An exciting adventure filled with fantastic creatures.   *ls*
Author from England

Ibbotson, Eva. **The Star of Kazan**. New York: Dutton Children's Books, a division of Penguin Young Readers Group, 2004. Originally published in Great Britain by Macmillan Children's Books in London, 2004. ISBN 0-525-47347-5. 405 p. (12 up). Novel.
    Annika, a 12-year-old foundling happily living with the cook and maid of three professors in Vienna in the early 1900s, still dreams of meeting her real mother one day. These dreams come true when Edeltraut von Trannenberg arrives with all of the proper documentation and sorrowful story as to why she had to give up her only daughter. Annika leaves her friends and the only family she knows to live the life of a proper lady at Frau Edeltrauts's estate, Spittal, in the German Empire. There she learns that food is scarce and all is not as it seems as she desperately tries to believe in her mother. When Annika discovers that she was the named recipient of the last will and testament of La Rondine, an old lady she spent time exchanging stories with, she realizes that her mother has been keeping many secrets from her. Strong character development and a passionate sense of place bring the reader into Annika's world where the beauty of Vienna prevails and true, honest friends are all the family this foundling needs. *School Library Journal Best Book of the Year 2004; Booklist Editor's Choice 2004; Fall 2004 Parents' Choice Gold Award Winner; ALA Notable Book 2005.   kmc*

Ibbotson, Eva. **Which Witch?** Illustrated by Annabel Large. New York: Dutton Children's Books, 1999. (New York: Puffin Books, 2000.) Originally published by Macmillan Children's Books in 1979. ISBN 0-525-46164-7. 231 p. (10 up). Novel.

Arriman the Awful, the Wizard of the North, decides he must have an heir. He invites the witches of Todcaster to enter a competition and he will marry the winner. Six witches enter the competition. Mabel Wrack is half mermaid. Old Mother Bloodwort often turns herself into a coffee table. The Shouter twins constantly bicker and argue. Madame Olympia is simply terrifying. Beautiful Belladonna is a white witch surrounded by flowers and gentle creatures. Belladonna befriends orphan Terrance Mudd and his pet earthworm, Rover, to make her magic more black. Arriman's dilemma only gets progressively worse as the competition proceeds. Finally, all is well. *ls*
Author from England

Inkpen, Mick. **Kipper's A to Z**. San Diego: Red Wagon/Harcourt, 2001. Originally published by Hodder Children's Books in 2000. ISBN 0-15-202594-4. 56 p. (3–6). Picture book.

Kipper, Inkpen's irresistibly cuddly dog, was created in England but became a star in the United States, thanks to a Nick, Jr. animated television series and spin-off books and videos. Here Kipper takes young readers through the alphabet, cleverly creating a small story that pulls the reader from one letter to the next and occasionally posing questions to the listener to provide an interactive experience. Among other Kipper books by Inkpen are *Kipper, Kipper's Birthday*, and *Kipper's Toybox*. *ss*

Jacques, Brian. **The Angel's Command: A Tale from the Castaways of the Flying Dutchman**. Illustrated by David Elliot. New York: Philomel Books, 2003. (New York: Ace Books, 2004). ISBN 0-399-23999-5. 374 p. (12 up). Novel.

In this sequel to *The Castaways of the Flying Dutchman*, Ben and his dog Ned arrive in Cartegena. At a dockside tavern they meet and join buccaneer Captain Raphael Thuron on his ship, La Petite Marie. Captain Thuron has made his fortune and intends to return to France. Two villainous pirates chase the La Petite Marie and her crew across the Atlantic to the French shore. At this point, a second adventure begins taking Ben and Ned into the French Pyrenees where they confront gypsies, evil sorcery, and avalanches. This is a swashbuckling and thrilling adventure where, once again, Ben and Ned help people in need. *ls*

Jacques, Brian. **Castaways of the Flying Dutchman**. Illustrated by Ian Schoenherr. New York: Philomel Books, 2001. (New York: Ace, 2002). ISBN 0-399-23601-5. 327 p. (12 up). Novel.

In 1620, Neb, a Danish boy who is mute, and his dog are aboard the ill-fated ship, the Flying Dutchman. While the ship and crew are fated to roam the seas forever, an avenging angel saves the two innocents who are to roam the world helping those in need. Neb can speak and communicate with his dog. First, they help Luis, an old shepherd, on Tierra del Fuego. Next, in 1896, Neb and his dog help preserve a vil-

SPOTLIGHT ON BRIAN JACQUES

Brian Jacques (pronounced "jakes") was born in Liverpool, England, in 1939. He grew up in the area around the Liverpool docks. His interest in adventure stories began at an early age and he counts Daniel Defoe, Arthur Conan Doyle, Sir Thomas Malory, Robert Louis Stevenson, and Kenneth Grahame among his favorite authors.

Dubbed a "master of the animal fantasy genre," by Sally Estes of Booklist Magazine, Jacques is most famous for his "Redwall" series that take place around the Redwall Abbey. The heroes are peace-loving mice, moles, shrews, squirrels, and their friends who exhibit human characteristics in a medieval setting. They face the dark side of the animal world, represented by rats, weasels, stoats, foxes, and their villain allies, in the day-to-day struggle of good versus evil, life versus death. He has received the Carnegie Medal nomination for *Redwall, Mossflower, Mattimeo, and Salamandastron*. Visit the author's homepage to learn more about the books at http://www.redwall.org/.

Two recent titles, *Castaways of the Flying Dutchman* and *The Angel's Command* demonstrate the author's love of high adventure.

Suggested Reading: Booklist, November 1, 1991; Contemporary Authors, Vol. 127; *Something About the Author*, Vol. 62 and 138.
Gauch, Patricia Lee. "Brian Jacques-Spinner of Yarns," *Language Arts,* v. 80. no. 5 (May 2003): 401–5.

Selected Works: *Redwall,* 1987; *Mossflower,* 1988; *Mattimeo,* 1989; *Mariel of Redwall,* 1991; *Salamastron,* 1992, *Martin the Warrior,* 1994; *The Bellmaker,* 1995; *Outcast of Redwall,* 1996; *Pearls of Lutra,* 1996; *The Long Patrol,* 1998; *Marlfox,* 1998; *The Legend of Luke,* 2000; *Lord Bocktree,* 2000; *Taggerund,* 2001; *Triss,* 2002; *Loamhedge,* 2003; *Rakkety Tam,* 2004.

lage from developers who want to create a quarry. An unusual, enticing story containing riddles, bullies, and humor with a touch of the supernatural. *ls*

Jacques, Brian. **The Great Redwall Feast**. Illustrated by Christopher Denise. New York: Philomel Books, 1996. ISBN 0-399-22707. 64 p. (10 up). Novel.
The creatures of Redwall Abbey are preparing a surprise feast for the abbot. The abbot decides to go on a Bobbaton Quest to Mossflower Wood with Constance, Matthias, and Foremole. The preparations proceed with song, confusion, and mishap. Bungo, a little mole is everywhere getting underfoot and tasting the pies, salads, and beverages. The feast is a great success. Finally, at the end, everyone finds out what a Bobbaton Quest is. The poetry and illustrations bring the world of Redwall to life. *ls*

Jacques, Brian. **The Legend of Luke**. Illustrated by Fangorn. New York: Philomel Books, 2000. (New York: Ace Books, 2001). Originally published by Hutchinson Children's Books in 1999. ISBN 0-399-23490-X. 374 p. (12 up). Novel.

While Redwall Abbey is being built, Martin the Warrior undertakes a journey to find out what happened to his father, Luke. When he reaches a red ship perched high between two rocks, Martin is given a book that recounts the story of how Luke the Warrior sailed away from the north coast to avenge the deaths of his wife and other families by the dreaded Sea Rogue, Vilu Dasker. This prequel to the Redwall series tells the legend of Luke and begins the story of Martin the Warrior and his famous sword. *ls*

Jacques, Brian. **Loamhedge**. Illustrated by David Elliot. New York: Philomel Books, 2003. ISBN 0-399-23724-0. 424 p. (12 up). Novel.

Martha, a young hare, is wheelchair bound. Her friends travel to Loamhedge to find a cure. Badger Lonna Bowstripe seeks to destroy the vermin Raga Bol and his Searats because they nearly killed him. When Raga Bol invades Redwall, the inhabitants put up a great defense, Martha finds the courage to use her legs, and Lonna Bowstripe gets his revenge. Riddles, ballads, feasting, and battles fill this Redwall saga where good and evil clash. *ls*

Jacques, Brian. **The Long Patrol**. Illustrated by Allan Curless. New York: Philomel Books, 1998. (New York: Ace, 1999). Originally published by Hutchinson Children's Books in 1997. ISBN 0-399-23165-X. 358 p. (12 up). Novel.

Tammo, a young hare, runs away from home to join the Long Patrol. The Long Patrol are the hares who live in Salamandastron, the badger stronghold. They patrol the countryside hunting vermin who are disturbing the peace. The vicious Rapscallion army is on the march. Their goal is to defeat Lady Cregga Rose Eyes, the Badger Lady, and take over Redwall Abbey. Meanwhile, at Redwall Abbey, the south wall is collapsing. The Redwallers make an amazing discovery when they investigate the cause of the collapse. This quick-paced action adventure tale is full of mystery and daring-do. *ls*

Jacques, Brian. **Lord Brocktree**. Illustrated by Fangorn. New York: Philomel Books, 2000. (New York: Ace Books, 2001). Originally published by Hutchinson Children's Books in 2000. ISBN 0-3992-3590-6. 370 p. (12 up). Novel.

A young hare named Dotti and Lord Brocktree, heir to Salamandastron, journey to the badger stronghold. Along the way, they discover that the mountain has been captured by wildcat Ungatt Trunn and his Blue Hordes. Reconquering Salamandastron requires the co-operation of squirrels, otters, hares, moles, and shrews. After Salamandastron is retaken, The Long Patrol is founded. The badger stronghold grows in strength welcoming all who come in peace. Gripping tale of bravery and courage fighting for one's home in spite of overwhelming odds. *ls*

Jacques, Brian. **Marlfox**. Illustrated by Fangorn. New York: Philomel Books, 1999. Originally published by Hutchinson Children's Books in 1998. ISBN 0-399-23307-5. 386 p. (12 up). Novel.

Villainous Marlfoxes have entered Mossflower Wood seeking treasure. They steal Redwall Abbey's one treasure, the tapestry of Martin the Warrior. Four young animals undertake a dangerous journey all the way to the Marlfox's isolated island to retrieve the tapestry. Along the way, they meet allies and enemies and discover the courage to complete their almost impossible quest. *ls*

Jacques, Brian. **Martin the Warrior**. Illustrated by Gary Chalk. New York: Philomel Books, 1994. (New York: Ace Books, 1995). Originally published by Hutchinson Children's Books in 1993. ISBN 0-399-22670-2. 376 p. (12 up). Novel.

Martin the Warrior is the mouse hero of Redwall Abbey, where a valued tapestry of Martin hangs. In this installment of the Redwall series, Martin's early story is told. Martin is held prisoner in Marshank, an evil fortress, by the tyrant stoat, Badrang. A young mouse, Rose, and her companion, Grumm, travel to Marshank to rescue her brother, Brome, from slavery. Martin and Rose team up with the other peace-loving animals to end Badrang's reign. This complex story is filled with fierce battles, colorful characters, and derring-do as good fights evil. *ls*

Jacques, Brian. **Outcast of Redwall**. Illustrated by Alan Curless. New York: Philomel Books, 1996. (New York: Puffin Books, 2004). Originally published by Hutchinson Children's Books in 1996. ISBN 0-399-22914-0. 360 p. (12 up). Novel.

The evil ferret, Swartt Sixclaw, and his hordes are on the rampage to kill Sunflash, the Badger Lord. Swartt abandons his son. The baby is found and taken to Redwall Abbey. Kindhearted Bryony names the ferret Veil. She raises him and is convinced that the goodness in him will prevail. When Veil commits an unforgivable crime, he is banished from Redwall. He meets up with his father's forces. Will he stay with his father or save someone who loves him? This epic adventure spans the lands around Redwall as the peaceful inhabitants must fight an evil foe. *ls*

Jacques, Brian. **Pearls of Lutra**. New York: Philomel Books, 1997. (New York: Ace, 1998). Originally published by Hutchinson Children's Books in 1996. ISBN 0-399-22946-9. 408 p. (12 up). Novel.

The Tears of All Oceans, six large rose-colored pearls, run through the adventures in this Redwall tale. Ublaz Mad Eyes, a pine marten who is the evil emperor of an island, wants them for his crown. He sends his minions out to find them. It is reported that the pearls are at Redwall Abbey. When the corsairs, searats, and monitor lizards kidnap Abbot Durral, Tansy, a young hedgemaid, is determined to find the pearls. High adventure, riddles, and humor work together for an exciting journey into the world that is Redwall. *ls*

Jacques, Brian. **A Redwall Winter's Tale**. Illustrated by Christopher Denise. New York: Philomel Books, 2001. ISBN 0-399-23346-6. 72 p. (10 up). Novel.

It's the last day of autumn and all the creatures of Redwall Abbey are preparing a huge feast. The festivities begin with songs, juggling, acrobatics, and magic by the Thistledown Troupe. When the feasting is done, the Abbybabes are sent to bed with Mighty Bullrock Badger telling the story of the Snow Badger. That night, the Snow Badger arrives and releases his snow hares who turn into snowflakes. Bungo, a little mole, wakes early and meets the Snow Badger, whom most of the creatures think of as a make believe figure, making the first day of winter a very special one indeed. Poetry and prose accompanied by warm and winsome illustrations show the magic of Redwall.   *ls*

Jacques, Brian. **Taggerung**. Illustrated by Peter Stanley. New York: Philomel Books, 2001. (New York, Firebird, 2003). Originally published by Hutchinson Children's Books in 2001. ISBN 0-399-23720-8. 438 p. (12 up). Novel.

The Juska band of Sawney Rath kidnaps a baby otter, a resident of Redwall Abbey. The omens say that he is the next Taggerung, a warrior hero. Since he is the only otter in the tribe, Taggerung never really fits in among the foxes, stoats, rats, and weasels. When ordered to skin alive a tribe member, Taggerung leaves the Juska to seek out his own adventures that lead him to Redwall Abbey and the sword of Martin the Warrior. Although it contains many of the qualities of most of the Redwall series—action-packed derring-do—this gentler tale is about finding one's destiny in the world.   *ls*

Jacques, Brian. **The Tale of Urso Brunov, Little Father of All Bears**. Illustrated by Alexi Natchev. New York: Philomel Books, 2003. ISBN 0-399-23762-3. 48 p. (4 up). Novel.

Urso Brunov, Little Father of All Bears, was the "strongest, cleverest, bravest, fiercest bear that ever lived," yet was smaller than the size of your thumb. When Urso awoke to find four of his tiny bears missing, having been taken to the zoo to be held captive by the mightiest of men, the Lord of All Sands, he immediately set out in pursuit. Rallied by the cry, "Believe me, for I am Urso Brunov!" the imprisoned creatures united with the small, mighty bear to gain their freedom. Their success returned them home, though not before teaching the Lord of All Sands a harsh lesson in humility and respect, and proving that bravery, determination, and heart outsize any bully.   *ank*

Jacques, Brian. **Triss**. Illustrated by David Elliot. New York: Philomel Books, 2002. (New York, Ace Books, 2003). ISBN 0-399-23723-2. 389 p. (12 up). Novel.

A brave squirrelmaid, Triss, escapes Riftgard where she was enslaved by the evil ferret King Agaru and his daughter, Princess Kurda. Pursued by Princess Kurda, Triss meets many creatures who help her along her way to Redwall Abbey where Triss is granted Matthew the Warrior's sword. After helping rid Mossflower Wood of adders, freebooters, and riftgarders, Triss returns to Riftgard to free the slaves so that they can live in the same peace and harmony that is enjoyed at Redwall Abbey. Another engrossing tale about Redwall and its inhabitants filled with ballads and feasts. *ls*

James, Simon. **The Day Jake Vacuumed**. Cambridge, MA: Candlewick, 2002. Originally published by J.M. Dent in 1989. ISBN 0-7636-1799-7 (paperback). 32 p. (4–7). Picture book.

James's cartoon-style illustrations are a good match for his outrageous story of a recalcitrant little boy who gets revenge when his mother makes him do the vacuuming. He begins by sucking the cat into the vacuum and then proceeds to larger quarry, including his mother, his sister, and his father. In each illustration, the machine expands, as does Jake's wicked grin. When the machine explodes, freeing his parents and sister, he finds himself sent to his room without supper. Jake gets the last laugh, though, as he realizes that vacuuming is one household chore he'll never be asked to do again. *ss*

Jarrett, Clare. **Best Picnic Ever**. Cambridge, MA: Candlewick, 2004. ISBN 0-76376-2370-9. 32 p. (3–5). Picture book.

When Jack and his mom take a picnic to the park, Jack finds a variety of obliging wild animals to play with and share the child-friendly lunch. A cumulative text and large, whimsical color pencil illustrations make this a fine book for reading aloud. The endpapers resemble a child's drawing of leaves and plants and set a happy mood for the story. *sg*
Author lives in England

Jarrett, Clare. **Catherine and the Lion**. Minneapolis: Carolrhoda, 1997. Originally published by HarperCollins, Ltd. in 1996. ISBN 1-57505-035-8. 26 p. (3–6). Picture book.

When Catherine wakes up in the morning, a friendly lion greets her. He joins her in her day's activities, at home and in school, where he listens to stories during circle time, gives rides to the children on the playground, and joins them in their after lunch nap. When a sleepy Catherine asks him at bedtime, "Will you always be here?" he replies, "Yes I will." Expressive line drawings with golden orange pastels give the book a warm and reassuring look, which reinforces the book's quiet tone as it depicts a child's world. This is her first children's book. *Kirkus Book Review Star. jvl.*
Author, a studio artist, lives in England

Kennemore, Tim. **Circle of Doom**. Pictures by Tim Archbold. New York: Farrar, Straus and Giroux, 2003. First published in Great Britain by Andersen Press, 2001. ISBN 0-374-31284-2. 203 p. Novel.

There's no such thing as magic, or is there? Thirteen-year-old Lizzie Sharp becomes convinced that she can do magic when she concocts a potion that

seemingly makes her cranky neighbor, Mrs. Potward, break her hip and then disappear. She convinces her skeptical brothers of the power of the potions, one set of coincidences leading to another until younger brother Max takes the potion to school to try out on a teacher. The consequences are more than the children bargain for. *Parent's Choice Award Silver 2003; Best Children's Books of the Year, 2004; Bank Street College.*   djg
Author lives in northwest London and was a runner-up for the British Library Association's Carnegie Medal in 1982.

Kessler, Liz. **The Tail of Emily Windsnap**. Cambridge, MA: Candlewick., 2004. ISBN 0-7636-2483-7. 209 p. (10–13). Novel.

Twelve-year-old Emily Windsnap discovers she is half mermaid when she swims for the first time in her seventh grade swim class. Despite her mother's warnings to stay away from the water, Emily secretly sneaks out to swim every night, and she soon stumbles upon a full mermaid, Shona. Shona takes Emily to Mermaid school, where Emily learns about the illegal love affairs between humans and merfolk and realizes that her long lost father must have been a merman. Through a series of coincidences and adventures, Emily discovers the location of the prison that houses her father and confronts Neptune to free her father and reunite her family.   aao
Author lives in England

King-Smith, Dick. **Lady Lollipop**. Illustrated by Jill Barton. Cambridge, MA: Candlewick Press, 2001. ISBN 0-7636-1269-3. (Paperback: Candlewick Press, 2003). Originally published in Great Britain in 2000. ISBN 0-7636-2181-1. 123 p. (8–12). Novel.

Princess Penelope is anything but charming. For her eighth birthday, the spoiled princess demands a pet pig. Despite disapproval from her parents, Penelope chooses Lollipop, the scruffy, yet clever companion of orphaned Johnny Skinner. Insistent that Lollipop becomes a palace-pig, Penelope causes a royal uproar, and it becomes Johnny's seemingly impossible task to train both Lollipop and the princess. In this endearing story of friendship, readers learn the importance of caring more about others than themselves, and the rewards of teamwork, creativity, and a good bit of patience. Jill Barton's enchanting illustrations capture the delightful characters, from the thunder of Princess Penelope, to the earnestness of Johnny Skinner and charm of Lady Lollipop. *NYPL Children's Books: 100 Titles for Reading and Sharing; ALA Notable Children's Books; Beverly Cleary Children's Choice Award. Clever Lollipop (2003) is the sequel.*   ank
Author from Gloucestershire, England

King-Smith, Dick. **The Nine Lives of Aristotle**. Illustrated by Bob Graham. Cambridge, MA: Candlewick Press, 2003. ISBN 0-7636-2260-5. 80 p. (6 up). Novel.

When Aristotle, the small, white kitten who's curiosity often overtakes good sense, goes to live with the kindhearted witch, Bella Donna, he learns promptly that he will need his nine lives. Bella Donna's cottage is a hazardous place for an audacious kitten, and Aristotle soon finds himself in some precarious predicaments. His first eight lives quickly disappear, despite Bella Donna's caring admonition and watchful eye. Humbled by his last misadventure, Aristotle finally settles down to enjoy a long last life with his good friend. Bob Graham's muted watercolor illustrations add charm and tenderness to the friendship of the old witch and her cat that sweetens with the passing of time. *New York Public Library Children's Books: 100 Titles for Reading and Sharing Children's Book Council Children's Choices.* The author's many animal stories include *Titus Rules* (2004), *Funny Frank* (2003), *Emily's Legs* (2002), and *I Love Guinea Pigs* (2001). *ank*
Author from Gloucestershire, England

Kitamura, Satoshi. **Comic Adventures of Boots**. New York: Farrar Straus Giroux, 2002. Originally published by Andersen Press Ltd. in 2002. ISBN 9-780374-314552. 32 p. (6–10). Novel.

Boots and his feline friends have three comic adventures. In "Operation Fish Biscuit," Boots regains his napping spot on the wall by spreading fish biscuits on the tin roof. In "Pleased to Meet You Madam Quark," Boots befriends a duck who teaches him how to swim. In "Let's Play a Guessing Game," Boots and his friends devise a game where one cat poses while the others guess who it is. Boots's adventures are clever, quick-paced, and funny. *ls*
Author from England

Laird, Elizabeth. **Beautiful Bananas**. Illustrated by Liz Pinchon. Atlanta: Peachtree. 2003. ISBN 1-56145-305-6. First published by Oxford University Press in Great Britain, 2003. 28 p. (4–8). Picture book.

Beatrice waves goodbye to Mama, she's on her way to see her granddad with a present—a beautiful bunch of bananas. But along the way she meets giraffe who flicks the bananas off her head into the stream—so sorry he gives her a beautiful flower instead. Trade after trade occurs on her journey through the jungle, until at last she arrives at grandad's with another beautiful bunch of bananas. Vivid paintings illustrate this playful tale.
This award-winning author has been shortlisted for the Carnegie Medal and has won the Smarties Young Judges prize. She is a specialist in African folklore.

Laird, Elizabeth. **The Garbage King**. Hauppauge: Barron's Educational Series, 2003. (ISBN 0-7641-2626-1). Originally published by Macmillan Children's Books in 2003. ISBN 0-7641-5679-9. 329 p. (12 up). Novel.

Mamo, a poor orphan, and Dani, a wealthy boy with a cruel father, meet in Addis Abba after they run away from desperate situations. They join a street gang

for protection and learn to survive by begging and scrounging. With the help of the gang, Mamo gets revenge on the man who sold him to a farmer. Dani's storytelling and writing abilities help to resolve his issues with his family. Mamo and Dani remain friends and both of them help the street gang to survive. A powerful and fascinating story. *ls*
Author from England has traveled widely in Ethiopia

Laird, Elizabeth, with Sonia Nimr. **A Little Piece of Ground**. London: Macmillan, 2003. (Hardcover: Macmillan, 2004). ISBN 0-330-43679-1. 214 p. (11 up). Novel.

Twelve-year-old Karim wants to be a champion soccer player, to be cooler and taller than his older brother, and—to invent a formula to dissolve steel in Israeli tanks. He lives in Ramallah. Regularly, his school days are disrupted by armed soldiers who impose curfews, strip grown men at blockades, and shoot at suspects. With his friends, he builds a secret soccer ground and hideout, and dreams of becoming a hero for Palestine. But when he is unable to hurry home before the curfew, he spends days hiding from soldiers and is shot in the leg. Though he returns to his family greeted as though he were a hero, the honor is bittersweet. This dramatic story gives voice to an often-unheard side in the conflict between Palestine and Israel. It will give readers deeper understanding of the emotional trauma of living with terror and war. *Hampshire Book Award (UK).* *mk*
Laird from UK; Nimr from Palestine

Langrish, Katherine. **Troll Fell**. New York: HarperCollins, 2004. Originally published by Collins in 2004. ISBN 0-06-058305-3. 264 p. (10 up). Novel.

After his father dies, Peer is taken to live with two lazy, greedy, identical-twin uncles in a rundown mill. The uncles plan to get troll gold by bringing a boy and a girl to the troll wedding to be held at Midwinter. At Midwinter, Peer finds himself inside Troll Fell with Hilde trying to rescue the twins, Sigrid and Sigurd. Peer learns the secret of troll beer and turns the tables on his evil uncles. Set in Northern England. *ls*
Author from England

Lawler, Janet. **If Kisses Were Colors**. Illustrated by Alison Jay. New York: Dial, 2003. ISBN 0-8037-2617-1. 24 p. (2–5). Picture book.

A text in rhymed couplets imagines the many forms kisses might take as a way to show the infinite amount of love a mother has for her child. "If kisses were pebbles, your beach would be lined with stones by the millions, of all shapes and kinds." Jay's soft, folk-art illustrations dominated by round shapes and pastel colors are quiet and comforting, evocative of the nursery. *ss*
Author from United States. Illustrator from England.

Lawrence, Caroline. **The Roman Mysteries**. Brookfield, CT: Roaring Brook Press, 2002 (Paperback: Puffin, 2004). Originally published in Great Britain by Orion Children's Books in 2001. ISBN 0-7613-1582-9. (9 up). Novels. Series.

As ten-year-old Flavia Gemina and her three friends encounter adventures, get caught in intriguing plots, and barely escape a natural disaster, they witness tragic events in ancient Rome during the first century AD. They meet the Roman admiral Pliny, escape the eruption of Mt. Vesuvius, uncover shady deals of kidnapping and slavery, and foil an assassination plot against a Roman emperor. In each of the books the children find themselves in danger but, by following clues and deductive reasoning, solve a mystery. These children may be the ancient forerunners of Nancy Drew and the Hardy Boys. *ok*
Author from England, grew up in California, lives in London

Lisle, Rebecca. **Copper**. New York: G.P. Putnam's Sons, 2004. Originally published by Andersen Press Ltd., 2002. ISBN 0-3992-4211-2.186 p. (10 up). Novel.

On her tenth birthday, Copper Beech must leave her home with her beloved Aunt Abby to travel to the Marble Mountains because "they" are after her. What "they" want is Copper's gold charm bracelet because it has magical powers. When Copper arrives at Spindlehouse, she has many questions but receives few answers. She discovers there is a feud between two clans, the Woods and the Rockers. Copper decides to take matters in her own hands to resolve the misunderstanding that began the feud and bring peace to the Marble Mountains. An exciting adventure filled with twists and turns and memorable characters. *ls*
Author from England

Marillier, Juliet. **Wolfskin**. New York: Tor, 2003. ISBN 0-765-30672-7. 493 p. (14 up). Novel. And sequel *Foxmask*. New York: Tor, 2004. ISBN 0-765-30674-3. 464 p. (14 up). Orkney Islands.

See Australia for description.

Mayo, Margaret. **Brother Sun, Sister Moon: The Life and Stories of St. Francis**. Illustrated by Peter Malone. Boston: Little, Brown, 2000. Originally published as *Brother Sun, Sister Moon: The Story of St. Francis* by Orion in 1999. ISBN 0-3165-6466-4. 70 p. (8–12). Picture book.

Both fact and legend are collected in this extensive picture book about St. Francis of Assisi. As a young man, Francis publicly gave up his wealth to follow God. As a friar, he was known for his peaceful nature and his ability to tame wild animals—according to story, wolves, birds, rabbits, and fish all understood and obeyed him. After Francis's death, his legacy lived on in the *Canticle of Brother Sun*, his poem praising creation; the Franciscan order; and the church built in his honor; as well as in the legends. Luminous paintings reminiscent of

late Medieval/early Renaissance religious art bring Francis to life, as well as the landscape and costumes of his time. *mk*
Author and illustrator from UK

McAllister, Angela. **Barkus, Sly and the Golden Egg**. Illustrated by Sally Anne Lambert. New York: Bloomsbury, 2002. First published as *The Baddies' Goodies* in England by St. Martin's Press in 2002. ISBN 1-5823-4764-6. 32 p. (4–8). Picture book.

Barkus Fox and his cousin Sly steal three chickens, but, tired, they decide to lock the hens in a shed and roast them the next day. The hens make their plan, led by Tweed who gives the admonition, "Pull yourselves together, ladies." They do and manage to trick the foxes into thinking that one of them has laid a golden egg, which will eventually hatch and lay golden eggs herself. The greedy foxes do what the hens ask of them, a mistake as the hens not only escape, but leave a trail of stolen cutlery that leads the farmer to all the loot the foxes had stolen. *jig*
Author and illustrator live in England

McAllister, Angela. **Harry's Box**. Illustrated by Jenny Jones. New York: Bloomsbury, 2003. ISBN 1-58234-772-7. 32 p. (5–8). Picture book.

Harry and his dog Wolfie use a cardboard box from the grocery store for a variety of imaginative games. In the garden the box becomes a lion's den; in the bathroom it becomes a pirate ship. Finally it becomes a castle in the bedroom, with Harry as king. A foe, his mother, enters bringing cookies to the king and thus they become friends. *jig*
Author lives in England. Illustrator lives in Wales.

McAllister, Angela. **The Little Blue Rabbit**. Illustrated By Jason Cockcroft. New York: Bloomsbury Children's Books, 2003. Published simultaneously in New York and London by Bloomsbury. ISBN 1-58234-834-0. 32 p. (3–5). Picture book.

Blue Rabbit doesn't mind sleeping in the huge bed because Boy is always there to cuddle and comfort him in this bedtime story with a reversal of roles. When Boy disappears, Blue Rabbit is forlorn and frightened to be alone. His friends help him search and even climb into bed with him, but not even the photograph of Boy provides solace. Only when Boy returns, tanned and larger, but still "soft and warm and stuffed with love," does Blue Rabbit feel secure. *jig*
Author and illustrator live in England

McAllister, Angela. **Night-Night, Little One**. Illustrated by Maggie Kneen. New York: Doubleday, 2003. ISBN 0-385-32732-3. 32 p. (3–5). Picture book.

Duffy, a baby rabbit, has trouble going to sleep. He rearranges the stuffed animals in bed with him, calls to his mother for a drink of water, sings so loudly

that his mother comes to quiet him, and declares that he is not tired. Each time his mother responds, telling him "Night-night, little one." Finally, after listening to his mother tell about nocturnal animals, he giggles as his mother says that Mrs. Badger tucks her youngster into bed and saying, "Day-day, little one," and falls asleep.
Author and illustrator live in England

McCaughrean, Geraldine. **Casting the Gods Adrift**. Illustrated by Patricia D. Ludlow. Chicago: Cricket Books, 2002. Originally published by A & C Black in 1998. ISBN 0-8126-2684-2. 103 p. (10 up). Novel.

When their reed boat sinks in the Nile, Tutmose, his brother Ibrim, and their father, Harkhuf, are rescued by the pharaoh Akhenaten's royal barge. They sail to El-Amarna where the boys are given training: Tutmose as a sculptor and Ibrim as a musician. Harkhuf is made the pharaoh's official animal collector but he cannot accept Akhenaten's new religion and wants to bring back the old ways. In despair, Harkhuf devises a plot to poison the pharaoh that Tutmose manages to undo quickly and cleverly. Egypt in the 14th-century B.C. provides an interesting setting. An observant, talented boy learns to think for himself and saves his family and the pharaoh from disaster. *ls*
Author from England

McCaughrean, Geraldine. **The Kite Rider**. New York: HarperCollins, 2002. First published in England by Oxford University Press in 2001. ISBN 0-06-623874-9. 272 p. (9–12). Novel.

Haoyou seeks friendship and freedom when apprenticed as a kite-rider in the Great Miao's Jade Circus. With Mipeng's help, he carries offerings to the spirits of 13th-century China and dazzles villagers with his acrobatics while strapped onto a brilliant scarlet kite. When Miao's life is threatened by Kubla Khan, the entire circus unites to save the circus master or die with him. Haoyou returns to his village and rescues his mother from a ruthless killer, showing wisdom and compassion beyond his twelve years. Marco Polo's journals inspired this novel. *2001 Nestle Smarties Book Prize Bronze Medal, 2002; Carnegie Medal shortlist. Geraldine McCaughrean's* Not the End of the World, *the tale of Noah's unwed daughter Timna, brings the author her third Whitbread children's book award in 17 years. nrn*
Author lives in Berkshire, England.

McCaughrean, Geraldine. **My Grandmother's Clock**. Illustrated by Stephen Lambert. New York: Clarion, 2002. ISBN 0618216952. First published in Great Britain by HarperCollins, 2002. 32 p. (4–8). Picture book.

Grandmother has a clock, but it does not go and when the little girl asks her why she doesn't get it fixed, she learns that Grandmother has plenty of other ways to tell the time. Seconds are counted by the beating of a heart and minutes are how long it takes to think a thought and put them into words. The soft watercolor illustrations depict an idyllic country setting and the warm relationship between grandparents and their grandchild.

McCaughrean, Geraldine. **The Stones Are Hatching**. New York: Harper Collins, 2000. Originally published by Oxford University Press, 1999. ISBN 0-0602-8765-9. 130 p. (10–14). Novel.

Phelim Green believes there may be a ghost cat in the old house he shares with his sister. Instead he meets Domovoy and a whole troop of dirty little "glashans" who are all terrified and want him to save them and the world from the Worm, asleep these 2000 years but now waking because of the din of war. Phelim, with three companions, Alexia the witch girl, Mad Sweeny, a Napoleonic War soldier, and Obby Oss (Hobby Horse), guide him through his quest. McCaughrean interweaves traditional folkloric characters, such as the washer of bloody shirts, an omen of death, into this modern anti-war allegory. The author won the Carnegie Award for her book, *A Pack of Lies*.   *jvl*
Author lives in UK

McCaughrean, Geraldine. **Stop the Train!** New York: HarperCollins, 2003. ISBN 0-060-50749-7. 292 p. (10 up). Novel.

Cissy Sissney, her parents, and tens of thousands of others, like "a colony of ants moving their nest" (5) hoped for a fresh start. As their train ambled along at the government-stipulated twelve miles per hour, Cissy dreamt of her past and future. Set during the 1893 Oklahoma land rush, this story narrates the desperate, but nonetheless hilarious efforts of Florence's settlers to convince the scoundrel owner of the Red Rock Runner railroad to fulfill his promise of a scheduled stop in their town. Along the way, this group of contentious merchants and farmers become a community. *2002 Smarties Prize-Bronze, 9-11; 2001 Carnegie Medal "Highly Commended."*   *lmp*
Author lives in England

McDonnell, Flora. **Flora McDonnell's A B C**. Illustrated by the author. Cambridge, MA: Candlewick Press, 1997. First published in England in 1997. ISBN 0-7636-0118-7. 36 p. (3–6). Picture book.

This alphabet book gives both upper and lower case letters and two objects, with the larger identified in upper case letters, the smaller in lower case letters, a BEAR and a butterfly, for example. Very clear, creative.   *jig*
Author lives in England

McDonnell, Flora. **Giddy-up! Let's Ride!** Illustrated by the author. Cambridge, MA: Candlewick Press, 2002. ISBN 0-7636-1778-4. 32 p. (3–5). Picture book.

Illustrations show how various people ride, from a jockey on a horse, to a rajah on an elephant, to a nomad on a camel, with the simple text on each double

page illustration also giving the sound made as the animal moves along. The knight in armor makes a "clanketty-clank" sound while the cowgirl shouts "Yee-ha!" The closing page shows how children ride—on a hobby horse, saying "Giddy-up!" The author explains that the book was inspired by the nursery rhyme, "This is the way the ladies ride," chanted by her grandmother as she gave a ride on her knee. *jig*
Author lives in England

McDonnell, Flora. **Sparky**. Illustrated by the author. Cambridge, MA: Candlewick Press, 2004. ISBN 0-7636-2208-7. 32 p. (3–5). Picture book.

Sparky the puppy is nervous after arriving at his new home, but when he and his new friend Mary begin having fun together, he relaxes. They dance, listen to music, play in the sandbox, and finally fall asleep in her bed. In the end, Sparky decides that this has been "the best day ever." *jig*
Author lives in England

McKay, Hilary. **Dolphin Luck**. New York: Margaret K. McElderry Books, 1999. Originally published in Great Britain by Hodder Children's Books in 1998. ISBN 0-689-82376-2. 153 p. (9–12). Novel.

Companion to *Dog Friday* and *The Amber Cat* this novel recounts the hilarious adventures of the Robinson children while their parents are vacationing. Quick-switching vignettes are used to present each of the four children's escapades in real time. As each child pursues their separate missions of devising traps to catch burglars, searching for an ancient magic sword with a dolphin hilt, and traveling on the train with a menagerie of illegitimately-gotten animals, the chaos builds to riotous eruption leaving the adults of the story breathless and flustered. Readers will close the book laughing and not wanting the story to end. *js*
Author lives in Lincolnshire, England

McKay, Hilary. **Saffy's Angel**. New York: Margaret K. McElderry Books, 2002. Originally published by Hodder Children's Books in 2001. ISBN 0-689-84933-8. 152 p. (11 up). Novel.

The Casson family is very creative, funny, and absolutely loveable. Mom and Dad pursue their artistic careers while the children explore their varied and unusual interests. Saffron discovers that she has been adopted by her aunt and uncle. Shortly after this, Saffron's grandfather dies leaving her feeling alone and bereft. Saffron discovers that her grandfather was going to get her stone angel from the garden in Siena where she had lived with her mother. Saffron makes friends with Sarah who is feisty and sometimes uses a wheelchair. Clever Sarah masterminds a trip to Siena so Saffy can retrieve her stone angel. Other events in the Casson family are interwoven with Saffy's quest that leads her to come to terms with her life through the support of her friends and family. *Whitbread*

Children's Book Award. The adventures of the Casson family continue in *Indigo's Star*, 2004. *ls*
Author from England

McKee, David. **The Conquerors**. New York: Handprint, 2004. Originally published in London by Andersen. ISBN 1-5935-4078-7. 32 p. (4–8). Picture book.

The general of a large and mighty country invades and conquers each of its neighboring countries, one by one. Eventually, all the countries in the world are conquered but one—and that one is so small it doesn't even have an army. And so, of course, when the day comes that the general is unable to resist invading the small country, the outcome is inevitable. Or is it? This profound story and delightful childlike pictures send a special message that is all the more effective for framing a quiet plea for peace (annotation from publisher).

McKee, David. **Elmer in the Snow**. New York: Lothrop, Lee & Shepard Books, 1994. Originally published in England in Great Britain by Andersen Press. ISBN 0-688-14934-0. 27 p. (3–6). Picture book.

Elmer, a colorful patchwork elephant, is expecting his cousin Wilbur, but when Wilbur arrives, Elmer and his gray elephant friends have to go hunting for him all over the jungle, which is lush with fantasy plants depicted in yellows, pinks, oranges, and purples. Wilbur, a ventriloquist, has them hunting for him for quite a while, until he reveals that he is stuck in a tree and the others rescue him. This playful series, which began in 1968 with *Elmer: The Story of a Patchwork Elephant,* stimulates observation and perception. It is popular with preschool children. Recent books in this series include *Elmer and the Kangaroo*, Harper-Collins 2000; *Elmer and the Lost Teddy,* Lothrop, Lee & Shepard, 1999; *Elmer in the Snow.* Lothrop, Lee & Shepard, 1995; *Hide and Seek Elmer,* Lothrop, Lee & Shepard, 1998 (a lift-the-flap book); *Elmer's New Friend*, Andersen Press, 2002 (a board book with mirror—the new friend is you). *IRA 1997 Children's Choice book. jvl*

Melnikoff, Pamela. **Prisoner in Time: A Child of the Holocaust**. Philadelphia: The Jewish Publication Society, 2001. Originally published by the Penguin Group in 1992. ISBN 0-8276-0735-0. 142 p. (12 up). Novel.

While twelve-year-old Jan is hiding from the Nazis in Prague in 1942, he finds a golden bird amulet, which allows him to travel back in time to sixteenth century Prague where Rabbi Loew is creating the Golem. Jan returns to 1942 Prague, gives himself up to the Nazis, and is taken to the model internment camp at Terezin. Jan learns how to survive in the camp and observes everything that is happening around him. He manages to survive until the day that his name appears on the transport list and finds that someone has stolen his golden bird. A convoluted story whose ending is stark and abrupt. *ls*
Author from England

Minchin, Adele. **The Beat Goes On**. New York: Simon & Schuster, Inc. Originally published in Great Britain by Livewire Books, The Women's Press, Ltd. in 2001. ISBN 0-689-86611-9. 212 p. (12 up). Novel.

Leyla's world is turned upside down when her dearest cousin, Emma, tests positive for HIV. Emma's mother knows, but she's not talking. Who else can the adolescents confide in? Leyla discovers a world of secrets that parallels a network of support as she learns more about HIV/AIDS and begins teaching drumming to fellow teens infected with the disease. A short section of teen HIV/AIDS resources is included at the back of the book. *Branford Boase Award for fiction.* nrn
Author lives in UK

Morpurgo, Michael. **Kensuke's Kingdom**. New York: Scholastic Press, 2003. First published in Great Britain by Heinemann, 1999. ISBN 439-38202-5. 164 p. (10–14). Novel.

On their around-the-world sailing trip, Michael and his dog are swept from the family yacht, and washed up on a small, unihabited island in the South Pacific. However, there is another resident, a Japanese naval doctor who has hidden there for almost 40 years, since the end of World War II. He, Kensuke, teaches Michael to survive and eventually helps in his rescue. An uneasy relationship slowly develops as they attempt to bridge cultural differencs. *Carnegie Medal, commeded list 2000.* mln
Author from Great Britain and has won many awards including the Whitbread Award and Smarties Prize. Michael Morpugo was named the Children's Laureate for the years 2003–2005.

Morpurgo, Michael. **Toro! Toro!** Illustrated by Michael Foreman. New York: HarperCollins, 2001. First published in hardback by HarperCollins, UK in 2001. ISBN 0-0071-0718-8 (pb). 127 p. (9–12). Novel.

When nine-year-old Antonitio helps his father birth a new bull and the mother dies, he becomes responsible for its care. His father warns him not to get attached; this is a bull destined for the ring. But the boy and the bull form a bond and Antonio pledges to keep Paco safe. Against the backdrop of this struggle for survival is the turmoil of the Spanish civil war, breaking out in their rural village. Countrymen fighting each other, who can understand it? Not Antonio, when he decides to sneak out of the house and lead his fathers heard of cattle away from the dangers of the bullring. But while he is on his mission of mercy, planes fly over his farm and village and begin dropping bombs. Morpurgo masterfully and unobtrusively weaves the historical details of a violent war into a narrative that is compelling, yet told with sensitivity to a child's sensibility. djg

Moss, Miriam. **Bad Hare Day**. Illustrated by Lynne Chapman. Simultaneously published by Bloomsbury USA and Bloomsbury London in 2003. ISBN 1-58234-785-9. 28 p. (4–7). Picture book.

The pun of the title acts as a punch line to the story of Herbert Hare, hairdresser extraordinaire. On the day in question, he has a full schedule of clients, each with different hair needs. Bear wants a wash and blow dry, Panda a perm, layers for Llama, and so forth. Unfortunately, this is also the day Herbert's niece Holly appears: "Mama says you should look after me while she goes shopping." While Herbert is in the back room attending to supplies, Holly decides to be helpful by finishing up his clients. As you can guess, none get the do they came in for, and Herbert declares Holly a "bad, bad hare." Humorous illustrations, while deliberately silly and full of their own punny details, capture the essence of salon culture quite accurately. *ss*

Naidoo, Beverley. **The Other Side of Truth**. New York: HarperCollins, 2001. First published in 2000 by Puffin Books in London, England. ISBN 0-06-029628-3. 248 p. (Paperback: Amistad Press, 2002). (12 up). Novel.

After Sade's mother is brutally murdered, her father continues to write the truth about human rights violations in Nigeria. He sends Sade and her young brother to England with the hope of reuniting with them one day.But they are abandoned at the London airport and unable to contact their uncle. They live as frightened refugees as they worry about their activist father at home. Sade campaigns to free her father and proclaim the truth of what really happened on the day her mother was killed. *2000 Nestle Smarties Silver Medal, 2002 Carnegie Medal, 2002 International Board on Books for Young People Honor Book, 2003 Sankei Children's Book Award*, and other distinguished honors. *sg and nrm*
Author from South Africa, lives in UK

Naidoo, Beverley. **Out of Bounds: Seven Stories of Conflict and Hope**. New York: HarperCollins, 2003. Originally published in 2001 by Puffin Books, England. ISBN 0-0605-0799-3. 176 p. (12 up). Short stories.

These stories are set in each decade from 1948 through 2000 and feature fictional characters caught up in the tumultuous times of the apartheid rule. Naidoo, who was born in South Africa and lived under the injustices says that her characters "inhabit a most beautiful land, but one that is full of barriers—real walls and those in the mind." The collection concludes with the story of Tohan and Soloni, two boys going out of bounds, taking risks to reach out across the boundaries out of compassion and in friendship—a story of hope for the future. A Timeline across apartheid is appended putting the stories in the context of the struggle toward hope. *2004 Children's Africana Book Award.* *djg*

Newsome, Jill. **Night Walk**. Illustrated by Claudio Munoz. New York: Clarion, 2003. Originally published by Andersen Press, Ltd., in 2002. ISBN 0-618-32458-5. 32 p. (4–6). Picture book.

Daisy the dog and Flute the cat live together happily but couldn't be more different. When adventuresome Daisy coaxes the placid, home-loving Flute out for

an evening stroll, adventures abound. Daisy chases away some strange cats and Flute bravely rescues Daisy from an aggressive stray cat. Flute enjoys the adventure, but still prefers the calm of a peaceful house at night. Interesting perspectives and wonderfully drawn animals, full of expression and movement, convey the excitement of the adventure. *sg*
Author lives in England

Nicholson, William. **Slaves of the Mastery**. With artwork by Peter Sis. New York: Hyperion, 2001. First published in the UK by Egmont Publishers. ISBN 0-7868-0570-6. 434 p. (9–12). Novel.

Nicholson,William. **Firesong**. With artwork by Peter Sis. New York: Hyperion, 2002. First published in the UK by Egmont Publishers. ISBN 0-7868-0571-4. 422 p. (9–12). Novel.
    The Wind on Fire Trilogy concludes with books two and three. Twins Bowman and Kestrel save their family and the rest of the Manth people from slavery and help bring about the downfall of the cruel city-state of the Mastery. Now they are free to seek the Promised land, but the journey is long, difficult, and dangerous. Good triumphs over evil in these dramatic tales of adventure. *djg*

Ormerod, Jan. **Emily and Albert**. Illustrated by David Slonim. San Francisco: Chronicle Books, 2004. ISBN 0-8118-3615-0. 42 p. (5–8). Picture book.
    Emily the ostrich and Albert the elephant are good friends, though Emily, somewhat lacking in insight and sensitivity, takes credit for attributes and achievements that are actually Albert's. For instance, she decides one day that he is unwell and has Albert stay indoors, lying down. When she leaves the house, Albert takes his bicycle for a spin, but when he returns in great spirits, she is convinced that it is she who cured him. The gentle irony must be deduced by the reader. The satisfying ending, however, has the two sharing an armchair as Albert reads to an appreciative Emily. *jvl*
Author from Australia, lives in England. Illustrator from United States.

Pearce, Philippa. **The Little Gentleman**. Drawings by Tom Pohrt. New York: Greenwillow Books/HarperCollins, 2004. ISBN 0-0607-3160-5. 200 p. (8–12). Novel.
    When Mr. Franklin breaks his leg he instructs Bet, a lonely little girl who lives next door with her grandparents, to read aloud from an unusual book about earthworms, Darwin and Tennyson. How strange, but stranger still is when he directs her to go out to the meadow and read in her loudest voice. Imagine her surprise when she soon discovers her audience, a little black mole. This Little Gentleman, she soon learns, has been bewitched and has played an amazing part in history. But Bet learns more of the power of friendship through her acquaintance with this

little fellow in this unusual fantasy story. Charming pen and ink drawings by an American artist open each chapter. *Publishers Weekly Starred Review.   djg*
Author is Carnegie Medal winner, Tom's Midnight Garden, *and* The Battle of Bubble and Squeak, *which received the Whitbread award, and* Mrs. Cockle's Cat *that received the Kate Greenaway Medal.*

Platt, Richard. **Pirate Diary: The Journal of Jake Carpenter**. Illustrated by Chris Riddell. Cambridge, MA: Candlewick, 2001. ISBN 0-7636-0848-3. 64 p. (9–12). Picture book.
   Nine-year-old Jake begins his diary as he and his uncle set sail from Holyoak, North Carolina, on a merchant ship in 1716. When their ship is taken over by pirates, he becomes one of them. His adventures include a near flogging by a brutal captain, a fierce storm, and a successful raid for Spanish treasure. He returns home with a small fortune and a taste for life at sea. Sailing on the high seas comes to life and the characters seem to leap off of the pages with these wonderfully detailed ink and watercolor illustrations. A few of the illustrations in this oversized book spread across two pages and include a cutaway view of the ship, a raging sea, and a battle between the two ships. "Notes for the Reader" provides a brief history of the American colonies, a map of Jake's journey, and a history of piracy. A glossary and index are appended. *Smarties Silver Medal, 2002 (ages 6–8).   kk Author lives in England*

Pratchett, Terry. **The Amazing Maurice and His Educated Rodents**. New York: HarperCollins, 2001. ISBN 0-06-001233-1. 241 p. (12 up). Novel.
   A talking cat recruits a group of intelligent rats and a boy with a pennywhistle to cash in on the Pied Piper legend in this laugh outloud fantasy. We meet Maurice, the cat, as he is explaining to the pennywhistle playing Keith why taking "government" money from the town officials to get rid of the rats (their cohorts Peaches, Dangerous Beans, and the rest of the rat gang) isn't really stealing. Fast paced and funny, this suspenseful adventure story has something for everyone. *2001 Carnegie Medal; ALA Best Book for Young Adults; New York Public Library Books for the Teen Age; VOYA Best Science Fiction, Fantasy, and Horror; ALA Top 10 Best Book for Young Adults.   djg*

Pratchett, Terry. **A Hat Full of Sky**. New York: HarperCollins, 2004. ISBN 0-06-058660-5. 278 p. (10 up). Novel.
   Tiffany Aching is an official witch-in-training. Mistress Weatherwax (the world's greatest witch) decided she should learn to control her prodigious innate talent after defeating the evil Queen of the elves. Now Tiffany is an apprentice with Miss Level, a rather hum-drum but dependable witch, if you disregard her expertise at bilocation. However, something invisible, something as ancient as creation—a hiver—is stalking Tiffany. Once again, Tiffany confronts a night-

marish world with only the Wee Free Men, and this time Mistress Weatherwax, as her allies. *lmp*
Author lives in England

Pratchett, Terry. **The Wee Free Men**. New York: HarperCollins, 2003. ISBN 0-06-001236-6. 320 p. (10 up). Novel.

Tiffany Aching is an ordinary nine-year-old who enjoys tickling trout and musing over unusual words. She recently decided she'll be a witch when she grows up. One day, as she's staring into a stream, Tiffany encounters two Nac Mac Feegle, nastiest of all the fairy tribes, who shriek a panic-stricken warning at her: "Crivens! Gang awa' oot o' here, ye daft wee hinny! 'Ware the green heid!" (4). Tiffany's subsequent adventures as she vanquishes the evil Queen of the Elves with her impressive, newly discovered magical talents are humorous and spine-chilling—but always totally electrifying. *lmp*
Author lives in England

Prue, Sally. **Cold Tom**. New York: Scholastic, 2003. Originally published by Oxford University Press in 2001. (Paperback: Scholastic, 2004). ISBN 0-439-48268-2. 187 p. (9–12). Novel.

Forced out of the Meadows by his elfin parents who have decided that, because he is different, he is a danger to the Tribe and must die, Tom flees to the city of human "demons." The heat, noises, and smells of the city and its inhabitants repulse and terrify him, but he has nowhere else to hide. When Anna, a young girl; Joe, her half-brother; and Edie Mackintosh, a neighbor, attempt to help Tom, he withdraws and fights to remain free of their human "bonds" as he struggles with the realization that he is part elf and part human "demon." This fantasy deals with the difficult search for identity and a place to belong, especially for those who are of two worlds. Complex and haunting, *Cold Tom* is reminiscent of Lois Lowry's *Gathering Blue* (Houghton Mifflin, 2000) or David Almond's *Skellig* (Delacorte, 1999). With references to the old Scottish ballad, Prue's first novel, "Tam Lin," this book is for the true fantasy aficionado. *Branford Bease Award; 2002 Smarties Silver Prize. kk and lmp*
Author lives in England

Prue, Sally. **The Devil's Toenail**. New York: Scholastic, 2004. ISBN 0-439-48634-3. 204 p. (12 up). Novel.

New to his school and desperate to find friends, Stevie Saunders, 13, is dared to set fire to a library wastebasket as his initiation into a gang. Terrified of fire, Stevie manages to postpone the deed until his family returns from their camping trip on the Bank Holiday. While walking on the beach, Stevie finds a fossil with the curious nickname of the devil's toenail. Stevie thinks the devil's toenail gives him power to do evil. While Stevie is wrestling with his thoughts, he reveals that

the bullying he received in his old school resulted in an incident where Stevie was set on fire. Stevie overcomes the influence of the devil's toenail and manages to figure out how cruel Daniel, the gang leader, is. Stevie saves asthmatic Ryan from inhaling aerosol spray as Daniel watches, egging Ryan on. The other gang members consider Stevie's actions heroic. A psychological thriller filler with drama and surprises. *ls*
Author from England

Pullman, Philip. **Lyra's Oxford**. New York: Alfred A. Knopf, 2003. ISBN 0-375-82819-2. 49 p. (13 up). Novel.

This short tale takes place about two years after the end of Pullman's *His Dark Materials* trilogy and features the main characters Lyra and her daemon Pantalaimon. It is a bit disjointed without the context of the trilogy and will make more sense to readers who are familiar with that work. One interesting inclusion in the book is a fold-out map of Oxford. *bn*
Author from UK

Puttock, Simon. **A Ladder to the Stars**. Illustrated by Alison Jay. New York: Henry Holt, 2001. Originally published by Frances Lincoln in 2001. ISBN 0-8050-6783-3. 26 p. (6–9). Picture book.

A seven-year-old girl wishes on a star that she sees out of her bedroom window, and the star hears her wish and enlists the other forces of heaven—the sun and moon, the clouds and wind—to make it come true. Her wish: to climb into the sky and dance with the star. The forces of heaven plant a seed next to her house, and the tree grows to majestic proportions. One hundred years later, she is an old woman, lying in the same bed, and the tree has touched the sky. The star invites her to climb the tree so they can dance. Whether read as an allegory of death or strictly as a fantasy, the text offers observations on the nature of time and change. One hundred years may be nothing to a star, but on earth trees grow, neighborhoods change, and people die. *ss*

Reeve, Philip. **Mortal Engines**. New York: HarperCollins, 2003. First published in the UK by Scholastic, 2001. ISBN 0-06-008208-9. 310 p. (12 up). Novel.

Set in the distant future on an Earth that has been destroyed by the Sixty Minute War, this thrilling and imaginative science fiction novel presents a world of motorized Traction Cities that prey on smaller suburbs and villages as they all move through a barren countryside. On the Traction City of London, Tom, a fifteen-year-old orphan and apprentice for the Historical Guild, saves his hero, Valentine, the Head Historian, from an attack by Hester, a young girl with a terrible scar running down the middle of her face. In the process both he and Hester find themselves plunging off the moving city into the barren Out-Country. In their attempt to catch up with London, they discover that the Lord Mayor of London, with the help of Valentine, has resurrected an ancient atomic weapon. Tom and Hester join

forces with the Anti-Traction League to prevent the Lord Mayor from using this weapon to destroy the Shield-Wall, built to protect the remaining "static" cities from Municipal Darwinism. *Nestle Smarties Book Prize Gold Award; Whitbread Children's Book Award Shortlist. kk*
Author lives in England

Roome, Diana Reynolds. **The Elephant's Pillow**. Pictures by Jude Daly. New York: Farrar, Straus and Giroux, 2003. First published in Great Britain, in somewhat different form by Frances Lincoln Ltd, 2003. ISBN 0-374-32015-2. 28 p. (5–8). Picture book.

Long ago in the city of Peking, there lived a boy named Sing Lo. His father was a rich merchant and he had everything he could want. Now there was in that same city an Imperial Elephant, who, lost in grief after the death of the Emperor, had not been able to sleep. Can a spoiled boy find a way to solve the problem of another? This simple fable is illustrated by South African Jude Daly in the distinctive style that has won her many awards. *djg*

Ross, Tony. **I Want My Pacifier**. La Jolla, CA: Kane/Miller, 2004. ISBN 1929132654. 24 p. Picture book.

The royal pacifier has mysteriously disappeared again. It always turns up, though, even if it is found in some very strange places. This book, companion to *I Don't Want to Go to Bed* (2004), features Tony Ross's comic watercolor illustrations. *Author was the 2004 Hans Christian Anderson Award Nominee from the United Kingdom.*

Rowe, John A. **Jasper the Terror**. New York: Michael Neugebauer/North-South, 2001. First published in Switzerland under the title *Theodor Terror*. ISBN 0-7358-1476-7. 32 p. (4–8). Picture book.

It's lunchtime in the forest and Jasper the Dragon would love nothing more than some burnt toast. But every time he goes to a friend to ask for some he has to sneeze and when he sneezes flames roared. Moles pants are burned in the first sneeze attach, but soon all the animals are suffering. So the animals take Jasper to the professor for a cure. Stylized illustrations done with paint, pen, and ink add wit and whimsy to the story. *djg*

Rowling, J.K. **Harry Potter and the Chamber of Secrets**. Illustrated by Mary Grandpre. New York: Arthur A. Levine Books, 1999. (New York: Scholastic, 2002). ISBN 0-439-13635-0. 341 p. (10 up). Novel.

After a miserable summer with the Dursleys, Harry Potter returns for his second year at Hogwarts School for Witchcraft and Wizardry by flying car. He must contend with the new Defense Against the Dark Arts teacher, conceited publicity-hound, Gilderoy Lockhart. As the school year progresses, a monster roams the school striking its victims senseless. Harry, Ron, and Hermione are determined to

discover what evil lurks in the Chamber of Secrets. Their search leads them into a bathroom occupied by Moaning Myrtle, following spiders into the Forbidden Forest and exploring Hogwarts drains. Lots of mystery, suspense, and adventures are packed into one school year.   *ls*
Author from England

Rowling, J.K. **Harry Potter and the Goblet of Fire**. Illustrated by Mary Grandpre. New York: Arthur A. Levine Books, 2000. (New York: Scholastic, 2002). ISBN 0-439-13959-7. 734 p. (10 up). Novel.

The Quidditch games at Hogwarts have been cancelled for the year because the Triwizard Tournament is to be held. Three champions, one from each of the wizarding schools of Beauxbatons, Durmstrang, and Hogwarts, are to compete. During the school year, the champions face three wizarding tasks. The prize is the Triwizard Cup and one thousand Galleons. The Goblet of Fire selects the champions. One from each school and—Harry Potter! How Harry's name was chosen is a complete mystery for he is underage. The thinking is that someone wants Harry to die. This year, Hermione is championing the rights of the house elves whom she considers to be enslaved. The tension and mystery increase through the school year that ends on a tragic note.   *ls*
Author from England

Rowling, J.K. **Harry Potter and the Order of the Phoenix**. Illustrations by Mary Grandpre. New York: Arthur A. Levine Books, 2003. (New York: Scholastic, 2004). ISBN 0-439-35806-X. 870 p. (12 up). Novel.

Sixteen-year-old Harry Potter is in his fifth year at Hogwarts. This year includes his O.W.L. exams, his first kiss, and bad press. The Dark wizard Voldemort is alive and gathering his forces. The Ministry of Magic chooses not to believe that he exists. As a result, Dumbledore creates the Order of the Phoenix, an organization of witches, wizards, and mythical creatures fighting to stop Voldemort's rise to power. At Hogwarts, the Ministry of Magic is interfering with all aspects of the school—curriculum, teachers, student activities. Harry Potter begins teaching willing students spells, charms, and jinxes to enable them to be prepared to fight Voldemort and his Death Eaters. A dark, menacing tale where evil attempts to overpower good.   *ls*
Author from England

Rowling, J.K. **Harry Potter and the Prisoner of Azkaban**. Illustrated by Mary Grandpre. New York: Arthur A. Levine Books, 1999. (New York: Scholastic, 2001). ISBN 0-439-13635-0. 435 p. (10 up). Novel.

When Aunt Marge comes to visit the Dursleys, Harry cannot tolerate living at four Privet Drive any longer. Harry catches the Knight Bus and runs away to the Leaky Cauldron in Diagon Alley. Harry learns that a dangerous prisoner, Sirius Black, has escaped from Azkaban, a wizard's prison. Harry is in great danger. The

soul-stealing dementors from Azkaban are guarding Hogwarts. When Harry does meet Sirius Black, he learns about his father's student days at Hogwarts and he receives an unexpected surprise. Harry's third year at Hogwarts is dark and menacing but it is filled with escapades with the Invisibility Cloak, magical creatures, and Quidditch games. *ls*
Author from England

Said, S.F. **Varjak Paw**. New York: Random House, 2003. First published in London: Davild Fickling, 2003. ISBN 0-385-75019-6. 256 p. (8–12). Novel.

Varjak, a dreamer and a do-er, is not considered a true Mesopotamian Blue by the rest of his pampered Paw (cat) family. When an evil intruder threatens to destroy all cats, Varjak responds with courage and some basic knowledge, which he learns in dream sequences. With the help of new found friends, the enemy is defeated. Graphic illustrator, David Mc Kean enriches this high adventure with bold ink sketches on half of its pages. *Nestle Smarties Gold Medal Book Prize, 2003. mln*

Stainton, Sue. **The Lighthouse Cat**. Illustrated by Anne Mortimer. New York: Katherine Tegen Books/HarperCollins, 2004. ISBN 0-0600-9604-7. 32 p. (5–9). Picture book.

At the top of the lighthouse, the twenty-four-candle lantern glows its warning without fail, until one stormy night, when the lighthouse keeper is unable to relight the candles after the wind blows them out. Shivering, the cat Mackerel, gazes hard out to sea and spies a fishing boat near the jagged-toothed rocks. His yellow eyes glow as he caterwauls and screams into the wind. Eleven cats, come slipping and tumbling down the Cliffside and join Mackerel, twenty-four eyes glowing in the dark night. The history of the early candlelit lighthouses on the treacherous Eddystone rocks south of Plymouth is appended and rich, luminous paintings add depth to this delightful tale. *djg*

Stewart, Paul. **The Birthday Presents**. Pictures by Chris Riddell. New York: HarperCollins, 1999. ISBN 0-06-028289-7. First published in Great Britain, 1999. 26 p. (4–8). Picture book.

In this sequel to *A Little Bit of Winter* (1998), the friends Rabbit and Hedgehog realize they have never celebrated their birthdays. Since they don't know their birth dates, they decide to celebrate the very next day. Cartoon style watercolor over detailed pen and ink drawings are the perfect complement to these sweet stories. Other books in the series include: *Rabbit's Wish* (2001) and *What Do You Remember* (2002).
Author and Illustrator live in England

Stewart, Paul, and Chris Riddell. **The Edge Chronicles Book 1: Beyond the Deepwoods**. New York: David Fickling Books, 2004. First published by Doubleday in 1998. ISBN 0-385-75068-4. 278 p. (10–12). Fantasy.

This is the first installment of a proposed six volume series. Book 1 introduces the character of Twig, a boy who discovers the Woodtrolls, whom he has been living among for twelve years, are not related to him. While setting off on a journey, and accidentally diverging from the path, Twig stumbles upon many adventures and ultimately finds his place in the chaos of the many societies he encounters. Books 2 and 3 continue Twig's adventures, while Book 4 goes back in time to the story of Twig's parents. Book 5 (2005) and Book 6 pick up again with the original characters. Highly detailed sketches appear on almost every page, bringing to life the descriptions of this unique fantasy world. *cbl*

Turnbull, Ann. **No Shame, No Fear**. Cambridge, MA: Candlewick Press, 2004. ISBN 0-7636-2505-1. 293 p. (12 up). Novel.

In 1662 Parliament passes the Quaker Act forbidding non-Anglican worship. William Heywood, son of a wealthy alderman, returns home from Oxford. As he prepares for a prestigious apprenticeship that ensures his future stature and wealth, he begins to question his beliefs. Susanna Thorn is a fifteen-year-old Quaker, the daughter of country weavers. She agrees to work for another Quaker who owns the town's printing press and bookshop. As William explores the Quaker faith and lifestyle, he falls deeply in love with Susanna. The two lovers are swept up in a maelstrom of religious persecution that threatens their very existence. *lmp*
Author lives in England

Voake, Charlotte. **Pizza Kittens**. Cambridge, MA: Candlewick Press, 2002. ISBN 0-7636-1622-2. 36 p. (4–8). Picture book.

Mom and Dad are trying to have a peaceful supper, but Lucy, Joe, and Bert are not having any of it. Comical watercolor illustrations depict the disastrous results. *Author has been shortlisted four times for the prestigious Kurt Maschler Award.*

Watkins-Pitchford, Denys. **The Little Grey Men: A Story for the Young in Heart** by BB. New York: HarperCollins, 2004. First published in 1942 by Eyre & Spottiswoode. ISBN 0-0605-5448-7. 294 p. (10–14). Novel.

Baldmoney, Sneezewort, Dodder, and Cloudberry are the last gnomes in Britain. But Cloudberry has disappeared and the remaining three build a boat to take them upstream on the Folly brook to try to find him. This fantasy, winner of the Carnegie Medal brought back into print, is full of magic and adventure. Pen and ink illustrations portray the Little People and their woodland home. *Carnegie Medal Winner 1942 United Kingdom.* *djg*

Waugh, Sylvia. **Earthborn**. New York: Delacorte Press, 2002. First published by Bodley Head in 2002. ISBN 0-3859-0060-0. 273 p. (8–10). Novel.

Twelve-year-old Nesta suddenly learns that her parents are from another planet and that they all will need to leave earth in seven days. Since she was born on earth, Nesta knows no other way of life and feels no connection to this other

planet. She decides to stay even if her parents go without her so she arranges to leave home until after the deadline. *bn*
Author from UK

Waugh, Sylvia. **Space Race**. New York: Delacorte, 2000. Originally published in Great Britain by the Bodley Head Children's Books in 2000. ISBN 0-385-37266-8. 241 p. (10 up). Novel.

Tonitheen, who's earth name is Thomas Derwent, and his father, Vateelin, alias Patrick Derwent, have been living on earth for five years. It is the only life that eleven-year-old Thomas remembers. With their mission completed, it is time to return to their home, Ormingat. Thomas is distraught, but resigns himself to the move. Then a funny thing happens on the way to their space ship. Thomas and Patrick are involved in a major traffic accident and separated. Their individual adventures while attempting to reunite and make their predetermined launch time create a suspenseful and humorous ending to the story. *js*
Author lives in the north of England

Wells, Philip. **Daddy Island**. Illustrated by Niki Daly. Cambridge, MA: Barefoot Books, 2001. ISBN 1-84148-197-1. 26 p. (4–7). Picture book.

A loving relationship between a father and his son is portrayed in playful, rhyming poetry and stylized watercolor illustrations. Standing tall on his daddy's knees, he is a tree, very still on daddy's lap, he is a rock. Like the bear, he is fierce and loving. This delightful picture book celebrates the father-son relationship. *djg*
Author from England. Illustrator from South Africa.

Whybrow, Ian. **Little Wolf, Pack Leader**. Illustrated by Tony Ross. Minneapolis: Carolrhoda, 2003. First published in England by HarperCollins in 2002. ISBN 1-57505-400-0. 126 p. (8–10). Novel.

In letters to his parents, complete with sketches and notes in his own handwriting, Little Wolf tells about his altercations with Spoiler, the leader of the RHYWP, the Really Harsh Young Wolf Pack. Arm burns are a regular event. Little Wolf explains, through easily decipherable but not standard spelling, how he is able to capture Mister Twister, get his little brother back, and become leader of his own pack, the SPOBBTHALOF, Small Pack of Brute Beasts That Have a Load of Fun. *jig*
Author lives in England

Willis, Jeanne. **I Want to Be a Cowgirl**. Illustrated by Tony Ross. New York: Henry Holt, 2002. Originally published by Andersen Press in 2001. ISBN 0-8050-6997-6. 24 p. (4–7). Picture book.

Simple, rhymed text tells only part of the story of a young city-dweller with a yen for the Wild West. Ross's cartoon-style drawings show the narrator in her western regalia—first the hat with turned-up brim (which turns out to be her father's good dress hat, to his dismay), then the lasso (once the clothesline), and finally the furry, sheepskin-like chaps (formerly part of a perfectly good living room rug). Her activities are juxtaposed against ongoing life in the city, which remains unspecified. Clever details in the illustrations (e.g., cloud formations in the shape of cacti, cattle, hats, and horses) abound to underscore the endless imagination of this single-minded little girl. *ss*

Willis, Jeanne. **Naked without a Hat**. New York: Delacorte Press, 2004. Originally published in Great Britain in 2003 by Faber and Faber Limited. ISBN 0-385-73166-3. 218 p. (14 up). Novel.

Nineteen year-old Will Avery moves out of his overprotective mother's house when her boyfriend Ray starts to spend too much time there. Agreeing with his mother to keep their special secret about his childhood, Will rents the attic of a flat and enjoys living with his landlord Chrissy and his unique roommates Rocko, and James. Will gets a job at the local park where he enjoys taking care of the animals. While working at the park Will meets and falls in love with Zara, an Irish gypsy, who is living with her family in a trailer at the park illegally. Life is good for Will until his mother learns that Zara is an Irish gypsy, refuses to allow them to marry and divulges Will's secret: he has Down Syndrome and had surgery as a child to conceal it. Learning this late in the novel explains Will's simplistic telling of the story and wide-eyed wonder of the world as well as the unusual antics of his roommates. *2003 Whitbread Children's Book Award shortlist.   kmc*
Author lives in London

Wilson-Max, Ken. **L Is for Loving: An ABC for the Way You Feel**. New York: Hyperion, 1999. ISBN 0-7868-0527-7. 32 p. (4–8). Picture book.

From Angelic to Zippy, each letter receives a one or two page spread in this oversized picture book featuring the full-faced children that have become this illustrator's trademark. Generous, happy, and kind counter greedy, jealous and miserable in this panoply of emotions. Wilson-Max has won international awards and is the illustrator for many books including: *I Hate to be Sick (2004), The Baby Goes Beep (2003), Tickle, Tickle (2002),* and *Good Night Monster (2001).   djg*
Author from Zimbabwe and studied art in Harare, Zimbabwe.
Now living in England he works as a freelance designer.

Winterson, Jeanette. **The King of Capri**. Illustrated by Jane Ray. New York: Bloomsbury USA Children's Books, 2003. ISBN 1-58234-830-8. 28 p. (5–8). Picture book.

Fortunes reverse when a tempest blows through the wealthy island of Capri, and everything gets blown across the bay to the poor city of Naples. Mrs. Jewel, a Neapolitan washerwoman, finds the King of Capri's treasures in her garden, and he is left with only his socks and a bathrobe. But unlike the greedy former ruler, generous Mrs. Jewel has something for everyone, even the impoverished king. Vivid, fantastical mixed-media illustrations give an imaginative spin to the Neapolitan coastline. However, the artwork also perpetuates the stereotype that

the wealthy have lighter skin than the poor, something that is not necessarily the rule in this region. *mk*
Author and illustrator from UK

Wishinsky, Frieda. **Jennifer Jones Won't Leave Me Alone**. Illustrated by Neal Layton. Minneapolis: Carolrhoda Book, 2003. First published by Transworld Publishers Ltd. London England. ISBN 0-87614-921-2. 28 p. (5–8). Picture book.

Jennifer Jones sits by his side and shouts in his ear, tells him she loves him and calls him "dear." Everyone thinks they make a cute pair, but he doesn't and wishes she'd move. But when Jennifer's mother is transferred and she moves away . . . he misses her! It's boring and lonely without her. She writes from exciting places and when the letter arrives telling him she's coming back in June, he takes just a minute to decide he'll tell his classmates before running out to buy a welcome home gift. This is another delightful treat from the author/illustrator team who also wrote *Nothing Scares Us* (2000). *djg*
Author lives in Toronto. Illustrator lives in Scotland.

Wormell, Mary. **Bernard the Angry Rooster**. New York: Farrar, Straus, and Giroux, 2001. ISBN 0-374-30670-2. unpaged. (4–7). Picture book.

Bernard, the speckled rooster, is normally happy, but he's out of sorts today. He chases the farmer's daughter, torments the sunning cat, pecks at the dog, and jumps on the pony. "What's the matter with you, Bernard? Why are you so cross?" they all ask in turn. The answer comes when the pony's kick sends Bernard flying onto the stable roof from which he climbs a tree that is higher than the new weather vane, once again establishing himself as lord of the barnyard. Careful readers will find many clues to the reasons for Bernard's annoyance; all will enjoy Wormell's bold linoleum cut prints and the reassuring reminder that we all have bad days.
Author lives in Scotland

Zephaniah, Benjamin. **Refugee Boy**. New York: Bloomsbury, 2001. ISBN 1-58234-763-8. 287 p. (10–14). Novel.

Fourteen-year-old Alem Kelo of Eritean (mother) and Ethiopian (father) descent is brought by his father to the UK to keep him safe from the civil war raging in his homeland. His father goes so far as to abandon him in the UK so that he can be declared a refugee, while the father returns to Africa to join his wife in working for peace. Alem faces many struggles and challenges despite help from the Refugee Council, caring foster parents, and a budding friendship with a schoolmate. He suffers two devastating losses but also receives overwhelming support from friends who seek political asylum for him in the face of the burecracy of the social services system. The final chapters are heart-rending and thought-provoking, revealing the soul of this fine young man. A short list of worldwide organizations that help refugees and asylum seekers is included. *bjk*
Author lives in UK

Related Information

Marsh Award for Children's Literature in Translation is administered by the National Centre for Research in Chidlren's Literature (University of Surrey, Roehampton, Digby Stuart College, London SW 15 5PH),
e-mail: G.Lathey@roehampton.ac.uk

With aims to encourage the translation of foreign children's books into English, this biennial award is open to British translators of books for 4–16 year olds, published in the UK by a British publisher. Any category will be considered with the exception of encyclopedias, reference books, or electronic books. The award is made to the translator.

Begun in 1996, the Award honors the translators of children's books by giving once every two years an honorarium of £3000. Anthea Bell was awarded the prize in 2003 for her translation of Hans magnus Enzensberger's *Where Were You Robert?* The 2005 recipient was Sarah Adams for her translation of *The Eye of the Wolf* from the French of Daniel Pennac, published by Walker Books.

Bookfair

Edinburgh International Book Festival
Edinburgh, Scotland
phone: 44 131 228 5444
e-mail: admin@edbookfest.co.uk
http://www.edbookfest.co.uk
August

CHILDE: Culture 2000 Project
http://www.bookchilde.org/About.htm

In November 2000 Buckinghamshire County Council Library Service received approval from the European Commission to lead a digitization and education project that would center around the creation of a Web site dedicated to the preservation and promotion of early children's book collections from across Europe.

The project, entitled CHILDE (Children's Historical Literature Disseminated throughout Europe) was developed in collaboration with the County Council's European Team and involves a number of other partners:

- Dublin City Public Libraries, Dublin, Ireland
- Institut fur Jugendbuchforshung, Frankfurt, Germany
- International Youth Library, Munich, Germany
- Koninklijke Bibliotheek, The Hague, The Netherlands
- La Baracca: Testoni Ragazzi, Bologna, Italy
- National Centre for Research in Children's Literature, University of Surrey, Roehampton, England
- Wandsworth Borough Council Library Service, London, England

YUGOSLAVIA

Mead, Alice. **Girl of Kosovo**. New York: A Dell Yearling Book, 2001. ISBN 0-440-41853-4. paperback. 113 p. (10 up). Novel.

Zana loves her life with her school friends in a small village in Kosovo. But Zana's family is Albanian. Her best friend, next door, is Serbian. The Serb police mistreat the Albanians. When the Serb forces massacre fifty-four members of one family, her family tries to run away. But bombs bring terror and tragedy and Zana is injured. She has to go away for treatment. She wonders why the world doesn't come to help them. Alice Mead has put a face on the ethnic cleansing in Kosovo. *jm*

Author from United States

Chapter 10

Global

MULTINATIONAL BOOKS

Ajmera, Maya, and Anna Rhesa Versola. **Children from Australia to Zimbabwe: A Photographic Journey around the World**. Watertown, MA: Charlesbridge Publishing, 1997. Originally published by SHAKTI for Children in 1996. ISBN 0-88106-999-X (hc). unpaged. (8–12). Informational book.

This ABC gazetteer of 25 countries, plus the imaginary country of Xanadu, features children beautifully photographed in a variety of their daily activities. Each entry begins with a greeting written phonetically in the country's dominant language and includes a relief map, a picture of the flag, and several full-colored photographs of children at work, at play, and celebrating festivals. The brief text is supplemented by a facts section that will appeal to children, including: the proportion of children to the total population, favorite sports, an environmental fact, and other countries beginning with the same letter of the alphabet. *rcb*
Authors from United States

Ajmera, Maya, and John D. Ivanko. **To Be an Artist**. Watertown, MA: SHAKTI for Children, 2004. ISBN 1-57091-503-2. 32 p. (5–10). Informational book.

Art is a universal language spoken around the world. This beautiful photo essay demonstrates this with photographs of children from thirty-five countries engaged in painting, singing, dancing, playing music, writing, acting, making sculptures, and many other ways that show how creatively children celebrate who they are and how they see the world around them. A map at the end of the book locates each of the countries included. *djg*
Authors from United States

Armstong, Jennifer, ed. **Shattered: Stories of Children and War**. New York: Alfred A. Knopf, 2002 (Paperback: Laurel-Leaf, 2003). ISBN 0-375-81112-5. 166 p. (12 up). Short stories.

This is a collection of twelve fictional short stories, written by well-established authors of young adult fiction. The time periods of the stories vary, as do the locations. The common thread that unites these separate and distinct stories is the perspective of a child. The editor's selection skillfully demonstrates that one can never fully understand all aspects of a war. Authors' notes at the end give the reader a glimpse into why each particular piece was written. Also, scrolled across the bottom of the pages are footnotes that give background information and/or statistics that enhance the story—all of which are documented in source notes. *ALA Best Books for Young Adults, 2003; Bank Street College of Education Best Children's Books of the Year, 2003; Notable Social Studies Trade Books for Young People, 2003.* *cbl*
Editor from United States

Fraustino, Lisa Rowe, ed. **Soul Searching: Thirteen Stories about Faith and Belief**. New York: Simon & Schuster, 2002. ISBN 0-689-83484-5. 267 p. (12 up). Anthology.

In her introduction written days after September 11, 2001, Fraustino writes that "we must fight the tendency to reduce the world's cultures to sound bites and remember that all religions in all countries are composed of real people . . . who all need the same basic things: food, shelter, friends." The stories in this collection represent the humanity in the world's religions. An unwed Amish mother, a Thai monk, Hindu traditions, and a lack of Christian faith as one loses all possessions in a massive flood among others, are brought to life in these stories reminding us that "we all gaze at the same sky . . ." *kmc*
Author from United States

Hollyer, Beatrice. **Let's Eat! What Children Eat around the World**. New York: Henry Holt in association with Oxfam, 2004. Originally published as *Let's Eat! Children and Their Food around the World* in the United Kingdom by Frances Lincoln, 2003. ISBN 0-8050-7322-1. 41 p. (8 up). Informational book.

Oxfam-sponsored *Let's Eat!* allows readers to peek into the lives of five children around the world and get nosy about customary meals. "Do they eat loads of weird stuff in other countries" (5) or do they love cookies and snacks too? Photographs catch children in school uniforms and ethnic garb; share highlights of family times; unveil the countryside; even explore local markets. Children prepare family meals and perform other chores like herding the sheep in Mexico. In Thailand, readers meet Kamalotas Sudasna who doesn't like spicy food! Recipes and a food glossary complete this international feast. *lmp*
Author lives in United States

How People Live. New York: Dorling Kindersley, 2003. ISBN 0-7894-9867-7. 304 p. (10 up). Informational book.

This accessible reference book begins with a world map and statistics and continent by continent gives a survey of the diverse cultures around the world. Appealing color photographs introduce daily lives, customs, languages, and religions. *djg*

Jackson, Ellen. **It's Back to School We Go! First Day Stories from around the World**. Illustrated by Jan Davey Ellis. Brookfield, CT: The Millbrook Press, 2003. ISBN 0-7613-2562-X. (lib. bdg.) ISBN 0-7613-1948-4 (tr.) 32 p. (7–10). Informational book.

Children from eleven countries are portrayed experiencing their first day of school. Each child's first person account is enhanced by a fact box that tells something about the culture. The author has tried to capture from rural Kenya to urban China, from northern Russia to southern Peru; children will begin to understand the diversity of the school experiences they share and to compare and contrast the lives of children from different cultures that emphasize their commonalities. *djg*
Author from United States

Kahn, Rukhsana. **Muslim Child: Understanding Islam through Stories and Poems**. Illustrated by Patty Gallinger. Sidebars by Irfan Allli. Morton Grove, IL: Albert Whitman, 2002. First published in Canada by Naploeon Publishing/ RendezVous Press, 1999. ISBN 0-8075-5307-7. 104 p. (7–10). Anthology.

The stories and poems in this collection are gathered to provide an overview of Islam as a whole. The eight stories are set in the United States, Pakistan, Canada, England, Nigeria, and Saudi Arabia. Combining stories, informational sidebars, and verses from the Quran, the authors explain many aspects of the Islamic religion. A craft, a recipe, and an Arabic pronunciation guide will make this a useful book. *djg*
Author from Pakistan, lives in Canada

Lewis, J. Patrick. **A World of Wonders: Geographic Travels in Verse and Rhyme**. Illustrated by Alison Jay. New York: Dial, 2002. ISBN 0-8037-2579-5. 34 p. (8–11). Poetry.

Using a variety of poetic forms (acrostics, quatrains, blank verse, concrete, and more), Lewis skillfully offers information about places around the world and some of the people known for exploring them. Countries, cities, and landscapes all provide opportunities for rhyming and often have the added benefit of indicating pronunciation: "Sri Lanka used to be Ceylon/Ancient Persia? Now Iran." Jay's stylistic oil paintings are rendered in muted shades of blue and gold overlaid with a cracked veneer to add an historical feel. Varied page designs sustain interest and emphasize the ideas presented. *ss*
Author from United States

Mason, Antony. **People around the World**. New York: Kingfisher, 2002. ISBN 0-7534-5497-1. 256 p. (10–14). Informational book.

Information about the cultural, social, and economic aspects of children's lives in many countries is attractively presented with beautiful full-color photographs. An index is appended.   *djg*
Author from England

The Milestones Project: Celebrating Childhood around the World. Photography by Dr. Richard Steckel and Michele Steckel. Berkeley: Tricycle Press, 2004. ISBN 1-58246-132-5. 64 p. (7–10). Informational book.

The Milestones Project is a comprehensive effort to document childhood experience in places far and wide. More than 23,000 photographs can be found at their website www.milestonesproject.com. This book gathers photographs of children and their writings to describe the milestone experiences of birthdays, losing teeth, first haircut, going to the doctor or dentist, getting glasses, early chores, and pets. Brief writings on each topic written by noted children's book authors and illustrators such as Joy Cowley of New Zealand, Uza Unobagha of Nigeria, and Daniel Möller of Sweden are included.   *djg*
Authors from United States

Montanari, Donata. **Children around the World**. New York: Kids Can Press, 2001. ISBN 1-5537-064-3. 32 p. (5–7). Picture book.

This charming informational picture book introduces young readers to 12 children from countries around the world: China, India, Greece, Tanzania, Australia, the Philippines, Morocco, Bolivia, Japan, Mexico, Canada, and the United States. The book opens with a world map, and each country is represented on a two-page spread. Montanari's attractive paper collage artwork and simple text will appeal to a young audience.   *djg*
Author from Canada

Under the Spell of the Moon: Art for Children from the World's Great Illustrators. Edited by Patsy Aldana. With a foreword by Katherine Paterson. Groundwood/Douglas & McIntyre, 2004. ISBN 0-88899-559-8. 80 p. (7–12). Illustrated book.

See Canada for description.

Voices: Poetry and Art from around the World. Selected by Barbara Brenner. Washington, DC: National Geographic Society, 2000. ISBN 0-7922-7071-1. 96 p. (8–12). Poetry.

The mix of contemporary and traditional poetry and artwork compiled here and organized by continent convey a distinct feeling of the places from which it comes. In an author's note, Brenner pays tribute to the role of the translator and

credits the translator of each chant, haiku, poem, or lyric contained in the book. Stunning artwork convey the power, beauty, and variety of the literature from North and South America, Europe, Africa, Asia, and Australia/Oceania. Credits and an index are appended in this valuable anthology that gives the reader a sense of the universality of the themes common to all mankind. *djg*
Author from United States

Vyner, Tim. **World Team**. First published in the United Kingdom in 2001 by Jonathan Cape, London. Brookfield, CT: Roaring Brook Press, 2001. ISBN 0-7613-2409-7. 32 p. (4–8). Picture book.

One big round world, one small round ball. Right now, more children than you can possibly imagine are playing soccer. Vyner shares his love of soccer through a brief sentence about one child playing or dreaming about their own participation in a World Cup game in thirteen different countries. A two-page color illustration depicts each child in their cultural setting. Country and the time of day are written in a sidebar on each page. *djg*
Author lives in England

GEOGRAPHY SERIES

A Child's Day in . . . New York: Marshall Cavendish. 32 p. (7–10). Informational books. Volumes currently available: Brazilian Village, Chinese City, Egyptian City, Ghanaian City, Indian Village, Nordic Village, Peruvian City, Russian City, South African City, Vietnamese City.

This series takes the reader through the typical day of a child living in a specific geographic region. Each volume opens with an author's note about the region, a map, and an introduction to the family featured in the book. Bright photographs and simple text follow each child as he or she attends school, spends time with family and friends, and attends to chores. Words from languages other than English are italicized and defined in the glossary. Concluding sections include brief information about the history, language, and religion of the region. *aao*

Colors of the World. Minneapolis: Carolrhoda Books, Inc. 24 p. (7–11). Volumes currently available: Australia, China, France, Germany, Ghana, India, Israel, Japan, Kenya, Mexico, Navajo, and Russia.

Colorful two-page spreads—each dedicated to a different color—are the canvas for one to three paragraphs about the subject. The featured color is tied to some aspect of history, culture, or geography. For example, in *Colors of India*, brown is the color of the spinning wheel that helped India gain independence from Britain, orange is the color of the Bengal tiger roaming the forests, and red is the color of a bride's sari. An introduction, map, and index are included. Despite its sometimes challenging vocabulary, the series' colorful format and unique organization may find readers spanning a wide range of ages. *aao*

Indigenous Peoples. New York: Weigl Publishers, Inc. 32 p. (9–12). Informational books.
Volumes currently available: Aboriginal Australians, Bushmen of Southern Africa, Inuit, Maasai, Maori, Mongols, Polynesians, Yanomami.
This series examines some of the world's earliest cultures in colorful, attractive volumes. Outstanding photographs, taken mainly of children, are featured on every page along with text boxes containing key information. Each volume takes the reader from the group's ancient history through modern culture, including the current issues facing the indigenous groups. Chapter titles include "Stories and Legends," "Dressing Up," "Food and Fun," "Great Ideas," and "Fascinating Facts." The appendix includes further reading, web resources, a glossary, an index, and photography credits. *aao*

Welcome to My Country. (Welcome to . . .) Milwaukee, WI: Gareth Stevens Publishing. 48 p. (7–10). Informational books.
Volumes currently available: Afghanistan, Argentina, Australia, Bosnia and Herzegovina, Brazil, Cambodia, Canada, Chile, China, Colombia, Costa Rico, Cuba, Democratic Republic of the Congo, Denmark, Ecuador, Egypt, England, Ethiopia, Finland, France, Germany, Greece, Haiti, Hungary, India, Indonesia, Iran, Iraq, Ireland, Israel, Italy, Japan, Kenya, Malaysia, Mexico, Morocco, Myanmar, Netherlands, New Zealand, Nigeria, Norway, Pakistan, Peru, Philippines, Poland, Portugal, Russia, Saudi Arabia, Scotland, Singapore, South Africa, South Korea, Spain, Sri Lanka, Sweden, Thailand, Turkey, Ukraine, United States of America, Vietnam.
Young readers can learn the essential facts about another country from the colorful and inviting pages of this series. Each book supplies basic information about the featured country's land, history, government and economy, people, language, arts, leisure activities, and food. A map, glossary, bibliography, index, and a "quick facts page" is included at the back of the books. Although the text is often dry, the format is appealing and the appendices are useful for school reports. *aao*

What Was It Like, Grandma? Brookfield, CT: Millbrook Press. 32 p. (6–9). Informational books.
Volumes currently available: African-American, Arab-American, British-American, Chinese-American, Hispanic-American, Jewish-American, Native American.
This scrapbook-style series provides a window into the experiences of different ethnic groups living in the United States. Each title features a grandmother spending time with her grandchildren and sharing the memories of her life as a little girl growing up in the United States. The history, customs, and present-day life of the ethnic group are presented through the photographs, memories, and

stories of an individual family. The photographs and text work well together in an attractive format, and each book includes a glossary, a cultural activity to try at home, an illustrated family tree, and genealogical activities that introduce young readers to researching their family history.   *aao*

The World's Children (Children of . . .) Minneapolis: Carolrhoda Books, Inc. 48 p. (7–10). Informational books.

Volumes currently available: Belize, Bolivia, China, Cuba, Dominica, Ecuadorian Highlands, Egypt, Guatemala, Hawaii, India, Ireland, Israel, Mauritania, Micronesia, Morocco, Nepal, Northern Ireland, Philippines, Puerto Rico, The Sierra Madre, Slovakia, Tlingit, Vietnam, Yukatan, The Grandchildren of the Incas, The Grandchildren of the Lakota, The Grandchildren of the Vikings.

Each volume provides basic information about the featured country while highlighting the lives of individual children and their families. The result is an informative book that also provides a window into the more personal daily lives of children. The authors make an effort to represent the many different groups living within the featured countries or regions. For example, in *Children of Israel*, Jewish and Muslim children from many geographical regions of Israel are represented. The authors use a story-like prose to describe the children's religious, academic, and playtime activities. Each title includes a brief "more about . . ." section, short pronunciation guide, and an index.   *aao*

Related Information

Online Resources

International Children's Digital Library

The ICDL is a public library for the world, and the collection reflects diverse cultures, perspectives, and historical periods. The mission of the ICDL is to select, collect, digitize, and organize children's materials in their original languages and to create appropriate technologies for access and use by children 3–13 years old. The creators of the site caution "some materials may not be appropriate for sensitive readers." Books are organized by age groups 3–6, 6–9, and 10–13 and are categorized by genre and length. Books in 27 languages are digitized. The International Children's Digital Library is a project of the University of Maryland. http://www.icdlbooks.org/icdl

International Children's Literature

The materials listed here are intended to provide an introduction to children's literature portraying people and cultures from around the world. They were assembled from the World Wide Web, ERIC Database, and a variety of other bibliographic resources. http://reading.indiana.edu/ieo/bibs/intlchlit.html

International Research Society for Children's Literature
The foundations of the IRSCL were laid at the Frankfurt Colloquium of 1969, which was organized by the members of the Institut für Jugendbuchforschung of the Goethe University in Frankfurt, Germany. Members of the Frankfurt Institute proposed that an international organization support and promote research in the field of literature for children and young people.
http://www.irscl.ac.uk/

Passport: International Children's Literature
This excellent website is maintained by Denise Matulka and provides an introduction to international children's literature. Bibliographies are arranged by continent. The section "geographic focus" provides links to informative websites by continent.
http://passport.imaginarylands.org/

Words Without Borders: The Online Magazine of International Literature
Words Without Borders undertakes to promote international communication through translation of the world's best writing—selected and translated by a distinguished group of writers, translators, and publishing professionals—and publishing and promoting these works (or excerpts) on the web. Words Without Borders also serve as an advocacy organization for literature in translation, producing events that feature the work of foreign writers and connecting these writers to universities and to print and broadcast media. The first issue devoted to Children's Literature was in November/December 2004. Look for another piece in the January issue. The back issues will be kept in perpetuity. Readers may search the site under the category "children's literature."
http://www.wordswithoutborders.org/

Print Resources

Bookbird: A Journal of International Children's Literature (ISSN 0006 7377)
This refereed journal is published quarterly by IBBY. It covers many facets of international children's literature and includes news from IBBY and IBBY National Sections. The editorial team, Evelyn B. Freeman, Barbara A. Lehman, Lilia Ratcheva-Stratieva, and Patricia L. Scharer, works in cooperation with an Editorial Review Board, guest reviewers, and Associate Editors who are nominated by IBBY National Sections. The editorial office is supported by the Mansfield Campus and College of Education of the Ohio State University, USA. Articles in *Bookbird* are regularly clustered around themes and issues of international interest. News of IBBY projects and events are highlighted in the Focus IBBY column. Other regular columns include author and illustrator profiles, book reviews and reviews of secondary literature. *Bookbird* also pays special attention to reading promotion projects worldwide.

The White Ravens: A Selection of International Children's and Youth Literature.
This guide is developed by a dedicated team of advisors at the International Youth Library. The catalog contains over 200 new titles from around the world that have been determined to be ideal for translation into English. It is published annually and available at the Children's Book Fair in Bologna. It is also available online at International Youth Library.

Freeman, Evelyn. **Global Perspectives in Children's Literature**. Boston: Allyn & Bacon, 2000. ISBN 0-2053-0862-7. 136 p. Informational book.
This book reviews the status of children's literature around the world and explains the benefits of international children's literature for both children's development and the curriculum. The book presents various genres such as picture books, fiction, informational books, and poetry. Issues in the field are covered and criteria for selecting books are provided. History and contemporary trends are discussed and numerous books are presented as they relate to theme studies, content areas, visual literacy, and language arts.

Part 3

RESOURCES

Chapter 11

Children's Book Awards

UNITED STATES
MILDRED BATCHELDER AWARD

This award, sponsored by the ALA's Association for Library Service to Children, is given to the American publisher of a children's book considered to be the most outstanding of those books originally published in a country other than the United States in a language other than English, and subsequently translated and published in the United States during the previous year. Before 1979, there was a lapse of two years between the original publication date and the award date; to convert to the new system, two awards were announced in 1979, one for 1978 and one for 1979. Beginning in 1994, honor recipients were also selected.

1968 **Knopf.** *The Little Man* by Erich Kästner, translated from German by James Kirkup. Illustrated by Rick Schreiter.

1969 **Scribner.** *Don't Take Teddy* by Babbis Friis-Baastad, translated from Norwegian by Lise Sömme McKinnon.

1970 **Holt.** *Wildcat under Glass* by Aliki Zei, translated from Greek by Edward Fenton.

1971 **Pantheon.** *In the Land of UR: The Discovery of Ancient Mesopotamia* by Hans Baumann, translated from German by Stella Humphries. Illustrated by Hans Peter Renn.

1972 **Holt.** *Friedrich* by Hans Peter Richter, translated from German by Edite Kroll.

1973 **Morrow.** *Pulga* by Siny Rose Van Iterson, translated from Dutch by Alexander and Alison Gode.

1974 **Dutton.** *Petro's War* by Aliki Zei, translated from Greek by Edward Fenton.

1975 **Crown**. *An Old Tale Carved Out of Stone* by Aleksander M. Linevski, translated from Russian by Maria Polushkin.

1976 **Walck**. *The Cat and Mouse Who Shared a House* by Ruth Hürliman, translated from German by Anthea Bell.

1977 **Atheneum**. *The Leopard* by Cecil Bödecker, translated from Danish by Gunnar Poulsen.

1978 No award.

1979 Two awards given:

    Watts. *Konrad* by Christine Nöstlinger, translated from German (Austrian) by Anthea Bell. Illustrated by Carol Nicklaus.

    Harcourt. *Rabbit Island* by Jörg Steiner, translated from German by Ann Conrad Lammers. Illustrated by Jörg Müller.

1980 **Dutton**. *The Sound of Dragon's Feet* by Alki Zei, translated from Greek by Edward Fenton.

1981 **Morrow**. *The Winter Time Was Frozen* by Els Pelgrom, translated from Dutch by Raphael and Maryka Rudnik.

1982 **Bradbury**. *The Battle Horse* by Harry Kullman, translated from Swedish by George Belcher and Lone Thygesen-Belcher.

1983 **Lothrop**. *Hiroshima No Pika* by Toshi Maruki, translated from Japanese through Kurita-Bando Literary Agency.

1984 **Viking**. *Ronia, the Robber's Daughter* by Astrid Lindgren, translated from Swedish by Patricia Crampton.

1985 **Houghton**. *The Island on Bird Street* by Uri Orlev, translated from Hebrew by Hillel Halkin.

1986 **Creative Education**. *Rose Blanche* by Christophe Gallaz and Roberto Innocenti, translated from French by Martha Coventry and Richard Graglia. Illustrated by Roberto Innocenti.

1987 **Lothrop**. *No Hero for the Kaiser* by Rudolf Frank, translated from German by Patricia Crampton.

1988 **McElderry**. *If You Didn't Have Me* by Ulf Nilsson, translated from Swedish by Lone Thygesen-Belcher and George Belcher. Illustrated by Eva Eriksson.

1989 **Lothrop**. *Crutches* by Peter Härtling, translated from German by Elizabeth D. Crawford.

1990 **Dutton**. *Buster's World* by Bjarne Reuter, translated from Danish by Anthea Bell.

1991 **Dutton**. *A Hand Full of Stars* by Rafik Schami, translated from German by Rika Lesser.

    Honor book:

    Houghton. *Two Short and One Long* by Nina Ring Aamundsen, translated from Norwegian by the author.

1992 **Houghton**. *The Man from the Other Side* by Uri Orlev, translated from Hebrew by Hillel Halkin.

1993 No award.

1994 **Farrar**. *The Apprentice* by Pilar Molina Llorente, translated from Spanish by Robin Longshaw. Illustrated by Juan Ramón Alonso.
Honor books:
> **Viking**. *Anne Frank: Beyond the Diary* by Ruud van der Rol and Rian Verhoeven, translated from Dutch by Tony Langham and Plym Peters.
>
> **Farrar**. *The Princess in the Garden* by Annemie and Margriet Heymans, translated from Dutch by Johanna H. Prins and Johanna W. Prins.

1995 **Dutton**. *The Boys from St. Petrie* by Bjarne Reuter, translated from Danish by Anthea Bell.

1996 **Houghton**. *The Lady with the Hat* by Uri Orlev, translated from Hebrew by Hillel Halkin.
Honor books:
> **Holt**. *Damned Strong Love: The True Story of Willi G. and Stephan K.* by Lutz Van Dijk, translated from German by Elizabeth D. Crawford.
>
> **Walker**. *Star of Fear, Star of Hope*, by Jo Hoestlandt, translated from French by Mark Polizzotti.

1997 **Farrar**. *The Friends* by Kazumi Yumoto, translated from Japanese by Cathy Hirano.

1998 **Holt**. *The Robber and Me* by Josef Holub, translated from German by Elizabeth D. Crawford.
Honor books:
> **Scholastic**. *Hostages to War: A True Story* by Tatjani Wassiljewa, translated from German by Anna Trenter.
>
> **Viking**. *Nero Corleone: A Cat's Story* by Elke Heidenrich, translated from German by Doris Orgel.

1999 **Dial**. *Thanks to My Mother* by Schoschana Rabinovici, translated from German by James Skofield.
Honor book:
> **Viking**. *Secret Letters from 0–10* by Susie Morgenstern, translated from French by Gill Rosner.

2000 **Walker**. *The Baboon King* by Anton Quintana, translated from Dutch by John Niewenhuizen.
Honor books:
> **Farrar**. *Collector of Moments* by Quint Buchholz, translated from German by Peter F. Neumeyer.
>
> **R&S Books**. *Vendela in Venice* by Christina Björk, translated from Swedish by Patricia Crampton. Illustrated by Inga-Karin Eriksson.
>
> **Front Street**. *Asphalt Angels* by Ineke Holtwijk, translated from Dutch by Wanda Boeke.

370   Chapter 11

2001   **Arthur A. Levine/Scholastic**. *Samir and Yonatan* by Daniella Carmi,
translated form Hebrew by Yael Lotan.
Honor book:
David R. Godine. *Ultimate Game* by Christian Lehmann, translated
from French by William Rodarmor.

2002   **Cricket Books/Carus Publishing**. *How I Became an American* by
Karin Gündisch. Translated from German by James Skofield.
Honor book:
Viking Press. *A Book of Coupons* by Susie Morgenstern, translated
from French by Gill Rosner. Illustrated by Serge Bloch.

2003   **The Chicken House/Scholastic**. *The Thief Lord* by Cornelia Funke,
translated from German by Oliver Latsch.
Honor book:
Godine. *Henrietta and the Golden Eggs* by Hanna Johansen, translated
from German by John Barrett. Illustrated by Käthi Bhend.

2004   **Walter Lorraine/Houghton Mifflin**. *Run, Boy, Run* by Uri Orlev,
translated from Hebrew by Hillel Halkin.
Honor book:
Chronicle. *The Man Who Went to the Far Side of the Moon: The Story
of Apollo 11 Astronaut Michael Collins* by Uusma Schyffert,
translated from Swedish by Emi Guner.

2005   **Delacorte/Random House**. *The Shadows of Ghadames* by Joëlle Stolz,
translated from the French by Catherine Temerson.
Honor books:
Farrar. *The Crow-Girl: The Children of Crow Cove* by Bodil
Bredsdorff, translated from the Danish by Faith Ingwersen.
Richard Jackson/Simon &Schuster's Atheneum Division.
Daniel Half Human and the Good Nazi by David Chotjewitz,
translated from the German by Doris Orgel.

JANE ADDAMS CHILDREN'S BOOK AWARDS

The Jane Addams Children's Book Awards are given annually to the children's
picture books and longer books published the preceding year that effectively
promote the cause of peace, social justice, world community, and the equality
of the sexes and all races as well as meeting conventional standards for excellence. The Awards have been presented annually since 1953 by the Women's International League for Peace and Freedom and the Jane Addams Peace Association. Beginning in 1993, a Picture Book category was created. Honor books
may be chosen in each category. http://home.igc.org/~japa/jacba/2004/2004_
winners_&_pr.html

1999–1953 may be viewed at http://home.igc.org/~japa/jacba/index_jacba.html

2000 Older *Through My Eyes* by Ruby Bridges. Scholastic.

Honor *The Birchbark House* by Louise Erdrich. Hyperion.

Kids on Strike! by Susan Campbell Bartoletti. Houghton Mifflin.

Picture *Molly Bannaky* by Alice McGill. Illustrated by Chris K. Soentpiet. Houghton Mifflin.

Honor *A Band of Angels* by Deborah Hopkinson. Illustrated by Raúl Colón. Anne Schwartz/Atheneum.

When Sophie Gets Angry—Really, Really Angry . . . by Molly Bang. Blue Sky Press/Scholastic.

2001 Older *Esperanza Rising* by Pam Muñoz Ryan. Scholastic.

Honor *The Color of My Words* by Lynn Joseph. Joanna Cotler/ HarperCollins.

Honor *Darkness over Denmark: The Danish Resistance and the Rescue of the Jews* by Ellen Levine. Holiday House.

Walking to the Bus-Rider Blues by Harriette Gillem Robinet. Jean Karl/Atheneum/Simon & Schuster.

Picture *The Composition* by Antonio Skármeta, illustrations by Alfonso Ruano. Groundwood.

Honor *The Yellow Star: The Legend of King Christian X of Denmark* by Carmen Agra Deedy. Illustrated by Henri Sorensen. Peachtree.

2002 Older *The Other Side of Truth* by Beverly Naidoo. HarperCollins.

Honor *A Group of One* by Rachna Gilmore. Holt.

True Believer by Virginia Euwer Wolf. Atheneum/S&S.

Picture *Martin's Big Words: The Life of Dr. Martin Luther King, Jr.* by Doreen Rappaport, art by Bryan Collier. Jump at the Sun/ Hyperion.

Honor *Amber Was Brave, Essie Was Smart* by Vera B. Williams. Greenwillow/HarperCollins.

2003 Older *Parvanna's Journey* by Deborah Ellis. Groundwood/Douglas & McIntyre.

Honor *The Same Stuff As Stars* by Katherine Paterson. Clarion.

When My Name Was Keoko by Linda Sue Parks. Clarion.

Picture *Patrol: An American Soldier in Vietnam* by Walter Dean Myers. Illustrated by Ann Grifalconi. HarperCollins.

Honor *¡Si, Se Puede! Janitor Strike in L.A.* by Diana Cohn. Illustrated By Francisco Delgado. Cinco Puntos Press.

Honor *The Village That Vanished* by Ann Grifalconi, illustrated by Kadir Nelson. Dial.

2004 Older *Out of Bounds: Seven Stories of Conflict and Hope* by Beverly Naidoo. Harper Collins.

Honor   *Getting Away with Murder: The True Story of the Emmett Till Case* by Chris Crowe. Phyllis Fogelman/Penguin.

Honor   *Shutting Out the Sky: Tenements of New York* by Deborah Hopkinson. Orchard/Scholastic.

Picture   *Harvesting Hope: The Story of Cesar Chavez* by Kathleen Kroll. Illustrations by Yuyi Morales. Harcourt.

Honor   *Girl Wonder: A Baseball Story in Nine Innings.* Illustrations by Terry Widener. Atheneum.

Honor   *Luba, the Angel of Bergen-Belsen* by Michelle R. McCann. Illustrations by Ann Marshall. Tricycle.

Special Commendation:
           The Breadwinner Trilogy by Deborah Ellis. Groundwood.

NOTABLE BOOKS FOR A GLOBAL SOCIETY

The Notable Books for a Global Society (NBGS) Committee, part of the International Reading Association Children's Literature and Reading Special Interest Group, selects each year a list of twenty-five outstanding trade books for enhancing student understanding of people and cultures throughout the world. Winning titles include fiction, nonfiction, and poetry written for students in grades K–12. To be eligible for selection a book must: portray cultural accuracy and authenticity of characters, be rich in cultural details, honor and celebrate diversity as well as common bonds in humanity, provide in-depth treatment of cultural issues, include characters within a cultural group or between two or more cultural groups who interact substantively and authentically, and include members of a "minority" group for a purpose other than filling a "quota." Lists of all winners from the years 1996–2004 are posted at:

http://www.csulb.edu/org/childrens-lit/proj/nbgs/intro-nbgs.html#about

INTERNATIONAL
ASTRID LINDGREN MEMORIAL AWARD

The Astrid Lindgren Memorial Award (ALMA) was established by the Swedish Government in 2002. The annual prize of SEK 5 million (equivalent to approx. USD 655,000 or 530,000 Euros) may be awarded to authors, illustrators, and promoters of reading whose work reflects the spirit of Astrid Lindgren. The aim of the award is to increase interest in children's and young people's literature, and to promote children's rights on a global level. The award is administered by The Swedish National Council for Cultural Affairs.
www.alma.se

2002 Author: Christine Nöstlinger (Austria) Illustrator: Maurice Sendak (USA)
2004 Author: Lygia Bounga Nunes (Brazil)

HANS CHRISTIAN ANDERSEN AWARD

This international award, sponsored by the International Board on Books for Young People, is given every two years to a living author and, since 1966, to a living illustrator whose complete works have made important international contributions to children's literature.
http://www.ibby.org/index.php?id=273

1956 Eleanor Farjeon (UK)
1958 Astrid Lindgren (Sweden)
1960 Erich Kästner (Germany)
1962 Meindert DeJong (USA)
1964 René Guillot (France)
1966 Author: Tove Jansson (Finland) Illustrator: Aloiw Carigiet (Switzerland)
1968 Authors: James Krüss (Germany) and José Maria Sanchez-Silva (Spain)
      Illustrator: Jirí Trnka (Czechoslovakia)
1970 Author: Gianni Rodari (Italy) Illustrator: Maurice Sendak (USA)
1972 Author: Scott O'Dell (USA) Illustrator: Ib Spang Olsen (Denmark)
1974 Author: Maria Gripe (Sweden) Illustrator: Farshid Mesghali (Iran)
1976 Author: Cecil Bödker (Denmark) Illustrator: Tatjana Mawrina (USSR)
1978 Author: Paula Fox (USA) Illustrator: Svend Otto S. (Denmark)
1980 Author: Bohumil Riha (Czechoslovakia) Illustrator: Suekichi Akaba
      (Japan)
1982 Author: Lygia Bojunga Nunes (Brazil) Illustrator: Zbigniew Rychlicki
      (Poland)
1984 Author: Christine Nöstlinger (Austria) Illustrator: Mitsumasa Anno
      (Japan)
1986 Author: Patricia Wrightson (Australia) Illustrator: Robert Ingpen
      (Australia)
1988 Author: Annie M.G. Schmidt (Netherlands) Illustrator: Dušan Kalláy
      (Czechoslovakia)
1990 Author: Tormod Haugen (Norway) Illustrator: Lisbeth Zwerger (Austria)
1992 Author: Virginia Hamilton (USA) Illustrator: Kveta Pacovská
      (Czechoslovakia)
1994 Author: Michio Mado (Japan) Illustrator: Jörg Müller (Switzerland)
1996 Author: Uri Orlev (Israel) Illustrator: Klaus Eniskat (Germany)

1998   Author: Katherine Paterson (USA) Illustrator: Tomi Ungerer (France)
2000   Author: Ana Maria Machado (Brazil) Illustrator: Anthony Browne (UK)
2002   Author: Aiden Chambers (UK) Illustrator: Quentin Blake (UK)
2004   Author: Martin Waddell (Ireland) Illustrator: Max Velthuijs
           (Netherlands)

JANUSZ KORCZAK LITERARY AWARD

Funded by the Ministy of Culture and the Arts of the initiative of the Polish section of IBBY, this award was established in 1979 in memory of the famous Polish writer and teacher who died in a Nazi concentration camp along with the orphaned children to whom he had dedicated his life. The prize is awarded biennially to living authors whose books for or about children contribute to international understanding among young people from all over the world. The awards are presented in two categories: books for children and books about children. After 1987, the award was temporarily suspended; it resumed in 1990, at which time additional books were named as distinctions.

1979   Astrid Lindgren (Sweden); Sergiej Michalkow (USSR); Bohumil Riha
           (Czechoslovakia)
1981   Michael Ende (Germany); Jan Navratil (Czechoslovakia); Katherine
           Paterson (USA)
1983   Ewa Nowacka (Poland); Dieo Dickman (Czechoslovakia); Mirjam
           Pressler (Germany)
1985   Luczezar Stanczew (Bulgaria); Maria Winn (USA)
1987   Maria Borowa (Poland); Albert Lichanow (USSR)
1990   Uri Orlev (Israel); Halina Filipczuk (Poland)
           Distinctions: Marion Dane Bauer (USA); Revan Inanishvili (USSR)
1992   Joanna Rudnianska (Poland); Robert Coles (USA)
           Distinction: "Guliwer," a periodical about children's books (Poland)
1994   Ofra Belbert-Avni (Israel); Mats Wahl (Sweden)
1996   Jostein Gaarder (Norway); Biliem Klimacek and Desider Toth (Slovak
           Republic); Gertruda Skotnicka (Poland)
           Distinction: Trude de John (Netherlands)
1998   Reinhardt Jung (Austria); Oleg F. Kurguzov (Russia)
           Special Awards: Lars H. Gustofsson (Sweden); Annouchka Gravel
           Caluchko (Canada)
           Distinctions: Murti Bunanta (Indonesia); Rukhsana Khan (Canada)
2000   Annika Thor (Sweden)
           Distinctions: Andri Snaer Magnason (Iceland); Bina Stampe Zmavc
           (Slovenia)
           The Prize was suspended in 2000 because of lack of funds.

NOMA CONCOURS FOR
CHILDREN'S PICTURE BOOK ILLUSTRATIONS

The biennial award is given to illustrators in Asia, Africa, Arab States, Oceana, Latin America, and the Caribbean to encourage them to show their works more widely. Sankei Award for Children's Books. Est. 1954.

UNESCO PRIZE FOR CHILDREN'S LITERATURE
IN THE SERVICE OF TOLERANCE

The United Nations Educational, Scientific, and Cultural Organization established this prize to carry the message of the United Nations Year for Tolerance beyond 1995. The prize is awarded every two years in recognition of works for the young that best embody the concepts and ideals of tolerance and peace and promote mutual understanding based on respect for other peoples and cultures. There are two categories: books for children under thirteen and those for thirteen- to eighteen-year-olds. The author of the prize-winning book in each category receives a cash award of US $8,000 donated by the Fundación Santa María/ Ediciones S.M. of Spain.
www.unesco.org/culture/toleranceliterature/

1997 **Under 13**: *Something Else* by Kathryn Cave (UK)
Honorable mentions: *To Bounce or Not to Bounce* by Naif Abdulrahman Al-Mutawa (Kuwait); *Le petit garçon bleu* (Little Blue Boy) by Fatou Keïta (Côte d'Ivoire); *The Primer of Children's Rights* by Ljubivoje Rsumovic (Yugoslavia).
13–18: *Neun Leben* (Nine Lives) by Chen Danyan (China)
Honorable mentions: *Samir und Jonathan* by Daniella Carmi (Israel); *Once There Was a Hunter* by Eleni Sarantiti (Greece); *On the Wings of Peace*, compiled by Sheila Hamanaka (USA)
1999 **Under 13**: *Sosu's Call* by Meshack Asare (Ghana)
Honorable mentions: *Hoe gaat het? Goed* (How Are You? Fine) by Anke Kranendonk (Netherlands); *Lines and Circles* by Fatma Al-Maadoul (Egypt); *Mon ami Jim* (My Friend Jim) by Kitty Crowther (Belgium).
13–18: *A Different Kind of Hero* by Anne R. Blakeslee (USA)
Honorable mentions: *Contact* by C.B. Peper (South Africa); *A Swallow in Winter* by Billi Economou-Rosen (Greece).
2001 **Under 13**: *La guerre* (The War) by Anaïs Vaugelade (France).
Honorable mentions: *My Brother is Different* and *My Friend*, a two-book series by Najla Nusayr Bashour (Lebanon); *La cosa più importante* (The Most Important Thing) by Antonella Abbatiello (Italy); *The A.O.K. Project* by Vivienne Joseph (New Zealand).

13–18: *Isthage Mir* (The Mir Space Station) by Violet Razeghpanah (Iran).

Honorable mentions: *Angela* by James Moloney (Australia); *La noche en que Vlado se fue* (The Night Vlado Left) by Manuel Quinto (Spain); *Café au lait et pain aux raisins* (Coffee with Mild and Raisin Rolls), the French version of a book originally written by German author Carolin Philipps, translated from the German by Jeanne Étoré (France).

2003   **Under 13:** *La composición* (The Composition) by Antonio Skármeta (Venezuela).

Honorable mentions: *Wir alle für immer zusammen* (Together Forever) by Guus Kuijer (Germany); *Meu Vô Apolinário* (My Grandpa Apolináro) by Daniel Munduruku (Brazil). *Huff Bluff* by Amal Farah (Egypt); *Nips XI* by Ruth Starke (Australia).

13–18: *Because Pula Means Rain* by Jenny Robson (South Africa).

Honorable mentions: *Caged Eagles* by Eric Walters (Canada); *Grenzen* (Borders) by Katrein Seynaeve (Belgium); *El diari lila de la Carlota* (Catalan) *El diario violeta de Carlota* (Spanish) by Gemma Lienas (Spain); *Le Meilleur Choix* by "Gardons contact" (Burundi).

Other prominent international awards include the Tehran International Biennal of Illustrations, the Biennale of Illustrations Brataslava, and the Bologna Book Fair Ragazzi awards.

Chapter 12

Organizations

While numerous organizations work on behalf of international literacy and children's literature, these are the most closely associated with USBBY in North America.

United States Board on Books for Young People (USBBY)
USBBY Secretariat
PO Box 8139
Newark, DE 19714-8139
E-mail: acutts@reading.org
Website: www.usbby.org

USBBY PATRONS

American Library Association
50 E. Huron, Chicago, IL 60611
Phone: 800-545-2433
Fax: 312-440-9374
E-mail: ala@ala.org
Website: www.ala.org

Children's Book Council
2 W. 37th Street, 2nd floor
New York, NY 10018-7480

Phone: 212-966-1990
Fax: 212-966-2073
E-mail: info@cbcbooks.org
Website: www.cbcbooks.org

International Reading Association
800 Barksdale Rd., Box 8139
Newark, DE 19714-8139
Phone: 302-731-1600
Fax: 302-731-1057
Website: www.reading.org

National Council of Teachers of English
1111 W. Kenyon Rd.
Urbana, IL 61801-1096
Phone: 800-369-6283
Fax: 217-328-9625
E-mail: public_info@ncte.org
Website: www.ncte.org

INTERNATIONAL

**International Board on Books
for Young People (IBBY)**
IBBY Secretariat
Nonnenweg 12, Fostfach
CH-4003 Basel, Switzerland
E-mail: ibby@eye.ch
Website: www.ibby.org

**IBBY Documentation Centre of
Books for Disabled Young People**
Box 1140, N-0317 Oslo, Norway
Fax: 47 22 85 80 02
Website:
www.ibby.org/index.php?id=271

International Youth Library
Schloss Blutenburg
D-81247 Munich, Germany
E-mail: bib@ijb.de
Website: www.ijb.de

**International Research Society
for Children's Literature**
Fax: 61 2 9514 5556
Website: www.irscl.ac.uk/

**The International Federation
of Library Associations and
Institutions**
Box 95312, 2509 CH The Hague,
Netherlands
Fax: 31 70 3834827
E-mail: IFLA@ifla.org
Website: www.ifla.org

**The International Library
of Children's Literature**
12-49 Ueno Park
Taito-ku Tokyo
110-0007 Japan
Tadao Ando 2002

Chapter 13

Publishers

The North American Publishers listed here have an international focus or consistently include international titles on their publishing lists. A more comprehensive list of names and addresses of children's book publishers can be obtained from the Children's Book Council (see chapter 12 for contact information). The addresses below are current at the time of publication but subject to change. For updated information, consult the current edition of *Books in Print* or *Literary Marketplace*, available in most libraries, or visit the Children's Book Council website.

Harry N. Abrams, Inc
Abrams Books for Young Readers
100 Fifth Avenue
New York, NY 10011
Phone: 212-206-7715
Fax: 212-645-8437
Website: www.abramsbooks.com
E-mail: online form
  As publisher of art books, this company publishes an outstanding selection of international children's picture books.

Barefoot Books
206 Massachusetts Avenue
Cambridge, MA 02140
Phone: 617-576-0660
Toll Free: 1-866-417-2369
Fax: 617-576-0049
Website: www.barefoot-books.com
E-mail: feedback@barefootbooks.com

The U.S. counterpart of a British company, Barefoot Books brings together art and story in thoughtfully prepared books by writers, artists, and storytellers from all over the world.

Bloomsbury Publishing
175 Fifth Avenue, Suite 712
New York, NY 10010
Fax: 212-982-2837
Website: www.bloomsburyusa.com
E-mail: bloomsburykids@bloomsburyusa.com

A leading independent publisher in the United Kingdom with offices in the United States for publishing U.S. editions.

Candlewick Press
2067 Massachusetts Avenue
Cambridge, MA 02140
Phone: 617-661-3330
Fax: 617-661-0565
Website: www.candlewick.com
E-mail: bigbear@candlewick.com

The U.S. branch of London-based Walker Publishers provides a vehicle for bringing the works of some of the best British authors and illustrators to this country.

Charlesbridge Publishing
85 Main Street
Watertown, MA 02472
Phone: 1-800-225-3214
Fax: 1-800-926-5775
Website: www.charlesbridge.com
E-mail: books@charlesbridge.com

As a publisher of educational books, Charlesbridge introduces the cultures of the world to children as well as the sciences.

Chicken House
2 Palmer Street
Frome
Somerset,
BA11 1DS
Phone: +44 (0)1373 454 488
Fax: +44 (0)1373 454 499
Website: www.doublecluck.com
E-mail: chickenhouse@doublecluck.com

An independent children's book publishing company in the United Kingdom with an enthusiasm for developing new writers, artists, and ideas that have worldwide popularity making an impact on an international scale.

Houghton Mifflin Company
Clarion Books
215 Park Avenue South
New York, NY 10003
Phone: 212-420-5800
Fax: 212-420-5855
Website: www.houghtonmifflinbooks.com/clarion
E-mail: children'sbooks@hmco.com
The late Dorothy Briley, a tireless promoter of internationalism, brought many authors and illustrators of note to this list.

The Creative Company
123 South Broad Street
P.O. Box 227
Mankato, MN 56001
Phone: 507-388-6273
Toll free: 1-800-445-6209
Fax: 507-388-2746
E-mail: creativeco@aol.com
This division of Creative Education regularly publishes a number of high quality international picture books, primarily from France and Germany.

DK Publishing
375 Hudson Street
New York, NY 10014
Phone: 212-213-4800
Fax: 212-689-4828
Website: www.dk.com
E-mail: ecommerce@penguingroup.com
DK, the U.S. sister company of Dorling Kindersley, England, specializes in beautifully photographed informational books in a variety of formats for all ages, many originating in England. DK also produces companion CD-ROMs and videos.

Farrar, Straus, and Giroux
19 Union Square West
New York, NY 10003
Phone: 212-741-6900

Fax: 212-633-2427
Website: www.fsgbooks.com
E-mail: childrens-marketing@fsgbooks.com

As a result of a translation and distribution agreement with the largest Swedish publisher of children's books, Rabén and Sjögren, this company publishes a number of translated Swedish picture books every year. In addition, the company publishes translated fiction for young adults.

Front Street Books
862 Haywood Road
Asheville, NC 28806
Phone: 828-221-2091
Fax: 828-221-2112
Website: www.frontstreetbooks.com

A small press that publishes a number of books in translation, including books from the Dutch publisher Lemniscaat.

David R. Godine, Publisher
9 Hamilton Place
Boston, MA 02108-4715
Phone: 617-451-9600
Fax: 617-350-0250
Website: www.godine.com
E-mail: info@godine.com

Godine's reputation for fine bookmaking extends to the choices he makes when publishing international books.

Groundwood Books
720 Bathurst Street
Suite 500
Toronto, Ontario
M5S 2R4 Canada
Phone: 416-537-2501
Fax: 416-537-4647
Website: www.groundwoodbooks.com
E-mail: susanm@groundwood-dm.com

A Canadian company, Groundwood also has a Latino imprint, Libros Tigrillo, dedicated to books from Spanish-speaking people living in this hemisphere.

Handprint Books
413 Sixth Avenue
Brooklyn, NY 11215-3310
Phone: 1-800-722-6657

Fax: 1-800-858-7787
Website: www.handprintbooks.com
E-mail: feedback@handprintbooks.com
This publishing firm also distributes Ragged Bear Books, a British publisher of books for the very young.

Kane/Miller Book Publishers
P.O. Box 8515
La Jolla, CA 92038
Phone: 1-800-968-1930
Fax: 858-456-9641
Website: www.kanemiller.com
E-mail: info@kanemiller.com
This small press specializes in children's picture books from around the world, both in translation and from English-language countries.

Lerner Publishing Group
Carolrhoda Books
Millbrook Press
1251 Washington Avenue North
Minneapolis, NN 55401-1607
Phone: 1-800-328-4929
Fax: 1-800-332-1132
Website: www.lernerbooks.com
Website: www.carolrhodabooks.com—under construction
These imprints publish international fiction and high-quality non-fiction for children in series.

Margaret K. McElderry Books/
Simon & Schuster
1230 Avenue of the Americas
New York, NY 10020
Website: www.simonsays.com
E-mail: consumer.customerservice@simonandschuster.com
Margaret K. McElderry, children's book publisher and editor, is recognized for her leadership in bringing international children's books to the United States.

Mondo Publishing
980 Avenue of the Americas
New York, NY 10018
Phone: 888-88-Mondo
Fax: 888-532-4492
Website: www.mondopub.com
E-mail: info@mondopub.com

Mondo's eclectic list contains selections from Australia, Canada, and New Zealand as well as an excellent series of folktales from around the world.

North-South Books
875 Sixth Avenue
New York, NY 10001
Phone: 212-706-4545
Fax: 212-868-5951
Website: www.northsouth.com
    North-South Books is the English-language imprint of Nord-Süd Velag, the Swiss children's book publisher. The company emphasizes high-quality multinational co-publications featuring lesser-known authors and illustrators, and regularly reissues older international titles. North-South also publishes the English-language editions of Michael Neugebauer Books, another Swiss publisher.

Soundprint Books
353 Main Avenue
Norwalk, CT 06851
Phone: 800-228-7839 or 203-838-6009
Website: www.soundprints.com
E-mail: online form
    Although the company publishes book-and-cassette packages and also specializes in stuffed toys, books are available separately.

Star Bright Books, Inc.
Star Building
4226 25th Street
Long Island City, NY 11101
Phone: 718-784-9112
Fax: 718-784-9012
Website: www.starbrightbooks.com
E-mail: info@starbrightbooks.com
    This small press publishes a few original titles and also distributes all Lothian books from Australia that have not been reprinted in U.S. editions.

Tundra Books of Northern New York
P.O. Box 1030
Plattsburgh, NY 12901
Phone: 416-598-4786—in Canada
Toll Free: 1-800-788-1074
Fax: 416-598-0247—in Canada
Website: www.tundrabooks.com
E-mail: tundra@mcclelland.com

A Canadian-owned and managed company with a New York State address, Tundra specializes in French-English bilingual, Canadian, and Native American books for children and exceptional picture book art.

Walker and Company
104 Fifth Avenue
New York, NY 10011
Phone: 212-727-8300
Fax: 212-727-0984
Website: www.walkerbooks.com
E-mail: orders@walkerbooks.com
This independent American publisher has no affiliation with the British publisher of the same name, and given their short annual lists, the proportion of international books is significant.

ONLINE PUBLISHERS

Words Without Borders
Words Without Borders/Bard College
c/o Susan Gillespie
Institute for International Liberal Education
Bard College
Annandale-on-Hudson, NY 12504-5000
Website: www.wordswithoutborders.org
E-mail: wwbinfo@bard.edu
An online magazine for international literature whose aim is to introduce distinguished translated works, including children's titles, to the general public.

African Review of Books
Kelsey Cottage
2 the Green
Laverstock, SP1 1QS
United Kingdom
Phone: +44 870 712 8932
Or in South Africa
P.O. Box 10024
Johannesburg, 2000
South Africa
Phone: +27 82 968 8955
Website: www.africanreviewofbooks.com
E-mail: mail@africanreviewofbooks.com
An independent online publication publicizing and reviewing African books, including children's titles, and debating issues in the African publishing industry.

Chapter 14

Sources for Foreign-Language and Bilingual Books

The following distributors and publishers are sources for children's books in other languages, most often imported from other countries but in some cases written and published in the United States to serve a distinct language community. These sources can be useful in finding books that have not been published in the United States as well as in locating the original language edition of a book published in translation or other books by the same author or illustrator. This list was compiled by the Children's Services Division of the San Francisco Public Library and is reproduced with the permission of Grace W. Ruth, Children's Materials Selection Specialist.

Abril Armenian Book Store (Armenian)
415 E. Broadway, #102
Glendale, CA 91205-1029
Phone: (818) 243-4112
Website: www.AbrilBooks.com

Arabic Book Outlet (Arabic)
P.O. Box 312, Don Mills
Ontario, CANADA M3C 2S7
Phone: (416) 466-4518
Fax: (416) 466-1754
E-mail: trans-tutorcom@on.aibn.com

Arkipelago Philippine Arts Books Crafts (Tagalog)
953 Mission Street
San Francisco, CA 94103
Phone: (415) 777-0108

Fax: (415) 777-0113
Website: www.arkipelagobooks.com
Contact: Marie Irving Romero

Balkatha (Indic Languages)
13042 Essex Lane
Cerritos, CA 90703
Phone: (562) 865-4633
Fax: (562) 403-0432
E-mail: sales@Balkatha.com
Website: www.balkatha.com

Bilingual Publications Company (Spanish)
270 Lafayette Street, Suite 705
New York, NY 10012
Phone: (212) 431-3500
Fax: (212) 431-3567
Contact: Linda Goodman; Approval plan

Books on Wings (Spanish)
Now **Brodart en Espanol**
Website: www.espanol.brodart.com

Casalini Libri (Italian)
Via Benedetto da Maiano, 3
50014 Fiesole
Firenze ITALY
E-mail: info@casalini.it
Website: www.casalini.it

Children's Book Press (Chinese, Korean, Spanish, Tagalog, Vietnamese)
2211 Mission Street
San Francisco, CA 94110
Phone: (415) 995-2200
Fax: (415) 995-2222
E-mail: info@childrensbookpress.ort
Website: www.childrensbookpress.org

Croatian Book Shop (Croatian)
6313 St. Clair Avenue
Cleveland, OH 44103
Phone: (216) 391-5350

Cypress Book (US) Company, Inc. (Chinese from People's Republic, using simplified characters)
360 Swift Avenue, #42
South San Francisco, CA 94080
Phone: (650) 872-7718
Fax: (650) 872-7808
E-mail: info@cypressbook.com; cypbook@pacbell.net
Website: www.cypressbook.com

Daya Imports & Exports, Inc. (Gujarati, Hindi, Tamil, Urdu—Books in Indic languages from India)
Toronto:
5863 Leslie Street, Suite 205
Toronto, Ontario, CANADA M2H 1J8

Vancouver:
6540 East Hastings Street, Suite 334
Burnaby, BC, CANADA V5B 4Z5
Phone: (416) 502-9083 (Toronto); (604) 293-0339 (Vancouver)
E-mail: daya@daya.com (Toronto); Krishna@daya.com (Vancouver)
Website: www.daya.com

Donars Spanish Books (Spanish)
P.O. Box 808
Lafayette, CO 80026-0808
Phone: (303) 666-9175
Fax: (303) 666-9043
E-mail: donars@prolynx.com

Eastwind Books & Arts, Inc. (Chinese from People's Republic, Hong Kong)
1435A Stockton Street
San Francisco, CA 94133
Phone: (415) 772-5888 (Chinese Books)
Fax: (415) 474-0630
E-mail: contact@eastwindbooks.com
Website: www.eastwindbooks.com

European Book Company (French, German)
925 Larkin Street
San Francisco, CA 94109
Phone: (415) 474-0626; 1-(877)-746-3666
Fax: 474-0630
E-mail: info@europeanbook.com

Far Eastern Books (Arabic, Bengali, Greek, Gujarati, Hindi, Punjabi, Tamil, Urdu, Vietnamese)
P.O. Box 846, Adelaide Street Station
Toronto, Ontario, CANADA M5C 2K1
Phone: (905) 477-2900; 1-(800)-291-8886
Fax: (905) 479-2988
E-mail: sales@febonline.com
Website: www.febonline.com

G.L.S. Books (German)
Headquarters in Berlin
U.S. Office in Cambridge, MA
Phone: (617) 497-0937
E-mail: 100074.1301@compuserve.com; glsbook@world.std.com
Website: www.galda.com

Globus: A Slavic Bookstore (Russian)
332 Balboa Street
San Francisco, CA 94118
Phone/Fax: (415) 668-4723
E-mail: globus@jps.net
Website: http://pweb.jps.net/~globus

Gozlan's Sefer Israel (Hebrew)
28 West 27th Street, Suite 402
New York, NY 10001
Phone: (212) 725-5890; Toll free (outside NY) 1-877-733-7019
Fax: (212) 689-6534
E-mail: marcgozlan@seferisrael.com
Website: www.seferisrael.com

Harrassowitz KG, Otto (German)
Booksellers & Subscription Agents
65174 Wiesbaden
GERMANY
Phone: +49-(0)611-530 0
Fax: +49-(0)611-530 560
In North America: Toll free: (800) 574-5732
Fax: (251) 342-5732
E-mail: service@harrassowitz.de
Website: www.harrassowitz.de

Irish Books & Media (Irish Gaelic)
1433 East Franklin Avenue
Minneapolis, MN 55404-2135
Phone: (612) 871-3505; (800) 229-3505
Fax: (612) 871-3358
E-mail: IrishBook@aol.com
Website: www.irishbook.com

Jeong-Eum-Sa Imports (Korean)
3921 Wilshire Blvd, Suite 501
Los Angeles, CA 90010
Phone: (213) 738-9140
Fax: (213) 738-9141
E-mail: jesimport@hotmail.com

Ketabsara Persian Bookstore & Publishers (Farsi)
1441 B Westwood Blvd.
Los Angeles, CA 90024
Phone: (888) 538-2272
Fax: (310) 477-4700
Website: www.ketabsara.com

Kinokuniya Bookstores of America Company, Ltd. (Japanese)
1581 Webster Street
San Francisco, CA 94115
Phone: (415) 567-7625
Fax: (415) 567-4109

10 West 49th Street
New York, NY 10020
Phone: (212) 765-7766
Fax: (212) 541-9335
Other stores: Seattle, WA; Beaverton,OR; San Jose, CA; Los Angeles, CA; Edge-
    water, NY; Costa Mesa, CA.
E-mail: sf@kinokuniya.com

Lectorum Publications, Inc. (Spanish)
A subsidiary of Scholastic
Business office/Public Libraries
205 Chubb Ave.
Lyndhurst, NJ 07071-3520
Phone: (800) 345-5946
Fax: (877) 532-8676

E-mail: lectorum@scholastic.com
Website: www.lectorum.com
Approval plan

Librairie Champlain (French)
468 rue Queen Street E
Toronto, Ontario, CANADA M5A 1T7
Phone: (416) 364-4345
Fax: (416) 364-8843
E-mail: info@librairiechamplain.com
Website: www.librairiechamplain.com

Libros Sin Fronteras (Spanish from Latin America)
Now part of **Baker & Taylor**
E-mail: libros@btol.com
Website: www.librossinfronteras.com

Luso-Brazilian Books (Portuguese)
560 West 180th Street, Suite 304
New York, NY 10033
Phone: (212) 568-0151; Outside NY (800) 727-LUSO
Fax: (212) 568-0147
E-mail: info@lusobraz.com
Website: www.lusobraz.com

Mandarin Language & Cultural Center (Chinese from Taiwan)
1630 Oakland Road, Suite A207
San Jose, CA 95131
Phone: (408) 441-9114
Fax: (408) 441-9116 (Mail order only; good for people who know Chinese. Best
   prices.)

Many Cultures Publishing/Study Center Press (Multicultural curriculum ma-
   terials, bilingual Southeast Asian folktales—Cambodian, Laotian, Tagalog,
   Vietnamese)
1095 Market Street, Suite 602
San Francisco, CA 94103
Phone: (415) 626-1650; Toll free: (888) 281-3757
Fax: (415) 626-7276
E-mail: rumi@studycenter.org
Website: www.studycenter.org

Mariuccia Iaconi Book Imports (Spanish)
970 Tennessee Street
San Francisco, CA 94107
Phone: (800) 955-9577; (415) 821-1216
Fax: (415) 821-1596
E-mail: mibibook@earthlink.net
Website: www.mibibook.com

Mo Inc. (Vietnamese)
774 Geary Street
San Francisco, CA 94109-7302
Phone: (415) 673-6838

Multi-Cultural Books and Videos, Inc. (Arabic, Chinese, French, Indic, Korean, Persian, Russian, Spanish, bilingual)
29280 Bermuda Lane
Southfield, MI 48076
Phone: (248) 948-9999
Fax: (248) 948-0030

1594 Caille Avenue
Belle Rover, Ontario, CANADA, N0R 1A0
Phone: (519) 727-4155
Fax: (519) 727-4199
Toll Free: (800) 567-2220
E-mail: service@multiculbv.com
Website: www.multiculbv.com

Pacific Books & Arts (Chinese, Hong Kong)
524A Clement Street
San Francisco, CA 94118
Phone: (415) 751-2238
Fax: (415) 751-0938

Pan Asian Publications, Inc. (Chinese, Hmong, Japanese, Khmer, Korean, Lao, Russian, Spanish, Vietnamese)
U.S. Office
29564 Union City Blvd.
Union City, CA 94587
Phone: (510) 475-1185
Fax: (510) 475-1489

Canadian Office
P.O. Box 131, Agincourt Station
Scarborough, Ontario M1S 3B4

Toll Free (US & Canada): 1-800-909-8088
E-mail: sales@panap.com
Website: www.panap.com

Perma-Bound (Spanish)
U.S. Office
617 E. Vandalia Road
Jacksonville, IL 62650
Phone: (800) 637-6581; (217) 243-5451
Fax: (800) 551-1169; (217) 243-7505
E-mail: books@perma-bound.com

Canadian Office
Box 517 Station A
Willowdale, Ontario M2N 5T1
Phone: (800) 461-1999; (705) 745-6908
Fax: (705) 876-9703
E-mail: perma-bound.ca@sympatico.ca
Website: www.perma-bound.com (search by Subject Heading—Spanish)

Polonia Bookstore, Inc. (Polish)
4738 N. Milwaukee Avenue
Chicago, IL 60630
Phone: (773) 481-6968; Toll free (866) 210-6451
Fax: (773) 481-6972
E-mail: books@polonia.com
Website: www.polonia.com

Rainbow Book Company (Spanish)
500 East Main Street
Lake Zurich, IL 60047
Phone: (800) 255-0965; (847) 726-9930
Fax: (847) 726-9935
E-mail: sales@rainbowbookcompany.com
Website: www.rainbowbookcompany.com

Schoenhof's Foreign Books (Many languages)
76A Mount Auburn Street
Cambridge, MA 02138
Phone: (617) 547-8855
Fax: (617) 547-8551
E-mail: info@schoenhofs.com
Website: www.schoenhofs.com

Shen's Books (Asian Languages)
40951 Fremont Blvd.
Fremont, CA 94538
Phone: (800) 456-6600; (510) 688-1898
Fax: (510) 668-1057
E-mail: info@shens.com
Website: www.shens.com

Siam Book Center (Thai)
5178 Hollywood Blvd.
Los Angeles, CA 90027
Phone: (323) 665-4236
Fax: (323) 665-0521

Sino-American Books & Arts (Chinese from Taiwan, books & videos)
751 Jackson Street
San Francisco, CA 94133
Phone: (415) 421-3345

South Pacific Books, Ltd. (Maori, Samoan, Tongan, etc.)
P.O. Box 3533
Auckland, NEW ZEALAND
Phone: 649 838 3821
Fax: 649 838 3822
E-mail: Sales@southpacificbooks.co.nz
Website: www.southpacificbooks.co.nz

Szwede Slavic Books (Czech, Polish, Russian)
1629 Main Street
Redwood City, CA 94063

Mailing address
P.O. Box 1214
Palo Alto, CA 94302
Phone: (650) 780-0966; (650) 851-0748
Fax: (650) 780-0967
E-mail: slavicbooks@szwedeslavicbooks.com
Website: www.szwedeslavicbooks.com

Tatak Pilipino (Tagalog)
1660 Hillhurst Ave.
Los Angeles, CA 90027
Phone: (323) 953-8660; Toll free: (800) 828-2577 (West Coast); (866) 828-2577
    (East Coast)

Other stores: San Diego, CA; Daly City, CA; Union City, CA; Vallejo, CA; Jersey City, NJ
E-mail: tatak@tatak.com
Website: www.tatakpilipino.com (click on PHILBOOKS)

Toan Thu Bookstore (Vietnamese, mail order, A-V materials also)
2115 Pedro Avenue
Milpitas, CA 95035
Phone: (408) 945-9959
Fax: (408) 942-6600
E-mail: toanthu@aol.com
Vietnamese speakers only, but via e-mail will receive help in English. (See www.sachVietnam.com for suggested children's titles)

V & W Cultural Company (Chinese)
18850 Norwalk Blvd.
Artesia, CA 90701-5973
Phone: (562) 865-8882
Fax: (562) 865-5542
(Mail order only, good source for Chinese-speaking)

Victor Kamkin Books (Russian)
220 Girard Street, Suite I
Gaithersburg, MD 20877
Phone: (301) 990-4010
Fax: (301) 990-4822
E-mail: kamkin@kamkin.com
Website: www.kamkin.com

Zoobooks (Spanish editions)
c/o Wildlife Education, Ltd.
12233 Thatcher Court
Poway, CA 92064-6880
Phone: (800) 477-5034
Fax: (858) 513-7660
E-mail: zoobooks@palmcoastd.com
Website: www.zoobooks.com

Author/Translator/Illustrator Index

Title Index

Subject Index

About the Editor

Doris Gebel is the head of Youth Services at the Northport-East Northport Public Library. She has taught as an adjunct professor of Children's Literature at The Palmer School of Library and Information Science and at St. Joseph's College, Patchogue, NY, where she has also taught courses devoted to International literature for children and storytelling. Mrs. Gebel served on the 2003 Mildred L. Batchelder Award Committee and served on the 2006 Newbery Committee. She has been a member of the United States Board on Books for Young People for many years.